UNDERSTANDING PARTNERSHIP AND LLC TAXATION
Third Edition

UNDERSTANDING PARTNERSHIP AND LLC TAXATION

THIRD EDITION

Jerold Friedland
Professor of Law
DePaul University College of Law

ISBN: 978-1-4224-9091-4 (print)
ISBN: 978-1-4224-8657-3 (eBook)

Library of Congress Cataloging-in-Publication Data

Friedland, Jerold A.
Understanding partnership and LLC taxation / Jerold Friedland. — 3rd ed.
p. cm.
Includes index.
ISBN 978-1-4224-9091-4
1. Partnership—Taxation—Law and legislation—United States. 2. Private companies—Taxation—Law and legislation—United States. I. Title.
KF6452.F764 2012
343.7305'2662—dc23   2011044690

NOTE TO USERS
To ensure that you are using the latest materials available in this area, please be sure to periodically check the LexisNexis Law School web site for downloadable updates and supplements at www.lexisnexis.com/lawschool.

Editorial Offices
121 Chanlon Rd., New Providence, NJ 07974 (908) 464-6800
201 Mission St., San Francisco, CA 94105-1831 (415) 908-3200
www.lexisnexis.com

MATTHEW◆BENDER

ACKNOWLEDGMENTS

My appreciation goes to the administration and staff of DePaul University College of Law for their support and to the excellent editing staff at LexisNexis for their work on this book.

Jerold Friedland

Wilmette, Illinois

November, 2011

TABLE OF CONTENTS

Chapter 1	INTRODUCTION TO TAXATION OF PARTNERSHIPS AND LIMITED LIABILITY COMPANIES	1

§ 1.01   OVERVIEW OF RULES GOVERNING TAXATION OF PARTNERSHIPS AND LIMITED LIABILITY COMPANIES 1

   [A]   Aggregate and Entity Principles of Subchapter K 1

   [B]   Computing and Reporting Income from Partnership or LLC Operations . . 2

   [C]   Determining Distributive Shares 3

   [D]   Contributions to Partnership or LLC 3

   [E]   Basis of Interest in Partnership or LLC 4

   [F]   Owner-Entity Transactions 5

   [G]   Distributions to Partners or Members 6

   [H]   Payments to Retiree or Deceased Owner's Estate 7

   [I]   Sale or Exchange of Partnership or LLC Interest 7

   [J]   Adjustments to Basis of Partnership or LLC Assets 8

   [K]   Termination of a Partnership or LLC 8

§ 1.02   DETERMINING THE FORM OF BUSINESS TO ADOPT 9

   [A]   Prevalent Business Forms 9

      [1]   C Corporation 9

      [2]   S Corporation 9

      [3]   Partnership 10

      [4]   Limited Partnership 11

      [5]   Limited Liability Partnership 11

      [6]   Limited Liability Company 11

      [7]   Co-ownership 12

   [B]   Factors to Consider in Choosing Business Form 12

      [1]   Nontax Factors 12

         [a]   Limited Liability 12

         [b]   Management and Control Arrangements 13

         [c]   Capital Structure 15

         [d]   Transferability of Interests 16

         [e]   Death or Other Withdrawal of Owner 16

      [2]   Tax Factors 18

         [a]   Tax Consequences of Capital Contributions 18

         [b]   Ownership Restrictions 18

         [c]   Taxability of Income and Loss 19

         [d]   Allocations of Income or Loss Items 20

         [e]   Basis Limitation on Deductibility of Losses 21

         [f]   Loss Limitations Under the At-Risk and Passive Activity Rules . . . 21

TABLE OF CONTENTS

[g]   Distributions   22

Chapter 2   **TAX CLASSIFICATION OF ECONOMIC**
                     RELATIONSHIPS **25**

§ 2.01   OVERVIEW OF TAX CLASSIFICATION ISSUES   25
§ 2.02   DETERMINING TAX CLASSIFICATION UNDER THE
          REGULATIONS   26
  [A]   Overview of the Classification Regulations   26
    [1]   Domestic Ventures   27
    [2]   Foreign Ventures   28
  [B]   Definition of Entity   29
  [C]   Definition of Business Entity   30
  [D]   Classification of a Domestic Business Entity   30
    [1]   Per Se Corporations   31
    [2]   Single-Owner Entities   32
    [3]   Entities With Two or More Owners   32
    [4]   Grandfather Rule for Domestic Entities   33
  [E]   Classification of a Foreign Business Entity   33
    [1]   Limited Liability Defined   34
    [2]   Per Se Foreign Corporations   34
    [3]   Grandfather Rule for Foreign Entities   34
    [4]   Single-Member Foreign Entities   35
    [5]   Foreign Entities With Two or More Owners   35
    [6]   Classification of Partnership That Terminates or Divides   36
  [F]   Election Procedures   36
  [G]   Change in Classification or Number of Members   37
    [1]   Elective Change in Classification   37
    [2]   Change in Number of Members   39
§ 2.03   DETERMINING WHETHER AN "ENTITY" EXISTS   40
§ 2.04   PUBLICLY TRADED PARTNERSHIPS TAXED AS
          CORPORATIONS   41
  [A]   Effective Date of Final Regulations   42
  [B]   Publicly Traded Partnership Defined   42
  [C]   Publicly Traded Partnership With Qualifying Passive-Type Income Not
          Taxed as a Corporation   43
  [D]   Publicly Traded Foreign Partnerships   43
§ 2.05   THE ANTI-ABUSE REGULATIONS   44
  [A]   Transactions Inconsistent With Intent of Subchapter K   45
  [B]   Facts and Circumstances Analysis   47
  [C]   The Abuse of Entity Rule   47
§ 2.06   ELECTING TO BE EXCLUDED FROM PARTNERSHIP TAX RULES .   48

TABLE OF CONTENTS

[A]   Overview 48

[B]   Entities Eligible for the Election 49

  [1]   Investment Partnerships 50

  [2]   Partnerships for Production, Extraction, or Use of Property 50

  [3]   Organizations of Securities Dealers 51

[C]   Effect of Election 51

[D]   Procedure for Making the Election 53

[E]   Election by Showing Intent 53

[F]   Election for Partial Exclusion 54

[G]   Effective Date and Revocation 54

§ 2.07   CLASSIFYING UNINCORPORATED ASSOCIATIONS — PRE-1997 RULES 55

Chapter 3   TAX ACCOUNTING FOR PARTNERSHIPS AND LIMITED LIABILITY COMPANIES 59

§ 3.01   OVERVIEW OF TAX ACCOUNTING 59

§ 3.02   COMPUTING TAXABLE INCOME 60

[A]   Items That Must Be Separately Stated 61

  [1]   Items Specified in I.R.C. Section 702 62

  [2]   Items Specified in the Regulations 63

  [3]   Items That Affect Partner's Tax Liability 64

  [4]   Items Subject to Limitations on Partner's Return 65

[B]   Determining Partner's Share of Partnership Gross Income 66

[C]   Level for Determining Character of Partnership Income 67

  [1]   Effect of Partnership-Level Characterization 68

  [2]   Character of Income if Partner Is Controlled Foreign Corporation ... 69

[D]   Character of Gain or Loss on Disposition of Certain Contributed Property 72

§ 3.03   ELECTIONS AFFECTING PARTNERSHIP OR LLC INCOME 75

[A]   Overview 75

[B]   Accounting Method 76

  [1]   Cash Method Not Allowed if C Corporation Is a Partner 77

  [2]   Cash Method Not Allowed if Partnership Is a Tax Shelter 77

  [3]   Cash Method Not Allowed to Farming Partnership With Corporate Partner 78

[C]   Amortization of Organization Expenses 78

[D]   Amortization of Start-Up Costs 78

[E]   Election to Expense Cost of Depreciable Property 78

[F]   Elections Made by Partners 79

  [1]   Foreign Tax Credit 80

  [2]   Discharge of Indebtedness 80

TABLE OF CONTENTS

[a]	Purchase Price Adjustment	81
[b]	Reduction of Tax Attributes	81
[c]	Election to Reduce Basis of Depreciable Property	81
[d]	Qualified Real Property Business Indebtedness	82
[e]	Debt-Discharge Rules Apply to Each Partner Separately	83
[f]	Partner's Election to Reduce Basis of Depreciable Property or Depreciable Real Property	83
[g]	Effect of Debt Discharge Income on Basis of Partnership Interest	85
[h]	Exchange of Partnership Interest for Discharged Debt	86

§ 3.04   PARTNERSHIP OR LLC TAX YEAR 86

[A]	Timing of Partner's Share of Partnership Income	87
[B]	Adoption or Change of Partner's or Member's Tax Year	89
[C]	Rules Governing Selection of Partnership Tax Year: I.R.C. Section 706	89
[1]	Majority-Interest Taxable-Year Rule	91
[2]	Principal-Partners Rule	92
[3]	Least-Aggregate-Deferral Rule	93
[D]	Business Purpose for Fiscal Tax Year	94
[1]	Natural Business Year-Gross-Receipts Test	95
[2]	Business Purpose When Gross-Receipts Test Not Satisfied	95
[E]	52-53-Week Tax Year	96
[F]	Election of Tax Year Other Than Year Required by I.R.C. Section 706	96

§ 3.05   SIMPLIFIED FLOW THROUGH FOR ELECTING LARGE PARTNERSHIPS 97

Chapter 4   **ACQUIRING A PARTNERSHIP OR LLC INTEREST BY CONTRIBUTION** **99**

§ 4.01   OVERVIEW OF GENERAL RULES 99

§ 4.02   CONTRIBUTING PROPERTY IN EXCHANGE FOR A PARTNERSHIP OR LLC INTEREST 102

[A]	General Rule: Gain and Loss Not Recognized	102
[B]	Definition of Property Under I.R.C. Section 721(a)	104
[1]	Installment Obligations	104
[2]	Right to Use Property	105
[3]	Cancellation of Partnership or LLC Debt	105
[4]	Assets Produced by Personal Services	106
[5]	Personal Notes	106
[C]	Gain Recognized on Contribution of Property to Investment Company	106

§ 4.03   BASIS, HOLDING PERIOD, AND CHARACTERIZATION RULES . . 108

[A]	Partner's or Member's Basis in the Partnership or LLC Interest	108
[B]	Partner's or Member's Holding Period for the Partnership or LLC	

TABLE OF CONTENTS

Interest 109

[C]   Partnership's or LLC's Basis and Holding Period in Contributed
Property 109

[D]   Character of Contributed Property 110

[E]   Allocation of Income, Gain, Loss, and Deduction Attributable to Contributed
Property 111

[F]   Distributions May Require Property Contributor to Recognize Gain . . . 112

§ 4.04   PARTNERSHIP OR LLC INTEREST ACQUIRED FOR CONTRIBUTION
OF PROPERTY SUBJECT TO A LIABILITY 112

[A]   General Treatment of Changes in Partners' or Members' Liabilities . . . 112

[B]   Effect of Change in Liabilities on the Noncontributing Partners or
Members 114

[C]   Effect of Change in Liabilities on the Partnership or LLC 114

[D]   Effect of Decrease in Contributing Partner's or Member's Individual
Liabilities 114

[E]   Gain Recognized When Liabilities Exceed Contributing Partner's or
Member's Basis 115

[F]   Assumption of Accounts Payable When Existing Business Is
Contributed 117

§ 4.05   PARTNERSHIP OR LLC INTEREST ACQUIRED FOR CONTRIBUTION
OF SERVICES 117

[A]   Overview 117

[B]   Receiving a Capital Interest for Services 120

    [1]   Value of Interest Received for Services 122

    [2]   Unvested Interests 122

    [3]   Electing to Include Income Under I.R.C. Section 83(b) 124

    [4]   Service Partner's Basis in Partnership Interest 125

    [5]   Deduction for Payment to Service Partner or Member 125

    [6]   Partnership May Recognize Gain or Loss 126

[C]   Receiving an Interest in Future Profits 127

    [1]   Background — The *Diamond* Decision 128

    [2]   Background — The *Campbell* Decision 129

    [3]   The Service's Current Position — Revenue Procedures 93-27 and
2001-43 131

§ 4.06   START-UP, ORGANIZATION, AND SYNDICATION EXPENSES . . . 133

[A]   Amortization of Start-Up Expenses 133

[B]   Amortization of Organization Expenses 135

[C]   Nondeductibility of Syndication Expenses 136

[D]   "Disguised" Organization and Syndication Expenses 136

TABLE OF CONTENTS

Chapter 5	BASIS IN PARTNERSHIP/LLC INTEREST 139

§ 5.01 OVERVIEW OF BASIS OF PARTNER'S OR MEMBER'S
INTEREST 139

[A] When Is Determination of Basis Required? 139

[B] Initial Basis — How it Is Determined 140

[C] Continuing Adjustments to Partner's Basis 143

[1] Basis Adjustment for Taxable Income or Loss 145

[2] Basis Increase for Tax-Exempt Income 146

[3] Basis Decrease for Nondeductible Expenditures 148

[4] Basis Decrease for Distributions 149

[5] Basis Increase for Depletion Deductions 150

[6] Basis Decrease for Depletion Deductions 151

[7] Basis Adjustment When Partnership Sells Corporate Partner's
Stock 151

[a] Limitation on Basis Adjustment if no I.R.C. Section 754 Election in
Effect 152

[b] Limitation on Basis Adjustment if Partnership Makes Distribution to
Another Partner 154

[D] Basis Adjustment When Partner or Partnership Debt Is Discharged ... 156

[E] Basis Adjustment on Sale, Exchange, or Liquidation of Partnership
Interest 157

[F] Order of Basis Adjustments 158

[1] Loss-Deduction Limitation 158

[2] Distributed Property 159

[3] Gain Recognized on Cash Distribution 160

[4] Marketable Securities 160

[5] Advance or Draw Taken 161

[6] Encumbered Property Contributed or Distributed 161

[G] Partnership's Basis in Its Assets — How it Is Determined 162

[H] "Inside Basis" and "Outside Basis" 163

[1] Events That Upset Equivalence of Inside Basis and Outside Basis .. 164

[2] Restoring Equivalence: I.R.C. Section 754 Election 166

[I] Relationship Between Partner's Basis and Capital Account 166

§ 5.02 ALTERNATIVE METHOD FOR DETERMINING BASIS: I.R.C. SECTION
705(b) 167

§ 5.03 EFFECT OF PARTNERSHIP LIABILITIES ON BASIS OF PARTNER'S
INTEREST IN PARTNERSHIP 168

[A] Overview of General Rules 168

[B] Nonrecourse Liabilities in Tax-Sheltered Investments 171

[C] Interaction With At-Risk and Passive Activity Rules 171

§ 5.04 PARTNERSHIP LIABILITIES DEFINED 172

TABLE OF CONTENTS

[A]	General Rules	172
[B]	Sham Liabilities	173
[C]	Contingent Liabilities	175
[D]	Obligations Treated As Liabilities Under Regulations Section 1.752-7	176
[E]	Loans Treated As Capital Contributions — "Thin" Partnerships	177
§ 5.05	GENERAL RULES GOVERNING PARTNER'S SHARE OF PARTNERSHIP LIABILITIES	178
[A]	Overview of Regulations	178
[B]	Interests of Related Persons	180
[C]	Assumption of Partnership or Partner Debt	180
§ 5.06	PARTNER'S SHARE OF RECOURSE LIABILITIES	180
[A]	Partner's Economic Risk of Loss	182
[B]	Partner's Payment Obligation	184
[C]	Anti-Abuse Rule	185
[D]	When Must Partner or Partnership Obligations Be Satisfied?	185
[E]	Obligation to Pay Interest on Nonrecourse Debt	186
[F]	Partner's Nonrecourse Loan to Partnership	186
§ 5.07	PARTNER'S SHARE OF NONRECOURSE LIABILITIES	186
[A]	Liability and Allocation Rules Coordinated	186
[B]	Computing a Partner's Share of Nonrecourse Liabilities	187
§ 5.08	CHANGES IN PARTNER'S SHARE OF PARTNERSHIP LIABILITIES	193
[A]	Events That Change Partner's Share of Liabilities	193
[B]	Changes in the Amount of Partnership Liabilities	193
[C]	Addition or Loss of a Partner	193
[D]	Contribution or Distribution of Encumbered Property	194
[1]	Contribution of Encumbered Property	194
[2]	Distribution of Encumbered Property	196
[3]	Encumbrance Limited to Value of Property	196
[4]	Payments Made on Excess Encumbrance	197
[E]	Sale or Exchange of Partnership Interest	197
Chapter 6	**DISTRIBUTIVE SHARES**	**199**
§ 6.01	OVERVIEW OF DISTRIBUTIVE SHARE RULES	199
[A]	General Rules	199
[B]	When Distributive Share Is Taxable	201
§ 6.02	ALLOCATIONS ATTRIBUTABLE TO CONTRIBUTED PROPERTY	202
[A]	Reasonable Allocation Methods	205
[1]	The Traditional Method	206
[2]	Traditional Method With Curative Allocations	211
[3]	Remedial Allocations	212

TABLE OF CONTENTS

[4]		Small Disparities and Aggregation Rules	214
[5]		Securities Partnerships	215
[B]		Distribution of Contributed Property to Noncontributing Partner	215
[1]		Basis Adjustments	216
[2]		Anti-Abuse Rule	217
[C]		Distributions to Contributing Partner	217
[1]		Special Rules for Computing Net Precontribution Gain	220
[2]		Distributions Not Subject to I.R.C. Section 737	221
[3]		Basis Adjustments	221
§ 6.03		ALLOCATIONS WHEN INTERESTS CHANGE	223
[A]		General Rules	224
[B]		Determining Distributive Shares Under the Varying-Interest Rule	225
[C]		Special Rule for Allocable Cash-Basis Items	227
[D]		Change of Interests in Tiered Partnerships	228
[E]		Change in Partners' Interests Under Partnership Agreement	229
§ 6.04		SPECIAL ALLOCATIONS — OVERVIEW	230
[A]		General Rules	231
[B]		Partnership Agreement Defined	232
[C]		Distributive Shares in Absence of Valid Partnership Agreement	232
§ 6.05		SUBSTANTIAL ECONOMIC EFFECT	233
[A]		Economic-Effect Test	235
[1]		Provisions Required in Partnership Agreement	235
[2]		Liquidating Distributions of Positive Capital Account Balances	236
[3]		Liquidation When Partner Has Deficit Capital Account	238
[a]		General Rule-Deficit Must Be Restored	239
[b]		Exceptions to Deficit-Restoration Requirement	240
[i]		Alternate Economic-Effect Test	240
[ii]		Partial Obligation to Restore Deficit	244
[iii]		Reduction of Deficit-Restoration Obligation	244
[4]		Economic-Effect Equivalence	245
[5]		Partial Economic Effect	246
[B]		Substantiality Test	246
[1]		After-Tax Economic Consequences Rule	247
[2]		Shifting Tax Consequences	248
[3]		Transitory Allocations	249
§ 6.06		CAPITAL ACCOUNT REQUIREMENTS	251
[A]		General Rules	252
[B]		Adjustments for Contributions and Distributions	253
[C]		Adjustments for Assumed Partnership Liabilities	255
[D]		Promissory Notes	256
[E]		Revaluations of Partnership Property	256

TABLE OF CONTENTS

[F]   Adjustments for Disparities Between Book Value and Tax Basis of
       Contributed or Revalued Property 260

[G]   Adjustments for Nondeductible, Noncapital Expenditures and Disallowed
       Losses 263

[H]   Adjustments for Guaranteed Payments and Employee Benefit Plan
       Contributions 263

§ 6.07 PARTNERS' INTERESTS IN THE PARTNERSHIP 263

[A]   General Rules 264

[B]   Factors Considered When Determining Partners' Interests in the
       Partnership 264

§ 6.08 ALLOCATIONS OF ITEMS ATTRIBUTABLE TO NONRECOURSE
        LIABILITIES 265

[A]   Overview of Regulations 268

[B]   Safe Harbor for Allocations of Nonrecourse Deductions 270

[C]   Partnership Minimum Gain 272

[D]   Nonrecourse Deductions 274

[E]   Partners' Shares of Partnership Minimum Gain 278

[F]   Distributions Allocable to Nonrecourse Borrowings 279

[G]   Minimum-Gain Chargeback 282

[H]   Nonrecourse Debt for Which Partner Bears Risk of Loss 285

§ 6.09 LIMITATIONS ON PARTNER'S AND LLC MEMBER'S DEDUCTION
        FOR LOSSES — I.R.C. SECTION 704(d) 286

[A]   General Rules 286

[B]   Effect of Sale, Death, Termination, or Gift 288

**Chapter 7   TRANSACTIONS BETWEEN PARTNERS/MEMBERS AND
                 PARTNERSHIP/LLC 289**

§ 7.01 OVERVIEW OF PARTNERSHIP TRANSACTIONS 289

[A]   Transactions in Which the Partner Acts in a Nonpartner Capacity 289

[B]   Transactions That May Be Recharacterized as Occurring Between the
       Partnership and a Partner Acting in a Nonpartner Capacity 290

[C]   Special Treatment of Losses and Capital Gains on Sales Between a
       Partnership and Persons With Controlling Interests 290

[D]   Accrual-Method Deductions Deferred Until Payment Occurs 291

[E]   Guaranteed Payments to a Partner Who Provides Services or Capital to the
       Partnership in a Partner Capacity 291

[F]   Partnership-Partner Transactions Treated as Contributions or Included in the
       Partner's Distributive Share 292

§ 7.02 DETERMINING WHETHER A PARTNER ACTS IN A PARTNER OR
        NONPARTNER CAPACITY 292

§ 7.03 GUARANTEED PAYMENTS FOR PARTNER'S SERVICES OR
        CAPITAL 294

TABLE OF CONTENTS

[A]   General Tax Consequences of Payments for Services or Use of
        Capital 294

[B]   Guaranteed Payments 296

[C]   Character of Guaranteed Payments for Use of Partner's Capital 300

[D]   Payments Computed from Gross Income 301

[E]   Draws, Bonuses, and Payments Dependent on Profits 302

§ 7.04 TRANSACTIONS IN WHICH PARTNER ACTS IN NONPARTNER
        CAPACITY 303

[A]   Loans and Leases 303

   [1] Bad Debts 304

[B]   Services 304

[C]   Sales 305

[D]   Contribution and Related Distribution Treated as Disguised Sale 305

   [1] Overview of Regulations 310

   [2] Tests for Determining Whether Disguised Sale Occurs 313

   [3] Payments not Included in Disguised Sale 323

   [4] Contribution of Encumbered Property Treated as Disguised Sale ... 323

      [a] Qualified Liabilities 324

      [b] Nonqualified Liabilities 326

   [5] Debt-Financed Disguised Sales 327

   [6] Disguised Sale by Partnership to Partner 330

   [7] Disguised Sale of Partnership Interest 331

   [8] Disclosure of Disguised Sale Transactions 332

[E]   Contribution and Related Income Allocation Treated as Disguised Payment
        for Services or Property 332

§ 7.05 SALES AND EXCHANGES INVOLVING CONTROLLED AND RELATED
        PARTNERSHIPS 334

[A]   Special Rules to Prevent Tax-Motivated Transactions Between a Partnership
        and Its Partners — An Overview 334

[B]   Definition of Control Under I.R.C. Section 707(b) 334

[C]   Limitation on Loss Deductions 336

[D]   Gain Treated as Ordinary Income if Property Is Not a Capital Asset to
        Purchaser 338

[E]   Gain Treated as Ordinary Income if Property Is Depreciable by
        Purchaser 338

[F]   Deductions for Accrued Expenses 339

Chapter 8   DISTRIBUTING PARTNERSHIP/LLC PROPERTY TO
             PARTNERS OR MEMBERS 341

§ 8.01 OVERVIEW OF DISTRIBUTION RULES 341

[A]   General Rules Applicable to Distributions 342

TABLE OF CONTENTS

[1]   Gain or Loss on Current or Liquidating Distribution 342

[2]   Basis of Distributee Partner's Interest in the Partnership 343

[3]   Basis of Distributed Property in the Distributee Partner's Hands 344

[4]   Character and Holding Period of Distributed Property 345

[5]   Distribution That Changes Partner's Share of I.R.C. Section 751
          Property 345

[6]   Partnership's Basis in Undistributed Property 345

[7]   Payments to a Retiring Partner or Deceased Partner's Successor 346

[B]   Distinction Between Current and Liquidating Distributions 346

§ 8.02   SPECIAL RULES FOR CERTAIN DISTRIBUTIONS 348

[A]   Distribution of Marketable Securities 348

[1]   Marketable Securities Defined 348

[2]   Money Distribution Reduced by Partner's Share of Appreciation . . . 349

[3]   Certain Distributions Not Subject to Gain Recognition Rule 350

[4]   Exception for Investment Partnerships 351

[5]   Basis Adjustments 351

[6]   Anti-Abuse Rule 352

[B]   Constructive Distribution of Money Upon Decrease in Partner's Share of
          Partnership Liabilities 353

[C]   Distributions Associated With Contribution of Property 355

[D]   Distribution of Stock to a Corporate Partner 356

§ 8.03   CURRENT (NONLIQUIDATING) DISTRIBUTIONS 357

[A]   Money Distribution 358

[B]   Advances or Draws Against a Partner's Expected Distributive Share . . 359

[C]   Property Distribution 360

[D]   Money and Property Distribution 362

[E]   Special Basis in Distributed Property Under I.R.C. Section 732(d) 363

[F]   Partnership Tax Consequences 364

§ 8.04   LIQUIDATING DISTRIBUTIONS 365

[A]   Recognizing Gain on Money Distribution 366

[B]   Recognizing Loss on Liquidating Distributions 367

[C]   Determining and Reporting Gain or Loss on a Series of Liquidating
          Distributions 368

[D]   Property Distribution 368

[E]   Allocating Basis to Distributed Property 370

§ 8.05   CHARACTERIZING PARTNER'S GAIN OR LOSS ON DISPOSITION OF
          DISTRIBUTED PROPERTY 372

[A]   Unrealized Receivables and Inventory 373

[B]   Recapture Property 375

§ 8.06   DISPROPORTIONATE DISTRIBUTIONS OF UNREALIZED
          RECEIVABLES AND INVENTORY 375

[A]   Transactions Not Treated as Disproportionate Distributions 380

TABLE OF CONTENTS

[B]		Computing Gain or Loss in a Disproportionate Distribution	380
	[1]	Computational Steps	380
	[2]	Noncash Distributions	385
	[3]	Constructive Distribution When Partner's Share of Partnership Liabilities Decreases	388
[C]		Distributions Involving Recapture Property	391
[D]		Distributions in Liquidation of Entire Partnership	392
§ 8.07		BASIS ADJUSTMENTS RELATED TO DISTRIBUTIONS	393
[A]		Computing and Allocating Basis Adjustments Under I.R.C. Section 754 Election	396
[B]		Illustrating Basis Adjustments	399
	[1]	Distributee Partner Recognizes Gain on Cash Distribution	399
	[2]	Distributee Partner Recognizes Loss on Liquidating Distribution	401
	[3]	Basis of Distributed Property Changes	402
	[4]	Elective Adjustment Under I.R.C. Section 732(d)	404
[C]		Unusable Basis Adjustments Carried Forward	405
[D]		Distributions By Tiered Partnerships	406
[E]		Basis Adjustment on Distributions Subject to I.R.C. Section 751(b)	407
[F]		Making a Basis-Adjustment Election	408

Chapter 9 — **FAMILY PARTNERSHIPS AND LIMITED LIABILITY COMPANIES** — **409**

§ 9.01		OVERVIEW OF FAMILY PARTNERSHIP RULES	409
§ 9.02		KEY ISSUES IN ESTABLISHING PARTNER STATUS IN A FAMILY PARTNERSHIP	410
[A]		Subjective Test of Partner Status: *Commissioner v. Culbertson*	411
[B]		Partner Status When Capital Is Material in Producing Income: I.R.C. Section 704(e)(1)	412
[C]		Partner Status When Capital Interest Is Acquired by Gift	414
	[1]	Donor Is the Real Owner	416
	[2]	Donee Is the Real Owner	419
	[3]	Limited Partnership Interest Acquired by Gift	421
	[4]	Tax-Avoidance Motive in Gift of Partnership Interest	421
§ 9.03		DETERMINING PARTNER STATUS OF TRUSTEES	422
§ 9.04		DETERMINING PARTNER STATUS OF MINOR CHILDREN	424
§ 9.05		SELLING A PARTNERSHIP INTEREST TO A FAMILY MEMBER: SALE OR GIFT?	425
§ 9.06		ALLOCATING PARTNERSHIP INCOME AMONG FAMILY MEMBERS	426
[A]		Intrafamily Sales Considered Indirect Gifts	428
[B]		Indirect Gifts	429
[C]		Reallocation for Reasonable Value of Donor's Services	429

TABLE OF CONTENTS

[D]	Reallocation for Disproportionate Allocation	431
[E]	Allocation in Year of Gift	432
§ 9.07	ESTATE AND GIFT TAX CONSIDERATIONS: EFFECT OF I.R.C. SECTIONS 2701–2704 ON TRANSFERS TO FAMILY MEMBERS	432

Chapter 10	**LIQUIDATING PAYMENTS TO A RETIRING PARTNER/ MEMBER OR A DECEDENT'S SUCCESSOR**	**437**

§ 10.01	OVERVIEW OF LIQUIDATING PAYMENTS — I.R.C. SECTION 736	437
[A]	Payments Governed by I.R.C. Section 736	438
[B]	Classification of Liquidating Payments	439
[C]	Payments for Partner's/Member's Interest in Partnership/LLC Property — I.R.C. Section 736(b) Payments	440
[1]	Valuing Partner's/Member's Share of Partnership/LLC Property	440
[2]	Limited Exclusion for Unrealized Receivables and Goodwill	441
[3]	Taxation of I.R.C. Section 736(b) Payments	444
[D]	Payments Exceeding Partner's/Member's Interest in Partnership/LLC Property — I.R.C. Section 736(a) Payment	448
[1]	Determining the Amount of I.R.C. Section 736(a) Payments	449
[2]	Taxation of I.R.C. Section 736(a) Payments	449
[3]	Summary — Steps in Determining Taxation Of Lump-Sum Liquidating Payment	452
§ 10.02	SERIES OF CASH LIQUIDATING PAYMENTS	452
[A]	Determining the I.R.C. Section 736(a) and I.R.C. Section 736(b) Portions of Each Payment	453
[B]	Computing Gain or Loss Recognized on the I.R.C. Section 736(b) Portion	457
[C]	Computing Gain or Loss Recognized on the I.R.C. Section 736(a) Portion	460
§ 10.03	NONCASH LIQUIDATING PAYMENTS	462

Chapter 11	**WHEN A PARTNER OR LLC MEMBER DIES**	**471**

§ 11.01	OVERVIEW OF STATE LAW AND TAX CONSIDERATIONS	471
[A]	State Law Considerations	471
[1]	General Partnership	471
[2]	Limited Partnership	472
[3]	Limited Liability Company	472
[B]	Tax Considerations — In General	473
[1]	Tax Year Closes for Deceased Partner or Member	473
[2]	Death of Partner or Member May Terminate Partnership or LLC	474
[3]	Basis of Successor's Partnership/LLC Interest	475

TABLE OF CONTENTS

[4]   Basis of Partnership/LLC Property 475

[5]   Value of Decedent's Interest Subject to Estate Tax 476

[6]   Liquidation of Interest of Deceased Partner or Member 476

[7]   Sale of Decedent's Interest to Remaining Partners or Members 477

[8]   Sale of Decedent's Interest to Third Party 478

[9]   Liquidation of Partnership or LLC 478

[10]   Successor Joins Partnership or LLC 479

§ 11.02   PRE-1998 RULES FOR ALLOCATING INCOME FOR YEAR OF
          PARTNER'S DEATH 479

§ 11.03   EFFECTS OF INCOME-IN-RESPECT-OF-A-DECEDENT (IRD)
          RULES 480

[A]   General Explanation of IRD Rules 480

[B]   IRD Attributable to a Partnership or LLC Interest 481

[1]   Liquidating Payments 481

[2]   Assets That Would Be IRD if Held by Decedent 482

§ 11.04   EFFECT OF PARTNER'S OR MEMBER'S DEATH ON BASIS 483

[A]   Successor's Basis for Partnership or LLC Interest 483

[B]   Basis of Partnership or LLC Property 484

[1]   I.R.C. Section 754 Election 484

[2]   I.R.C. Section 732(d) Election for Distributed Property 485

[3]   Summary of Effect of Partner's or Member's Death on Basis of
        Partnership/LLC Interests and Partnership/LLC Property 487

§ 11.05   ESTATE TAXATION: DETERMINING THE VALUE OF A
          PARTNERSHIP/LLC INTEREST 490

[A]   Effects of Partnership/LLC Agreements 491

[1]   Insurance-Funded Cross-Purchase Agreements 492

[2]   Insurance-Funded Redemption Agreements 493

[B]   Special Valuation Rules — I.R.C. Section 2032A 494

**Chapter 12   SELLING OR EXCHANGING A PARTNERSHIP OR LLC
                   INTEREST 495**

§ 12.01   OVERVIEW 495

§ 12.02   COMPUTING SELLING PARTNER'S OR MEMBER'S GAIN OR
          LOSS 497

[A]   Seller's Amount Realized 497

[B]   Seller's Basis 499

[C]   Sale of Portion of Partner's Interest 500

[D]   Abandoned or Worthless Interest: Character of Loss 501

[E]   Deficit-Capital-Account Effect on Amount Realized 503

[F]   Tax Rate and Holding Period Applied to Seller's Capital Gain or Loss . 504

§ 12.03   CHARACTERIZING SELLER'S GAIN OR LOSS: ORDINARY INCOME
          RECOGNIZED ON I.R.C. SECTION 751 PROPERTY 505

TABLE OF CONTENTS

[A]		Defining I.R.C. Section 751 Property	506
[1]		Unrealized Receivables	506
[2]		Inventory	509
[B]		Reporting Requirements	510
§ 12.04		DETERMINING EFFECTS OF SALE OR EXCHANGE ON PARTNERSHIP TAX YEAR	510
§ 12.05		DETERMINING EFFECTS OF SALE OR EXCHANGE ON PARTNER'S LOSS DEDUCTIONS	511
§ 12.06		EXCHANGE OF PARTNERSHIP INTERESTS IN NONRECOGNITION TRANSACTION	512
[A]		Exchanging Interests in the Same Partnership	512
[B]		Converting Partnership's Interests to LLC Interests and Vice-Versa	513
[C]		Exchanging Interests in Different Partnerships	514
[D]		Contributing a Partnership or LLC Interest to a Corporation	514
[E]		Conversion of a Corporation to a Partnership or LLC	515
[F]		Contributing a Partnership or LLC Interest to Another Partnership	515
[G]		Distribution of a Partnership or LLC Interest by a Corporation	517
[H]		Distribution of a Partnership or LLC Interest by a Partnership	517
[I]		Distribution of a Partnership or LLC Interest by a Trust or Estate	518
[J]		Transferring a Partnership Interest at Partner's Death	518
[K]		Gifting a Partnership or LLC Interest	518
[L]		Making a Charitable Contribution	519
§ 12.07		RECHARACTERIZING SALE OR EXCHANGE OF A PARTNERSHIP INTEREST	520
§ 12.08		ADJUSTING BASIS OF PARTNERSHIP OR LLC PROPERTY	523
[A]		General Rule: Sale or Exchange of Interest Does Not Affect Basis of Partnership or LLC Property	523
[B]		Electing to Adjust Basis of Partnership or LLC Property	524
[C]		Determining Whether Basis Adjustment Rules Apply	525
[D]		Computing the I.R.C. Section 743(b) Basis Adjustment	527
[E]		Transferring an Interest in a Tiered Partnership	531
[F]		Allocating Basis Adjustments Among Partnership Assets	532
[1]		Income in Respect of a Decedent	535
[2]		Carryover Basis Transaction	536
[G]		Contribution of Basis Adjusted Property to a Partnership or Corporation	539
[H]		Allocations to Goodwill	540
[I]		Computing Tax Consequences of I.R.C. Section 743(b) Basis Adjustment	543
[1]		Effect of Basis Adjustment on Partner's Income, Gain, or Loss	544
[2]		Effect of Basis Adjustment on Partner's Cost Recovery, Amortization and Depletion Deductions	544

TABLE OF CONTENTS

[J]   Distributing Property for Which I.R.C. Section 743(b) Adjustment Has Been Made 548

[K]   Sale of Partnership Interests Between Members of Affiliated Group of Corporations 550

[L]   Transfer Terminating a Partnership 551

[M]   Making and Reporting the I.R.C. Section 754 Election 553

§ 12.09 ADJUSTING BASIS OF PROPERTY DISTRIBUTED TO PURCHASING PARTNER: I.R.C. SECTION 732(d) ELECTION 553

[A]   Effect of Election on Disproportionate Distributions of I.R.C. Section 751 Property 555

[B]   Making the Election 556

[C]   Mandatory I.R.C. Section 732(d) Adjustments 556

Chapter 13   **TERMINATING A PARTNERSHIP OR LLC** **559**

§ 13.01 OVERVIEW OF EVENTS TERMINATING A PARTNERSHIP OR LLC 559

§ 13.02 CEASING PARTNERSHIP BUSINESS OR FINANCIAL ACTIVITIES 561

§ 13.03 CHANGING BUSINESS FORM 561

[A]   Changing to a Sole Proprietorship 562

[B]   Changing to a Corporation 564

[C]   Converting Interests in the Same Partnership 565

[D]   Converting a Partnership to an LLC and Vice Versa 566

§ 13.04 SELLING OR EXCHANGING 50 PERCENT OR MORE OF INTERESTS IN PARTNERSHIP OR LLC PROFITS AND CAPITAL 566

[A]   Sale or Exchange Requirement 568

  [1]   Transfers Not Causing Termination 568

  [2]   Nontaxable Transfers Considered Exchanges Under Termination Rules 570

  [3]   Tiered Partnerships 571

[B]   Determining Whether 50 Percent of Profits and Capital Are Transferred 572

  [1]   Determining Capital Interest 572

  [2]   Determining Profits Interest 573

§ 13.05 MERGING, CONSOLIDATING, DIVIDING, AND CONVERTING PARTNERSHIPS OR LLCS 573

[A]   Continuing or Terminating Partnership or LLC in Merger or Consolidation 573

[B]   Tax Consequences of Merger or Consolidation 576

[C]   Dividing a Partnership or LLC 583

§ 13.06 TAX CONSEQUENCES OF PARTNERSHIP TERMINATION 587

[A]   Partnership Tax Year Closes 587

TABLE OF CONTENTS

[B]   Elections 588
[C]   Cessation of Business — Assets Deemed Distributed 589
[D]   Termination by Sale or Exchange — Assets Deemed Contributed to New
        Partnership 589
[E]   Holding Period for Partnership Assets Following Termination 592
[F]   Character of Partnership Property Following Termination 593
[G]   Suspended Losses 593

Table of Cases **TC-1**

Table of Statutes **TS-1**

Table of Administrative Pronouncements **TOA-1**

Table of Regulations **TOR-1**

Index **I-1**

Chapter 1

INTRODUCTION TO TAXATION OF PARTNERSHIPS AND LIMITED LIABILITY COMPANIES

§ 1.01   OVERVIEW OF RULES GOVERNING TAXATION OF PARTNERSHIPS AND LIMITED LIABILITY COMPANIES

Subchapter K of the Internal Revenue Code contains the rules governing the taxation of partners and partnerships. Ordinarily, a limited liability company (LLC) with more than one member is treated as a partnership for tax purposes. Therefore, Subchapter K generally governs the taxation of LLCs and their members. Unless otherwise noted, references to partnerships and partners throughout this text also refer to LLCs and their members.

The following sections provide a broad overview of the basic principles and rules of subchapter K. Detailed analysis of these provisions is provided in the other chapters of this book.

[A]   Aggregate and Entity Principles of Subchapter K

The first and most basic rule set forth in Subchapter K is that a partnership is not a taxable entity.[1] A partnership serves as a conduit through which its income, gains, losses, deductions, and credits pass directly to its partners. Each partner reports his share of the partnership's income or loss on his individual tax return, and his personal tax liability correspondingly increases or decreases.[2] Thus, for reporting and paying tax liabilities, a partnership is treated as an aggregate of individuals who provide capital and services to a joint enterprise, rather than as a separate entity.

For computing the amount and timing of the income or loss passed through to its partners, however, a partnership is considered an entity that is separate and distinct from its members.[3] For example, partnership income is determined using a method of accounting and taxable year the partnership selects, and most tax elections affecting the amount and timing of the income and deductions are made at the partnership level.[4] Similarly, each partnership income or loss item generally

---

[1]   I.R.C. § 701.

[2]   I.R.C. § 701.

[3]   *See* U.S. v. Basye, 410 U.S. 441 (1973).

[4]   I.R.C. § 703(b).

is reported pro rata by each partner and retains the same character it had when the partnership earned or incurred it.[5] The concept of a partnership as an entity also is reflected in (1) the requirement that every partner maintain a basis for his partnership interest that is distinct from the basis of the partnership's property,[6] and (2) the rules permitting some partner-partnership transactions to be taxed as if they occur between unrelated parties.[7]

[B]   Computing and Reporting Income from Partnership or LLC Operations

Although a partnership is not a taxable entity, it must compute and characterize the amount of income that passes through it to be reported on its partners' returns.[8] For this purpose, a partnership adopts its own tax year and accounting method. With important exceptions, a partnership must adopt the same tax year as the partners who own a majority of its interests.[9] A partnership computes its taxable income in the same manner that an individual does, except that it may not claim certain deductions that are allowed on a partner's return (*e.g.*, the standard deduction and personal exemptions).[10] Not included in overall partnership taxable income are partnership items that may be subject to special tax treatment on any partner's return, such as capital gains or interest; these items are accounted for and stated separately.[11]

Each partner reports his distributive share of partnership income, gain, loss, deduction, or credit on his tax return for the year in which, or with which, the partnership's year ends, regardless of whether any amounts are distributed to him.[12] Each item generally must be reported with the same character it had when the partnership earned or incurred it.[13] A partner may not deduct his distributive share of partnership losses that exceed the basis of his partnership interest at the close of the partnership's tax year.[14] Losses that cannot be deducted because of this basis limitation are carried over to subsequent years. Deductions for partnership losses also may be restricted by rules outside of subchapter K, *i.e.*, the at-risk rules of I.R.C. Section 465 and the passive loss rules of I.R.C. Section 469.

---

[5] I.R.C. § 702(b).

[6] I.R.C. §§ 705, 722, 733, 742.

[7] *See* I.R.C. § 707(a), (c).

[8] The partnership reports its income or loss to the Service on an information return, Form 1065, and notifies each partner of his distributive share of these amounts on Schedule K-1.

[9] I.R.C. § 706(b).

[10] I.R.C. § 703(a)(1), (2).

[11] I.R.C. § 703(a)(1).

[12] I.R.C. § 706(a).

[13] I.R.C. § 702(a), (b).

[14] I.R.C. § 704(d).

[C] Determining Distributive Shares

Each partner's distributive share of any item of partnership income, gain, loss, or deduction ordinarily is determined from the allocations the partners establish in their partnership agreement.[15] An allocation of any item in the agreement is disregarded if it fails to satisfy the substantial economic effect test described in the regulations.[16] Affected items are reallocated among the partners according to their actual interest in the partnership, as determined from all the facts and circumstances.[17] Tax items attributable to contributed property must be allocated in a manner that accounts for any difference between the value and basis of the property when it was contributed.[18] For example, when a partnership sells contributed property, the contributing partner must be allocated all of the gain up to the amount of appreciation inherent in the property at the time of the contribution.

The amount of income or loss allocated to a partner must reflect his varying interests in each portion of the year, if his interest in the partnership increases or decreases during the year.[19] This rule prevents partnership items from being retroactively allocated to partners who join the partnership or who increase their interests late in the partnership tax year.

[D] Contributions to Partnership or LLC

When a partner contributes property to a partnership in exchange for a partnership interest, he generally does not recognize gain or loss.[20] The contributed property has the same basis for the partnership that it had in the hands of the contributing partner.[21] A partner's initial basis in his partnership interest is the total of cash plus the basis of any property he contributes.[22]

In connection with a contribution to a partnership, a partner may recognize gain or loss in the following circumstances:

(1) A partner recognizes income if he exchanges his services for an interest in partnership capital.[23] The partner reports the value of the partnership interest as ordinary compensation income when he receives it.[24] In the year that the partner reports it as income, the partnership deducts or capitalizes the value of the interest given for the partner's services.[25]

---

[15] I.R.C. § 704(a).

[16] I.R.C. § 704(b); Treas. Reg. § 1.704-1(b).

[17] *Id.*

[18] I.R.C. § 704(c).

[19] I.R.C. § 706(d).

[20] I.R.C. § 721(a).

[21] I.R.C. § 722.

[22] I.R.C. § 723.

[23] Treas. Reg. § 1.721-1(b).

[24] I.R.C. § 83.

[25] *Id.*

(2) A partner who contributes property encumbered by a liability is deemed to receive a cash distribution equal to the transferred debt.[26] If the deemed cash distribution exceeds the basis of his partnership interest, the partner recognizes gain.

(3) A partner who contributes property and receives a related distribution may be treated as if he sold, rather than contributed, the property to the partnership.[27]

(4) A partner recognizes gain if he contributes property to an investment company partnership.[28]

(5) Special rules apply to prevent a contribution from changing the character of income inherent in contributed property. Any unrealized receivables, inventory, or capital loss property contributed to a partnership retain the same character in the partnership that they had in the hands of the contributing partner.[29] Thus, a partnership recognizes ordinary income or loss on a disposition of contributed receivables or inventory. The partnership recognizes a capital loss if it sells or exchanges property that was contributed with a built-in capital loss within five years of the contribution.

[E]   Basis of Interest in Partnership or LLC

Each partner has a basis in his partnership interest that is separate from the partnership's basis in its assets.[30] In this respect, a partnership interest is treated as an interest in a separate entity comparable to stock in a corporation. A partner must know the basis for his interest for a number of tax purposes, including:

(1) computing his gain or loss when he sells the interest;

(2) computing his gain or loss on a distribution from the partnership;

(3) determining his basis in property distributed by the partnership; and

(4) determining the maximum amount of partnership losses he may deduct.

A partner's initial basis for his interest depends on how he acquires it. The basis of an interest acquired in exchange for a capital contribution is the contributed cash plus the partner's basis in any contributed property.[31] The basis of an interest acquired from another partner by purchase, gift, or inheritance is determined under the general basis rules of the Code.[32]

---

[26] I.R.C. § 752(b).

[27] I.R.C. § 707(a).

[28] I.R.C. § 721(b).

[29] I.R.C. § 724.

[30] I.R.C. § 705.

[31] I.R.C. §§ 722, 723.

[32] I.R.C. §§ 742, 1011–1023.

Each partner is deemed (1) to make a cash contribution to the partnership that is equal to any increase in his share of partnership liabilities, and (2) to receive a cash distribution that is equal to any decrease in his share of liabilities.[33] Thus, when partnership liabilities change, the bases of the partners' interests also change. Each partner's basis also changes continually to reflect his share of partnership income and loss and any distributions he receives or additional contributions he makes.[34]

[F]   Owner-Entity Transactions

The tax treatment of a transaction between a partnership and one of its partners depends on the capacity in which the partner acted. A transaction between a partnership and a partner who does not act in a partner capacity generally is taxable as if it occurred between unrelated parties.[35] For example, a partnership may deduct payments it makes to a partner for services unrelated to his partner status, and the partner reports the payments as compensation. In determining the amount, timing, and character of the deduction and the income, both the partnership and the partner use their own tax accounting method and their own tax year. To prevent abusive arrangements, an allocation and related distribution by a partnership to a partner may be recharacterized by the Service as a payment to a nonpartner.[36]

Payments by a partnership for services or capital a partner provides in a partner capacity are guaranteed payments if the amount is not measured as a percentage of partnership income.[37] Guaranteed payments are deductible from partnership ordinary income or are capitalized, depending on the nature of the service or expense.[38] For example, a partnership may deduct guaranteed payments for a partner's services in managing partnership operations but must capitalize guaranteed payments for brokerage services related to acquiring partnership assets. Guaranteed payments are ordinary income for the partners and are recognized in the year the partnership deducts or capitalizes them.[39] A payment to a partner for services or capital that is measured as a percentage of partnership income is included in the partner's distributive share.

Special anti-abuse rules apply to transactions between partnerships and their controlling partners and between partnerships under common control.[40] No loss may be recognized on a sale or exchange of property between (1) a partnership and a partner who directly or indirectly owns more than 50 percent of the partnership's capital or profits, or (2) between two parties in which the same parties directly or

---

[33] I.R.C. § 752.

[34] I.R.C. § 705.

[35] I.R.C. § 707(a).

[36] I.R.C. § 707(a)(2)(A), (B).

[37] I.R.C. § 707(c).

[38] *Id.*

[39] *Id.*

[40] I.R.C. §§ 707(b), 267.

indirectly own more than 50 percent of the capital or profits.[41] A similar rule denies capital gain treatment on a sale or exchange of property that is not a capital asset in the hands of the purchaser.[42]

[G] Distributions to Partners or Members

A partner generally may receive distributions of partnership property without recognizing gain or loss. The distribution is treated as a nontaxable withdrawal of the partner's invested capital up to the basis of his partnership interest.[43] This rule applies to distributions that liquidate a partner's entire partnership interest and to current distributions (*i.e.*, nonliquidating distributions).

A partner recognizes gain on a current or liquidating distribution, however, to the extent that the amount of cash he receives exceeds the basis in his partnership interest.[44] A partner cannot recognize a loss on a current distribution,[45] but he may recognize a loss on a liquidating distribution that consists solely of cash, unrealized receivables, and inventory.[46] The loss is the difference between the partner's basis for his interest and the sum of the distributed cash plus the partnership's basis in the distributed inventory and receivables. Any recognized gain or loss is treated as if it was realized on a sale of a partnership interest, and it ordinarily results in a capital gain or loss.[47]

A partner generally does not recognize gain or loss when he receives a current or liquidating distribution of property other than cash. If the distribution is current, the partner takes the property with the same basis that it had in the partnership, but the amount is limited to the basis in his partnership interest at the time of distribution less any cash distributed to him at that time.[48] If the distribution is liquidating, the total basis of all the property the partner receives equals the basis in his partnership interest less any cash distributed to him at that time.[49] Specific rules apply in allocating that basis over the distributed assets.[50] Gain a partner recognizes on a subsequent disposition of distributed unrealized receivables must be reported as ordinary income.[51] A disposition of distributed inventory within five years of the distribution also generates ordinary income.[52]

Special rules are provided to prevent distributions from being used to shift capital gain and ordinary income among partners. Under I.R.C. Section 751(b), a

---

[41] I.R.C. § 707(b).

[42] *Id.*

[43] I.R.C. § 731.

[44] I.R.C. § 731(a).

[45] I.R.C. § 731(a), (b).

[46] I.R.C. § 731(a)(2).

[47] I.R.C. § 741.

[48] I.R.C. § 732(a).

[49] I.R.C. § 732(b).

[50] I.R.C. § 732(c).

[51] I.R.C. § 735(a).

[52] I.R.C. § 735(b).

distributee partner or the partnership may recognize gain or loss on a distribution that changes any partner's proportionate interests in certain ordinary income property (*e.g.*, I.R.C. Section 751 property). These transfers are treated as if the distributee partner exchanged a portion of his interest in the I.R.C. Section 751 property for an increased share of other partnership assets or vice versa.[53] The partner or partnership can recognize gain or loss on this hypothetical exchange.

[H]   Payments to Retiree or Deceased Owner's Estate

Payments a partnership makes to completely liquidate the interest of a retiring or deceased partner are subject to special rules that allow the partnership a great deal of flexibility in planning for a partner's withdrawal.[54] The liquidating payments are divided into two classes: (1) amounts deemed to be for the partner's interest in partnership property,[55] and (2) other payments that represent the partner's distributive share of partnership income or guaranteed payments.[56] Payments to a partner for his share of partnership property are taxable under the rules applicable to distributions. For certain partnerships, these payments do not include amounts paid for a partner's share of goodwill unless specifically required by the partnership agreement, nor any amounts paid for his share of unrealized receivables.[57] Other liquidating payments are included in the partner's distributive share of partnership income to the extent that they are computed as a percentage of partnership income.[58] These payments cannot be deducted by the partnership. The timing for recognition and the character of the income the partner reports is determined at the partnership level. Amounts computed without regard to partnership income are treated as guaranteed payments.[59] These amounts may be deducted by the partnership and reported by the partner as ordinary income.

[I]   Sale or Exchange of Partnership or LLC Interest

A partner who sells or exchanges his partnership interest generally is deemed to transfer a discrete asset rather than his share of each item of partnership property. A partnership interest ordinarily is a capital asset; therefore, a partner realizes capital gain or loss on its sale.[60] I. R.C. Section 751, however, provides rules designed to prevent conversion of the selling partner's share of the partnership's unrealized ordinary income into capital gain. Under I.R.C. Section 751, a sale of a partnership interest is divided into two parts:

(1)   the seller recognizes ordinary income or loss on the portion of the sale attributable to his share of the partnership's unrealized receivables and

---

[53] *See* Treas. Reg. § 1.751-1(b).

[54] I.R.C. § 736.

[55] I.R.C. § 736(b).

[56] I.R.C. § 736(a).

[57] I.R.C. § 736(b)(2).

[58] I.R.C. § 736(a)(1).

[59] I.R.C. § 736(a)(2).

[60] I.R.C. § 741.

substantially appreciated inventory (*i.e.*, I.R.C. Section 751 property);[61] and

(2)   the seller recognizes capital gain or loss on the portion of the sale attributable to his share of all other partnership property.[62]

[J]   Adjustments to Basis of Partnership or LLC Assets

A partner's basis for a partnership interest acquired by sale or exchange is its cost. A partner's basis for a partnership interest acquired by inheritance is the interest's value on the date of death. Because these transfers do not affect the partnership's basis for its assets,[63] a disparity arises between the new partner's basis for his interest and his share of the basis of the partnership's property. To eliminate this disparity, the partnership may elect under I.R.C. Section 754 to adjust the basis of the new partner's share of partnership property to reflect its value when acquired.[64]

Disparities between the partners' bases for their partnership interests and the basis of partnership property also may arise as a result of certain distributions (*e.g.*, if a partner recognizes gain or loss on a distribution or if the distribution causes a change in the basis of distributed property). The same I.R.C. Section 754 basis adjustment election applicable to transfers of partnership interests applies to eliminate disparities caused by distributions.[65]

Once an I.R.C. Section 754 election is made, it cannot be revoked without the Service's consent. Any subsequent transfer or distribution may trigger a basis adjustment, whether or not the partner or partnership desires it.

[K]   Termination of a Partnership or LLC

A partnership may terminate for tax purposes even though it continues under state law. A termination occurs when (1) a partnership ceases conducting its operations in a partnership form, or (2) 50 percent or more of the interests in partnership capital and profits are sold or exchanged within a 12-month period.[66] When a partnership terminates because it ceases operations, its tax year closes and a liquidating distribution of all its assets is deemed to occur.[67] A partnership that terminates under the sale or exchange rule is deemed to contribute all its assets to a new partnership and then make a liquidating distribution of its interests in the new partnership.[68] If two or more partnerships merge or consolidate, the partnership whose members own a majority of the new entity's capital and profits

---

[61] I.R.C. § 751.

[62] I.R.C. § 741.

[63] I.R.C. §§ 743(a), 734(a).

[64] I.R.C. §§ 754, 743(b).

[65] I.R.C. § 734(b).

[66] I.R.C. § 708(b).

[67] I.R.C. § 706(c).

[68] Treas. Reg. § 1.708-1(b)(1)(iv).

continues; all other partnerships terminate.[69] A similar rule applies in determining whether a divided partnership continues or terminates for tax purposes.[70]

§ 1.02 DETERMINING THE FORM OF BUSINESS TO ADOPT

[A] Prevalent Business Forms

Determining whether a partnership or LLC is the appropriate business form for a jointly owned endeavor requires careful consideration of a number of tax and nontax factors. This decision usually is made by comparing the relative advantages and disadvantages of conducting the venture as a partnership or LLC with the consequences of operating it as a regular corporation or as an S corporation.[71] A business or property that is jointly owned also may be organized as a co-ownership, a trust, a real estate investment trust (REIT), or a real estate mortgage investment company (REMIC).

[1] C Corporation

A corporation is established when its owners file articles of incorporation in accordance with state law. Generally, corporations are taxable under Subchapter C of the Internal Revenue Code, and thus often are referred to as "C" corporations.[72] Most of the rules governing corporate management, capital structure, and shareholder rights are codified in extensive and well-understood state laws. The most significant nontax aspect of a corporation is that its owners ordinarily are not personally liable for corporate debts. This feature makes the corporate format attractive to parties who wish to limit their potential losses to the capital that they invest in the venture.

The most important tax aspect of a C corporation is that its income and gains are subject to two levels of taxation (1) when the income and gains are earned by the corporation and (2) when a distribution is made to corporate shareholders. Corporate losses are deductible only against corporate income and do not pass through to the shareholders.

[2] S Corporation

An S corporation is an incorporated entity whose shareholders elect to have the venture taxed under Subchapter S of the Internal Revenue Code instead of under Subchapter C. Many corporations are not eligible for this election because the number and the kind of shareholders that S corporations may have is significantly limited. An eligible corporation can elect Subchapter S treatment at its inception, or

---

[69] I.R.C. § 708(b)(2)(A).

[70] I.R.C. § 708(b)(2)(B).

[71] *See, e.g.*, Holbrook-Lawrence, *Choice of Entity for Holding and Operating Real Estate: A Comparison of S Corporations and Partnerships*, 26 J. Real Est. Tax n 22 (Fall 1998).

[72] Certain publicly traded partnerships also are taxable under Subchapter C and an unincorporated business entity may elect that tax treatment.

it may operate as a C corporation and convert to an S corporation later. Similarly, a corporation that operates under Subchapter S may terminate its election and convert to a C corporation.

For nontax purposes, S and C corporations are treated in the same manner and are subject to the same state laws. Thus, shareholders of S corporations are not personally liable for corporate obligations. A significant difference between S and C corporations is that an S corporation is limited to one class of stock,[73] whereas a C corporation may issue various stock classes.

The main tax effect of a Subchapter S election is that the corporation's income, deductions, gains, and losses generally are not subject to taxation at the corporate level. Instead, these tax items pass through to the shareholders, who report their shares of each corporate item on their personal tax returns. A corporate level tax may be imposed, however, on certain income of S corporations that formerly operated as C corporations.

In many respects, shareholders of S corporations are taxable in the same manner as the partners of a partnership. As discussed below, however, a number of important differences between partnership and S corporation taxation exist.

[3] Partnership

Unincorporated ventures with multiple owners typically are considered partnerships for state law and tax purposes. Most partnerships are general partnerships, meaning that each partner is an agent for the venture whose actions may bind the other partners.[74] Every general partner is personally liable for all partnership obligations; a general partner's personal assets are potentially at risk if the venture is unsuccessful.[75] Partners may organize and operate their partnership informally pursuant to an unwritten understanding, or they may formalize their arrangement through a written partnership agreement.

General partnerships are taxable under Subchapter K of the Internal Revenue Code. The main tax feature of a partnership is that no tax is imposed at the partnership level. Instead, each partner reports his share of each item of the partnership's gain, loss, income, deduction, or credit on his personal tax return. Joint ventures engaged in specific types of activities may elect to be excluded from the tax rules of Subchapter K; these ventures are treated as co-ownerships.[76] Certain publicly traded partnerships are excluded from Subchapter K and are taxable as C corporations.[77]

---

[73] I.R.C. § 1361.

[74] U.P.A. §§ 13, 14.

[75] U.P.A. § 15.

[76] I.R.C. § 761(a).

[77] I.R.C. § 7704.

[4] Limited Partnership

A second kind of partnership is a limited partnership, which is formed by executing and filing a written instrument in accordance with state statutes.[78] A limited partnership must have at least one general partner that bears personal liability for partnership obligations.[79] The limited partner's status is similar to that of a corporate shareholder: limited partners cannot directly manage partnership business affairs; they cannot bind the partnership; and their liability for partnership obligations is limited to the capital they have invested. Limited partnerships are taxable under Subchapter K in the same manner as general partnerships.

[5] Limited Liability Partnership

Many states have enacted statutes that permit a general partnership to register as a limited liability partnership (LLP) or registered limited liability partnership (RLLP).[80] Members of a partnership that registers as an LLP or RLLP are not personally liable for certain kinds of partnership debts. Although the scope of liability protection differs considerably from state to state, most LLP statutes shield partners from personal liability for (1) the negligence, malpractice, malfeasance, and wrongdoing of other partners or of persons under other partners' supervision and control, and (2) indirect liability to other partners through contribution, indemnification, or assessment. Some states extend liability protection to other partnership debts and obligations. Partners continue to be personally liable, however, for their own negligence or misconduct and for wrongful conduct or negligence of persons under their direct supervision or control.

[6] Limited Liability Company

All states have enacted statutes that permit the formation of a business entity called a Limited Liability Company (LLC). The LLC combines the limited liability of a corporation with the flexibility and tax advantages of a partnership. If the LLC is properly formed and operated under state law, its members are not personally liable for the entity's debts and obligations. An LLC that has at least two members is classified as a partnership for federal tax purposes unless the members elect to be taxed as a corporation. An LLC's income, gain, loss and deduction flow through to its members who report their distributive shares of these items in the same manner as partners of a partnership.

Generally, a member's rights concerning matters such as the LLC's governance, operations, transfer of interests, income, distributions, and liquidation are set forth in an operating agreement that is similar to a partnership agreement. The members of an LLC may manage the business directly or they may delegate some or all managerial functions to other members or to hired managers. Unlike a limited partnership, an LLC member who participates in management does not forfeit limited liability under state law.

---

[78] *See* U.L.P.A. § 2; R.U.L.P.A. § 201.

[79] U.L.P.A. § 1; R.U.L.P.A. § 101.

[80] See, for example, the Illinois LLP statute in 805 ILCS 205/8.1–205/15. *See also* Rev. Rul. 95-55, 1995-2 C.B. 313 (New York general partnership registered as RLLP).

[7] Co-ownership

In a co-ownership, each co-owner is deemed to own an undivided portion of the mutually held property. One co-owner is not an agent for other co-owners and cannot bind or create obligations for them. An arrangement is considered a co-ownership if it involves the passive holding of property and if the owners do not engage in any significant business activities. If the owners actively participate in operating the property, their arrangement is likely to be considered a partnership for state law and tax purposes.

A co-ownership arrangement can have markedly different tax consequences than a partnership. For example, most tax elections in a partnership are made at the partnership level and bind all of the partners.[81] These elections include the use of installment-method reporting, selection of the partnership's tax accounting method, and the election of nonrecognition on like-kind exchanges. In contrast, each co-owner is free to make his own elections on the tax treatment of various items, which may result in each of the co-owners using a different method. Unlike a partnership, co-owners share most tax items in proportion to their interests in the property; they cannot contractually allocate various income and loss items among themselves.

[B] Factors to Consider in Choosing Business Form

In choosing the appropriate form for a business venture, investors must consider a number of nontax factors relating to its organization and operation. In some situations, these nontax objectives mandate the kind of entity that must be used. Frequently, more than one kind of entity can be used to meet the investors' goals. For example, an enterprise that requires limited liability can be structured as a C corporation, an S corporation, a limited liability company, a registered limited liability partnership or a limited partnership with a corporate general partner. When more than one form of organization meets the investors' goals, tax considerations become paramount in determining the choice of entity.

[1] Nontax Factors

[a] Limited Liability

Business owners often wish to protect their personal assets from business creditors' claims. Typically, this goal is attained by organizing the venture under a state law that limits the owners' liability to the amount of capital they have invested in the entity. The broadest form of statutory limited liability from all creditors is afforded to shareholders of a corporation (taxable under either Subchapter C or S) and to members of a limited liability company (LLC).[82] Many states have enacted statutes permitting a general partnership to register with a designated state office as a limited liability partnership (LLP). Although the scope of liability protection

---

[81] I.R.C. § 703(b).

[82] An LLC formed under one state's laws may not have limited liability for operations in another state unless it takes all necessary steps to qualify for doing business in that jurisdiction.

varies from state to state, partners of a registered LLP typically are not liable for debts arising from torts but remain liable for other partnership obligations.

In some business situations, complete limited liability is not possible. Although many states permit professionals to operate their practices as a corporation, LLC or LLP, the professionals generally remain personally liable for their own malpractice and for the acts of persons under their direct control. These entities can, however, provide liability protection against the malpractice of other professionals and against debts to general creditors. Owners of a closely held business often cannot insulate themselves from business debts because creditors demand personal guarantees for their obligations.

In many situations, investors can insulate their personal assets from business debts by operating as a limited partnership. In a partnership, all partners other than limited partners are jointly liable for partnership obligations and are jointly and severally liable for obligations that arise from another partner's wrongful act or breach of trust.[83] Under state law, limited partners are not liable for partnership obligations that exceed their capital contributions. This protection against personal liability is not available to limited partners who participate in managing the partnership's business affairs.[84] A limited partnership must have at least one general partner whose individual assets may be reached by partnership creditors. Many ventures reduce the total amount of nonbusiness assets at risk in the enterprise by having a corporation act as the general partner. This arrangement limits the total liability of all investors to the amount of capital invested in the partnership and the capital owned by the corporate general partner.

[b]   Management and Control Arrangements

Business owners should consider how each business form affects the way they may operate and control their enterprise. Corporations are centrally managed by a board of directors that acts in a representative capacity for the shareholders who elect them.[85] Thus, shareholders generally lack direct, immediate control over corporate operations and managerial decisions. Shareholders of closely held corporations, however, can directly control corporate operations by serving as directors and officers.

General partnerships usually allow more flexibility than corporations in structuring management and control arrangements because partners can specify each party's managerial role through appropriate provisions in the partnership agreement. The agreement may grant any partner or group of partners control over all business affairs, or it may limit their discretion to particular kinds of decisions. For example, the partnership agreement can ensure a dominant role for minority partners by giving them control over certain key business decisions. In contrast, a similar corporate arrangement for minority shareholders would require complex voting agreements or voting trusts.

---

[83] U.P.A. §§ 13, 14, 15.

[84] U.P.A. § 7; R.U.L.P.A. § 303(a).

[85] *See, e.g.*, Model Business Corporation Act § 35.

The control and management of a limited partnership is closer to the corporate structure than that of a general partnership because the general partners provide central management for the limited partners. Management by general partners is required because if a limited partner participates directly in partnership business affairs, he becomes personally liable for partnership obligations.[86] Limited partners may vote on, and thereby control, however, a number of important partnership business activities without losing their limited liability status.[87] For example, limited partners may consult and advise the general partners about the partnership's business and may propose, approve, or disapprove of actions, such as making changes in the nature of the partnership's business and incurring debts outside the ordinary course of partnership business.[88] Unlike limited partners, all members of an LLC may participate directly in management without losing their limited liability protection. The governance of a member-managed LLC is similar to a general partnership. Alternatively, the LLC operating agreement may require governance by hired managers who are not members. Governance of a hired-manager LLC is similar to a corporation and members exercise indirect control through their selection of the outside managers.

PRACTICE NOTE:

An LLC may be *member-managed* or *manager-managed*. Ordinarily, an LLC is member-managed if it operates in a manner similar to a partnership, with active participation of its members. By contrast, large, complex LLCs that operate like a corporation usually are manager-managed.

The management method and rights, duties and powers of members and managers should be clearly stated in the LLC Operating Agreement. In drafting the agreement, the following issues should be considered:

- In a manager-managed LLC, the manager's authority and responsibilities can be set forth in the operating agreement, subject to amendment through a process set forth in bylaws governing management. The operating agreement should state that its provisions control if the bylaws conflict with the operating agreement.

- An LLC having more than one manager should clearly define the authority of each manager and the decision-making procedure for important LLC actions.

- The operating agreement of a manager-managed LLC should clearly state that non-manager members lack authority to bind the LLC.

---

[86] *See* U.L.P.A. §§ 7, 9; R.U.L.P.A. §§ 303, 403.

[87] *See, e.g.*, R.U.L.P.A. § 303(b).

[88] *Id.*

- The operating agreement may provide that LLC operations will be directed by designated officers in the same fashion as a corporation. In that case, the agreement should describe the officers and their duties.

- The operating agreement should specify the extent to which managers, officers, or members may delegate responsibilities and authority.

- The standard of care for managers and members should be clearly defined in the operating agreement. This standard may vary with regard to each person's management role, level of responsibility, and compensation.

- The operating agreement should specify any indemnification officers, managers or members are entitled to for their actions on behalf of the LLC.

- The operating agreement should define voting rights and procedures and the vote levels required for each important LLC action.

[c] Capital Structure

Investors should consider how the capital structure of each business form affects the way they share its income, profits, capital, and losses. Partnerships and limited liability companies generally provide the most flexibility in allocating these items among business owners because partners and LLC members may contractually agree to share any item of partnership gain, loss, income, or expense to best meet the individual partners' financial and tax goals. For example, one partner may be given a greater share of the appreciation (and corresponding depreciation) of certain partnership assets, while another partner may obtain a larger share of the partnership's operating income or loss. The sharing arrangement the partners express in their partnership agreement ordinarily is respected under state law.[89] An allocation in the partnership agreement is respected for tax purposes if it has substantial economic effect; that is, it substantially affects the values of the partners' interests independent of tax consequences.[90]

Somewhat less flexibility is available in allocating the economic consequences of corporate activities among shareholders. A regular corporation can create different interests in its capital appreciation and operating income by issuing various classes of common stocks, preferred stocks, debt instruments, and hybrid securities. An S corporation is even more restrictive, because its capital structure is limited to one class of common stock, and no hybrid securities are permitted.[91]

---

[89] *See* U.P.A. § 18; U.L.P.A. § 14; R.U.L.P.A. § 503.

[90] I.R.C. § 704(b).

[91] I.R.C. § 1361.

[d]   Transferability of Interests

Owners of business or investment interests should consider how the choice of business form affects their ability to sell or otherwise transfer their interests. Partnership interests, other than limited partnership interests, ordinarily are not readily transferable because all general partners must consent to the transfer. This feature protects the continuing partners against unwanted new partners whose actions can bind the partnership. Although a partner may assign his right to receive his share of partnership profits and capital, the assignee does not become a partner with rights to participate in partnership management unless all of the other partners consent.[92]

Most constraints on transferability do not apply to limited partnership interests. Limited partners may freely assign their interests, and the assignee obtains the assignor's right to share in partnership profits.[93] Because limited partners do not participate in partnership management, an assignment of a limited partner's interest in partnership profits is equivalent to a sale of the interest. Also, the partnership agreement may allow an assignee to become a substitute limited partner, with rights to inspect partnership books and to vote on certain matters, without the consent of the other partners.[94]

Corporate stock theoretically is a more liquid form of investment than a partnership interest because shareholders may transfer their shares without anyone's consent, and the transferee obtains all the transferor's rights and interests. In a closely held corporation, however, a shareholder's right to transfer his shares is likely to be subject to substantial contractual or statutory restrictions.[95] These restrictions usually preclude stock transfers that affect control of corporate affairs; therefore, little difference exists between the liquidity of closely held corporate stock and partnership interests.

The limited liability company provides a great deal of flexibility in determining the transferability of members' interests. Generally, transfer rights are governed by the LLC operating agreement. The agreement can provide that a transferee of an interest automatically is admitted as a substitute member, or it may require the consent of some or all members for the transferee to be admitted. A member who cannot transfer his interest to a new member may freely assign it; the assignee obtains the assignor's right to share in profits but does not receive any other membership rights.

[e]   Death or Other Withdrawal of Owner

Investors should consider the consequences of any member's death, disability, or retirement. In a partnership, a partner's withdrawal causes a dissolution that negates every partner's authority to act as the partnership's agent except in

---

[92] U.P.A. § 27.

[93] U.L.P.A. § 19; R.U.L.P.A. §§ 702, 704.

[94] *Id.*

[95] *See, e.g.*, Delaware General Corporation Law § 347.

matters relating to the wind up of its affairs.[96] The dissolution generally protects the withdrawing partner, or his successor, from personal liability for future obligations incurred by the other partners.[97]

A dissolution does not terminate the partnership's business, however; the remaining partners may continue its operations.[98] The continuing partners' obligations to liquidate or to purchase the interest of a deceased or retiring partner are usually specified in a buy-sell agreement. The parties also may agree in advance that a deceased partner's successor may join the partnership in continuing its business.

The effect of a member's withdrawal from a limited liability company is similar to a partnership. Generally, a limited liability company dissolves under state law upon the death, retirement, resignation, expulsion, bankruptcy, or dissolution of a member or whenever a member's interest in the LLC terminates. However, most states permit the remaining members to elect to continue the LLC's business. If only one member remains, the LLC will no longer be taxable as a partnership unless a new member is admitted.

A corporation does not dissolve or terminate when a shareholder dies or otherwise withdraws. In a closely held corporation, however, the lack of a ready market for the corporation's stock often means that the practical effect of a shareholder's withdrawal is the same as a partner's withdrawal from a partnership. Thus, the corporation's business will terminate unless the other owners are willing and able to continue its operations. As in a partnership, the obligation of the continuing shareholders to liquidate or to purchase the stock of a deceased or retired shareholder may be specified in a buy-sell agreement.

A limited partnership does not dissolve or terminate when a limited partner withdraws. The partnership agreement typically specifies the time when a withdrawing limited partner is entitled to receive a distribution of the value of his interest. If the agreement is silent, the limited partner must receive a distribution of his capital after six months' notice to the other partners.[99] The partnership agreement may contain a provision allowing a limited partner to designate his estate or other successor as a substitute limited partner.[100] Withdrawal of less than all of the general partners does not dissolve a limited partnership if the remaining general partners are authorized to continue partnership business operations.[101]

---

[96] U.P.A. § 33.

[97] *But see* U.P.A. § 35 (partnership may be bound after dissolution with respect to certain third parties without notice of dissolution).

[98] U.P.A. § 38.

[99] U.L.P.A. § 16(2); R.U.L.P.A. § 603.

[100] U.L.P.A. § 2(1)(a); R.U.L.P.A. § 201(a)(7).

[101] U.L.P.A. § 20, R.U.L.P.A. § 801. The authority may be in the partnership agreement or may be provided by consent of all the members of the partnership.

[2]   Tax Factors

[a]   Tax Consequences of Capital Contributions

The tax treatment of cash contributions to corporations and partnerships[102] is similar. No gain or loss is recognized, and the contributor's basis for the stock or interest he receives equals the amount of cash he contributes.

If property is contributed, however, the tax consequences to corporations and partnerships can differ significantly. In a partnership, any gain or loss inherent in contributed property is deferred until the partnership sells the asset or the contributing partner sells his partnership interest. The contributing partner does not recognize gain or loss at the time of contribution, regardless of his percentage of ownership in the partnership.[103] The contributor's basis for the property carries over to the partnership,[104] and it also becomes the basis for the partnership interest he receives.[105] When the partnership sells the contributed property, the gain or loss that was not recognized at the time of contribution is recognized and allocated to the contributing partner.[106]

In contrast, a transfer of appreciated property to a regular or S corporation in exchange for stock is a taxable transaction unless the transferor, together with other parties making contributions at the same time, controls the corporation through ownership of at least 80 percent of its stock.[107] If the transfer satisfies this control requirement, no gain or loss is recognized, the contributing shareholder's basis for the property carries over to the corporation, and it becomes the basis for the stock he receives.[108] In a C corporation, the corporation is taxable on any gain or loss when it disposes of the contributed property, and there are no current tax consequences to the shareholders. In an S Corporation, gain or loss that the corporation recognizes when it disposes of the property passes through to the shareholders in proportion to their stock ownership.[109] Unlike what happens in a partnership, the gain or loss is not allocated to the contributing shareholder.

[b]   Ownership Restrictions

An entity, including a limited liability company, may be a partnership for tax purposes regardless of the nature or the number of its partners or the kind of activities in which it engages. Thus, its partners or members may consist of any

---

[102] It is important to keep in mind that all tax rules applicable to partnerships and partners apply equally to limited liability companies and their members.

[103] I.R.C. § 721.

[104] I.R.C. § 723.

[105] I.R.C. § 722.

[106] I.R.C. § 704(c)(1)(A). The contributing partner also recognizes gain or loss if the partnership distributes the contributed property to another partner within five years of the contribution date. I.R.C. § 704(c)(1)(B).

[107] I.R.C. § 351.

[108] I.R.C. §§ 358, 362.

[109] I.R.C. § 1366.

number of domestic or foreign individuals, corporations, trusts, estates, tax-exempt organizations, or other partnerships. Generally, an unincorporated business entity with more than one owner is taxed as a partnership unless it elects to be treated as a corporation (see classification rules in Chapter 2). Certain joint ventures involving passive property ownership or natural resource extraction, however, may elect to be excluded from the Subchapter K rules and treated as co-ownerships.[110]

As is the case in a partnership, no restrictions are imposed on the nature and number of shareholders of C corporations; these corporations may engage in any kind of activity their charters permit. Taxation under Subchapter C is not elective for any entity that is incorporated under local law, but certain unincorporated entities may elect to be treated as a corporation. (*See* Chapter 2). Eligible corporations may be excluded from the rules of Subchapter C by electing to be taxed under Subchapter S.

Subchapter S corporations are subject to important limitations on the number and the kind of shareholders they may have. No more than 100 shareholders are permitted, and all shareholders must be individuals who are U.S. citizens or residents, estates, or certain kinds of trusts.[111] Thus, S corporations exclude an important segment of potential investors, including venture capital firms, ESOPS, and foreign nationals. Although a C corporation cannot own S corporation stock, an S corporation is permitted to have wholly-owned C corporation subsidiaries.[112] An election to be taxable under Subchapter S requires the unanimous consent of the corporation's shareholders.[113]

[c]   Taxability of Income and Loss

For tax purposes, a partnership or LLC is not a separate tax-paying entity.[114] Each partner or member is separately and individually taxable on his share of partnership or LLC profits, losses, deductions, and credits.[115] Each partner or member reports his share of each tax item, and each item retains the same character it had when earned or incurred by the partnership or LLC.[116] The pass-through of items to partners and LLC members means that income avoids the double tax imposed on corporate income and that losses may offset income the partner or member has from other sources.

In contrast, a C corporation is a separate, tax-paying entity. Thus, its income and profits are taxed at the corporate level when earned, and these amounts are subject to a second tax when distributed to shareholders as dividends. Dividends

---

[110] I.R.C. § 761.

[111] Changes to the S Corporation eligibility rules enacted in 2004 increased the total number of allowable shareholders from 75 to 100 and permit certain family members to elect to be treated as one shareholder. I.R.C. § 1361(c)(1); 1361(b)(1)(A).

[112] I.R.C. § 1361(b)(2).

[113] I.R.C. § 1362.

[114] I.R.C. § 701.

[115] I.R.C. §§ 701, 702.

[116] I.R.C. § 702(b).

always are taxable as ordinary income, regardless of the source of the earnings at the corporate level.[117]

The taxation of S corporations is similar to the treatment of partnerships. An S corporation is not a taxable entity; it serves as a conduit through which its income and losses pass through to shareholders.[118] Each shareholder reports his share of each tax item on his tax return, and these items retain the same character they had when they were earned or incurred by the S corporation.[119] Although a partnership is never treated as a taxable entity, an S Corporation may be taxable if it once operated as a C corporation. Corporate-level taxation may result if excessive passive-type income is generated by corporate assets[120] or if the corporation disposes of assets that had built-in gain when the S election occurred.[121]

[d]   Allocations of Income or Loss Items

The partnership and LLC provide the most flexibility for allocating income, losses, deductions, and credits among the partners or members in accordance with their individual investment and tax goals. The owners may establish their shares of each partnership or LLC item through appropriate provisions in their partnership or operating agreement.[122] An allocation set forth in the agreement is respected for tax purposes unless tests contained in the regulations determine that it lacks substantial economic effect.[123] Because a carefully drafted agreement ordinarily satisfies these tests, most allocations of partnership or LLC tax items are valid.

Investors in a C corporation can create some flexibility for allocating income and capital appreciation among themselves by issuing different classes of common and preferred stock and sophisticated debt instruments.

Little flexibility is available to S corporations. Unlike C corporations, S corporations are permitted only one class of common stock. Although voting rights may differ, preferred stock cannot be used to create different interests in corporate capital and income. Some differences in the cash flow allocated among S corporation shareholders can be effected if a portion of their capital is provided as loans rather than as capital contributions. Because the use of sophisticated hybrid securities may be characterized as a prohibited second class of stock, their use is precluded.

---

[117] I.R.C. § 301.

[118] I.R.C. § 1366.

[119] *Id.*

[120] I.R.C. § 1375.

[121] I.R.C. § 1374.

[122] I.R.C. § 704(a).

[123] I.R.C. § 704(b); Treas. Reg. § 1.704-1(b).

[e]   Basis Limitation on Deductibility of Losses

Taxpayers who wish to use losses from a business or investment activity to offset their income from other sources must structure the venture to be taxable as a partnership (which includes an LLC) or S corporation. A partner generally may deduct his share of losses up to the basis of his partnership interest and an S corporation shareholder may deduct losses up to the basis for his stock. In contrast, losses of a C corporation do not pass through to the shareholders; they must be carried back or carried over to offset future corporate income.

For ventures that use significant amounts of borrowed funds, a partnership or LLC is the preferred organization form because the basis of a partner's interest increases by his share of the partnership's liabilities.[124] Each partner is treated as if he personally borrowed his share of the partnership's obligations and contributed that amount of cash to the partnership, even if the partnership debt is nonrecourse (*i.e.*, no partner is personally liable for repayment of the debt). The resulting basis increase enables partners to deduct losses attributable to funds the partnership borrows.

In contrast, a shareholder's basis for stock in an S corporation does not include corporate liabilities, other than loans the shareholder makes directly to the corporation;[125] therefore, corporate obligations to third parties do not increase a shareholder's basis. A shareholder can increase the basis of his stock by borrowing funds personally and lending or contributing the proceeds to the corporation. When the loan must be directly secured by corporate assets, however, this transaction is not possible in practice. Highly leveraged ventures usually are organized as limited partnerships or LLCs because partners can deduct significantly greater losses than S corporation shareholders who make the same out-of-pocket investment.

[f]   Loss Limitations Under the At-Risk and Passive Activity Rules

Tax provisions outside of Subchapters K and S may bar certain deductions even if a partner, LLC member or shareholder has sufficient basis in his partnership interest or stock. Losses may be restricted under I.R.C. Section 465 to the extent that they are attributable to nonrecourse liabilities. I.R.C. Section 465 limits a taxpayer's deductions for losses from an activity to the amount he has at risk in the activity at the end of the tax year (*i.e.*, his capital contribution plus liabilities for which he bears personal liability). This limitation does not apply to qualified

---

[124] I.R.C. §§ 752, 722.

[125] I.R.C. § 1366(d). *See* Uri v. Comm'r, 949 F.2d 371 (10th Cir. 1991) (shareholders who personally guarantee S corporation loan cannot increase basis in stock by pro rata amount of guarantee); Estate of Leavitt v. Comm'r, 90 T.C. 206 (1988), *aff'd*, 875 F.2d 420 (4th Cir.), *cert. denied*, 493 U.S. 958 (1989); Brown v. Comm'r, 706 F.2d 755, 756 (6th Cir. 1983); Goatcher v. U.S., 944 F.2d 747 (10th Cir. 1991); Harris v. U.S., 902 F.2d 439 (5th Cir. 1990). *But see* Selfe v. U.S., 778 F.2d 769 (11th Cir. 1985) (pro-rata inclusion of personal loan guarantees in shareholder's stock basis allowed where lender looked primarily to shareholder for repayment).

nonrecourse financing used in real estate activities. The at-risk rules apply to certain closely held C corporations.[126]

Under I.R.C. Section 469, certain taxpayers cannot deduct losses incurred in passive activities that exceed their income from other passive activities. Taxpayers subject to these limitations include individuals, estates, trusts, closely held C corporations, and personal service corporations.[127] An activity is passive for these taxpayers if it is a trade or business in which they do not materially participate.

The passive loss rules are applied to partners, LLC members and S corporation shareholders in a similar manner. Based on his participation in each partnership or corporate activity, each partner or shareholder separately determines if his income or loss from the activity is passive. With important exceptions, a limited partner's share of all partnership income or loss is passive.[128] The passive loss rules apply only in a modified form to closely held C corporations. (A C corporation is closely held if, at any time during the last half of its taxable year, five or fewer individuals directly or indirectly owned more than 50 percent of the value of its stock.)[129] Closely held corporations may not use passive losses and credits to offset portfolio income but may use them to offset income from an active business.

The passive loss limitations fully apply to personal service corporations. A C corporation is a personal service corporation if (1) its principal activity is performing personal services that employee-owners substantially performed,[130] and (2) all of the employee-owners together own more than 10 percent of the value of the corporation's stock.[131]

[g]   Distributions

A liquidating or nonliquidating distribution from a partnership to a partner generally is treated as a nontaxable return of the partner's capital. The partner recognizes no gain until he receives cash exceeding the basis of his partnership interest.[132] The partner recognizes no gain on noncash property distributions. The partner defers any gain not recognized when the distribution occurs and recognizes it when he subsequently disposes of the distributed property.[133] A partner may recognize a loss on a liquidating distribution if the only property he receives consists of cash, unrealized receivables, or inventory.[134] These rules also apply to limited liability companies.

Like partnership distributions, cash distributions from an S corporation

---

[126]   I.R.C. § 465(a).

[127]   I.R.C. § 469(a)(2). Personal service corporations are defined under I.R.C. § 469(j)(2).

[128]   I.R.C. § 469(e)(1).

[129]   Treas. Reg. § 1.469-1T(g)(2)(i).

[130]   I.R.C. § 469(j)(2), citing to I.R.C. § 269A(b)(2).

[131]   I.R.C. § 469(j)(2)(B).

[132]   I.R.C. § 731(a)(1).

[133]   Gain or loss may be recognized under I.R.C. § 751(b), however, if the distribution changes a partner's share of certain partnership ordinary income property.

[134]   I.R.C. § 731(a)(2).

generally are considered a nontaxable return of capital up to the shareholder's basis for his stock; the excess is considered capital gain.[135] An S corporation's property distributions, however, are treated quite differently than a partnership's property distributions. The S corporation is deemed to sell the distributed property to the shareholder, and the corporation recognizes any gain or loss inherent in the property when the distribution occurs.[136] That gain passes through to the shareholders and is taxable to them in the year the distribution occurs.[137]

Cash distributions from C corporations are taxable to the shareholders as dividends to the extent of the corporation's earnings and profits.[138] Therefore, corporate earnings are subject to double taxation: (1) they are taxable for the corporation when earned, and (2) they are taxable for the shareholder when distributed. A similar double tax is imposed when a C corporation distributes appreciated property; the transaction is treated as if the corporation sold the property for its value and distributed the cash proceeds to the shareholder.[139]

---

[135] I.R.C. § 1368(b). Certain cash distributions may be taxable, however, if attributable to earnings and profits accumulated under Subchapter C before the corporation elected to be taxed under Subchapter S. I.R.C. § 1368(e).

[136] I.R.C. §§ 311, 1371(a).

[137] I.R.C. § 1366. However, gain "built-in" to corporate assets when it converts from a C to an S corporation is taxable at the corporate level. I.R.C. § 1374.

[138] I.R.C. § 301.

[139] I.R.C. §§ 311, 312.

Chapter 2

TAX CLASSIFICATION OF ECONOMIC RELATIONSHIPS

§ 2.01 OVERVIEW OF TAX CLASSIFICATION ISSUES

The tax consequences of a joint economic relationship depend on whether the relationship is classified for tax purposes as a partnership or as some other arrangement, such as a corporation, sole proprietorship, trust, or co-ownership. Ventures classified as partnerships are governed by the complex rules of Subchapter K, while other joint endeavors are taxed under other rules, based on the enterprise's classification. The classification of an economic relationship is determined under federal tax rules and not under state or local law.

The significance of classification is illustrated by assuming that two persons jointly own income-producing property. If the arrangement between the parties is a partnership, the character and timing of each partner's income or loss is determined at the partnership level and the partnership makes most tax elections affecting the property. In contrast, if the two parties hold the property as co-tenants, each party separately determines the time and character of his income, and each party is free to make his own elections for the co-owned property.

This chapter describes the criteria for determining whether a joint economic relationship is a partnership for tax purposes. The discussion focuses on the following areas:

The current classification regulations. Classification regulations that became effective on January 1, 1997, provide rules for determining whether an economic venture is taxable as a partnership or corporation. Certain domestic and foreign entities are automatically classified as corporations. An unincorporated business entity (*i.e.*, an entity that is not a trust), such as a partnership or limited liability company, may choose to be taxed either as a partnership or as a corporation. Special treatment applies to single-member entities. These rules are described in § 2.02, *infra*.

Cases and rulings on whether an entity exists. Under the regulations, the first step in the classification process is to determine if the venture is an "entity" for federal tax purposes. The regulations provide little guidance as to what constitutes an "entity" other than to state that the determination is made under federal tax law rather than state or local law. Presumably, whether an entity exists is decided under principles similar to those applied in pre-1997 federal tax cases and rulings on whether a joint economic arrangement created a partnership. These rules are described in § 2.03, *infra*.

Publicly traded partnerships. The classification regulations do not apply to entities that are subject to classification under specific provisions of the Internal Revenue Code. Under the publicly traded partnership rules of I.R.C. Section 7704, a partnership is treated as a corporation for tax purposes if its interests are readily tradable on securities markets. A partnership is exempt from this treatment if it derives substantially all of its income from certain qualifying passive investment sources or if it was in existence before the effective date of I.R.C. Section 7704. The rules for determining if a partnership is publicly traded and for determining if it is exempt from corporate taxation are described in § 2.04, *infra*.

The anti-abuse rule. The regulations establish an "anti-abuse" rule designed to prevent taxpayers from using Subchapter K for tax avoidance. If a partnership transaction violates the anti-abuse rule, the Service can:

(1)   disregard the existence of the partnership;

(2)   treat the taxpayer as a non-partner;

(3)   change the method of accounting used by the partnership or a partner;

(4)   reallocate partnership income and loss among the partners; or

(5)   otherwise adjust the claimed tax treatment.

The anti-abuse rule is described in § 2.05, *infra*.

The election to be excluded from the partnership tax rules of Subchapter K. This election is available to partnerships engaged in investment activities, production, extraction, or use of certain kinds of property and to certain partnerships of securities dealers. This chapter explains the rules applicable to the election, including eligibility for the election, how the election is made, and what effect the election has on Code sections outside of Subchapter K. The election rules are discussed in § 2.06, *infra*.

The pre-1997 classification rules. Under the classification regulations in effect before 1997, an unincorporated entity, such as a limited liability company or limited partnership, was considered an association taxable as a corporation if it had more than two of four specific corporate characteristics: centralized management, freely transferable interests, continuity of life, and limited liability. A venture that lacked at least two of these characteristics ordinarily was classified as a partnership. Because these rules apply to years before 1997, they are described in § 2.07, *infra*.

§ 2.02   DETERMINING TAX CLASSIFICATION UNDER THE REGULATIONS

[A]   Overview of the Classification Regulations

Regulations that became effective January 1, 1997, provide a simple method for determining whether a venture is taxable as a partnership or subject to other tax rules.[1] Under these regulations, entities incorporated under state or federal

---

[1] Treas. Reg. §§ 301.7701-1 through 301.7701-3.

statutes and certain other specified organizations are automatically taxable as corporations. Most other domestic business organizations that have more than one member, including limited liability companies, are taxable under the partnership rules,[2] unless the entity files an election to be classified as a corporation. Special classification rules apply to foreign organizations.

NOTE:

A taxpayer's attempt to invalidate the current regulations, referred to as the "check-the-box" rules, was rejected by the Sixth Circuit Court of Appeals.[3] The taxpayer was the sole member of several limited liability companies that were classified as disregarded entities under the default rule of the regulations. Such classification caused the taxpayer to be liable for the LLC's employment taxes.

The taxpayer asserted that issuance of the regulations exceeded the Treasury Department's authority to provide interpretive rules under I.R.C. Section 7805. He also argued that the IRS must recognize the separate existence of the LLCs under state law. The Appeals Court concluded that the regulations were a reasonable exercise of regulatory authority and that state law provisions affect, but do not control, federal tax provisions.

---

[1] Domestic Ventures

The proper tax classification of a domestic[4] organization may be determined in the following manner:

(1) *Determine whether the venture is an "entity" under the Federal tax rules.* A joint undertaking may be an entity for tax purposes even though it is not treated as an entity under state law.[5] Conversely, an organization recognized as a separate entity under state law may not be considered an entity for tax purposes. (*See* § 2.03, *infra.*)

(2) *Determine whether the entity is a "business entity." An entity is a business entity unless it is a trust.*[6] Generally, trusts have neither associates nor an objective to carry on business for profit. An entity

---

[2] The regulations define a partnership as a business entity that has at least two members and which is not a per se corporation under the regulations. Treas. Reg. § 301.7701-(2)(c)(1).

[3] Littriello v. U.S., 484 F.3d 372 (6th Cir. 2007); cert denied, 128 S. Ct. 1290 (2008).

[4] An entity is a domestic entity if it is created or organized in the United States or under the law of the United States or of any state, including the District of Columbia. Treas. Reg. § 301.7701-1(d), (e). However, the Treasury is authorized to issue regulations that may classify certain entities as foreign even though organized in the United States. I.R.C. § 7701(a)(4), as amended by the Taxpayer Relief Act of 1997.

[5] Treas. Reg. § 301.7701-1(a)(2).

[6] For definition of trust, see Treas. Reg. § 301.7701-4.

classified as a trust is taxed under the trust rules of Subchapter J.

(3)   ***Determine whether the business entity is automatically classified as a corporation for tax purposes (a per se corporation).*** This group includes: (1) any organization actually incorporated under state, federal or Indian tribe law, and (2) any other organization specifically listed in the regulations. (*See* § 2.02[C][1], *infra.*) These business entities are taxable as corporations. Any business entity that is not automatically classified as a corporation is referred to as an "eligible entity."

(4)   ***Determine the tax classification if the eligible entity has only one member.*** A single member entity cannot be taxable as a partnership. If the sole member is an individual, the venture is taxed as a sole proprietorship (*i.e.*, the entity is disregarded), unless the member elects to have the entity taxed as a corporation. If the sole member is not an individual (*e.g.*, it is a corporation), the venture is treated as a branch or division of the owner (*i.e.*, the entity is disregarded), unless the member elects to have the entity taxed as a corporation. (*See* § 2.02[F], *infra.*)

(5)   ***Determine the tax classification if the eligible entity has at least two members.*** An eligible entity with more than one member automatically is classified as a partnership unless it files an election to be taxed as a corporation. (*See* § 2.02[F], *infra.*)

[2]   Foreign Ventures

The regulations contain rules for determining the U.S. tax classification of business organizations created and governed by foreign law.[7] The classification of a foreign organization for tax purposes may be determined in the following manner:

(1)   ***Determine if the regulations include this type of entity in the list of per se corporations.*** A foreign entity is automatically taxed as a corporation if the type of organization is included in an extensive list of foreign business forms set forth in the regulations. A venture that is not on the list is a "foreign eligible entity." (*See* § 2.02[E][2], *infra.*)

(2)   ***Determine the tax classification if the foreign eligible entity has only one member.*** Generally, a foreign entity that provides limited liability for all its owners is classified as a corporation. If the sole member lacks limited liability, the entity is disregarded for tax purposes unless the member files an election to be taxed as a corporation. Partnership tax status is not available to single member entities. A member of a foreign entity has limited liability if the member lacks personal liability for the entity's debts and obligations by reason of being a member. (*See* § 2.02[E][1], *infra.*)

(3)   ***Determine the tax classification if the foreign eligible entity has at least two members.*** If at least one member lacks limited liability, the entity is treated as a partnership unless it files an election to be taxed as

---

[7] The Treasury is authorized to issue regulations that may classify certain entities as foreign even though organized in the United States. I.R.C. § 7701(a)(4), as amended by the Taxpayer Relief Act of 1997.

a corporation. If all members have limited liability, the venture is taxable as a corporation unless it files an election to be classified as a partnership. (*See* § 2.02[F], *infra*.)

[B] Definition of Entity

A venture can be classified as a partnership or corporation for tax purposes only if it is an "entity" that is separate from its owners. Whether an organization is a separate entity is determined under federal tax law and does not depend upon whether it is recognized as an entity under local law.[8] For tax purposes, a joint venture or contractual relationship may be a separate entity if the participants carry on a trade, business, financial operation or venture and divide the realized profits.[9]

The regulations do not provide guidelines for determining whether an arrangement constitutes an entity. The sole example in the regulations states that a separate entity may be created when co-owners of an apartment building lease space and also provide services to the occupants either directly or through an agent.[10] A joint undertaking merely to share expenses, however, does not create a separate entity. For example, adjacent landowners who jointly construct a ditch to drain surface water from their properties do not create a separate entity. Similarly, co-owners who maintain, repair, rent or lease their property do not constitute an entity for tax purposes. Thus, no separate entity is formed when tenants in common merely lease property to a third party without providing significant services in connection with the lease.

Certain organizations may not be considered entities for tax purposes even though formed and recognized under local or federal law.[11] For example, an organization wholly owned by a state is not treated as a separate entity if it is an integral part of the state, nor are Native American tribes incorporated under specified federal statutes.[12] Similarly, an arrangement that is a "qualified cost sharing arrangement" as defined in the tax regulations[13] is not a separate entity for classification purposes.[14] Most important, a single owner organization that is considered a separate entity under state law, such as a one member limited liability company, is disregarded for tax purposes unless it elects to be classified as a corporation.[15]

---

[8] Treas. Reg. § 301.7701-1(a)(1).

[9] Treas. Reg. § 301.7701-1(a)(2).

[10] *Id.*

[11] Treas. Reg. § 301.7701-1(a)(3).

[12] *Id.*

[13] *See* Treas. Reg. § 1.482-7.

[14] Treas. Reg. § 301.7701-1(c).

[15] Treas. Reg. § 301.7701-1(a)(4). See discussion of single member organizations in § 2.02[D][2], *infra*.

[C] Definition of Business Entity

Once it is determined that a venture constitutes an entity for tax purposes, the next step is determine if it is a "business entity." An entity is a business entity unless it is trust (as defined in the regulations), or it is subject to special tax treatment under specific provisions of the Internal Revenue Code (*e.g.*, a real estate investment trust). The term business entity includes single owner entities, even though such entities may choose to be disregarded for tax purposes.

The exclusion of trusts from the definition of business entities applies only to "ordinary" trusts and certain "investment" trusts. A trust is an ordinary trust if its purpose is to make trustees responsible for protecting and conserving property for beneficiaries who cannot share in this responsibility.[16] In that case, the beneficiaries are not considered associates in a joint enterprise to conduct a business for profit. This kind of trust is taxable under Subchapter J of the Internal Revenue Code.

In an investment trust, the beneficiaries, referred to as certificate holders, form the trust to facilitate the management of their investments. Generally, this arrangement is classified as a trust if there is only one class of ownership interest representing undivided beneficial interests in the trust assets and the trust agreement does not allow the certificate holders to vary their investments. An investment trust is treated as a business entity rather than a trust if the trust agreement permits the certificate holders to vary their interests,[17] or if there are multiple classes of ownership interests.[18]

A third type of trust, called a "business" trust, is considered a business entity rather than a trust for tax purposes. Although called a trust because legal title to property is conveyed to trustees for beneficiaries, the purpose is to carry on a profit-making business that ordinarily would be conducted by a corporation or partnership.[19] This kind of business entity includes Massachusetts business trusts and the Illinois land trusts.

[D] Classification of a Domestic Business Entity

A domestic entity is an entity created or organized in the United States or under any Federal or state law.[20] The basic rules for classifying a domestic business entity are summarized as follows:

(1) Certain entities, called per se corporations, are automatically classified as corporations for tax purposes. A per se corporation may have one owner or multiple owners.

(2) A business entity that is not a per se corporation is an "eligible entity." An

---

[16] Treas. Reg. § 301.7701-4(a).

[17] Treas. Reg. § 301.7701-4(c). *See* Comm'r v. North American Bond Trust, 122 F.2d 545 (2d Cir. 1941), *cert. denied*, 314 U.S. 701 (1942).

[18] Treas. Reg. § 301.7701-4(c).

[19] Treas. Reg. § 301.7701-4(b).

[20] Treas. Reg. § 301.7701-1(d). This includes the District of Columbia. Treas. Reg. § 301.7701-1(e).

eligible entity may file an election to be classified as a corporation or it may accept the "default" classification provided in the regulations. The default classification available to an eligible entity depends upon whether it has a single owner or multiple owners.

(3)   The default classification for a single owner business entity is a sole proprietorship if the owner is an individual, or a branch or division of the owner if not an individual.

(4)   The default classification for an entity with at least two owners is a partnership.

(5)   An eligible entity that was in existence before 1997 retains its classification and need not make any election unless requesting a change in classification. However, a single-owner entity that was classified as a partnership before 1997 is considered an entity separate from its owner.[21]

[1] Per Se Corporations

The following domestic business entities are automatically classified as corporations for tax purposes:[22]

(1)   an entity organized under a Federal or State statute, or a statute of a federally recognized Indian tribe, if the statute describes or refers to the entity as incorporated, a corporation, body corporate, or body politic;

(2)   an association — this group includes any unincorporated entity that has elected to be taxable as a corporation. Certain entities are deemed to elect association status:

    (a)   A tax-exempt entity (under I.R.C. Section 501(a)) is deemed to make an election to be classified as an association as of the first day for which the exemption is claimed or determined to apply. The deemed election remains in effect until exempt status is withdrawn, rejected, or revoked and a new classification is elected.[23]

    (b)   An entity that elects to be treated as a real estate investment trust (REIT) under I.R.C. Section 856(c)(1) is deemed to elect association tax status as of the first day it is treated as a REIT.[24]

(3)   an entity organized under a State statute that describes or refers to the entity as a joint-stock company or joint-stock association;

(4)   an insurance company;

(5)   a state-chartered bank if any of its deposits are insured under the Federal Deposit Insurance Act or a similar federal statute;

(6)   a business entity wholly owned by a state or its political subdivision; and

---

[21] Treas. Reg. § 301.7701-3(b)(3).

[22] Treas. Reg. § 301.7701-2(b).

[23] Treas. Reg. § 301.7701-3(c)(v)(A).

[24] Treas. Reg. § 301.7701-3(c)(v)(B).

(7)   a business entity that is taxable as a corporation under any other specific provision of the Internal Revenue Code (*e.g.*, a publicly traded partnership;[25] or a taxable mortgage pool[26]).

[2]   Single-Owner Entities

A single-owner domestic business entity that is not a per se corporation is an "eligible entity" that may choose one of two tax classifications:

(1)   The entity may choose to be disregarded for tax purposes. This is the "default" classification for domestic single member business entities, meaning that no election need be filed to obtain this status.[27] If the sole owner is an individual, the venture will be taxable as a sole proprietorship. If the owner is not an individual (*e.g.*, it is a corporation), the venture is treated as a branch or division of the owner.

The default classification can be very advantageous for a single owner limited liability company. For an individual, an LLC provides limited liability without the operating restrictions applicable to S corporations. An individual can form separate LLCs for different enterprises to insulate the assets of one venture from the creditors of another. Because each LLC is disregarded for tax purposes, separate tax returns are not required.

A corporation that operates more than one enterprise may wish to form separate LLCs rather than subsidiary corporations. Because each LLC is considered a branch, or division for tax purposes, the parent corporation obtains limited liability for each business operation while avoiding the complexity of filing consolidated returns with subsidiaries. Indeed, the parent corporation may itself be an S corporation, thereby providing the shareholders with pass-through tax treatment for all the businesses the corporation operates.

An LLC may be preferable to a corporate subsidiary when the parent wishes to sell the business operation. Sale of an LLC subsidiary is treated as a sale by the parent of the LLC's assets. The parent recognizes gain on the appreciation in the LLC assets and the purchaser obtains a cost basis. In contrast, the sale of stock of a corporate subsidiary can result in multiple taxation to the seller or no cost basis to the purchaser unless the complex requirements of I.R.C. Sections 338 and 336 are satisfied.

(2)   A single-owner eligible business entity that does not wish to be disregarded for tax purposes may file an election to be treated as an association taxable as a corporation. (See election procedure at § 2.02[F], *infra*.)

[3]   Entities With Two or More Owners

A domestic business entity that has two or more owners that is not a per se corporation is an "eligible entity" that may choose one of two tax classifications:

---

[25] I.R.C. § 7704.

[26] I.R.C. § 7701(i).

[27] Treas. Reg. § 301.7701-3(a).

(1)   The entity may choose to be taxable as a partnership. This is the "default" classification for domestic business entities with more than one owner, meaning that no election need be filed to obtain this status.[28]

(2)   If the entity does not wish to be taxed as a partnership, it may file an election to be treated as an association taxable as a corporation. (See election procedure at § 2.02[F], *infra*.)

[4]   Grandfather Rule for Domestic Entities

Most domestic business entities[29] that adopted a tax classification before the effective date of the regulations (*i.e.*, January 1, 1997) may retain that classification if the following three conditions are met:[30]

(1)   The entity had a reasonable basis[31] for its claimed classification.

(2)   The entity and all its members recognized the federal tax consequences of any change in tax classification within the sixty months prior to January 1, 1997.

(3)   Neither the entity nor any member was notified in writing on or before May 8, 1996, that the entity's classification was under examination.

[E]   Classification of a Foreign Business Entity

A foreign entity is an entity that is not created or organized in the United States or under any Federal or state law.[32] The basic rules for classifying a foreign business entity are summarized as follows:[33]

(1)   Certain foreign entities are per se corporations that are automatically classified as corporations for tax purposes. A per se corporation may have one member or multiple members.

(2)   A foreign business entity that is not a per se corporation is a "foreign eligible entity." A foreign eligible entity may accept the default classification provided in the regulations or it may elect the alternative classification. The default classification of a foreign eligible entity depends upon two factors: (a) whether it has a single member or more than one member, and (b) whether any member lacks limited liability under local law (as defined below).

(3)   If the sole member of a foreign entity has limited liability, the default classification is an association taxable as a corporation. The sole member may elect to have the entity disregarded for tax purposes.

---

[28] Treas. Reg. § 301.7701-3(a).

[29] The grandfather rule does not apply to per se corporations under the current regulations described in Treas. Reg. § 301.7701-2(b)(1), (3), (4), (5), (6), or (7).

[30] Treas. Reg. § 301.7701-3(f).

[31] Within the meaning of I.R.C. § 6662.

[32] Treas. Reg. § 301.7701-1(d).

[33] Treas. Reg. § 301.7701-3(b)(2).

(4)   If the sole member of the foreign entity lacks limited liability, the default classification is to disregard the entity for tax purposes. The sole member may elect association status; in that case, the venture is taxable as a corporation.

(5)   If the entity has two or more members and all members have limited liability, the default classification is association taxable as a corporation. The entity may elect to be treated as a partnership for tax purposes.

(6)   If the entity has two or more members and at least one member lacks limited liability, the default classification is taxation as a partnership. The entity may elect to be classified as an association taxable as a corporation.

[1]   Limited Liability Defined

The regulations define limited liability as follows:

> [A] member of a foreign eligible entity has limited liability if the member has no personal liability for the debts of or claims against the entity by reason of being a member. This determination is based solely on the statute or law pursuant to which the entity is organized, except that if the underlying statute or law allows the entity to specify in its organizational documents whether the members will have limited liability, the organizational documents may also be relevant. . . . [A] member has personal liability if the creditors of the entity may seek satisfaction of all or any portion of the debts or claims against the entity from the member as such. A member has personal liability . . . even if the member makes an agreement under which another person (whether or not a member of the entity) assumes such liability or agrees to indemnify that member for any such liability.[34]

[2]   Per Se Foreign Corporations

The regulations set forth an extensive list of foreign entities that are automatically treated as corporations for United States tax purposes. Apparently, the Treasury believes that the similarity between these entities and United States corporations warrants automatic classification. The list includes business entities of ninety different nations.[35]

[3]   Grandfather Rule for Foreign Entities

Under a "grandfather" rule, a foreign entity included on the list of per se corporations need not change to corporate tax status if the entity was in existence on May 8, 1996, and satisfies a number of other conditions set forth in the regulations.[36]

---

[34] Treas. Reg. § 301.7701-3(b)(2)(ii).

[35] Treas. Reg. § 301.7701-2(b)(8)(i).

[36] Treas. Reg. § 301.7701-2(d).

[4] Single-Member Foreign Entities

A single-owner foreign business entity that is not a per se corporation is a "foreign eligible entity" that may choose one of two tax classifications:

(1)   If the sole member of the foreign entity lacks limited liability, the entity may be disregarded for tax purposes. The venture is treated as a sole proprietorship if the owner is an individual, or as a branch or division of the owner if not an individual. This is the default classification, meaning that no election is required to obtain this tax status. The entity may elect to be considered an association taxable as a corporation.

(2)   If the sole member has limited liability, the default classification is association taxable as a corporation. The member may elect to have the entity disregarded for tax purposes.

The fact that a wholly owned foreign entity may be disregarded for United States tax purposes can be advantageous in structuring foreign operations.[37] For example, a United States parent corporation may form a U.S. limited liability company or corporate subsidiary to own all the interests in a foreign entity. The foreign entity may be disregarded and treated as a division of the parent for U.S. tax purposes, either by default or by affirmative election. The domestic LLC or subsidiary insulates the parent from liability arising from foreign operations. Although the foreign earnings are currently included in the parent's income, that income is largely offset by the pass-through of the tax credit for taxes paid to the foreign country.

[5] Foreign Entities With Two or More Owners

A foreign business entity that has at least two owners and is not a per se corporation is a foreign eligible entity that may choose either of the following tax classifications:

(1)   If all members have limited liability, the entity may be classified as an association taxable as a corporation. This is the default classification, meaning that no election is required to obtain this tax status. The entity may affirmatively elect to be treated as a partnership for tax purposes.

(2)   If at least one member of the foreign entity lacks limited liability, the default classification is taxation as a partnership. The entity may elect to be classified as an association taxable as a corporation.

---

[37] *But see* Rev. Proc. 99-7, 1999-1 I.R.B. 226 (Service will not issue advance ruling on classification of foreign entity if classification is inconsistent with purposes of U.S. tax law).

[6] Classification of Partnership That Terminates or Divides

Under Subchapter K, a partnership terminates for tax purposes if at least 50 percent of the total interests in partnership capital and profits are sold or exchanged within a twelve month period.[38] Following this termination, a new partnership is deemed to be formed with the old entity's assets. The classification regulations state that the new entity deemed to arise after the termination is considered a partnership by default without requiring an election. For example, if a foreign entity that elected partnership classification terminates under the 50-percent sale rule, the new entity is considered a partnership even though a new election is not filed.[39]

Subchapter K also provides that if a partnership divides into two or more entities, a resulting partnership is considered a continuation of the prior partnership if its members owned more than 50 percent of the interests in the prior partnership.[40] The classification regulations state that if the former partnership elected partnership tax status, the continuing partnership retains that tax classification without filing a new election.[41]

[F] Election Procedures

A domestic or foreign eligible entity that is satisfied with its default tax classification need not file any election to obtain that status.[42] If the entity desires a different initial classification or to change its current tax status, it must file Form 8832, "Entity Classification Election," with the service center designated on the form. The election must provide all the information required by the form and instructions, including the entity's taxpayer identification number.[43]

An eligible entity that elects to change its classification cannot make another election during the 60 months following the first election's effective date.[44] This limitation period does not apply to the election an existing entity made to change its classification as of the regulations' effective date (January 1, 1997). The Internal Revenue Service may waive the 60-month limitation by letter ruling, but only if 50 percent of the entity's ownership interests are held by persons that did not own any interests on the filing date or effective date of the prior election.[45]

---

[38] I.R.C. § 708(b)(1)(B).

[39] Treas. Reg. § 301.7701-3(e).

[40] I.R.C. § 708(b)(2)(B).

[41] Treas. Reg. § 301.7701-3(e).

[42] According to the preamble to the regulations, protective elections are permitted. This may be advisable if uncertainty about the entity's status exists.

[43] Treas. Reg. § 301.7701-3(c).

[44] Presumably, any number of elections can be made if the 60 months have elapsed between each election. Treas. Reg. § 301.7701-3(c)(1)(iv).

[45] Treas. Reg. § 301.7701-3(c)(1)(iv).

[G]   Change in Classification or Number of Members

[1]   Elective Change in Classification

The Treasury has issued proposed regulations addressing the tax consequences of elective changes in entity classification.[46] The proposed regulations minimize the tax consequences of these elective classification changes by characterizing the changes as follows:[47]

(1)   An association that elects to be classified as a partnership is deemed to liquidate by distributing its assets and liabilities to its shareholders and then the shareholders are deemed to contribute all of the distributed assets and liabilities to the partnership.[48]

(2)   A partnership that elects to be classified as an association is deemed to contribute all of its assets and liabilities to the association in exchange for stock and then the partnership is deemed to liquidate by distributing stock in the association to its partners.[49]

(3)   An association that elects to be disregarded as an entity separate from its owner is deemed to liquidate by distributing its assets and liabilities to its sole owner.[50]

(4)   An entity disregarded as separate from its owner that elects to be classified as an association is deemed to have its owner contribute all of the entity's assets and liabilities to the association in exchange for stock.[51]

Example:[52] Arlen is sole owner of Apco Company, which is classified as a disregarded entity for tax purposes. On January 1, 2000, Bea purchases a 50 percent interest in Apco from Arlen. Although a partnership is the default classification for Apco when Bea acquires her interest, Arlen and Bea elect to have the entity classified as an association effective on January 1, 2000.[53] Arlen is treated as if he contributed all Apco's assets and liabilities to the newly formed Apco association on December 31, 1999. Bea is treated as if she purchased 50 percent of the shares of Apco stock from Arlen on January 1, 2000. Because Arlen does not retain control of the association as required for nonrecognition under I.R.C. Section 351, Arlen's contribution is taxable and he recognizes gain or loss as if he sold each asset

---

[46] Treas. Reg. § 301.7701-3(g).

[47] Treas. Reg. §§ 301.7701-2, -3; T.D. 8844, 2001-12 I.R.B. 917, *modified*, 2002-2 I.R.B. 281.

[48] Treas. Reg. § 301.7701-3(g)(1)(i). This characterization is consistent with Rev. Rul. 63-107 (1963-1 C.B. 71).

[49] Treas. Reg. § 301.7701-3(g)(1)(ii). This does not affect Rev. Rul. 84-111 (1984-2 C.B. 88), in which the IRS ruled that it would respect the form used by the taxpayers when a partnership converts to a corporation.

[50] Treas. Reg. § 301.7701-3(g)(1)(iii).

[51] Treas. Reg. § 301.7701-3(g)(1)(iv).

[52] Treas. Reg. § 301.7701-3(f)(4), Ex. (1).

[53] This election is treated as a change in classification so that no classification change election is allowed during the sixty months succeeding the effective date of the election. *See* § 2.02[F], *infra*.

for its fair market value. Apco's basis in the assets deemed contributed by Arlen is their fair market value and that is Arlen's basis in his Apco stock. Arlen has no additional gain upon the sale of stock to Bea, and Bea takes a cost basis in the stock purchased from Arlen.

Timing of elective changes. Under the proposed regulations, an election to change an entity's classification is effective at the start of the day for which the election is effective.[54] Any transactions deemed to occur because of the classification change are considered to happen immediately before the close of the day before the election is effective. For example, if an association elects to convert to a partnership on January 1, the association's tax year closes on December 31 and the first day of the partnership's tax year is January 1.[55] Each person who was an owner on the date that a classification change is deemed to occur, and who is not an owner when the election is filed, must also sign the election.[56]

Basis adjustments. A partnership that elects to be taxed as an association is treated as if it contributed all its property to a newly formed corporation in a transaction that is nontaxable under I.R.C. Section 351. Generally, the corporate transferee's basis in the property deemed transferred to it by the partnership is the same as the partnership's basis in the property. Proposed regulations provide that a corporate transferee's basis in property transferred by a partnership in an I.R.C. Section 351 transfer includes any special basis adjustment under I.R.C. Section 743.[57] Any gain the partnership may recognize as a result of the deemed transfer of its property to the association is determined without reference to any special basis adjustment. However, the partner with the special basis adjustment can use the special basis adjustment to reduce its share of gain the partnership recognizes.[58] The special basis adjustment is also taken into account in determining the partner's basis in the stock received in the exchange.[59]

> **Example:** The AB Partnership owns Property X. AB's basis in Property X is $100. Partner A has a $5 special basis adjustment in Property X under I.R.C. Section 743(b). The partnership elects to be classified as an association for tax purposes. AB is deemed to contribute all of its assets and liabilities to the association in exchange for stock, and to immediately liquidate by distributing the stock to its partners. Under the proposed regulations, the association's basis in Property X is $105, which includes Partner A's $5 special basis adjustment. Partner A's basis in the association's stock also increases by the $5 special basis adjustment for Property X.

---

[54] Treas. Reg. § 301.7701-3(c). The tax treatment of an elective change in an entity's classification is determined under all relevant provisions of the Internal Revenue Code and general principles of tax law, including the step transaction doctrine. Treas. Reg. § 301.7701-3(g)(2).

[55] Treas. Reg. § 301.7701-3(g)(3).

[56] Treas. Reg. § 301.7701-3(c)(2)(iii).

[57] Prop. Treas. Reg. § 1.743-2(a).

[58] Prop. Treas. Reg. § 1.743-2(b).

[59] Prop. Treas. Reg. § 1.743-2(c).

The Treasury Department has issued proposed regulations designed to prevent taxpayers from changing a foreign entity's classification in order to generate U.S. tax benefits that would otherwise be unavailable.[60] The proposed regulations are directed at classification changes that create disregarded entities and partnerships for the purpose of avoiding tax rules relating to international transactions.[61] Under the proposed regulations, a foreign entity's election to change its classification from association (taxable as a corporation) to disregarded entity may be retroactively invalidated in certain circumstances.[62]

[2]   Change in Number of Members

Regulations address the consequences of a change in the number of members of the entity, holding that such membership changes do not affect the entity's classification. However, an entity initially classified as a partnership that subsequently has only one member (and continues to be an entity under local law), will be disregarded as an entity separate from its owner.[63] Additionally, a single-member disregarded entity that subsequently has more than one member will be classified as a partnership as of the date it has more than one member.[64] These automatic classifications can be changed by election if the entity is not subject to the 60-month limitation on elections (*see* § 2.02[F], *supra*).

Example (1):[65] On April 1, 2000, Dwight and Edith, both U.S. persons, form Detco, a foreign entity. Under the default rules for foreign entities, Detco is classified as an association and it does not elect to be classified as a partnership. Dwight subsequently purchases all of Edith's interest in Detco. Detco continues to be classified as an association and no classification election is deemed to occur. Detco may subsequently elect to be treated as a disregarded entity without regard to the sixty month limitation.

Example (2):[66] On April 1, 2000, Fran and Gary, U.S. persons, form Frago, a foreign entity. Under the default rules for foreign entities, Frago is classified as an association and it does not elect to be classified as a partnership. On January 1, 2001, Frago elects to be classified as a partnership effective on that date. Under the sixty month limitation, Frago cannot elect to be classified as an association until January 1, 2006 (*i.e.*, sixty months after the effective date of the election to be classified as a partnership).

---

[60]   Prop. Reg. §§ 301.7701-2, -3, 64 Fed. Reg. 66,591 (Nov. 29, 1999).

[61]   For example, I.R.C. §§ 861–865 (rules governing source of income), I.R.C. § 904 (foreign tax credit limitation categories), I.R.C. §§ 951–964 (disposition of ownership interests under Subpart F), and I.R.C. § 367 (outbound transfers).

[62]   Prop. Treas. Reg. § 301.7701-3(h). An invalid election is deemed not to have been made for purposes of the 60-month limitation on such elections. *See* § 2.02[F], *supra*.

[63]   Treas. Reg. § 301.7701-3(f)(2).

[64]   *Id.*

[65]   Treas. Reg. § 301.7701-3(f)(4), Ex. (2).

[66]   Treas. Reg. § 301.7701-3(f)(4), Ex. (3).

On June 1, 2001, Fran purchases all of Gary's interest in Frago. Because Frago has only one member, it is no longer classified as a partnership but, pursuant to the default rules, is treated as a disregarded entity. This is not considered a change in classification for purposes of the sixty month rule and Frago cannot elect to be classified as an association until January 1, 2006 (*i.e.*, sixty months after the January 1, 2001, election to be classified as a partnership).

The Service has issued two rulings addressing the tax consequences of a change in classification resulting from an increase or decrease in the number of an entity's members. Revenue Ruling 99-5[67] describes the consequences when a single-member limited liability company that is disregarded as a separate entity transforms to a multi-owner entity classified as a partnership for tax purposes. Revenue Ruling 99-6[68] concerns the consequences when one person purchases all the interests in a limited liability company causing the LLC's partnership status to terminate.[69]

§ 2.03   DETERMINING WHETHER AN "ENTITY" EXISTS

As described in § 2.02, above, the regulations provide that an economic arrangement may be classified as a partnership only if it is a business "entity" that is separate from its owners. Whether an arrangement constitutes a separate entity is decided under federal tax law and not under state or local law.[70] The regulations do not establish criteria for determining whether an entity exists. The only guidance is the following paragraph:

> A joint venture or other contractual arrangement may create a separate entity for federal tax purposes if the participants carry on a trade, business, financial operation, or venture and divide the profits therefrom. For example, a separate entity exists for federal tax purposes if co-owners of an apartment building lease space and in addition provide services to the occupants either directly or through an agent. Nevertheless, a joint undertaking merely to share expenses does not create a separate entity for federal tax purposes. For example, if two or more persons jointly construct a ditch merely to drain surface water from their properties, they have not created a separate entity for federal tax purposes. Similarly, mere co-ownership of property that is maintained, kept in repair, and rented or leased does not constitute a separate entity for federal tax purposes. For example, if an individual owner, or tenants in common, of farm property lease it to a farmer for a cash rental or a share of the crops, they do not necessarily create a separate entity for federal tax purposes.[71]

---

[67] 1999-6 I.R.B. 8.

[68] 1999-6 I.R.B. 6.

[69] Under I.R.C. § 708(b)(1)(A). *See* § 14.03, *infra*.

[70] Treas. Reg. § 301.7701-1(a)(1).

[71] Treas. Reg. § 301.7701-1(a)(2).

The term entity encompasses many economic arrangements that would not be taxable as partnerships under the former regulations. Although state law is not controlling, the vast majority of partnerships, limited partnerships and limited liability companies set up under state business organization statutes are entities for tax purposes. It is also likely that many economic ventures not formally organized under state law are taxable as partnerships under the default classification rules. A venture that is considered a partnership, whether by default or affirmative election, is subject to all partnership tax rules, including filing requirements and associated penalties.

Although the term entity is not well defined, evidence of its meaning is found in the tax cases and rulings defining the term "partnership." Under the pre-1997 classification rules, a venture was taxable under Subchapter K only if it met the tax definition of a "partnership" established by the former I.R.C. Sections 761 and 7701 regulations. (For discussion of the pre-1997 rules, see § 2.07, *infra*.) The definition of a partnership in those regulations is similar to the current description of an entity.[72] Presumably, determining if an arrangement is an entity under the current regulations involves criteria similar to those used for determining whether a partnership was created under the former rules.

§ 2.04   PUBLICLY TRADED PARTNERSHIPS TAXED AS CORPORATIONS

Before 1987, many entities were considered partnerships for tax purposes even though their interests were traded on securities markets in the same manner as corporate stock is traded. These ventures, often referred to as "master limited partnerships," were distinguished from associations taxable as corporations under the corporate resemblance test applied by the pre-1997 classification regulations.[73]

Congress determined that most publicly traded limited partnerships should be taxed as corporations without regard to the classification regulations. This action was deemed necessary to forestall the increasing use of these partnerships to avoid corporate-level taxation.[74]

I.R.C. Section 7704 was enacted in 1987 to ensure that a publicly traded partnership (PTP) is taxable as a corporation unless it comes under a specific exception in the statute, even though the entity would otherwise be classified as a partnership. I.R.C. Section 7704 applies to any domestic or foreign entity taxable as a partnership, including limited liability companies.[75]

A PTP subject to corporate taxation under I.R.C. Section 7704 is deemed to transfer all of its assets and liabilities to a newly formed corporation in exchange for

---

[72] *See* former Treas. Reg. § 1.761-1(a).

[73] Former Treas. Reg. § 301.7701-2. For discussion of the former regulations, see § 2.07, *infra*.

[74] *See* H.R. Rep. No. 391, 100th Cong., 1st Sess. 1063 (1987). Earnings of a limited partnership are taxed only at the partner level while corporate earnings are taxed at the corporate level and again at the shareholder level when distributed as dividends.

[75] Treas. Reg. § 1.7701-1 *et. seq. See* Rev. Proc. 95-10, 1995-1 C.B. 501.

stock which is then distributed to its partners in liquidation of the partnership.[76] These transactions are deemed to occur on the first day that the partnership is treated as a corporation under the statute.[77] The tax consequences of the constructive transfer and liquidation (including any recapture of tax benefits) are determined under the general tax rules of I.R.C. Sections 351, 731, and 732.[78] (For discussion of tax consequences of incorporating a partnership, see § 12.06, *infra*.)

I.R.C. Section 7704(c) provides a major exception for publicly traded partnerships that derive substantially all income from passive sources such as interest, dividends, and rent. Another major exception applies to certain PTPs that were in existence before December 17, 1987, the effective date of the statute.[79] However, partners in PTPs that are exempt from corporate taxation are subject to special limitations under the passive loss rules of I.R.C. Section 469.[80]

[A]   Effective Date of Final Regulations

The rules described in the following sections are set forth in final regulations that generally are effective for tax years beginning in 1996 and thereafter.[81] Under a grandfather provision, a venture that was actively engaged in an activity before December 4, 1995 is not subject to these regulations until of the first tax year beginning in 2006, unless it adds a "substantial new line of business."[82] A grandfathered entity may rely on the earlier rules provided in Notice 88-75.[83] If the entity adds a substantial new line of business, however, the regulations apply to tax years beginning on or after the date new line is added.[84] A technical termination under I.R.C. Section 708(b)(1)(B) is disregarded in determining whether an existing entity comes under the grandfather exception.[85]

[B]   Publicly Traded Partnership Defined

The publicly traded partnership (PTP) rules apply to any domestic or foreign entity that would be taxable as a partnership under the classification rules of I.R.C. 7701. (*See* § 2.02, *supra*.) This includes partnerships, limited liability companies and business trusts.[86] A venture is a PTP taxable as a corporation if its interests are publicly traded and no statutory exception applies. Interests in a partnership (or LLC) are publicly traded if they are (1) traded on an established securities

---

[76] I.R.C. § 7704(f).

[77] I.R.C. § 7704(f).

[78] *See* H.R. Rep. No. 391, 100th Cong., 1st Sess. 1071 (1987).

[79] Revenue Act of 1987, Pub. L. No. 100-203, 100th Cong., 1st Sess., § 10211(c)(2)(A) (Dec. 22, 1987).

[80] I.R.C. § 469(k).

[81] Treas. Reg. § 1.7704-1(l).

[82] As defined in Treas. Reg. §§ 1.7704-2(c), (d) (using 12/4/95 as the applicable date). Treas. Reg. § 1.7704-1(*l*)(3).

[83] 1988-2 C.B. 386.

[84] Treas. Reg. § 1.7704-1(l)(2).

[85] Treas. Reg. § 1.7704-1(l)(4).

[86] Treas. Reg. § 1.7701-1 et seq. *See* Rev. Proc. 95-10, 1995-1 C.B. 501.

market, or (2) readily tradable on a secondary market or on the substantial equivalent of a secondary market.[87]

[C] Publicly Traded Partnership With Qualifying Passive-Type Income Not Taxed as a Corporation

I.R.C. Section 7704(c) provides an important exception to the general rule that publicly traded partnerships (PTPs) are taxable as corporations.[88] Under the exception, a PTP is not treated as a corporation if 90 percent or more of its gross income is "qualifying" passive-type income.

The legislative history indicates that this exception was enacted to permit partnership status for ventures engaged in investment activities because the tax benefits their partners receive could also be obtained if the partners purchased the investments directly. In contrast, PTPs engaged in business activities are treated as corporations under I.R.C. Section 7704(a) because these ventures are normally conducted in corporate form and are subject to corporate-level taxation.

A PTP is exempt from corporate treatment if at least 90 percent of its gross income for the taxable year is "qualifying" as defined in I.R.C. Section 7704(d). The partnership must satisfy this gross-income test in the first tax year that it becomes a PTP and in every subsequent tax year.[89] For example, a partnership that first becomes a PTP in Year 1 cannot be exempt under the 90 percent test in Year 3 unless it satisfied the gross-income test in Years 1 and 2.

[D] Publicly Traded Foreign Partnerships

Temporary regulations have been issued to preclude the use of publicly traded foreign partnership to avoid application of the *surrogate foreign corporation* rules of I.R.C. Section 7874.[90] I.R.C. Section 7874 applies to "inversion" transactions in which a U.S. parent corporation of a multinational corporate group is replaced by a foreign entity. The section is intended to curtail transactions that utilize a minimal presence in the foreign country of incorporation to avoid U.S. tax.[91] In many cases, the new foreign entities conduct business in the same manner as before the inversion but the group that includes the inverted entity avoids U.S. tax on its foreign operations and may engage in various techniques to avoid U.S. tax on its U.S. operations.

---

[87] I.R.C. § 7704(b); Treas. Reg. § 1.7704-1(a).

[88] The passive-type income exception is not available to a partnership that is registered under the Investment Company Act of 1940. I.R.C. § 7704(c)(3). This means that the exception does not apply to a partnership that would be a regulated investment company under I.R.C. § 851(a) if it was a domestic corporation. However, future regulations may permit this kind of a partnership to qualify for the passive-type income exception if one of its principal activities is buying and selling commodities, options, futures or forward contracts with respect to commodities. *See* H.R. Rep. No. 495, 100th Cong., 1st Sess. 946 (1987).

[89] I.R.C. § 7704(c)(1).

[90] Temp. Treas. Reg. § 1.7874-2T, T.D. 9265 (June 6, 2006).

[91] See H.R. Conf. Rep. No. 108-755, 108th Cong., 2d Sess., at 568 (Oct. 7, 2004); S. Rep. No. 108-192, 108th Cong., 1st Sess., at 142 (Nov. 7, 2003).

Under I.R.C. Section 7874, a foreign corporation is treated as a surrogate foreign corporation if, pursuant to a plan or a series of related transactions, it acquires substantially all the properties of a domestic corporation or partnership and after the acquisition, at least 60 percent of the foreign corporation's stock is held by former shareholders of the domestic corporation. Income of a surrogate foreign corporation is subject to U.S. tax, in whole or part depending on the level of owner continuity.

The temporary regulations target transactions designed to avoid application of I.R.C. Section 7874 by using a foreign partnership with publicly traded interests, rather than a corporation, to acquire the properties of a domestic corporation or partnership. Certain publicly traded foreign partnership can utilize the same U.S. tax avoidance opportunities as a foreign corporation by avoiding classification as a corporation for U.S. tax purposes under the exception for partnerships that derive 90 percent or more of their gross income from passive income such as dividends.[92] The temporary regulations ensure that I.R.C. Section 7874 is not avoided in this manner by providing that a publicly traded foreign partnership not classified as a corporation under I.R.C. section 7704 will be treated as a foreign corporation for purposes of applying I.R.C. Section 7874 to determine if the acquiring foreign entity is a surrogate foreign corporation.

The regulations define a publicly traded foreign partnership as any foreign partnership that would, but for the application of I.R.C. Section 7704(c), be classified as a corporation at any time during the two-year period following the partnership's completion of an acquisition. In that case, the foreign partnership will be considered a foreign corporation in determining whether it is a surrogate foreign corporation, applying the ownership percentage tests of I.R.C. Section 7874. These rules apply to foreign entities considered partnerships under both foreign and U.S. law and foreign entities that are considered corporate entities under foreign law but treated as partnerships for U.S. tax purposes.[93]

§ 2.05 THE ANTI-ABUSE REGULATIONS

The "anti-abuse" regulations under I.R.C. Section 701 are intended to prevent taxpayers from using the partnership tax rules of Subchapter K for tax avoidance purposes.[94]

These regulations grant the Commissioner of Internal Revenue broad authority to disregard or recast transactions engaged in by an entity taxable under Subchapter K. In effect, the Commissioner is authorized to modify the operation and interpretation of any Code section or regulation relevant to a partnership transaction to prevent tax avoidance. Although the regulations assert that the

---

[92] I.R.C. § 7704(c).

[93] Temp. Treas. Reg. § 1.7874-2T(e).

[94] Treas. Reg. § 1.701-2. Generally, the regulations are effective for transactions on or after May 12, 1994. The abuse of entity rule in Treas. Reg. § 1.701-2(e) is effective for transactions on or after January 3, 1995. Treas. Reg. § 1.701-2(g). The regulations apply only to income taxes under subtitle A of the Internal Revenue Code. Treas. Reg. § 1.701-2(h).

anti-abuse rule will affect a relatively small number of partnership transactions,[95] the actual scope and impact of these rules is yet to be determined.

The anti-abuse rule consists of two parts, summarized below.

Intent of Subchapter K rule. The Commissioner may recast a transaction that reduces partners' aggregate tax liability in a manner that is "inconsistent with the intent of Subchapter K." The regulations describe the legislative intent for the partnership tax rules and set forth tests a partnership transaction must satisfy to be consistent with this intent. If the transaction is inconsistent, the Commissioner may disregard the partnership, disregard a taxpayer's status as a partner, adjust the partnership's or partner's accounting method, reallocate partnership income or loss, or otherwise change the claimed tax treatment.

Abuse of entity rule. The Commissioner may treat a partnership as an aggregate of its partners, rather than as a separate entity, to the extent needed to carry out the purpose of any provision of the Code or regulations. This treatment may apply regardless of the taxpayer's intent in structuring the transaction. The Commissioner may not apply this rule, however, if a provision of the Code or regulations prescribes entity treatment and contemplates the ultimate tax results.

The anti-abuse regulations do not provide clear, unambiguous standards for determining when and how they will apply to a partnership transaction. Application of the regulations often requires a subjective analysis of the taxpayer's purpose or intent for forming a partnership or engaging in a particular transaction. Taxpayers and Service personnel also must make subjective determinations about whether the drafters of a statute or regulation clearly contemplated its application to a partnership and the ultimate tax consequences. The uncertainties created by these regulations are likely to continue until standards are developed through case law and administrative rulings (or the regulations are determined to be invalid).

[A]   Transactions Inconsistent With Intent of Subchapter K

According to the regulations, "Subchapter K is intended to permit taxpayers to conduct joint business (including investment) activities through a flexible economic arrangement without incurring an entity-level tax."[96] To be consistent with this intent, the following three requirements must be satisfied:

(1)   The partnership must be bona fide and each of its transactions must have a substantial business purpose.

(2)   The form of each partnership transaction must conform with its substance.

(3)   Each partner's tax consequences from partnership operations and from transactions with the partnership must accurately reflect the economic agreement among the partners and clearly reflect each partner's income (*i.e.*, there must be a "proper reflection of income"). Income is deemed properly reflected if the application of a tax provision to a transaction and

---

[95]   Treas. Reg. § 1.701-2 (preamble).

[96]   Treas. Reg. § 1.701-2(a).

the ultimate tax results were clearly contemplated when the provision was enacted. Whether these factors were clearly contemplated in connection with a particular transaction is determined from all the facts and circumstances.

The premise of the regulations is that tax provisions are intended to reflect the true economic arrangement between parties unless Congress or the Treasury wished to effectuate some other policy. If the tax provision in question has a policy objective, the regulations do not require proper reflection of income if that outcome was "clearly contemplated" by the provision. The regulations provide little guidance as to how taxpayers must determine whether a tax provision "clearly contemplated" a particular outcome. Presumably, the determination is made by analyzing each provision's legislative history.

The regulations authorize the Commissioner to recast a partnership transaction for tax purposes if:

(1)   the partnership was formed or availed of for a transaction having a principal purpose[97] to substantially reduce the present value of the partners' aggregate tax liability; and

(2)   the transaction attains the tax reduction in a manner that is inconsistent with the intent of Subchapter K.[98]

A transaction may be recharacterized to obtain tax results that are consistent with the intent of Subchapter K, even though the transaction falls within the literal words of a statute or regulation. To obtain the appropriate tax results, the Commissioner may:[99]

(1)   disregard the partnership, in whole or in part, and consider the partnership's assets and activities to be owned and conducted by one or more of its partners;

(2)   disregard one or more person's tax status as a partner;

(3)   adjust the partnership's or any partner's method of accounting to reflect clearly the partnership's or the partner's income;

(4)   reallocate the partnership's items of income, gain, loss, deduction, or credit among the partners; or

(5)   otherwise adjust or modify the claimed tax treatment.

---

[97] The regulations apply if tax avoidance is one principal purpose even though other business purposes are more important to the transaction.

[98] Treas. Reg. § 1.701-2(b).

[99] *Id.*

[B] Facts and Circumstances Analysis

Whether a transaction violates the anti-abuse rule is determined from all of the facts and circumstances.[100] The most important analysis appears to involve a comparison of the purported business purpose for a transaction with the claimed tax benefits. The regulations list seven factors that are "illustrative" of when the anti-abuse rule may apply:[101]

(1) The present value of the partners' aggregate federal tax liability is substantially less than it would be if the partners directly owned partnership assets and conducted partnership activities.

(2) The present value of the partners' aggregate tax liability is substantially less than it would be if separate transactions designed to achieve a particular result are treated as steps in a single transaction.

(3) A partner who obtains the claimed tax results has a nominal interest in the partnership, bears no meaningful risk of loss, or has little participation in partnership profits other than a preferred return for the use of his capital.

(4) Substantially all of the partners are directly or indirectly related to one another.

(5) Partnership allocations literally comply with the regulations under I.R.C. Section 704(b) but the results are inconsistent with the rules' purpose. This is particularly important if income or gain is specially allocated to a partner that is effectively exempt from taxation (*e.g.*, a foreign person, an exempt organization, an insolvent taxpayer, or a taxpayer with unused carryovers for net operating losses, capital losses, or foreign tax credits).

(6) The benefits and burdens of ownership of property nominally contributed to the partnership are substantially retained by the contributor or a related party.

(7) The benefits and burdens of ownership of partnership property are substantially shifted to a distributee.

[C] The Abuse of Entity Rule

Under the abuse-of-entity rule, the Commissioner may treat a partnership as an aggregate of its partners, rather than as a separate entity, as appropriate to carry out the purpose of any provision of the Code or regulations.[102] This authority does not exist if the Code or regulation specifically prescribes treating the partnership as an entity and clearly contemplated the ultimate tax results.[103]

---

[100] Treas. Reg. § 1.701-2(c).

[101] The regulations warn that these factors "may be indicative, but do not necessarily establish," that a partnership violated the anti-abuse rule. These are not the only factors taken into account and the weight given to any factor depends on all the facts and circumstances. The presence or absence of any does not create any presumption. Treas. Reg. § 1.701-2(c).

[102] Treas. Reg. § 1.701-2(e).

[103] Treas. Reg. § 1.701-2(e)(2).

It is unclear how to determine whether a statute or regulation outside of Subchapter K "clearly contemplated" its application to a partnership or the ultimate tax results. Presumably, the rules of Subchapter K are specifically designed to provide either entity or aggregate treatment in the partnership context and their intended application and tax results always are contemplated. Provisions outside of Subchapter K, however, are generally not drafted with partnerships in mind and their application and tax results in the partnership context are rarely contemplated.

§ 2.06 ELECTING TO BE EXCLUDED FROM PARTNERSHIP TAX RULES

[A] Overview

In limited situations, I.R.C. Section 761(a) permits a venture classifiable as a partnership (*e.g.*, a partnership or limited liability company) to elect to be excluded from all or some of the Subchapter K's partnership taxation provisions.[104] The election is restricted to organizations that are used for one of the following purposes:

(1)   for investment purposes only and not for the active conduct of a business;

(2)   for the joint production, extraction, or use of property, but not for selling services or property produced or extracted; or

(3)   by securities dealers for a short period to underwrite, sell, or distribute a particular issue of securities.[105]

All members of the organization must agree to the election,[106] and it must be possible to adequately determine the members' incomes without first computing partnership taxable income.[107] No election is permitted by an entity that would be treated as a corporation for tax purposes under the classification regulations.[108]

A venture may wish to be excluded from the partnership tax rules for the following purposes:

• to avoid the restrictive rules governing the taxable years of a partnership and its partners[109] (*see* Chapter 3);

• to allow each investor to make certain elections separately rather than have elections at the partnership level bind all partners.[110] These elections

---

[104] I.R.C. § 761(a).

[105] *Id.*

[106] Treas. Reg. § 1.761-2(b)(2)(i).

[107] Treas. Reg. § 1.761-2(a)(1).

[108] *Id.*

[109] *See* I.R.C. § 706(b).

[110] *See* I.R.C. § 703(b); Treas. Reg. § 1.703-1(b)(1). Generally, elections required to be made by the partnership under Treas. Reg. § 1.703-1(b)(1) are made by the individual partners if an election is made.

include accounting methods (*see* Chapters 3, 8),[111] depreciation and cost-recovery methods (*see* Chapters 3, 8),[112] installment reporting (*see* Chapter 7),[113] and nonrecognition of gain on an involuntary conversion (*see* Chapters 8, 12);[114]

- to allow for a nontaxable like-kind exchange of property. Although the like-kind exchange rules of I.R.C. Section 1031 do not apply to exchanges of partnership interests, this limitation does not apply to an interest in a partnership that makes an election under I.R.C. Section 761(a); an interest in an electing partnership is treated as an interest in each of the partnership's assets and not as an interest in the partnership;[115]

- to provide certainty regarding the tax treatment of a venture where uncertainty exists as to whether it is a partnership for tax purposes. For example, a group of investors may wish to file an election if it is unclear whether their arrangement is a co-ownership or investment partnership; and

- to avoid the complexity and expense involved in maintaining partnership records and preparing and filing partnership tax returns.

[B]   Entities Eligible for the Election

A partnership may not elect to be excluded from the partnership tax rules of Subchapter K, unless it is:

(1)   an investment partnership;

(2)   a partnership for the production, extraction, or use of property; or

(3)   a partnership that is an organization of securities dealers.

NOTE:

Under I.R.C. Section 761(f),[116] a *qualified joint venture* is not treated as a partnership for tax purposes if it is conducted by a husband and wife who file a joint return for the tax year. Under this provision, all items of income, gain, loss, deduction, and credit are divided between the spouses according to their interests in the venture and each spouse takes into account his or her share of these items as if they were attributable to a

---

See Rev. Rul. 83-129, 1983-2 C.B. 105. *Cf.* Rev. Rul. 81-261, 1981-2 C.B. 60.

[111]   I.R.C. § 446.

[112]   I.R.C. §§ 167, 168.

[113]   I.R.C. § 453.

[114]   I.R.C. §§ 1031, 1033.

[115]   I.R.C. § 1031(a), as amended by the Revenue Reconciliation Act of 1990.

[116]   As amended by the Small Business and Work Opportunity Act of 2007 (Pub. L. No. 110-28) § 8215(a).

trade or business conducted by the spouse as a sole proprietor. Each spouse reports his or her share on the appropriate tax form (e.g., a Schedule C).

A *qualified joint venture* is a joint venture involving the conduct of a trade or business if:

- the only members of the joint venture are a husband and wife, both spouses *materially participate*[117] in the trade or business, and

- both spouses elect to apply this treatment. If the election is made, each spouse's share of income or loss from the qualified joint venture is taken into account under the above rules in determining the spouse's net earnings from self-employment and social security benefits.[118]

[1] Investment Partnerships

Partnerships used for investment purposes only and not for the active conduct of a business may elect to be excluded from the partnership tax rules. The participants must jointly purchase, retain, sell, or exchange investment property, and they must:[119]

(1) own the investment property as co-owners;

(2) reserve the right separately to take or dispose of their shares of any acquired or retained property; and

(3) not actively conduct a business or irrevocably authorize a representative to purchase, sell, or exchange the investment property; however, each participant can authorize a representative to deal with his share of the investment property for his account, but this authority cannot continue for more than one year.[120]

In many situations, this kind of venture would be considered a co-ownership rather than a partnership. If uncertainty about the venture's tax status exists, an election may be advisable.

[2] Partnerships for Production, Extraction, or Use of Property

An election is permitted by partnerships used for the joint production, extraction, or use of property, but not for selling services or property produced or extracted.[121] The participants in the joint production, extraction, or use of property

---

[117] Under the passive loss rules of I.R.C. § 469(h), without regard to the rule considering participation by one spouse as participation by the other.

[118] I.R.C. § 1402(a)(17).

[119] Treas. Reg. § 1.761-2(a)(2).

[120] Treas. Reg. § 1.761-2(a)(2)(iii).

[121] I.R.C. § 761(a)(2); Treas. Reg. § 1.761-2(a)(3).

must:

(1)   own the property as co-owners either in fee or under lease or other form of contract granting exclusive operating rights;

(2)   separately reserve the right to take in kind or dispose of their shares of any property produced, extracted, or used;[122] and

(3)   not jointly sell services or the property produced or extracted.

Each participant may delegate authority to sell his share of the property for his account, but not for a period in excess of the minimum needs of the industry, and in no event for more than one year.[123] An organization that cycles, manufactures, or processes materials for persons who are not members of the organization may not elect to be excluded from partnership treatment.[124]

Special requirements apply to co-producers of natural gas subject to a joint operating agreement.[125] To make or maintain an election under I.R.C. Section 761, the co-producers must use one of two permissible methods described in the regulations in reporting income from gas sales and certain related deductions and credits.

[3]   Organizations of Securities Dealers

An organization of securities dealers can elect exclusion from partnership treatment if it is established (1) for a short period of time, and (2) to underwrite sell, or distribute a particular issue of securities.[126] This provision was added to protect syndicates of securities dealers that were formed to underwrite the sale or distribution of a single issue from the I.R.C. Section 6698 penalty for not filing a partnership return.

[C]   Effect of Election

A partnership that makes an election under I.R.C. Section 761(a) is exempt from the specific tax rules in Subchapter K. Thus, partnership income or loss need not be computed, and no partnership tax returns must be filed.

An election may have adverse tax consequences if it results in a deemed dissolution of an existing partnership. This may occur if the election is made for a venture that was taxable as a partnership in prior years. The dissolution may cause the partners to recognize gain under I.R.C. Section 731 if the amount of cash the partnership is deemed to distribute to them upon the dissolution exceeds the bases of their partnership interests. (*See* Chapter 8.) An election should be made for an

---

[122] *See* Ltr. Rul. 8226014 (joint venture not eligible for election where only some participants had right to take share of production in kind and one participant had right of first refusal on organization's production).

[123] Treas. Reg. § 1.761-2(a)(3)(iii).

[124] Treas. Reg. § 1.761-2(a)(3).

[125] Treas. Reg. § 1.761-2(d).

[126] I.R.C. § 761(a)(3).

existing partnership only after it is determined that the deemed cash distribution will not exceed any partner's basis.

An election is not considered a disposition or distribution of partnership property that triggers gain or loss under I.R.C. Section 704(c) to a partner who contributed property to the partnership in a pre-election year.[127] As discussed in Chapter 4, I.R.C. Section 704(c) requires that a partner recognize the gain or loss built into contributed property if the partnership (1) disposes of the property, or (2) distributes it to another partner within seven years of the contribution date.

Although an electing partnership is exempt from Subchapter K, it is treated as a partnership under all Code sections outside Subchapter K.[128] For example, the Service ruled that an electing joint venture was a partnership for purposes of limiting the investment tax credits that its partners were allowed.[129] The Tax Court took the same position in *Bryant v. Commissioner*,[130] holding that the I.R.C. Section 761(a) election is restricted by its own terms to Subchapter K and that it does not otherwise affect the treatment of an organization.

The Service has indicated that, in some cases, an I.R.C. Section 761(a) election may exempt a partnership from Code sections outside Subchapter K. Revenue Ruling 83-129 holds that partners of an electing partnership can make inconsistent elections, rather than a single election as a partnership, for mining development expenditures.[131]

The Service attempted to explain its position in this ruling by stating that it will determine the effect of an election in each case by ascertaining if a non-Subchapter K rule can apply "without doing violence to the concept of electing out of Subchapter K."[132] Apparently, the Service will treat each partner in an electing partnership as the direct owner of a proportionate share of partnership assets rather than as the owner of a separate partnership interest.[133]

---

[127] H.R. Rep. No. 795, 100th Cong., 2d Sess. 1358 (1988); H.R. Rep. 101-247, 101st Cong., 1st Sess. 1358.

[128] Bryant v. Comm'r, 46 T.C. 848 (1966), *aff'd*, 399 F.2d 800 (5th Cir. 1968); Rev. Rul. 65-118, 1965-1 C.B. 30.

[129] Rev. Rul. 65-118, 1965-1 C.B. 30. *See* Rev. Rul. 82-213, 1982-2 C.B. 31 (investment credit property owned by electing partnership used by partnership not partners); Rev. Rul. 80-219, 1980-2 C.B. 19 (investment credit recaptured). *But see* Madison Gas & Electric Co. v. Comm'r, 72 T.C. 521 (1979), *aff'd*, 633 F.2d 512 (7th Cir. 1980), in which the Tax Court suggested that it based its holding in *Bryant* upon specific partnership limitations in the investment credit provisions, and that a different result may be reached when no specific reference to partnerships exists in the statute or regulations.

[130] 46 T.C. 848 (1966), *aff'd*, 399 F.2d 800 (5th Cir. 1968). *See* Cokes v. Comm'r, 91 T.C. 222 (1988) (individuals subject to self-employment tax as partners remain so if partnership elects out of Subchapter K).

[131] 1983-2 C.B. 105. *But see* Madison Gas & Electric Co. v. Comm'r, 72 T.C. 521 (1979), *aff'd*, 633 F.2d 512 (7th Cir. 1980), where the Service argued that an election does not preclude partnership treatment in determining whether a taxpayer may deduct a trade or business expense that would require capitalization at the partnership level.

[132] GCM 39043.

[133] The scope of this ruling is suggested by TAM 9214011, in which the Service treats the sale of an interest in a partnership that elected under I.R.C. § 761(a) as a sale of the partner's proportionate interest in each partnership asset.

[D] Procedure for Making the Election

The election to be completely excluded from the partnership tax provisions of Subchapter K is made by filing a properly executed partnership tax return (Form 1065) containing only the names, addresses, and taxpayer identification numbers of the organization and all its members and the following attached or incorporated statements:

(1)   The organization qualifies for exemption as an investing partnership, operating partnership, or organization of securities dealers.

(2)   All of its members elect to have the organization excluded from partnership treatment.

(3)   If a copy of the organization's operating agreement is obtainable or, if the agreement is oral, the person from whom the provisions of the agreement can be obtained.[134]

The Service assumes that an election to be excluded from the partnership tax provisions is consented to by all members of an organization unless a member notifies the Service in writing that (1) he does not consent to the exclusion, and (2) he sent the same notification to all other members of the organization by registered or certified mail. This notice must be filed within 90 days after the organization is formed. Because a valid election requires the consent of all members, one member's properly filed objection precludes exclusion from partnership tax treatment.

[E] Election by Showing Intent

An organization that qualifies for, but fails to make, an effective election for complete exclusion from Subchapter K is deemed to have made an election if the facts and circumstances show that its members intended, at the time of its formation, to secure exclusion beginning with the organization's first taxable year.[135] Either of the following factors may demonstrate the necessary intent:

(1)   at the time the organization was formed, the members agreed that it be excluded from partnership treatment; or

(2)   beginning with the organization's first taxable year, the members owning substantially all of its capital interests report their shares of its income and other tax items on their returns in a manner consistent with the organization's exclusion from partnership treatment.[136]

---

[134] Treas. Reg. § 1.761-2(b)(2)(i).

[135] Treas. Reg. § 1.761-2(b)(2)(ii).

[136] Treas. Reg. § 1.761-2(b)(2)(ii)(a), (b).

[F]   Election for Partial Exclusion

An organization may request to be excluded from only certain sections of the partnership tax provisions if (1) it qualifies for complete exclusion from these rules, and (2) all of its members consent to the requested exclusion.[137] The exclusion is not effective until approved by the Service, and it is subject to any conditions the Service imposes.[138] The Service will not approve an organization's election to be excluded from the rules governing the required partnership taxable year[139] or to the rule limiting a partner's loss deduction to the basis in his partnership interest.[140]

A request for partial exclusion must be made no later than 90 days after the beginning of the taxable year for which the partial exclusion is to begin. The request must:

(1)   state that all of the organization's members consent to the election;

(2)   state that the organization qualifies for complete exclusion from partnership treatment; and

(3)   specify the partnership provisions from which exclusion is sought.[141]

[G]   Effective Date and Revocation

An election for complete exclusion is effective beginning with the taxable year for which the election is filed.[142] For example, if an organization would otherwise be required to file a partnership tax return for the calendar year 1990 by April 15, 1991, an election filed on or before that date is effective for the 1990 taxable year. A deemed election for complete exclusion is effective with the organization's first taxable year.[143] An election for partial exclusion is effective only when approved by the Service.[144]

An election continues in effect until the organization no longer qualifies for the exclusion or until the election is revoked.[145] An election cannot be revoked without the Service's consent.[146] An application for permission to revoke is made to the Commissioner no later than 30 days following the beginning of the taxable year to which the revocation is to apply.[147]

---

[137]   Treas. Reg. § 1.761-2(c).

[138]   *Id.*

[139]   Rev. Rul. 57-215, 1957-1 C.B. 208. *See* I.R.C. § 706(b).

[140]   Rev. Rul. 58-465, 1958-2 C.B. 376. *See* I.R.C. § 704(b).

[141]   Treas. Reg. § 1.761-2(c).

[142]   *See* Treas. Reg. § 1.761-2(b)(2)(i), (3).

[143]   *See* Treas. Reg. § 1.761-2(b)(2)(ii), (3).

[144]   *See* Treas. Reg. § 1.761-2(c).

[145]   Treas. Reg. § 1.761-2(b)(3).

[146]   *Id.*

[147]   *Id.*

§ 2.07 CLASSIFYING UNINCORPORATED ASSOCIATIONS — PRE-1997 RULES

As described in § 2.02, *supra*, the regulations currently governing the classification of entities for tax purposes became effective on January 1, 1997. These rules replace the vastly different classification criteria established by the former regulations in 1960. Because the former regulations are relevant to pre-1997 transactions, their basic principles are summarized in this section.

The discussion in this section is of historical importance only. The regulations and rulings do not apply to the classification of entities after 1996. (For analysis of the current regulations, see § 2.02, *supra*.)

Under the former regulations, a venture was not considered a partnership if it met the tax definition of a corporation.[148] Because the Code defines the term corporation to include unincorporated "associations,"[149] an organization could be classified as a corporation for tax purposes even though considered a partnership under local law. In this situation, the association was taxable under the corporate tax rules of Subchapter C rather than under the partnership rules of Subchapter K.

Because the Code failed to provide criteria for classifying associations as corporations, guidelines evolved through case law, regulations, and administrative rulings. The Supreme Court established the basic test in *Morrissey v. Commissioner*,[150] holding that an unincorporated association was taxable as a corporation if it more closely resembled a corporation than any other kind of entity. This resemblance was determined by comparing the characteristics of the association in question with typical corporate characteristics.

In 1960, the Treasury issued regulations that partially adopted the *Morrissey* corporate-resemblance test for classifying associations.[151] According to the former regulations, an entity was classified as a corporation if it exhibited a majority of the corporate characteristics described in *Morrissey*:

(1)   the presence of associates;

(2)   a business objective and profit motive;

(3)   centralized management;

(4)   continuity of life;

(5)   limited liability; and

(6)   free transferability of interests.

---

[148] I.R.C. § 761(a). *Cf.* I.R.C. § 7701(a). An organization classified as an association that changes its corporate characteristics to require reclassification as a partnership is deemed to liquidate. If the change occurs involuntarily (as by amendment to the regulations), the change is not a liquidation and no tax is incurred. Rev. Rul. 63-107, 1963-1 C.B. 71.

[149] I.R.C. § 7701(a)(3).

[150] 296 U.S. 344 (1935).

[151] Former Treas. Reg. § 301.7701-2(a)(1). In *Morrissey*, the court noted that the Treasury was permitted to issue different rules defining the term association and may clarify or change these rules. *See* 296 U.S. at 354.

Because the first two factors, associates and a profit objective, are common to corporations and partnerships, the regulations did not count them in distinguishing a partnership from an association.[152] Thus, an unincorporated association was classified as a corporation for tax purposes only if it exhibited more than two of the remaining characteristics — centralized management, continuity of life, limited liability, and free transferability of interests.[153] Each of these characteristics was given equal weight in determining an entity's classification.[154]

The test in the former regulations differed significantly from the analysis the Court used in *Morrissey. Morrissey* involved an overall evaluation of the similarity between the entity in question and a corporation. In contrast, the 1960 regulations simply required counting the number of corporate characteristics the entity exhibited, without weighing the degree of corporate similarity each factor contributes.[155]

Thus, an organization that lacked two or more corporate characteristics was classified as a partnership even though its overall nature was more like a corporation. The regulations were purposely skewed this way to prevent unincorporated professional practices from adopting corporate pension plans which, at that time, provided far greater tax benefits than were available to professional partnerships.[156]

Although the Service eventually abandoned its attempt to bar corporate pension plans for professionals,[157] the anti-corporation slant of the regulations continued to allow ventures to be classified as partnerships even though they granted investors most of the important benefits of corporate status. This result contributed to a proliferation of tax shelters organized as limited partnerships.

The Service's attempts to curb limited partnership tax shelters through litigation[158] and administrative rulings[159] related to the classification issue were unsuccessful.[160] Therefore, Congress attacked those tax shelters by enacting legislation that eliminated most of the tax benefits limited partnerships formerly provided to

---

[152] Former Treas. Reg. § 301.7701-2(a)(2).

[153] Former Treas. Reg. § 301.7701-2(a)(2).

[154] Former Treas. Reg. §§ 301.7701-2(a)(3), 301.7701-3(b)(2), Example (2); Larson v. Comm'r, 66 T.C. 159, 185 (1976), *acq.* 1979-1 C.B. 1.

[155] In Larson v. Comm'r, 66 T.C. 159, 185 (1976), the Tax Court suggested that it would have classified the entity in question as a corporation if the regulations permitted applying different weights to the corporate characteristics.

[156] The Service's litigation had failed to prevent professional groups from being characterized as associations taxable as corporations. *See* U.S. v. Kintner, 216 F.2d 418 (9th Cir. 1954), *aff'g* 107 F. Supp. 976 (D. Mont. 1952).

[157] Rev. Rul. 70-101, 1970-1 C.B. 278.

[158] *See* Zuckman v. U.S., 524 F.2d 729 (Ct. Cl. 1975); Larson v. Comm'r, 66 T.C. 159 (1976), *acq.* 1979-2 C.B. 2.

[159] *See, e.g.*, Rev. Proc. 72-13, 1972-1 C.B. 735, and Rev. Proc. 74-17, 1974-1 C.B. 438, establishing rigorous criteria for obtaining an advance ruling classifying an entity as a limited partnership. In 1977, the Treasury issued new classification regulations, Prop. Treas. Reg. § 301.7701, 42 Fed. Reg. 1038 (Jan. 5, 1977), but these were immediately withdrawn. 42 Fed. Reg. 1489 (Jan 7, 1977).

[160] In 1982, the Service announced that it was reevaluating the classification rules. IR 82-145 (Dec 16,

investors. This legislation included the passive-loss rules of I.R.C. Section 469 and the publicly traded partnership rules of I.R.C. Section 7704, as well as a number of stringent reporting and penalty provisions. (*See, e.g.*, I.R.C. §§ 6662, 6698, 6700.)

However, perhaps a more important factor was the diminished attractiveness of most tax-sheltered investments due to lower tax rates, elimination of the investment tax credit, and the reduction in allowable deductions for items such as depreciation and interest. The demise of the tax shelter industry allowed the Treasury to issue the flexible, taxpayer friendly, "check-the-box" classification regulations in 1996 and eliminate the complexities and uncertainties created by the former regulations. (*See* § 2.02, *supra*.)

Although the classification of a venture was governed by the tax regulations, local law applied in determining whether the legal relationships referred to in the regulations existed.[161] Local law was examined to determine if a particular corporate characteristic was present in an organization. The regulations indicated that general partnerships organized under the Uniform Partnership Act (U.P.A.) did not generally exhibit any of the pertinent corporate characteristics.[162]

Similarly, limited partnerships subject to the Uniform Limited Partnership Act (U.L.P.A.), the Revised Uniform Limited Partnership Act (R.U.L.P.A.),[163] or state statutes corresponding to these uniform acts, generally lacked the characteristics of continuity of life and centralized management.[164] Therefore, ventures subject to these statutes ordinarily were classified as partnerships.

1982). That study was completed in 1988 without indicating that these rules will be changed. Ann. 88-118, 1988-2 C.B. 450.

[161] Former Treas. Reg. § 301.7701-1(c). *See* Richlands Medical Ass'n v. Comm'r, T.C. Memo. 1990-660 (professional association taxable as corporation where state law provided entity with continuity of life, centralized management, and limited liability).

[162] Former Treas. Reg. § 301.7701-1(c). *See, e.g.*, Foster v. Comm'r, 80 T.C. 34, 184–90 (1983). The Uniform Partnership Act has been adopted by all states except Louisiana, as well as by the District of Columbia and the Virgin Islands.

[163] Although the regulations refer to partnerships formed under statutes corresponding to the Uniform Limited Partnership Act, an amendment in 1983 provides that these references are deemed to refer to R.U.L.P.A. as well.

[164] Former Treas. Reg. § 301.7701-2(a), (b), (c). A limited partnership with a corporate general partner may possess centralized management regardless of state law if limited partners own substantially all the interest in the general partner. Former Treas. Reg. § 301.7701-2(c)(4).

Chapter 3

TAX ACCOUNTING FOR PARTNERSHIPS AND LIMITED LIABILITY COMPANIES

§ 3.01 OVERVIEW OF TAX ACCOUNTING

An entity taxable as a partnership (including a limited liability company) is not itself a taxpayer; rather, the entity serves as a conduit through which its income, gains, losses, deductions, and credits pass directly to the partners or members.[1] Each partner or member reports its share of the entity's income or loss on its individual tax return and its personal tax liability increases or decreases correspondingly. In this sense, a partnership or LLC is treated as an aggregate of individuals for tax purposes, rather than as a separate business entity.

A partnership or LLC is treated as an entity, however, when computing the amount and timing of the income or loss passed through to the partners or members.[2] The entity's income is determined using its own method of accounting and tax year. Most elections affecting the amount and timing of the entity's income and deductions are made at the entity level.[3] Partners or members generally must report their shares of each item of partnership or LLC income or loss as having the same character (*e.g.*, capital gain or loss) it had when earned or incurred by the partnership or LLC.[4]

With some exceptions, a partnership or LLC computes its taxable income or loss in the same manner as an individual. Certain items, however, are not aggregated with the entity's income; they must be segregated and accounted for separately.[5] (*See* § 3.02[A], *infra*.) The partnership or LLC reports its taxable income or loss and separately stated items to the Service on an information return (Form 1065) and notifies each partner or member of his distributive share of these amounts (on Schedule K-1).

Each partner or member reports his distributive share of the entity's taxable income or loss and separately stated items on the appropriate schedule of his

---

[1] I.R.C. § 701. But see § 3.05, *infra*, regarding electing large partnerships, which may be a taxpayer in certain situations.

[2] The principle that a partnership is treated as an entity for purposes of computing income and loss was reaffirmed by the Supreme Court in U.S. v. Basye, 410 U.S. 441 (1973). *See* Rev. Rul. 75-113, 1975-1 C.B. 19.

[3] I.R.C. § 703(b).

[4] I.R.C. § 702(b). A partner who treats a partnership item in a manner inconsistent with the treatment of the item on the partnership's return must notify the IRS of the inconsistency. I.R.C. § 6222.

[5] These items are specified in I.R.C. §§ 702 and 703 and the regulations thereunder.

individual tax return for the tax year during which the partnership or LLC tax year ends.[6] A partner or member must report his distributive share of partnership or LLC income even if no money or property was actually distributed to him during the year.

A partner's or member's deduction for his share of entity losses may be limited on his personal tax return if specific statutory restrictions apply (*e.g.*, the at-risk rules, the passive loss limitation, or the I.R.C. Section 704(d) basis limitation). (See discussion of the at-risk rules and the passive loss rules in Chapter 6, and the I.R.C. Section 704(d) basis limitation in Chapter 5.)

This chapter describes the general rules governing tax accounting for partnership income or loss and the specific rules for computing, characterizing, and reporting partnership tax items. These rules are equally applicable to limited liability companies classified as partnerships and their members. The discussion is organized as follows:

(1)   Section 3.02 discusses the computation of partnership taxable income and the items that must be accounted for separately on the partnership return. This section also covers related issues, including partnership gross income, character of partnership income, income earned by partnership agents or from nonpartnership sources, and the effect of nonpartnership tax rules on partnership tax accounting.

(2)   Section 3.03 describes the tax elections that affect the treatment of partnership tax items. Included are the elections that the partnership must make, as well as the elections partners make individually.

(3)   Section 3.04 describes the rules governing adoption and change of a partnership's tax year. It covers determining the tax year mandated by statute, the factors that establish a business purpose for adopting a fiscal tax year, and the fiscal-year election allowed to partnerships that make certain required payments to the government.

§ 3.02   COMPUTING TAXABLE INCOME

Although a partnership is not a taxpaying entity, its net ordinary income or loss from operations and investments is referred to as its taxable income or loss.[7] A partnership determines its taxable income or loss in two steps:

(1)   The partnership segregates all income and loss items that must be accounted for and stated separately.[8] These items are excluded from the computation of partnership taxable income.

(2)   The partnership aggregates all remaining income and deductions and computes its net income or loss in much the same manner as an individual

---

   [6]   I.R.C. § 706.

   [7]   I.R.C. § 702(a)(8); Treas. Reg. § 1.702-1(a). But see special rules for electing large partnerships in § 3.05, *infra*.

   [8]   I.R.C. § 702(a); Treas. Reg. § 1.702-1(a).

taxpayer.[9]

Each partner includes his distributive share of partnership taxable income or loss in the gross income on his individual tax return and includes his share of each separately stated item on the appropriate schedule of his return.[10]

In computing its taxable income, a partnership may not claim any personal exemptions[11] nor deduct the following items:[12]

(1)   taxes paid to foreign countries and U.S. possessions;[13]

(2)   charitable contributions;[14]

(3)   net operating losses;[15]

(4)   itemized personal expenses such as alimony and medical expenses;[16] and

(5)   oil and gas depletion.[17]

Although the partnership does not deduct these expenses in computing its taxable income, they are reflected in the partners' distributive shares of separately stated partnership items. Therefore, each partner's share of these expenses is reflected on the appropriate schedule of his tax return, subject to any limitations on their deductibility. For example, each partner combines his share of the partnership's charitable contributions with contributions he made outside the partnership. This total is used to determine the charitable contribution deduction the partner is allowed on his individual tax return.

[A]   Items That Must Be Separately Stated

Any item of income or deduction that may be subject to special tax treatment by any partner is not included in computing the partnership's taxable income; it must be accounted for and stated separately. Each partner combines his distributive share of separately stated items with similar items from nonpartnership sources on his individual tax return. Income or loss items that must be separately stated fall under four categories:

(1)   items specified in the Code;

(2)   items specified in the regulations;

(3)   any item that would cause any partner's income tax liability to differ from the amount that would result if he did not take the item into account

---

[9]   I.R.C. §§ 702(a), 703(a); Treas. Reg. §§ 1.702-1(a), 1.703-1(a).

[10]   *See* I.R.C. § 706(a); Treas. Reg. § 1.706-1(a).

[11]   I.R.C. § 151.

[12]   I.R.C. § 703(a)(2).

[13]   I.R.C. §§ 164(a), 901.

[14]   I.R.C. § 170.

[15]   I.R.C. § 172.

[16]   Part VII of Subchapter B, I.R.C. § 212 *et seq.*

[17]   I.R.C. § 611.

separately;[18] or

(4)   any item that is subject to limitations on the amount a partner may deduct or exclude from income.

These four categories are discussed in the subsections below.

[1]   Items Specified in I.R.C. Section 702

Under I.R.C. Section 702(a), a partnership must separately state and account for the following items discussed below.

Short-term and long-term capital gains and losses. The partnership does not list individual transactions involving capital assets but nets its long-term capital gains with long-term losses, and its short-term capital gains with short-term losses.[19] Only the net long-term gain or loss and the net short-term gain or loss are separately stated by the partnership. Each partner combines his distributive share of these net amounts with his long- and short-term capital gains or losses from other sources. A partner's share of partnership long-term capital gain or loss retains its long-term character, even though the partner has owned his partnership interest less than the long-term holding period.[20]

Under capital gains provisions enacted in 1997, the tax rate applicable to a long-term capital gain depends on how long property is held before being sold or exchanged. The rates may differ for property held for 12 months, 18 months, or five years.[21] Thus, partnerships and LLCs must keep track of the gains from property with each holding period and separately pass these amounts through to partners.

Gains and losses from property used in a trade or business and involuntary conversionsns. The partnership must separately state its net gain or loss from sales, exchanges, and involuntary conversions of property described in I.R.C. Section 1231.[22] Each partner takes into account his distributive share of each of these items and combines them on his tax return with similar items from nonpartnership sources.

Charitable contributions. Under I.R.C. Section 170, individual taxpayers may deduct charitable contributions, subject to "contribution-base" limitations (*i.e.*, their adjusted gross income computed without regard to any net operating loss carryback). Some kinds of contributions cannot exceed 50 percent of the individual's contribution base, while other types of contributions are deductible only up to 30 percent of the individual's contribution base.[23] To preserve these limitations, a partnership must separately state the amounts contributed in each category. Each partner takes into account his distributive share of each contribution category in

---

[18]   Treas. Reg. § 1.702-1(a)(8), (ii).

[19]   Treas. Reg. § 1.702-1(a)(1), (2).

[20]   Rev. Rul. 68-79, 1968-1 C.B. 310.

[21]   I.R.C. § 1(h).

[22]   Treas. Reg. § 1.702-1(a)(3). See Schedule K-1, which requires gains and losses from involuntary conversions to be reported separately from other I.R.C. § 1231 gains and losses.

[23]   I.R.C. § 170(b)(1)(B).

determining the limitations on his own charitable contribution deduction.[24]

Dividends qualifying for deduction. [25] Under I.R.C. Sections 243–246, corporations may deduct a portion of the dividends they receive on stock owned in other corporations. To permit the computation of this deduction, a partnership must separately state any dividend income that may give rise to a deduction.

Foreign taxes. A partner may elect either (1) to deduct his share of taxes paid or accrued to foreign countries or U.S. possessions under I.R.C. Section 164(a), or (2) to treat this amount as a credit under I.R.C. Section 901. Because this choice is made at the partner level, the partnership must separately state these taxes.[26]

[2] Items Specified in the Regulations

The regulations require partnerships to separately state the following items:[27]

(1) recoveries of tax benefit items (*i.e.*, bad debts, prior taxes, and delinquency amounts under I.R.C. Section 111);

(2) gains and losses from wagering (I.R.C. § 165(d));

(3) soil and water conservation expenditures (I.R.C. § 175);

(4) nonbusiness expenses (I.R.C. § 212);

(5) medical expenses and dental payments (I.R.C. § 213);

(6) expenses for care of certain dependents;[28]

(7) alimony payments (I.R.C. § 215);

(8) amounts for taxes and interest paid to cooperative housing corporations (I.R.C. § 216);

(9) intangible drilling and development costs (I.R.C. § 263(c));

(10) certain mining exploration costs (I.R.C. § 617);

(11) gain or loss attributable to disproportionate distributions to partners that are subject to I.R.C. Section 751(b); and

(12) any item of income, gain, loss, deduction, or credit subject to a special allocation under the partnership agreement that differs from the general

---

[24] Under Treas. Reg. § 1.170A-1(h)(7), a partner's distributive share of charitable contributions actually paid by a partnership during its tax year may be allowed as a deduction in the partner's separate return for the partner's tax year with or within which the partnership year ends. The partner's share is aggregated with his other contributions in applying the limitations of I.R.C. § 170(b). *See* Rev. Rul. 96-11, 1996-1 C.B. 140.

[25] Part VIII of Subchapter B. This provision applies to corporate dividend-received deductions. Dividend exclusions for individual taxpayers were repealed in the Tax Reform Act of 1986.

[26] Treas. Reg. § 1.702-1(a)(6). *See* Rev. Rul. 71-141, 1971-1 C.B. 211 (corporate partner entitled to its share of partnership's foreign tax credit).

[27] Treas. Reg. § 1.702-1(a)(8)(i).

[28] The regulations refer to I.R.C. § 214, which has been repealed and replaced with I.R.C. § 21 (providing for a credit).

allocation of partnership income or loss (see discussion of special allocations in Chapter 4).

[3]　Items That Affect Partner's Tax Liability

Partnerships must separately state, and each partner must separately take into account, his distributive share of any partnership item that, if separately taken into account by any partner, would result in an income tax liability for that partner different from the liability that would result if that partner did not take the item into account separately.[29]

The regulations state that an item must be accounted for separately if that treatment by any partner would change that partner's tax liability or the tax liability of "any other person."[30] Addition of the reference to "any other person" is designed to ensure specific treatment of partnership gross income subject to the special rules applicable to controlled foreign corporations.

A number of these items are listed in the regulations or cited in the directions to Schedule K of the partnership information return. These include:

(1)　amounts received as pensions, annuities, or retirement income for purposes of the tax credit for the elderly;[31]

(2)　income and deductions subject to the hobby loss limitation;[32]

(3)　earned income if

　　(a)　an individual partner resides outside the United States (for purposes of the exclusion of foreign source income under I.R.C. Section 911),[33]

　　(b)　a partner is a child of 14 years or less (for purposes of determining the net unearned income subject to taxation at his parents' tax rate),[34] or

　　(c)　a partner has a qualified pension or profit-sharing plan (for determining the allowable contribution deduction);[35]

(4)　U.S. source income allocated to nonresident alien or foreign corporate partners subject to a 30 percent tax rate;[36]

---

[29]　Treas. Reg. § 1.702-1(a)(8), (ii).

[30]　Treas. Reg. § 1.702-1(a)(8)(ii) issued in T.D. 9008 (July 23, 2002). This restates the position taken in the proposed regulations issued in 2000 in 65 Fed. Reg. 56,836.

[31]　*See* Treas. Reg. § 1.702-1(a)(8), (ii). The regulations refer to I.R.C. § 37, which has been changed to I.R.C. § 22.

[32]　*See* Treas. Reg. § 1.702-1(a)(8), (ii). The regulations refer to I.R.C. § 270, which has been changed to I.R.C. § 183.

[33]　*See* Treas. Reg. § 1.702-1(a)(8), (ii). I.R.C. § 911(d)(2) defines earned income as ". . . wages, salaries, or professional fees, and other amounts received as compensation for personal services actually rendered."

[34]　I.R.C. § 1(g).

[35]　I.R.C. §§ 401(c), 404(a).

[36]　I.R.C. §§ 871, 881.

(5)   Subpart F income if any partner is a controlled foreign corporation;[37]

(6)   depreciation or depletion deductions if an estate or trust is a partner;[38]

(7)   tax preference items subject to the alternative minimum tax;[39]

(8)   nonbusiness deductions of individuals for determining a noncorporate partner's net operating loss;[40]

(9)   net earnings or loss from self-employment;[41]

(10)   corporate tax preference items;[42]

(11)   deductible or capitalized guaranteed payments to partners;[43]

(12)   gross income from farming or fishing;

(13)   income from debt cancellation;[44]

(14)   tax-exempt interest or income;[45] and

(15)   nonbusiness bad debts.[46]

Example: Alan, Barbara, and Carl are equal members in the ABC limited liability company. Alan is a resident of a foreign country and, pursuant to I.R.C. Section 911, may exclude part of his foreign-source earned income from his distributive share of partnership income. As a result, Alan's share of ABC's income will differ depending upon whether earned income is separately stated or included in ABC's overall taxable income. Therefore, earned income must be excluded from the computation of ABC's taxable income and must be separately stated for all the members.

[4]   Items Subject to Limitations on Partner's Return

Partnership items that may require separate statement because of limitations on the amount deductible or excludable by a partner include the following:

(1)   expensing of business property;[47]

---

[37] Treas. Reg. 1.702-1(a)(8)(ii). *But see* Brown Group v. Comm'r, 77 F.3d 217 (8th Cir. 1996), *vacating and remanding* 104 T.C. 105 (1995).

[38] I.R.C. §§ 167(h) and 611(b); *See* Rev. Rul. 74-71, 1974-1 C.B. 158 (separate statement required if tax liability of estate or trust would change).

[39] I.R.C. § 57.

[40] I.R.C. § 172(d)(4).

[41] I.R.C. § 1402.

[42] I.R.C. § 291.

[43] I.R.C. §§ 707(c), 162, 263.

[44] I.R.C. § 108.

[45] I.R.C. § 103.

[46] I.R.C. § 166(d).

[47] I.R.C. § 179. A partner's basis in his partnership interest decreases by his entire distributive share of partnership expenditures for depreciable assets deducted under I.R.C. § 179; Rev. Rul. 89-7, 1989-1

(2) oil and gas income, for purposes of the depletion deduction;[48]

(3) investment income and expenses, for the investment interest limitation;[49]

(4) partnership losses subject to the at-risk limitations;[50]

(5) partnership income and losses subject to passive loss limitations, with separate statement of amounts from rental activities and portfolio income;[51]

(6) income and losses from rental real estate activities for the $25,000 exemption from the passive loss limitation;[52]

(7) payments to Keogh plans for partners;[53] and

(8) expenditures subject to the uniform capitalization rules.[54]

Example: Carla owns a 50-percent interest in the CD Partnership. In 19X1, the partnership has total investment income of $80,000 and total investment interest expenses of $60,000. These items are not included in CD's taxable income but are separately stated.

Carla incurred nonpartnership investment interest expenses of $20,000 in 19X1 but had no other investment income. No deduction is allowed at the partnership level for the investment interest expense, and Carla includes her $30,000 share of that expense (one half of $60,000) and her $40,000 share of partnership investment income (one-half of $80,000) on her individual tax return. Under the investment interest limitation rules,[55] Carla cannot deduct $10,000 of her investment interest expense in 19X1 (the excess of her $50,000 total investment interest expense over her $40,000 of investment income).

[B] Determining Partner's Share of Partnership Gross Income

Whenever it is necessary for a partner to determine his gross income for any income tax purpose, the computation must include his distributive share of the partnership's gross income.[56] A partner may be required to compute his gross

---

C.B. 178. This is true even if the partner cannot use the entire deduction on his individual tax return because of the limitation on such deductions.

[48] I.R.C. § 613.

[49] I.R.C. § 163(d); Rev. Rul. 86-138, 1986-2 C.B. 84, holds that a multi-tiered partnership must separately state investment interest and expense if any partner of any partnership is affected by the I.R.C. § 163(d) limitation.

[50] I.R.C. § 465.

[51] I.R.C. § 469.

[52] I.R.C. § 469. The individual income and expense items are reported on Form 8825.

[53] I.R.C. § 469.

[54] I.R.C. § 263A; *See* Temp. Treas. Reg. § 1.263A-1T; 1988-2 C.B. 422, Notice 88-99.

[55] I.R.C. § 163(d).

[56] I.R.C. § 702(c). Although the regulations do not address the issue, it appears logical to determine a partner's share of gross income using the same ratio as for determining his taxable income.

income to determine:[57]

(1)   whether filing a tax return is required (I.R.C. § 6012(a));

(2)   whether an exemption may be claimed for certain dependents (I.R.C. § 151(c));

(3)   gross income received from certain U.S. possessions (I.R.C. § 931);

(4)   whether the partner may exclude foreign source income (I.R.C. § 911);

(5)   the gross income from farming that limits soil and water conservation deductions (I.R.C. § 175);

(6)   adjusted gross income for purposes of the percentage limitations on miscellaneous itemized deductions (I.R.C. § 67), charitable contribution deductions (I.R.C. § 170), and medical expense deductions (I.R.C. § 213);

(7)   whether a corporation is a personal holding company (I.R.C. § 542);

(8)   whether a corporation is a controlled foreign corporation (I.R.C. § 954);

(9)   the unrelated-business income of a tax-exempt organization (I.R.C. § 512(c)); and

(10)   whether a partner who is a child of 14 years or less is subject to taxation at his or her parents' tax rate (under I.R.C. § 1(j)).

[C]   Level for Determining Character of Partnership Income

Although the Code is somewhat ambiguous, the character of each item of partnership income, gain, loss, deduction, or credit is generally determined based on the partnership's activities, not the activities of each individual partner.[58] Each partner reports his distributive share of each partnership item as retaining the same character it was determined to have at the partnership level. For example, a partner reports capital gain or loss when a partnership sells property that is a capital asset in its hands, even though it would be classified as ordinary-income property in the partner's hands. As discussed below, however, this partnership-level characterization rule may not apply to a controlled foreign corporation's share of partnership Subpart F income (*see* § 3.02[C][2], *infra*) or to certain property contributed by a partner (*see* § 3.02[D], *infra*).

Regulations and rulings suggest that the Treasury is inclined to characterize income at the partner (rather than partnership) level in a number of situations. For example, the preamble to recent proposed regulations under I.R.C. Section 702 maintains that the character of a partner's distributive share is the character that "best serves" the Code or regulations section at issue.[59] Applying this rationale,

---

[57] *See* Treas. Reg. § 1.702-1(c)(1).

[58] *See* Treas. Reg. § 1.702-1(b); Podell v. Comm'r, 55 T.C. 429 (1970); Resnik v. Comm'r, 66 T.C. 74 (1976), *aff'd*, 555 F.2d 634 (7th Cir. 1977); Davis v. Comm'r, 74 T.C. 881 (1980), *aff'd*, 746 F.2d 357 (6th Cir. 1984); Rev. Rul. 77-304, 1977-2 C.B. 59; Rev. Rul. 68-79, 1968-1 C.B. 216; Rev. Rul. 67-188, 1967-1 C.B. 216.

[59] Prop. Treas. Reg. § 1.702-1(a)(8), (ii).

the proposed regulations state that the legislative intent of Subpart F precludes allowing a controlled foreign corporation (CFC) to avoid Subpart F treatment simply by receiving income as distributive share of partnership income, rather than directly.[60]

A similar approach is taken in recently issued final regulations under I.R.C. Section 1032.[61] Under I.R.C. Section 1032, a corporation does not recognize gain or loss on a sale of its own stock. Applying an aggregate approach, regulations extend this nonrecognition treatment to a corporate partner's share of gain or loss realized from a partnership that sells the corporate partner's stock.[62] Recently issued final regulations state that aggregate theory of partnership taxation is applied in determining the adjustments that must be made to the corporate partner's basis for its partnership interest.[63] Using the aggregate approach, the corporate partner must increase (or decrease) the basis of its partnership interest by the amount of gain (or loss) not recognized.[64] (For complete discussion of basis adjustment required by I.R.C. Section 1032, see § 5.01[C][7], *infra*.)

[1] Effect of Partnership-Level Characterization

Partnership-level characterization affects the manner in which partners report their shares of the following items of partnership income, gain, loss, or deduction:

(1) whether gain or loss on a sale or exchange of partnership property is capital or ordinary gain or loss;[65]

(2) whether partnership gross income and deductions are attributable to business or nonbusiness activities, for computing a partner's net-operating-loss deduction;[66]

(3) whether a partnership is carrying on a trade or business, for computing a partner's deductions for trade or business expenses;[67]

(4) whether a bad debt is a business or nonbusiness bad debt;[68]

(5) whether interest is classified as trade or business interest, investment

---

[60] *See* Prop. Treas. Reg. § 1.952-1(g)(1).

[61] Treas. Reg. § 1.1032-3(a); T.D. 8883, 2000-2 C.B. 115.

[62] Treas. Reg. § 1.1032-3(a).

[63] Treas. Reg. § 1.705-2(a); T.D. 8986, 2001-4 I.R.B. 424.

[64] *See* Rev. Rul. 99-57, 1999-2 CB 678.

[65] Davis v. Comm'r, 74 T.C. 881 (1980), *aff'd*, 746 F.2d 357 (6th Cir. 1984); Podell v. Comm'r, 55 T.C. 429 (1970).

[66] Treas. Reg. § 1.702-2; *See* I.R.C. § 172. *See also* Campbell v. U.S., 813 F.2d 694 (5th Cir. 1987) (taxpayer's net operating loss carryback does not include his share of losses from partnership not carrying on a trade or business).

[67] *See* Madison Gas & Electric Co. v. Comm'r, 72 T.C. 521 (1979), *aff'd*, 633 F.2d 512 (7th Cir. 1980) (partnership required to capitalize expenditures even though payments would constitute deductible business expenses if incurred by partners). *See also* Rev. Rul. 75-523, 1975-2 C.B. 257 (classification of partnership expenditures as investment expense passes through to partners).

[68] I.R.C. § 166. *See* Cole v. Comm'r, T.C. Memo. 1962-287; Sales v. Comm'r, 37 T.C. 576 (1961). Nonbusiness bad debts are treated as short-term capital losses under I.R.C. § 166(d).

interest, portfolio interest, qualified residence interest, or personal interest, for determining any limitations on a partner's interest deduction;[69]

(6)　whether income is classified as portfolio income, for computing any limitations on a partner's deduction for passive losses;[70] and

(7)　whether income or loss is classified as passive or active, for determining any limitations on a partner's deduction for passive losses — the classification as passive or active depends on two factors: (a) whether the partnership is carrying on a trade or business, and (b) whether the partner in question materially participates in that activity.[71]

Example: George, a real estate dealer, forms a limited liability company with Hilary, who is not a dealer. The LLC is formed to acquire real estate for investment. The members invest cash that is then used to acquire a parcel of realty. Upon sale of the realty, the character of the income, determined at the entity level, is capital gain. On their individual tax returns, both George and Hilary recognize capital gain income, even though if George had sold the parcel as an individual, it would have been ordinary income for him. Similarly, interest paid on funds borrowed to obtain and carry the realty is characterized as investment interest expense subject to limitations on deductibility under I.R.C. Section 163(d).

[2]　Character of Income if Partner Is Controlled Foreign Corporation

Certain United States shareholders of a controlled foreign corporation (CFC) are currently taxable on their share of the CFC's foreign source income specified in Subpart F[72] of the Code (Subpart F income)[73] even though no amounts are distributed to them. A characterization issue arises when a CFC is a partner in a partnership that has foreign source income. If the income is characterized at the partnership level, the CFC partner's distributive share is not currently taxable to its shareholders as Subpart F income because the partnership is not a CFC. If characterization is at the partner level, however, the CFC's distributive share of partnership income constitutes Subpart F income currently taxable to its shareholders.

---

[69]　I.R.C. § 163; Temp. Treas. Reg. §§ 1.163-8T, 1.163-9T.

[70]　I.R.C. § 469(e)(1).

[71]　I.R.C. § 469(c).

[72]　I.R.C. §§ 951–964.

[73]　The Subpart F rules are designed to eliminate specific tax advantages that U.S. shareholders would otherwise obtain by organizing their corporations in foreign countries that have relatively low tax rates. Subpart F income is defined in I.R.C. § 952(a) to include "foreign base company income" (FBCI), as defined in I.R.C. § 954. FBCI includes foreign base company sales income" (FBCSI) which is any income derived from the purchase or sale of personal property if (1) the purchase or sale is to, from, or on behalf of a related party, (2) the property is manufactured, produced, grown or extracted outside the country under whose laws the CFC is created or organized, and (3) the property is purchased or sold for use, consumption or disposition outside the CFC's country of organization. I.R.C. § 954(a).

Recent developments have created a great deal of uncertainty in this area. This note provides a chronology of these developments:

In Revenue Ruling 89-72,[74] the Service ruled that the character of a CFC partner's distributive share is determined for Subpart F income purposes at the CFC level. The ruling considers a U.S. parent machinery manufacturer corporation (P) that owns all the stock of CFC organized in country Y. CFC is a 25 percent partner in the PRS partnership, organized in country X. PRS purchases machines from P and sells them in country X. If CFC directly sold the machines for use in country X, the income would be currently taxable to its shareholders under Subpart F.[75] On these facts, the Service concludes that CFC's share of partnership income from PRS is Subpart F income that is currently taxable to shareholder P. In effect, the ruling treats the partnership as an "aggregate" of individual owners rather than as a separate entity.[76]

In Brown *Group v. Commissioner*,[77] the Tax Court initially disagreed with Revenue Ruling 89-72, holding that the character of a CFC's distributive share of a foreign partnership's income is determined at the partnership level (*i.e.*, the partnership is considered a separate "entity"). Because the partnership was not a CFC, its income was not Subpart F income.

Responding to criticism from the tax bar, the Tax Court withdrew its decision for reconsideration. The court subsequently reversed itself, now holding that a CFC's distributive share of partnership income is Subpart F income if it would be Subpart F income if directly earned by the CFC (*i.e.*, the partnership is considered an "aggregate" of its owners).[78] Upon appeal, the Eighth Circuit reversed the Tax Court, holding that the character of partnership income is determined at the "entity" level and that separate characterization tests are not applied for each partner.[79]

Dissatisfied with the *Brown Group* decision, in early 1998, the Treasury Department issued temporary and proposed regulations[80] providing two sets of provisions:

(1)   Rules relating to the treatment of a CFC's distributive share of partnership income under Subpart F; and

---

[74] 1989-1 C.B. 257.

[75] The income would be FBCSI because derived from the sale of machines bought from a related party (P) and sold for use in a country other than the CFC's country of organization. I.R.C. § 954(a).

[76] *But see* FSA 1998-389 (Jan 1, 1992) at 98 TNT 220-83 (CFC must treat partnership distribution as foreign base company services income if CFC had no employees, owned no equipment, and used related corporation to perform services on behalf of partnership).

[77] 102 T.C. 616 (1994), *withdrawn and reconsidered*, 104 T.C. 105 (1995), *vacated and remanded*, 77 F.3d 217 (8th Cir. 1996).

[78] 104 T.C. 105 (1995).

[79] 77 F.3d 217 (8th Cir. 1996).

[80] 63 Fed. Reg. 14613 (Mar. 26, 1998).

(2) Rules designed to curtail the use of "hybrid branch" arrangements to avoid Subpart F.[81] The Treasury defines a hybrid branch as one that is considered part of the CFC for U.S. tax purposes (*i.e.*, it is "fiscally transparent"), but is considered a separate entity (*i.e.*, not fiscally transparent) in the country where the CFC is incorporated.[82] In response to Congressional demands, however, the Treasury quickly withdrew the new rules. The regulations were withdrawn in Notice 98-35,[83] which also announced that the IRS intended to issue new regulations in both areas.[84]

Final regulations address the main issues raised in the *Brown Group* case — the appropriate treatment of a CFC's distributive share of partnership income under Subpart F. The regulations provide rules for determining whether a CFC partner's distributive share of partnership income is Subpart F income.[85] The regulations also cover treatment of a CFC partner's distributive share of foreign personal holding company income, foreign base company sales income, foreign base company services income, and earnings invested in United States property under certain provisions of Subpart F.

These regulations maintain that the character of a partner's distributive share is the character that "best serves" the Code or regulations section at issue.[86] Using this approach, the regulations assert that it is contrary to the legislative intent of Subpart F to allow a CFC to avoid Subpart F treatment simply by receiving income as a distributive share of partnership income, rather than directly.

The regulations under I.R.C. Section 702 indicate that an item must be separately taken into account if separate accounting by any partner would change the tax liability of that partner or of any other persons.[87] The regulations amend the existing regulations to require separate accounting for an item if that treatment changes the tax liability of a partner or "any other persons." This is the position taken in Revenue Ruling 86-138,[88] holding that a subsidiary partnership in a multi-tiered arrangement must separately state items that change a partner's tax liability if separately accounted for by any partner in the multi-tiered arrangement.

Thus, if any partner is a CFC, income items that would be Subpart F income if separately taken into account by the CFC must be separately stated for all partners. Such treatment means that U.S. shareholders of the CFC must include their pro rata share of the income in their gross income under the rules of Subpart F.

---

[81] The hybrid branch rules were also issued as temporary regulations. T.D. 8767, 1998-27 I.R.B. 35.

[82] *See* 1998-2 C.B. 34, Notice 98-35.

[83] 1998-2 C.B. 34.

[84] 1996-2 C.B. 209, Notice 96-39. *See also* 1998-1 C.B. 433, Notice 98-11 (partnership arrangements that raise issues similar to hybrid branch arrangements will be addressed in separate regulations).

[85] T.D. 9008 (July 23, 2002). The final regulations adopt most of the rules set forth in proposed regulations issued in 2000. 65 Fed. Reg. 56836. The regulations apply to tax years beginning on or after July 23, 2002.

[86] Preamble to regulations issued in T.D. 9008 (July 23, 2002).

[87] Treas. Reg. § 1.702-1(a)(8), (ii).

[88] 1986-2 C.B. 84.

[D] Character of Gain or Loss on Disposition of Certain Contributed Property

The general rule that the character of partnership income, gain, loss, deductions, or credit is determined at the partnership level (*see* § 3.02[C], *supra*) does not apply to gain or loss that a partnership realizes when it disposes of certain property contributed by a partner. Under I.R.C. Section 724, a partnership recognizes ordinary income or loss when it disposes of contributed property that constituted either (1) unrealized receivables,[89] or (2) inventory[90] in the hands of the contributing partner at the time of contribution. If the partnership disposes of contributed property that had a built-in capital loss at the time of contribution, it recognizes capital loss. Thus, the character of the gain or loss on disposition of these types of contributed property is determined at the contributing partner, rather than the partnership, level.

For inventory and capital-loss property, this special treatment applies only if the partnership disposes of the property within five years of the date it was contributed. No time limitation applies to the characterization of income or loss on disposition of contributed receivables.

This partner-level characterization rule precludes taxpayers from converting potential ordinary income to capital gain or potential capital loss to ordinary loss by contributing inventory, receivables, or capital-loss property to a partnership.[91] If the partnership disposes of contributed inventory or receivables, the amount of ordinary income or loss inherent in the property at the time of contribution is allocated to the contributing partner under the I.R.C. Section 704(c) allocation rules for contributed property.

Any additional income or loss is allocated among the partners as ordinary income or loss in accordance with their distributive shares under the partnership agreement.[92] Upon a disposition of contributed capital-loss property, the built-in loss is allocated to the contributing partner as a capital loss, and any additional loss is characterized at the partnership level and allocated among the partners in accordance with their distributive shares.[93] The amount of loss allocated to the contributing partner cannot exceed the loss the partnership actually realizes. Thus, if the property increases in value but is still sold at a loss, only the amount of the partnership loss is allocated to the contributing partner.

A partnership realizes ordinary income or loss whenever it disposes of contributed property that was an unrealized receivable in the hands of the

---

[89] As defined in I.R.C. § 751(c).

[90] As defined in I.R.C. § 751(d)(2).

[91] Under I.R.C. § 1237, subdivided real estate held primarily for sale to customers may be treated as a capital asset if the taxpayer holds it for five years, does not own any other realty, and does not improve the property.

[92] *See* I.R.C. § 704(c)(1)(A).

[93] I.R.C. § 704(b). If the partnership agreement is silent or makes an allocation that lacks substantial economic effect, the partners' distributive shares are determined in accordance with their interests in the partnership. For discussion of distributive shares, see Chapter 6.

contributing partner.[94] For this purpose, an unrealized receivable is (1) any right to payment for goods (other than capital assets) or services that was not previously includable in the contributing partner's income, and (2) the gain inherent in contributed property that is subject to recapture as ordinary income.[95] The amount of ordinary income is not limited to the gain inherent in the receivables when contributed but applies to any gain the partnership recognizes on a disposition of the property.

The partnership realizes ordinary income or loss when it disposes of property that was inventory in the hands of the contributing partner if the disposition occurs within five years of the date of contribution.[96] For this purpose, inventory includes stock in trade, items held primarily for sale to customers in the ordinary course of a trade or business, and any other item that would generate ordinary income if sold by the partner immediately before the contribution.[97] The ordinary-income rule is not limited to the amount of gain inherent in the inventory when contributed but applies to any gain the partnership recognizes on a disposition of the property during the five-year period.[98]

> **Example:** Irwin and John form the IJ Limited Liability Company as equal members. Irwin, a real estate dealer, contributes a parcel of land that he holds as ordinary-income property; John contributes cash. The LLC is not a dealer in real estate and holds the land for investment. At the time of contribution, the land is worth $30,000, and Irwin's basis in the property is $20,000. Three years later, the LLC sells the realty for $40,000. The LLC recognizes $20,000 of ordinary income ($40,000 sales price less $20,000 basis carried over from Irwin). Irwin is allocated $15,000 of this income — $10,000 under I.R.C. Section 704(c) (representing the precontribution appreciation) and $5,000 as his 50-percent distributive share of the LLC's income. John is allocated $5,000 of ordinary income as his distributive share. If the LLC holds the land for six years before selling it for $40,000, Irwin is allocated $15,000 of long-term capital gain and John is allocated $5,000 of long-term capital gain.

A partnership that disposes of property contributed with a built-in capital loss realizes a capital loss if the disposition occurs within five years of the date of contribution.[99] The partnership's capital loss is limited to the amount of loss built in to the property at the time of contribution. A contributed capital asset has a built-in loss to the extent that the contributing partner's basis in the property exceeds its fair market value immediately before the contribution.[100]

---

[94] I.R.C. § 724(a).

[95] I.R.C. § 751(c). The recapture items subject to this rule are set forth in the statute.

[96] I.R.C. § 724(b).

[97] I.R.C. §§ 724(b), 751(d), 1221. The I.R.C. § 724 characterization rules do not apply to contributed trade or business property described in I.R.C. § 1231, even if the property was not held for the long-term holding period by the contributing partner.

[98] I.R.C. § 724(b).

[99] I.R.C. § 724(c).

[100] *Id.*

Example: Joan and Ken form the JK Partnership as equal partners to engage in the business of developing and selling real estate. Joan, who is not a dealer in realty, contributes a tract of land to the partnership. She purchased the land two years earlier for $10,000; its value at the time of contribution is $8,000. Two years after Joan contributes the land, the partnership sells it for $7,000. The partnership realizes a $2,000 capital loss (the amount built in at the time of contribution) and a $1,000 ordinary loss (representing the post-contribution decline in value). Joan is allocated the entire $2,000 capital loss, and Joan and Ken are each allocated $500 of the ordinary loss.

If the land is sold for $7,000 six years after it is contributed, the partnership realizes a $3,000 ordinary loss.[101] Joan is allocated $2,500 of that loss, and Ken is allocated $500 of loss.

To prevent tax avoidance, the characterization rules for contributed property also apply to property acquired in exchange for such property in certain nontaxable transactions. If contributed receivables, inventory, or capital-loss property is transferred to another person in a nonrecognition transaction (or in a series of nonrecognition transactions), any substituted-basis property received by the partnership or by the transferee[102] is subject to the characterization rules described above.[103] For this purpose, substituted-basis property is property with a basis determined in whole or in part by reference to the transferor's basis.[104] However, this taint does not apply when a partnership receives stock in a C corporation in exchange for a capital contribution if the transaction is not currently taxable under I.R.C. Section 351.[105]

Example: Lester, a real estate dealer, contributes Tract A, a parcel of land that he holds as inventory, to the LM Partnership. One year later the partnership, which is not a dealer in real estate, enters into a nontaxable like-kind exchange with Nora, and receives Tract B for Tract A. Under I.R.C. Section 1031(d), both the partnership and Nora have a basis in the land received that is the same as the basis in the land given up in the exchange. If the partnership sells Tract B within five years of the date that Tract A was contributed, it realizes ordinary gain or loss. Similarly, if Nora disposes of Tract A within five years of the contribution, she realizes ordinary gain or loss, regardless of the fact that the property is not inventory in her hands.

---

[101] In both situations, $2,000 of loss is allocated to Joan under I.R.C. § 704(c). However, the character of the loss differs.

[102] H.R. Rep. No. 432, 98th Cong., 2d Sess. 1223 (1984); S. Rep. No. 169, 98th Cong., 2d Sess. 234 (1984).

[103] I.R.C. § 724(d)(3)(A).

[104] I.R.C. § 7701(a)(42).

[105] I.R.C. § 724(d)(3)(B). I.R.C. § 351 provides that gain or loss is not recognized when property is transferred to a corporation solely in exchange for stock and the persons transferring the property control the corporation immediately after the exchange.

§ 3.03   ELECTIONS AFFECTING PARTNERSHIP OR LLC INCOME

[A]   Overview

Any election affecting the computation of a partnership's taxable income is made by the partnership, not by the partners individually.[106] Partnership elections are binding on all the partners as to their shares of partnership income, but they do not apply to a partner's tax items from nonpartnership sources.[107] Elections made at the partnership level include the following:[108]

(1)   the choice of accounting, depreciation, cost-recovery, and inventory methods;[109]

(2)   the election to defer recognition of gain attributable to an involuntary conversion under I.R.C. Section 1033;

(3)   the election not to use installment reporting for an installment sale under I.R.C. Section 453;[110]

(4)   the election to expense depreciable business assets under I.R.C. Section 179;

(5)   the election to deduct research and development expenses under I.R.C. Section 174;[111]

(6)   the election to deduct intangible drilling and development costs of oil and gas properties under I.R.C. Section 263(c);

(7)   the election to treat operating mineral interests as separate properties under I.R.C. Section 614;[112]

(8)   the election to adjust the basis of partnership property under I.R.C. Section 754;

---

[106]   I.R.C. § 703(b).

[107]   Treas. Reg. § 1.703-1(b)(1). *See* Beilke v. Comm'r, T.C. Memo. 1963-5.

[108]   A partnership-level election in I.R.C. Section 108(i) allowed partnerships and other businesses to make an irrevocable election to defer recognition of income from the cancellation of business debt reacquired in 2009 or 2010. That income is deferred until the 5th year after the reacquisition (fourth year for a reacquisition in 2010). The deferred amount is then included in the taxpayer's income ratably over the following five years.

[109]   I.R.C. §§ 446, 167, 168, 472. *See* Rev. Rul. 81-261, 1981-2 C.B. 60 (election to use ADR class life system made by partnership).

[110]   *See, e.g.*, Priv. Ltr. Rul. 199935075 (partnership may file late election not to use installment method if good cause shown).

[111]   The deduction under I.R.C. § 174 is allowed only if the partnership engages in a profit-seeking activity and conducts a trade or business. *See, e.g.*, Universal Research & Dev. Partnership No. 1 v. Comm'r, T.C. Memo. 1991-437; Active Lipid Dev. Partners, Ltd. v. Comm'r, T.C. Memo. 1991-522; Diamond v. Comm'r, 930 F.2d 372 (4th Cir. 1991).

[112]   Rev. Rul. 84-142, 1984-2 C.B. 117.

(9)   the election to amortize partnership organization expenses under I.R.C. Section 709;

(10)   the election to amortize start-up costs under I.R.C. Section 195;

(11)   the election of a partnership tax year under I.R.C. Section 706(b), if a satisfactory business purpose exists;[113]

(12)   the election for mixed straddles under I.R.C. Sections 1092 and 1256;[114]

(13)   the election to deduct soil and water conservation expenditures under I.R.C. Section 175; and

(14)   the election to amortize pollution control facilities under I.R.C. Section 169.

It is important to be sure that the partnership, rather than any individual partner, makes the required elections. For example, if partnership property is involuntarily converted (as by condemnation or fire), the I.R.C. Section 1033 election to defer the gain must be made by the partnership, and the qualifying replacement property must be acquired by the partnership.[115]

In *Estate of Goldstein v. Commissioner*,[116] the court disallowed an election made by a 95-percent partner who had reinvested his share of a condemnation award in qualifying property. The court maintained that the election and reinvestment had to be made by the partnership.

[B] Accounting Method

With limited exceptions, a partnership may use any method of tax accounting that clearly reflects its income.[117] Although a partnership's accounting method may differ from the methods used by the partners, it cannot choose a method that distorts any partner's income.[118] A partner must report his distributive share of partnership income as determined under the partnership's accounting method, even though he would not recognize the income under his own accounting method.[119]

---

[113] See discussion at § 3.04[D], *infra*.

[114] A mixed straddle is a straddle that consists partly of a futures contract subject to I.R.C. § 1256 (an I.R.C. Section 1256 contract).

[115] Demirjian v. Comm'r, 54 T.C. 1691 (1970), *aff'd*, 457 F.2d 1 (3d Cir. 1972); Myers v. U.S., 72-2 U.S.T.C. § 9669 (S.D. Cal. 1972); Varner v. Comm'r, T.C. Memo. 1973-27; McManus v. Comm'r, 65 T.C. 197 (1975), *aff'd*, 583 F.2d 443 (9th Cir. 1978); Fuchs v. Comm'r, 80 T.C. 506 (1983).

[116] T.C. Memo. 1976-19.

[117] I.R.C. § 446(c).

[118] Rev. Rul. 75-113, 1975-1 C.B. 19; Fong v. Comm'r, T.C. Memo 1984-402.

[119] *See, e.g.*, Wilson v. Comm'r, T.C. Memo. 1964-71.

[1] Cash Method Not Allowed if C Corporation Is a Partner

A partnership that has a C corporation as a partner generally may not compute its taxable income using the cash method of accounting or using a hybrid accounting method that records some transactions under the cash method.[120] This rule prevents a C corporation, which could not itself use the cash method, from obtaining the advantages of the cash method through its ownership of a partnership interest.[121] The prohibition also applies to partnerships in which a C corporation indirectly owns an interest.[122] For example, if a C corporation is a partner in a partnership that owns an interest in another partnership, neither partnership may use the cash method.

[2] Cash Method Not Allowed if Partnership Is a Tax Shelter

A partnership classified as a "tax shelter" is barred from using the cash method of accounting or a hybrid accounting method that records some transactions under the cash method.[123] A partnership may be considered a tax shelter if it is in one of the following categories:[124]

(1)   Interests in the partnership have been offered for sale at any time in an offering required to be registered with any federal or state agency having authority to regulate security offerings.

(2)   More than 35 percent of the partnership's losses during the tax year are allocable to limited partners or limited entrepreneurs (including members of a limited liability company).[125]

(3)   The partnership's principal purpose is the avoidance or evasion of federal income tax.

A partnership that must change from the cash method of accounting because of these rules may take any resulting adjustments into account over a period that cannot exceed four years.[126]

---

[120] I.R.C. § 448(a)(2). Temp. Treas. Reg. § 1.448-1T(a)(4).

[121] *See* Staff of the Joint Committee on Taxation, General Explanation of the Tax Reform Act of 1986, at 476.

[122] Temp. Treas. Reg. § 1.448-1T(a)(3).

[123] I.R.C. § 448(a); Temp. Treas. Reg. § 1.448-1T(a)(4).

[124] I.R.C. §§ 448(d)(3), 461(i)(3), (4), 464(c), 6662(d)(2)(C)(ii).

[125] A limited entrepreneur is a person who does not actively participate in business management. I.R.C. § 464(e)(2). *See* Priv. Ltr. Rul. 9321047 (1993). *See also* Priv. Ltr. Rul. 9501033 (1995), Priv. Ltr. Rul. 9407030 (1993).

[126] I.R.C. § 448(d)(7). The timing is determined under the rules of Rev. Proc. 84-74, 1984-2 C.B. 736.

[3] Cash Method Not Allowed to Farming Partnership With Corporate Partner

I.R.C. Section 447 provides that a partnership with a corporate partner engaged in farming must use the accrual method of tax accounting and must capitalize its "preproductive period expenses," as described in I.R.C. Section 263A. These rules do not apply to S corporations or to corporations that meet the gross-receipts test of I.R.C. Section 447(d).

[C] Amortization of Organization Expenses

A partnership may elect to amortize organization expenses over a period of not less than 60 months, starting with the month in which the partnership begins business.[127] The amortization election is made by attaching a statement to the partnership's tax return for its first year in business.[128] The return and statement must be filed by the appropriate due date for the return (including any extensions of time for filing), although an amended return and statement may be filed later to include any organizational expenses omitted from the original statement. The statement must describe each organizational expense (whether or not paid), including the amount of the expense and the date it was incurred.[129] (For discussion of organization costs, see Chapter 3.)

[D] Amortization of Start-Up Costs

A partnership may elect to amortize expenditures it incurs to start its trade or business ratably over a period that is not less than 60 months.[130] The election is made by attaching a statement to the partnership return for the year in which the partnership's trade or business begins.[131] (For discussion of start-up costs, see Chapter 3.)

[E] Election to Expense Cost of Depreciable Property

A partnership may elect, under I.R.C. Section 179, to treat part of its cost for certain property as a deductible expense rather than as a capital expenditure. Property qualifies for this treatment if it is depreciable property purchased for use in an active trade or business.[132]

The amount deductible for any tax year is limited to the purchaser's taxable income from active trade or business sources.[133] This limitation applies to a partnership as well as to each partner.[134] Thus, the total amount of expense

---

[127] I.R.C. § 709(b).

[128] Treas. Reg. § 1.709-1(c).

[129] *Id.*

[130] I.R.C. § 195(b); *See* Rev. Rul. 81-150, 1981-1 C.B. 119.

[131] I.R.C. § 195(d).

[132] I.R.C. § 179(d)(1).

[133] I.R.C. § 179(b)(3)(A).

[134] I.R.C. § 179(d)(8).

deductions a partnership may allocate to its partners cannot exceed the partnership's taxable income, and each partner's deduction is limited to his individual taxable income.[135] A partner's share of the expense deductions is allowed in the partner's year in which the partnership's year ends.[136] Nondeductible amounts may be carried over to subsequent years.[137] The total deduction allowed in any taxable year is limited to a spefic dollar amount. The partnership reduces the basis of its I.R.C. Section 179 property in the year of the election by the full amount it elects to expense even if all or part of the deduction must be carried forward by the partnership or by any partner.[138]

[F] Elections Made by Partners

Five elections affecting the treatment of partnership income are made separately by each partner rather than at the partnership level. These are:

(1) the election under I.R.C. Section 901 allowing a taxpayer to treat his share of taxes paid or accrued to foreign countries or U.S. possessions as a credit rather than as a deduction under I.R.C. Section 164(a);[139]

(2) the election under I.R.C. Section 617 relating to deduction and recapture of mining exploration expenditures;[140]

(3) the election under I.R.C. Section 108 regarding exclusion of income from discharge of debt;[141]

(4) the election under I.R.C. Section 871(d) that allows a nonresident alien partner to treat his share of partnership income from U.S. real estate as being "effectively connected" with the conduct of a U.S. trade or business;[142] and

(5) the election under I.R.C. Section 59(e) to amortize expenditures for circulation, research and experimentation, intangible drilling and development, and mining development and exploration.[143]

---

[135] Treas. Reg. § 1.179-2(c)(2). This regulation was held valid in Hayden v. Commr, 204 F.3d 772 (7th Cir. 2000).

[136] Treas. Reg. § 1.179-2(b)(3)(iv).

[137] I.R.C. § 179(b)(3)(B).

[138] Treas. Reg. § 1.179-1(f)(2).

[139] I.R.C. § 703(b)(3).

[140] I.R.C. § 703(b)(2).

[141] I.R.C. § 703(b)(1).

[142] Treas. Reg. § 1.703-1(b)(2)(iii), referring to the election in Treas. Reg. § 1.871-10.

[143] I.R.C. § 59(e)(4)(C), relating to elections for expenditures under I.R.C. §§ 173, 174(a), 263(c), 616(a), and 617(a).

[1] Foreign Tax Credit

Each partner may elect whether to treat his share of the partnership's foreign taxes as either a deduction against his income or a credit against his tax liability.[144] The credit allowed is the partner's proportionate share of the taxes paid or accrued by the partnership to a foreign country or a possession of the United States.[145] This rule applies only to partners who are:

(1)   citizens of the United States;

(2)   domestic corporations;[146]

(3)   residents of the United States or Puerto Rico; and

(4)   alien residents of the United States or Puerto Rico.[147]

Nonresident alien individual and foreign corporate partners are permitted a foreign tax credit for taxes on income effectively connected with the conduct of a U.S. trade or business.[148]

[2] Discharge of Indebtedness

A taxpayer generally realizes income to the extent that his debts are forgiven, canceled, or otherwise discharged without payment.[149] Exceptions to this rule are provided under I.R.C. Section 108(a), which permits a taxpayer to exclude income from a discharge of his debt if:

(1)   The discharge occurs when he is insolvent.[150] The insolvency exclusion is limited to the amount by which the taxpayer is insolvent, and he realizes income to the extent that the debt discharge makes him solvent.[151]

(2)   The discharge is granted in Title 11 bankruptcy proceedings.

(3)   The debt discharged was incurred in certain farming activities.

(4)   The discharged debt is qualified real property business indebtedness.[152]

---

[144] I.R.C. §§ 164(a), 901.

[145] I.R.C. § 901(b)(5).

[146] Although I.R.C. § 901(b)(5) refers to partners who are "individuals," case law and rulings indicate that corporate partners are entitled to claim a credit for foreign taxes paid by the partnership. Arundel Corp. v. U.S., 102 F. Supp. 1019 (Ct. Cl. 1952); Rev. Rul. 71-41, 1971-1 C.B. 211.

[147] Arundel Corp. v. U.S., 102 F. Supp. 1019 (Ct. Cl. 1952); Rev. Rul. 71-41, 1971-1 C.B. 211.

[148] I.R.C. §§ 901(b)(4), 906(a).

[149] I.R.C. § 61(a)(12); U.S. v. Kirby Lumber Co., 284 U.S. 1 (1931).

[150] As defined in I.R.C. § 108(d)(3). In determining whether a partner is insolvent, assets that are exempt from creditor's claims under state law are excluded. See Priv. Ltr. Rul. 9130005. See also Hunt v. Comm'r, T.C. Memo. 1989-335.

[151] I.R.C. § 108(a)(3). In Rev. Rul. 92-53, 1992-2 C.B. 48, the Service limits the amount of a nonrecourse debt that may be taken into account in determining a taxpayer's insolvency.

[152] I.R.C. § 108(a)(1)(D), added by the Revenue Reconciliation Act of 1993.

[a]   Purchase Price Adjustment

A reduction in all or part of a solvent purchaser's purchase-money obligation to a seller is not treated as a debt discharge but rather as a reduction in the purchase price for the property securing the debt.[153] The price adjustment reduces the basis of the property but does not generate cancellation of debt income. A bankrupt or insolvent partnership may treat a debt reduction by the seller as a purchase price adjustment if all partners report the transaction in the same manner as the partnership.[154]

[b]   Reduction of Tax Attributes

Although insolvent, bankrupt, or farming taxpayers do not realize discharge-of-indebtedness income, they must reduce certain of their tax attributes by the amounts discharged. The attributes are reduced in the following order:[155]

(1)   net operating losses;

(2)   general business credit carryovers allowable under I.R.C. Section 38;

(3)   capital loss carryovers;

(4)   the basis of the taxpayer's property (in accordance with the rules of I.R.C. Section 1017); and

(5)   foreign tax credit carryovers allowable under I.R.C. Section 27.

In applying the attribute-reduction rule, the taxpayer's net operating losses, capital loss carryovers, and basis are reduced by one dollar for each dollar of debt discharged. However, the business credit and foreign tax credit carryovers are reduced by one dollar for each three dollars of discharge.[156]

[c]   Election to Reduce Basis of Depreciable Property

In place of the attribute reduction, a taxpayer may elect, under I.R.C. Section 108(b)(5), to apply all or any portion of the amount discharged to reduce the basis of his depreciable property under I.R.C. Section 1017.[157]

Cancellation of debt income does not arise when property encumbered by a nonrecourse liability is transferred to the lender in exchange for discharge of the

---

[153] I.R.C. § 108(e)(5). Rev. Rul. 92-99, 1992-2 C.B. 35, holds that the reduction of an undersecured nonrecourse debt by a debtholder other than the seller is not a purchase price adjustment. The ruling rejects contrary holdings in a number of cases decided during the 1940s.

[154] Rev. Proc. 92-92, 1992-2 C.B. 505.

[155] I.R.C. § 108(b). For the order of reduction, see Treas. Reg. § 1.1017-1(a).

[156] I.R.C. § 108(b)(3).

[157] The election to reduce the basis of depreciable property under I.R.C. § 108(b)(5) by a bankrupt, insolvent or farm debtor is made on Form 982. Treas. Reg. § 1.108-4. Form 982 can also be used by a debtor to elect to treat real property held for sale as depreciable property. Treas. Reg. § 1.1017-1(f). Form 982 must be attached to the debtor's timely (including extensions) federal income tax return for the tax year in which the debtor realized the excluded COD income. The election cannot be revoked without IRS consent.

debt.[158] The transaction is considered a sale of the property for the principal amount of the debt, regardless of whether the transfer occurs pursuant to a bankruptcy, foreclosure, or deed in lieu of foreclosure, and even though the property is worth less than the debt.[159] In contrast, cancellation of debt income arises when a debt is discharged without any related property transfer.[160] If the reduced debt is a purchase-money obligation to the property's seller, however, the transaction is treated as a reduction in the purchase price rather than a debt cancellation.[161]

If property is transferred in exchange for discharge of a recourse debt, the transaction is treated (1) as a sale to the extent of the value of the property, and (2) as a cancellation of indebtedness to the extent that the amount of discharged debt exceeds the property's value.[162] For example, a transfer of property worth $10,000 having an $8,000 basis in exchange for discharge of a $12,000 recourse debt results in $2,000 of gain from the sale portion of the transaction and $2,000 of cancellation of debt income.[163]

[d]   Qualified Real Property Business Indebtedness

Under I.R.C. Section 108(c), a taxpayer other than a C corporation may elect to exclude certain income from a discharge of qualified real property business indebtedness (QRPBI).[164] The exclusion is limited to the basis of the taxpayer's depreciable real property held immediately before the discharge. The taxpayer reduces the basis of his depreciable real property by the amount excluded.

QRPBI is debt incurred or assumed in connection with real property used in a trade or business and secured by the property.[165] To qualify as QRPBI, the debt must have been incurred or assumed before 1993 or, if later, incurred or assumed to acquire, construct, reconstruct, or substantially improve the secured real property.[166] The debtor must elect to treat the debt as QRPBI.

---

[158] *See* 2925 Briarpark, Ltd. v. Comm'r, 163 F.3d 313 (5th Cir. 1999), *aff'g* T.C. Memo. 1997-298 (partnership income from discharge of nonrecourse loans treated as gain from transfer of property under I.R.C. § 61(a)(3), not discharge-of-indebtedness income under I.R.C. § 61(a)(12)); FSA 1999-873 (undated) (foreclosure of property results in gain from sale of property and not income from discharge of indebtedness excludable under I.R.C. § 108).

[159] Comm'r v. Tufts, 461 U.S. 300 (1983); I.R.C. § 7701(g); Treas. Reg. § 1.1001-2(a)(4). See discussion in Chapter 12.

[160] Gershkowitz v. Comm'r, 88 T.C. 984 (1987); Rev. Rul. 91-31, 1991-1 C.B. 19.

[161] I.R.C. § 108(e)(5).

[162] Treas. Reg. § 1.1001-2(a)(2) states that the amount realized on a disposition of property securing a recourse liability does not include amounts that are cancellation of debt income.

[163] Rev. Rul. 90-16, 1990-1 C.B. 12.

[164] I.R.C. § 108(c)(1). The election is made on Form 982 attached to a timely (including extensions) tax return for the year in which the taxpayer has excludible discharge of indebtedness income. Treas. Reg. § 1.108(c)-5.

[165] I.R.C. § 108(c)(3)(A).

[166] I.R.C. § 108(c)(4), (3)(B).

[e]   Debt-Discharge Rules Apply to Each Partner Separately

When a partnership debt is discharged without payment, the rules of I.R.C. Section 108 described in the preceding section apply to each partner separately, not at the partnership level.[167] This rule holds even if the partnership is the subject of bankruptcy proceedings.[168] The amount of income the partnership realizes from the cancellation of its debt passes through to the partners as a separately stated item, and each partner treats his distributive share of that income in the same manner as he would treat cancellation of a debt he owed as an individual.[169]

Each partner's treatment of the income depends on whether he is solvent, insolvent, or in bankruptcy when he realizes the income. Solvent partners are taxed on their shares of the debt discharge as ordinary income, while insolvent or bankrupt partners exclude these amounts and either reduce their tax attributes or elect to reduce the basis in their depreciable assets.[170]

> **Example:** David, Edward, and Freda are equal partners in the DEF Partnership. As the result of a bankruptcy proceeding, the partnership is discharged of a $30,000 liability.
>
> David has had all his individual debts discharged in a separate bankruptcy case. Therefore, he excludes his $10,000 allocable share of the partnership's debt discharge and reduces his tax attributes or elects to reduce his basis in depreciable property by that amount.
>
> Edward is insolvent to the extent of $5,000 before the partnership's debt discharge. Therefore, he excludes $5,000 of income and reduces his tax attributes or elects to reduce his basis in depreciable property by that amount. He reports the remaining $5,000 as debt-discharge income.
>
> Freda, a solvent partner, reports her $10,000 distributive share of the debt discharge as income.

[f]   Partner's Election to Reduce Basis of Depreciable Property or Depreciable Real Property

General rules. As noted above, a debt discharge is excluded from income if one of the exceptions of I.R.C. Section 108(a) applies. Insolvent, bankrupt, or farming taxpayers must either reduce certain tax attributes by the amount discharged or

---

[167] I.R.C. § 108(d)(6). This rule was added by the Bankruptcy Tax Act of 1980 to overrule the prior law established in Stackhouse v. United States, 441 F.2d 465 (5th Cir. 1971). In *Stackhouse*, a debt discharge for an insolvent partnership was not deemed to generate cancellation of debt income for its partners. The Tax Court rejected the *Stackhouse* decision in Gershkowitz v. Comm'r, 88 T.C. 984 (1987), holding that the insolvency exception applies at the partner, rather than partnership, level. In Estate of Newman v. Comm'r, 934 F.2d 426 (2d Cir. 1991), *rev'g* T.C. Memo. 1990-230, the Second Circuit adopted the *Stackhouse* approach for pre-Bankruptcy Tax Act cases, holding that the insolvency exception applies at the partnership level.

[168] I.R.C. § 1399 provides that no separate taxable entity results from the commencement of a bankruptcy case against a partnership.

[169] S. Rep. No. 1035, 96th Cong., 2d Sess. 21 (1980).

[170] I.R.C. § 108(a), (b).

elect under I.R.C. Section 108(b)(5) to reduce the basis of their depreciable property. A taxpayer whose debt discharge income is excluded under the I.R.C. Section 108(c) qualified real property business indebtedness exception must reduce the basis of his depreciable real property.

Under the basis reduction election, a taxpayer decreases the basis of property he holds by the amount of excluded debt discharge income on the first day of the tax year following the tax year of the exclusion. Basis is reduced (but not below zero) in the following order:[171]

(1) trade or business or investment real property (other than property held as inventory) that secured the discharged debt immediately before the discharge;

(2) trade or business or investment personal property (other than inventory), accounts receivable and notes receivable, that secured the discharged debt immediately before the discharge;

(3) remaining property (other than inventory), accounts receivable, notes receivable and realty (other than property held as inventory);

(4) inventory accounts receivable, notes receivable and realty (other than property held as inventory); and

(5) property neither used in a trade or business nor held for investment.

Special basis adjustment election for discharged partnership debt. A partner treats his distributive share of partnership debt discharge income as attributable to a discharged debt secured by the partner's interest in the partnership.[172] If the partner makes an election under I.R.C. Section 108(b)(5) (or I.R.C. Section 108(c)), he treats his partnership interest as depreciable property (or depreciable real property) to the extent of his share of the property owned by the partnership.[173] This treatment is allowed only if the partnership makes a corresponding reduction in the basis of its depreciable property (or real property) for that partner's interest (*i.e.*, to reduce the partner's share of the partnership's depreciable basis in its property).[174]

Generally, the basis reduction election is a matter of agreement between the partner and the partnership; a partner may choose whether to ask a partnership to reduce the basis of partnership property and the partnership may grant or withhold its consent. A partnership's consent is not required to reduce the basis of the partnership's depreciable property (or depreciable real property) if a partner reduces the basis in its partnership interest under I.R.C. Section 108(b)(2)(E) (related to reduction in tax attributes). However, a partnership is required to consent to the election if consent is requested by (1) partners owning (directly or indirectly) an aggregate of more than 80 percent of partnership capital and profits

---

[171] Treas. Reg. § 1.1017-1(a), (c).

[172] Treas. Reg. § 1.1017-1(g).

[173] Treas. Reg. § 1.1017-1(c). A taxpayer may elect to treat real property held as inventory as depreciable property. Treas. Reg. § 1.1017-1(f).

[174] Treas. Reg. § 1.1017-1(g). *See* § 12.08, *infra.*

interests, or (2) five or fewer owning partners (directly or indirectly) an aggregate of more than 50 percent of partnership capital and profits interests.[175]

A partner must request a partnership's consent if, at the time of the discharge, he owns (directly or indirectly) a greater than 50-percent interest in partnership capital and profits, or if reductions to the basis of the partner's depreciable property (or depreciable real property) are being made that affect the partner's distributive share of partnership debt discharge income.[176]

[g]   Effect of Debt Discharge Income on Basis of Partnership Interest

The discharge of a partnership liability causes two concurrent adjustments to a partner's basis in his partnership interest. The partner's basis increases by the amount of cancellation of debt income included in his distributive share of partnership income.[177] His basis decreases by the amount of cash deemed distributed to him (under I.R.C. Section 752(b)) as a result of the reduction in his share of partnership liabilities. The increase in basis for the partner's distributive share and the decrease in basis for the distribution both take place at the end of the partnership's tax year.[178] Thus, no net change in a partner's basis occurs if his distributive share of cancellation of debt income is the same as his share of the discharged partnership liability under I.R.C. Section 752 (*i.e.*, the basis increase for the income equals the basis decrease for the distribution).[179]

> **Example:** George and Harriet each contribute $10,000 for equal interests in the GH Partnership. GH purchases property for $100,000, using its $20,000 of cash and $80,000 borrowed from a bank. Each partner has an equal share of the debt under I.R.C. Section 752.[180] The loan increases each partner's basis in his partnership interest to $50,000 ($10,000 cash contribution + $40,000 share of the partnership liability).
>
> In Year 2, a decline in the value of the property induces the bank to cancel $20,000 of the debt. The partnership has no other transactions during the year. Each partner's distributive share of partnership income in Year 2 consists of $10,000 of cancellation of debt income and each partner's basis in his partnership interest increases by that amount at the end of the partnership tax year. At the same time, each partner is deemed to receive a cash distribution equal to the $10,000 reduction in his share of the partnership debt and the basis in his interest decreases by that amount. At the end of Year 2, each partner's basis in his partnership interest is $40,000

---

[175]   Treas. Reg. § 1.1017-1(g)(2).

[176]   Treas. Reg. § 1.1017-1(g)(2)(ii)(B).

[177]   I.R.C. §§ 705(a), 733. The basis increase occurs even if the partner excludes the income on his individual return under the bankruptcy or insolvency exceptions. I.R.C. § 705(a)(1).

[178]   Rev. Rul. 92-97, 1992-2 C.B. 124.

[179]   Legislative history suggests that Congress believed that the basis increases and decreases caused by discharge of partnership indebtedness would offset each other.

[180]   I.R.C. § 752; Treas. Reg. § 1.752-2. Under the regulations, each partner's share of the recourse debt equals the economic risk of loss he bears for it. *See* § 5.06, *infra.*

($10,000 cash contribution + $30,000 share of partnership liability + $10,000 distributive share of income - $10,000 deemed cash distribution).

The result might differ if a partner's distributive share of cancellation of debt income differs from his share of the partnership liability that was discharged.[181] In that situation, the basis adjustments are not equal and the partner's basis in his partnership interest increases or decreases. If the deemed cash distribution from the reduction in the partner's share of the partnership debt exceeds the basis in his partnership interest (after the increase for his distributive share of cancellation of debt income), he recognizes gain equal to the excess amount.[182]

[h] Exchange of Partnership Interest for Discharged Debt

Under IRC Section 108(e)(8), a partnership that transfers a capital or profits interest in the partnership to a creditor in satisfaction of a partnership debt generally recognizes cancellation of indebtedness income.[183] The amount of income is the amount that would be recognized if the debt were satisfied with money equal to the fair market value of the partnership interest. The income is allocated among the partners who held interests in the partnership immediately before the satisfaction of the debt.[184]

§ 3.04 PARTNERSHIP OR LLC TAX YEAR

A partnership (or LLC) must adopt a tax year for computing and reporting the income or loss and separately stated items that pass through to its partners (or members). Each partner reports his share of partnership tax items on his individual tax return for his tax year during which the partnership year ends (see § 3.04[A], infra). Complex rules limit the tax year a partnership may select to a year that either (1) conforms to the year used by as many partners as possible, or (2) is

---

[181] This assumes that a partner may be allocated a share of debt-cancellation income that differs from the share of the debt included in the basis of his partnership interest under I.R.C. § 752. Rev. Rul. 92-97, 1992-2 C.B. 124, holds that such allocations of debt-cancellation income are invalid (under the economic effect test of I.R.C. § 704(b)) unless the partners are unconditionally obligated to restore a deficit in their capital accounts when their interests are liquidated. If no unconditional obligation exists, each partner's share of cancellation of debt income must equal the decrease in his share of the debt (i.e., the amount of cash deemed distributed to him under I.R.C. § 752). The ruling concludes that a special allocation of cancellation of debt income is valid only if the deficit restoration obligation requires a partner to contribute funds needed to satisfy another partner's right to receive his positive capital account balance. An allocation is not valid if the deficit restoration obligation is limited to amounts needed to pay partnership creditors or if the obligation only arises under a qualified income offset provision.

[182] I.R.C. § 731(a). See, e.g., Gershkowitz v. Comm'r, 88 T.C. 984 (1987) (pre-Bankruptcy Tax Act case). But see Estate of Newman v. Comm'r, 934 F.2d 426 (2d Cir. 1991), rev'g T.C. Memo. 1990-230 (pre-Bankruptcy Tax Act). See also Priv. Ltr. Rul. 8348001.

[183] This provision was enacted by the American Jobs Creation Act, Pub. L. No. 108357 (2004), and applies to cancellations of indebtedness on or after October 22, 2004.

[184] The Service has issued proposed regulations regarding the determination of cancellation of indebtedness (COD) income of a partnership that transfers a partnership interest to a creditor in satisfaction of the partnership's indebtedness (debt-for-equity exchange). Prop. Treas. Reg. § 1.704-1(b)(2).

necessitated by a valid business purpose (*see* § 3.04[C], [D], *infra*). Certain partnerships may elect to avoid these tax-year limitations by making "required payments" specified in I.R.C. Section 444 to the Treasury (*see* § 3.04[F], *infra*).

[A] Timing of Partner's Share of Partnership Income

Each partner includes his distributive share of partnership taxable income or loss and separately stated items on his individual tax return for the year within which the partnership's tax year ends.[185] A partner must recognize his distributive share whether or not any amounts actually are distributed to him during the year.[186]

> **Example (1):** Anne, an individual who uses a calendar tax year, owns interests in the AB and the AD Partnerships. AB Partnership uses a tax year that ends on September 30; AD Partnership's tax year ends on November 30. On her tax return for Year 2, Anne reports her share of AB's income for the period October 1, Year 1, through September 30, Year 2; and her share of AD's income for the period December 1, Year 1, through November 30, Year 2.

> **Example (2):** Carl, who uses a calendar tax year, owns an interest in the CD Limited Liability Company which uses a tax year ending on June 30. In Year 2, CD changes to a calendar year, so that its next tax year ends on December 31, Year 2. Carl reports 18 months of LLC income on his Year-2 tax return — 12 months of income from the LLC tax year July 1, Year 1 through June 30, Year 2; and six months of income from the short LLC tax year July 1, Year 2, through December 31, Year 2.

Ordinarily, each partner's distributive share is determined at the close of the tax year the partnership has adopted, using the partnership's tax-accounting method.[187] However, the partnership's tax year is deemed to close for a partner on the day he sells, exchanges, or liquidates his entire partnership interest.[188] The partner reports his share of partnership income up to the date of the sale, exchange, or liquidation on his return for the year in which the disposition occurs.[189]

> **Example:** David, a calendar-year taxpayer, is a partner in the DE Partnership, which uses a tax year ending on October 30. David sells his entire partnership interest on August 15, Year 2. Since DE's tax year is deemed to close for David on August 15, David includes his distributive share of partnership income for the period November 1, Year 1, through August 15, Year 2, on his Year 2 tax return.

If David sells his interest on November 15, Year 2, his Year-2 tax return

---

[185] I.R.C. § 706(a). A partnership may have a short tax year. Linsmayer v. Comm'r, T.C. Memo 1995-437. *See* Lenard L. Politte, M.D., Inc. v. Comm'r, 101 T.C. 359 (1993).

[186] Treas. Reg. § 1.702-1(a).

[187] I.R.C. § 706(c)(2).

[188] I.R.C. § 706(a). For discussion of the sale or exchange of partnership interest, see Chapter 12. For discussion of liquidations of partnership interests, see Chapter 10.

[189] I.R.C. §§ 702, 703, 706; Rev. Rul. 56-233, 1956-1 C.B. 51 (cash-method partner includes partnership income computed under accrual method).

should include his distributive share of partnership income for the normal partnership tax year November 1, Year 1, through October 30, Year 2; and his share of income for the period November 1, Year 2, through November 15, Year 2.

Guaranteed payments. Certain payments to a partner for his services or for the use of his capital are treated as "guaranteed payments" if the amount paid is not determined based on the partnership's income.[190] The partner recognizes a guaranteed payment as income in his year that includes the end of the partnership year during which the partnership deducts or capitalizes the payment as an expense.[191] If the partnership uses the accrual method, the partner is taxable when the partnership accrues the guaranteed payment, even though he uses the cash method of accounting and has not yet received payment.[192] A partner is taxable on the full amount of a guaranteed payment (as ordinary income), even if the partnership cannot deduct it. Thus, the partner is taxable on the full payment, even though the nature of the payment requires capitalization by the partnership (*e.g.*, a payment related to acquiring an asset).[193] (For discussion of guaranteed payments, see Chapter 8.)

> **Example:** Frank, George, and their FG Limited Liability Company all use a calendar tax year. The LLC accrues a $10,000 business expense in Year 1 for a guaranteed payment owed to Frank. Frank agrees to defer receipt of the payment until Year 2, when the LLC's cash flow improves. Even though Frank uses the cash method, he includes the $10,000 guaranteed payment in his Year-1 income, because that is the period when the partnership accrued a liability for the payment. Frank includes the $10,000 payment in his income, even if the partnership must capitalize rather than deduct the payment.

A partner who transacts business with his partnership in a nonpartner capacity reports any income or gain in accordance with general tax-accounting rules and under his own method of tax accounting.[194] Special rules limit the deductibility of losses and may change the character of gain realized in a transaction between a partner and his partnership. (For discussion of partner-partnership transactions, see Chapter 7.)

The Service has issued a Revenue Procedure that allows certain partnerships that invest in tax exempt bonds to make an election enabling their money market fund partners to account for their shares of partnership income on a monthly basis rather than at the normal year end.[195]

---

[190] I.R.C. § 707(c).

[191] Treas. Reg. § 1.707-1(c).

[192] *Id.*; Pratt v. Comm'r, 64 T.C. 203 (1975), *rev'd on other grounds*, 550 F.2d 1023 (5th Cir. 1977). *See* S. Rep. No. 1622, 83d Cong., 2d Sess. 387 (1954).

[193] Gaines v. Comm'r, T.C. Memo. 1982-731; Rev. Rul. 80-234, 1980-2 C.B. 203. *See* Jolin v. Comm'r, T.C. Memo. 1985-287.

[194] I.R.C. § 707(a).

[195] Rev. Proc. 2002-16, 2002-9 I.R.B. 572.

The election is designed to accommodate money market fund partners that receive tax-exempt interest payment from the partnership on a monthly basis. The Revenue Procedure affects many regulated investment companies' (RIC) money market funds that are required to distribute tax-exempt interest earnings each year.[196] Without the election, a money market fund partner with a tax year that differs from the bond partnership will have a mismatch between its monthly distribution of income and the year-end inclusion of its distributive share of partnership income under I.R.C. Section 706(a). This may cause a distribution of tax exempt income to a partner to be treated as return of capital or result in total income that is more than the actual amount distributed.

[B] Adoption or Change of Partner's or Member's Tax Year

A new taxpayer may adopt any permissible tax year on his first tax return without obtaining prior approval from the IRS.[197] A partner may not change his tax year without IRS permission, even if he is changing to the same year his partnership uses.[198] The IRS will not approve a change in a partner's tax year unless he shows a satisfactory business purpose for the change.[199] Failure to obtain IRS approval results in disallowance of the change.[200]

[C] Rules Governing Selection of Partnership Tax Year: I.R.C. Section 706

To prevent a deferral of the time at which partnership income is taxed, I.R.C. Section 706(b)(1)(B) provides rules that restrict a partnership's choice of tax year to one that conforms to the year used by as many partners as possible.[201] A partnership must adopt or change its tax year in accordance with these rules, unless it can establish, to the Service's satisfaction, that it has a business purpose for using a different year.[202] A partnership that uses an invalid tax year must recompute its income and its partners' distributive shares based upon the proper tax year.[203]

Unless a partnership establishes a business purpose for having a tax year that is not prescribed by I.R.C. Section 706(b)(1)(B), the partnership determines the tax year it must adopt or change to under one of three methods listed in that Code

---

[196] *See* I.R.C. § 103(a).

[197] Temp. Treas. Reg. § 1.441-1T(b)(2).

[198] Although the language in the Code suggests that a principal partner may change to his partnership's tax year without the Service's consent, the regulations indicate that a change in any partner's tax year requires prior approval. I.R.C. §§ 442, 706(b)(2); Treas. Reg. §§ 1.442-1(b)(2)(ii), 1.706-1(b)(2).

[199] I.R.C. § 706(b)(2).

[200] Treas. Reg. § 1.442-1(b)(1).

[201] S. Rep. No. 313, 99th Cong., 2d Sess. 165 (1986).

[202] I.R.C. § 706(b)(1)(C).

[203] Clapp v. Comm'r, 36 T.C. 905 (1961), *aff'd on another issue*, 321 F.2d 12 (9th Cir. 1963).

section.[204] These methods are used in the following order of priority:[205]

The following tests require a partnership to determine the partners' interests in partnership profits and capital. Proposed regulations have been issued to clarify the meaning of a partner's interest in partnership profits and capital for purposes of these tests.[206] Under the proposed regulations, a partner's profits interest equals his share of partnership taxable income, rather than book income. A partner's profits interest is determined annually based on the manner in which the partnership expects to allocate its income for the year. A partnership that does not expect to have income in the current year determines profits interests based on the manner in which it expects to allocate income in the first tax year in which it expects to have income.

Generally, a partner's capital interest is determined by reference to the partnership assets he would be entitled to receive upon withdrawal from, or liquidation of, the partnership. Ordinarily this would require a valuation of the partnership's assets. To ease the administrative burden of such valuations, the proposed regulations provide that partnerships that maintain capital accounts in accordance with the regulations under I.R.C. Section 704(b)[207] may assume that a partner's interest in partnership capital is the ratio of the partner's capital account to all partners' capital accounts.

(1) *Majority-interest taxable-year rule.* A partnership must use the same tax year that is used by the partners whose aggregate interests exceed 50 percent of all interests in partnership capital and profits (*see* § 3.04[C][1], *infra*).

(2) *Principal-partners rule.* If the majority-interest taxable-year rule cannot apply because partners owning more than 50 percent of partnership profits and capital do not have the same tax year, the partnership must use the tax year used by all of its principal partners (*see* § 3.04[C][2], *infra*).

(3) *Least-aggregate-deferral rule.* If the majority-interest taxable-year rule does not apply, and the principal partners do not have the same tax year, the partnership must use the tax year that results in the least aggregate deferral of income to its partners (*see* § 3.04[C][3], *infra*).[208] In determining whether a partnership must change its tax year, any changes in the tax years of its partners must be taken into account.[209] Interests held by tax-exempt partners are not counted unless their income is subject to the unrelated business tax.[210]

Special rule for foreign partners. Proposed regulations would require a partnership to determine its tax year by disregarding the interests of foreign

---

[204] I.R.C. § 706(b)(1)(B), (C).

[205] I.R.C. § 706(b)(1)(B).

[206] Prop. Treas. Reg. § 1.706-1(b)(4).

[207] Prop. Treas. Reg. § 1.704-1(b)(2)(iv).

[208] Temp. Treas. Reg. § 1.706-1T(a)(1).

[209] I.R.C. § 706(b)(5).

[210] Temp. Treas. Reg. § 1.706-3T.

partners who are not subject to U.S. taxation on their shares of partnership income.[211] Generally, a foreign partner is a partner that is not a U.S. person (as defined in I.R.C. § 7701(a)(30)).[212] However, controlled foreign corporations (CFCs) and foreign personal holding companies (FPHCs) are not treated as foreign partners because the U.S. owners of such entities may be currently taxable on income from these entities. Generally, a foreign partner's interest would be disregarded unless his distributive share of partnership income includes gross income that is effectively connected with a U.S. trade or business (*effectively connected taxable income* (ECTI)).[213] If the foreign partner is subject to a U.S. income tax treaty, his interest would be disregarded unless his share of income includes gross income attributable to a *permanent establishment* in the U.S.[214] A foreign partner's interest would not be disregarded if he is allocated gross income that is ECTI (or attributable to a permanent establishment) even if the partner incurs a net loss from the partnership and does not actually pay U.S. tax.[215]

[1] Majority-Interest Taxable-Year Rule

A new or existing partnership must adopt or change to the tax year that is used by the partners who own an aggregate interest of more than 50 percent of partnership profits and capital.[216] A partnership determines its majority-interest tax year (if any) on the first day of the tax year.[217] For an existing partnership, that day is the first of the year it currently uses.[218] A partnership that must change its tax year to satisfy the majority-interest taxable-year rule is not required to change to another tax year for either of the two tax years following the year of change.[219]

> **Example (1):** Alpha Corp, Beta Corp, and Cappa Corp form the ABC Partnership. Alpha owns 40 percent of partnership profits and capital and uses a June 30 tax year. Beta owns 30 percent of partnership profits and capital and also uses a June 30 tax year. Cappa owns 30 percent of partnership profits and capital and uses a September 30 tax year. ABC must adopt a June 30 tax year because that is the year used by partners owning a majority of the interests in its capital and profits.

> **Example (2):** Assume the same facts as in Example (1). In Year 2, Beta Corp sells its entire partnership interest to Delta Corp (which uses a September 30 tax year). Because Cappa and Delta are on the same September 30 tax year and own a majority of partnership interests, the

---

[211] Prop. Treas. Reg. § 1.706-4.

[212] Prop. Treas. Reg. § 1.706-4(c).

[213] Prop. Treas. Reg. § 1.706-4(a)(1).

[214] Prop. Treas. Reg. § 1.706-4(a)(2).

[215] This differs from the treatment of a tax-exempt partner whose interests are disregarded unless a tax liability actually is incurred. *See* Temp. Treas. Reg. § 1.706-3T.

[216] I.R.C. § 706(b)(1)(B)(i), (b)(4)(A)(i).

[217] I.R.C. § 706(b)(4)(A)(i)(I), (II).

[218] *Id.*

[219] I.R.C. § 706(b)(4)(B).

partnership must change to a September 30 year. Because this change is required under the majority-interest rule, the partnership will not be required to change to another tax year for either of the two tax years following the year the partnership changes to the September 30 year.

The two-year no-change rule does not apply to a continuing partnership that is treated as a new partnership following a constructive termination under I.R.C. Section 708.[220] Thus, the "new" partnership must adopt the year used by its majority partners. As discussed in Chapter 13, a partnership is deemed to terminate if 50 percent or more of the interests in its capital and profits are sold or exchanged within a 12-month period. The "new" partnership must make all required elections and adopt an initial tax year.

Example (3): Assume the same facts as in Example (2) and that, within 12 months of Beta's sale to Delta, Cappa sells its partnership interest to Elco Corp, which uses a June 30 tax year. Since 60 percent of the interests in partnership capital and profits have been sold in that period, the partnership terminates under I.R.C. Section 708. (For discussion of the I.R.C. Section 708 termination rules, see Chapter 13.) The partnership of Alpha, Delta, and Elco is now treated as a new partnership for tax purposes and must adopt an initial tax year. Under the majority-interest rule, the partnership must use the June 30 tax year followed by a majority of its partners.

[2] Principal-Partners Rule

If partners owning a majority of partnership profits and capital (*see* § 3.04[C][1], *supra*) do not have the same tax year, the partnership must adopt the tax year used by all of its principal partners. A principal partner is a partner who owns an interest of 5 percent or more in partnership profits or capital.[221]

Example: The FGX Limited Liability Company has 22 members. Following is a summary of member interests and year-ends:

No. of Partners	Percent of Ownership	End of Tax Year
2	40% (20% each)	June 30
10	40% (4% each)	December 31
10	20% (2% each)	September 30

In this case, the majority-interest rule does not apply because partners owning a majority of interests do not use the same tax year. Therefore, the partnership must follow the principal-partners rule and adopt a June 30 tax year, the year used by both of its principal partners.

---

[220] Treas. Reg. § 1.708-1(b).

[221] I.R.C. § 706(b)(1)(B)(ii), (b)(3).

[3] Least-Aggregate-Deferral Rule

If the majority-interest and principal-partner rules cannot be applied (*see* § 3.04[C][1], [2], *supra*), a partnership must adopt the tax year used by one or more of the partners that results in the least "aggregate deferral" of income to the partners.[222] The aggregate deferral for a tax year is determined by adding together the products obtained by multiplying (1) the months of deferral for each partner that the choice of tax year would generate by (2) each partner's interest in partnership profits for the year. Deferral to each partner is measured by the number of months from the end of the partnership's tax year forward to the end of the partner's tax year. The partnership must adopt the tax year that produces the lowest sum.[223]

Example: Argo Corp, which uses a June 30 tax year, forms an equal partnership with Bango Corp, which uses a July 31 tax year. Because the majority-interest and principal-partner rules do not apply, the partnership must adopt either Argo's or Bango's tax year, depending on which results in the least aggregate deferral of income.

The aggregate deferral of income that would result from the partnership's adopting Argo's June 30 tax year is:

	Year-end	Profit Interest	Month × Deferred	=	Interest Deferral
Argo	June 30	.5	0		0.0
Bango	July 31	.5	1		0.5
Aggregate deferral					0.5

The aggregate deferral of income that would result from using Bango's July 31 tax year is:

	Year-end	Profits Interest	Month × Deferred	=	Interest Deferral
Argo	June 30	.5	11		5.5
Bango	July 31	.5	0		0.0
Aggregate deferral					5.5

The partnership must adopt June 30 as its tax year because that year results in the least aggregate deferral of income.[224]

---

[222] I.R.C. § 706(b)(1)(B)(iii); Temp. Treas. Reg. § 1.706-1T(a)(1).

[223] Temp. Treas. Reg. § 1.706-1T(a)(2).

[224] Temp. Treas. Reg. § 1.706-1T(d), *Example (1)*.

If more than one tax year results in the same aggregate deferral, the partnership may select any one of the years. However, if one of the qualifying years is the year the partnership currently uses, the partnership must continue to use that year.[225]

The year that results in the least aggregate deferral is generally determined at the beginning of the partnership's current year. However, the IRS District Director may require a different determination date if it more accurately reflects the ownership of the partnership and the partners' aggregate deferral of income. This will occur if the partners engage in a tax-motivated transaction, such as a temporary shift in the ownership of partnership interests to avoid the least-deferral-of-income rules.[226]

A special *de minimis* rule applies if the tax year that results in the least aggregate deferral produces an aggregate deferral that is less than.5 (five-tenths) when compared with the aggregate deferral produced by the partnership's current tax year.[227] In that case, the partnership must continue to use its current year.[228]

> **Example:** The XY Partnership currently uses a September 30 tax year. Following the sale of a partnership interest, XY finds that there is no tax year used by the partners owning a majority of its interests nor by all of its principal partners. A March 31 tax year produces a least aggregate deferral of 1.45, while the current September 30 year results in an aggregate deferral of 1.05. Because the difference between the least aggregate deferral and the aggregate deferral of the current year is less than.5 (1.45 - 1.05 =.4), the partnership must continue to use the September 30 tax year.[229]

[D] Business Purpose for Fiscal Tax Year

A partnership may adopt a tax year different from that required by the majority-interest, principal-partner, or least-deferral rules only if it establishes, to the Service's satisfaction, that a business purpose exists for using another year.[230] A partnership satisfies the business-purpose requirement if it adopts a tax year that coincides with its "natural business year."[231] (*See* § 3.04[D][1], *infra.*) In a business that has peak and slack periods, the natural business year usually ends at, or soon after, the close of the peak period.[232] For example, a ski resort is likely to have a natural business year ending in the early spring, while a beach resort will have a natural business year ending after the summer. A partnership that lacks a

---

[225] Temp. Treas. Reg. § 1.706-1T(d), *Example (1)*.

[226] Temp. Treas. Reg. § 1.706-1T(d), *Example (1)*.

[227] Temp. Treas. Reg. § 1.706-1T(a)(4).

[228] Temp. Treas. Reg. § 1.706-1T(a)(4). The *de minimis* rule does not apply to the partnership's first tax year beginning after 1986.

[229] Temp. Treas. Reg. § 1.706-1T(d), *Example (6)*.

[230] I.R.C. § 706(b)(1)(C).

[231] Treas. Reg. § 1.706-1(b)(4)(iii).

[232] Rev. Proc. 74-33, 1974-2 C.B. 489.

natural business year must establish a 'compelling" nontax reason for a fiscal tax year (see § 3.04[D][2], infra).

[1] Natural Business Year-Gross-Receipts Test

A partnership may establish the existence of a natural business year by meeting a gross-receipts test.[233] Under this test, a partnership is considered to have a natural business year if 25 percent or more of its gross receipts for a 12-month period are recognized in the last two months of that period.[234] This requirement must be satisfied for the three consecutive 12-month periods ending with the last month of the natural business year.

[2] Business Purpose When Gross-Receipts Test Not Satisfied

A partnership wishing to retain, or change to, a fiscal year that does not satisfy the gross-receipts test for a natural business year (see § 3.04[D][1], supra) must establish some other "business purpose" for its requested year. The IRS determines whether the stated business purpose is satisfactory based on its consideration of all the facts and circumstances, including the tax consequences that will result if the requested year is permitted [235] These tax consequences include (1) any deferral or shift in a substantial portion of a partner's income or deductions from one year to another that substantially reduces his tax liability, and (2) the creation of a short period in which there is a substantial net operating loss.[236]

The following nontax factors ordinarily are not sufficient to satisfy the business-purpose requirement:[237]

(1) the use of a particular year for regulatory or financial accounting purposes;

(2) the hiring patterns of a particular business (i.e., the fact that a firm typically hires staff during certain times of the year);

(3) the use of a particular year for administrative purposes, such as the admission or retirement of partners or shareholders, promotion of staff, and compensation or retirement arrangements with staff, partners, or shareholders; and

(4) the fact that a particular business involves the use of price lists, a model year, or other items that change on an annual basis.

The IRS will not approve a fiscal tax year that defers or distorts a partner's income unless "compelling reasons" are shown.[238] Thus, approval will not be granted merely because a fiscal year is more convenient to the partnership or

---

[233] Rev. Proc. 2002-38, 2002-22 I.R.B. 103.

[234] Id. See Rev. Proc. 83-25, 1983-1 C.B. 689. But see Rev. Proc. 74-33, 1974-2 C.B. 489.

[235] Rev. Rul. 87-57, 1987-2 C.B. 117.

[236] Id.

[237] H.R. Rep. No. 841, 99th Cong., 2d Sess. II-319 (1986); Rev. Proc. 2002-39, 2002-22 I.R.B. 1046.

[238] Rev. Rul. 87-57, 1987-2 C.B. 117.

partners. In effect, the Service's position is that a fiscal year is allowable only if the partnership (1) satisfies the gross-receipts test for a natural business year, or (2) shows that its failure to satisfy that test resulted from extenuating circumstances.

[E]   52-53-Week Tax Year

A partnership or partner may have an annual accounting period end on the same day of the week (e.g., the last Friday in June) by adopting a tax year that varies between 52 and 53 weeks.[239] To adopt, change to or from, or retain a 52-53-week tax year, the partnership and its partners must determine their taxable incomes as if their tax years ended on the last day of the calendar month preceding the end of the 52-53-week year.[240] Neither a partnership nor a partner may use a 52-53-week year if the principal purpose is tax avoidance.[241]

[F]   Election of Tax Year Other Than Year Required by I.R.C. Section 706

The tax-year rules of I.R.C. Section 706(b) restrict a partnership's choice of year to one that conforms to the year used by as many partners as possible.[242] The purpose of this restriction is to preclude the deferral of income that occurs when a partnership uses a tax year that differs from the year used by its partners.

Because most partnerships are owned by individuals using the calendar tax year, these rules require many partnerships to use a calendar year. However, in response to protests by accountants and tax return preparers about the substantially increased number of calendar-year tax returns, Congress enacted rules permitting partnerships to elect a fiscal year. The election, however, limits the number of months of income-deferral partners may obtain from the fiscal year, and requires the partnership to make refundable, non-interest-bearing payments to the Treasury to eliminate the tax benefit of income deferral.[243]

Under I.R.C. Section 444(b)(1), a new partnership may elect to adopt a tax year other than the year required by I.R.C. Section 706(b) only if the selected year does not create a "deferral period" longer than three months. A deferral period is the number of months from the beginning of the selected tax year forward to the close of the tax year that the partnership would otherwise be required to use under I.R.C. Section 706(b).[244]

An existing partnership may elect to use a tax year that does not create a deferral period exceeding the lesser of (1) the deferral period of the tax year that

---

[239] I.R.C. § 441(f)(1).

[240] Temp. Treas. Reg. § 1.441-3T(d)(1)(ii).

[241] I.R.C. § 441(f)(3); Temp. Treas. Reg. § 1.441-3T(c)(2)(i).

[242] I.R.C. § 706(b)(1)(B); S. Rep. No. 313, 99th Cong., 2d Sess. 165 (1986). Similar limitations apply to the choice of tax year by S corporations and personal service corporations.

[243] The election is permitted under I.R.C. § 444. The required payment rules are provided in I.R.C. § 7519. Both sections were enacted in the Revenue Act of 1987.

[244] I.R.C. § 444(b)(4). The required year is determined by assuming that no business purpose exists for a fiscal year.

is being changed, or (2) three months.[245] The deferral period of the tax year being changed is the deferral period of the tax year immediately preceding the year for which the I.R.C. Section 444 election is being made. In effect, an existing partnership cannot make an election that will increase the deferral period the partnership currently enjoys.

For any year that an I.R.C. Section 444 election is in effect, a partnership must make a "required payment" to the IRS.[246] Required payments are intended to compensate the Treasury for the value of the partners' tax deferral that results from the partnership's using a tax year other than the year required by I.R.C. Section 706(b).

PRACTICE NOTE:

An election under I.R.C. Section 444 allows partners to defer tax on partnership income for up to three months. To obtain this benefit, the partnership must make an interest-free deposit of funds with the government that is supposed to approximate the total amount of tax the partners deferred. This tax deferral is computed by assuming that (1) each partner is taxable at a rate 1 percent above the highest tax rate on individuals, and (2) partnership income for the current year will equal its income in the prior year.

If partnership income does not increase substantially from year to year, any cash-flow benefit the partners obtain by deferring tax on partnership income is likely to be exceeded by the lost earnings on the required payment. If partnership income is expected to increase substantially, however, the required payments based on the lower income of prior years may be much less than the tax liability the partners actually defer.

As a practical matter, most partnerships are unlikely to obtain any tax advantages from an election under I.R.C. Section 444. Thus, the decision to make the election is usually based on nontax considerations, such as more desirable dates for taking inventories, closing books and records, and preparing financial statements and tax returns.

---

§ 3.05   SIMPLIFIED FLOW THROUGH FOR ELECTING LARGE PARTNERSHIPS

Large entities with 100 or more members may elect a simplified form of partnership tax reporting.[247] An electing large partnership is permitted to substantially reduce the number of tax items that must be separately reported to its many members. Most items of income, deduction, credit and loss are combined at the

---

[245] I.R.C. § 444(b)(2); Temp. Treas. Reg. § 1.444-1T(b)(2)(iii).

[246] I.R.C. § 7519.

[247] I.R.C. §§ 771–777.

entity level and the net amounts passed through to the members. This simplified reporting method is intended to facilitate tax reporting by large entities and their members and to improve IRS audit procedures.

Generally, an entity may elect this simplified tax reporting if it is classified as a partnership for tax purposes and had 100 or more members in the preceding tax year. However, entities engaged in a services business are ineligible for the election, as are commodity pools. Unlike other partnerships, an electing large partnership does not terminate for tax purposes if 50 percent or more of its interests are sold or exchanged within a 12-month period.

Chapter 4

ACQUIRING A PARTNERSHIP OR LLC INTEREST BY CONTRIBUTION

§ 4.01 OVERVIEW OF GENERAL RULES

Under general tax law principles, a taxpayer recognizes gain or loss when he exchanges an interest in property he owns for an interest in other property.[1] I.R.C. Section 721(a) provides an important exception to this general rule when the property the taxpayer receives in the exchange is an interest in a partnership (*i.e.*, the property is "contributed" for the partnership interest). The regulations suggest that the rationale for this nonrecognition rule is that the transaction merely changes the contributing partner's form of ownership, because he continues to have a substantial investment in the property through his interest in the partnership.[2]

> **Example (1):** For equal interests in the AB Partnership, Allen contributes $10,000 in cash and Betty contributes land worth $10,000 with a basis of $4,000. Under general tax principles, this transaction could be characterized as a sale by Betty of a half-interest in the land to Allen for $5,000. Because her basis in half the land is $2,000, Betty would recognize a $3,000 gain. The sale aspect of the transaction is illustrated by the fact that, on a liquidation of the partnership, Betty would receive $5,000 in cash and a one-half interest in the land she contributed. The other half-interest in the land would be distributed to Allen. Under I.R.C. Section 721(a), however, Betty does not recognize any gain on her contribution of the land to the partnership.

The rule permitting nontaxable contributions of property for partnership interests is significantly broader than the corresponding rule of I.R.C. Section 351 governing exchanges of property for corporate stock. Under I.R.C. Section 351, the exchange is fully taxable, unless the persons contributing the property control 80 percent of the corporation's stock immediately after the transaction. The absence of an ownership requirement in the partnership context allows a nontaxable exchange of property for a partnership interest regardless of how large or small an interest the partner receives. Thus, no gain or loss is recognized, even though the transaction substantially changes the partner's interest in the transferred property; that is, his continuing interest in the property is relatively small in comparison with the interest he acquires in other partnership assets.

> **Example (2):** Using the facts in Example (1), assume that one year later

---

[1] I.R.C. § 1001.

[2] Treas. Reg. § 1.1002-1(c).

Carol obtains a 10-percent interest in the partnership by contributing equipment worth $2,000 with a $1,000 basis. Under I.R.C. Section 721(a), Carol does not recognize any gain on the contribution. However, if Carol had contributed the equipment to a corporation in exchange for 10 percent of its stock, she would have recognized a $1,000 gain because she would not control 80 percent of the corporation's stock after the transaction.

The nonrecognition rule of I.R.C. Section 721(a) defers, but does not discharge, the tax consequences of the gain or loss inherent in property contributed to a partnership. The following basis and allocation rules ensure that the gain or loss "built in" to the property at the time of contribution is ultimately taken into account:

(1)   I.R.C. Section 723 provides that a partnership's basis in contributed property is the same as the contributing partner's basis when the contribution occurs. Thus, any gain or loss built-in to the contributed property will be recognized when the partnership disposes of the asset. Under I.R.C. Section 704(c)(1)(A), gain, loss, and other tax items attributable to contributed property must be allocated in a manner that takes account of the difference between the property's fair market value and its tax basis at the time of contribution. Consequently, the built-in gain or loss the partnership recognizes will be allocated to the contributing partner and included in his share of partnership income. Although the character of the built-in gain or loss is not necessarily preserved, I.R.C. Section 724 sets forth rules to prevent contributions from changing the character of income or loss attributable to receivables, inventory, and capital-loss property.

(2)   Special rules prevent partnerships from shifting the gain or loss "built-in" to contributed property from the contributing partner to other partners. I.R.C. Section 704(c)(1)(B) requires the contributing partner to recognize the built in gain or loss if the contributed property is distributed to another partner within seven years of the contribution date. Under I.R.C. Section 737, the contributing partner recognizes the gain built-in to the contributed property if other partnership property is distributed to him within seven years. (*See* Chapter 4.)

(3)   Under I.R.C. Section 722, a partner's basis for a partnership interest acquired in exchange for a contribution equals the amount of money the partner contributes plus his basis in any contributed property. This correlation between a partner's basis in contributed property and the basis of his partnership interest ensures that any gain or loss that was deferred at the time of contribution is recognized when the partner disposes of his partnership interest.

Example (3): Under the facts in Example (1), the partnership's basis for the land Betty contributed is $4,000, and Betty's basis for her partnership interest is $4,000. The partnership's balance sheet for tax and "book" purposes is as follows:

Asset	Tax Basis	Book Value
Cash	$10,000	$10,000
Land	4,000	10,000
	$14,000	$20,000
Partners' Capital		
Allen	$10,000	$10,000
Betty	4,000	10,000
	$14,000	$20,000

If the partnership sells the land for its $10,000 book value, it recognizes a $6,000 tax gain, even though it has not realized an economic gain by selling the property for its book value. Because the entire gain is attributable to precontribution appreciation, I.R.C. Section 704(c)(1)(A) requires the $6,000 to be allocated to Betty for tax purposes. The partnership's balance sheet after the sale is as follows:

Asset	Tax Basis	Book Value
Cash	$20,000	$20,000
Partners' Capital		
Allen	$10,000	$10,000
Betty	10,000	10,000
	$20,000	$20,000

Assume that the partnership does not sell the land but instead, Betty sells her partnership interest to Carl for its $10,000 value. Because Betty's basis in her partnership interest is $4,000, she recognizes a $6,000 gain on the sale.

Because gain is not recognized on a contribution of property for a partnership interest, it is often necessary to distinguish contributions from other partner-partnership transactions. Subchapter K contains two specific rules designed to prevent a purported property contribution from "disguising" a transaction that is, in substance, a sale or exchange of the property transferred to the partnership. Under I.R.C. Section 721(b), a partner recognizes gain on a contribution of appreciated property to a partnership "investment company." This rule is designed to preclude taxpayers from transferring appreciated investments to a partnership to obtain tax-free diversification of their portfolios. Under I.R.C. Section 707(a)(2)(B), a transfer of property to a partnership is treated as a sale rather than a contribution if the transferor receives a distribution from the partnership that is equivalent to a payment for the property.

In determining the tax consequences of a contribution, the effect of any changes in the partners' shares of partnership liabilities must be taken into account. Changes in liabilities generally occur when a partner contributes encumbered property to a partnership (because the contributing partner's individual liabilities are shifted to the other partners) and when a new partner joins a partnership with existing debts (because partnership liabilities are shifted from the existing partners to the new partner). Under I.R.C. Section 752, a partner whose share of partnership liabilities increases is deemed to contribute money to the partnership, and a partner whose share of liabilities decreases is deemed to receive a distribution of money. A partner who contributes encumbered property may recognize gain, if the cash distribution he is deemed to receive on the transfer of his individual liabilities to the partnership exceeds the basis of his partnership interest.[3] (The treatment of contributions that shift partnership liabilities is discussed in § 4.05, *infra*.)

A services partner who receives an unrestricted partnership interest is taxable when he receives it if the interest has an ascertainable fair market value at that time. The value of an interest acquired for services depends on whether the partner is entitled to a portion of existing partnership capital or merely allowed to share in future partnership profits. The value of a capital interest is readily determined by reference to the amount of capital shifted to the services partner from the other partners. In contrast, the present value of an interest in future profits usually cannot be determined because the amount of profits is speculative. Thus, in typical situations, a services partner is not taxable when he receives a profits interest but simply reports his share of the profits as earned by the partnership. (*See* § 4.06, *infra*.)

§ 4.02 CONTRIBUTING PROPERTY IN EXCHANGE FOR A PARTNERSHIP OR LLC INTEREST

[A] General Rule: Gain and Loss Not Recognized

No gain or loss is recognized by a partner or partnership when money or other property is contributed to the partnership in exchange for a partnership interest. This nonrecognition rule under I.R.C. Section 721(a) applies to a partner's initial contribution to a newly formed or existing partnership and to contributions a partner makes after he has joined the partnership.[4] Unlike the rule governing contributions to corporations,[5] gain or loss is not recognized, even though the contributing partner does not control the partnership after the contribution.

The following statutory exceptions to the nonrecognition rule may apply:

(1)   A partner recognizes gain but not loss when he exchanges appreciated property for an interest in a partnership classified as an "investment company" under I.R.C. Section 721(b). (*See* § 4.02[C], *infra*.)

(2)   I.R.C. Section 721(c) authorizes the IRS to issue regulations requiring gain to be recognized when appreciated property is contributed to a partnership if the built-in gain otherwise would be transferred to a foreign partner.[6] This provision replaces the former excise tax imposed on

---

[3] I.R.C. § 731. *See* Chapter 8.

[4] Treas. Reg. § 1.721-1(a).

[5] I.R.C. § 351.

[6] This section was added by the Taxpayer Relief Act of 1997, H.R. 2014. The regulations have not yet been issued.

contributions to foreign partnerships under I.R.C. Section 1491.[7]

(3) I.R.C. Section 721(d) authorizes the IRS to issue regulations treating a deemed royalty arising from the contribution of an intangible to a foreign partnership as ordinary income.[8] The deemed royalty is to be treated as foreign source income only to the extent as would an actual royalty. This provision replaces the pre-1997 rule that treated the deemed royalty as U.S. source income.[9]

(4) Proposed regulations under the corporate liquidation rules may require a corporate partner to recognize gain on a contribution of appreciated property to a partnership that owns stock or other equity interests in the corporate partner or its affiliates.[10] This treatment applies if the transaction is economically equivalent to the corporate partner exchanging its interest in the appreciated property for an interest in its own stock. A similar recognition rule may apply if the partnership distributes the corporate partner's stock to that partner; the corporate partner is considered to redeem its stock for a portion of its partnership interest and recognizes any gain inherent in that interest. (*See* § 8.02, *infra.*)

Gain or loss may be recognized if the Service recharacterizes a partner's purported property contribution to the partnership as some other kind of transaction. For example, a transfer of money to a partnership that is, in substance, a loan, rent, or payment for partnership property or services, is not treated as a contribution, regardless of the form of the transaction.[11] The Service may recharacterize a purported contribution as a sale between a partner and partnership if the contributing partner receives a distribution of partnership assets that is related to his contribution,[12] or if the contributing partner receives an allocation of partnership income that is related to his contribution.[13]

Even if a contribution is not taxable under the general nonrecognition rule, the contributing partner may recognize gain under collateral tax rules. A partner who contributes property encumbered by a mortgage or other liability recognizes gain to the extent that the liability he transfers to the partnership exceeds the basis in his partnership interest.[14] The property contribution itself does not result in a gain for the partner. The gain comes from the cash distribution he is deemed to receive from the partnership when the partnership becomes liable for his individual debt.

---

[7] I.R.C. §§ 1491–1494 were repealed as of August 5, 1997.

[8] The regulations will follow the treatment afforded transfers of intangibles to a foreign corporation under I.R.C. § 367(d)(2).

[9] The provision is effective August 5, 1997. Treas. Regulations have not yet been issued.

[10] Prop. Treas. Reg. § 1.337(d)-3. *See* 1989-1 C.B. 679, Notice 89-37; Notice 93-2, 1993-1 C.B. 292.

[11] Treas. Reg. § 1.707-1(a).

[12] I.R.C. § 707(a)(2)(B).

[13] I.R.C. § 707(a)(2)(A).

[14] I.R.C. §§ 731, 752(b).

Noncontributing partners may recognize gain or loss when another partner contributes money or property to acquire or increase an interest in the partnership. The noncontributing partners are deemed to receive cash distributions from the partnership to the extent that the contributing partner becomes liable for, or increases his share of, existing partnership debts. If any partner's deemed distribution exceeds the basis in his partnership interest, he recognizes gain.[15] The Service has ruled that noncontributing partners may recognize gain or loss as a result of a contribution in which the contributing partner acquires (or increases) his interest in the partnership's ordinary income property and becomes liable for a share of partnership liabilities.[16] The ruling holds that each noncontributing partner is taxable under I.R.C. Section 751 as if he received a distribution of a portion of the ordinary income property and then sold it back to the partnership in exchange for a reduction in his share of partnership debt.[17]

[B]   Definition of Property Under I.R.C. Section 721(a)

Legislative history, regulations, and case law do not adequately define "property" as used in the partnership context of I.R.C. Section 721. Consequently, the meaning of the term "property" is often defined by reference to decisions under I.R.C. Section 351 on contributions of property to a corporation in exchange for stock. Although I.R.C. Sections 721 and 351 are not identical, the meaning of property in the partnership context is analogous to its meaning in the corporate context. Property comprises tangibles such as money, realty, and other personal assets and intangibles such as contract rights,[18] notes,[19] accounts receivable,[20] and installment obligations. Reg. § 1.721-1(a). An interest in a partnership constitutes property that may be contributed to another partnership without recognition of gain.[21]

[1]   Installment Obligations

A contribution of an unrelated party's installment obligation to a partnership is not a disposition of the obligation requiring immediate recognition of the unreported gain. The partnership reports the gain as it receives payments on the obligation.[22] However, a disposition occurs if the partnership itself is the obligor on

---

[15] I.R.C. §§ 731, 752(b).

[16] The property subject to this treatment, referred to as "I.R.C. § 751 property," includes "unrealized receivables" and "substantially appreciated inventory."

[17] Rev. Rul. 84-102, 1984-2 C.B. 119. *But see* Rev. Rul. 84-115, 1984-2 C.B. 118.

[18] Ambrose v. Comm'r, T.C. Memo. 1956-125 (contract for purchase of wine); Dillon v. U.S., 84-2 U.S.T.C. ¶ 9921 (S.D. Tex. 1981) (contractual right to participate in another partnership).

[19] Priv. Ltr. Rul. 8117210 concludes that a third party's demand note is property under I.R.C. § 721.

[20] Hempt Bros., Inc. v. U.S., 490 F.2d 1172 (3d Cir.), *cert. denied*, 419 U.S. 826 (1974); Rev. Rul. 80-198, 1980-2 C.B. 113. Under I.R.C. § 704(c), however, the income recognized when the receivables are collected must be allocated to the contributing partner.

[21] Rev. Rul. 84-115, 1984-2 C.B. 118, holding that a transfer of a partnership interest for an interest in another partnership is a nontaxable contribution rather than a taxable exchange.

[22] Treas. Reg. § 1.453-9(c)(2). Under I.R.C. § 704(c) the precontribution gain must be allocated to the contributing partner.

the note.[23] The contributing partner recognizes gain equal to the difference between the value of the partnership interest he receives and his basis in the contributed obligation.[24]

[2] Right to Use Property

A right to use property does not qualify as a property contribution under I.R.C. Section 721; the partnership must receive an ownership interest in the contributed item.[25] For example, a partnership's use of a partner's personal property to obtain credit or to secure existing debt is considered a right rather than a contribution.[26] If, however, the partnership obtains the benefits of ownership, the transaction may be treated as a contribution, even if the partner retains legal title to the property. Thus, a long-term lease,[27] a right to extract specific mineral reserves,[28] a nonexclusive license to use a patented process,[29] and a right to royalties carved out of a larger oil payment interest have been treated as property.[30]

[3] Cancellation of Partnership or LLC Debt

Cancellation of a partnership debt by a creditor in exchange for a partnership interest is a property contribution if the debt arose from a loan or sale of property. In effect, the partnership receives a contribution of the amount it owes to the creditor. Because the debt is contributed rather than cancelled, the partnership should not recognize cancellation of indebtedness income. If the debt was incurred for services performed for the partnership, however, the creditor will be considered to have received his partnership interest for services and not for property.[31] In that case, the creditor recognizes compensation income equal to the value of the interest he receives and the partnership recognizes income as if it transferred undivided interests in partnership property in exchange for the services.

A partnership interest acquired by a creditor in exchange for cancellation of a partnership debt is treated as I.R.C. Section 1245 property, and the aggregate amount of ordinary loss and bad-debt deductions claimed by the creditor is treated as if it were depreciation. When the creditor later disposes of the partnership interest, a portion of any gain realized is recaptured as ordinary income.[32]

---

[23] I.R.C. § 453B(f).

[24] I.R.C. § 453B(a).

[25] The transaction is treated as if it were between the partnership and a nonpartner under I.R.C. § 707(a). Treas. Reg. § 1.721-1(a), Treas. Reg. § 1.707-1(a)(1).

[26] Treas. Reg. § 1.707-1(a).

[27] Ltr. Rul. 8225069.

[28] Ltr. Rul. 8301001.

[29] E. I. du Pont de Nemours & Co. v. U.S., 471 F.2d 1211 (Ct. Cl. 1973) (contribution of property under I.R.C. § 351).

[30] H B Zachry Co. v. Comm'r, 49 TC 73 (1967) (contribution of property under I.R.C. § 351).

[31] Treas. Reg. § 1.721-1(b)(1).

[32] I.R.C. § 108(e)(7). For application to partnerships, see I.R.C. § 108(e)(7)(E).

[4]   Assets Produced by Personal Services

Property does not include services rendered for the partnership; a partner generally is taxed on the fair market value of a partnership interest received for services and the partnership may deduct or capitalize that amount. However, assets produced by the personal efforts of a contributing partner (e.g., professional goodwill,[33] technical know-how,[34] trade secrets,[35] and contract rights)[36] constitute property that may be contributed to a partnership tax free under I.R.C. Section 721.

[5]   Personal Notes

A partner may receive a partnership interest in exchange for his own note payable to the partnership. The partner's basis in his personal note, and in the partnership interest he receives for it, is zero.[37] The contributing partner increases the basis in his partnership interest when, and to the extent that, he makes payments on the note.[38]

Although a partner's basis increases as he pays the principal on the note, the treatment of interest payments is uncertain. A simple and appropriate approach is to treat the interest payments as additional capital contributions governed by I.R.C. Section 721, and the partner's basis increases as he makes the payments. If the interest is not considered an additional contribution, the payments are included in the partnership's income, and the partner has a corresponding interest expense subject to the limitations on deductibility of personal, investment, and passive activity interest.

[C]   Gain Recognized on Contribution of Property to Investment Company

The general nonrecognition rule of I.R.C. Section 721(a) does not apply if property is contributed to a partnership that, "would be treated as an investment company (within the meaning of I.R.C. Section 351) if it were incorporated."[39] This exception, under I.R.C. Section 721(b), is designed to preclude taxpayers from

---

[33] Rev. Rul. 70-45, 1970-1 C.B. 17.

[34] Rev. Rul. 64-56, 1964-1 C.B. 133. See U.S. v. Rees, 295 F.2d 817 (9th Cir. 1961).

[35] Rev. Rul. 71-564, 1971-2 C.B. 179.

[36] Dillon v. U.S., 84-2 U.S. Tax Cas. ¶ 9921 (S.D. Tex. 1981) (contract right to participate in another partnership); U.S. v. Stafford, 727 F.2d 1043 (11th Cir. 1984), rev'g and rem'g 552 F. Supp. 311 (M.D. Ga. 1982), on remand from 611 F.2d 990 (5th Cir. 1980), rev'g and rem'g 435 F. Supp. 1036 (M.D. Ga. 1977) (letter of intent to provide financing for real estate development). But see U.S. v. Frazell, 335 F.2d 487 (5th Cir. 1964), cert. denied, 380 U.S. 961, 85 S. Ct. 1104, 14 L. Ed. 2d 152 (1965), suggesting that contribution of an unvested partnership interest to a corporation is not property under I.R.C. § 351 if the partnership interest is to be received for services.

[37] Oden v. Comm'r, T.C. Memo. 1981-184, affd in unpublished opinion, 679 F.2d 885 (4th Cir. 1982); accord Bussing v. Comm'r, 88 T.C. 449 (1987).

[38] Rev. Rul. 80-235, 1980-2 C.B. 229.

[39] Partnership investment companies are defined by reference to the regulations under I.R.C. § 351 applicable to corporate investment companies. S. Rep. No. 938, pt. 2, 94th Cong., 2d Sess. 43 (1976).

transferring appreciated investments to a partnership to obtain tax-free diversification of their portfolios. According to I.R.C. Section 721(b), a partner recognizes gain (but not loss),[40] if:

(1) the partner contributes appreciated property to a partnership investment company; and

(2) the contribution results in a direct or indirect diversification of his interests.[41]

A partnership is an investment company if, after the partner's contribution, more than 80 percent of the value of its assets[42] consist of the following "listed" items: money; stocks and other equity interests in a corporation; evidences of indebtedness, options, forward or futures contracts, notional principal contracts, and derivatives; foreign currency; interests in precious metals (unless used in an active trade or business after the contribution); interests in a regulated investment company (RIC) or a real estate investment trust (REIT), common trust funds, and publicly traded partnerships (as defined in Code Section 7704(b)); or other interests in noncorporate entities that are convertible into or exchangeable for any of the listed assets.

Other assets counted toward the 80-percent test are interests in an entity if substantially all of its assets are listed assets, and as provided in regulations, interests in other entities to the extent of the value of the interest attributable to listed assets. The IRS has regulatory authority to add other assets to the list.

A partnership holding these assets is an investment company only if the following requirements also are met:

(1) the assets must be held for investment purposes;[43]

(2) for the 80-percent test, a partnership that owns a 50-percent or greater interest in a corporation or partnership is deemed to own its pro rata share of that entity's marketable stocks and securities;[44]

(3) the investment company determination must consider any plan regarding the partnership's assets in existence immediately after the transfer;[45] and

(4) the property contribution must result directly or indirectly in diversification.[46]

A property contribution ordinarily results in diversification of a partner's interests if "two or more persons transfer nonidentical assets" to the partnership.[47]

---

[40] Although I.R.C. § 721(b) applies to gains only, I.R.C. § 351(e)(1) causes shareholders to recognize both gains and losses on transfers to corporate investment companies. Treas. Reg. § 1.351-1(c)(1).

[41] Treas. Reg. § 1.351-1(c)(5). *See also* S. Rep. No. 938, pt. 2, 94th Cong., 2d Sess. 44 (1976).

[42] Treas. Reg. § 1.351-1(c)(1)(ii).

[43] Treas. Reg. § 1.351-1(c)(4).

[44] Treas. Reg. § 1.351-1(c)(4).

[45] Treas. Reg. § 1.351-1(c)(2).

[46] Treas. Reg. § 1.351-1(c)(1)(i).

[47] Treas. Reg. § 1.351-1(c)(5).

A *de minimis* rule states that diversification does not occur if the contributed assets differ only slightly. Diversification probably does not occur when the partnership agreement allocates gains and losses from specific contributed property to the contributing partner, and requires that the property be returned to that partner when he withdraws from the partnership.[48]

A partner's basis in his partnership interest increases by the amount of any gain recognized under I.R.C. Section 721(b).[49]

§ 4.03 BASIS, HOLDING PERIOD, AND CHARACTERIZATION RULES

[A] Partner's or Member's Basis in the Partnership or LLC Interest

A partner's initial basis in a partnership interest acquired in exchange for a contribution is the amount of money he contributes plus his basis in any contributed property (*i.e.*, substituted basis)[50] according to I.R.C. Section 722.

If the partnership is an investment company, the partner's basis is increased by any gain recognized under I.R.C. Section 721(b). Gain a partner recognizes in connection with a contribution of property encumbered by a liability does not increase his basis, because that gain results from the cash distribution the partner is deemed to receive when the partnership becomes liable for his individual debts, rather than from the contribution itself.

> **Example:** On July 1, Year 1, Arthur and Barbara form the AB Partnership, each receiving a 50-percent interest in the capital and profits of the newly formed partnership. Arthur contributes undeveloped real estate that was purchased two years earlier for $50,000. The property has a fair market value of $60,000 at the time of contribution. Barbara contributes $60,000 in cash. Neither the partnership nor either of the partners recognizes any gain as a result of this transaction, in accordance with the general rule of I.R.C. Section 721(a).
>
> Under I.R.C. Section 722, Arthur's basis in his partnership interest is $50,000, which is the substituted basis for the contributed real estate. Arthur's capital account, however, is credited with $60,000, the fair market value of the contributed real estate. The basis for Barbara's partnership interest and her capital account are both $60,000. AB Partnership's basis for the real estate is $50,000, its carryover basis, according to I.R.C. Section 723.

---

[48] S. Rep. No. 938, pt. 2, 94th Cong., 2d Sess. 44 (1976).

[49] I.R.C. § 722. Similarly, the partnership's basis in the contributed property increases by the amount of gain that the partner recognized. I.R.C. § 723.

[50] A partnership's basis in contributed personal-use property that is converted to business or investment use is the lesser of the property's basis or fair market value when contributed.

[B]   Partner's or Member's Holding Period for the Partnership or LLC Interest

A partner's holding period for a partnership interest that was received in exchange for capital assets and depreciable trade or business property, as defined in I.R.C. Section 1231, includes his holding period for the contributed property.[51] For contributions of other kinds of assets, such as inventory or accounts receivable, the holding period for the partnership interest begins on the date of the transfer.[52] The Code and regulations do not indicate how the holding period for a partnership interest is determined when mixed assets with different holding periods are contributed. Perhaps no definitive answer is necessary because the issue becomes moot once the partnership interest has been held for the long-term holding period. Arguably, a partner who sells his partnership interest before it qualifies for long-term holding period treatment may fragment the sale and report part of his gain or loss as long term and part as short term.[53]

> **Example:** On July 1, Year 1, Robert and Sara form the RS LLC as equal members to hold and invest in real estate. Robert, who is not a dealer in real estate, contributes land that he purchased on May 1, Year 1. Sara, a real estate dealer, contributes land from her inventory that she purchased two years earlier. The land that Robert contributes is a capital asset with a holding period of two months; that holding period transfers to the LLC and to his LLC interest. The land that Sara contributes is ordinary income property in her hands and, therefore, the holding period for Sara's LLC interest begins on July 1, Year 1. Although the real estate Sara contributes is a capital asset in the hands of the LLC, the LLC's holding period also begins on July 1, Year 1.

[C]   Partnership's or LLC's Basis and Holding Period in Contributed Property

The gain or loss that is not recognized when property is contributed to a partnership is deferred until the partnership disposes of the property. The amount of potential gain is preserved at the partnership level by I.R.C. Section 723, which provides that the partnership's basis in contributed property is the same as the partner's basis at the time of the contribution, (*i.e.*, a carryover basis). If a partner contributes personal-use property that is being converted to a business or investment asset, such as a personal residence or automobile, the partnership's basis for determining loss and depreciation deductions is the property's basis or its fair market value when contributed, whichever is less.[54]

---

[51] I.R.C. § 1223(1).

[52] Treas. Reg. § 1.1223-1(a).

[53] *Cf.* I.R.C. § 1223(1); Runkle v. Comm'r, 39 B.T.A. 458 (1939).

[54] Au v. Comm'r, 40 T.C. 264 (1963), *aff'd per curiam*, 330 F.2d 1008 (9th Cir. 1964); Treas. Reg. §§ 1.165-9(b), 1.167(g)-1.

If the partnership is an investment company, basis is increased by any gain the contributing partner recognizes under I.R.C. Section 721(b).[55]

In determining whether partnership capital gains and losses are long or short term, the partnership's holding period for contributed property includes the contributing partner's holding period.

[D]   Character of Contributed Property

The character of gain or loss a partnership recognizes when it sells contributed property generally depends on the character of the property in the hands of the partnership.[56] However, I.R.C. Section 724 provides exceptions to this rule to prevent taxpayers from using partnerships to convert ordinary income into capital gain or to convert capital loss into ordinary loss.[57] The same character of gain or loss that the contributing partner would realize is carried over to a partnership when it disposes of contributed unrealized receivables, inventory items, or "built-in" capital-loss property.[58] A partnership always realizes ordinary income when it disposes of contributed receivables, or when it disposes of contributed inventory within five years of the contribution; a partnership realizes a capital loss to the extent of the loss inherent in the property at the time of contribution if, within five years of the contribution, it sells property that would have generated a capital loss to the contributing partner.[59]

These characterization rules also apply to substituted-basis property that the partnership acquires in a nonrecognition transaction (or a series of nonrecognition transactions) in exchange for contributed receivables, inventory, or capital-loss property.[60] Property is "substituted-basis property" if the partnership's basis is determined from:

(1)   the property's basis in the hands of the transferor, or

(2)   the partnership's basis in the property it transfers in exchange for the property it acquires.[61]

The "taint" from the characterization rules does not apply to stock in a subchapter C corporation received for partnership property in a nonrecognition transaction under I.R.C. Section 351.[62]

---

[55] I.R.C. § 723.

[56] I.R.C. §§ 702, 703.

[57] *See* Staff of Joint Committee on Taxation, General Explanation of the Revenue Provisions of the Deficit Reduction Act of 1984, at 234–35 (1984). I.R.C. § 735 applies similar rules to characterize gain or loss when a partner disposes of receivables or inventory distributed to him by a partnership.

[58] I.R.C. § 724(d)(3).

[59] I.R.C. § 724(c).

[60] I.R.C. § 724(d)(3).

[61] I.R.C. § 7701(a)(42).

[62] I.R.C. § 724(d)(3)(B).

[E] Allocation of Income, Gain, Loss, and Deduction Attributable to Contributed Property

Under I.R.C. Section 704(c)(1)(A), partnership income, gain, loss, and deductions attributable to contributed property must be allocated among the partners by taking into account the difference between the basis and the fair market value of the property at the time it was contributed to the partnership. This requirement prevents a contributing partner from shifting to the other partners the tax consequences attributable to precontribution changes in the value or basis of contributed property. The allocation rules for contributed property are discussed in Chapter 6.

Each of the assets contributed to a partnership must be accurately valued in order to comply with I.R.C. Section 704(c). This valuation can be a difficult task, particularly if the assets of an existing business are transferred to a partnership. For example, if two accountants, each in their own practice, decide to join together in a partnership, they must appraise the value of any furniture, equipment, accounts receivable, work in progress, and goodwill that they are contributing to the new partnership. They must determine and record the difference between the value and adjusted basis of each of these assets at the time of contribution.

If only a "small disparity" exists between the book value and tax basis of property contributed by a partner in a single partnership tax year, the partnership may elect to disregard the I.R.C. Section 704(c) rules or to apply these rules only when it disposes of the property.[63]

A small disparity exists if the difference between the book value and tax basis of property contributed by one partner during a tax year is not greater than 15 percent of its tax basis and the total gross disparity does not exceed $20,000.

The following types of property may be aggregated in making allocations under I.R.C. Section 704(c), if contributed by one partner during a partnership tax year:[64]

(1) *Depreciable property.* All depreciable property, other than real property, that is included in the same general asset account under I.R.C. Section 168.

(2) *All zero-basis property, other than real property.*

(3) *Inventory of a partnership that does not use a specific identification method of accounting (other than securities and similar investment assets).*[65]

---

[63] Treas. Reg. § 1.704-3(e).

[64] Treas. Reg. § 1.704-3(e)(2).

[65] As defined in Treas. Reg. § 1.704-3(e)(3)(ii).

[F]   Distributions May Require Property Contributor to Recognize Gain

Under I.R.C. Section 704(c)(1)(B), a partner recognizes gain or loss if property he contributed to the partnership is distributed to another partner within seven years of the contribution. A similar rule under I.R.C. Section 737 requires a contributing partner to recognize gain if other partnership property is distributed to him within seven years of the contribution. (For discussion of these provisions, see Chapters 6 and 8.)

§ 4.04   PARTNERSHIP OR LLC INTEREST ACQUIRED FOR CONTRIBUTION OF PROPERTY SUBJECT TO A LIABILITY

The following sections describe the tax consequences of a contribution of encumbered property to a partnership or LLC. The most significant consequences are attributable to the changes in the partners' shares of partnership liabilities that occur when the liability for the property is shifted from the contributing partner to the partnership. Although this chapter provides a general overview of the rules for determining each partner's share of a liability, the in-depth analysis and illustration of these rules is found in Chapter 5.

[A]   General Treatment of Changes in Partners' or Members' Liabilities

A partnership or limited liability company often becomes responsible for paying liabilities related to contributed property. For example, real estate or equipment may be contributed subject to a mortgage or purchase money obligation, or a partner or member may transfer all the assets and liabilities of an existing business to the partnership or LLC. As a result, individual liabilities of the contributing partner or member are shifted to the partnership or LLC and, in turn, to all of its partners or members. These shifts occur even though no partner or member is personally obligated for payment of the debt, *i.e.*, the debt is nonrecourse.

When a new person joins a partnership or LLC, a portion of the continuing partners' liabilities are shifted to that new partner or member,[66] and when a new partner or member transfers property and liabilities to a partnership or LLC with existing debts, liabilities are shifted both to and from the new and continuing partners and members. The tax treatment of these shifts in responsibility for partnership liabilities is based on two general rules of I.R.C. Section 752:

(1)   Under I.R.C. Section 752(a), each partner is deemed to contribute cash to the partnership to the extent that

---

[66] Section 17 of the Uniform Partnership Act states that: "A person admitted as a partner into an existing partnership is liable for all the obligations of the partnership arising before his admission as though he had been a partner when such obligations were incurred, except that this liability shall be satisfied only out of partnership property."

(a)   his share of the partnership's liabilities increases; or

(b)   he becomes individually liable for partnership liabilities.

(2)   Under I.R.C. Section 752(b), a partner is deemed to receive a cash distribution from the partnership to the extent that

(a)   his share of the partnership's liabilities decreases; or

(b)   his individual liabilities are shifted to the partnership.

A partnership or LLC is considered liable for an encumbrance on contributed property under I.R.C. Sections 752(a) and (b), regardless of whether it assumes the liability or merely takes the property subject to the liability.[67] Similarly, the contributing partner is deemed to be relieved of liabilities on transferred property even if he was not personally obligated for the debt (*i.e.*, it is a nonrecourse liability). However, the amount of a nonrecourse liability deemed transferred to the partnership is limited to the fair market value of the contributed property.[68]

Example: In exchange for an LLC interest, Edward contributes a building worth $120,000 that is subject to a $150,000 mortgage. The mortgage is nonrecourse and, therefore, neither Edward nor the LLC has any personal liability for its payment. Because the LLC takes title to the building, the mortgage liability is deemed to be transferred from Edward to the LLC. However, in determining the amount of any constructive cash contributions by the members under I.R.C. Section 752(a), the LLC liabilities are increased only $120,000 — the fair market value of the property, and the constructive cash distribution to Edward under I.R.C. Section 752(b) also is limited to $120,000.

A partner generally does not recognize gain or loss as a result of an actual or constructive contribution to, or distribution from, the partnership. The only tax consequence of a contribution or distribution is an adjustment to the basis of the partner's partnership interest.[69] However, I.R.C. Section 731(a) requires a partner to recognize gain to the extent that the amount of cash distributed to him exceeds the adjusted basis for his partnership interest immediately before the distribution. This rule prevents cash distributions from reducing a partner's basis below zero — a result that is not permitted.[70] The gain is treated as if it were derived from a sale of a portion of the partnership interest and, therefore, is generally characterized as

---

[67] I.R.C. § 752(c).

[68] I.R.C. § 752(c) applies only to limit the amount of liability deemed transferred when encumbered property is contributed to a partnership or distributed from a partnership to a partner. The statute is not relevant in determining the amount realized by a partnership when it is relieved of liability in connection with a sale or other disposition of its property. Comm'r v. Tufts, 461 U.S. 300 (1983).

[69] I.R.C. §§ 722, 731(a). See Chapter 5 generally for discussion of rules used to determine a partner's basis in his partnership interest.

[70] I.R.C. § 733. Because the reduction of a partner's individual liabilities is considered a constructive cash distribution, a decrease in liabilities that exceeds the partner's basis results in taxable gain. I.R.C. § 731(a).

capital gain.[71]

[B]   Effect of Change in Liabilities on the Noncontributing Partners or Members

When a partnership takes contributed property subject to a liability, or the partnership otherwise assumes a contributing partner's liability, each partner is deemed to make a cash contribution to the partnership in an amount equal to his share of the liability.[72] This constructive capital contribution results in a corresponding increase in each partner's basis in his partnership interest.[73] Each partner's share of the debt is determined after the contribution is made, in order to take into account the new partner's share of all of the partnership's liabilities. For complete discussion and examples, see Chapter 5.

[C]   Effect of Change in Liabilities on the Partnership or LLC

The assumption of a mortgage or other liability does not effect the partnership's basis in contributed property. Therefore, the partnership's basis in the property is the same as its basis in the hands of the contributing partner,[74] even if the contributing partner recognizes gain under I.R.C. Section 731 as a result of being relieved of a liability that exceeds the basis in his partnership interest.[75] However, under I.R.C. Section 754, the partnership may elect to increase the basis of its assets, including assets other than the encumbered property, by the amount of the I.R.C. Section 731 gain.

[D]   Effect of Decrease in Contributing Partner's or Member's Individual Liabilities

Although a partner who transfers encumbered property to a partnership is relieved of the entire debt, he also becomes liable for a share of the liability through his status as a partner. As a result, the contributing partner receives a constructive cash distribution equal to the net amount of the liability that has been shifted to the other partners.[76] If this constructive distribution does not exceed the partner's basis in his partnership interest, no gain is recognized and the partner reduces his basis by the amount of the distribution.[77]

---

[71] I.R.C. § 741. However, ordinary income treatment may result from the collapsible partnership provisions of I.R.C. § 751.

[72] I.R.C. § 752(a).

[73] I.R.C. § 722.

[74] I.R.C. § 723.

[75] I.R.C. § 723 was amended in 1984, with retroactive effect to 1976, to make it clear that the basis of contributed property is increased only by gain recognized under I.R.C. § 721(b).

[76] Temp. Treas. Reg. § 1.752-1T(j)(3). *See also* Rev. Rul. 79-205, 1979-2 C.B. 255; Rev. Rul. 87-120, 1987-2 C.B. 161. The partner is deemed to make an additional cash contribution if the increase in his share of partnership liabilities exceeds the decrease in his individual liabilities.

[77] I.R.C. § 733.

Example: Kevin and Lester form the KL Partnership. In exchange for a two-thirds interest in partnership capital and profits, Kevin contributes a building with a fair market value of $60,000 that is subject to a $30,000 recourse mortgage that is assumed by the partnership. The adjusted basis for the building at the time of contribution is $40,000. Lester contributes $15,000 in cash for a one-third partnership interest.

The basis for Kevin's partnership interest is $30,000, computed as follows:

Basis of contributed building		$40,000
Less net decrease in liability treated as cash distribution-		
Decrease in personal liability	(30,000)	
Assumption of 2/3 of partnership liabilities	$20,000	
		(10,000)
Adjusted basis		$30,000

The basis for Lester's partnership interest is $25,000, computed as follows:

Cash contribution		$15,000
Plus net "cash" contribution under I.R.C. Section 752(a)		
Decrease in personal liabilities	0	
1/3 of partnership liabilities	$10,000	
		10,000
Adjusted basis		$25,000

The partnership's basis for the building is $40,000, carried over from Kevin.

[E] Gain Recognized When Liabilities Exceed Contributing Partner's or Member's Basis

A partner recognizes gain, according to I.R.C. Section 731(a), to the extent that the amount of cash distributed to him exceeds the adjusted basis for his partnership interest immediately before the distribution. Because the reduction of a partner's individual liabilities is considered a constructive cash distribution, a decrease in liabilities that exceeds the partner's basis results in taxable gain. The gain is treated as if it were derived from a sale of the partnership interest and generally is characterized as capital gain.[78] A partner does not increase the basis in his partnership interest by the amount of gain recognized under I.R.C. Section 731(a) and, therefore, his basis is zero following the constructive distribution.[79]

Example: Harold, Irma, and John form a partnership in which each has a

---

[78] I.R.C. § 741. However, ordinary income treatment may result from the collapsible partnership provisions of I.R.C. § 751.

[79] I.R.C. § 722 was amended in 1984 to make it clear that a partner's basis in his partnership interest is increased only by gain recognized under I.R.C. § 721(b), which deals with transfers to investment company partnerships.

one-third interest in capital and profits. Harold and Irma each contribute $60,000 in cash for their interests. John contributes a building worth $150,000 that is subject to a $90,000 recourse mortgage that is assumed by the partnership. John's basis in the building is $50,000.

John recognizes $10,000 of gain, determined as follows:

Basis of property contributed	$15,000
Constructive distribution under Section 752(b)	
(2/3 x $90,000 liability shifted to the other partners)	(60,000)
Cash distribution in excess of basis	($10,000)
(Basis may not be less than 0)	
Gain recognized under Section 731	$10,000

A gain on the sale or exchange of a partnership interest is characterized generally under I.R.C. Section 741 as capital gain. Because the building John contributes is a depreciable trade or business asset under I.R.C. Section 1231, the holding period the partnership uses to determine if the gain is long or short term is the same as the holding period the building had in John's hands.

Both Harold and Irma add $30,000 to the basis of their partnership interests (1/3 * $90,000 mortgage assumed by the partnership). Therefore, each of them has a basis of $90,000 ($60,000 + $30,000).

The basis of the building to the partnership is $50,000 (carried over from John).

The partnership's balance sheet is as follows:

Assets	Basis	Fair Market Value
Cash	$120,000	$120,000
Building	50,000	150,000
	$170,000	$270,000
Liabilities		$90,000
Capital		
Harold	$90,000	$60,000
Irma	$90,000	$60,000
John	0	60,000
	$180,000[80]	$180,000

---

[80] Note that the total basis in all the partnership interests ("outside basis") does not match the total basis in the partnership's assets ("inside basis"). This problem can be resolved by an election under I.R.C. § 754, which would result in a $10,000 increased basis for the partnership's building.

[F] Assumption of Accounts Payable When Existing Business Is Contributed

A cash-basis partnership's accrued but unpaid expenses and accounts payable are not liabilities for I.R.C. Section 752 purposes.[81] Therefore, a transfer of accounts payable to a partnership in connection with a contribution of the assets and liabilities of an ongoing business is not treated as a constructive distribution to, or contribution by, any partner. When the partnership pays the expense, the deduction will be allocated to the contributing partner and the basis in his partnership interest decreases at that time under I.R.C. Section 705.[82]

The rules for contributions of accounts payable do not override the assignment-of-income doctrine in situations in which it would ordinarily apply to a cash-method partner's contribution of accrued but unpaid items.[83] Legislative history refers to Revenue Ruling 80-198,[84] and the cases cited therein, as examples of circumstances when assignment-of-income principles might continue to apply.

§ 4.05 PARTNERSHIP OR LLC INTEREST ACQUIRED FOR CONTRIBUTION OF SERVICES

[A] Overview

The nonrecognition rules of I.R.C. Section 721 are limited to exchanges of property for partnership interests and thus do not apply when a partner receives an interest for his past or future services to a partnership.[85] A partner who receives a partnership interest for services generally is taxable when he receives it if the interest has an ascertainable fair market value at that time.[86]

The value of an interest acquired for services depends upon whether the partner is entitled to a portion of existing partnership capital or merely allowed to share in future partnership profits.[87] Ordinarily, the value of an interest in partnership capital can be determined by reference to the amount of capital shifted to the

---

[81] Rev. Rul. 88-77, 1988-2 C.B. 129.

[82] Under I.R.C. § 705(a)(2), the basis in a partner's partnership interest is reduced by his distributive share of partnership losses. See discussion of basis in Chapter 5, generally.

[83] Conf. Rep. on the Tax Reform Act of 1984, H.R. Rep. No. 861, 98th Cong., 2d Sess. 856-57 (1984). *See* Staff of Joint Committee on Taxation, General Explanation of the Revenue Provisions of the Deficit Reduction Act of 1984, p. 215 (1984).

[84] 1980-2 C.B. 113.

[85] I.R.C. §§ 61, 83; Treas. Reg. § 1.721-1(b)(1). *Cf.* Prop. Treas. Reg. 1.721-1(b)(1)(i) (1971).

[86] *Id.*

[87] Although regulations under I.R.C. § 721 suggest that transfers of partnership capital interests are treated differently than transfers of profits interests, case law indicates that a partner may be taxable on receipt of either kind of interest. *See, e.g.,* U.S. v. Frazell, 335 F.2d 487 (5th Cir. 1964), *cert. denied*, 380 U.S. 961 (1965); Diamond v. Comm'r, 56 T.C. 530 (1971), *aff'd*, 492 F.2d 286 (7th Cir. 1974). *But see* Campbell v. Comm'r, 943 F.2d 815 (8th Cir. 1991), *rev'g* T.C. Memo. 1990-162 (government appears to concede that receipt of partnership profits interest for services not taxable); National Oil Co. v. Comm'r, T.C. Memo. 1986-596 (same).

services partner from the other partners.[88] In contrast, an interest in future profits usually lacks an ascertainable present value because the amount of profits are speculative.[89] Typically, a services partner is not taxable when he receives an interest in partnership profits but simply reports his share of the profits as earned by the partnership.[90]

In Revenue Procedure 93-27,[91] the Service provides a safe harbor for ensuring that a partner is not taxable when he receives an interest in partnership profits in exchange for services. The procedure states that ordinarily a taxable event does not occur when a person provides past or future services to or for a partnership, in a partner capacity or in anticipation of becoming a partner, in exchange for an interest in future partnership profits. This safe harbor does not apply if:

(1)   the profits interest relates to a substantially certain and predictable income stream from partnership assets, such as income from high-quality debt securities or a high-quality net lease;

(2)   the partner disposes of the profits interest within two years of receipt; or

(3)   the profits interest is a limited partnership interest in a "publicly traded partnership" under I.R.C. Section 7704(b).

If a partner receives a partnership interest in a taxable exchange for services, the timing of the partner's compensation income and any corresponding partnership deduction is determined under the rules of I.R.C. Section 83.[92] Under that section, a partner is taxed on the fair market value of an interest received for services in the year he receives it unless the interest is subject to a substantial risk of forfeiture in the hands of the service partner or a transferee of the service partner. If these restrictions apply to the service partner's interest, taxation is deferred until the year in which the restrictions lapse, and the partner is taxable on the value of the interest at that time.[93] However, I.R.C. Section 83(b) allows a partner to elect to include the current value of the interest in his income in the year it is received, even if the interest is subject to a substantial risk of forfeiture or is nontransferable.

---

[88] Treas. Reg. § 1.721-1(b)(1). *See* U.S. v. Frazell, 335 F.2d 487, 489 (5th Cir. 1964), *cert. denied*, 380 U.S. 961 (1965).

[89] Campbell v. Comm'r, 943 F.2d 815 (8th Cir. 1991), *rev'g* T.C. Memo. 1990-162; Diamond v. Comm'r, 492 F.2d 286 (7th Cir. 1974). *See* U.S. v. Pacheco, 912 F.2d 297 (9th Cir. 1990).

[90] *See* Kenroy, Inc. v. Comm'r, T.C. Memo. 1984-232; St. John v. U.S., 84-1 U.S.T.C. ¶ 9158 (C.D. Ill. 1983). For unusual circumstances in which a partner was taxed on receipt of profits interest, see Diamond v. Comm'r, 56 T.C. 530 (1971), *aff'd*, 492 F.2d 286 (7th Cir. 1974).

[91] 1993-2 C.B. 343.

[92] Although the legislative history to I.R.C. § 83 indicates that Congress was particularly concerned about transfers of corporate stock for services, there is no suggestion that transfers of partnership interests are exempted from I.R.C. § 83. H.R. Rep. No. 413 (pt. 1), 91st Cong., 1st Sess. 61 (1969); S. Rep. No. 552, 91st Cong., 1st Sess. 119 (1969).

[93] I.R.C. § 83(a), (c).

NOTE:

The Service has issued proposed regulations governing the tax treatment of partnerships interests issued in exchange for the performance of services (*compensatory partnership interests*).[94] The proposed regulations provide that such tax treatment is determined under the rules of I.R.C. Section 83, not I.R.C. Section 721.[95] In connection with these proposed regulations, the Service also published Notice 2005-43,[96] announcing a proposed revenue procedure that would provide an elective safe harbor permitting compensatory partnership interests to be valued by reference to their liquidation value. The proposed regulations would apply to transfers on or after the date they are finalized and the proposed revenue procedure would become effective at the same time. Until then, taxpayers may rely on current law, but cannot utilize the safe harbor election of the proposed revenue procedure.[97]

The proposed regulations provide that the tax treatment of compensatory partnership interests is determined under the rules of I.R.C. Section 83, not I.R.C. Section 721.[98] Such treatment applies to both capital and profits interests in a partnership.[99] Generally, this means that the service provider will recognize income equal to the value of the interest he/she receives and the partnership will be allowed a corresponding deduction for compensation paid. The rules of I.R.C. Section 721, however, will apply for the limited purpose of avoiding recognition to the partnership in connection with the transfer, vesting, or forfeiture of a compensatory partnership interest.[100]

A partnership that transfers an interest to a partner in a taxable exchange for services deducts or capitalizes the same amount that the service partner reports as income in the same year that he reports it. Because a transfer of appreciated property to pay an obligation is equivalent to the sale of the property, the partnership recognizes gain or loss to the extent that it is deemed to transfer a portion of each of its assets to a partner as payment for his services.

When a partnership interest is received for services performed for another partner individually, rather than for the partnership, the transaction is deemed to

---

[94] 70 F.R. 29675 (May 23, 2005).

[95] Prop. Treas. Reg. § 1.83-3(e); Prop. Treas. Reg. § 1.721-1(b)(1).

[96] 2005-24 I.R.B. 1221.

[97] This material goes in a text box so should be tagged as a comment.

[98] Prop. Treas. Reg. § 1.83-3(e), Prop. Treas. Reg. § 1.721-1(b)(1).

[99] The preamble to the proposed regulations states the capital and profits interests are property for purposes of I.R.C. § 83.

[100] Prop. Treas. Reg. § 1.721-1(b)(2).

occur outside the partnership.[101] The transferring partner is treated as if he sold a portion of his partnership interest, and the gain or loss he recognizes is the difference between the value of the services he receives and the basis allocable to the transferred interest.[102] The service partner reports the value of the interest he receives as compensation income, and he is deemed to contribute that amount to the partnership for his partnership interest.[103]

[B]   Receiving a Capital Interest for Services

A capital interest represents the owner's share of the value of partnership assets that he would receive if the partnership sold all its assets at fair market value and then liquidated.[104] The value of the capital interest includes the partner's share of the unrealized appreciation in partnership assets, accounts receivable, work in progress or similar items, regardless of whether they appear on the partnership's books.[105] A partner may be taxable on receipt of a capital interest if he is entitled to receive a portion of the unstated appreciation in partnership assets, even though nothing is credited to his capital account.[106]

> **Example (1):** Alice and Bob each contribute $15,000 to the AB Partnership in exchange for equal partnership interests. The partnership uses the $30,000 to purchase an asset. Each partner's capital account is credited with $15,000. In a later year, Alice and Bob admit Carl as a partner in exchange for services he performs for the partnership. The partnership agreement states that the three partners will share partnership distributions equally after Alice and Bob receive distributions equal to the amount in their capital accounts. At the time Carl is admitted, the partnership's only asset is worth $60,000.
>
> Following Carl's admission, the partnership's books appear as follows:

	Capital Account
Alice	$15,000
Bob	$15,000
Carl	0

> Carl recognizes $10,000 of compensation income at the time he is

---

[101]   *See* I.R.C. § 707(a).

[102]   McDougal v. Comm'r, 62 T.C. 720 (1974), *acq.* 1975-1 C.B. 2.

[103]   *Id.*

[104]   Rev. Proc. 93-27, 1993-2 C.B. 343; Mark IV Pictures, Inc. v. Comm'r, T.C. Memo. 1990-571. *See* Treas. Reg. § 1.704-1(e)(1)(v).

[105]   *See* Hearings on Advisory Group Recommendations on Subchapters C, J, and K before the Ways and Means Committee, 86th Cong., 2d Sess. 55 (1959), Hearings before Senate Finance Committee, 86th Cong., 2d Sess. 63, 97, 106 (1959), S. Rep. No. 1616, 86th Cong., 2d Sess., Vol. 4, 84-84 (1960).

[106]   Although I.R.C. § 704(c) requires any gain or loss "built in" to contributed property to be allocated to the contributing partner, no section requires gain or loss built in to partnership property to be allocated to the existing partners. A partnership may elect to make this allocation by revaluing its property when a new partner joins the partnership in accordance with the regulations under I.R.C. § 704(b).

admitted to the partnership, because that amount is the value of the interest in partnership capital the other partners have given up in his favor. Because Alice and Bob are entitled to preferential distributions totaling $30,000, the value of the remaining partnership assets (attributable to the unrealized appreciation that is not reflected on the partnership's books) is $30,000. Carl is taxable on the $10,000 value of his one-third share of that appreciation.

Capital accounts should be revalued when a new partner is admitted to the partnership to reflect the value of partnership assets at the time of admission. If the other partners do not intend to currently shift portions of their capital interests to the service partner (*e.g.*, he will be rendering services to the partnership in the future), the continuing partners' capital accounts should be credited with their shares of the current value of partnership assets. The service partner's capital account should be credited with only the value of property he actually contributes.

Example (2): Assume the same facts as in Example (1), above. Carl, the service partner, would not recognize income if, upon his admission to the partnership, the partners' capital accounts were restated as follows to reflect the current value of partnership assets:

	Capital Account
Alice	$30,000
Bob	$30,000
Carl	0

These capital account balances show that Carl has an interest only in the appreciation of partnership property that will occur after the date of his entry.

If the existing partners intend to compensate the service partner by a current shift in capital interests (*e.g.*, for services already performed), the capital accounts of all the partners should be credited with amounts that reflect the current value of their shares of partnership assets. However, a service partner who recognizes income on receipt of a partnership interest must pay the resulting tax liability even though he has not received any cash. If the new partner does not have other liquid assets, this outcome may be undesirable.

Example (3): Assume the same facts as in Example (2), above. If Carl is to receive a capital interest worth $10,000 in exchange for his services, the capital accounts should be as follows:

	Capital Account
Alice	$25,000
Bob	$25,000
Carl	10,000

These capital account balances reflect the fact that Carl has received a share of the current value of the partnership's assets.

[1] Value of Interest Received for Services

The fair market value of a partnership interest is the amount that a willing buyer would pay a willing seller if neither is acting under a compulsion to buy or sell and both know all relevant facts.[107] Fair market value is determined by an appraisal of the partnership's assets or by an agreement between parties who have adverse interests and who deal at arm's length. The value agreed on for a service partner's partnership interest ordinarily is the amount credited to his capital account.

If a partnership interest is subject to a restriction on transferability that will never lapse (e.g., the transferee is only allowed to sell the property at a formula price, or must first offer it to the partnership or other partners), the value of the interest is reduced to reflect the restriction.[108] When the value of the partnership interest cannot be determined directly, it may be determined by the value of the services a partner performs for it.[109]

[2] Unvested Interests

Under I.R.C. Section 83, a partner receiving an interest in partnership capital in connection with the performance of services reports the value of the interest (less any amount he paid for it) as compensation income in the year it is "substantially vested."[110] A partnership interest is not vested if it is subject to a substantial risk of forfeiture in the hands of the service partner or a transferee of the service partner.[111] Therefore, a restricted interest is not taxable until the year in which the risk of forfeiture lapses and the interest becomes freely transferable.[112] A requirement that the new partner perform future services in exchange for his partnership interest creates a substantial risk of forfeiture, and the new partner does not recognize income until the services are performed.[113] The partnership interest is valued at the time it is included in income, not at the time it was received.[114]

---

[107] Treas. Reg. § 20.2031-3. See Palmer v. Comm'r, 523 F.2d 1308 (8th Cir. 1975).

[108] I.R.C. § 83(d).

[109] Hensel Phelps Constr. Co. v. Comm'r, 74 T.C. 939 (1980), aff'd, 703 F.2d 485 (10th Cir. 1983).

[110] Proposed regulations under I.R.C. § 721 were issued in 1971 stating that transfers of partnership capital interests for services after June 30, 1969 are subject to I.R.C. § 83. Although these Proposed regulations have not been finally adopted, it appears well established that I.R.C. § 83 applies to compensatory transfers of partnership capital interests. Hensel Phelps Constr. Co. v. Comm'r, 74 T.C. 939 (1980), aff'd, 703 F.2d 485 (10th Cir. 1983).

[111] I.R.C. § 83(a), (c).

[112] Treas. Reg. § 1.721-1(b)(1) provides rules that are significantly different than those under I.R.C. § 83 for determining the amount and timing of a service partner's income. Because the regulations under I.R.C. § 721 were written prior to the enactment of I.R.C. § 83, any conflicting portions should be considered pre-empted and no longer applicable. See Prop. Treas. Reg. § 1.721-1(b)(1).

[113] Treas. Reg. § 1.83-3(c).

[114] If the property is subject to restrictions that will never lapse and allow the transferee to sell the property only at a formula price, that price will determine the property's value.

Until a restricted partnership interest vests, the service partner is not actually treated as a partner for tax purposes.[115] Therefore, the partnership's income is fully taxable to the other partners during the period that the service partner's interest is subject to a risk of forfeiture or is nontransferable. Any payments made to the service provider before his interest vests are taxable as ordinary compensation income (*i.e.*, as if he is a partnership employee), and the partnership deducts or capitalizes these amounts under general tax rules governing compensation. Other possible consequences of nonpartner status include:

(1) The service partner may become liable for partnership debts under state law but may not be allowed to include his share of the liabilities in the basis of his partnership interest for tax purposes.

(2) The service partner may not be allowed to deduct any share of partnership losses.

(3) No partnership may be deemed to exist at all for tax purposes if the service partner is one member of a two-person partnership, or if he is the sole general partner of a limited partnership.

These consequences are avoided if the service partner elects to include the value of his partnership interest in income under I.R.C. Section 83(b). In that case, the person making the election is considered a partner immediately.

Example: Michael and Nat form the MN Partnership. Michael contributes $500,000. The funds are used to purchase a shopping center. Michael receives a 90-percent interest in partnership capital and profits. Nat does not contribute capital, but he agrees to manage the shopping center in exchange for a 10 percent interest in partnership capital and profits.

If Nat's capital account is credited with $50,000, he has received a partnership capital interest for his services. Nat reports $50,000 as compensation income, because that is the amount he would receive if the partnership were liquidated.

In contrast, Nat is not taxable if the partnership agreement provides that Nat's partnership interest will be forfeited if he does not render services for at least two years. If, at the end of the second year, the shopping center is worth $900,000, Nat reports $90,000 ($900,000 * 10%) as compensation income at the end of that year, on the day that the risk of forfeiture of his partnership interest lapses.

Until his interest vests, Nat is not considered a partner for tax purposes. That means that he is not taxable on any distributive share of partnership income during the unvested period-the share he would receive is included in the other partners' distributive shares. Any distributions the partnership makes to Nat during the unvested period are treated as compensation for Nat's services; Nat includes them as compensation income, and the partnership may deduct them as business expenses.

---

[115] Treas. Reg. § 1.83-1(a).

[3] Electing to Include Income Under I.R.C. Section 83(b)

A partner receiving a partnership interest for services may elect to include its current value in income in the year it is received under I.R.C. Section 83(b), even if the interest is subject to a substantial risk of forfeiture or is nontransferable. The property is valued without taking into account the presence of any restrictions other than restrictions that will never lapse. The election must be made within 30 days of the transfer, and it may not be revoked without permission from the Service. If the property is subsequently forfeited, however, the partner may not claim a loss deduction for the amount he included in his income.

The election under I.R.C. Section 83(b) is advisable if the partnership interest is expected to appreciate substantially in value. When the service partner recognizes the interest at its current value, he defers recognition of any appreciation until he disposes of his partnership interest, at which time he reports the appreciation as capital gain. If the partner does not elect I.R.C. Section 83(b) treatment, he reports any increase in the value of his partnership interest as ordinary income at the time that the restriction or risk of forfeiture lapses. However, I.R.C. Section 83(b) treatment accelerates the time when the partner is taxable on the current value of the property. The advantages and disadvantages of accelerating, deferring, and changing the character of income must be carefully determined before deciding whether to make the election.

> **Example:** Assume the same facts as in the Example above. If Nat makes an I.R.C. Section 83(b) election, he reports compensation income of $50,000 at the time he receives the interest. Nat is immediately considered a partner for tax purposes, even though he may subsequently forfeit his partnership interest. At the end of Year 2, the shopping center has increased in value, and Nat's partnership interest is valued at $90,000. If Nat sells his partnership interest after Year 4 for $90,000, he realizes a $40,000 capital gain ($90,000 realized less $50,000 adjusted basis for his partnership interest).

Therefore, by making the election:

(1)   Nat pays a tax on $50,000 of ordinary income when he receives the partnership interest;

(2)   he has deferred recognition of $40,000 of income for two years;

(3)   the character of the $40,000 income on the appreciation of the value of the shopping center has changed from ordinary income to capital gain; and

(4)   Nat is taxable on his distributive share of partnership income and loss and includes his share of partnership liabilities in the basis of his interest.

If Nat did not elect I.R.C. Section 83(b) treatment, no income is recognized in Year 1, and $90,000 is taxable as ordinary income after Year 2.

If Nat elects I.R.C. Section 83(b) and leaves the partnership after only one year, he forfeits his partnership interest. Although he reported the $50,000 value of the interest as income, Nat is not allowed any deduction as a result of the forfeiture. Because the partnership has not actually transferred an interest to Nat for his services, it must include in current income any amount deducted in the year Nat made the I.R.C. Section 83(b) election.

[4] Service Partner's Basis in Partnership Interest

The receipt of a partnership interest for services is actually treated as a two-step transaction:

Step (1).   The partnership is deemed to transfer an interest in each of its assets as compensation for the partner's services. The partnership recognizes gain if it owns appreciated property because a transfer of property to satisfy an obligation is treated as a sale for tax purposes.[116]

Step (2).   The partner is deemed to immediately contribute these assets back to the partnership in exchange for his partnership interest. The amount of income the partner recognizes is his "cost" of acquiring the partnership interest, and that amount becomes the basis in his interest.[117] The partnership obtains a corresponding increase in the basis of the assets deemed contributed by the services partner.

[5] Deduction for Payment to Service Partner or Member

The partnership's treatment of the payment to a service partner depends on the nature of the services he renders. If the services are performed in connection with the acquisition of an asset, the partnership must capitalize the payment and treat it as part of the asset's cost. If the services are an ordinary and necessary business expense, the partnership may deduct the payment as a current business expense.[118] The partnership deducts or capitalizes the same amount that the service partner reports as income in the same year that he reports it.[119] If the partner makes an election under I.R.C. Section 83(b) to include the current value of restricted property, the partnership is allowed a deduction corresponding to the partner's income. If the partner subsequently forfeits the interest, however, the partnership must include the amount previously deducted in income or reduce the basis of the capitalized assets.[120]

---

[116] Treas. Reg. § 1.83-6(b) states that the transferor of property for services ". . . recognizes gain to the extent that the transferor receives an amount that exceeds the transferor's basis in the property."

[117] I.R.C. § 1012.

[118] Treas. Reg. § 1.83-6(a). *See also* Treas. Reg. § 1.721-1(b)(1); I.R.C. § 707(c).

[119] Treas. Reg. § 1.721-1(b)(2) states that the value of an interest is treated as a guaranteed payment under I.R.C. § 707(c), which allows a partnership to deduct its salary expenses in the partnership's year that they are paid or accrued.

[120] Treas. Reg. § 1.83-6(c).

[6] Partnership May Recognize Gain or Loss

The tax consequences of a taxable exchange of a partnership interest for services are the same as when:

(1)   the partnership transfers an interest in all of its property as payment for the partner's services; and

(2)   the partner contributes the same property back to the partnership for his interest.

For tax purposes, a transfer of appreciated property to pay for services or other obligations is equivalent to the property's sale.[121] Therefore, the partnership recognizes gain or loss to the extent that it is deemed to transfer a portion of each of its assets to a partner as payment for his services.[122] The character of the gain or loss depends on the character of the assets in the partnership. Because the service partner's basis in the assets when recontributed equals their fair market value, the partnership's basis in each asset is adjusted correspondingly.[123]

> **Example:** Carla receives a one-third capital and profits interest in the AB partnership in exchange for her agreement to manage the partnership's real estate. The partnership's only asset is a building worth $210,000, which was purchased five years earlier for $180,000. Because $60,000 of depreciation has been deducted, the partnership's adjusted basis in the building is $120,000.
>
> The partnership is treated as if it transferred a one-third interest in the building to Carla as a $70,000 payment for her services. Because the partnership's basis in one-third of the building is $40,000, the partnership recognizes gain of $30,000, which is taxable to Partners A and B. The character of the gain depends on the character of the building in the hands of the partnership.
>
> The effects of this transaction are:
>
> (1)   The partnership deducts the $70,000 payment from ordinary income as a business expense; the expense should be allocated to A and B.
>
> (2)   Carla is taxed as if she directly received a one-third interest in the building in payment for her services. Therefore, she reports $70,000 as compensation income.
>
> (3)   Carla's basis in the interest in the building is also $70,000; she is deemed to contribute her interest in the building to the partnership for a one-third interest in partnership capital and profits. Carla's basis for her partnership interest is $70,000, the same as her basis in the contributed property.

---

[121] U.S. v. Davis, 370 U.S. 65 (1962). Treas. Reg. § 1.83-6(b).

[122] It has been suggested, however, that it is proper to treat the exchange as if the service partner purchased the partnership interest for cash and the partnership used the cash to pay his compensation. Because no appreciated property is transferred, no gain is recognized. *See* Coven, *The Federal Tax Consequences of the Admission of a New Partner*, 31st Wm. & Mary Tax Conf. 149 (1985).

[123] I.R.C. § 723.

(4)   The partnership's basis in the building is $150,000 ($70,000 basis in the one-third interest "contributed" by Carla and $80,000 basis in the two-thirds interest retained by AB.)

[C]   Receiving an Interest in Future Profits

A profits interest represents a partner's right to share in future partnership profits as distinguished from a partner's share of assets the partnership currently owns.[124] In theory, there is no reason to treat a partner who receives an interest in future partnership profits for his services differently than a partner who receives a capital interest. However, taxing a partner currently on profits he expects to derive from a partnership in the future creates two difficult, practical problems:

(1)   it usually is not possible to ascertain the present value of speculative future profits; and

(2)   taxing a partner on the present value of future profits requires complex rules to ensure that the same income is not taxed a second time when it actually is earned.

Although the caselaw on this issue (described below) has been inconsistent and confusing, the courts generally have concluded that an interest in future partnership profits lacks an ascertainable present value because the amount of profits is speculative.[125] Typically, a services partner is not taxable when he receives an interest in partnership profits but simply reports his share of the profits as earned by the partnership.[126]

Many of the uncertainties on this issue were diminished by the Service's publication of Revenue Procedure 93-27[127] and Revenue Procedure 2001-43.[128] Revenue Procedure 93-27 provides a safe harbor for ensuring that a partner will not be taxable when he receives an interest in partnership profits in exchange for services. The procedure states that ordinarily a taxable event does not occur when a person provides past or future services to or for a partnership, in a partner capacity or in anticipation of becoming a partner, in exchange for an interest in future partnership profits. Revenue Procedure 2001-43 provides that whether or not an interest is a profits interest is determined when the interest is granted, even if it is substantially unvested (under I.R.C. Section 83). (*See* § 4.05[B][2], *infra*.)

---

[124] *See* Treas. Reg. §§ 1.704-1(e)(1)(v), 1.721-1(b)(1). Rev. Proc. 93-27, 1993 C.B. 343, defines a profits interest as any partnership interest other than a capital interest. A capital interest is defined as an interest that would give the holder a share of the proceeds if the partnership's assets were sold at fair market value and then the proceeds were distributed in a complete liquidation of the partnership.

[125] Campbell v. Comm'r, 943 F.2d 815 (8th Cir. 1991), *rev'g* T.C. Memo. 1990-162; Diamond v. Comm'r, 492 F.2d 286 (7th Cir. 1974). *See* U.S. v. Pacheco, 912 F.2d 297 (9th Cir. 1990).

[126] *See* Kenroy, Inc. v. Comm'r, T.C. Memo. 1984-232; St. John v. U.S., 84-1 U.S.T.C. ¶ 9158 (C.D. Ill. 1983). For unusual circumstances in which a partner was taxed on receipt of profits interest, see Diamond v. Comm'r, 56 T.C. 530 (1971), *aff'd*, 492 F.2d 286 (7th Cir. 1974).

[127] 1993-2 C.B. 343.

[128] 2001-43 I.R.B. 191.

[1]   Background — The *Diamond* Decision

For many years, the practical difficulties described above led practitioners to assume that a partner did not recognize income when he received an interest in partnership profits.[129] The profits were reported as the partner's distributive share of partnership income when they were earned. This view is supported by the Treasury regulations, which imply that receipt of a profits interest for services is treated differently than receipt of a capital interest.[130]

However, the decision in *Diamond v. Commissioner*,[131] proved this assumption to be incorrect when a partner receives a profits interest with an ascertainable value. The taxpayer in *Diamond* provided services when he obtained financing for a person who owned an option to purchase a building. The parties formed a joint venture when the building was acquired, and Diamond received a 60-percent interest in the building's profits after the optionholder recovered his capital investment. Three weeks after he entered the joint venture, Diamond sold his profits interest for $40,000, and he reported a short-term capital gain on the sale of a partnership interest. Diamond used this gain to offset a large capital-loss carryover.

Because the sale showed that the value of the profits interest he received was $40,000, the Tax Court held that he must report that amount as ordinary compensation income. The Court broadly maintained that I.R.C. Section 721 does not apply when a taxpayer performs services and is compensated with an interest in a partnership that is later formed.[132] Although the Seventh Circuit affirmed, its opinion is based on narrower grounds. The appellate court indicates that a profits interest is taxable only if it has a determinable market value and that usually these interests have only speculative value.[133]

Until the Service issued Revenue Procedure 93-27 in 1993, the *Diamond* decision seemed to establish that the nonrecognition rules of I.R.C. Section 721 do not apply when a partner receives a partnership interest for services, regardless of whether the interest is in partnership capital or profits.[134] In the absence of a nonrecognition

---

[129]   This position appears to have been accepted by the Tax Court before its holding in *Diamond. See* Hale v. Comm'r, T.C. Memo. 1965-224.

[130]   Treas. Reg. § 1.721-1(b)(1) states that the nonrecognition provisions of I.R.C. § 721 do not apply ". . . [T]o the extent that any of the partners gives up any part of his right to be repaid his contributions (as distinguished from a share in partnership profits) in favor of another partner as compensation for services . . .".

[131]   56 T.C. 530 (1971), *aff'd*, 492 F.2d 286 (7th Cir. 1974).

[132]   It is possible, therefore, that the *Diamond* decision is limited to situations in which a profits interest is received for past, rather than future, services.

[133]   492 F.2d 286, 290 (7th Cir. 1974).

[134]   The Eighth Circuit's opinion in Campbell v. Comm'r, 943 F.2d 815 (8th Cir. 1991), *rev'g* T.C. Memo. 1990-162, explains the result in *Diamond* without accepting the express holdings of the Tax Court and Seventh Circuit that a services partner is taxable on receipt of a profits interest if the interest has a determinable present value. The court proposes that Diamond was taxable because he did not intend to function or remain as a partner and thus was not acting in a partner capacity when he received the profits interest.

provision, the services partner would be taxable under the general rules of the Internal Revenue Code.

[2] Background — The *Campbell* Decision

The few profits interest cases decided after *Diamond* have been subject to I.R.C. Section 83, which governs the tax treatment of all compensatory property transfers — including transfers of partnership interests.[135] Although it has been suggested that profits interests are not "property" for I.R.C. Section 83,[136] the few cases that have considered the issue do not adopt that view.[137]

The major uncertainty about the tax consequences of receiving a profits interest for services had concerned the value of the interest when it is transferred to the partner. In *Diamond*, the value of the profits interest was readily determinable because the taxpayer sold the interest shortly after he received it. However, subsequent cases suggest that the value of the profits interest is limited to the amount that the service partner would receive from the partnership if his interest were liquidated immediately after he receives it.[138] Because a profits interest only entitles the service partner to participate in future profits, the liquidation value of the interest is always zero when it is received. Although receipt of a profits interest theoretically may be taxable under I.R.C. Section 83, the zero value the courts have placed on the interest means that there is no actual tax liability.

The initial Tax Court decision in *Campbell v. Commissioner*,[139] however, refused to apply the liquidation method to determine the value of a profits interest a partner received for his services in organizing a syndicated real estate partnership. Instead, the court computed the current value of the interest by projecting the future benefits the partner expected to receive from the partnership as set forth in the partnership prospectus. A major portion of these expected benefits consisted of projected cash flow and tax deductions, even though a substantial risk existed that the Service would eventually disallow the tax items. The court concluded that the value of the profits interest was not speculative because similar interests were sold to investors at concrete prices on the same day the service partner received his interest.

---

[135] I.R.C. § 83 was enacted after the year in issue in *Diamond* and thus was not applicable to the decision. Diamond was required to include the value of the interest he received in his income pursuant to the general definition of gross income set forth in I.R.C. § 61(a) ("gross income means income from whatever source derived, including . . . (1) Compensation for services . . .").

[136] Treas. Reg. § 1.83-3(e) states that an unfunded and unsecured promise to pay compensation in the future is not property for purposes of I.R.C. § 83.

[137] St. John v. U.S., 84-1 U.S.T.C. ¶ 9158 (C.D. Ill. 1983) (although profits interest may be taxable, facts indicated that interest had no value when received); Kenroy, Inc. v. Comm'r, T.C. Memo. 1984-232 (same); Kobor v. U.S., 88-2 U.S.T.C. ¶ 9477, 62 A.F.T.R.2d 5047 (C.D. Cal. 1987); Campbell v. Comm'r, 943 F.2d 815 (8th Cir. 1991), *rev'g* T.C. Memo. 1990-162 (financial and tax benefits allocable to profits interest too speculative to have current value).

[138] St. John v. U.S., 84-1 U.S.T.C. ¶ 9158 (C.D. Ill. 1983); Kenroy, Inc. v. Comm'r, T.C. Memo. 1984-232. *See* Campbell v. Comm'r, 943 F.2d 815 (8th Cir. 1991), *rev'g* T.C. Memo. 1990-162.

[139] T.C. Memo. 1990-162, *rev'd*, 943 F.2d 815 (8th Cir. 1991).

The Eighth Circuit reversed the Tax Court, holding that Campbell was not taxable because the profits interest he received had only a speculative value.[140] The Tax Court's valuation was deemed incorrect because:

(1)   the value of the profits interest could not be determined from the price paid by investors because the investor's interests carried superior rights to cash flow and capital return;

(2)   the value of the tax benefits was speculative because the partnership was taking untested positions that were likely to be challenged and disallowed by the Service; and

(3)   the statements in the partnership's offering memoranda regarding the expected success and profitability of the venture were merely speculative predictions.

Although the Court of Appeals disagreed with the Tax Court's valuation method, it did not offer an alternative method; the decision merely concludes that Campbell's profits interest was "without fair market value" when received.[141]

The tax treatment of partners who perform services in exchange for an interest in future partnership profits remains unclear. Although the Eighth Circuit's decision in *Campbell* is consistent with other post-*Diamond* cases that determined that a profits interest has no value when received, the following two aspects of the case should be noted:

(1)   Dictum in the opinion indicates the court's belief that a service partner is not taxable on receipt of a profits interest if he intends to remain in the partnership rather than immediately dispose of his interest. The court supports this view as follows:

  (a)   Although I.R.C. Section 721 mandates taxation of a services partner who receives a capital interest, different treatment is justified for a partner who receives a profits interest. The taxable event is the shift in capital to the services partner from the other partners. Because no capital is shifted to a partner who receives a profits interest, current income recognition is not required.

  (b)   Under I.R.C. Section 707, a partner is not taxable on compensation he receives from a partnership for his services unless he renders the services in a nonpartner capacity.[142] The court observes that Diamond was properly taxable on receipt of his profits interest because he did not perform services while acting in a partner capacity. Because he acquired the interest solely to sell it for an immediate

---

[140]   943 F.2d 815 (8th Cir. 1991).

[141]   The court may have used hindsight to determine that Campbell's profits interest had no value when received: the interest ultimately became worthless and the projected tax benefits were disallowed. *See Eighth Circuit Further Confuses* Diamond *Issue in* Campbell, 52 Tax Notes 1353 (Sept. 16, 1991).

[142]   I.R.C. § 707(a) generally provides that a partner who engages in transactions with his partnership while acting in a nonpartner capacity is taxable as if the partnership is a separate entity. I.R.C. § 707(c) provides special treatment for compensatory payments to a partner acting in a partner capacity if the payments are not measured by reference to partnership income.

capital gain, he never intended to "function as or remain a partner." In contrast, Campbell was not taxable on receipt of the profits interest because he intended to remain a partner, as evidenced by the fact that his interest was not transferable and was unlikely to generate an immediate profit.

(2)   In the *Campbell* appeal, the Service apparently conceded that the receipt of a profits interest is not taxable. Instead, the Service argued that the taxpayer received his partnership interest for services he rendered to his employer rather than for services to the partnership. The court refused to consider this new ground because it was not properly raised in the Tax Court. The Service's concession on this issue presaged its holding in Revenue Procedure 93-27,[143] that receipt of a profits interest is generally nontaxable.

[3]   The Service's Current Position — Revenue Procedures 93-27 and 2001-43

The Service has issued two Revenue Procedures to provide guidance about the treatment of partners who receive interests in future partnership profits in exchange for services. Revenue Procedure 93-27[144] provides that the receipt of a profits interest is not taxable if a safe harbor test regarding the current value of the interest is met. Revenue Procedure 2001-43[145] clarifies the prior procedure by providing that the Service will determine whether an interest is a profits interest at the time it is granted, even if the interest is substantially unvested for purposes of I.R.C. Section 83. Thus, the transfer of partnership profits interest that satisfies the requirements of both revenue procedures is not a taxable event for the partner or partnership when received or when the interest subsequently becomes vested.

As noted above, Revenue Procedure 93-27[146] provides a safe harbor for ensuring that a partner will not be taxable when he receives an interest in partnership profits in exchange for services. Under the Revenue Procedure, if a person receives a profits interest for services to or for the benefit of a partnership, in a partner capacity or in anticipation of becoming a partner, the IRS will not treat the interest's receipt as a taxable event for the partner or the partnership. The safe harbor does not apply, however, if:

(1)   the profits interest relates to a substantially certain and predictable stream of income from partnership assets, such as income from high-quality debt securities or a high-quality net lease;

(2)   within two years of receipt, the partner disposes of the profits interest; or

(3)   the profits interest is a limited partnership interest in a publicly traded partnership within the meaning of I.R.C. Section 7704(b). (See § 2.04,

---

[143] 1993-2 C.B. 343.

[144] *Id.*

[145] 2001-34 I.R.B. 191.

[146] 1993-2 C.B. 343.

supra, for discussion of publicly traded partnerships.)

A profits interest is defined as a partnership interest other than a capital interest. A capital interest is defined as an interest that would give the holder a share of the proceeds if the partnership sold its assets at fair market value and then distributed the proceeds in a complete liquidation of the partnership. Generally, this determination is made when the partnership interest is received.

In Revenue Procedure 2001-43,[147] the IRS describes the tax treatment of partners who receive unvested profits interests in partnerships in exchange for services. The determination of whether the interest is a profits interest is made when the interest is received, even if it is substantially unvested at that time under I.R.C. Section 83. If the requirements of the procedure are satisfied, the services partner does not recognize income when he receives the unvested profits interest nor when the interest vests. This is true even if no election is made under I.R.C. Section 83(b). For discussion of I.R.C. Section 83 and the election under I.R.C. Section 83(b), see § 4.05[B][3], *supra*.

To fall under the safe harbor of Revenue Procedure 2001-43, the following conditions must be satisfied:

(1)   The services partner must be treated as the owner of the partnership interest by all parties from the date it is granted, and the partner must take into account the distributive share of partnership income, gain, loss, deduction, and credit associated with his partnership interest for the entire period that he holds the interest;

(2)   Neither the partnership nor any partner deducts any amount (as wages, compensation or otherwise) for the fair market value of the interest when the interest is granted or when it becomes vested; and

(3)   All other conditions of Revenue Procedure 93-27 are satisfied.

The effect of the safe harbor is that the IRS will not tax the services partner when he receives the unvested profits interest, nor when the event occurs that causes the partner to be substantially vested in the profits interest.

Despite all the cases, rulings, and commentary[148] on this issue, the fact remains that Sol Diamond is the only person actually taxed on receipt of a profits interest. The unique facts in *Diamond* should be kept in mind (and avoided). The taxpayer received a profits interest for past services he performed for the partnership and sold the interest soon after he received it. His goal in the transaction appears to have been to convert ordinary compensation income to capital gain. The profits interest represented a share of future rent from a partnership-owned building that was fully occupied by financially secure tenants under long-term leases. These factors are reflected in the first two exceptions to the safe harbor established in Revenue Procedure 93-27.

---

[147]   2001-34 I.R.B. 191.

[148]   *See, e.g.*, Hoberman, Receipt of Partnership Interest in Exchange for Services: Still Polishing the *Diamond*, 15 J. Partnership Tax'n 336 (Winter 1999).

It is unlikely that the Service ever will try to tax receipt of profits interests in partnerships primarily engaged in performing services, such as law, accounting, or medical firms. Although these interests undoubtedly have value when received (why else would practitioners strive so hard to obtain them), that value is based upon conjecture about future individual accomplishments, rather than upon the value of fixed assets. A profits interest received for future services should not be taxable if the value of the interest depends upon the value of the unperformed services. Moreover, the tax consequences to the professional partnership would be staggering and administratively infeasible.

Other types of partnerships, such as those using profits interests to pay for services of investment bankers, promoters, developers, or attorneys, should be more wary. These arrangements will not fall under the safe harbors of Revenue Procedures 93-27 and 2001-43 if they provide the service partner with a certain and predictable stream of income from partnership assets. If future litigation arises, note that the basis for the Eighth Circuit's decision in *Campbell* is that the profits interest had only speculative value when received. The court did not reject the view that receipt of a profits interest may be taxable; it held that the Tax Court had incorrectly determined the value of the interest.

§ 4.06   START-UP, ORGANIZATION, AND SYNDICATION EXPENSES

[A]   Amortization of Start-Up Expenses

Before a partnership creates a new business or acquires an existing one, it may incur expenses to investigate the feasibility of the business and to get its operations started. These "start-up" costs are not deductible but are treated as capital expenditures incurred to acquire the new business according to I.R.C. Section 195(a).[149] However, I.R.C. Section 195(b) allows the partnership to elect to amortize qualified start-up costs over a period of not less than 60 months, beginning with the month in which the active trade or business begins.[150] I.R.C. Section 195 does not require capitalization of the following expenses:

(1)   interest subject to I.R.C. Section 163(a);

(2)   taxes subject to I.R.C. Section 164;

(3)   research and development subject to I.R.C. Section 174.

These costs are deductible under the specific rules of the related statutes.

The amortization deduction is allowed to the taxpayer who incurs the start-up expenses and enters the trade or business.[151] If a partnership incurs start-up expenses, the partnership must make the election and must take into account the

---

[149]   I.R.C. § 195 was enacted in 1980 and extensively amended by the 1984 Tax Reform Act.

[150]   The election must be made on return filed in a timely manner for the year in which the business begins. I.R.C. § 195(d).

[151]   S. Rep. No. 1036, 96th Cong., 2d Sess. 13 (1980).

amortization deductions in computing its taxable income.[152] If an individual general partner incurs a qualified expense in investigating whether to acquire a partnership interest, that partner must personally make the election and personally take the amortization deductions.[153] A limited partner, however, may not amortize investigatory expenses personally because he will not actively participate in the management of the partnership's business.[154] If the trade or business is completely disposed of before the end of the amortization period, expenses that have not yet been deducted are deductible as a loss under I.R.C. Section 165.

A start-up expenditure qualifies for amortization only if it would be currently deductible if it were incurred in connection with the operation of an existing trade or business.[155] The expenditure must also be paid or incurred:

(1)   to investigate the creation or acquisition of an active trade or business;

(2)   to create an active trade or business; or

(3)   for an activity engaged in for profit and production of income before the day on which the active trade or business begins, in anticipation of the activity becoming an active trade or business.

Qualified start-up expenses include those incurred to investigate a prospective business, such as costs to analyze potential markets, labor supply, and transportation facilities, and expenses incurred to start business operations, such as costs of advertising, employee training, lining up distributors, suppliers, and customers.[156]

Expenses related to starting up an investment activity that is not an active trade or business may not be amortized.[157] The expense must be one that would be deductible as a trade or business expense under I.R.C. Section 162 and not an expense incurred for the production of income under I.R.C. Section 212. A partnership engaged in rental activities is not in an active trade or business, unless the partnership furnishes "significant services" incident to the rental.[158] Operation of an apartment complex, office building, or shopping center generally constitutes an active trade or business.

---

[152] Except to the extent that it must be separately stated under I.R.C. § 702(a)(7). S. Rep. No. 1036, 96th Cong., 2d Sess. 13 (1980).

[153] S. Rep. No. 1036, 96th Cong., 2d Sess. 13 (1980).

[154] *Id.* The limited partner is allowed his share of the partnership's amortization deductions. *See* Rev. Rul. 81-150, 1981-1 C.B. 119.

[155] I.R.C. § 195(c).

[156] S. Rep. No. 1036, 96th Cong., 2d Sess. 13 (1980).

[157] *Id.*

[158] *Id.*

[B]   Amortization of Organization Expenses

Partners usually incur legal, accounting, and similar expenses when a new partnership is organized. They also may incur substantial costs to promote and sell partnership interests (*i.e.*, syndication fees), if the interests are marketed to the public. The general rule of I.R.C. Section 709(a) is that amounts paid or incurred to organize a partnership or to promote the sale of partnership interests are not deductible by the partners or the partnership.[159] However, I.R.C. Section 709(b) allows the partnership to elect to amortize certain organization expenses — but not syndication costs — over a period of not less than 60 months, beginning with the month in which the partnership begins doing business.[160] A partnership using the cash method of tax accounting cannot amortize unpaid amounts, but it may claim the previously nondeductible portion of the expense in the year payment is made.[161] If the partnership is liquidated before the end of the amortization period, expenses that have not yet been recovered are deductible as a loss under I.R.C. Section 165.[162]

Organizational expenses covered by I.R.C. Section 709(b) are expenditures that are:

(1)   "incident" to the creation of the partnership;[163]

(2)   chargeable to the partners' capital accounts; and

(3)   the kind that could be amortized over the life of the partnership if the partnership were organized for a definite period.

These expenses include legal fees for the organization of the partnership (*e.g.*, for negotiating and preparing a partnership agreement), accounting fees for setting up the partnership's books, and filing fees.[164] Expenses that may not be amortized include expenditures for acquiring assets or for transferring assets to the partnership, expenses connected with the admission or the removal of partners other than at the partnership's inception, expenses for contracts related to the

---

[159] Prior to the enactment of I.R.C. § 709 in 1976, the proper treatment of organization and syndication costs was uncertain. Although many syndicated limited partnerships deducted amounts paid to their promoters for organizational and marketing expenses, the IRS and the Tax Court treated the payments as nondeductible capital expenditures. *See* Staff of Joint Committee on Taxation, General Explanation of the Tax Reform Act of 1976, at 89 (1976); Cagle v. Comm'r, 63 T.C. 86 (1974), *aff'd*, 539 F.2d 409 (5th Cir. 1976).

[160] The date on which a partnership begins business is determined in light of the circumstances of each case. Ordinarily, the date is when the partnership starts its business operations and not when the partnership agreement is signed. However, acquisition of the operating assets needed in the partnership's business may constitute the beginning of business. Treas. Reg. § 1.709-2(c).

[161] Treas. Reg. § 1.709-1(b)(1).

[162] However, no deduction is allowed for capitalized syndication costs. Treas. Reg. § 1.709-1(b)(2).

[163] The regulations state that an expenditure is incident to the creation of a partnership only if it is incurred during the time period beginning within a reasonable time before the partnership begins business and ending on the due date (without extensions) for the partnership's tax return for the year in which it begins business. Treas. Reg. § 1.709-2(a).

[164] Treas. Reg. § 1.709-2(a).

operation of the partnership's business, and all syndication expenses.[165]

[C]   Nondeductibility of Syndication Expenses

A partnership's syndication expenses are the expenses it incurs to sell or to promote the sale of its partnership interests. These expenses are nonamortizable capital expenditures and, according to I.R.C. Section 709, no deduction is allowed when they are paid during the lifetime of the partnership or when the partnership is liquidated.[166] The syndication expenses do not reduce a partner's basis in his partnership interest and, therefore, the partner recognizes less gain when he sells his interest or when the partnership liquidates.[167]

Syndication expenses are defined as expenses connected with the issuing and marketing of interests in the partnership.[168] These expenses include:

(1)   brokerage fees;

(2)   registration fees;

(3)   legal fees of the underwriter or placement agent;

(4)   legal fees of the general partner or the partnership for securities advice;

(5)   legal fees for advice about the adequacy of the tax disclosures in the prospectus or placement memorandum for securities laws purposes; and

(6)   printing costs of the prospectus or other promotional materials.[169]

[D]   "Disguised" Organization and Syndication Expenses

To prevent partnerships from using allocations of partnership income to avoid the rules requiring capitalization of certain partnership expenses, I.R.C. Section 707(a)(2)(A) was enacted in 1984. Although the statute applies to a variety of transactions, Congress was particularly concerned about allocations used to pay partnership organization and syndication fees.[170] A partnership can obtain a tax benefit equivalent to a current deduction of these expenses by allocating partnership income to a partner who performed its organizing or syndicating services. The allocation is equivalent to a deduction because it reduces the amount of partnership income taxable to the remaining partners. Because the organizer-

---

[165] *Id.*

[166] Treas. Reg. § 1.709-1(b)(2); Rev. Rul. 85-32, 1985-1 C.B. 186.

[167] I.R.C. § 705(a)(2)(B) provides that a partner reduces the basis in his partnership interest by his share of partnership expenditures that are not deductible and not chargeable to his capital account. However, syndication costs are charged to the capital accounts and therefore do not cause a basis adjustment. In effect, the expenses of selling partnership interests are treated as the partnership's cost of raising its capital. *See* Rev. Rul. 85-32, 1985-1 C.B. 186; Rev. Rul. 81-153, 1981-1 C.B. 387; Priv. Ltr. Rul. 8028113.

[168] Treas. Reg. § 1.709-2(b).

[169] *Id.*

[170] H.R. Rep. No. 432, pt. 2 98th Cong., 2d Sess. 1219 (1984); S. Rep. No. 169, 98th Cong., 2d Sess. 224 (1984).

syndicator partner receives cash distributions from the partnership corresponding to his income allocation, the transaction is economically equivalent to a direct payment for services.

I.R.C. Section 707(a)(2)(A) provides that, in appropriate circumstances, a distributive share allocated to a partner may be recharacterized as a payment to a nonpartner. If the recharacterized payment is for a partner's services in organizing or syndicating the partnership, I.R.C. Section 709 applies, and the expense must be capitalized. An allocation will be recharacterized under the statute if:

(1)   a partner provides services for a partnership;

(2)   the partnership makes a related direct or indirect allocation and distribution to that partner; and

(3)   when viewed together the performance of services and the allocation and distribution are properly characterized as a transaction between the partnership and a nonpartner.

The statute directs the Treasury to issue regulations describing the criteria it will use in determining when a partnership allocation will be characterized as a payment to a nonpartner.[171]

---

[171] Although regulations under I.R.C. § 707(a)(2) have been issued, they do not address disguised payments for services. Treas. Reg. § 1.707-2 is reserved for rules governing disguised payments for services.

Chapter 5

BASIS IN PARTNERSHIP/LLC INTEREST

§ 5.01 OVERVIEW OF BASIS OF PARTNER'S OR MEMBER'S INTEREST

For most tax purposes, a partner or limited liability company member is not considered to have a direct interest in the partnership's or LLC's property, but rather to own a separate asset, the partnership or LLC interest, which represents the right to share in the partnership's or LLC's capital, profits, gains, and losses.[1] Each partner or member has a basis for his partnership or LLC interest that is distinct from the basis of the partnership or LLC assets. A partner's basis for his interest is important for a number of reasons, including:

(1) determining the maximum amount of partnership losses he may deduct;

(2) computing his gain or loss on a sale of the interest; and

(3) determining the tax consequences of distributions of money or property he receives from the partnership.

A partner's or member's basis includes his share of the partnership's or LLC's liabilities. Thus, a partner requiring additional basis to deduct his full share of partnership losses may obtain it by increasing his share of partnership liabilities. This is true even if the partnership's liabilities are nonrecourse, meaning that the partner does not bear any risk of loss on the debt. This chapter describes how a partner's basis in his partnership interest is determined. The discussion covers computation of the partner's initial basis and the subsequent basis adjustments that are required to reflect the partner's share of income and losses, and distributions he receives. A detailed analysis is provided of the complex rules governing a partner's share of recourse and nonrecourse partnership liabilities.

[A] When Is Determination of Basis Required?

A partner must determine the basis of his interest only when it is necessary to calculate his individual tax liability.[2] Basis must be determined in the following instances:

(1) *To calculate the amount of gain or loss realized when the interest is*

---

[1] Under the Uniform Partnership Act, however, each partner is a co-owner of partnership property and also owns a separate partnership interest representing his share of capital and profits. U.P.A. §§ 25, 26.

[2] Treas. Reg. § 1.705-1(a)(1).

sold or exchanged. The gain or loss is the difference between the amount realized and the partner's basis in his partnership interest[3] (*see* Chapter 12).

(2)   *To determine the maximum partnership loss that may be deducted each year.* Under I.R.C. Section 704(d), a partner's deduction for his distributive share of losses is limited to the basis in his interest at the end of the partnership year (*see* Chapter 12).

(3)   *To determine whether the partner recognizes gain when the partnership distributes cash.* Under I.R.C. Section 731(a), a partner recognizes gain to the extent that the amount of cash distributed exceeds the basis in his partnership interest (*see* § 5.01[F][3], *infra*; Chapter 8).

(4)   *To determine the partner's basis in distributed partnership property.* Under I.R.C. Section 732(a), a partner's total basis in property received in a nonliquidating distribution cannot exceed the basis in his partnership interest (*see* Chapter 8). Under I.R.C. Section 732(b), a partner's total basis in all property received in a liquidating distribution is limited to the basis of his partnership interest.

(5)   *To determine whether the partner recognizes a loss when his interest is liquidated.* Under I.R.C. Section 731(a)(2), a partner recognizes a loss on a liquidating distribution only if:

(a)   no property other than cash, inventory, or unrealized receivables is distributed to him; and

(b)   the basis in his partnership interest exceeds the sum of the cash and the partnership's basis in the distributed assets (*see* Chapter 8).

(6)   *To determine the adjustments to the basis of partnership property resulting from an I.R.C. Section 754 basis-adjustment election.* A partnership that makes this election must adjust the basis of its property whenever a difference arises between the partnership's basis in its property and the bases of the individual partners' interests because of transfers of interests or distributions of property (*see* § 5.01[H][2], *infra*, and Chapter 8).

When determining the allowable limit on loss deductions under I.R.C. Section 704(d), a partner determines the basis in his interest at the end of the partnership's tax year. In all other situations, a partner determines his basis immediately before he transfers his interest or receives a distribution.[4]

[B]   Initial Basis — How it Is Determined

A partner's initial basis in a partnership interest depends upon how the interest is acquired. If the interest is acquired in exchange for a contribution to the partnership, the initial basis equals the amount of cash paid, plus the partner's

---

[3] I.R.C. § 1001(a).

[4] Treas. Reg. §§ 1.705-1(a)(1), 1.731-1(a), 1.732-1(a).

basis in any property he contributes.[5] If the interest is acquired in exchange for a partner's promissory note, the basis of the interest is zero, because a taxpayer's basis for his own promissory note is zero.[6] However, the basis increases as the partner makes principal payments on the note.[7] (See discussion of partner's contribution obligations in § 5.06[D], *infra*.)

> **Example:** Sidney contributes $1,000 in cash, his personal note for $2,000, and property worth $20,000, with a basis of $15,000, to the ST Partnership in exchange for a partnership interest. Sidney's basis in his partnership interest is $16,000, computed as follows:

Asset	Basis	Fair Market Value
Cash	$1,000	$1,000
Personal Note	0	2,000
Property	15,000	20,000
	$16,000	$23,000

If a partner receives a partnership interest in exchange for forgiving a partnership debt to him, his basis in the interest equals his basis in the canceled obligation (ordinarily, the face amount), limited to the value of the interest when acquired.[8] The partner may deduct the difference between his basis in the debt and the value of the partnership interest as a bad debt.[9]

A creditor who receives a partnership interest from a partner in exchange for canceling the partner's debt takes a basis for the interest equal to the value of the canceled obligation, limited to the value of the acquired interest. The value of the interest will equal the amount of the canceled debt only if the transaction is at arm's-length and the partnership's business is profitable at that time.[10] If the interest is worth less than the canceled debt, the difference may be deducted as a bad debt.

A partner is considered to contribute money to a partnership in an amount equal to his share of the partnership liabilities, and his basis in the partnership interest increases by that amount.[11] Conversely, if the partnership assumes or takes contributed property subject to a partner's liability, the partner is considered to receive a cash distribution equal to the liability, and the basis in his interest decreases by that amount.[12] (See discussion and examples concerning inclusion of

---

[5] I.R.C. § 722.

[6] Rev. Rul. 80-235, 1980-2 C.B. 229 (partner has zero basis in own promissory note); Oden v. Comm'r, T.C. Memo. 1981-184, *aff'd, in unpublished opinion*, 679 F.2d 885 (4th Cir. 1982); Levy v. Comm'r, 732 F.2d 1435 (9th Cir. 1984); Gemini Twin Fund III v. Comm'r, T.C. Memo. 1991-315. *See* Priv. Ltr. Rul. 8448002.

[7] Rev. Rul. 80-235, 1980-2 C.B. 229.

[8] Shaheen v. Comm'r, T.C. Memo. 1982-445. *See* I.R.C. §§ 742, 1001.

[9] I.R.C. § 166.

[10] Sargent v. Comm'r, T.C. Memo. 1970-214.

[11] I.R.C. §§ 752(a), 722.

[12] I.R.C. §§ 752(b), 733.

partnership liabilities in basis in § 5.03, *infra*.)

A partner who performs services in exchange for a partnership interest is treated as if he (1) received an undivided interest in the partnership's property equal to the value of his services, and (2) contributed that property in exchange for his partnership interest. The partner reports the value of the partnership property he is deemed to receive as compensation income; his basis in the property also equals that value. The net effect of these hypothetical transactions is that the service partner's initial basis in his partnership interest equals the amount of compensation income he reports. (See discussion and examples concerning receipt of a partnership interest for services in Chapter 4.)

The basis of an interest acquired by any other means is determined under the general basis rules of the Internal Revenue Code.[13] Hence, the initial basis for an interest:

(1) purchased from another partner is its cost, including the selling partner's liabilities that the purchaser assumes or takes the interest subject to;[14]

(2) acquired from a decedent is its fair market value at the time of the partner's death or at the alternate valuation date;[15]

(3) acquired by gift is the lesser of the donor's basis in the interest (increased by any federal gift taxes he paid) or its fair market value.[16]

A partner who acquires a partnership interest in a nontaxable exchange determines his basis under the specific tax rules governing the exchange. For example, a parent corporation that receives a partnership interest through a nontaxable liquidation of an 80 percent-owned subsidiary takes the interest with a carryover basis from the subsidiary.[17] Similarly, a corporation's basis in a partnership interest contributed by a shareholder carries over from the shareholder/partner.[18]

The nonrecognition rules for like-kind exchanges do not apply to exchanges of partnership interests, even though both partnerships own similar property.[19] Therefore, a partner must recognize gain or loss when he exchanges one partnership interest for another, and adjust his basis in the interest.[20]

---

[13] I.R.C. § 742. These general rules are found in Part II of Subchapter O (I.R.C. §§ 1011–1023).

[14] I.R.C. § 1012.

[15] I.R.C. § 1014.

[16] I.R.C. § 1015.

[17] I.R.C. §§ 332, 334(b), 1223(2).

[18] I.R.C. §§ 351, 362.

[19] I.R.C. § 1031(a)(2)(D).

[20] I.R.C. § 1012.

Determining Initial Basis of Partner's Interest:

Method of Acquisition	Basis
Purchase	Purchase price plus buyer's share of partnership liabilities.
Contribution	Amount of cash plus contributor's basis for contributed property; cash contribution includes share of partnership liabilities; if encumbered property contributed, basis decreases by net reduction in contributor's share of partnership liabilities.
Cancellation of Partner's Debt	Creditor's basis in canceled debt, limited to value of the interest.
Performance of Services	Amount of compensation income reported.
Nontaxable Exchange	Under specific nonrecognition rules governing the transaction.
Gift	Lesser of donor's basis plus gift taxes or value of interest.
Inheritance	Value of interest on date of death or alternate valuation date.

[C]   Continuing Adjustments to Partner's Basis

Each partner's basis in his partnership interest is continually adjusted to reflect his share of the partnership's income, expenditures, and distributions. Basis is increased by:

(1)   Additional contributions made to the partnership. The increase equals the amount of cash given and the partner's basis in property contributed.[21] A partner is deemed to contribute an amount of cash equal to any increase in the partner's share of partnership liabilities, and the basis of his partnership interest increases by that amount.[22]

(2)   The partner's distributive share of partnership taxable income.[23] This includes both his share of overall taxable income and his share of all taxable items required to be separately stated under I.R.C. Section 702(a).

(3)   The partner's distributive share of partnership tax-exempt income.[24]

(4)   The partner's share of depletion deductions in excess of his share of the partnership's basis for depletable property.[25]

---

[21] I.R.C. § 722. For contributions to investment company partnerships, basis also increases by gain the contributing partner recognizes under I.R.C. § 721(b).

[22] I.R.C. §§ 752(a), 722.

[23] I.R.C. § 705(a)(1)(A).

[24] I.R.C. § 705(a)(1)(B).

[25] I.R.C. § 705(a)(1)(C).

The basis of each partner's interest is decreased, down to, but not below, zero, by:

(1)   Distributions received from the partnership. The decrease equals the amount of cash and/or the partnership's basis in the distributed property.[26] A partner is considered to receive a cash distribution equal to the amount of any decrease in the partner's share of partnership liabilities, and the basis of his partnership interest decreases by that amount).[27]

(2)   The partner's distributive share of partnership losses.[28]

(3)   The partner's distributive share of nondeductible partnership expenses that are not capital expenditures.[29]

(4)   Depletion deductions for partnership oil and gas property, up to each partner's proportionate share of the partnership's adjusted basis for its depletable properties.[30]

Example: On January 1, Edward and Frank formed the EF Partnership, each partner contributing $10,000 for equal interests in partnership capital and profits. Both partners and the partnership are calendar-year taxpayers. Partnership taxable income during the year is $16,000. On December 31, the partnership distributes $5,000 to Edward, but makes no distribution to Frank.

At the end of the year, Edward's adjusted basis in his partnership interest is $13,000, determined as follows:

Initial basis	$10,000
Plus distributive share of taxable income	8,000
Less cash distribution	(5,000)
Adjusted basis at end of year	$13,000

Frank's adjusted basis is $18,000:

Initial basis	$10,000
Plus distributive share of taxable income	8,000
Adjusted basis at end of year	$18,000

For most purposes, partners need only compute the bases of their interests at the close of the normal partnership tax year. A basis computation may be required during the year if:

(1)   The partnership tax year closes for a partner before its normal end because the partner sold or liquidated his entire partnership interest. In

---

[26] I.R.C. §§ 705(a)(2), 733.

[27] I.R.C. §§ 752(b), 733.

[28] I.R.C. § 705(a)(2)(A).

[29] I.R.C. § 705(a)(2)(B).

[30] I.R.C. § 705(a)(3).

that situation, the partner must compute his year-end basis as of the sale or liquidation date.

(2)   A partner must know the basis of his partnership interest before the end of the partnership tax year to determine the consequences of a distribution. The partner is taxable to the extent that a cash distribution exceeds the basis of his partnership interest immediately before the distribution. A partner who receives a property distribution cannot take a basis in the property that exceeds the basis of his partnership interest when the distribution occurs. In these situations, the partner computes the basis of his interest immediately before the distribution by taking into account any contributions or distributions (including constructive contributions or distributions resulting from liability changes) and any basis transfers (for example, sales or gifts) occurring up to that time.

[1]   Basis Adjustment for Taxable Income or Loss

A partner's basis in his partnership interest increases or decreases by his distributive share of the partnership's taxable income or loss.[31] This basis adjustment occurs at the end of the partnership's tax year.[32] A partner's basis is increased by his share of income because he is taxed on that amount regardless of whether any money is distributed to him.[33] Correspondingly, a partner's basis is reduced by his share of partnership losses because the losses are reportable on the partner's individual tax return.[34]

In effect, the partner adjusts his basis as though he directly earns or incurs his share of partnership income or loss. If these basis adjustments were not required, the partner would realize the income or loss a second time when he sells or liquidates his partnership interest.

Generally, under I.R.C. Section 703(a), partnership taxable income or loss is computed in the same manner as that of an individual. However, certain income or loss items specified in I.R.C. Section 702 are not included in the computation and must be accounted for separately. (See discussion of computation of partnership income in Chapter 3.) Thus, a partner's basis in his interest is subject to multiple adjustments reflecting his share of partnership taxable income or loss determined under I.R.C. Section 703(a) and his share of each item separately stated under I.R.C. Section 702.

Example: Fred is an equal partner in the FG Partnership, and his basis in his partnership interest at the beginning of the tax year is $50,000. For the current year, the partnership reports the following tax items:

---

[31] I.R.C. § 705(a)(1).

[32] Treas. Reg. § 1.705-1(a)(1).

[33] I.R.C. §§ 702, 706(a).

[34] *Id.*

$20,000	net income from operations
$8,000	long-term capital gain
$2,000	short-term capital loss
$1,000	dividend income

Assuming no other transactions, Fred's basis in his partnership interest at the close of the tax year is $63,500, determined as follows:

Beginning basis	$50,000
Distributive share of net income	10,000
Distributive share of LTCG	4,000
Distributive share of dividends	500
Distributive share of STCL	(1,000)
	$63,500

Although a partner decreases the basis in his partnership interest by his distributive share of partnership losses, basis may not be reduced below zero.[35] Under I.R.C. Section 704(d), a partner may not deduct partnership losses that exceed the basis in his partnership interest at the end of the partnership's tax year. The effect of these rules is that a partner's deduction for his share of partnership losses is limited to the positive basis in his partnership interest at the end of the year. Losses that cannot be deducted because a partner's basis is zero carry over, and may be deducted at the end of a subsequent year, if the partner has sufficient basis at that time.[36]

> **Example:** eorge is a 50-percent partner in the GH Partnership, and his basis in his partnership interest at the beginning of the tax year is $40,000. During the year, the partnership's sole tax item is an operating loss of $100,000. Although George's distributive share of the loss is $50,000, the deduction on his individual tax return for the year is limited to $40,000 (the basis of his partnership interest). This reduces George's basis in his partnership interest to zero; the $10,000 loss in excess of his basis carries over to the next year.
>
> If the partnership has $8,000 of taxable income in the subsequent year, George's basis in his partnership interest at the close of the year (before the deduction for losses) will be $4,000. George may then deduct $4,000 of the carried over loss, again reducing the basis in his partnership interest to zero. The $6,000 remaining loss carries over to the next year.

[2] Basis Increase for Tax-Exempt Income

A partner's basis increases by his distributive share of the partnership's tax-exempt income. This adjustment is needed to prevent that income from being taxed when it is distributed to the partner or when he sells or liquidates his

---

[35] I.R.C. §§ 705(a)(2), (a)(3), 731(a)(1), and 732(a)(2) all provide that a partner's basis cannot be reduced below zero.

[36] Treas. Reg. § 1.704-1(d)(1).

partnership interest. Although I.R.C. Section 705(a)(1)(B) allows the basis adjustment for "income of the partnership exempt from tax under this title," neither the Code nor the regulations define the scope of that phrase. Apparently it includes the following items:

(1)   life insurance proceeds and certain death benefits;[37]

(2)   interest on state and municipal obligations;[38]

(3)   income from discharge of indebtedness, if the partner is bankrupt or insolvent, and reduces other tax attributes;[39]

(4)   recovery of amounts deducted in prior years, to the extent that these items did not previously reduce the amount of income taxes paid;[40]

(5)   income from sources within U.S. possessions;[41]

(6)   gifts and inheritances;[42]

(7)   compensation for injuries or sickness;[43]

(8)   amounts received under accident and health plans;[44]

(9)   tax-exempt scholarship and fellowship grants;[45] and

(10)   other receipts specifically excluded from taxable income (*e.g.*, income taxes paid by a lessee corporation[46] and certain fringe benefits).[47]

Example: Greta and Harold are equal partners in the GH Partnership. At the beginning of the year, the partnership's balance sheet appeared as follows:

Assets:	Adjusted Basis	Fair Market Value
Real Estate	$30,000	$30,000
Municipal Bonds	20,000	20,000
	$50,000	$50,000
Capital:		
Greta	$25,000	$25,000
Harold	25,000	25,000
	$50,000	$50,000

---

[37] I.R.C. § 101.

[38] I.R.C. § 103.

[39] I.R.C. § 108.

[40] I.R.C. § 111.

[41] I.R.C. § 931.

[42] I.R.C. § 102.

[43] I.R.C. § 104.

[44] I.R.C. § 105.

[45] I.R.C. § 117.

[46] I.R.C. § 110.

[47] I.R.C. § 132.

During the year, the partnership earns $8,000 from real estate rentals and $2,000 of tax-exempt bond interest. Although each partner's distributive share of partnership taxable income is only $4,000, the basis of each of their interests increases by $5,000. The balance sheet now appears as follows:

Assets:	Adjusted Basis	Fair Market Value
Cash	$10,000	$10,000
Real Estate	30,000	30,000
Municipal Bonds	20,000	20,000
	$60,000	$60,000
Capital:		
Greta	$30,000	$30,000
Harold	30,000	30,000
	$60,000	$60,000

If Greta sells her partnership interest for $45,000 (assuming that the real estate and bonds have appreciated), she realizes $15,000 of taxable gain. Note that if there had not been an increase in basis reflecting her share of the tax-exempt income, Greta's basis at the time of sale would be $29,000, and she would receive a $16,000 taxable gain — $1,000 of which is attributable to the tax-exempt income.

[3]   Basis Decrease for Nondeductible Expenditures

A partner decreases the basis in his partnership interest by his distributive share of partnership expenditures that are "not deductible in computing its taxable income and not properly chargeable to capital account."[48] This rule ensures that a partner does not eventually obtain a tax benefit for the expenditure by decreasing the gain (or increasing the loss) he realizes when he sells or liquidates his partnership interest. Thus, the rule applies only to expenses that reduce the value of partnership assets and not to capital expenditures which merely change the kind of assets the partnership owns.

Although the regulations do not specifically describe the expenditures that require a basis reduction, the following items apparently are included:

(1)   Premiums on life insurance policies that is not deductible under I.R.C. Section 264.[49]

(2)   Charitable contributions.[50]

(3)   Nondeductible political contributions.

---

[48] I.R.C. § 705(a)(2)(B). *See* Rev. Rul. 96-10, 1996-1 C.B. 138 (partners' bases in partnership interests decreased for losses on sale of partnership property to a related partnership that are disallowed under I.R.C. § 707(b)(1); partners' bases increased by gain from the sale of partnership property not recognized under I.R.C. §§ 267(d) and 707(b)(1)).

[49] *Accord* Rev. Rul. 89-7, 1989-1 C.B. 178 (nondeductible start-up expenditures reduce basis of partnership interest).

[50] I.R.C. § 702(a)(4).

(4)   Expenses and interest related to the production of tax-exempt income that are not deductible under I.R.C. Section 265.

(5)   Losses, expenses, and interest incurred in transactions with related persons that are disallowed under I.R.C. Section 267.

Example: Marvin and Neil each contribute $10,000 in cash for equal interests in the MN Partnership. The partnership's opening balance sheet is as follows:

Assets:	Basis	Fair Market Value
Cash	$20,000	$20,000
	$20,000	$20,000
Capital:		
Marvin	$10,000	$10,000
Neil	10,000	10,000
	$20,000	$20,000

During its first tax year, the partnership has no income, and its only expenditure is $2,000 for premiums on term life insurance policies covering each partner. Because the premiums are nondeductible under I.R.C. Section 264, each partner's distributive share of partnership income or loss is zero. Under I.R.C. Section 705(a)(2)(B), however, each partner's basis in his partnership interest decreases by $1,000, his distributive share of the nondeductible expenditure. The partnership's balance at the end of year 1 is as follows:

Assets:	Adjusted Basis	Fair Market Value
Cash	$18,000	$18,000
	$18,000	$18,000
Capital:		
Marvin	$9,000	$9,000
Neil	9,000	9,000
	$18,000	$18,000

The impact of the basis reduction is illustrated by assuming that Marvin sells his partnership interest at the beginning of the next year for its $9,000 value. If no basis adjustment were required, Marvin's basis would be $10,000, and he would realize a $1,000 loss and thereby obtain a tax benefit for the nondeductible premium.

[4]   Basis Decrease for Distributions

When a partner receives a distribution from the partnership, the basis in his partnership interest decreases by (1) the amount of cash he receives, and (2) the partnership's basis in any other distributed property.[51] A distribution cannot reduce a partner's basis below zero. If the partner receives a cash distribution exceeding the basis in his partnership interest, his basis decreases to zero, and he recognizes

---

[51] I.R.C. § 733.

the amount that exceeds his basis as taxable gain[52] (*see* § 5.01[F][3], *infra*).

If property other than cash is distributed, the partner does not recognize gain, even if the partnership's basis in the property exceeds the partner's basis in his partnership interest.[53] Generally a partner's basis in distributed property is the same as the partnership's basis immediately before the distribution.[54] However, the partner's basis cannot exceed the basis in his partnership interest at that time.[55] If cash and other property are distributed in the same transaction, the cash is deemed to be distributed first.[56]

> **Example (1):** Larry's basis in his partnership interest is $10,000. If the partnership distributes $12,000 in cash to him, Larry's basis in his partnership interest is reduced to zero, and he recognizes $2,000 of taxable gain.

> **Example (2):** Mary's basis in her partnership interest is $10,000. The partnership distributes real estate worth $10,000 to Mary. The partnership's basis in the property is $6,000. As a result, Mary's basis in her partnership interest decreases to $4,000; her basis in the real estate is $6,000.

> **Example (3):** Assume the same facts as in Example (2), except that Mary's basis in her partnership interest is $5,000 when the distribution occurs. Mary's basis in her partnership interest decreases to zero, and her basis in the distributed real estate is limited to $5,000. (Note that $1,000 of the partnership's basis in the real estate disappears. However, if an election under I.R.C. Section 754 is in effect, the disappearing basis may be restored through an increase in the basis of undistributed partnership assets (*see* § 5.01[H][2], *infra*).)

[5]   Basis Increase for Depletion Deductions

A partner increases the basis in his partnership interest by the excess of his share of the partnership's depletion deductions over its basis in depletable property.[57] This adjustment is necessary because a taxpayer's total percentage depletion deductions for an oil- or gas-producing property are permitted to exceed his basis in the property.[58] Thus, depletion deductions are allowable in full even though prior depletion has reduced the basis in the depletable property to zero.[59]

---

[52] I.R.C. § 731.

[53] I.R.C. § 731(a)(1).

[54] I.R.C. § 732(a)(1).

[55] I.R.C. § 736(a)(2).

[56] *Id.*

[57] Treas. Reg. § 1.613A-3(e)(1).

[58] I.R.C. §§ 611, 613A.

[59] The basis in the property is not reduced below zero.

[6]   Basis Decrease for Depletion Deductions

Each partner's share of depletion deductions for partnership oil or gas properties is determined separately from his share of the partnership's taxable income or loss. This rule assures partners the same tax treatment they would obtain if they owned direct interests in the properties. In a direct investment, a taxpayer reduces his basis in depletable property by the amount of depletion he has deducted. I.R.C. Section 705(a)(3) provides similar treatment for partners by decreasing the basis in each partnership interest by each partner's share of depletion deductions.

Because a taxpayer in a direct investment reduces the basis in depletable property only to zero, a partner reduces the basis in his partnership interest for depletion deductions only up to his share of the partnership's basis in its depletable property.

[7]   Basis Adjustment When Partnership Sells Corporate Partner's Stock

Under I.R.C. Section 1032, a corporation does not recognize gain or loss on a sale of its own stock. In specific situations, regulations extend this nonrecognition treatment to a corporate partner's share of gain or loss realized from a partnership that sells the corporate partner's stock.[60] This treatment also applies to transactions in which the acquiring entity obtains the issuing corporation's stock indirectly in any combination of exchanges under I.R.C. Sections 721 and 351.

The transaction is treated as if, immediately before the sale, the partnership contributed cash equal to the value of the stock to the corporation in exchange for the stock.[61] The corporate partner increases (or decreases) the basis of its partnership interest by the amount of gain (or loss) not recognized.

This treatment applies only if, pursuant to a plan to acquire money or other property:

(1)   the partnership acquires the stock (directly or indirectly) from the issuing corporation in a carry-over basis transaction (determined under I.R.C. Section 723);

(2)   the partnership immediately transfers the stock to another person to acquire money or other property;

(3)   the person receiving the stock acquires it in a taxable transaction (*i.e.*, no substituted basis); and

(4)   the stock is not exchanged for stock of the issuing corporation.[62]

Example:[63] XCorp owns all of the stock of YCorp. YCorp is a partner in the YZ Partnership. YZ agrees to acquire a truck from Charlene in exchange

---

[60]   Treas. Reg. § 1.1032-3(a).

[61]   Treas. Reg. § 1.1032-3(b).

[62]   Treas. Reg. § 1.1032-3(c).

[63]   *See* Treas. Reg. § 1.1032-3(e), *Example (5)*.

for 10 shares of XCorp stock worth $10,000. XCorp transfers that amount of its stock to YCorp for that purpose and YCorp immediately contributes the X stock to YZ (in what would be a carryforward basis transaction under I.R.C. Section 723). YZ immediately transfers the X stock to Charlene for the truck.

YZ does not recognize gain or loss on the disposition of the XCorp stock. The transaction is treated as if YZ purchased the stock from XCorp immediately before the stock sale for $10,000 cash (which had been indirectly contributed to YZ by X through intermediate YCorp). YCorp's basis in its partnership interest in YZ increases by $10,000,[64] and XCorp's basis in its YCorp stock increases by $10,000.[65]

Generally, the corporate partner increases the basis of its partnership interest (under I.R.C. Section 705) by the amount of gain (or loss) not recognized (under I.R.C. Section 1032).[66] As noted in the sections below, however, the amount of the basis increase or decrease may be limited in some circumstances.[67]

The IRS may apply nonrecognition treatment under I.R.C. Section 1032 even if the partnership does not immediately transfer the stock to another person for money or other property. In Revenue Ruling 99-57,[68] for example, the Service held a corporate partner does not recognize gain or loss in the following situation:

Example: For equal interests in the ST partnership, Star Corporation contributes 100 shares of its own stock worth $100,000 (having a zero basis) and Tom contributes $100,000 in cash. In year two, when the value of the stock has increased to $120,000, ST transfers the stock to a third party in exchange for business property. ST realizes $120,000 of gain and allocates $100,000 of that gain to S (under I.R.C. Section 704(c) and the remaining $20,000 of gain equally between Star Corporation and Tom. Star Corporation does not recognize its share of the gain under I.R.C. Section 1032 and increases the basis for its interest by $110,000.

[a]   Limitation on Basis Adjustment if no I.R.C. Section 754 Election in Effect

Recent regulations under I.R.C. Section 705 coordinate the basis adjustment rules of I.R.C. Section 705 with the nonrecognition treatment afforded by I.R.C. Section 1032.[69] Importantly, the regulations do not permit a corporate partner to increase the basis of its interest by the full amount of unrecognized gain if the corporation acquired its interest in the partnership holding its stock when an I.R.C. Section 754 basis adjustment election was not in effect. (For discussion of the effect of an I.R.C. Section 754 election when a partnership interest is

---

[64] *See* I.R.C. § 722.

[65] *See* I.R.C. § 358.

[66] Rev. Rul. 99-57, 1999-2 C.B. 678.

[67] *See* Treas. Reg. § 1.705-2; Prop. Treas. Reg. § 1.705-2(a).

[68] 1999-2 C.B. 678.

[69] Treas. Reg. § 1.705-2; T.D. 8986 (Mar. 29, 2002).

purchased, see § 12.08, *infra*.) The regulations indicate that I.R.C. Section 705 is intended to preserve equality between a partner's basis for his partnership interest (outside basis) and his share of the basis of the partnership's assets (inside basis). This basis equality is not maintained, however, when a partner acquires a partnership interest at a time that the partnership does not have an I.R.C. Section 754 election in effect. In this situation, the regulations hold that it is "inconsistent with the intent" of I.R.C. Sections 705 and 1032 to increase the basis of the corporation's partnership interest by the full amount of gain not recognized under I.R.C. Section 1032.

The regulations provide the following example to illustrate when a basis increase is not appropriate:[70]

> **Example (1):** Zylo Corporation purchases a 50-percent interest in the XYZ Partnership for $100,000. The partnership's only asset is Zylo stock with a basis of $100,000 and a value of $200,000. XYZ does not have an I.R.C. Section 754 election in effect. If the partnership sells the stock for $200,000, Zylo would be allocated $50,000 of gain that would not be taxable under I.R.C. Section 1032. Under the general rules of I.R.C. Section 705(a)(1), the allocation of gain to Zylo would increase the basis of its partnership interest to $150,000. If Zylo then sold its partnership interest for its $100,000 value, it would recognize a $50,000 loss. The regulations maintain that increasing the corporate partner's basis for gain not recognized under I.R.C. Section 1032 is "inconsistent with the intent of section 705" because it creates a tax loss (or reduces gain) where no economic loss was incurred and no offsetting tax gain was previously recognized.[71]

This rule of the regulations will apply if:

(1)   a corporation acquires an interest in a partnership that owns its stock (or the partnership subsequently acquires its stock in an exchanged basis transaction);

(2)   the partnership does not have an I.R.C. Section 754 election in effect when the corporation acquires its interest; and

(3)   the partnership later sells or exchanges the stock.

Upon the partnership's sale of the stock, the corporate partner will increase (or decrease) the basis of its partnership interest by the amount of gain (or loss) it would be allocated (ignoring I.R.C. Section 1032) if the partnership had an I.R.C. Section 754 election effect when it acquired its interest.[72]

> **Example (2):** The MNO Partnership has $90,000 of contributed capital which it uses to purchase stock in the Perlo Corporation for $30,000 and land for $60,000. When the stock has appreciated to $120,000 and the land appreciated to $150,000, Partner M sells his one-third partnership interest to Perlo for $90,000. No I.R.C. Section 754 election is in effect. The

---

[70]   T.D. 8986 (Mar. 29, 2002).

[71]   Treas. Reg. § 1.705-2(a).

[72]   Treas. Reg. § 1.705-2(b).

partnership later sells the Perlo stock for $150,000, realizing a gain of $120,000. Although Perlo's share of the gain is $40,000, that gain is not recognized under I.R.C. Section 1032.

If an I.R.C. Section 754 election was in effect in the year Perlo acquired its partnership interest, Perlo would have obtained a $60,000 basis increase (under I.R.C. Section 743(b)) for its share of partnership property. This adjustment would have been allocated $30,000 to the stock and $30,000 to the land (under I.R.C. Section 755). Therefore, had the election been in effect, Perlo would be allocated only $10,000 of gain when the partnership sold the stock. Accordingly, Perlo increases the basis of its partnership interest by $10,000 as a result of the stock sale.

The regulations contain an anti-abuse rule to prevent avoidance through tiered partnerships or similar devices. The rule applies if:

(1)   a corporation acquires an indirect interest in its own stock through a chain of two or more partnerships, and

(2)   the corporation is subsequently allocated gain or loss from the sale of the stock.

In that case, the bases of the interests in the partnerships included in the chain must be adjusted in a manner that is ". . . consistent with the purpose of the regulations." The proposed regulations provide extensive examples to illustrate the kinds of adjustments that would be required.[73]

The regulations apply to gain or loss allocated in sales or exchanges of stock occurring after December 6, 1999.[74]

[b]   Limitation on Basis Adjustment if Partnership Makes Distribution to Another Partner

The Service has issued proposed regulations that limit the basis increase allowed to a corporate partner for gain not recognized under I.R.C. Section 1032 where another partner has received a distribution from the partnership that resulted in recognition of gain. These proposed regulations apply to situations in which

(1)   a corporation owns an interest in a partnership that owns its stock,

(2)   the partnership distributes money to another partner who recognizes gain (under I.R.C. Section 731) in a year when no I.R.C. Section 754 election is in effect, and

(3)   the partnership subsequently sells or exchanges the stock.[75]

For the reasons described in the preceding section, the Service maintains that it is "inconsistent with the intent of Sections 705 and 1032" to increase the basis of the

---

[73] Treas. Reg. § 1.705-2(c).

[74] Treas. Reg. § 1.705-2(e).

[75] 67 Fed. Reg. 15132 (Mar. 29, 2002).

corporate partner's interest in the partnership by the full amount of gain from the stock sale that it does not recognize under I.R.C. Section 1032.[76] Accordingly, the proposed regulations limit the increase (or decrease) to the corporate partner's basis in its partnership interest from the stock sale to the amount of gain (or loss) it would have recognized (ignoring I.R.C. Section 1032) if an I.R.C. Section 754 election had been in effect, for the year in which the partnership made the distribution.[77]

> **Example:**[78] Albert, Betty, and Casco Corporation form partnership ABC. Albert and Betty each contribute $10,000 and Casco contributes $20,000 for their partnership interests. ABC purchases Casco stock for $10,000, which appreciates in value to $70,000. ABC distributes $25,000 to Albert in complete liquidation of his partnership interest in a year when an I.R.C. Section 754 election is not in effect. ABC later sells the Casco stock for $70,000, realizing a gain of $60,000. Casco's share of the gain is $40,000, but under I.R.C. Section 1032, it does not recognize that gain.
>
> If ABC had an I.R.C. Section 754 election in effect when it made the distribution to Albert, Casco would increase the basis of its interest in the ABC partnership by its $40,000 share of gain from the subsequent sale of its stock. That would occur because ABC would increase the basis of partnership property[79] by the $15,000 gain Albert recognized on the distribution.[80] The basis increase would have been allocated to the Casco stock, increasing its basis to $25,000.[81]
>
> In that case, ABC would have recognized $45,000 ($70,000 minus $25,000 basis in the Casco stock) when it later sold the stock and Casco's share would have been only $30,000 (not recognized under I.R.C. Section 1032). Since Casco's share of the gain from the stock sale would be $30,000 if the partnership had an I.R.C. Section 754 election in effect when the distribution to Albert occurred, Casco's basis increase from the subsequent sale of the stock is limited to $30,000.
>
> The proposed regulations also apply to tiered partnership arrangements.[82] Thus, the basis limitation applies if a corporation indirectly owns an interest in its own stock through a chain of two or more partnerships, and a partnership in the chain distributes money to a partner that recognizes gain on the distribution during a year in which the partnership does not have an I.R.C. Section 754 election in effect. Upon a subsequent sale of the stock, the bases of the interests in the partnerships in the chain are adjusted in a consistent manner.

---

[76] Prop. Treas. Reg. § 1.705-2(a).

[77] Prop. Treas. Reg. § 1.705-2(b)(2)(i).

[78] Prop. Treas. Reg. § 1.705-2(b)(2)(ii).

[79] I.R.C. § 734(b)(1)(A).

[80] I.R.C. §§ 731(a), 734(b)(1)(A).

[81] Treas. Reg. §§ 1.734-1(b), 1.755-1(c)(1)(ii).

[82] Prop. Treas. Reg. § 1.705-2(c)(1).

Generally, the proposed regulations apply to sales or exchanges of stock occurring on or after March 29, 2002.[83]

[D] Basis Adjustment When Partner or Partnership Debt Is Discharged

Generally, a taxpayer recognizes income to the extent that his debts are discharged without payment. If a partnership debt is discharged, the partnership separately accounts for the debt discharge, and each partner is allocated his distributive share of that income.[84] Inclusion of debt-discharge income in a partner's distributive share results in a corresponding increase in the basis of his partnership interest.

No debt-discharge income is recognized by a taxpayer who is insolvent or bankrupt.[85] In lieu of income recognition, the taxpayer (1) reduces certain tax attributes (such as net operating loss and capital loss carryovers and unused credits) by the amount of the canceled debt, and (2) uses any remaining amount to decrease his basis in his depreciable property.[86]

Alternatively, the taxpayer may elect to reduce his basis in depreciable property before reducing his tax attributes. For this purpose, a partner who is insolvent or bankrupt when a partnership debt or his individual liability is canceled may treat the basis of his partnership interest as depreciable property to the extent of his share of the partnership's depreciable property.[87] This treatment is allowed only if the partnership makes a corresponding reduction in the basis of its depreciable property for that partner. Similar rules apply if the debt is a qualified real property business indebtedness (*see* Chapter 3).

When a partnership debt is discharged, the income exclusions, tax attribute, and basis-reduction rules apply to each partner separately, not at the partnership level.[88] The partnership separately accounts for the debt-discharge income, and each partner's distributive share of that income is allocated to him.[89] Solvent partners are taxed on their allocable share of the debt-discharge income, while insolvent or bankrupt partners exclude these amounts and either reduce their tax attributes, or elect to reduce the basis of their depreciable assets. (For additional discussion of debt-discharge income, see Chapter 3.)

When a partnership debt is canceled, each partner is deemed to receive a cash distribution equal to the decrease in his share of partnership liabilities.[90] The amount of cash the partner is deemed to receive generally equals the basis increase

---

[83] Prop. Treas. Reg. § 1.705-2(e).

[84] I.R.C. § 702.

[85] I.R.C. §§ 61, 108.

[86] I.R.C. § 108(b).

[87] I.R.C. § 1017(b)(3)(C).

[88] I.R.C. § 108(d)(6).

[89] I.R.C. § 702.

[90] I.R.C. § 752(b).

from his share of the partnership's debt-discharge income. Therefore, no net change in the basis of his interest occurs.[91] This is not true; however, if the partner's share of partnership income differs from his share of partnership liabilities.

> **Example:** Sam is a general partner who owns 90 percent of the profits and losses of the ST Partnership. The basis in his partnership interest is $20,000. Toni is a limited partner who owns 10 percent of partnership profits and losses, and the basis of her interest is zero. As the result of a bankruptcy proceeding, a $10,000 recourse partnership debt is discharged. Sam is allocated $9,000 of debt-discharge income, and the basis in his partnership interest increases to $29,000. Because Sam is the sole general partner, the entire recourse debt is included in the basis of his interest, and he is deemed to receive a $10,000 cash distribution when the liability is extinguished. (For discussion of partner's share of liabilities, see § 5.05, *infra*.) The $10,000 deemed-cash distribution decreases Sam's basis in his interest to $19,000. Toni is allocated $1,000 of debt-discharge income, and the basis in her interest increases to $1,000. As a limited partner, she does not share in recourse partnership debt, and she is not deemed to receive any cash distribution when the liability decreases.

[E]   Basis Adjustment on Sale, Exchange, or Liquidation of Partnership Interest

On the day a partner sells, exchanges, or liquidates his entire partnership interest, the partnership's tax year closes for him. The selling partner must determine his distributive share of partnership income or loss up to that date and report it on his individual tax return.[92] (See discussions of sale of a partnership interest at Chapter 12 and liquidation of a partnership interest in Chapters 10 and 13.)

In determining the tax consequences of the sale, exchange, or liquidation, the partner's basis in his partnership interest increases or decreases to reflect his distributive share as well as any other adjustments required for the portion of the year preceding the disposition.[93]

> **Example:** The NP Partnership and all of its partners use a calendar tax year. On July 1, 19X1, Nora sells her entire partnership interest to Quentin for $20,000 in cash. On the date of the sale, Nora's basis in her partnership interest is $5,000, and her distributive share of partnership income up to July 1, 19X1 is $12,000. Nora must report $12,000 of income from NP on her 19X1 tax return. The basis in her partnership interest increases to $17,000 on the date of sale to reflect her $12,000 share of partnership income.

---

[91] *See* S. Rep. No. 1035, 96th Cong., 2d Sess. 22 (1980).

[92] I.R.C. § 706(a), (c)(2)(A).

[93] Treas. Reg. §§ 1.705-1(a)(1), 1.706-1(c)(2). The partner determines his share of partnership income up to the date of sale or liquidation closing the partnership books on that date or prorating partnership income for the entire year.

The partnership's tax year does not close for a partner selling less than his entire partnership interest. To determine his gain or loss, the selling partner computes the basis in his entire interest on the date of the sale as if he were selling his entire interest.[94] He then allocates a portion of that basis to the portion of the partnership interest that was sold.

> **Example:** Assume the facts in the preceding example, except that Nora only sells half of her partnership interest to Quentin for $10,000. The partnership tax year does not close for Nora on July 1, 19X1, and her basis does not increase by any portion of her distributive share of partnership income for the year. Thus, the basis for her entire interest on July 1, 19X1 is $5,000. Nora's basis for the half interest she sells to Quentin is $2,500 on the date of sale.

[F] Order of Basis Adjustments

The order in which the basis adjustments required under I.R.C. Section 705 are made is important because specific tax benefits are limited by each partner's basis in his partnership interest. A partner's basis limits:

(1) the deduction for his share of partnership losses (*see* § 5.01[F][1], *infra*);

(2) his basis in any property distributed to him by the partnership (*see* § 5.01[F][2], *infra*);

(3) the amount of cash he may receive from the partnership without recognizing taxable gain (*see* § 5.01[F][3], *infra*).

Any negative adjustments made before basis is determined for these purposes can have adverse tax consequences.

[1] Loss-Deduction Limitation

A partner may deduct his distributive share of partnership losses only to the extent of the basis in his partnership interest at the end of the partnership's tax year.[95] To determine his year-end basis for this purpose, a partner:

(1) increases his basis by his distributive shares of partnership taxable income, tax-exempt income, and excess depletion, for the current year and all prior years; and

(2) decreases his basis by

(a) all distributions he received,

(b) his share of noncapital, nondeductible expenses,

(c) his share of depletion deductions, and

(d) his share of partnership losses, except for the current year's losses and losses carried over from a prior year.

---

[94] Treas. Reg. § 1.705-1(a)(1).

[95] I.R.C. § 704(d).

The effect of this ordering is that a partner's basis increases and decreases to reflect all adjustments required by I.R.C. Section 705(a), except for his share of the current year's losses and losses carried over from prior years.

[2]   Distributed Property

A partner's basis in property he receives from the partnership in a nonliquidating distribution generally is the same as the partnership's basis in the property.[96] However, a partner's basis in the distributed property cannot exceed the basis in his partnership interest immediately before the distribution.[97] To determine that basis, contributions the partner made and distributions he received up to that time are taken into account. If cash and property are distributed in the same transaction, the cash is deemed to be distributed first.[98] Because basis adjustments for a partner's distributive share of partnership items such as income or loss, tax-exempt income, and depletion are made at the close of the tax year, they do not affect basis for distributions made during the year.

> **Example:** Peter, a calendar-year taxpayer, is a partner in the PQ Partnership, which also uses the calendar year. At the beginning of the current year, Peter's basis in his partnership interest is $10,000. On July 1, the partnership distributes a parcel of undeveloped land to Peter in which the partnership's basis is $6,000. On September 1, the partnership distributes $2,000 in cash and some machinery to him. The partnership's basis in the machinery is $3,000.

The distributions are recorded as follows:

Peter's basis at the beginning of year	$10,000
July 1, land distributions	(6,000)
	$4,000
September 1, cash distribution	(2,000)
	$2,000
September 1, machinery distribution	(2,000)
(Peter's basis in machinery is $2,000)	
Peter's basis after the distributions	$0

The result of the July 1 distribution is that Peter's basis in the land is $6,000 (the same as the partnership's basis), and the basis in his partnership interest decreases to $4,000. Although the partnership's basis in the machinery distributed on September 1 is $3,000, Peter's basis in it is limited to $2,000, because his $4,000 basis at the time of the distribution must first be reduced by the $2,000 cash distributed at the same time.[99]

---

[96] I.R.C. § 732(a).

[97] I.R.C. § 732(a)(2).

[98] I.R.C. § 732(a).

[99] If the partnership has an I.R.C. § 754 election in effect when the distribution occurs, the basis of its assets increases by the $1,000 basis that seems to disappear as a result of the distribution.

[3] Gain Recognized on Cash Distribution

A partner is taxable on a cash distribution to the extent that the amount of cash he receives exceeds the basis in his partnership interest immediately before the distribution.[100] In this situation the partner determines his basis before the distribution as he would when determining the basis of distributed property, discussed in the preceding section. If cash and property are distributed in the same transaction, the cash is considered to be distributed first.

> **Example:** Assume the same facts as in the Example above, except that $5,000 in cash is distributed to Peter on September 1 instead of $2,000. Peter's basis at the time of the distribution is only $4,000, so he must recognize $1,000 of gain. Because the cash distribution reduces Peter's basis in his partnership interest to zero, his basis in the distributed machinery is zero.

The distributions are recorded as follows:

Peter's basis at the beginning of year	$10,000
July 1, land distributions	(6,000)
	$4,000
September 1, cash distribution	(5,000)
(Peter recognizes $1,000 of gain)	$0
September 1, machinery distribution	$0
(Peter's basis in machinery is zero)	
Peter's basis after the distributions[101]	$0

[4] Marketable Securities

Under I.R.C. Section 731(c), a partner recognizes gain on certain distributions of marketable securities. However, the partner's basis in his partnership interest and the partnership's adjusted basis in its remaining assets are determined without regard to this provision.[102] The rules for determining the distributee partner's basis in its partnership interest are applied as if no gain is recognized, and no adjustment is made to the basis of the distributed securities. Any basis increase or decrease for undistributed property under I.R.C. Section 734 (if the partnership has an I.R.C. Section 754 election in effect) is made as if no gain is recognized and no basis adjustment made to the property. (For discussion of I.R.C. Section 731(c), see Chapter 8.)

---

[100] I.R.C. § 731(a).

[101] If the partnership has an I.R.C. § 754 election in effect when the distribution occurs, the basis of its assets increases by the $1,000 gain the partner recognizes on the distribution and by the $3,000 of basis "lost" on the distribution of the machinery.

[102] I.R.C. § 731(c)(5).

[5]   Advance or Draw Taken

An advance or draw of money or property against a partner's distributive share of partnership income is not treated as an immediate distribution, but rather as a distribution occurring on the last day of the partnership's tax year.[103] The partner's basis in his partnership interest immediately before this year-end distribution increases by his distributive share of partnership income for the year. This rule allows a partner to withdraw cash from the partnership without being taxed on the distribution.

> **Example:** George's basis in his partnership interest at the beginning of the partnership tax year is $3,000. He withdraws $3,000 each month during the year as an advance against his expected share of partnership income; he is obligated to repay any excess. George's distributive share of partnership income for the year is $40,000, increasing the year-end basis in his partnership interest to $43,000. His monthly withdrawals, totaling $36,000, are deemed to have been distributed on the last day of the year. Since the basis in his partnership interest at that time exceeds the distributions, George is not taxed on the withdrawals.
>
> If the withdrawals are not treated as advances, the first $3,000 distribution would reduce the basis in his partnership interest to zero, and the remaining $33,000 in distributions would be taxable under I.R.C. Section 731(a) as cash distributions in excess of basis.[104]

[6]   Encumbered Property Contributed or Distributed

Contributions and distributions of encumbered property usually result in multiple adjustments to the basis of the contributing partner's partnership interest. The partner is considered to have received a cash distribution equal to the entire amount of the liability he transfers to the partnership, and to have contributed cash equal to the amount by which his share of partnership liabilities increases.[105] Conversely, a partner who receives a distribution of encumbered property is considered to have contributed cash equal to the entire amount of the debt the partnership transfers to him, and to have received a cash distribution equal to the amount by which his share of partnership liabilities decreases.[106]

In both situations, the constructive cash contribution and distribution are deemed to have occurred simultaneously, and only the net change in the partner's liabilities is taken into account.[107] This net cash contribution or distribution, and the resulting basis increase or decrease, are deemed to occur immediately before the

---

[103]   Treas. Reg. § 1.731-1(a)(1)(ii).

[104]   Under I.R.C. § 705(a), the basis in a partnership interest is not increased as the partnership earns income, but only at the end of the year by the partner's distributive share of partnership income for the entire year. The only exception is if the partner's entire interest has been sold or liquidated during the year, in which case his basis increases by his share of income up to the time of the sale or liquidation. Treas. Reg. § 1.705-1(a)(1).

[105]   I.R.C. § 752.

[106]   I.R.C. § 752.

[107]   Rev. Rul. 79-205, 1979-2 C.B. 255. *See* Rev. Rul. 87-120, 1987-2 C.B. 161.

encumbered property is contributed or distributed.

[G] Partnership's Basis in Its Assets — How it Is Determined

Although this chapter focuses on the partner's basis in his partnership interest, it is important to note that the partnership must separately determine the basis in its assets. The partnership must know the basis in each of its assets to:

(1)   compute the amount of its allowable depreciation, amortization, or similar deductions;

(2)   determine the amount of gain or loss it realizes on a sale or other disposition of the property; and

(3)   determine a partner's basis in property the partnership distributes to him. (Generally, a partner's basis in distributed property is the same as the partnership's basis at the time of the distribution).

A partnership's initial basis in an asset depends on how it is acquired. A partnership's basis in contributed property is the same as the contributing partner's basis immediately before the contribution.[108] The basis of property acquired in other ways is determined under the general tax basis rules of the Internal Revenue Code. Accordingly, the partnership's basis in purchased property is its cost;[109] its basis in property received as a gift is the donor's basis;[110] and its basis in property acquired from a decedent equals the value of the property when the decedent died.[111] This initial basis is adjusted under the general rules of the Code to reflect depreciation, depletion, deferred expenses, partial dispositions, and similar items.[112]

Generally, events that change a partner's basis in his partnership interest do not affect the partnership's basis in its assets. However, this is not the case if the partnership has made an election under I.R.C. Section 754. In that situation, the basis of partnership property is adjusted:

(1)   When a partnership interest is transferred by sale or exchange, or upon the death of a partner. The basis of partnership property is adjusted to reflect differences between a new partner's basis in his partnership interest and his proportionate share of the total basis of the partnership's assets.

(2)   When a partnership distributes cash or property with a basis exceeding the recipient partner's basis in his partnership interest. The basis of assets retained by the partnership is adjusted to reflect any gain the partner recognizes on a cash distribution and any reduction in the basis of

---

[108] I.R.C. § 723.

[109] I.R.C. § 1012.

[110] I.R.C. § 1015.

[111] I.R.C. § 1014.

[112] I.R.C. § 1016.

distributed property. (See discussion of the I.R.C. Section 754 election in § 5.01[H][2], *infra*.)

[H] "Inside Basis" and "Outside Basis"

A partner's basis in his partnership interest is often referred to as "outside" basis, while the partnership's basis in its assets is called "inside" basis. When a partnership begins, each partner's basis in his partnership interest equals the basis in the property he contributes, and the partnership's basis in the contributed property carries over from the partners.[113] Consequently, the partnership's total "inside" basis for its assets equals the sum of all the partners' "outside" bases. In many partnerships, this equality between total inside and outside basis continues from year to year because the various adjustments to the basis of partnership assets resulting from its operations are the same as the adjustments to the basis of the partners' partnership interests.[114]

> **Example:** Arthur and Betty each contribute $150,000 to the newly formed AB partnership in exchange for a 50-percent interest in capital and profits. The partnership uses $200,000 of contributed capital to purchase a building. At this time, the partnership's total inside basis for its assets is $300,000, which equals the partners' total outside basis in their partnership interests. This is reflected on the partnership's balance sheet as follows:
>
> | Assets: | Adjusted Basis | Fair Market Value |
> |---|---|---|
> | Cash | $100,000 | $100,000 |
> | Building | 200,000 | 200,000 |
> | | $300,000 | $300,000 |
> | Capital: | | |
> | Arthur | $150,000 | $150,000 |
> | Betty | 150,000 | 150,000 |
> | | $300,000 | $300,000 |

In its first year, the partnership earns $20,000 from operations and is allowed a $6,000 depreciation deduction for the building. The partnership's basis in the building decreases to $194,000, and it has $20,000 of additional cash. Each partner's distributive share of partnership income is $7,000 ([$20,000 earned – $6,000 depreciation] x.50). Each partner's basis in his partnership interest is adjusted to reflect his distributive share of partnership income or loss, and inside basis equals outside basis. The AB balance sheet now appears as follows:

---

[113] I.R.C. §§ 722, 723.

[114] The required adjustments to the basis of partnership interests are found in I.R.C. § 705(a).

Assets:	Adjusted Basis	Fair Market Value
Cash	$120,000	$120,000
Building	$200,000	$200,000
	(6,000) depr	(6,000) depr
	$194,000	$194,000
	$314,000	$314,000
Capital:		
Arthur	$157,000	$157,000
Betty	157,000	157,000
	$314,000	$314,000

[1] Events That Upset Equivalence of Inside Basis and Outside Basis

The equivalence between the partnership's inside basis and the partners' total outside basis is upset when the following events occur:

(1) *A partner acquires a partnership interest through a sale or exchange.* The new partner's basis in his partnership interest is its cost, and outside basis increases or decreases to reflect his share of the current value of partnership assets. This change in outside basis does not affect the inside basis of the partnership's assets.

Example: Using the facts in the example in § 5.01[8], above, assume that Charles purchases Betty's partnership interest at the beginning of Year 2 for $160,000. Charles's basis in his partnership interest is his cost of $160,000; the total outside basis of $317,000 ($157,000 + $160,000) now exceeds the inside basis of $314,000. The balance sheet appears as follows:

Assets:	Adjusted Basis	Fair Market Value
Cash	$120,000	$120,000
Building	$200,000	$200,000
	(6,000) depr	(6,000) depr
	$194,000	$194,000
	$314,000	$314,000
Capital:		
Arthur	$157,000	$157,000
Charles	160,000	160,000
	$317,000	$317,000

(2) *A partner dies.* A successor's basis in a partnership interest received from a deceased partner equals the value of the interest at the time of the partner's death.[115] Although the successor's outside basis increases or decreases to reflect his share of the current value of partnership assets, a partner's death does not affect the partnership's inside basis in its assets.

---

[115] I.R.C. § 1014.

Example: Use the same facts as in the example above, but assume that Betty dies and Charles inherits Betty's partnership interest. Charles's basis in the partnership interest is $160,000, its fair market value at Betty's death. As in the example above, total inside basis is $314,000, while total outside basis is $317,000.

(3)   ***A partnership distributes cash or property with a basis exceeding the recipient partner's basis in his partnership interest.*** Although the total basis of partnership assets decreases by its basis in the distributed property, the recipient partner's basis cannot decrease below zero.[116] Therefore, the decrease in the partnership's inside basis exceeds the decrease in the partner's outside basis.

Example: Donald and Edward are equal partners in the DE partnership. The partnership and both partners use a calendar tax year. On December 31, the partnership distributes $300,000 of its cash to Donald. Immediately before the distribution, the partnership's balance sheet is as follows:

Assets:	Adjusted Basis	Fair Market Value
Cash	$400,000	$400,000
Land	100,000	100,000
	$500,000	$500,000
Capital:		
Donald	$250,000	$250,000
Edward	250,000	250,000
	$500,000	$500,000

The distribution decreases Donald's basis in his partnership interest to zero, and he recognizes gain of $50,000 — the amount by which the cash distribution ($300,000) exceeds his basis ($250,000). The partners' total outside basis now exceeds the partnership's total inside basis by $50,000. Here is the balance sheet:

Assets:	Adjusted Basis	Fair Market Value
Cash	$100,000	$100,000
Land	100,000	100,000
	$200,000	$200,000
Capital:		
Donald	$0	$100,000
Edward	250,000	100,000
	$250,000	$200,000

---

[116] I.R.C. § 733.

[2]   Restoring Equivalence: I.R.C. Section 754 Election

Most disparities between the partnership's inside and the partners' total outside basis are eliminated if the partnership has a basis-adjustment election (under I.R.C. Section 754) in effect when the transfer or distribution creating the disparity occurs. Under the election, the bases of partnership assets are adjusted under I.R.C. Section 743(b) (for transfers of interests) or I.R.C. Section 734(b) (for distributions) in a manner that restores equality between inside and outside basis. For discussion of basis adjustments relating to distributions, see § 8.07, *infra*.

If no I.R.C. Section 754 election is made, disparities between inside and outside basis change the timing and character of a partner's income. A partner whose outside basis exceeds his proportionate share of the partnership's inside basis generally realizes more taxable income from partnership operations than he would if no disparity existed. This occurs because the lower basis of partnership assets results in smaller depreciation deductions and more gain when partnership assets are sold. However, the partner's increased income is offset when he disposes of his partnership interest. Because the basis in his partnership interest is increased by his distributive share of partnership income, he realizes less gain (or a greater loss) when he sells or liquidates the interest.

Although the partner's total gain or loss may be the same, he loses the time value of his tax dollars. In addition, because the sale or liquidation of a partnership interest generally is treated as the sale of a capital asset,[117] the partner may be limited to a capital loss when he sells his partnership interest, even though his earlier distributive share of partnership income was ordinary.

[I]   Relationship Between Partner's Basis and Capital Account

A partnership keeps track of each partner's economic investment in the partnership through a financial record called a capital account. Although capital accounts are maintained for financial purposes, the amount and timing of adjustments to these accounts usually are governed by tax, rather than financial accounting, rules. Tax rules are used because the Service will not respect partnership agreement provisions allocating income or loss items among partners unless their capital accounts are maintained in accordance with detailed tax regulations under I.R.C. Section 704(b).[118]

A partner's opening capital account generally equals the value of his contribution to the partnership (*e.g.*, cash plus the net value of any contributed property). As the partnership continues in existence, the capital account increases or decreases to reflect the partner's share of partnership income or loss and withdrawals. Ordinarily, capital accounts are not adjusted when the value of partnership assets changes and therefore, they do not reflect the current value of the partnership interests. The value of a partnership interest can be determined by

---

[117] Under I.R.C. § 741, a sale of a partnership interest is treated as a sale of a capital asset except to the extent that I.R.C. § 751 applies.

[118] Treas. Reg. § 1.704-1.4.

assuming a hypothetical sale of the partnership assets and then crediting the partners' accounts for the cash that would be received. In limited circumstances, a partnership may adjust its capital accounts to reflect the current value of partnership property if necessary for certain business purposes described in the regulations.[119]

§ 5.02   ALTERNATIVE METHOD FOR DETERMINING BASIS: I.R.C. SECTION 705(b)

A partner must know the basis in his partnership interest only in certain circumstances. Many partners do not keep track of the basis adjustments resulting from partnership operations. Therefore, over time, it may be difficult — or impossible — for some partners to reconstruct these adjustments. In those situations, the regulations under I.R.C. Section 705(b) prescribe rules allowing a partner to determine the basis in his partnership interest by reference to his proportionate share of the basis of the partnership's assets.

For purposes of I.R.C. Section 705(b), a partner's proportionate share of the basis of partnership property is determined by reference to the basis of the assets that would be received if the partnership were liquidated. For example, a partner entitled to receive 25 percent of partnership assets on liquidation has a basis in his partnership interest equal to 25 percent of the basis of partnership assets.[120]

If the partnership has liabilities, a partner's proportionate share of the basis of partnership property is computed net of the liabilities.[121] The partner's basis is then increased by his share of the partnership liabilities as determined under the rules of I.R.C. Section 752 (see § 5.03, infra). This procedure is necessary because a partner's share of partnership liabilities may differ from the share of partnership assets that the partner is entitled to receive in a liquidation.

The alternative rule for determining basis in a partnership interest may be used if:

(1)   a partner cannot practically determine his basis under the general rules of I.R.C. Section 705(a); or

(2)   in the IRS' opinion, it is reasonable to conclude that the results of using the alternative method will not vary substantially from the results that would be obtained under the general rules.[122]

A partner seeking to use the alternative rule must show why the general method of I.R.C. Section 705(a) is impractical and provide satisfactory evidence of the

---

[119] Treas. Reg. § 1.704-1(b)(2)(iv)(f) specifies when and how capital accounts may be revalued to reflect the current value of partnership property. *See* Chapter 4.

[120] Treas. Reg. § 1.705-1(b), *Example (1)*.

[121] Treas. Reg. § 1.705-1(b), *Example (3)*.

[122] Treas. Reg. § 1.705-1(b). *See, e.g.*, Long v. Comm'r, 77 T.C. 1045 (1981) (alternate method allowed to show that partner's basis equaled his negative capital account plus share of liabilities). *But see* Priv. Ltr. Rul. 8314039 (IRS refused to rule on correctness of basis computed as negative capital account plus liabilities).

partnership's basis in its assets.[123] If the partnership has been operating for a number of years, it should not be difficult to show that it is impractical to reconstruct the basis adjustments under I.R.C. Section 705(a). However, in other situations, the effort required to show that the alternate method produces substantially the same results as the general rule may make it simpler to use the general-rule method from the outset.

§ 5.03 EFFECT OF PARTNERSHIP LIABILITIES ON BASIS OF PARTNER'S INTEREST IN PARTNERSHIP

[A] Overview of General Rules

Any change in a partner's share of partnership liabilities causes a corresponding change in the basis of his partnership interest.[124] This correlation between liabilities and basis exists because a partner is deemed to:

(1)   contribute money to the partnership when his share of partnership liabilities increases or he individually assumes a partnership debt;[125] and

(2)   receive a distribution of money from the partnership when his share of partnership liabilities decreases or the partnership becomes liable for his individual debt.[126]

The partner's basis increases by the amount of money he is deemed to contribute[127] and decreases by the amount of money deemed distributed to him.[128]

Example (1): Allen and Barbara are equal partners in the AB general partnership. The partnership obtains a $12,000 recourse loan from a bank, payable in ten equal monthly installments. When the liability is incurred, each partner's share of partnership liabilities increases by $6,000. Therefore, each partner is deemed to contribute $6,000, cash, to the partnership, and each partner's basis in his partnership interest increases by that amount. One month later, AB pays $2,000 against the outstanding loan balance, and each partner's share of partnership liabilities decreases by $1,000. Allen and Barbara each are deemed to receive a $1,000 cash distribution, and the bases of their partnership interests decrease by that amount.

Example (2): Continuing the previous example, assume that Carl now contributes $20,000, cash, to the partnership in exchange for a 20-percent

---

[123] Coloman v. Comm'r, 540 F.2d 427 (9th Cir. 1976), aff'g T.C. Memo. 1974-78. The court refused to estimate the basis of the partnership's assets under the rule in Cohan v. Comm'r, 39 F.2d 540 (2d Cir. 1930).

[124] A partner has a single basis in a partnership interest even if he is both a general and limited partner. Rev. Rul. 84-53, 1984-1 C.B. 159. See also Priv. Ltr. Rul. 8350006.

[125] I.R.C. § 752(a); Treas. Reg. § 1.752-1(b).

[126] I.R.C. § 752(b); Treas. Reg. § 1.752-1(c).

[127] I.R.C. §§ 705, 722.

[128] I.R.C. §§ 705, 733.

interest in capital and profits. Because Carl's share of partnership liabilities increases by $2,000 (20 percent of $10,000 loan balance), he is deemed to contribute an additional $2,000 in cash. The additional cash contribution increases Carl's basis for his partnership interest to $22,000. Both Allen's and Barbara's shares of partnership liabilities decrease by $1,000, and each is deemed to receive a $1,000 cash distribution; the bases of their partnership interests decrease by that amount.

A purported partnership liability does not increase a partner's basis if, in substance, no current obligation exists. Thus, sham, contested, speculative, or contingent partnership liabilities may be disregarded. Similarly, a purported partnership debt to a partner is not characterized as a partnership liability if it more closely resembles a capital contribution than a loan.

In Notice 2000-44,[129] the Service warns that it will disallow losses and impose penalties on participants and promoters involved in arrangements that purport to give taxpayers artificially high basis in partnership interests to generate deductible losses on disposition of the interests.[130] The following example illustrates one type of transaction that may be subject to IRS scrutiny:

> **Example:** XCo borrows $3,000,000 in cash under a loan agreement that provides for an inflated stated rate of interest and a stated principal amount of only $2,000,000. XCo contributes the $3,000,000 to the XY Investment Partnership, and XY assumes the indebtedness. Upon XCo's later sale of its interest in XY for a nominal amount, XCo claims a loss deduction of $1,000,000.

The Service would disallow the loss, maintaining that a loss attributable to an artificially overstated basis in a partnership interest is not deductible because no actual economic consequences exist.[131] The Notice indicates that the Service believes that this kind of arrangement is being marketed to individual taxpayers wishing to avoid large capital gains from unrelated transactions, often by netting gains and losses through grantor trusts. The Service warns that willful concealment, or advising such concealment, in this manner may result in criminal prosecution.

A partner's basis is affected by a partnership liability only if his "share" of the liability increases or decreases. The rules for determining a partner's share of a liability are set forth in complex regulations under I.R.C. Section 752. These rules are summarized as follows:

(1) A partner's share of a partnership liability depends on whether the obligation is recourse or nonrecourse. A liability is recourse to the extent

---

[129] 2000-2 C.B. 255.

[130] 2000-2 C.B. 255. See 1999-2 C.B. 761, Notice 99-59, for a similar warning concerning corporate transactions.

[131] Notice 2000-44 cites the following authorities for the principle that an artificial loss lacking economic substance is not allowable: ACM Pshp. v. Comm'r, 157 F.3d 231, 252 (3d Cir. 1998), *cert. denied*, 526 U.S. 1017 (1999); Scully v. U.S., 840 F.2d 478, 486 (7th Cir. 1988); Shoenberg v. Comm'r, 77 F.2d 446, 448 (8th Cir. 1935). Notice 2000-44 states that such losses also may be disallowed under specific anti-abuse rules in the Code and regulations, particularly I.R.C. § 752 and Treas. Reg. § 1.701-2.

that any partner (or person related to a partner) bears the economic risk of loss for the debt if the partnership cannot pay it.[132] Conversely, a liability is nonrecourse to the extent that no partner (or related person) bears the economic risk of loss.[133]

(2) A partner's share of a recourse partnership liability is the economic risk of loss he bears for the debt.[134] This amount is what he would be obligated to pay a partnership creditor or contribute to the partnership to satisfy the debt, without reimbursement, if

   (a) all partnership liabilities become due;

   (b) all partnership assets become worthless;

   (c) the partnership sells all its assets for no consideration other than relief of its liabilities; and

   (d) the partnership liquidates all the partners' interests.[135]

(3) Each partner's share of nonrecourse partnership liabilities equals the sum of the following items[136]

   (a) the partner's share of partnership minimum gain, determined pursuant to the regulations under I.R.C. Section 704(b).[137]

   (b) the amount of gain allocable to the partner under

      (i) I.R.C. Section 704(c) regarding property the partner contributed to the partnership (I.R.C. Section 704(c) property), and

      (ii) rules similar to I.R.C. Section 704(c) regarding property the partnership revalued on its books (reverse I.R.C. Section 704(c) property),[138] if all partnership property subject to nonrecourse liabilities were sold for the amount of the liabilities.

   (c) The partner's share of excess nonrecourse liabilities (i.e., nonrecourse liabilities remaining after subtracting (a) and (b) above). This share may be determined:

      (i) from the partner's proportionate share of partnership profits; or

      (ii) in the manner that the deductions attributable to the nonrecourse liabilities are reasonably expected to be allocated.

---

[132] Treas. Reg. § 1.752-1(a)(1).

[133] Treas. Reg. § 1.752-1(a)(2).

[134] Treas. Reg. § 1.752-2(a).

[135] Treas. Reg. § 1.752-2(b)–(j).

[136] Treas. Reg. § 1.752-3(a).

[137] See Treas. Reg. §§ 1.704-1(b)(4)(iv)(f), 1.704-2.

[138] These rules are found at Treas. Reg. § 1.704(b)(1)–(2)(iv).

Excess nonrecourse liabilities may first be allocated to a partner up to his share of "excess" built-in gain from I.R.C. Section 704(c) property and reverse I.R.C. Section 704(c) property subject to the liability.[139]

[B] Nonrecourse Liabilities in Tax-Sheltered Investments

Under I.R.C. Section 704(d), a partner's deductions for partnership losses cannot exceed the basis in his partnership interest. A partner requiring additional basis to deduct his full share of losses may obtain it by contributing cash or property to the partnership or through the constructive contribution that occurs when his share of partnership liabilities increases.

A partner may prefer to acquire basis through an increase in partnership liabilities because this increases his allowable deductions without requiring any additional out-of-pocket investment in the partnership. If the partnership incurs nonrecourse liabilities, a partner increases his allowable deductions under I.R.C. Section 704(d) even though he does not bear an economic risk of loss on the debt.

The inclusion of nonrecourse liabilities in the basis of partnership interests was a significant factor in the proliferation of syndicated limited partnership tax shelters that occurred before the 1986 Tax Reform Act. Partnerships with substantial nonrecourse liabilities attracted many high-bracket investors by promising tax deductions greatly in excess of the investors' cash investments. The high basis attributable to the debt allowed limited partners to deduct large partnership losses, reducing the tax on their income from other sources. A partner's investment was relatively free of risk because, under state law, a limited partner's liability to partnership creditors is limited to the partner's capital contribution.

Many of the issues discussed in this chapter arose in connection with partnerships incurring large nonrecourse liabilities in order to generate high basis and large tax deductions for limited partners. When considering these issues, keep in mind the effect of legislation designed to reduce the attractiveness of these highly leveraged tax shelters. The most important provisions are the passive loss limitation rules of I.R.C. Section 469 and the at-risk rules of I.R.C. Section 465. Both statutes restrict a partner's deductions for partnership losses, regardless of whether he has sufficient basis for purposes of I.R.C. Section 704(d), as discussed below.

[C] Interaction With At-Risk and Passive Activity Rules

Although a partner properly includes a share of nonrecourse debt in the basis of his partnership interest under I.R.C. Section 752, he may be barred from taking deductions attributable to that debt by the at-risk rules of I.R.C. Section 465. The statute limits a taxpayer's deductions from an activity to the amount he has at risk in it. This amount includes only out-of-pocket contributions plus the share of debt

---

[139] Treas. Reg. § 1.752-3(a)(3), as amended by T.D. 8906 (Oct. 31, 2000). The amendment, which added the allocation method in paragraph (c) is effective October 31, 2000. For complete discussion, see § 5.07[B], *infra*.

for which the partner has personal liability. Real estate activities generally are exempted from many of the at-risk rules, and nonrecourse debt continues to be quite important to those partnerships.

The failure of the at-risk rules to curb tax shelters resulted in enactment of the passive loss limitation rules in the 1986 Tax Reform Act. Under I.R.C. Section 469, a taxpayer may deduct losses from passive activities only up to the amount of his income from passive sources. Income or loss generally is passive if it is generated by a trade or business in which the taxpayer does not materially participate. A taxpayer materially participates if he has a substantial operating role in the activity. Because limited partners do not ordinarily participate in partnership operations, their partnership losses are passive and cannot offset income from an active trade or business or from portfolio investments. (See discussion of passive loss rules in Chapter 6.)

§ 5.04   PARTNERSHIP LIABILITIES DEFINED

[A]   General Rules

The constructive contribution and distribution rules of I.R.C. Section 752 apply only to the extent that a partnership commitment creates a genuine debt. A purported partnership liability may be disregarded or recharacterized for tax purposes if, in substance, no current obligation exists. For example, a debt will be ignored as a sham if the facts indicate that the parties never intended that the liability be repaid. Similarly, partners may not include a liability in basis if the likelihood of its being repaid is speculative or contingent upon the partnership's success. A purported loan to a partnership by a partner may be recharacterized as a capital contribution if it more closely resembles an equity investment than true debt. Partnership liabilities do not include obligations that the partnership is contesting.[140]

A cash-basis partnership's accrued but unpaid expenses and accounts payable are not partnership liabilities under I.R.C. Section 752.[141] This rule applies to obligations the partnership incurs and to obligations transferred to it by a cash-method taxpayer in connection with the contribution of the assets and liabilities of an established business.[142] In the case of a contribution, the expenses must be allocated to the contributing partner, who will be allowed the deduction when the partnership pays the expenses.

> **Example:** Charles and Damon are partners in the CD General Partnership, which uses the cash method of accounting. At the close of its tax year, CD has accrued interest expense of $1,000 and accounts payable of $500 for services performed for the partnership. The interest and accounts payable are not partnership liabilities for I.R.C. Section 752.

---

[140] Long v. Comm'r, 71 T.C. 1 (1978), *on reconsideration*, 71 T.C. 724 (1979), *remanded*, 660 F.2d 416 (10th Cir. 1981).

[141] Rev. Rul. 88-77, 1988-2 C.B. 128.

[142] H.R. Rep. No. 861, 98th Cong., 2d Sess. 856 (1984).

A partner is not considered obligated for a recourse partnership debt unless (1) the existence and amount of the partnership liability can be determined with reasonable certainty, and (2) it is not subject to contingencies that make it unlikely that the debt will be discharged.[143] Similarly, an obligation is not recognized if the facts and circumstances indicate that a plan exists to circumvent or avoid it.[144]

A debt is taken into account only once, even though a person bears liability for an obligation individually as well as in his capacity as a partner.[145]

A partner's share of partnership liabilities must be determined whenever necessary to determine his, or any other person's, tax liability.[146] In general, this determination is required whenever a partner's basis in his partnership interest must be known under I.R.C. Section 705.[147]

[B] Sham Liabilities

A liability may be disregarded for tax purposes if it is incurred in a tax-motivated transaction lacking economic substance.[148] Many sham liability cases involve nonrecourse debt incurred by a partnership to purchase property for a price greatly exceeding the property's actual value. The debt substantially increases the partners' bases in their partnership interests, allowing them to deduct the inflated depreciation and interest expenses generated by the property.

Because the liabilities are nonrecourse, the partners obtain these tax benefits even though they are unlikely to pay the excessive acquisition price. The seller often agrees to take the nonrecourse note, even though it will not be satisfied, if he receives the actual value of the property through the down payment or other payments from the partnership.

Recently enacted I.R.C. Section 7701(o), codifies the judicially-created economic substance doctrine and adds substantial penalties for transactions that lack economic substance.[149] Generally, the economic substance doctrine provides that a taxpayer may not obtain the tax benefits of a transaction that lacks a realistic

---

[143] *See* Treas. Reg. § 1.752-2(b)(4).

[144] Treas. Reg. § 1.752-2(b)(5). *See* Treas. Reg. § 1.752-2(j)(3).

[145] Treas. Reg. § 1.752-4(c).

[146] Treas. Reg. § 1.752-4(d).

[147] *See* Treas. Reg. § 1.705-1(a); § 5.01[A], *supra.*

[148] If the transaction is a "sham," all tax benefits may be disallowed, including depreciation deductions attributable to the taxpayer's cash investment and recourse liabilities. Cooper v. Comm'r, 88 T.C. 84 (1987); Falsetti v. Comm'r, 85 T.C. 332 (1985); Grodt & McKay Realty, Inc. v. Comm'r, 77 T.C. 1221 (1981). In Rice's Toyota World v. Comm'r, 752 F.2d 89 (4th Cir. 1985), *aff'g in part* 81 T.C. 184 (1983), the Tax Court disallowed both depreciation and interest deductions attributable to a recourse debt. The Fourth Circuit reversed the disallowance of the interest deduction, holding that the note represented a genuine obligation of the taxpayer even though it could not be considered part of the purchase price of property for depreciation purposes. *See* Agro Science Co. v. Comm'r, 934 F.2d 573 (5th Cir.), *cert. denied*, 502 U.S. 907 (1991) (partnership not allowed deduction for notes paid to Brazilian company when debt was sham created to generate tax benefits); Sterenbuch v. Comm'r, T.C. Memo. 1991-505; Janklow v. Comm'r, T.C. Memo. 1988-46.

[149] The Health Care and Education Reconciliation Act of 2010, Pub. L. No. 111-152 (Mar. 30, 2010).

possibility of profit and does not change the taxpayer's economic position independent of tax consequences. The economic substance test is closely related to the business purpose test, which disallows tax benefits that do not arise from a transaction entered into for business purposes.[150] The new statute addresses a difference between the circuit courts of appeal regarding application of the doctrine. Prior to the statute, a majority of the courts applied a conjunctive test under which a transaction lacked economic substance if it did not satisfy either of two separate tests:[151]

- An objective economic substance test requiring a realistic possibility of a profit in the transaction; and

- A subjective business purpose test requiring that the taxpayer engaged in the transaction for a business purpose other than tax avoidance.

Several courts, however, applied a disjunctive test holding that a transaction would be respected for tax purposes if it had either economic substance or a business purpose.[152]

The new statute clearly requires application of the conjunctive, two-prong, test, providing that the tax benefits from a transaction are not allowed if the transaction does not have economic substance *or* lacks a business purpose.[153] Both requirements must be met to avoid application of the economic substance doctrine. Accordingly, avoidance of the economic substance doctrine requires a showing that (1) the transaction changed the taxpayer's economic position in a meaningful way and (2) that taxpayer had a substantial business purpose for entering into the transaction. Under the statute, the economic substance doctrine will continue to be applied in the same manner as if I.R.C. Section 7701(o) had never been enacted. Thus, the new section does not change existing standards other than to clarify that the test is conjunctive rather than disjunctive.

I.R.C. Section 7701(o) does not affect the tax treatment of basic business transactions taxpayer's engage in because of a comparative tax advantage.[154] For example, the doctrine does not necessarily apply merely because a taxpayer chooses to capitalize a venture with debt rather than equity, uses a foreign rather than domestic business entity, or uses a particular reorganization form under subchapter C.

The economic substance doctrine does not apply if the taxpayer has a substantial non-tax purpose for engaging in a transaction. In this regard, a taxpayer may rely on the potential for profit from a transaction only if the present

---

[150] See Lipton, Codification of the Economic Substance Doctrine — Much Ado About Nothing?, J. Tax'n, June 2010.

[151] See, e.g., Coltec Indus. v. U.S., 454 F.3d 1340 (Fed. Cir. 2006); UPS of Am. v. Comm'r, 254 F.3d 1014 (11th Cir. 2001); ACM Pshp. v. Comm'r, 157 F.3d 231 (3d Cir. 1998).

[152] See, e.g., Rice's Toyota World v. Comm'r, 752 F.2d 89 (4th Cir. 1985).

[153] I.R.C. § 7701(o)(5)(A), (B). In 2010-40 I.R.B. 411, Notice 2010-62, the Service provides interim guidance regarding codification of the economic substance doctrine for transactions after March 31, 2010.

[154] Staff of the Joint Committee on Taxation, Technical Explanation of the Revenue Provisions of the "Reconciliation Act of 2010" (JCX-18-10, Mar. 21, 2010).

value of the reasonably expected pre-tax profits is substantial in relation to the present value of the expected tax benefits from the transaction. Fees and other expenses must be taken into account as expenses in determining pre-tax profits.

The economic substance doctrine does not apply to an individual's personal transactions and is limited to transactions connected to a trade or business or profit-seeking activity. Accordingly, estate and gift planning transfers are not affected. It is likely that personal tax planning related to investments are subject to the doctrine. Substantial non-tax purpose does not include state tax savings or financial accounting benefits relating to reduction of tax.

A key aspect of the new law is the penalty imposed on transactions that lack economic substance. Under amended I.R.C. Section 6662, a penalty of 20 percent is imposed on an underpayment of tax attributable to claimed tax benefits that are disallowed because a transaction lacked economic substance or failed to meet the requirements of a similar rule of law. The penalty is increased to 40 percent for an underpayment attributable to a transaction found to lack economic substance if the facts affecting the tax treatment of the transaction are not adequately disclosed in the return or in a statement attached to the return.

[C] Contingent Liabilities

Contingent liabilities are not included in the basis of a partnership's property or in a partner's basis in his partnership interest. A liability is contingent if, based on the facts and circumstances when it is incurred, it appears that debt will not be satisfied unless improbable future events occur.[155] Most contingent liability cases involve notes that are to be paid out of the future income or cash flow of a speculative business or investment activity. These notes are deemed to represent contingent rather than current liabilities because they will be satisfied only if the venture produces more income than realistically can be expected.

A liability is not contingent if it is secured by property approximately equal in value to the amount of the debt, because it is reasonable to assume that the debt will be repaid.[156] In determining the value of the security, the present value of the future income it will generate may be included if that amount can be realistically predicted.[157] Future income may not be taken into account if the amount is unproven or speculative.

---

[155] Gibson Products Co. v. U.S., 460 F. Supp. 1109 (N.D. Tex. 1978), aff'd, 637 F.2d 1041 (5th Cir. 1980); Estate of Baron v. Comm'r, 83 T.C. 542 (1984), aff'd, 798 F.2d 65 (2d Cir. 1986); Saviano v. Comm'r, 765 F.2d 643 (7th Cir. 1985); Brountas v. Comm'r, 692 F.2d 152 (1st Cir. 1982), rev'g 73 T.C. 491 (1979); HGA Cinema Trust v. Comm'r, 950 F.2d 1357 (7th Cir. 1991) (notes not valid indebtedness despite potential effects of a bankruptcy because no evidence shown that bankruptcy was realistic or anticipated event when incurred). See also Treas. Reg. § 1.752-2(b)(4).

[156] Bolger v. Comm'r, 59 T.C. 760 (1973), acq. 1976-2 C.B. 1; Jackson v. Comm'r, 86 T.C. 492 (1986); Dillingham v. U.S., 81-2 U.S.T.C. ¶ 9601 (W.D. Okla. 1981).

[157] In determining the value of property purchased with a nonrecourse note, the IRS will not include estimates of potential future value nor values projected on the basis of assumed rates of inflation. Rev. Rul. 84-5, 1984-1 C.B. 32, corrected in Ann. 84-102, 1984-45 I.R.B. 21.

[D] Obligations Treated As Liabilities Under Regulations Section 1.752-7

The Service has issued final regulations designed to curb certain abusive tax shelter transactions involving partnership assumptions of partner obligations designed to accelerate or duplicate losses.[158] Generally, these transactions involve contingent obligations that reduce the actual value of the property subject to the obligation but are not included in the basis of the property for tax purposes. The kind of abuse in question is illustrated in Notice 2000-44,[159] involving a taxpayer that contributes a purchased option to a partnership and writes an option that is assumed by the partnership. The taxpayer asserted that its basis for its partnership interest increased by the cost of the purchased call option but does not decrease under I.R.C. Section 752 when the partnership assumes the written call option obligation. When the partnership interest is sold for a low amount (because of the decreased value associated with the call option obligation), the taxpayer claims a tax loss even though no corresponding economic loss is incurred. The partnership also may claim a deduction when it incurs a loss on the option obligation.

The supporting rationale for this transaction, sometimes called a "Son of Boss" transaction, was the assertion that the obligation assumed by the partnership was not a liability for purposes of I.R.C. Section 752. Although the Code does not define the term "liability," case law and rulings generally provide that it includes only an obligation that creates or increases the partnership's basis for any asset (including cash attributable to borrowing), gives rise to a current partnership deduction, or, currently decreases a partner's basis in its partnership interest (under I.R.C. Section 705(a)(2)(B).[160] Accordingly, a liability for purposes of I.R.C. Section 752 generally does not include an obligation that gives rise to a deduction only when it is actually paid.

The new regulations are designed to preclude this kind of duplicative loss transaction. The regulations respond to a Congressional legislative mandate issued in connection with enactment of new I.R.C. Section 358(h).[161] That law requires taxpayers to reduce the basis of stock received in a corporate nonrecognition transaction by the amount of any liability assumed in the exchange and directed

---

[158] T.D. 9207, 70 Fed. Reg. 30334 (May 26, 2005), replacing proposed and temporary regulations issued in T.D. 9062, 68 Fed. Reg. 37414 (June 24, 2003). The regulations are generally effective for transactions after June 23, 2003. Special rules apply to assumptions of liabilities occurring after October 18, 1999, and before June 24, 2003. Treas. Reg. § 1.752-6(d)(1). Retroactive application of these regulations was sustained in Cemco Investors, LLC v. U.S., 515 F.3d 749 (7th Cir. 2008).

[159] 2000-2 C.B. 255.

[160] See, e.g., Rev. Rul. 88-77, 1988-2 C.B. 129; Salina Partnership L.P. v. Comm'r, T.C. Memo. 2000-352; COLM Producer, Inc. v. U.S., 460 F. Supp. 2d 713 (N.D. Tex. 2006); Rev. Rul. 95-26, 1995-1 C.B. 131; see also Marriott Int'l Resorts, L.P. v. U.S., 83 Fed. Cl. 291 (2008), aff'd, 586 F.3d 962 (Fed. Cir. 2009) (under pre-1995 law, taxpayer had indirect notice that obligation to close short sale might give rise to liability under I.R.C. § 752 for purposes of calculating partnership basis).

[161] Community Renewal Tax Relief Act of 2000, Pub. L. No. 106-554, 106th Cong., 2d Sess. (Dec. 21, 2000). Certain regulations apply only to assumptions of liabilities by a partnership after October 18, 1999, and before June 24, 2003. All other final regulations as well as the temporary regulations under I.R.C. Section 358, generally apply to liabilities assumed on or after June 24, 2003.

the Treasury to provide similar rules for partnership transactions. The new regulations relate to a partnership's assumption of certain fixed and contingent obligations in connection with issuance of a partnership interest.[162]

These regulations expand upon Notice 2000-44,[163] in which the Service warned that it will disallow losses and impose penalties on participants and promoters in arrangements that purport to give taxpayers artificially high bases in partnership interests in order to generate deductible losses on disposition of the interests. The following example illustrates one type of transaction that is subject to IRS scrutiny:

> **Example:** XCo borrows $3,000,000 in cash under a loan agreement that provides for an inflated stated rate of interest and a stated principal amount of only $2,000,000. XCo contributes the $3,000,000 to the XY Investment Partnership, and XY assumes the debt. Upon XCo's later sale of its interest in XY for a nominal amount, XCo claims a loss deduction of $1,000,000.

The Service would disallow the loss, maintaining that a loss attributable to an artificially overstated basis in a partnership interest is not deductible because no actual economic consequences exist.[164] The Service believes that this kind of arrangement is being marketed to individual taxpayers wishing to avoid large capital gains from unrelated transactions, often by netting gains and losses through grantor trusts. Taxpayers are warned that willful concealment, or advising such concealment, in this manner may result in criminal prosecution.

[E] Loans Treated As Capital Contributions — "Thin" Partnerships

A "loan" by a partner to his partnership may be recharacterized as an equity investment if that is the substance of the transaction.[165] The lending partner is then deemed to have made a capital contribution of the funds advanced to the partnership, and the basis of his partnership interest is increased by that amount.

---

[162] Treas. Reg. § 1.752-6.

[163] 2000-36 I.R.B. 255. See 1999-52 I.R.B. 761, Notice 99-59, for a similar warning concerning corporate transactions.

[164] Notice 2000-44 cites the following authorities for the principle that an artificial loss lacking economic substance is not allowable: ACM Pshp v. Comm'r, 157 F.3d 231, 252 (3d Cir. 1998); Scully v. U.S., 840 F.2d 478, 486 (7th Cir. 1988); Shoenberg v. Comm'r, 77 F.2d 446, 448 (8th Cir. 1935); Jade Trading, LLC v. U.S., 80 Fed. Cl. 11 (2007).

[165] Hambuechen v. Comm'r, 43 T.C. 90 (1964).

§ 5.05 GENERAL RULES GOVERNING PARTNER'S SHARE OF PARTNERSHIP LIABILITIES

[A] Overview of Regulations

Under the regulations in effect before 1989, partners shared recourse partnership liabilities in the ratio that they shared partnership losses, and nonrecourse liabilities in the ratio that they shared partnership profits. A debt was recourse if any partner was personally liable, and nonrecourse if no partner had personal liability. These regulations generated uncertainty and frequent litigation because they did not account for lending practices and financing techniques, such as guarantees, assumptions, and indemnities, that shift the risk of loss for a debt among partners without regard to whether the partnership borrowed on a recourse or nonrecourse basis.

In 1984, Congress directed the Treasury to revise its regulations to provide that a partner's share of each recourse partnership liability equals his economic risk of loss for the debt, taking into account current commercial lending practices. In December, 1991, the Treasury issued final regulations under I.R.C. Section 752 governing partners' shares of partnership liabilities.

Each partner's share of a recourse partnership liability equals the portion of the economic risk of loss he bears for the debt.[166] A partner bears the economic risk of loss for a liability to the extent that he or a related person would be obligated either to pay a partnership creditor or to contribute funds to the partnership to satisfy the debt, without reimbursement, if the partnership engaged in a hypothetical transaction called a "constructive liquidation."[167]

In a constructive liquidation, all partnership debts are presumed to be due and all partnership assets are assumed to be worthless. The effect of these rules is that a partner's share of a recourse partnership liability is the amount the partner would be obligated to pay from his personal funds if the partnership became completely unable to satisfy the debt.

The regulations coordinate the rules for determining a partner's share of nonrecourse partnership liabilities with the rules governing allocations of partnership gain or loss under I.R.C. Sections 704(b) and 704(c).[168] Each partner's share of nonrecourse partnership liabilities equals the sum of the following items:[169]

(1)   The partner's share of partnership minimum gain, determined pursuant to the regulations under I.R.C. Section 704(b).[170]

(2)   The partner's share of I.R.C. Section 704(c) minimum gain. This equals

---

[166]   Treas. Reg. § 1.752-2(a).

[167]   Treas. Reg. § 1.752-2(b).

[168]   Under the I.R.C. § 704(b) regulations. For discussion of the I.R.C. § 704(b) allocation rules and the definition of partnership minimum gain, see Chapter 4.

[169]   Treas. Reg. § 1.752-3(a).

[170]   *See* Treas. Reg. § 1.704-1(b)(4)(iv)(f).

gain that would be allocated to the partner

(a)   under I.R.C. Section 704(c) for contributed property (I.R.C. Section 704(c) property), and

(b)   in the same manner as under I.R.C. Section 704(c) for property the partnership revalued on its books (reverse I.R.C. Section 704(c) property),[171]

if all partnership property subject to nonrecourse liabilities were sold for the amount of the debts.

(3)   The partner's share of excess nonrecourse liabilities (i.e., total partnership nonrecourse liabilities remaining after subtracting the amounts determined under (1) and (2) above). A partner's share of the excess liabilities is computed by multiplying the partnership's total excess nonrecourse liabilities by the partner's percentage interest in partnership profits. Alternatively, the partnership may allocate the excess nonrecourse liabilities in the manner it reasonably expects that the deductions attributable to those liabilities will be allocated.

Excess nonrecourse liabilities may first be allocated to a partner up to his share of "excess" built-in gain from I.R.C. Section 704(c) property and reverse I.R.C. Section 704(c) property subject to the liability.[172] This "excess" built-in gain equals the amount by which such gain exceed the partner's share of I.R.C. Section 704(c) minimum gain computed under paragraph (2) above.

The effect of these rules is to increase a partner's share of nonrecourse liabilities by the nonrecourse deductions allocated to him (i.e., deductions attributable to nonrecourse partnership debts), and the proceeds of nonrecourse borrowings distributed to him. (See discussion of minimum gain in Chapter 6.) The resulting basis increase allows the partner (1) to deduct his share of partnership losses without limitation under I.R.C. Section 704(d) (which limits a partner's deduction for partnership losses to the basis of his partnership interest — see Chapter 6), and (2) to receive distributions derived from nonrecourse borrowings without recognizing gain under I.R.C. Section 731(a) (which provides that a partner recognizes gain when cash distributed to him exceeds the basis of his partnership interest).

If a single transaction causes a partner's share of partnership liabilities to both increase and decrease, only the net change is taken into account; the increase and decrease are presumed to occur simultaneously.[173] A simultaneous increase and decrease in a partner's share of liabilities usually occurs when he contributes, or receives a distribution of, property encumbered by a liability because the partnership's liabilities and the partner's individual liabilities both change.

---

[171]   See Treas. Reg. § 1.704-1(b)(4)(iv)(f), (r).

[172]   Treas. Reg. § 1.752-3(a)(3), as amended by T.D. 8906 (Oct. 31, 2000). The amendment, which added the allocation method in paragraph (c), is effective October 31, 2000.

[173]   Treas. Reg. § 1.752-1(f).

[B]   Interests of Related Persons

A partner's share of partnership liabilities is determined by presuming he has all the rights and obligations of certain related persons. For example, a partner bears the economic risk of loss for a liability to the extent that a person related to him bears that risk. Thus, the interests of parties related to a partner or partnership must be taken into account before determining whether a liability is recourse or nonrecourse or computing the partners' shares of the liability. The rules determining who is a related party are set forth in the regulations.[174]

[C]   Assumption of Partnership or Partner Debt

A partner is deemed to contribute cash to a partnership if he assumes a partnership liability, and he is deemed to receive a cash distribution from a partnership that assumes his individual liability.[175] Under the regulations, a liability is assumed to the extent that the assuming person is personally obligated to pay the debt.[176] Two additional criteria apply if a partner or related person assumes a partnership liability:[177]

(1)   the person to whom the liability is owed must know of the assumption and be able to enforce directly the partner's (or related person(s) obligation for the debt; and

(2)   no other partner (or person related to another partner) bears the economic risk of loss for the debt immediately after the assumption.

§ 5.06   PARTNER'S SHARE OF RECOURSE LIABILITIES

A debt is a recourse partnership liability to the extent that any partner bears the economic risk of loss if the partnership fails to satisfy the obligation.[178] Each partner's share of a recourse partnership liability equals the portion of the economic risk of loss he bears for the debt.[179]

The following sections analyze, in detail, the rules governing the determination of a partner's economic risk of loss for a partnership liability. These rules are summarized as follows:

(1)   A partner bears the economic risk of loss to the extent that he or a related person would be obligated either to pay a partnership creditor or to contribute funds to the partnership to satisfy the debt, without reimbursement, if the partnership engages in a hypothetical transaction called a "constructive liquidation." In a constructive liquidation, the following

---

[174]   Treas. Reg. § 1.752-4(b)(2).

[175]   I.R.C. § 752(a), (b).

[176]   Treas. Reg. § 1.752-1(d)(1).

[177]   Treas. Reg. § 1.752-1(d)(2).

[178]   Treas. Reg. § 1.752-1(a).

[179]   Treas. Reg. § 1.752-2(a).

events are deemed to occur simultaneously:[180]

    (a)   all partnership liabilities become due;

    (b)   all partnership assets become worthless;

    (c)   the partnership sells all its assets for no consideration other than relief of its liabilities;

    (d)   all income and loss items from the deemed disposition of partnership assets are allocated among the partners; and

    (e)   the partnership liquidates all the partners' interests.

(2)   A partner's share of partnership liabilities is determined by presuming that he has all the rights and obligations of certain related persons. Thus, a partner bears the economic risk of loss for a liability to the extent that a person related to him bears that risk. Whether a partner is related to a person is determined under the rules of I.R.C. Sections 267(b) and 707(b)(1), with certain modifications.

(3)   The surrounding facts and circumstances determine whether a partner is obligated for a partnership debt.[181] All statutory and contractual obligations relating to the partnership liability are taken into account, including nonpartnership contractual obligations (*e.g.*, guarantees, indemnifications, and reimbursement agreements) and obligations imposed by the partnership agreement or by state law.

(4)   A payment obligation is disregarded if it is subject to contingencies that make it unlikely that the obligation will be discharged.[182] An obligation that will arise only after the occurrence of an uncertain future event is ignored until the event actually occurs.

(5)   A partner's payment obligation is reduced to the extent that he is entitled to reimbursement from another partner (or person related to another partner).[183]

(6)   Each partner's payment obligation is determined by assuming that all other partners and related persons will perform their payment obligations, regardless of their actual net worth.[184]

(7)   A partner who pledges his individual property as security for a partnership liability bears the economic risk of loss for the debt up to the value of the pledged assets.[185] A partner is deemed to indirectly pledge property he contributes to the partnership solely as security for a partnership liabil-

---

[180] Treas. Reg. § 1.752-2(b)(1).

[181] Treas. Reg. § 1.752-2(b)(3).

[182] Treas. Reg. § 1.752-2(b)(4).

[183] Treas. Reg. § 1.752-2(b)(5).

[184] Treas. Reg. § 1.752-2(b)(6).

[185] Treas. Reg. § 1.752-2(h)(1).

ity.[186]

(8)   A partner who guarantees the payment of 25 percent of the total interest on an otherwise nonrecourse partnership liability may be considered to bear the economic risk of loss for a portion of the debt.[187]

(9)   A partner bears the entire economic risk of loss for a nonrecourse loan he (or a related person) makes to the partnership.[188] An exception to this treatment is provided for certain nonrecourse loans if the partner has only a *de minimis* interest in the partnership.[189]

(10)   Under an anti-abuse rule, a payment obligation may be disregarded or considered another person's obligation if a principal purpose of the arrangement is to misrepresent whether a partner bears the economic risk of loss for an obligation.[190] This rule specifically applies if the arrangement is tantamount to a guarantee of an obligation or if a plan to circumvent or avoid the obligation exists.[191]

[A]   Partner's Economic Risk of Loss

Each partner's share of a recourse partnership liability equals the portion of the economic risk of loss he bears for the debt.[192] In general, a partner bears the economic risk of loss to the extent that he (or a person related to him) would be obligated to make a payment to a creditor or a contribution to the partnership for a partnership liability if the partnership constructively liquidated.[193]

In a constructive liquidation, the following events are deemed to occur:[194]

(1)   All partnership assets (except property partners contributed solely to secure payment of partnership liabilities) become worthless.

(2)   All partnership liabilities become due and payable in full.

(3)   In taxable transactions, the partnership sells all its assets. The partnership is deemed to sell its property securing nonrecourse debts (*i.e.*, liabilities for which the creditor's rights are limited to partnership assets) for the amount of the liability. All other assets are deemed sold for no consideration. In computing the partnership's gain or loss on these sales, the following rules apply:[195]

---

[186] Treas. Reg. § 1.752-2(h)(2).

[187] Treas. Reg. § 1.752-2(e).

[188] Treas. Reg. § 1.752-2(c).

[189] Treas. Reg. § 1.752-2(d).

[190] Treas. Reg. § 1.752-2(j).

[191] Treas. Reg. § 1.752-1(j)(2), (3).

[192] Treas. Reg. § 1.752-2(a).

[193] Treas. Reg. § 1.752-2(b).

[194] Treas. Reg. § 1.752-2(b)(1)(i)–(v).

[195] Treas. Reg. § 1.752-2(b)(2).

(a)   The partnership's gain or loss on the deemed sale of property securing nonrecourse liabilities equals the difference between the amount of the liability and the property's tax basis. Book value rather than tax basis is used if the property was contributed by a partner or revalued on the partnership's books.[196]

(b)   For all other assets, the partnership is deemed to recognize a loss equal to its tax basis for the property. The loss is deemed to be the book value of any contributed or revalued assets.

(4)   Each partner is allocated his distributive share of partnership income, gain, loss, and deduction generated by the deemed sale of assets, and his capital account is adjusted accordingly.

(5)   All the partners' interests in the partnership are liquidated.

Example (1):[197] Gary and Helen each contribute $10,000 to form the GH General Partnership. The partnership purchases an office building for $100,000, giving the seller $20,000 in cash and an $80,000 recourse note. The partnership agreement allocates all items to the partners equally except losses, which are allocated 90 percent to Gary and 10 percent to Helen. The agreement requires capital accounts to be maintained in accordance with the regulations under I.R.C. Section 704(b), and both partners are obligated to restore any deficit capital account upon liquidation.

If the partnership constructively liquidates, the following is deemed to occur:

*   The $80,000 liability becomes due.

*   The building and other partnership assets are deemed worthless.

*   The building is sold for its zero value, resulting in a $100,000 loss.

*   The partners' capital accounts are adjusted to reflect their distributive shares of the partnership's loss on the sale, as follows:

	Gary	Helen
Initial capital account	$10,000	$10,000
Loss on deemed sale	(90,000)	(10,000)
	($80,000)	-0-

The partnership liquidates, and Gary is obligated to pay the partnership $80,000 to restore his deficit capital account balance. The partnership then can apply the $80,000 of contributed funds to satisfy its liability.

Because no other contractual or statutory payment obligations exist, Gary's share of the partnership liability is $80,000 — the amount he must contribute to the partnership as a result of the constructive liquidation. Helen's share of the liability is zero because she has no payment obligation

---

[196] Contributed property is subject to I.R.C. § 704(c) and revalued property subject to Treas. Reg. § 1.701-1(b)(4)(i).

[197] Treas. Reg. § 1.752-2(f), *Example (1)*.

as a result of the constructive liquidation.

Example (2):[198] Assume the same facts as Example (1), except that the partnership agreement allocates all profits and losses 40 percent to Gary and 60 percent to Helen.

If the partnership constructively liquidates, the $80,000 note is deemed due, and the partnership is deemed to sell all its property for zero consideration, resulting in a $100,000 loss. After the deemed sale, the partners' capital accounts would appear as follows:

	Gary	Helen
Initial capital account	$10,000	$10,000
Loss on deemed sale	(40,000)	(60,000)
	($30,000)	($50,000)

Gary's share of the partnership liability is $30,000 — the amount he must contribute to the partnership as a result of the constructive liquidation. Helen's share of the liability is $50,000 — the amount she must contribute as a result of the constructive liquidation.

[B]   Partner's Payment Obligation

A partner bears the economic risk of loss for a liability to the extent that he or a related person would be obligated to pay a creditor or to contribute funds to the partnership because the liability became due pursuant to the partnership's constructive liquidation.[199] No payment obligation exists to the extent that the partner or related person is entitled to reimbursement from another partner or from a person related to another partner.[200]

Assumption that payment obligations will be satisfied. Each partner's payment obligation and risk of loss is determined by assuming that all other partners and related persons will perform their payment obligations, regardless of their actual net worth.[201] This assumption does not apply if a plan to circumvent or avoid the obligation exists.

Contingent obligations not recognized. A payment obligation is disregarded if the facts and circumstances show that it is subject to contingencies making it unlikely that the obligation ever will be discharged.[202] A payment obligation that will arise only after a future event occurs which is not reasonably certain is ignored until the event occurs.

De minimis exception. A partner (or related person) is not considered to bear the economic risk of loss for a partnership nonrecourse liability he guarantees if:

---

[198] *See* Treas. Reg. § 1.752-2(f), *Example (2)*.

[199] Treas. Reg. § 1.752-2(b)(1).

[200] Treas. Reg. § 1.752-2(b)(1), (5).

[201] Treas. Reg. § 1.752-2(b)(6).

[202] Treas. Reg. § 1.752-2(b)(4).

(1)   the guarantor's direct or indirect interest in each partnership item of income, gain, loss, deduction, or credit for every tax year that he is a partner is 10 percent or less; and

(2)   the loan would be qualified nonrecourse financing under I.R.C. Section 465(b)(6), determined without regard to the type of activity financed.[203] Generally, qualified nonrecourse financing means financing obtained from a governmental agency or from a person actively and regularly engaged in lending money.[204]

[C]   Anti-Abuse Rule

The final regulations provide an "anti-abuse" rule under which the payment obligation of a partner or related person may be disregarded or treated as another person's obligation in determining the economic risk of loss for a debt.[205] This rule applies if the facts and circumstances show that a principal purpose of the parties to the arrangement is (1) to eliminate a partner's economic risk of loss for the obligation, or (2) to create the appearance that the partner or related person bears the economic risk of loss for a liability when, in fact, the substance of the arrangement is otherwise.[206]

[D]   When Must Partner or Partnership Obligations Be Satisfied?

The regulations provide time-value-of-money rules that reduce a partner's economic risk of loss for a partnership debt to reflect any delay in the time he is permitted to satisfy the obligation.[207] These rules apply if the partner is not required to satisfy his payment obligation within the following time periods:

(1)   A payment obligation (*i.e.*, an obligation other than an obligation to contribute funds to the partnership) must be satisfied within a "reasonable time" after the liability becomes due.

(2)   An obligation to make a contribution to the partnership must be satisfied by the later of

     (a)   the end of the partnership tax year in which the partner's interest in the partnership is liquidated; or

     (b)   90 days after his interest is liquidated.

---

[203] Treas. Reg. § 1.752-2(d)(2).

[204] *See* I.R.C. § 49(a)(1)(D)(iv); Chapter 6.

[205] Treas. Reg. § 1.752-2(j)(1).

[206] Treas. Reg. § 1.752-2(j)(1). The temporary regulations did not provide this general anti-abuse rule.

[207] Treas. Reg. § 1.752-2(g)(1).

[E]   Obligation to Pay Interest on Nonrecourse Debt

A partner who guarantees payment of interest on a nonrecourse partnership liability may be considered to bear the economic risk of loss for a portion of the debt.[208] The debt is treated as two separate partnership liabilities: (1) a recourse liability equal to the present value of the guaranteed interest, and (2) a nonrecourse liability equal to the remainder of the debt principal.

The recourse portion is allocated to the partners who guarantee the interest, and the nonrecourse portion is allocated under the rules governing nonrecourse liabilities.

[F]   Partner's Nonrecourse Loan to Partnership

In general, a partner who makes or acquires an interest in a nonrecourse loan to his partnership is considered to bear the economic risk of loss for the entire amount owed to him.[209] This is also true if a person related to the partner makes the nonrecourse loan.

> **Example:** John and Zeta Corporation each contribute $100,000 for equal interests in the JZ General Partnership. The partnership purchases a hotel using its $200,000 of capital and a $1.8 million nonrecourse loan from Vargo Corp, a bank that is a wholly owned subsidiary of Zeta. Because the nonrecourse debt is owed to a person related to Zeta, Zeta bears the economic risk of loss for the entire loan.

§ 5.07   PARTNER'S SHARE OF NONRECOURSE LIABILITIES

[A]   Liability and Allocation Rules Coordinated

A partnership liability is nonrecourse if no partner bears the economic risk of loss for the debt;[210] that is, if no partner is obligated to pay a partnership creditor or to contribute funds to the partnership to satisfy the liability if the partnership constructively liquidates. The regulations under I.R.C. Section 752 coordinate the rules for determining a partner's share of nonrecourse partnership liabilities with the rules governing allocations of partnership gain or loss under I.R.C. Sections 704(b) and 704(c).

Coordination of the liability-sharing rules with the allocation rules ensures that a partner's share of a nonrecourse liability includes an amount equal to his share of any losses and distributions attributable to the liability. For example, a partner who is allocated a $100 loss attributable to property subject to a nonrecourse liability also is allocated a $100 share of the debt. Because the basis of the partner's interest increases by his $100 share of the nonrecourse liability, he can fully deduct

---

[208] Treas. Reg. § 1.752-2(e).

[209] Treas. Reg. § 1.752-2(c)(1).

[210] Treas. Reg. § 1.752-1(a)(2).

the $100 loss without limitation under the I.R.C. Section 704(d) rule that restricts a partner's loss deductions to the basis of his partnership interest (*see* Chapter 6). Similarly, a partner who receives a $100 cash distribution attributable to nonrecourse partnership borrowings is allocated a $100 share of the debt and obtains a corresponding basis increase. The basis increase allows the partner to receive the distribution without recognizing gain under I.R.C. Section 731(a).

[B]   Computing a Partner's Share of Nonrecourse Liabilities

Each partner's share of nonrecourse partnership liabilities equals the sum of the following items:[211]

(1)   ***The partner's share of partnership minimum gain.*** This amount is determined pursuant to the regulations under I.R.C. Section 704(b) governing allocations of deductions attributable to nonrecourse liabilities[212] (*see* Chapter 6). In general, partnership minimum gain equals the amount of gain the partnership would realize if it sold all its assets subject to nonrecourse liabilities for the amount of the debts. Partnership losses and deductions for a year are "nonrecourse deductions" (*i.e.*, attributable to nonrecourse liabilities) to the extent that partnership minimum gain increases during the year. Each partner's share of partnership minimum gain equals the aggregate amount of (a) nonrecourse deductions allocated to him, and (b) proceeds of nonrecourse loans distributed to him.

By increasing the basis of a partner's interest by nonrecourse liabilities equal to his share of minimum gain, the I.R.C. Section 752 regulations allow a partner to

(a)   Deduct his share of partnership losses without limitation under I.R.C. Section 704(d), which provides that a partner's deduction for partnership losses cannot exceed the basis of his partnership interest. In effect, the basis increase a partner obtains for his share of liabilities under I.R.C. Section 752 equals the amount of losses allocated to him under I.R.C. Section 704(b).

(b)   Receive distributions of cash the partnership derived from nonrecourse borrowings without recognizing gain. Under I.R.C. Section 731(a), a partner recognizes gain to the extent that the amount of cash distributed to him exceeds the basis of his partnership interest. In effect, the partner's basis increases under I.R.C. Section 752 by the amount of nonrecourse debt proceeds distributed to him.

(2)   ***The partner's share of I.R.C. Section 704(c) minimum gain.*** This equals the amount of taxable gain that would be allocated to the partner

(a)   under I.R.C. Section 704(c) for property he contributed to the

---

[211]   Treas. Reg. § 1.752-3(a).

[212]   Treas. Reg. § 1.752-3(a)(1).

partnership (I.R.C. Section 704(c) property; *see* Chapter 4); or

(b) in the same manner as under I.R.C. Section 704(c) for property the partnership revalued on its books (reverse I.R.C. Section 704(c) property, if the partnership sold all its property subject to nonrecourse liabilities for no consideration other than satisfaction of the liabilities.[213]

Nonrecourse liabilities equal to a partner's share of I.R.C. Section 704(c) minimum gain are included in the basis of his partnership interest to allow the partner to avoid recognizing gain on a contribution of property subject to a nonrecourse liability in excess of the property's basis. Excluding the liability from the contributing partner's basis could cause the partner to recognize gain under I.R.C. Section 731(a) if the deemed cash distribution resulting from the decrease in his individual liabilities exceeds the basis of his partnership interest.

In calculating the partnership's I.R.C. Section 704(c) minimum gain, a partnership holding multiple properties subject to a single liability may allocate the debt among the properties based on any reasonable method.[214] (This situation typically arises when a partnership refinances several properties secured by individual liabilities with a single nonrecourse liability.) For example, the liability may be allocated among properties based on their relative fair market values. A method is not reasonable if the amount allocated to any property exceeds its value. The portion of the nonrecourse liability allocated to each property is treated as a separate loan. Reductions in the debt's principal are allocated among the properties in the proportion that the principal was originally allocated to the properties. *See* Example (5), *infra*.

(3) ***The partner's share of the partnership's excess nonrecourse liabilities.*** A partnership's excess nonrecourse liabilities equals the total amount of nonrecourse liabilities remaining after subtracting the amounts determined under paragraphs (1) and (2) above.[215] A partner's share of the excess liabilities may be computed by either of two methods:[216]

(a) By multiplying the partnership's total excess nonrecourse liabilities by the partner's percentage interest in partnership profits. In general, a partner's profits interest is determined from the facts and circumstances relating to the economic arrangement between the partners.[217] However, a provision in the partnership agreement specifying the partners' profits interests for allocating excess nonrecourse liabilities is respected if reasonably consistent with

---

[213] Treas. Reg. § 1.752-3(a)(2).

[214] Treas. Reg. § 1.753-3(b), as amended by T.D. 8906 (Oct. 31, 2000). The amendment is effective October 31, 2000.

[215] Treas. Reg. § 1.752-3(a)(3).

[216] Excess nonrecourse liabilities need not be allocated under the same method each year. Treas. Reg. § 1.752-3(a)(3).

[217] Treas. Reg. § 1.752-3(a)(3).

valid allocations of another significant item of partnership income or gain (*i.e.*, allocations that satisfy the substantial economic-effect test of the I.R.C. Section 704(b) regulations).

(b)   By allocating the excess nonrecourse liabilities among the partners in the same manner that the deductions attributable to the liabilities are reasonably expected to be allocated.[218] Thus, a partnership may allocate its excess nonrecourse liabilities among partners in the same proportion that it allocates its nonrecourse deductions as long as the deduction allocation is permitted under I.R.C. Sections 704(b) and 704(c).

Excess nonrecourse liabilities may first be allocated to a partner up to his share of "excess" built-in gain from I.R.C. Section 704(c) property and reverse I.R.C. Section 704(c) property that is subject to the liability.[219] This "excess" built-in gain equals the amount by which such gain exceeds the partner's share of I.R.C. Section 704(c) minimum gain computed under paragraph (2) above. If the entire amount of the excess nonrecourse liability is not allocated to the contributing partner, the remaining amount of the excess nonrecourse liability must be allocated under one of the other methods described above.

This "third tier" allocation was modified by recent regulations to allow a liability attributable to contributed property to be more fully allocated to the contributing partner. This change is designed to prevent the "ceiling rule" limitation on deductions for contributed property from shifting liabilities from the contributing partner to a non-contributing partner. Such a liability shift could create a constructive cash distribution to the contributing partner resulting in gain recognition under I.R.C. Section 731(a).

Example (1):[220] Orville and Rose each contribute $10,000 to form the OR Partnership. The partnership purchases depreciable property for $100,000, giving the seller a nonrecourse note for the entire purchase price. No principal payments are due on the purchase money note for five years. The partnership agreement allocates all partnership items to the partners equally.

Immediately after the purchase, Orville and Rose share the nonrecourse liability equally because they have equal interests in partnership profits. Thus, each partner is deemed to contribute $50,000 to the partnership to reflect the increase in his share of partnership liabilities (from $0 to $50,000). The partners' capital accounts and tax bases are as follows:

---

[218] Treas. Reg. § 1.752-3(a)(3). This alternative method was not provided for in the former temporary regulations.

[219] Treas. Reg. § 1.752-3(a)(3), as amended by T.D. 8906 (Oct. 31, 2000). The amendment, which added the allocation method in paragraph (c), is effective October 31, 2000.

[220] Treas. Reg. § 1.752-3(b), *Example (1)*.

	Tax Basis		Capital Account	
	Orville	Rose	Orville	Rose
Cash	$10,000	$10,000	$10,000	$10,000
Share of liability	50,000	50,000	0	0
	$60,000	$60,000	$10,000	$10,000

In Year 1, the partnership is allowed a $20,000 cost-recovery deduction for the property, reducing its tax basis for the asset to $80,000. The deduction causes partnership minimum gain for the year to increase by $20,000 ($20,000 minimum gain at year end [the gain the partnership would realize on a sale of the property for the $100,000 outstanding debt principal] less zero minimum gain at the beginning of the year). The cost recovery is a nonrecourse deduction, and, pursuant to the partnership agreement, each partner is allocated $10,000 of nonrecourse deductions for the year. Orville and Rose each have a $10,000 share of partnership minimum gain at the end of Year 1. Thus, at the end of the year, each partner is allocated $10,000 of the nonrecourse liability to match his share of partnership minimum gain. The remaining $80,000 of the nonrecourse liability is allocated equally between Orville and Rose in proportion to their equal shares of partnership profits.

The partners' year-end capital accounts and tax bases are as follows:

	Tax Basis		Capital Account	
	Orville	Rose	Orville	Rose
Cash	$10,000	$10,000	$10,000	$10,000
Share of Losses	(10,000)	(10,000)	(10,000)	(10,000)
Share of liability	50,000	50,000	0	0
	$50,000	$50,000	$0	$0

Example (2): Assume the same facts as Example (1), except that the partnership agreement allocates all cost-recovery deductions to Orville and all other partnership items are shared equally. Assuming that the special allocation is valid under I.R.C. Section 704(b), all $20,000 of nonrecourse deductions in Year 1 are allocated to Orville. Thus, Orville's share of partnership minimum gain at the end of Year 1 is $20,000, and Rose's share is zero. Orville is allocated a $20,000 share of the nonrecourse liability to match his share of the minimum gain. The remaining $80,000 of the nonrecourse liability is allocated equally between Orville and Rose in proportion to their equal shares of partnership profits.

The partners' year-end capital accounts and tax bases are as follows:

	Tax Basis		Capital Account	
	Orville	Rose	Orville	Rose
Cash	$10,000	$10,000	$10,000	$10,000
Share of Losses	(20,000)	0	(20,000)	0
Share of liability	60,000	40,000	0	0
	$50,000	$50,000	($10,000)	$10,000

Example (3):[221] Assume the same facts as Example (1), except that the partnership agreement allocates all cost-recovery deductions to Orville and allocates all excess nonrecourse liabilities in the same manner that the deductions attributable to the liabilities are reasonably expected to be allocated. Assuming that the special allocation of cost recovery is valid under I.R.C. Section 704(b), Orville's share of the nonrecourse liability is $100,000 immediately after the property is purchased.

The partners' capital accounts and tax bases are as follows:

	Tax Basis		Capital Account	
	Orville	Rose	Orville	Rose
Cash	$10,000	$10,000	$10,000	$10,000
Share of liability	100,000	0	0	0
	$110,000	$10,000	$10,000	$10,000

All $20,000 of nonrecourse deductions in Year 1 are allocated to Orville. Orville is allocated a $20,000 share of the nonrecourse liability to match his share of the minimum gain. The remaining $80,000 of the nonrecourse liability also is allocated to Orville to match the expected allocations of the future deductions attributable to the liability. The partners' year-end capital accounts and tax bases are as follows:

	Tax Basis		Capital Account	
	Orville	Rose	Orville	Rose
Cash	$10,000	$10,000	$10,000	$10,000
Share of Losses	(20,000)	0	(20,000)	0
Share of liability	100,000	0	0	0
	$90,000	$10,000	($10,000)	$10,000

Example (4): In exchange for equal interests in the ST General Partnership, Steve contributes an apartment building worth $120,000 with a $60,000 basis, subject to a $70,000 nonrecourse loan; Tania contributes $50,000 in cash. Steve is allocated $10,000 of the nonrecourse liability because he would be allocated that amount of taxable gain under I.R.C. Section 704(c) if the partnership sold the building to satisfy the debt ($70,000 realized on satisfaction of loan less $60,000 basis). The remaining $60,000 liability ($70,000 debt less $10, 000 I.R.C. Section 704(c) gain) is allocated equally between the partners in accordance with their equal interests in partnership profits. Steve's share of the nonrecourse liability is $40,000 ($10,000 share of I.R.C. Section 704(c) minimum gain plus $30,000 share of the excess), and Tania's share is $30,000, her share of the excess.

Although Steve's share of partnership liabilities increases by $40,000, his individual liabilities decrease by $70,000 when the encumbered property is transferred to the partnership. The $30,000 net reduction in Steve's

---

[221] Treas. Reg. § 1.752-3(b), *Example (2).*

liabilities is treated as a cash distribution to him. (See discussion of contribution of encumbered property in § 5.08[D], *infra*.)

In Revenue Ruling 95-41,[222] the Service concluded that the partners' shares of nonrecourse liabilities for property contributed subject to a nonrecourse liability will differ depending on whether the partnership uses the traditional, curative or, remedial allocation method described in the regulations under I.R.C. Section 704(c) (for discussion of the I.R.C. Section 704(c) allocation rules, see § 6.02, *infra*.) The ruling suggests that use of the remedial allocation method may increase the contributing partner's share of nonrecourse liabilities for the contributed property under I.R.C. Section 752.

Example (5):[223] For equal interests in the EF Partnership, Enid contributes $70 of cash and Fred contributes two assets:

- Property X — value of $70, basis of $40, subject to a $50 nonrecourse liability; and

- Property Y — value $120, basis of $40, subject to a $70 nonrecourse liability.

Immediately after the contributions, EF refinances the two separate liabilities with a single $120 nonrecourse liability. All of the built in gain attributable to Property X ($30) and Property Y ($80) is allocable to Fred under I.R.C. Section 704(c).

First tier allocation: Because the $120 nonrecourse liability is less than the $190 total book value of all properties subject to the liability, no partnership minimum gain exists and no portion of the liability is allocated under the first tier.

Second tier allocation: EF allocates the nonrecourse liability evenly between Properties X and Y, so that each property is deemed to be subject to a separate $60 nonrecourse liability. Fred is allocated $20 of the liability from each property (the I.R.C. Section 704(c) gain from each property — $60 liability - $40 adjusted basis), for a total of $40 under the second tier.

Third tier allocation: EF has $80 of excess nonrecourse liability to allocate under the third tier ($120 total liability - $40 allocated under the first and second tiers).

EF first allocates this amount up to each partner's share of the remaining I.R.C. Section 704(c) gain for the properties, and then equally to Enid and Fred (consistent with their equal interests in partnership profits). Fred has $70 of remaining Section 704(c) gain ($10 on Property X and $60 on Property Y), and is allocated $70 of the liability. The remaining $10 is divided equally between Enid and Fred.

The overall allocation of the $120 nonrecourse liability is as follows:

---

[222] 1995-1 C.B. 132.

[223] *See* Treas. Reg. § 1.752-3(c), *Example (3)*.

	Tier 1	Tier 2	Tier 3	Total
Enid	$0	$0	$5	$5
Fred	0	40	75	115

§ 5.08   CHANGES IN PARTNER'S SHARE OF PARTNERSHIP LIABILITIES

[A]   Events That Change Partner's Share of Liabilities

A partner's basis in his partnership interest increases or decreases whenever his share of the partnership's liabilities changes.[224] The partners can change their shares of partnership liabilities by agreement (*e.g.*, by adjusting the ratio for sharing profits and losses). Transactions at both the partnership and the partner level also change the partners' shares of liabilities. These transactions include:

(1)   changes in the liabilities as they are paid off or incurred;

(2)   the addition or loss of a partner;

(3)   a partner's contribution of encumbered property;

(4)   the distribution of encumbered property to a partner; and

(5)   the sale of a partnership interest.

These transactions are discussed in the following subsections.

[B]   Changes in the Amount of Partnership Liabilities

A partner's share of partnership liabilities generally increases when the partnership incurs obligations and decreases as its obligations are satisfied.[225] Therefore, a partner's basis in his partnership interest may increase when the partnership borrows funds to purchase assets or finance its operations and decreases as the debts are repaid.

[C]   Addition or Loss of a Partner

Each partner's share of partnership liabilities generally decreases when a new partner is admitted and increases when an old one withdraws. Therefore, a change in a partnership's membership results in constructive cash contributions or distributions and corresponding basis adjustments.

> **Example:** Sandra and Thelma each own a 50-percent interest in the capital and profits of the ST Partnership. The partnership's only liability is a $30,000 recourse debt owed to a bank; each partner's share of the debt is $15,000. ST admits Richard to the partnership, with the result that each

---

[224] This results from the constructive cash contributions and distributions that occur under I.R.C. § 752.

[225] An increase in partnership liabilities that does not affect his share of liabilities will not affect the partner's basis in his partnership interest.

partner now has an equal one-third interest in the RST Partnership. Both Sandra and Thelma's shares of the partnership liabilities are reduced to $10,000 from $15,000, and each is deemed to receive a $5,000 cash distribution. The basis of each of their partnership interests is also reduced $5,000. The basis in Richard's partnership interest increases by his $10,000 share of partnership liabilities.

[D]   Contribution or Distribution of Encumbered Property

[1]   Contribution of Encumbered Property

When a partner contributes encumbered property to a partnership, the partnership is considered to assume the debt up to the value of the property at the time of contribution.[226] At the same time, the partner assumes a share of the partnership's liabilities, including the liability he just transferred. The partner is deemed to receive a cash distribution from the partnership equal to the amount by which the decrease in his individual liabilities exceeds the increase in his share of partnership liabilities (*i.e.*, the net decrease).[227]

The constructive distribution occurs immediately after the property is contributed. Each of the other partners is deemed to make a cash contribution to the partnership equal to his share of the debt transferred to the partnership.

Example (1): For equal interests in the AB Partnership, Allen contributes $1,000 in cash and Betty contributes property worth $3,500, with a basis of $2,000 and subject to a $2,500 nonrecourse debt. The partnership is considered to assume the liability, decreasing Betty's individual indebtedness by $2,500. At the same time, Betty's share of partnership liabilities increases by $2,000: $1,500 of I.R.C. Section 704(c) gain allocable to her, plus a $500 (one-half) share of the amount by which the partnership liability exceeds that gain. The $500 net reduction of Betty's share of the liabilities is treated as a cash distribution to her. Betty's basis in her partnership interest is $1,500 ($2,000 basis in the contributed property less the $500 cash distribution she is deemed to receive).

Allen's share of the nonrecourse debt is $500 (one-half of the amount by which the liability exceeds the minimum gain and I.R.C. Section 704(c) gain allocated to Betty), and the basis in his partnership interest increases to $1,500 ($1,000 cash contribution plus $500 share of partnership liabilities). The partners' bases in their partnership interests may be summarized as follows:

---

[226] Treas. Reg. § 1.752-1(e).

[227] Treas. Reg. § 1.752-1(f). *See also* Rev. Rul. 79-205, 1979-2 C.B. 255; Rev. Rul. 87-120, 1987-2 C.B. 161. The partner is deemed to make an additional cash contribution if the increase in his share of partnership liabilities exceeds the decrease in his individual liabilities.

	Allen's Basis	Betty's Basis
Cash contributed	$1,000	$0
Property contributed	0	2,000
Deemed cash distribution	0	(2,500)
Share of nonrecourse debt	500	2,000
	$1,500	$1,500

The presumption that the partnership assumes an encumbrance on contributed property applies only in determining the increase or decrease in the partnership's and the partners' liabilities. It does not apply in determining which partners bear the economic risk of loss for a recourse debt. If the contributing partner continues to bear the economic risk of loss for the liability transferred to the partnership, no net change in his share of liabilities occurs.

Example (2):[228] For equal interests in the AB General Partnership, Ben contributes $500 in cash and Arthur contributes property worth $2,000, with a basis of $1,000 that is subject to a $1,500 recourse debt. Although the partnership does not actually assume the liability, it is deemed to assume it for purposes of determining that Arthur's individual liabilities decrease by $1,500 and that partnership liabilities increase by that amount. If Arthur retains personal responsibility and economic risk of loss for the entire debt (*i.e.*, no other partners incur any economic risk of loss under state law or by agreement), his share of partnership liabilities is $1,500. Because no net change in his share of partnership liabilities and individual liabilities occurs, Arthur is not deemed to make a cash contribution to, or receive a cash distribution from, the partnership. Therefore, his basis in his partnership interest is $1,000 (the basis for the contributed property).

Example (3): Assume the same facts as in Example (2), except that the partnership actually assumes Arthur's liability to the creditor.[229] If AB were to constructively liquidate, both partners would be obligated to contribute $750 to the partnership to satisfy its liability. Therefore, each partner bears the economic risk of loss for $750. Because the $1,500 decrease in Arthur's individual liabilities exceeds the $750 increase in his share of partnership liabilities, he is deemed to receive a cash distribution equal to the $750 difference. The basis in Arthur's partnership interest immediately before the distribution is $1,000 (his basis in the contributed property); the distribution decreases the basis in his interest to $250. The basis of Ben's partnership interest is $1,250 after the contribution ($500 actual cash contribution plus $750 deemed cash contribution).

Example (4): Assume the same facts as in Example (3), except that Arthur's basis for the contributed property is $500. Because the $750 cash distribution he is deemed to receive exceeds the $500 basis in his interest,

---

[228] *See* Treas. Reg. § 1.752-1(g), *Example.*

[229] As discussed in § 5.05[C], *supra*, the regulations provide that a liability is assumed to the extent that the assuming person is personally obligated to pay the liability. Treas. Reg. § 1.752-1(d)(1).

Arthur recognizes a $250 gain. The basis in his partnership interest is zero.[230]

[2] Distribution of Encumbered Property

A partner who receives a distribution of encumbered property is considered to assume the liability up to the value of the property when the distribution occurs.[231] At the same time, the partner's share of the partnership's liabilities decreases by his share of the liability transferred to him.

The partner is deemed to contribute cash to the partnership equal to the amount by which the increase in his individual liabilities exceeds the decrease in his share of partnership liabilities (*i.e.*, the net increase).[232] The constructive contribution occurs immediately after the property is distributed to him. All other partners are deemed to receive a cash distribution from the partnership equal to the decrease in their shares of partnership liabilities, and the bases in their partnership interests decrease by that amount. If a partner's constructive distribution exceeds the basis in his partnership interest, he recognizes gain equal to the excess amount.[233]

[3] Encumbrance Limited to Value of Property

When a partner contributes encumbered property, the partnership is deemed to assume the debt only up to the value of the property at the time of contribution.[234] Similarly, a partner who receives a distribution of encumbered property is considered to assume the liability only up to value of the property when the distribution occurs.[235]

This limitation applies in determining the cash contributions and distributions deemed to occur when encumbered property is contributed to, or distributed by, a partnership.[236] It does not apply when determining the amount a partner realizes on a sale of his partnership interest or the amount the partnership realizes when it sells the encumbered property.[237]

> **Example:** Roger contributes $5,000 cash and undeveloped realty he purchased for $8,000 to the RS Partnership for a 50-percent partnership interest. The realty is worth $6,000, subject to an $8,000 nonrecourse mortgage. Steve contributes $3,000 in cash for his 50-percent interest.
>
> Roger's contribution decreases his individual liabilities by the $6,000 value of the encumbered realty. Because there is no partnership minimum gain or

---

[230] I.R.C. § 733 provides that a partner's basis cannot be less than zero.

[231] Treas. Reg. § 1.752-1(e).

[232] Treas. Reg. § 1.752-1(f). *See also* Rev. Rul. 79-205, 1979-2 C.B. 255; Rev. Rul. 87-120, 1987-2 C.B. 161.

[233] I.R.C. § 731(a).

[234] I.R.C. § 752(c); Treas. Reg. § 1.752-1(e).

[235] *Id.*

[236] I.R.C. § 752(a) or (b).

[237] I.R.C. § 7701(g); Comm'r v. Tufts, 461 U.S. 300, *reh'g denied*, 463 U.S. 1215 (1983); Treas. Reg. § 1.752-1(c).

I.R.C. Section 704(c) gain, Roger's share of the partnership's liability is $3,000 (in accord with his 50-percent profits interest). The $6,000 decrease in Roger's individual liabilities exceeds the $3,000 increase in his share of partnership liabilities; thus, he is deemed to receive a cash distribution equal to the $3,000 difference. Steve is deemed to make a $3,000 cash contribution to the partnership as a result of his increased share of partnership liabilities.

[4]   Payments Made on Excess Encumbrance

A partner who contributes property subject to a liability greater than its value continues to be the debtor on the excess portion of the debt that is not transferred to the partnership.[238] Any payments made after the partnership pays off the total assumed liability reduce the contributing partner's individual liabilities. Therefore, they constitute constructive cash distributions to the partner who contributed the property.[239]

> **Example:** Using the facts of the Example above, assume that the value of the land Roger contributed increases to $10,000 and that the encumbrance is paid off at the rate of $2,000 each year. At the end of the third year, the entire $6,000 liability deemed transferred to the partnership under I.R.C. Section 752(c) is satisfied. Therefore, the $2,000 principal payment in the fourth year is treated as a constructive distribution to Roger.

A partnership that distributes property subject to an encumbrance is considered liable for the portion of the debt that exceeds the property's value. A partner's payments of debt principal made after the entire assumed liability is paid off reduce the partnership's liability and, therefore, are treated as cash contributions to the partnership by the partner.[240]

[E]   Sale or Exchange of Partnership Interest

Liabilities in a sale or exchange of a partnership interest are treated in the same manner as liabilities in any other sale or exchange of property.[241] Under general tax law principles, the amount realized on a sale of property includes the liabilities of which the seller is relieved,[242] whether or not the seller has any personal liability for the debt.[243] The regulations implement this rule by providing that when a partnership interest is sold or exchanged, the selling partner's amount realized includes any reduction in his share of partnership liabilities.[244]

---

[238]   I.R.C. § 752(c). That section merely limits the amount of debt transferred in a contribution or distribution; it does not extinguish any portion of the debt.

[239]   I.R.C. § 752(b).

[240]   I.R.C. § 752(a).

[241]   I.R.C. § 752(d); Treas. Reg. § 1.752-1(h).

[242]   U.S. v. Hendler, 303 U.S. 564 (1937).

[243]   Crane v. Comm'r, 331 U.S. 1 (1947).

[244]   Treas. Reg. § 1.752-1(h). The regulations refer to the seller's amount realized under I.R.C. § 1001 and the regulations thereunder.

Because the selling partner includes his share of partnership liabilities in the basis of his interest under I.R.C. Sections 752(a) and 705(a), the additional amount realized does not generate additional taxable gain. The purchaser's basis in his partnership interest is its cost, which includes his share of partnership liabilities.[245]

> **Example:** Ted, a 25-percent partner in the TU Partnership, sells his partnership interest to Walter for a $15,000 cash payment. At the time of the sale, Ted's share of the partnership's liabilities is $5,000; these liabilities are transferred to Walter when he acquires the interest. Ted's amount realized on the sale is $20,000: $15,000 cash plus $5,000 relief of his share of partnership liabilities. Because Ted's basis in his interest includes $5,000 of the partnership liabilities, the $5,000 increase in the amount realized does not generate additional gain on the sale. Walter's basis in his partnership interest equals its $20,000 cost.

---

[245] I.R.C. § 742. A taxpayer who inherits a partnership interest takes a basis equal to the fair market value of the interest increased by the decedent partner's share of partnership liabilities on the date of death or alternate valuation date. *See* FSA 199935053.

Chapter 6

DISTRIBUTIVE SHARES

§ 6.01 OVERVIEW OF DISTRIBUTIVE SHARE RULES

[A] General Rules

The Code uses the term "distributive share" to describe the portion of partnership income or loss on which a partner is taxable each year. Each partner's distributive share includes his share of overall partnership income or loss as well as his share of each item of income, loss, deduction, or credit that is separately accounted for under I.R.C. Section 702 (See Chapter 3 for discussion of the computation of partnership taxable income and separately stated items.) Because of the pass-through nature of partnership and limited liability company taxation, a partner or LLC member is taxable on his distributive share, whether or not any amounts actually are distributed to him.[1] Each partner or member must report his distributive share on his personal tax return for the year in which (or with which) the partnership's or LLC's tax year ends.[2] (*See* § 6.01[A], *infra.*)

A partner's distributive share of overall partnership income or loss and share of any specific tax item are determined from the partnership agreement, subject to the limitations described in items (1) through (5) below.[3] Thus, within those limitations, partners are free to allocate the economic and tax consequences of partnership operations and transactions among themselves in a manner that takes into account their individual financial goals and tax situations.

The partners' freedom to set their distributive shares in the partnership agreement is subject to the following significant restrictions:

(1) All income, gain, loss, deduction, or credit that is attributable to property a partner contributes to the partnership must be shared among the partners in a manner that accounts for any difference between the fair market value and tax basis of the property when contributed (I.R.C. Section 704(c)). This rule applies to the amount of gain or loss inherent in the contributed property and to any deductions the property generates (*e.g.*, depreciation). The purpose of this rule is to ensure that tax consequences attributable to the pre-contribution appreciation or

---

[1] In U.S. v. Basye, 410 U.S. 441 (1973), the Supreme Court held that a partner is taxable on his distributive share of partnership income even though it is paid directly to a trust, cannot be withdrawn until retirement, and is forfeited if the partner terminates his relationship with the partnership.

[2] I.R.C. § 706(a).

[3] I.R.C. § 704(a).

depreciation in contributed property are allocated to the contributing partner and not shifted to other partners. (*See* § 6.02, *infra.*)

(2) If any partner's interest in the partnership changes during the partnership's tax year, each partner's distributive share is determined under a method that accounts for his varying interests during the year (I.R.C. Section 706(d)(1)). The partner's distributive share is computed separately for the periods before and after the change in his interest occurs. This rule prevents income or loss attributable to the first portion of a partnership year from being retroactively allocated to partners who enter (or increase their interests in) the partnership later in the year. (*See* § 6.03, *infra.*)

(3) If any partner's interest in the partnership changes during the partnership's tax year, each partner's distributive share of partnership "allocable cash basis items" is determined on a daily basis (I.R.C. Section 706(d)(2)). "Allocable cash basis items" are current expense items (*e.g.*, interest, taxes, compensation, rent) that the partnership accounts for under the cash method. A pro rata portion of these items is assigned to each day of the year to which they are economically attributable. The prorated amount is then allocated to the partners in proportion to their interests in the partnership during each day of the year. This rule prevents deductions that are economically attributable to an early part of the year from being allocated to a partner who enters (or increases his interest in) the partnership before the underlying expense is paid. (*See* § 6.03[C], *infra.*)

(4) An allocation in the partnership agreement is disregarded for tax purposes if it lacks "substantial economic effect" (I.R.C. Section 704(b)(2)). This rule invalidates allocations that are advantageous for tax purposes but that do not substantially affect the partners' economic interests in the partnership. Ordinarily, the economic effect of an allocation is determined by reference to its impact on the partners' capital accounts, and the regulations contain elaborate rules regarding the maintenance of these capital accounts. If an allocation is invalid, each partner's distributive share is determined in accordance with his "interest in the partnership" as determined from all the facts and circumstances. (*See* § 6.05, *infra.*)

(5) A partner who received his interest as a gift must decrease his distributive share of income to the extent that (a) it has been computed without allowing for reasonable compensation for services to the partnership by the person who gave him the interest, and (b) it is proportionately greater than the share of partnership capital he was given (I.R.C. Section 704(e)). These rules are designed to prevent gifts of small interests in partnership capital from being used to shift large amounts of partnership income to family members in lower tax brackets.

[B] When Distributive Share Is Taxable

A partner or LLC member generally reports his distributive share of partnership or LLC tax items on his tax return for the year in which (or with which) the partnership or LLC tax year normally ends.[4] The partnership's tax year is deemed to close for a partner on the date he sells, exchanges, or liquidates his entire partnership interest (*i.e.*, before the normal year end), and he reports his share of partnership tax items up to that date on his return for the year in which the disposition occurs.[5]

> **Example (1):** Arthur, Betty, and Clara, all calendar-year taxpayers, are partners in the ABC Partnership, which is permitted to use a fiscal tax year ending on October 31. All partners report their distributive shares of partnership income for the partnership tax year November 1, Year 1, through October 31, Year 2, on their personal tax returns for calendar Year 2.

> **Example (2):** Using the facts in Example (1), assume that on November 30, Year 2, Arthur sells his entire partnership interest to Don. The partnership tax year closes for Arthur on November 30, and he reports his distributive share of partnership income for the period November 1 through November 30, Year 2, on his personal tax return for Year 2. He also reports his share of partnership income for the partnership tax year November 1, Year 1, through October 31, Year 2 on his Year 2 return.

If a partnership terminates, the partnership's tax year closes for all partners, and each partner reports his distributive share of partnership items up to the termination date, on his tax return for the year in which the termination occurs.[6] A partnership terminates:

(1)   when it ceases doing business in partnership form; or

(2)   when 50 percent or more of the interests in the partnership are sold or exchanged within a 12-month period.[7]

A partnership terminated under the 50 percent sale or exchange rule is deemed to continue as a new partnership for tax purposes. (For complete discussion of terminations, see Chapter 13.)

---

[4] I.R.C. § 706(a).

[5] I.R.C. § 706(c)(2)(A). *But see In re* LaBrum & Doak LLP, 237 B.R. 275 (E.D. Pa. 1999) (dissolving law firm in bankruptcy proceedings may allocate its tax recapture liability under I.R.C. § 467 to all present and former partners who received benefit of the recapture, not only to only partners remaining at dissolution).

[6] I.R.C. § 706(c)(1).

[7] I.R.C. § 708(b)(1).

§ 6.02 ALLOCATIONS ATTRIBUTABLE TO CONTRIBUTED PROPERTY

Partnership income, gains, losses, and deductions that are attributable to property contributed by a partner must be allocated in a manner that takes account of the difference between the value and basis of the property when it is contributed.[8] This allocation requirement (under I.R.C. Section 704(c)(1)(A)) was enacted in 1984 to ensure that the tax consequences of pre-contribution appreciation or depreciation of contributed property are allocated to the contributing partner — not shifted to other partners.[9] As illustrated below, the potential for shifting income and deductions arises because a partner's capital account is credited with the fair market value of property he contributes, whereas the partnership's basis for the property carries over from the contributing partner.

NOTE:

A special rule under IRC Section 704(c)(1)(C) restricts the transfer of any loss built-in to contributed property from the contributing to non-contributing partners.[10] Under that section, a built-in loss (meaning the excess of the property's adjusted basis over its fair market value when contributed) is taken into account only in determining the items allocated to the partner who contributed the loss property. In determining amounts allocated to other partners, however, the basis of the contributed loss property to the partnership is deemed to equal its fair market value when contributed.[11]

A partnership determines the economic effect of its transactions by reference to the book value of contributed property (book income or loss) and separately determines the tax consequences of the transactions by reference to its tax basis for the property (taxable income or loss). Ordinarily, the amount of a tax item allocated to a partner must match the corresponding economic allocation (book item) included in the partner's capital account. For example, an increase in a partner's capital account to reflect his share of partnership income (book income) will equal his distributive share of partnership income, and the corresponding increase in the basis of his partnership interest, as computed for tax purposes (tax income). In other words, the tax allocation generally follows the book allocation. The equivalence of book and tax items is lost, however, when property is contributed with a tax basis that differs from its value.

Example: For equal interests in the AB Partnership, Alex contributes $5,000 in cash and Barbara contributes property worth $5,000, in which her

---

[8] I.R.C. § 704(c)(1)(A).

[9] H.R. Rep. No. 98-861, 98th Cong., 2d Sess. 857 (1984).

[10] I.R.C. § 704(c)(1)(C)(i), as amended by the American Jobs Creation Act (AJCA), Pub. L. No. 108-357 (2004). The new rules apply to contributions after October 22, 2004.

[11] I.R.C. § 704(c)(1)(C)(ii).

basis is $1,000. Each partner's capital account is credited with $5,000, the value of their contributions. Alex's basis for his partnership interest is $5,000, and Barbara's basis for her interest is $1,000. The partnership's basis for the property contributed by Barbara is $1,000. If the partnership sells the property for $5,000, the partnership recognizes a $4,000 tax gain, even though it has no "book" gain or loss on the sale (*i.e.*, it sold the property for its $5,000 book value).

Alex's capital account is unaffected by the sale of the contributed property because the partnership did not realize any book income on the sale. If I.R.C. Section 704(c) did not apply, each partner would be allocated $2,000 of the partnership's tax gain in accordance with their equal interest in partnership profits. In effect, Barbara could shift half the pre-contribution gain to Alex. To prevent this income shift, I.R.C. Section 704(c) requires the partnership to allocate the entire $4,000 tax gain to Barbara.

Reasonable allocation method required. I.R.C. Section 704(c)(1)(A) is designed to prevent tax consequences attributable to a difference between the value and basis of contributed property from being shifted from the contributing partner to noncontributing partners.[12] A partnership must allocate all items of income, gain, loss and deduction from contributed property using a "reasonable" method that is consistent with this statutory purpose.[13] Although no specific method is mandated, the regulations describe three allocation methods that are generally considered reasonable.

Separate allocations made for each property. The required allocations are determined separately for each contributed property.[14] Therefore, gains and losses built-in to different contributed properties cannot be aggregated in determining if a book value/tax basis difference exists. Different allocation methods may be used for different contributed items if the method used for each property is applied consistently and the overall method or combination of methods is reasonable under the facts and circumstances.[15] If a partnership terminates under I.R.C. Section 708(b)(1)(B) (*i.e.*, because 50 percent of its interests were sold within a 12-month period), the new partnership that arises need not use the same allocation method as the terminated partnership.[16]

I.R.C. Section 704(c) property defined. The allocation rules apply to "Section 704(c) property," defined as contributed property having an adjusted tax basis that differs from its book value (*i.e.*, fair market value) when contributed.[17] I.R.C. Section 704(c) property does not include assets sold to a partnership,[18] but does encompass accounts payable and receivable and other accrued but unpaid items of

---

[12] Treas. Reg. § 1.704-3(a)(1).

[13] *Id.*

[14] Treas. Reg. § 1.704-3(a)(2).

[15] *Id.*

[16] *Id.*

[17] Book value is determined under Treas. Reg. § 1.704-1(b)(2)(iv) or using a book capital account based on the same principles. Treas. Reg. § 1.704-3(a)(3)(i).

[18] This includes disguised sales under I.R.C. § 707. Treas. Reg. § 1.704-3(a)(5).

a cash method contributor.[19] When the contributed property is itself a partnership interest, the contributor's built-in gain or loss attributable to that interest is proportionate to his share of the partnership's entire built-in gain or loss.[20] Property acquired in exchange for contributed property in a non-taxable transaction also is I.R.C. Section 704(c) property.[21]

Transferred interests. When a partner who contributed property with built-in gain or loss transfers his partnership interest, the built-in gain or loss is allocated to the transferee partner as it would have been to the transferor. If a portion of the interest is transferred, a proportionate share of built-in gain or loss is allocated to the transferee.[22]

Tiered partnerships. A special rule applies to tiered partnerships when property contributed to one partnership (upper tier) is in turn contributed to another partnership (lower tier). Allocations to partners of the lower tier partnership must account for the differences between the value and basis of the contributed property, and these allocations are again made among the contributor and the other partners of the upper tier partnership.[23]

Revaluations. The I.R.C. Section 704(c) regulations also govern special allocations under I.R.C. Section 704(b) when capital accounts are adjusted to reflect revaluations of partnership property (*see* § 6.06, *infra*).[24] Tax items attributable to the revalued property must be allocated "in the same manner" as under I.R.C. Section 704(c) to account for disparities between the value and basis of the property caused by the revaluation.

Anti-abuse rule. An allocation method is not deemed reasonable if the contribution and allocation is made "with a view" to shifting the tax consequences of built-in gain or loss among the partners so that the present value of the partners' aggregate tax liability is substantially reduced.[25]

NOTE:

A partnership that sells IRC Section 704(c) property in an installment sale[26] must treat the installment obligation received as IRC Section 704(c) property having the same amount of built-in gain or loss as the sold property. The built-in gain or loss is adjusted for any gain or loss recognized on the installment sale. The method for allocating the gain or

---

[19] Treas. Reg. § 1.704-3(c)(4).

[20] Treas. Reg. § 1.704-3(a)(7).

[21] Treas. Reg. § 1.704-3(a)(8).

[22] Treas. Reg. § 1.704-3(a)(7).

[23] Treas. Reg. § 1.704-3(a)(9).

[24] Treas. Reg. § 1.704-1(b)(4)(i).

[25] Treas. Reg. § 1.704-3(a)(10). This is similar to the "substantiality" test in the regulations under I.R.C. § 704(b).

[26] Defined in I.R.C. § 453(b).

loss from the instalment obligation must be consistent with the allocation method chosen for the original property.[27]

[A] Reasonable Allocation Methods

A partnership must allocate tax items from contributed property among partners using a reasonable method that prevents pre-contribution gain or loss from being shifted among the partners. The regulations describe three allocation methods that generally are reasonable: the traditional method, the traditional method with curative allocations, and the remedial allocation method. Although other allocation methods may be allowed in appropriate circumstances, it is likely that most allocations will accord with the three methods sanctioned by the regulations. An allocation method is not unreasonable merely because another method would result in a higher total tax liability.[29]

The regulations under IRC Section 704(c) implement a strong anti-abuse allocations affecting built-in gain or loss property contributed to a rship.[30] These regulations were issued in response to a recommendation by nt Committee on Taxation that the partnership tax rules be strengthened to e that the allocation rules in the regulations under IRC Section 704(c) are not to generate unwarranted tax benefits.[31]

Under the anti-abuse rule:

- An allocation method is not reasonable if a contribution of property and corresponding allocation of tax items with respect to the property are made with a view to shifting the tax consequences of built-in gain or loss among the partners in a manner that substantially reduces the present value of the partners' aggregate tax liability.

- For purposes of this anti-abuse rule, the term partners includes both direct and indirect partners.[32]

- An allocation method under IRC Section 704(c) cannot be used to achieve tax results inconsistent with the intent of Subchapter K of the Code; and

- The Service may recast a transaction to achieve tax results that are consistent with the intent of Subchapter K.

---

[27] Treas. Reg. § 1.704-3(a)(8)(i); T.D. 9193 (Mar. 22, 2005). The regulations are effective November 2 2003.

[28] The regulations indicate that without specific published guidance, an allocation method unreasonable if the basis of contributed property is increased (or decreased) to reflect built-in gain loss), or if the partnership creates tax allocations without corresponding book allocations. Treas. § 1.704-3(a)(1).

[29] Treas. Reg. § 1.704-3(a)(1).

[30] T.D. 9485 (June 9, 2010). This Treasury decision adopts prior proposed regulations substantive change. The regulations apply to taxable years beginning after June 9, 2010.

[31] Report of Investigation of Enron Corporation and Related Entities Regarding Federa Compensation Issues, and Policy Recommendations (JCS-3-03) Feb. 2003 at 220.

[32] Treas. Reg. § 1.704-3(a)(10).

loss from the installment obligation must be consistent with the allocation method chosen for the original property.[27]

[A] Reasonable Allocation Methods

A partnership must allocate tax items from contributed property among partners using a reasonable method that prevents pre-contribution gain or loss from being shifted among the partners. The regulations describe three allocation methods that generally are reasonable: the traditional method, the traditional method with curative allocations, and the remedial allocation method. Although other allocation methods may be allowed in appropriate circumstances, it is likely that most allocations will accord with the three methods sanctioned by the regulations.[28] An allocation method is not unreasonable merely because another method would result in a higher total tax liability.[29]

Recent regulations under IRC Section 704(c) implement a strong anti-abuse rule for allocations affecting built-in gain or loss property contributed to a partnership.[30] These regulations were issued in response to a recommendation by the Joint Committee on Taxation that the partnership tax rules be strengthened to ensure that the allocation rules in the regulations under IRC Section 704(c) are not used to generate unwarranted tax benefits.[31]

Under the anti-abuse rule:

- An allocation method is not reasonable if a contribution of property and corresponding allocation of tax items with respect to the property are made with a view to shifting the tax consequences of built-in gain or loss among the partners in a manner that substantially reduces the present value of the partners' aggregate tax liability.

- For purposes of this anti-abuse rule, the term partners includes both direct and indirect partners.[32]

- An allocation method under IRC Section 704(c) cannot be used to achieve tax results inconsistent with the intent of Subchapter K of the Code; and

- The Service may recast a transaction to achieve tax results that are consistent with the intent of Subchapter K.

---

[27] Treas. Reg. § 1.704-3(a)(8)(i); T.D. 9193 (Mar. 22, 2005). The regulations are effective November 23, 2003.

[28] The regulations indicate that without specific published guidance, an allocation method is unreasonable if the basis of contributed property is increased (or decreased) to reflect built-in gain (or loss), or if the partnership creates tax allocations without corresponding book allocations. Treas. Reg. § 1.704-3(a)(1).

[29] Treas. Reg. § 1.704-3(a)(1).

[30] T.D. 9485 (June 9, 2010). This Treasury decision adopts prior proposed regulations without substantive change. The regulations apply to taxable years beginning after June 9, 2010.

[31] Report of Investigation of Enron Corporation and Related Entities Regarding Federal Tax and Compensation Issues, and Policy Recommendations (JCS-3-03) Feb. 2003 at 220.

[32] Treas. Reg. § 1.704-3(a)(10).

[1] The Traditional Method

The traditional method is based on the principle that disparities between the book value and tax basis of contributed property are eliminated by allocating gain, loss, depreciation, depletion and amortization from these assets to the non-contributing partners as if no book-tax disparity existed.[33] Put another way, tax items from contributed property are first allocated to the non-contributing partners up to the value of their book items; any remaining tax items are then allocated to the contributing partner.

Allocating gain or loss. The gain or loss a partnership recognizes on a disposition of contributed property is allocated to the contributing partner up to the amount of gain or loss inherent in the property when it was contributed.[34] Each partner's capital account is adjusted to reflect his share of partnership "book" gain or loss (*i.e.*, gain or loss as computed from the fair market value of the property when contributed), while the tax consequences are determined from the property's tax basis. Any gain or loss that exceeds the amount built-in at the time of contribution (*i.e.*, post-contribution gain or loss) is allocated among the partners according to their partnership agreement.[35]

> **Example (1):** Charles and Don are equal members of the CD Limited Liability Company. Charles contributes $20,000 in cash and Don contributes land worth $20,000, with a tax basis of $10,000. Each member's capital account is credited with the $20,000 value of his contribution. Charles' basis in his LLC interest is $20,000 and Don's basis is $10,000.[36] The LLC's basis in the land is $10,000.[37] Following the contribution, the LLC's tax and book capital account records are as follows:

	Charles		Don	
	Tax	Book	Tax	Book
Initial capital account	$20,000	$20,000	$10,000	$20,000

If the LLC sells the land for $25,000, the $10,000 of built-in gain it realizes is allocated to Don and included in his distributive share. This allocation under I.R.C. Section 704(c) eliminates the initial difference between the book value of the property credited to Don's capital account ($20,000) and the tax basis in his LLC interest ($10,000). The remaining $5,000 of post-contribution gain is allocated equally to Charles and Don for book and tax purposes in accordance with their operating agreement.

---

[33] The rule is called "traditional" because it was the method in effect under the I.R.C. § 704(c) regulations before the 1984 Act.

[34] Treas. Reg. § 1.704-3(b)(1).

[35] I.R.C. § 704(b).

[36] Under I.R.C. § 722, a partner's basis in his partnership interest generally equals the amount of money he contributes plus his basis in any property he contributes.

[37] Under I.R.C. § 723, the partnership generally takes the same basis in contributed property that it had in the hands of the contributing partner.

[1]   The Traditional Method

The traditional method is based on the principle that disparities between the book value and tax basis of contributed property are eliminated by allocating gain, loss, depreciation, depletion and amortization from these assets to the non-contributing partners as if no book-tax disparity existed.[33] Put another way, tax items from contributed property are first allocated to the non-contributing partners up to the value of their book items; any remaining tax items are then allocated to the contributing partner.

Allocating gain or loss. The gain or loss a partnership realizes on a disposition of contributed property is allocated to the contributing partner the amount of gain or loss inherent in the property when it was contributed to the partner's capital account is adjusted to reflect his share of partnership "Each or loss (*i.e.*, gain or loss as computed from the fair market value of the gain when contributed), while the tax consequences are determined from the property tax basis. Any gain or loss that exceeds the amount built-in at the time contribution (*i.e.*, post-contribution gain or loss) is allocated among the part according to their partnership agreement.[35]

> **Example (1):** Charles and Don are equal members of the CD Limited Liability Company. Charles contributes $20,000 in cash and Don contributes land worth $20,000, with a tax basis of $10,000. Each member's capital account is credited with the $20,000 value of his contribution. Charles' basis in his LLC interest is $20,000 and Don's basis is $10,000.[36] The LLC's basis in the land is $10,000.[37] Following the contribution, the LLC's tax and book capital account records are as follows:
>
> | | Charles | | Don | |
> | --- | --- | --- | --- | --- |
> | | Tax | Book | Tax | Book |
> | Initial capital account | $20,000 | $20,000 | $10,000 | $20,000 |

the LLC sells the land for $25,000, the $10,000 of built-in gain it realizes is ed to Don and included in his distributive share. This allocation under I.R.C. 704(c) eliminates the initial difference between the book value of the credited to Don's capital account ($20,000) and the tax basis in his LLC 0,000). The remaining $5,000 of post-contribution gain is allocated arles and Don for book and tax purposes in accordance with their ement.

is
or
eg.
             "traditional" because it was the method in effect under the I.R.C. § 704(c) Act.

1).

ithout

Tax and

's basis in his partnership interest generally equals the amount of n any property he contributes.

ip generally takes the same basis in contributed property that it partner.

arising from the contribution over the depreciable life of the contributed property.

Example (3): Assume the same facts in Example (1), except that Don contributes equipment valued at $20,000, in which his adjusted basis is $10,000, and that the remaining depreciation deduction allowable for the equipment is 20 percent of its basis per year. Book depreciation is $4,000 per year (20 percent of $20,000 book value). Charles's one-half share of that book depreciation is $2,000. Because the tax depreciation allowable for the equipment is only $2,000 per year (20 percent of $10,000 tax basis), Charles is allocated the entire $2,000 tax depreciation deduction. Don's share of the tax depreciation is zero.

The total decrease in Don's depreciation deductions from the contributed property equals the gain built into the property when he contributed it. In effect, Don is taxed on that built-in gain over the property's remaining depreciable life. Don's lost tax depreciation also eliminates the disparity between his capital account and the tax basis in his LLC interest.[42] This is illustrated by assuming that the LLC's total income over the remaining five-year life of the equipment exceeds its losses, other than depreciation, by $20,000:

	Charles		Don	
	Tax	Book	Tax	Book
Initial capital account	$20,000	$20,000	$10,000	$20,000
Share of income	10,000	10,000	10,000	10,000
Depreciation ($2,000 x 5 years)	(10,000)	(10,000)	0	(10,000)
Capital account (end of year 5)	$20,000	$20,000	$20,000	$20,000

Example (4): Assume the same facts, except that Don's basis for the equipment is $12,000, and the depreciation deduction allowable is 20 percent of basis per year ($2,400). Because Charles's book allocation for depreciation is $2,000, he will be allocated $2,000 of the depreciation deduction each year. The remaining $400 of tax depreciation each year is allocated to Don. Again, assume that the LLC's total income over the remaining five-year life of the equipment exceeds its losses, other than depreciation, by $20,000:

	Charles		Don	
	Tax	Book	Tax	Book
Initial capital account	$20,000	$20,000	$12,000	$20,000
Share of income	10,000	10,000	10,000	10,000
Depreciation ($2,400 x 5 years)	(10,000)	(10,000)	(2,000)	(10,000)
Capital account (end of year 5)	$20,000	$20,000	$20,000	$20,000

---

[42] I.R.C. § 705(a).

Effect of the ceiling rule. Ordinarily, the noncontributing partners' share of book deductions from the contributed property (computed from its value when contributed) are matched by an equal share of tax deductions from the property (computed from the contributor's tax basis when contributed). This equivalence is lost, however, if the "ceiling rule"[43] causes the tax deductions allocated to the noncontributing partners to be less than their share of book deductions. The ceiling rule limits the total amount of deductions allocated to partners to the amount allowed at the partnership level. The ceiling rule also prevents the disparity between the book value of the contributing partner's capital account and its tax basis from being eliminated over the depreciable life of the contributed property; the disparity is not eliminated until the partner sells or liquidates his interest in the partnership.

Example (5): Again, assume the facts in Example (1), except that Don's basis in the contributed equipment is only $8,000. Although Charles's book depreciation each year is $2,000 (50 percent of $20,000 * 20% allowable depreciation), the ceiling rule limits his tax depreciation allocation to $1,600 — the amount of depreciation allowed to the LLC ($8,000 * 20%). Because of the ceiling rule, Charles "loses" $400 of depreciation each year. Note that the ceiling rule prevents the book value/tax-basis disparity from being eliminated over the life of the contributed property:

	Charles		Don	
	Tax	Book	Tax	Book
Initial capital account	$20,000	$20,000	$8,000	$20,000
Share of income	10,000	10,000	10,000	10,000
Depreciation ($1,600 x 5 years)	(8,000)	(10,000)	0	(10,000)
Capital account (end of year 5)	$22,000	$20,000	$18,000	$20,000

Charles will obtain the tax benefit of the lost deductions when he sells or liquidates his partnership interest. If he sells his interest for its $20,000 fair market value at the end of Year 5, he recognizes a $2,000 loss, which offsets the total depreciation he was unable to deduct under the ceiling rule. However, the loss is a capital loss, even though the depreciation deductions were ordinary in character. In effect, Charles' current ordinary loss deductions are converted to a deferred capital loss.

Don recognizes a $2,000 tax gain if he sells his interest for its $20,000 value. This equals the amount of gain Don did not recognize over the depreciable life of the property because of the ceiling rule. Because the gain is a capital gain, Don has effectively converted current ordinary income to a deferred capital gain.

---

[43] Treas. Reg. § 1.704-3(b)(1).

[2] Traditional Method With Curative Allocations

A partnership using the traditional method may correct distortions created by the ceiling rule by making reasonable "curative" allocations to noncontributing partners. A curative allocation is an allocation of income, gain, loss, or deduction for tax purposes that differs from the allocation of the corresponding book item.[44] For example, if a noncontributing partner is allocated less tax depreciation than book depreciation because of the ceiling rule, the partnership can allocate tax depreciation from another item of partnership property to make up the difference. The curative tax allocation is allowed even though the contributing partner is allocated the corresponding book depreciation.

Curative allocations may be limited to one or more particular tax items (*e.g.*, depreciation from a specific property or properties) even if these allocations do not fully offset the ceiling rule limitation.[45] A partnership must apply its curative allocations to each property consistently from year to year.[46]

A curative allocation is considered reasonable if it satisfies the following requirements:

(1)   The allocation must be expected to consist of tax items that will have substantially the same effect on the partners' tax liability as the item limited by the ceiling rule.[47] For example, if the ceiling rule limits an ordinary deduction, a curative allocation of income to the contributing partner must be expected to have substantially the same effect as an allocation of ordinary income.[48] An exception to this character rule applies if the item limited by the ceiling rule is depreciation. In that case, the partnership agreement may allocate gain from the sale of the contributed property to the contributing partner even if the character differs.[49]

(2)   Generally, an allocation is not reasonable to the extent that it exceeds the amount necessary to offset a ceiling rule limitation in the current tax year.[50] A curative allocation relating to a prior year may be reasonable, however, if

    (a)   The allocation consists of gain from the disposition of the contributed property subject to the ceiling rule limitation; or

    (b)   In the year the property was contributed, the partnership agreement required curative allocations over a reasonable time period — such as the property's economic life.

Example (1): Frank and George form the equal FG partnership. Frank

---

[44] Treas. Reg. § 1.704-3(c)(1).

[45] Treas. Reg. § 1.704-3(c)(1).

[46] Treas. Reg. § 1.704-3(c)(2).

[47] Treas. Reg. § 1.704-3(c)(3)(iii).

[48] *Id.*

[49] The allocation provision must be in the partnership agreement in the year the property was contributed. Treas. Reg. § 1.704-3(c)(3)(iii).

[50] Treas. Reg. § 1.704-3(c)(3).

contributes Property X with a value of $10,000 and a $4,000 adjusted basis. George contributes $10,000 of cash, which is used to purchase Property Y. Both properties are depreciable over 5 years, using the straight line method. Under the ceiling rule, George's share of tax depreciation from Property X each year is $800, which is $200 less than his corresponding share of book depreciation ($1,000). The partnership agreement provides a curative allocation of an additional $200 per year of tax depreciation from Property Y to offset this ceiling rule limitation. Assuming that partnership operating income equals its operating expense, allocations for Year 1 is:

	Frank		George	
	Tax	Book	Tax	Book
Initial capital account	$4,000	$10,000	$10,000	$10,000
Depreciation Property X	0	(1,000)	(800)	(1,000)
Depreciation Property Y	(800)	(1,000)	(1,200)	(1,000)
Capital account (end of year 1)	$3,200	8,000	$8,000	$8,000

Example (2): Use the same facts except that the contributed cash is used to purchase inventory and that the partnership has $1,000 of sales income. The regulations indicate that the ceiling rule limitation may be offset by a curative allocation of $200 of additional taxable sales income to Frank.

	Frank		George	
	Tax	Book	Tax	Book
Initial capital account	$4,000	$10,000	$10,000	$10,000
Depreciation Property X	0	(1,000)	(800)	(1,000)
Sales income	700	500	300	500
Capital account (end of year 1)	$4,700	$9,500	$9,500	$9,500

[3] Remedial Allocations

The remedial allocation method may be used whenever the ceiling rule causes a book allocation to a noncontributing partner to differ from the corresponding tax allocation.[51] In that case, the partnership can eliminate the book/tax disparity through (1) a remedial allocation to the noncontributing partner of the appropriate amount and kind of income, deduction, loss, or gain and (2) a simultaneous offsetting remedial allocation to the contributing partner. In effect, the remedial allocation method eliminates ceiling rule distortions by creating "notional" tax items that are allocated among the partners.[52] Although these notional items shift tax items among the partners, they do not affect their book capital accounts, or change

---

[51] Treas. Reg. § 1.704-3(d).

[52] The remedial allocation method is the only reasonable method permitting the creation of artificial tax items. Treas. Reg. § 1.704-3(d)(5). Similarly, the IRS cannot require a partnership to use the remedial allocation method or any other method involving the creation of artificial tax items.

partnership taxable income or the basis of partnership property.[53]

To apply the remedial allocation method, depreciation for a contributed property is computed as if two separate assets are involved:[54]

(1)   A portion of the property's book value equal to its tax basis is recovered in the same manner and amount as allowed for tax purposes (*i.e.*, over the property's remaining depreciation period). This depreciation is allocated among the partners using the traditional method.

(2)   The remaining book value (the excess of the property's book over tax basis) is recovered using any depreciation method and recovery period that would be allowed if the partnership purchased the property on the contribution date.

In the year that a non-contributing partner is subject to a ceiling rule limitation, a sufficient remedial allocation is made to eliminate the effect of the limitation. A simultaneous, offsetting remedial allocation is made to the contributing partner.

The remedial allocations must have the same tax attributes (*i.e.*, source and character) as the item limited by the ceiling rule.[55] For example, if the ceiling rule limits depreciation from contributed rental property, the noncontributing partner's remedial allocation is depreciation from rental property and the contributing partner's offsetting remedial allocation must be ordinary income from rental property. Similarly, if the ceiling rule limits a loss from the sale of contributed property, the contributing partner's offsetting remedial allocation must be gain from the sale of that property.

> **Example:** [56] Heidi and Jane form the equal HJ Limited Liability Company. Heidi contributes depreciable property with a tax basis of $4,000 and a value of $10,000. Jane contributes $10,000 in cash. The contributed property has a 4-year remaining depreciable life to Heidi, using the straight line method. However, it would have a 10-year depreciable life (straight line) if newly purchased.
>
> Under the remedial allocation method, book depreciation is determined separately for the book value equal to the property's tax basis ($4,000 depreciated over 4 years) and for the excess book value ($6,000 depreciated over 10 years). In years 1 through 4, total book depreciation is $1,600 ($1,000 from the portion of book value equal to tax basis and $600 from the portion of book value in excess of basis). Book depreciation for years 5 through 10 is $600. Actual tax depreciation from the property is $1,000 a year over 4 years.
>
> Under the traditional rule, the allocations for Year 1 are:

---

[53] Treas. Reg. § 1.704-3(d)(4).

[54] Treas. Reg. § 1.704-3(d)(2).

[55] Treas. Reg. § 1.704-3(d)(3).

[56] *See* Treas. Reg. § 1.704-3(d)(7), *Example (1)*.

| | Heidi | | Jane | |
	Tax	Book	Tax	Book
Initial capital account	$4,000	$10,000	$10,000	$10,000
Depreciation Year 1	(200)	(800)	(800)	(800)
Capital account (end of year 1)	$3,800	$9,200	$9,200	$9,200

Remedial allocations are not required in years 1 through 4 because the traditional method does not create a ceiling rule limitation (*i.e.*, Jane's book and tax allocations are equal). However, ceiling rule distortions do appear in years 5 through 10. These distortions are eliminated by remedial allocations of tax depreciation to Jane and offsetting ordinary income allocations to Heidi in each year:

| | Heidi | | Jane | |
	Tax	Book	Tax	Book
Capital account (end of year 4)	$3,200	$6,800	$6,800	$6,800
Depreciation Year 5	0	(300)	0	(300)
Remedial allocation	300	0	(300)	0
Capital account (end of year 5)	$3,500	$6,500	$6,500	$6,500

[4] Small Disparities and Aggregation Rules

Small disparities. If only a "small disparity" exists between the book value and tax basis of property contributed by a partner in a single partnership tax year, the partnership may elect to disregard the I.R.C. Section 704(c) rules or to apply these rules only when it disposes of the property.[57] A small disparity exists if the difference between the book value and tax basis of property contributed by one partner during a tax year is not greater than 15 percent of its tax basis and the total gross disparity does not exceed $20,000. Certain types of property may be aggregated in making allocations under I.R.C. Section 704(c), if contributed by one partner during a partnership tax year.[58]

Aggregation of similar properties. The following types of property may be aggregated in making allocations under IRC Section 704(c), if contributed by one partner during a partnership tax year:[59]

- Depreciable property. All depreciable property, other than real property, that is included in the same general asset account under IRC Section 168.

- All zero-basis property, other than real property.

- Inventory of a partnership that does not use a specific identification method of accounting (other than securities and similar investment assets).[60]

---

[57] Treas. Reg. § 1.704-3(e).

[58] Treas. Reg. § 1.704-3(e)(2).

[59] *Id.*

[60] As defined in Treas. Reg. § 1.704-3(e)(2)(i), (ii), (iii).

[5] Securities Partnerships

Special rules are provided for securities partnerships.[61] These rules are designed to limit the administrative burdens that I.R.C. Section 704(c) would otherwise impose because of the large number of assets and frequent revaluations in these business operations.

[B] Distribution of Contributed Property to Noncontributing Partner

Under I.R.C. Section 704(c)(1)(B), a partner that contributes I.R.C. Section 704(c) property to a partnership recognizes gain or loss if the property is distributed to another partner within seven years[62] of the contribution date.[63] The amount recognized equals the gain or loss that would have been allocated to the partner under I.R.C. Section 704(c) if the partnership sold the property to the distributee partner for its fair market value at the time of the distribution. The character of the gain or loss recognized by the contributing partner is determined in the same manner.[64]

I.R.C. Section 704(c) property is contributed property having an adjusted tax basis that differs from its book value (*i.e.*, fair market value) when contributed.[65] Property deemed contributed to a new partnership following a technical termination under I.R.C. Section 708(b)(1)(B) is I.R.C. Section 704(c) property only to the extent it was such property in the terminated partnership immediately before the termination.[66]

I.R.C. Section 704(c)(1)(B) was enacted in 1989 to preclude the use of property distributions to shift gain or loss among partners.[67] The following example illustrates the type of transaction that the statute is designed to prevent:

> **Example:** Before the enactment of I.R.C. Section 704(c)(1)(B), Carol contributes land to the CD Partnership in Year 1. The land is worth $20,000 and has a $10,000 basis when contributed. Donald contributes $10,000 in cash. In Year 4, the partnership distributes the land to Donald. Donald recognizes no gain on the distribution, and his basis in the property is $10,000. If Donald sells the land for $20,000, he recognizes a $10,000 gain. The effect of the transaction is that Carol's $10,000 of precontribution gain is shifted to Donald.

The shift in gain is temporary. Because the distribution decreases the basis

---

[61] Treas. Reg. § 1.704-3(e)(3).

[62] The seven-year period applies to property contributed after June 8, 1997. Property contributed before that date is subject to a five-year period. Generally, the seven-year period begins on and includes the date of contribution. Treas. Reg. § 1.704-4(a)(4)(i).

[63] I.R.C. § 704(c)(1)(B); Treas. Reg. § 1.704-4(a). Generally, the seven-year period begins on and includes the date of contribution. Treas. Reg. § 1.704-4(a)(4)(i).

[64] Treas. Reg. § 1.704-4(b).

[65] Treas. Reg. § 1.704-3(a)(3)(i).

[66] Treas. Reg. § 1.704-3(a). *See* Treas. Reg. § 1.708-1(b)(4).

[67] S. Rep. No. 101-56, 101st Cong., 1st Sess. 268 (1989).

of Donald's partnership interest by $10,000, he will incur an additional $10,000 of gain when he sells or liquidates his partnership interest. However, the partners obtain a current tax benefit from the income shift while the offsetting tax burden may occur in the distant future.

If I.R.C. Section 704(c)(1)(B) applies, $10,000 of gain is recognized at the time of the distribution and allocated to Carol. Thus, no income shifting or tax deferral occurs.

[1] Basis Adjustments

Contributing partner's basis in the partnership interest. The contributing partner increases or decreases the basis in his partnership interest by the amount of gain or loss he recognizes.[68] This increase or decrease is taken into account in determining (1) the contributing partner's basis for any other property distributed to him in the same distribution (other than like-kind property, see below) and (2) the amount of gain the partner recognizes under I.R.C. Sections 731 or 737.[69] The partnership's basis in the distributed property increases or decreases immediately before the distribution by the gain or loss the contributing partner recognizes; that increase or decrease is taken into account in determining the distributee partner's basis in the property distributed to him.[70] If the partnership has an election in effect under I.R.C. Section 754, any basis adjustments to partnership property (including the distributed I.R.C. Section 704(c) property) under I.R.C. Section 734(b) are made after the preceding adjustments.[71]

> **Example:** For equal interests in the EF Partnership, Edgar contributes realty worth $50,000 with a $20,000 basis, and Frank contributes $50,000 in cash. The partnership distributes the realty to Frank in Year 4, when the property is worth $60,000. The partnership is deemed to sell the realty to Frank for $50,000, and Edgar recognizes the $30,000 of gain that was "built in" to the realty when he contributed it. Edgar increases the basis of his partnership interest by the $30,000 of gain he recognizes. The partnership's basis in the land increases from $20,000 to $50,000 immediately before the distribution to Frank. Assuming Frank's basis in his partnership interest is at least $50,000, his basis in the land is $50,000, the same as the partnership's basis. Thus, Frank recognizes $10,000 of gain if he subsequently sells the land for $60,000. If the basis in his partnership interest is less than $50,000, his basis in the land is limited to the basis in his interest.

Transferee of contributing partner's interest. A transferee of all or a portion of a contributing partner's interest is treated as the contributing partner for purposes of I.R.C. Section 704(c)(1)(B), to the extent of the share of built-in gain or loss

---

[68] I.R.C. § 704(c)(1)(B)(iii); Treas. Reg. § 1.704-4(e). These basis adjustments are not elective and must be made regardless of whether the partnership has an election in effect under I.R.C. § 754.

[69] Under I.R.C. § 731, a partner recognizes gain if the money distributed to him exceeds the basis of his partnership interest. I.R.C. § 737 applies when a partner receives a distribution of property he previously contributed.

[70] I.R.C. § 704(c)(1)(B)(iii); Treas. Reg. § 1.704-4(e).

[71] Treas. Reg. § 1.704-4(e)(3).

allocated to the transferee.[72] Thus, the new partner steps into the contributing partner's shoes for purposes of the distribution rules.

The regulations provide a number of exceptions and special rules that allow distributions of contributed property without gain recognition.[73]

[2]   Anti-Abuse Rule

The regulations under I.R.C. Section 704(c)(1)(B) provide a specific anti-abuse rule for distributions of contributed property.[74] That rule provides that if a principal purpose of a transaction is to achieve a tax result that is inconsistent with the purpose of the statute, the IRS can recast the transaction for tax purposes to achieve tax results consistent with the statutory purpose. The preamble to the regulations describes that purpose as preventing partners from circumventing the built-in gain or loss rules of I.R.C. Section 704(c). Whether a tax result is inconsistent with the statute's purpose is determined from all the facts and circumstances.

An example from the regulations illustrates the one type of transaction that may be subject to the anti-abuse rule.[75] In the example, a partnership is about to liquidate when the partners become aware of potential gain recognition under I.R.C. Section 704(c)(1)(B). With a principal purpose of avoiding that gain, the partners amend the partnership agreement and take other steps to shift the benefits and burdens of ownership of the contributed property to the noncontributing partners until the seven-year statutory period expires.[76] The property is then distributed to the noncontributing partners. The example concludes that the amendment to the partnership agreement and other steps taken by the partnership were the "functional equivalent" of a distribution. Thus, the distribution occurred "in substance" within the seven-year period, and the contributing partner recognizes gain under I.R.C. Section 704(c)(1)(B) at that time. The example indicates that the anti-abuse rule would not apply if the partners merely delayed the distribution without amending the partnership agreement or changing their economic interests in the property.

[C]   Distributions to Contributing Partner

Under I.R.C. Section 737, a partner recognizes the gain built into property he contributed if he receives a distribution of other partnership property within seven years of the contribution.[77] This provision is designed to prevent partnerships from

---

[72] Treas. Reg. § 1.704-4(d)(2).

[73] Treas. Reg. § 1.704-4(c).

[74] Treas. Reg. § 1.704-4(f).

[75] Treas. Reg. § 1.704-4(f)(2), *Example (1)*.

[76] The actual example uses a five-year period. However, the statutory period was extended to seven years in 1997.

[77] I.R.C. § 737 is applicable to distributions on or after June 25, 1992. The seven-year period applies to property contributed after June 8, 1997. Property contributed before that date is subject to a five-year period.

avoiding the rules of I.R.C. Section 704(c) requiring allocation of built-in gain or loss to the contributing partner.[78]

The amount of gain the partner recognizes equals the lesser of the excess distribution or the net precontribution gain, defined as follows:

(1) **The excess distribution.** [79] This is defined as the excess of the fair market value[80] of the distributed property (other than money) over the distributee partner's basis for his partnership interest before the distribution[81] (reduced by the amount of money distributed in the same transaction). For this purpose, the distributee's partner's basis includes any basis adjustment resulting from the distribution (*e.g.*, adjustments for liabilities under I.R.C. Section 752) and from any other associated distribution except

(a) the basis increase for the gain recognized under I.R.C. Section 737;[82] and

(b) the basis decrease under I.R.C. Section 733(2) for property distributed to the partner (other than property that partner previously contributed).

Example: [83] In Year 1, Judy, Karen, and Len form the equal JKL Partnership. Judy contributes nondepreciable Property A, with a fair market value of $10,000 and a tax basis of $4,000. Karen and Len each contribute $10,000 in cash. The partnership purchases nondepreciable Property B for $9,000, subject to a $9,000 nonrecourse liability. Under I.R.C. Section 752, the partners share the liability equally so that the basis for each partner's partnership interest increases by $3,000.

At the end of Year 3, $2,000 cash and Property B, subject to the $9,000 liability, are distributed to Judy in a current distribution.

To determine Judy's excess distribution, the basis of her partnership interest increases to $11,000 ($7,000 initial basis — $2,000 cash distribution — $3,000 decrease in her share of the $9,000 partnership liability + $9,000 increase in her individual liabilities). Because the $11,000 basis for Judy's interest exceeds the $9,000 fair market value of the distributed property, the excess distribution is zero. Judy recognizes no gain under I.R.C. Section 737.

---

[78] *See* Senate Finance Committee, Technical Explanation of Revenue Act of 1992, 104.

[79] Treas. Reg. § 1.737-1(b)(1).

[80] Treas. Reg. § 1.737-1(b)(2).

[81] The distributee partner's basis in the partnership interest is determined as of the last day of the partnership's tax year if the is properly characterized as an advance or drawing against the partner's distributive share of income. Treas. Reg. § 1.737-1(b)(3)(ii). In that situation, the partner's basis includes his share of partnership income or loss and other basis adjustments for the entire tax year.

[82] Under I.R.C. § 737(c)(1).

[83] Treas. Reg. § 1.737-1(e), *Example (2)*.

(2) ***The partner's net precontribution gain.*** [84] Net precontribution gain is the net gain the distributee partner would recognize under I.R.C. Section 704(c)(1)(B) if all the property contributed by that partner within seven years of the distribution and currently held by the partnership were distributed to another partner.[85] As discussed in § 6.02, *supra*, I.R.C. Section 704(c)(1)(B) requires a partner to recognize gain when property he contributed is distributed to another partner in the amount that would be allocated to him if the property were sold rather than distributed.[86]

Any gain recognized under I.R.C. Section 737 is in addition to any gain recognized under I.R.C. Section 731.[87] The character of the gain is determined by reference to the character of the net precontribution gain.[88]

Example: [89] In Year 1, Louis, Mary and Nat form the LMN Limited Liability Company. Louis contributes depreciable Property A, having a value of $30,000 and adjusted basis of $20,000. Mary contributes nondepreciable Property B, having a value and basis of $30,000. Nat contributes $30,000 in cash.

Property A has a 10 year remaining depreciable life using the straight-line method. Allocations for the contributed property are made under the traditional method. Thus, Property A generates $3,000 per year of book depreciation — allocated $1,000 to each partner — and $2,000 per year of tax depreciation — allocated $1,000 each to Mary and Nat.

At the end of Year 3, Property B, worth $30,000, is distributed to Louis in complete liquidation of his LLC interest. At that time, Louis's basis in his LLC interest is $20,000, Property A's book value is $21,000 ($30,000 initial book value — $9,000 total book depreciation) and its adjusted basis is $14,000 ($20,000 initial basis — $6,000 total tax depreciation).

Louis recognizes $7,000 of gain on the distribution, the lesser of the excess distribution and the net precontribution gain. The excess distribution is $10,000 ($30,000 fair market value of the Property B — $20,000 basis for Louis's LLC interest). Louis's net precontribution gain is $7,000, ($21,000 book value of Property A — $14,000 tax basis for the property).

---

[84] I.R.C. § 737(a); Treas. Reg. § 1.737-1(c).

[85] Other than a partner who owns, directly or indirectly, more than 50 percent of the capital or profits interest in the partnership. Treas. Reg. § 1.737-1(c)(1).

[86] The allocation of built-in gain is governed by I.R.C. § 704(c)(1)(A).

[87] I.R.C. § 731 requires a partner to recognize gain to the extent that he receives a cash distribution that exceeds the basis in his partnership interest.

[88] I.R.C. § 737(a).

[89] Treas. Reg. § 1.737-1(e), *Example (1)*.

[1] Special Rules for Computing Net Precontribution Gain

(1) **Basis adjustments under I.R.C. Section 734(b)(1)(A).** If, in the same transaction, money and property subject to I.R.C. Section 737 are distributed to a partner when the partnership has an I.R.C. Section 754 election in effect, the distributee's net precontribution gain is reduced by any basis increase (under I.R.C. Section 734(b)(1)(A)) to I.R.C. Section 704(c) property contributed by the distributee partner.)[90] This gain reduction reflects the fact that the partner has recognized some built-in gain on the cash distribution under I.R.C. Section 731.

(2) **Transfers of a partnership interest.** The transferee of all or part of a contributing partner's interest succeeds to the transferor's net precontribution gain in an amount proportionate to the transferred interest.[91]

(3) **I.R.C. Section 704(c)(1)(B) gain recognized in related distribution.** If, in the same transaction as the distribution subject to I.R.C. Section 737, I.R.C. Section 704(c) property is distributed to another partner, net precontribution gain is computed after adjustments are made for gain or loss the contributing partner recognizes under I.R.C. Section 704(c)(1)(B) (or that would have been recognized except for the like-kind exception).[92] This adjustment is required to avoid gain recognition under both I.R.C. Sections 704(c)(1)(B) and 737 for the same built-in gain.

(4) **Actual distribution required.** Net precontribution gain is determined without regard to I.R.C. Section 704(c)(2) if property contributed by the distributee partner is not actually distributed to another partner in a distribution related to the I.R.C. Section 737 distribution.[93]

(5) **Character of gain.** The character of the distributee partner's gain under I.R.C. Section 737 is determined by, and is proportionate to, the character of the partner's net precontribution gain.[94] The character of the net precontribution gain is determined by netting all gains and losses of the same character from I.R.C. Section 704(c) property. Any character class with a net negative amount is disregarded. The character of the partner's gain under I.R.C. Section 737 is in proportion to the character classes with net positive amounts.

Character is determined at the partnership level by presuming that all its I.R.C. Section 704(c) property is sold to an unrelated party at the time of the distribution.[95] Accordingly, any rules for determining the character of gain or loss on a sale apply in determining the character of net precontribution gain.

---

[90] Treas. Reg. § 1.737-1(c)(2)(ii).

[91] Treas. Reg. § 1.737-1(c)(2)(iii).

[92] Treas. Reg. § 1.737-1(c)(2)(iv).

[93] Treas. Reg. § 1.737-1(c)(2)(v).

[94] I.R.C. § 737(a); Treas. Reg. § 1.737-1(d).

[95] This includes any item that must be separately accounted for by the contributing partner under I.R.C. § 702(a).

[2]   Distributions Not Subject to I.R.C. Section 737

The gain recognition rules of I.R.C. Section 737 do not apply in the following situations:

(1)   Property contributed on or before October 3, 1989.[96]

(2)   Technical partnership termination under I.R.C. Section 708(b)(1)(B).[97]

(3)   Certain transfers to another partnership.[98]

(4)   Certain partnership divisions.

(5)   Certain partnership incorporations.[99]

(6)   Certain previously contributed property.[100]

[3]   Basis Adjustments

Distributee partner's basis. The contributing partner's basis for his partnership interest increases by the amount of gain the partner recognizes under I.R.C. Section 737.[101] This basis increase is not taken into account in determining the amount of gain the partner recognizes under I.R.C. Sections 737 or 731 (if money is distributed in the same transaction). The basis increase is included, however, for purposes of determining the partner's basis in the property received in the distribution under I.R.C. Section 732.[102] If the partner's previously contributed property is distributed in the same transaction, the partner's basis for that property is determined as if it were received in a prior distribution without regard to I.R.C. Section 737.[103]

> **Example:** [104] In Year 1, Beth, Chris, and Dave form the equal BCD Partnership. Beth contributes nondepreciable Property A (fair market value of $10,000 and a tax basis of $5,000). Chris contributes nondepreciable Property B (fair market value and tax basis of $10,000). Dave contributes $10,000 cash.
>
> In Year 3, Property B is distributed to Beth in complete liquidation of her partnership interest. Beth recognizes $5,000 of gain under I.R.C. Section 737 (her excess distribution is $5,000 [$10,000 value of Property B — $5,000 basis in Beth's partnership interest] and her net precontribution gain is $5,000 [$10,000 value of Property A — $5,000 tax basis for that property]).
>
> The basis of Beth's partnership interest increases by the $5,000 of

---

[96]   Treas. Reg. § 1.737-1(c)(2)(i).

[97]   Treas. Reg. § 1.737-2(a).

[98]   Treas. Reg. § 1.737-2(b)(1).

[99]   Treas. Reg. § 1.737-2(c).

[100]   Treas. Reg. § 1.737-2(d)(1), (2).

[101]   Treas. Reg. § 1.737-3(a).

[102]   Treas. Reg. § 1.737-3(b)(1).

[103]   Treas. Reg. § 1.737-3(b)(2).

[104]   Treas. Reg. § 1.737-3(e), *Example (1)*.

recognized gain to $10,000. Because this increase is taken into account in determining Beth's basis in the distributed property, her basis in Property B is $10,000 (under I.R.C. Section 732(b)).

Partnership's basis. The partnership's basis in property previously contributed by the distributee partner increases by the amount of gain that partner recognizes under I.R.C. Section 737.[105] This basis increase is limited to "eligible property," defined as partnership property that:

(1)   was included in calculating the distributee's net precontribution gain;

(2)   has a value greater than its basis;

(3)   is of the same character as the gain recognized by the distributee; and

(4)   was not distributed to another partner in the same (or a related) transaction.

The basis increase is allocated among the partnership's eligible property as follows:[106]

(1)   Eligible property of the same character is treated as a single group.[107]

(2)   Each group is allocated its proportionate share of gain of the same character recognized by the distributee under I.R.C. Section 737.

(3)   Within each group, the basis increase is allocated among property in the order contributed by the partner to the partnership, starting with the earliest contribution. The amount allocated to a property equals the difference between the property's value and basis at the time of the distribution. The bases of properties contributed in the same (or a related) transaction increase in proportion to their respective amounts of unrealized appreciation at the time of the distribution.

These basis adjustments to partnership property are not elective and must be made regardless of whether the partnership has an I.R.C. Section 754 election in effect.[108] If an I.R.C. Section 754 election is in effect, basis adjustments (under I.R.C. Section 734(b)(1)(A)) attributable to money distributions in the same transaction are made before the basis adjustments attributable solely to gain under I.R.C. Section 737. Any other basis adjustments to partnership property under I.R.C. Section 734(b) are made after and take into account the I.R.C. Section 737 adjustments.

Any basis increase to partnership property is treated as a new property depreciable under any applicable method and period available to the partnership for newly purchased property of the type adjusted that is placed in service at the time

---

[105] Treas. Reg. § 1.737-3(c).

[106] Treas. Reg. § 1.737-3(c)(3).

[107] Character is determined in the same manner as the character of the recognized gain is determined under Treas. Reg. § 1.737-1(d).

[108] Treas. Reg. § 1.737-3(c)(4).

of the distribution.[109]

§ 6.03   ALLOCATIONS WHEN INTERESTS CHANGE

A partner's or LLC member's interest in a partnership or limited liability company may change during a tax year as a result of events such as an increase or decrease in the number of partners or members, or a sale, exchange, or liquidation of all or part of the interest. Under the "varying interest" rule of I.R.C. Section 706(d), a partner's distributive share for a year in which his interest changes must be determined by taking into account his different interests in the partnership during the periods before and after the change.[110]

The partner's interests during each period may be determined either: (1) by an interim closing of the partnership books on the date his interest changes, or (2) by prorating the share of partnership items he would have been allocated if his interest did not change before the end of the year.[111] Special rules apply to allocations of certain expenses of cash-method partnerships (allocable cash-basis items).[112] Each partner's share of these items is computed as if the partnership paid a ratable portion of the expense on each day to which it is economically attributable.[113] If the change in a partner's interest results from a sale, exchange, or liquidation of his entire interest, the partnership's tax year closes for that partner on the date of the transaction, and his share of partnership items is determined for the "short" tax year ending on that date.[114] (See discussion of sale or exchange of partner's interest in Chapter 12 and discussion of liquidation of partner's interest in Chapter 10.) If the partnership terminates, all partners' interests are deemed to be completely liquidated and each partner's share of partnership items is determined for the short tax year ending on the termination date.[115] (For discussion of partnership termination, see Chapter 13.) Any other change in a partner's interest does not close the partnership tax year, and the partner's share of partnership items must be computed by taking into account his different interests before and after the change.[116]

---

[109] Treas. Reg. § 1.737-3(d).

[110] I.R.C. § 706(d)(1). The Treasury has issued proposed regulations governing the determination of partners' distributive shares of partnership items when a partner's interests vary during a partnership tax year. 74 Fed. Reg. 17119-01 (Apr. 14, 2009).

[111] Treas. Reg. § 1.706-1(c)(2)(ii).

[112] I.R.C. § 706(d)(2).

[113] I.R.C. § 706(d)(2)(A)(i).

[114] I.R.C. § 706(c)(1).

[115] I.R.C. §§ 706(c)(1), 708(b).

[116] I.R.C. § 706(c)(2)(B); Treas. Reg. § 1.706-1(c)(2)(ii).

[A] General Rules

When a partner's interest in a partnership changes during the year, his distributive share of partnership tax items is determined for each portion of the year based upon his interest during that particular period.[117] This "varying interest" rule applies to changes in partners' interests arising from the following events:

(1) ***The admission of a new partner in exchange for a capital contribution.*** The new partner's distributive share and any decreases in the continuing partners' shares are determined by taking into account the partners' different percentages of interest in the partnership before and after the admission date.[118]

The partnership may use a mid-month convention to determine the admission date. Under this convention, partners admitted during the first 15 days are deemed admitted on the first day of the month, and partners admitted after the 15th day are deemed admitted on the 16th day.[119] The convention cannot be used if the partnership determines the partners' varying interests by the proration method.[120] The Treasury is authorized to issue regulations allowing conventions other than the mid-month convention, if no tax abuse potential exists.[121]

(2) ***An increase in a partner's interest in exchange for an additional capital contribution.*** The distributive shares of the partners whose interests increase or decrease as a result of the contribution are determined by taking into account their varying partnership interests before and after the contribution.[122]

(3) ***A transfer by sale, exchange, liquidation or upon death of a partner's entire interest.*** The partnership tax year closes for the deceased or withdrawing partner on the disposition date, and he is allocated his share of partnership tax items up to that time.[123] In the case of a sale, the purchaser is allocated his share of partnership items for the period from the date of purchase to the end of the partnership's tax year. In the case of a death or liquidation, the partners compute their shares of partnership items by taking into account their exact interests before and after the death or liquidation date. The mid-month convention (described in (1),

---

[117] I.R.C. § 706(d). *See* Melone, *Distributive Shares and the Varying Interests Rule: Planning Ideas and Open Issues*, 14 J. Partnership Tax'n 339 (Winter 1998).

[118] I.R.C. § 706(d); Treas. Reg. § 1.706-1(c)(2)(ii).

[119] I.R. 84-129 (Dec. 13, 1984).

[120] *Id.*

[121] H.R. Rep. No. 861, 98th Cong., 2d Sess. 858–59 (1984). *See* Staff of the Joint Committee on Taxation, General Explanation of the Tax Reform Act of 1984, 98th Cong., 2d Sess. 221–22 (1984).

[122] Rev. Rul. 77-310, 1977-2 C.B. 217; Lipke v. Comm'r, 81 T.C. 689 (1983), interpreting I.R.C. § 706(c)(2)(B), *amended and redesignated as* I.R.C. § 706(d) by Pub. L. No. 98-369, 98th Cong., 2d Sess. § 72(a) (July 18, 1984); S. Rep. No. 196, 98th Cong., 2d Sess. 219 (1984).

[123] Treas. Reg. § 1.706-1(c)(2).

above) may not be used in this situation.[124]

(4) *A sale, exchange, or liquidation of a portion of a partner's interest.* The partnership tax year does not close for any partner who gives up only a portion of his interest.[125] When this portion is given up by a sale or exchange, the seller determines his distributive share by taking into account his different interests before and after the disposition; the purchaser computes his share for the period after the date of purchase. The mid-month convention (described in (1), above) may be used to determine the purchaser's admission date.[126] When the portion being given up results from a liquidation, both the partner whose interest decreases and the partners whose interests increase, compute their distributive shares by taking into account their different interests before and after the liquidation date.

(5) *A partner's making or receipt of a gift of a partnership interest.* Both the donor and the donee generally determine their distributive shares by taking into account their different interests before and after the gift. In computing the donee's distributive share (for the year of the gift and subsequently), the following special rules apply:

(a) Allowance must be made for reasonable compensation to the donor for services he renders to the partnership.[127]

(b) The donee's share of income attributable to partnership capital cannot be proportionately greater than the donor's share of income attributable to partnership capital.[128] (For a full discussion of family partnership rules, see Chapter 9.)

[B] Determining Distributive Shares Under the Varying-Interest Rule

A partner's share of partnership tax items for the portion of the year before and after his interest in the partnership changes may be determined under either of the following methods:[129]

(1) *An interim closing of the partnership books on the date the partner's interest changes.* This method is used unless the partners agree to use another valid method.

(2) *Prorating the share of partnership items the partner would have been allocated if his interest had not changed before the end of the year.* The

---

[124] Staff of the Joint Committee on Taxation, General Explanation of the Tax Reform Act of 1984, 98th Cong., 2d Sess. 221–22 (1984).

[125] I.R.C. § 706(c)(2)(B).

[126] Staff of the Joint Committee on Taxation, General Explanation of the Tax Reform Act of 1984, 98th Cong., 2d Sess. 221–22 (1984).

[127] I.R.C. § 704(e)(2).

[128] *Id.*

[129] Treas. Reg. § 1.706-1(c)(2)(ii).

proration may be based on the number of days in the partnership tax year before and after the change in the partner's interest occurs. Partners also may use any other reasonable proration method, such as the ratio of sales before or after the change to total sales for the year.

If the change in the partner's interest results from a transfer of all or part of his interest, both the transferor and transferee must use the same method to determine their distributive shares.[130]

Example: Lewis, a one-third partner in the LMN Partnership (which uses a calendar tax year), sells his entire partnership interest to Peter on June 30. Up to the date of sale, LMN has $120,000 of ordinary income and $60,000 of capital gain. The partnership generates an additional $90,000 of ordinary income and $30,000 of capital gain from the date of sale through the end of the year.

Different results may be obtained under the two accepted methods, as follows:

Interim-Book-Closing Method

$120,000	LMN's ordinary income, 1/1 to 6/30
x 1/3	Lewis's interest
$40,000	Lewis's share of LMN's ordinary income
$60,000	LMN's capital gain
x 1/3	Lewis's interest
$20,000	Lewis's share of LMN's capital gain

Proration Method

$120,000	LMN's ordinary income, 1/1 to 6/30
+ 90,000	LMN's ordinary income, 7/1 to 12/31
$210,000	LMN's ordinary income for the year
x 1/3	Lewis's interest
$70,000	
x 1/2	Prorated for one-half of the year
$35,000	Lewis's share of LMN's ordinary income
$60,000	LMN's capital gain for 1/1 to 6/30
+ 30,000	LMN's capital gain for 7/1 to 12/31
$90,000	LMN's capital gain for year
x 1/3	Lewis's interest
$30,000	
x 1/2	Prorated for one-half of the year
$15,000	Lewis's share of LMN's capital gain

Whichever method is used for Lewis must be used to compute Peter's distributive share for the remainder of the year.

---

[130] Treas. Reg. § 1.706-1(c)(2)(ii).

[C]   Special Rule for Allocable Cash-Basis Items

The interim-book-closing or proration method, used in determining a partner's distributive share when his interest in the partnership changes, does not apply to certain expenses of cash-method partnerships that the Code terms "allocable cash basis items."[131] Instead, each partner's share of these items is computed as if the partnership paid a ratable portion of the expense on each day to which it is economically attributable. Therefore, these deductions are allocated among partners based on their interests in the partnership for each day of the year, regardless of when the partnership actually paid the underlying expense. This rule precludes newly admitted partners from receiving retroactive allocations of deductions attributable to the period before they joined the partnership.

The allocable cash-basis items subject to this rule are interest, taxes, payments for services (*e.g.*, compensation or fees), payments for the use of property (*e.g.*, rent or lease payments), and any other item that may be specified in regulations so as to avoid significant misstatements of partners' income.[132] The regulations provide that a deduction for a payment to a related person that is deferred under I.R.C. Section 267(a)(2) is treated as an allocable cash-basis item in the year the deduction is allowed.[133]

The amount of cash-basis items allocated to each partner is determined as follows:

(1)   A portion of each item is assigned to each day to which it is economically attributable. For example, if the partnership leases property for the entire year, 1/365 of the rent paid at year-end is economically attributable to each day of the year. If the property is leased only for the month of June, 1/30 of the rent is allocated to each day of that month.

(2)   The amount assigned to each day is allocated among the partners in proportion to their interests in the partnership at the close of the day.[134] The mid-month convention may be used to determine the date that a partner's interest changes.[135]

Example (1): Edith and Fred are equal partners in the EF Partnership, which uses the cash method and a calendar tax year. Rent for the partnership's office space is $36,000 a year and is paid at the end of the year. On December 1, Year 1, Gary joins the partnership as an equal one-third partner. Both Edith and Fred are allocated $17,500 of the partnership's rental-expense deduction, representing their one-half interest in the partnership for 11 months and one-third interest for one month ($3,000 per month x 11 months x 1/2 = $16,500, plus $3,000 x 1 month x 1/3 = $1,000). Gary's distributive share of the partnership's rental deduction for Year 1 is

---

[131] I.R.C. § 706(d)(2).

[132] I.R.C. § 706(d)(2)(B).

[133] Temp. Treas. Reg. § 1.706-2T, *citing* I.R.C. § 267(a)(2).

[134] I.R.C. § 706(d)(2)(A).

[135] Staff of the Joint Committee on Taxation, General Explanation of the Tax Reform Act of 1984, 98th Cong., 2d Sess. 221–22 (1984).

$1,000 (his one-third interest in the $3,000 rent expense attributable to the one-month period he owned his partnership interest).

Allocable cash-basis items are not assigned to any part of a tax year, unless the expense actually is paid during the year. An item that is economically attributable to a prior year but paid in the current year is assigned to the first day of the year in which it is paid.[136] The item is then allocated among the persons who were partners on the days of the prior year in which the expense was incurred, in proportion to their interests in the partnership on each day.[137] Amounts allocable to a person who was a partner in the prior year but who is no longer a partner in the year the item is paid may not be deducted by anyone. These amounts are capitalized and added to the basis of partnership assets.[138] The basis increase is allocated among partnership assets under the rules applicable to optional basis adjustments.[139]

> **Example (2):** Assume the facts in Example (1), except that: (a) Edith leaves the partnership on December 31, Year 1, and (b) the rent is not paid until January 31, Year 2. The $36,000 rental payment is deemed to be paid on January 1, Year 2, because it is economically attributable to a prior year. Therefore, as in Example (1), Fred is allocated $17,500, and Gary is allocated $1,000 of the expense. However, because Edith is no longer a partner on January 1, Year 2, she cannot be allocated any deduction for the rent attributable to the period she was a partner. The $17,500 deduction she would have been allowed (her interest in the Year 1 was the same as Fred(s) is capitalized and added to the basis of the partnership's assets.

An allocable cash-basis item paid in a year before the period to which it is economically attributable is assigned to the last day of the year of payment.[140] Partners on that day are allocated their shares of the expense. However, the deductibility of these items is likely to be limited by nonpartnership rules that preclude cash-method taxpayers from deducting prepaid expenses.[141]

[D] Change of Interests in Tiered Partnerships

A tiered partnership exists when one partnership (parent partnership) owns an interest in another partnership (subsidiary partnership).[142] Before the Tax Reform Act of 1984, tiered partnerships often were used to retroactively allocate the subsidiary's losses to partners of the parent partnership. Taxpayers purchased interests in a parent partnership late in the parent's tax year, but before the subsidiary's tax year ended. When the subsidiary's year closed, the parent partnership was allocated its share of the subsidiary's losses. These losses were, in

---

[136] I.R.C. § 706(d)(2)(C)(i).

[137] I.R.C. § 706(d)(2)(D)(i).

[138] I.R.C. § 706(d)(2)(D)(ii).

[139] *Id. See* I.R.C. § 755.

[140] I.R.C. § 706(d)(2)(C)(ii).

[141] *See, e.g.*, I.R.C. §§ 461(g) (prepaid interest expenses), 461(i) (prepaid expenses of tax shelters).

[142] *See, e.g.*, I.R.C. § 706(d)(3).

turn, allocated to the partners of the parent partnership.

The 1984 Act provided the following rules to prevent retroactive allocations through tiered partnerships:

(1)   When a parent partnership's interest in a subsidiary changes during the year, the parent's distributive share of the subsidiary's tax items is determined under the same varying-interest rule applicable to other shifts in partnership interests.[143]

(2)   When a partner's interest in the parent partnership changes, his distributive share of all parent-partnership tax items (not just cash-basis items) attributable to the subsidiary partnership is computed under the rules used to determine his share of allocable cash-basis items.[144] The allocation is made as follows:

(a)   The subsidiary assigns a portion of each item to each day to which it is economically attributable. Non-cash-basis items (*e.g.*, depreciation) may be prorated over the entire period.[145]

(b)   The parent partnership's share of the amount assigned to each day is allocated among its partners based on each partner's interest in the parent at the close of that day.[146] A subsidiary-partnership item paid in the current year that is economically attributable to a prior or subsequent year is allocated under rules analogous to those for allocable cash-basis items.[147]

[E]   Change in Partners' Interests Under Partnership Agreement

The varying-interest rule does not apply to partners who adjust their distributive shares of partnership items by an amendment to the partnership agreement or by a provision in the agreement that alters their shares when a specified event occurs.[148] For this purpose, the partnership agreement includes any modifications made up to or at the time for filing the partnership's tax return (not including extensions).[149] Therefore, partners may retroactively change their shares of partnership items if the modification is not related to an additional capital contribution by a new or existing partner, or a transfer or liquidation of all or part of a partner's interest.

---

[143] I.R.C. § 706(d)(3).

[144] *Id.*

[145] *See* H.R. Rep. No. 98-861, 98th Cong., 2d Sess. 858–59 n.4 (1984); Staff of the Joint Committee on Taxation, General Explanation of the Tax Reform Act of 1984, 98th Cong., 2d Sess. 221 (1984).

[146] *See* H.R. Rep. No. 98-861, 98th Cong., 2d Sess. 858–59 n.4 (1984); Staff of the Joint Committee on Taxation, General Explanation of the Tax Reform Act of 1984, 98th Cong., 2d Sess. 221 (1984).

[147] I.R.C. § 706(d)(3).

[148] S. Rep. No. 196, 98th Cong., 2d Sess. 219 (1984).

[149] I.R.C. § 761(c); Treas. Reg. § 1.761-1(c). The modification must be adopted in the manner provided for in the partnership agreement or it must be agreed to by all partners.

Example: The ABC Limited Partnership was formed in January, Year 1 and uses a calendar tax year. The partnership agreement allocates 95 percent of partnership net losses to the limited partners and 5 percent of its losses to the general partners until the first month in which the partnership earns a net profit. At that time, the sharing ratio changes to allocate 50 percent of all profits and losses to the general partners and 50 percent to the limited partners. ABC has net losses in all months until May, Year 3. Although the partners' interests change during the year, neither the varying-interest rule nor the allocable cash-basis-expense rule applies in determining their distributive shares for Year 3.

§ 6.04 SPECIAL ALLOCATIONS — OVERVIEW

The term "special allocation" generally refers to an allocation of a partnership or LLC item that is disproportionate to the partners' or members' capital contributions or to their ratio for sharing other partnership or LLC items. I.R.C. Section 704(b) provides the general rule that allocations in a partnership agreement are respected for tax purposes if they have "substantial economic effect." Regulations define this to mean that the tax consequences of an allocation must be incurred by the same partner who incurs the economic benefit or burden of the allocation. In other words, partners cannot share tax items differently than they share economic items. For example, a partner who receives a disproportionately large share of partnership income must be allocated that income for tax purposes. Similarly, a partner cannot be allocated a disproportionately high share of depreciation deductions for partnership assets unless he also bears the economic consequences of the decline in value of the assets.

The regulations create a two-part, safe-harbor test for determining whether an allocation has substantial economic effect. The first part of the test requires the allocation to have an "economic effect" that increases or decreases the dollar value of the partners' capital accounts (i.e., the amount they would receive upon a liquidation). This test ordinarily cannot be satisfied unless the partnership maintains the partners' capital accounts in accordance with elaborate rules set forth in the regulations. To ensure that the changes in the partners' capital accounts actually affect the amounts that they receive from the partnership, the regulations generally require the partnership agreement to contain provisions that: (1) require the partnership to make liquidating distributions that conform with the partners' positive capital account balances (see § 6.05[A][1], infra), and (2) require partners with deficit capital account balances to restore the deficits when their interests are liquidated (see § 6.05[A][2], infra).[150]

The second part of the safe-harbor test requires the economic effect of the allocation to be "substantial." In general, this means that a reasonable possibility must exist that the allocation will significantly change the dollar amounts the partners will receive from the partnership (i.e., the value of their capital accounts) without regard to tax consequences.[151] Thus, an allocation that changes the value of

---

[150] Treas. Reg. § 1.704-1(b)(2)(ii)(b).

[151] Treas. Reg. § 1.704-1(b)(2)(iii)(a).

a partner's capital account is not substantial, if the economic effect is offset by tax factors.

Different rules apply to special allocations of losses and deductions attributable to a partnership's nonrecourse liabilities (nonrecourse deductions). An example of a nonrecourse deduction is depreciation claimed for property acquired subject to a nonrecourse mortgage. These allocations cannot satisfy the economic-effect test because the creditor, rather than any partner, bears the economic burden if the value of the property securing the liability decreases below the amount of the debt. The regulations permit special allocations of nonrecourse deductions only if the partnership agreement contains specified provisions requiring partners to be allocated gain equal to their nonrecourse deductions (minimum gain) when the property securing the debts is disposed of. A partnership generally realizes gain on these dispositions even if no money is received because the full amount of the nonrecourse liability is included in its amount realized.[152] (See § 6.08, infra.)

The general rule that a partner's distributive share of partnership tax items is determined by the partnership agreement does not apply to allocations that are invalid because they lack substantial economic effect.[153] In that situation, each partner's share of the unallocated item is computed from his "interest in the partnership" as determined by taking into account all facts and circumstances that relate to the economic arrangement between the partners.[154]

[A] General Rules

A partnership or LLC agreement may (1) allocate overall income or loss in a manner that differs from the partners' or members' proportionate capital contributions, and (2) allocate specific items of income, gain, loss, deduction, and credit in a manner that differs from the partners' or members' overall profit and loss ratios. These "special allocations" allow partners and members a great deal of flexibility in determining how they will share the risks and benefits associated with particular partnership or LLC assets or operations. They also allow specific tax items, such as capital gains or depreciation, to be allocated to the partners and members who can use them most advantageously.

A special allocation in the partnership agreement is valid for tax purposes if it meets any of the following requirements:[155]

(1) *The allocation satisfies a "substantial economic effect" test set forth in the regulations.* This test consists of two parts:

    (a) An *economic effect test* requiring the economic benefit or burden corresponding to the tax allocation to be reflected in the partners' capital accounts (*i.e.*, increase or decrease the amount they will receive on a liquidation of their interest). The partners' capital

---

[152] I.R.C. § 7701(g); Comm'r v. Tufts, 461 U.S. 300 (1983).

[153] I.R.C. § 704(b).

[154] I.R.C. § 704(b); Treas. Reg. § 1.704-1(b)(3).

[155] Treas. Reg. § 1.704-1(a).

accounts must be maintained in accordance with detailed rules in the regulations.

(b) *A substantiality test* requiring the economic effect of the allocation to be substantial when compared with the shift in tax consequences it causes.

(2) *The allocation corresponds to the partner's economic "interest in the partnership," as determined from all the facts and circumstances.* This rule applies if the partnership agreement fails to allocate an item or if an allocation in the agreement is invalid because it lacks substantial economic effect.

(3) *The allocation is deemed to correspond to the partner's interest in the partnership.* [156] This rule applies to items that have no economic effect apart from their tax consequences (*e.g.*, tax credits, percentage depletion, deductions attributable to nonrecourse liabilities, recapture income, and tax preference items).

[B] Partnership Agreement Defined

For purposes of determining whether an allocation has substantial economic effect, the partnership or LLC agreement includes all oral and written agreements among the partners/members or between any partners/members and the partnership or LLC.[157] For example, the extent of a partner's obligation to restore a deficit capital account balance takes into account any direct or indirect arrangements that limit his obligation, such as puts, options, buy-sell agreements, and stop-loss arrangements.[158] The partnership agreement also includes, for this purpose, provisions of federal, state, or local law that govern partnership affairs or are incorporated by reference into the agreement.[159]

[C] Distributive Shares in Absence of Valid Partnership Agreement

The general rule that a partner's distributive share is determined by the partnership agreement does not apply if:

(1) the agreement fails to allocate overall or specific items of income, gain, loss, deduction, or credit; or

(2) an allocation in the agreement does not have substantial economic effect.[160]

In these situations, the partner's distributive share of any unallocated amounts is determined from his "interest in the partnership," which is his share of the

---

[156] Treas. Reg. § 1.704-1(b)(1)(i).

[157] Treas. Reg. § 1.704-1(b)(2)(ii)(h).

[158] Treas. Reg. § 1.704-1(b)(2)(ii)(h).

[159] *Id.*

[160] I.R.C. § 704(b).

economic benefit or burden of each partnership item as determined from the facts and circumstances.[161] In the unusual case when neither the taxpayer nor the IRS can establish facts and circumstances regarding the partners' interests in the partnership, the partners are presumed to have equal interests.[162]

A partner's interest in the partnership is determined separately for each item of income, deduction, credit, gain, or loss. Ordinarily, his interest in any particular item may differ from his overall interest in the partnership.[163] For example, a partner may have a 90-percent interest in a cost-recovery deduction and a 50-percent interest in overall profits. However, this flexibility as to a partner's interest in particular items does not apply to partnership items that cannot have economic effect, such as deductions attributable to the partnership's nonrecourse liabilities. These items must be allocated in accordance with a partner's overall interest in the partnership, or the allocations must satisfy rules under which they are deemed to accord with the partner's overall interest.[164]

§ 6.05 SUBSTANTIAL ECONOMIC EFFECT

The substantial economic effect test creates a safe harbor for establishing the validity of partnership or LLC allocations. The test consists of two parts, both of which must be satisfied:[165]

(1) An **economic effect test** requiring the partner that receives the allocation, bear the economic burden or obtain the economic benefit corresponding to the allocation. The economic effect of an allocation is determined from its impact on the partners' capital accounts, which must be maintained in accordance with detailed rules in the regulations.

Three alternative tests may be used to establish the economic effect of an allocation:

(a) The economic effect test is satisfied if the partnership agreement contains all of the following provisions:

(i) A provision requiring capital accounts to be maintained for partners in accordance with the rules set forth in the regulations. The purpose for these capital account rules is to ensure that allocations of partnership tax items match the corresponding economic allocations (book items) included in the partners' capital accounts; that is, the tax allocation must follow the book allocation. For example, if a partner's capital account is reduced by $100 to reflect his share of depreciation for a partnership

---

[161] Treas. Reg. § 1.704-1(b)(3)(i). *See, e.g.,* Mammoth Lakes Project v. Comm'r, T.C. Memo. 1991-4 (partnership losses allocated in accord with partner's interest in partnership where partnership agreement is silent).

[162] Treas. Reg. § 1.704-1(b)(3)(i).

[163] *Id.*

[164] *Id.*

[165] Treas. Reg. § 1.704-1(b)(2)(i).

asset, the partner must be allocated a $100 depreciation deduction for tax purposes. (The capital account rules are discussed in detail at § 6.06, *infra*.) Different capital account requirements apply to allocations related to property contributed to the partnership or which is revalued on the partnership's books. Because the book value of such property differs from its tax basis, book items for the property (such as depreciation) cannot match the corresponding tax item.

(ii)   A provision that liquidating distributions to all partners will be made in accordance with the partners' positive capital account balances. This provision ensures that any change in a partner's capital account will actually affect the amount he receives from the partnership.

(iii)   A provision unconditionally obligating the partner receiving the allocation to restore any deficit balance in his capital account when his partnership interest is liquidated.[166] This provision ensures that a partner cannot avoid the economic effect of a decrease in his capital account by withdrawing from the partnership when he has a deficit capital account.

(b)   The alternate economic-effect test requires the partnership agreement to contain the first two provisions required by the general economic-effect test but, in place of the provision obligating partners to restore deficit capital accounts, the agreement must include a "qualified-income-offset" provision.[167] An allocation is valid under this test only if the partner is not reasonably expected to have a deficit capital account. A qualified-income offset provides that a partner who unexpectedly incurs a deficit capital account will be allocated partnership income and gain to eliminate the deficit "as quickly as possible."[168] The alternative economic-effect test may be used to validate special allocations to partners, particularly limited partners who are not obligated by their partnership agreement or state law to restore any deficit in their capital accounts.

(c)   The economic equivalence test requires partners to demonstrate that the economic effect of an allocation is equivalent to the results that would be obtained under the general economic-effect test. This test may be useful for a partnership that has not followed the capital account rules of the regulations but can establish that its partners will always be entitled to the same liquidating distributions as under the general test.

(2)   A **substantiality test** requiring the economic effect of the allocation to be substantial when compared with the shift in tax consequences it causes.

---

[166]   Treas. Reg. § 1.704-1(b)(2)(ii)(b).

[167]   Treas. Reg. § 1.704-1(b)(2)(ii)(d)(1), (2), (3).

[168]   *Id.*

The economic effect of an allocation is generally substantial if a reasonable possibility exists that it will significantly change the dollar amounts the partners will receive from the partnership without regard to tax consequences.[169] The economic effect of an allocation generally is not substantial if:

(a) The allocation enhances one partner's after-tax economic position but is not likely to diminish substantially any other partner's after-tax economic position.[170]

(b) The allocation is likely to shift tax consequences among the partners without substantially changing their economic consequences.[171]

(c) The allocation is transitory, because its effect is likely to be offset by a subsequent allocation.[172]

[A] Economic-Effect Test

[1] Provisions Required in Partnership Agreement

An allocation has economic effect if the partner receiving it obtains the economic benefit or bears the economic burden corresponding to the allocated item.[173] The allocation must affect the dollar amount that the partner will receive from the partnership.[174]

To ensure that allocations have economic effect, the regulations require the inclusion of specific provisions in the partnership agreement during the full term of the partnership. The required provisions are as follows:

(1) Capital accounts will be maintained for all partners in accordance with the rules set forth in the regulations

(2) Liquidating distributions to all partners will be made in accordance with the partners' positive capital account balances.

(3) The partner receiving the allocation is unconditionally obligated to restore any deficit balance in his capital account when his partnership interest is liquidated.[175] (Exceptions to the rule requiring an unlimited deficit-restoration obligation are discussed at § 6.05[A][3][b], *infra.*)

Example: Lester and Marie each contribute $50,000 to form the LM Limited Liability Company, and the LLC uses the entire $100,000 to purchase depreciable equipment. The operating agreement provides that

---

[169] Treas. Reg. § 1.704-1(b)(2)(iii)(a).

[170] *Id.*

[171] Treas. Reg. § 1.704-1(b)(2)(iii)(b).

[172] Treas. Reg. § 1.704-1(b)(2)(iii)(c).

[173] Treas. Reg. § 1.704-1(b)(2)(ii)(a).

[174] Staff of the Joint Committee on Taxation, General Explanation of the Tax Reform Act of 1976, 94th Cong., 2d Sess. 94 (1976).

[175] Treas. Reg. § 1.704-1(b)(2)(ii)(b).

both members share LLC taxable income and loss equally, except that all cost-recovery deductions for the equipment are allocated to Lester. The agreement also provides that capital accounts will be properly maintained, that liquidating distributions will be made in accordance with the members' positive capital account balances, and that each member is obligated to restore any deficit balance in his capital account. In Year 1, Lester is allocated a $5,000 cost-recovery deduction, which satisfies the economic-effect test. The fact that Lester bears the economic burden of the depreciation deduction allocated to him may be demonstrated by assuming that: (1) the LLC has no income or loss other than depreciation during the year, and (2) it liquidates at the end of the year:

	Lester		Marie	
	Tax	Book	Tax	Book
Initial capital account	$50,000	$50,000	$50,000	$50,000
Depreciation	(5,000)	(5,000)	0	0
Capital account, end of year 1	$45,000	$45,000	$50,000	$50,000

The liquidating distribution Lester receives is $5,000 less than the distribution Marie receives. This amount corresponds to the depreciation (*i.e.*, the decline in value) of LLC assets he agreed to bear. Note that the economic effect of the allocation is determined by presuming that LLC assets actually decline in value by the amount of depreciation reflected in the members' capital accounts.

[2] Liquidating Distributions of Positive Capital Account Balances

An allocation lacks economic effect unless the partnership agreement provides, during the full term of the partnership, that liquidating distributions to partners will accord with their positive capital account balances.[176] This provision must apply both on the liquidation of an individual partner's interest and when the entire partnership liquidates.

The distribution must be made by the later of (1) the end of the partnership tax year in which the liquidation occurs, or (2) 90 days after the liquidation date.[177] This requirement is not met if the partnership delays liquidating after its primary business activities have ceased in order to defer the date when a partner's capital account balance must be distributed to him.[178]

The partners' capital account balances are determined after making all adjustments for the partnership tax year in which the liquidation occurs.[179] These adjustments do not include adjustments that are attributable to the liquidating

---

[176] Treas. Reg. § 1.704-1(b)(2)(ii)(b)(2).

[177] *Id.*

[178] Treas. Reg. § 1.704-1(b)(2)(ii)(g).

[179] Treas. Reg. § 1.704-1(b)(2)(ii)(b)(2).

distribution itself or to contributions other partners must make to restore their deficit capital accounts.[180]

Example (1): Burt and Carol each contribute $40,000 to form the BC Partnership; each partner's capital account is credited with $40,000. The partnership uses the entire $80,000 to purchase equipment that is depreciable ratably over 4 years. Under the partnership agreement, Burt and Carol share partnership income and loss equally, except that all depreciation allowed for the equipment is allocated to Burt. The partnership agreement also provides that capital accounts will be maintained in accordance with the regulations, but that upon liquidation, partnership assets will be distributed equally between the partners regardless of their capital account balances. Because liquidating distributions need not accord with the partners' capital accounts, the depreciation allocation fails the economic-effect test and is disregarded for tax purposes.

To illustrate that this allocation lacks economic effect, assume that, in Year 1, partnership income equals expenses (except for the $20,000 depreciation deduction allocated to Burt), and that, after Year 1, the partnership sells the equipment for its $60,000 book value and liquidates. On liquidation, pursuant to the equal-distribution provision in the partnership agreement, Burt and Carol each receive $30,000. Both partners contributed $40,000 to the partnership and, therefore, each sustains a $10,000 economic loss fully attributable to depreciation of the equipment. Because Burt was allocated $20,000 in depreciation and his ending capital account balance is $20,000 less than Carol's, the $30,000 distribution means that Burt bears only one-half of the economic loss attributable to the decline in value of the equipment. Carol actually bears the other half of the loss.[181]

Following is a summary of the two partners' capital accounts:

	Burt	Carol
Capital contribution	$40,000	$40,000
Depreciation deduction	(20,000)	0
Balance, end of Year 1	$20,000	$40,000
Cash distribution on liquidation	30,000	30,000
Gain (loss) on liquidation	$10,000	($10,000)

Because Burt does not incur the economic effect of the depreciation allocation, the allocation is not respected for tax purposes. The depreciation will be reallocated in accordance with the partners' interests in the partnership.

Example (2): Assume the same facts as in Example (1), except that the partnership agreement provides that liquidation proceeds will be distributed in accordance with capital account balances if the partnership is liquidated during its first five years, but that they will be distributed

---

[180] *Id.*

[181] Treas. Reg. § 1.704-1(b)(5), *Example (1)(i).*

equally to partners if the partnership is liquidated after that time. This allocation fails the economic-effect test and is disregarded, because the agreement does not provide that liquidating distributions must follow positive capital account balances during the entire term of the partnership.[182]

Example (3): Assume the same facts as in Example (1), except that the partnership agreement provides that liquidation proceeds will be distributed in accordance with capital account balances whenever the partnership or any partner's interest is liquidated. The allocation of depreciation deductions to Burt satisfies the economic-effect test and is valid for tax purposes (assuming that the substantiality test also is met).

To see the economic effect of the allocation, assume that the partnership liquidates at the end of Year 2. Burt has been allocated a total of $40,000 in depreciation, and the balance of his capital account is zero. Carol's capital account is $40,000. The equipment, which is the partnership's sole asset, is presumed worth $40,000. Upon a liquidating distribution in accordance with the partners' capital accounts, Carol receives assets worth $40,000 and Burt receives nothing. Therefore, Burt has sustained the entire $40,000 economic loss attributable to the equipment's depreciation.

[3] Liquidation When Partner Has Deficit Capital Account

The regulations provide a general rule that a partner who receives a special allocation must be unconditionally obligated to restore any deficit balance in his capital account when his partnership interest is liquidated.[183]

The requirement that partners be obligated to restore deficit capital accounts upon liquidation of their interests is subject to three exceptions:

(1)   A partner may limit his deficit-restoration obligation to a specific amount by contributing a promissory note to the partnership or by agreeing to make a specified future capital contribution. In either of these situations, allocations are valid to the extent that they do not create a deficit capital account that exceeds the amount of the partner's obligation.[184]

(2)   Under an alternate economic effect test, an allocation is valid if (a) it does not create or increase a deficit in the partner's capital account, and (b) the partnership agreement contains a qualified-income-offset provision.[185] In determining whether the allocation creates or increases a deficit, the partner's capital account is adjusted to reflect certain reasonably anticipated increases or decreases. A qualified-income offset provides that a partner whose capital account becomes negative as a result of certain unexpected adjustments or distributions will be allocated sufficient partnership income to eliminate the deficit as quickly as possible.

---

[182]   Treas. Reg. § 1.704-1(b)(5), *Example (1)(ii)*.

[183]   *See, e.g.*, Rev. Rul. 92-97, 1992-2 C.B. 124.

[184]   Treas. Reg. § 1.704-1(b)(2)(ii)(c).

[185]   Treas. Reg. § 1.704-1(b)(2)(ii)(d).

(3) A partner may eliminate or reduce his obligation to restore all or part of any future deficit in his capital account.[186] Eliminating or reducing a future deficit-restoration obligation does not invalidate any prior allocations, if the partner continues to be obligated to restore any existing deficit in his capital account.

[a] General Rule-Deficit Must Be Restored

An allocation to a partner generally lacks economic effect unless the partnership agreement obligates the partner to restore a deficit balance in his capital account when his partnership interest is liquidated.[187] This provision ensures that a partner cannot avoid the economic effect of a decrease in his capital account by liquidating his interest in the partnership when he has a deficit capital account. If the partner's capital account deficit is not restored upon liquidation, the economic burden of the losses, deductions, and distributions that created the deficit are shifted to the other partners.[188]

> **Example (1):** Claire contributes $75,000 and Dell contributes $25,000 to form the CD Partnership. The partnership agreement provides that all income, gain, loss, and deduction will be allocated equally between the partners, that capital accounts will be maintained under the rules in the regulations, and that liquidating distributions will be made in accordance with the partners' positive capital account balances. Neither partner is obligated to restore a deficit capital account following a liquidation of his interest. The equal income and loss allocation fails the economic-effect test and is disregarded.
>
> To illustrate that the allocation lacks economic effect, assume that the partnership incurs a $20,000 loss in each of its first three years, reducing the book value of partnership assets to $40,000 ($100,000 contributed capital less $60,000 in losses). If the allocation in the agreement were respected, the partnership losses would create the following capital accounts:
>
> | | Claire | Dell |
> | --- | --- | --- |
> | Initial capital account | $75,000 | $25,000 |
> | Losses, Years 1, 2, 3 | (30,000) | (30,000) |
> | Gain (loss) on liquidation | $45,000 | ($5,000) |
>
> If the partnership liquidates, Claire receives only $40,000 from the partnership, even though her capital account is $45,000. Although Dell does not receive a distribution, his $30,000 in tax losses exceeds his economic loss by $5,000. In effect, Claire bears the economic burden of $5,000 of partnership loss deducted by Dell.

---

[186] Treas. Reg. § 1.704-1(b)(2)(ii)(f).

[187] Treas. Reg. § 1.704-1(b)(2)(ii)(b)(3).

[188] *See, e.g.*, Rev. Rul. 92-97, 1992-2 C.B. 124 (allocation of cancellation of debt income lacks economic effect unless partners are unconditionally obligated to restore deficit needed to satisfy another partner's right to receive positive capital account balance).

Example (2): Assume the same facts as in Example (1), except that the partners are obligated to restore their deficit capital account balances when the partnership liquidates. The income and loss allocation in the partnership agreement is valid for tax purposes (assuming that the substantiality test is also met).

To illustrate the economic effect of this allocation, assume the partnership liquidates at the end of Year 3. Dell's capital account balance is a deficit $5,000 and, because he is obligated to restore a deficit balance, he must pay $5,000 to the partnership. After Dell makes his payment, partnership assets total $45,000, which is the balance of Claire's capital account, and Claire receives the entire $45,000. The result: Dell bears the entire economic burden of the partnership losses allocated to him.

A partner must be required to restore a deficit capital account balance by the later of (1) the end of the partnership tax year in which the liquidation occurs, or (2) 90 days after the liquidation date.[189] This requirement is not satisfied if the partnership delays liquidation after its primary business activities has ceased, in order to defer the date when a partner must restore his deficit capital account balance.[190]

A partner is not considered obligated to restore a deficit capital account if his obligation is not legally enforceable or if a plan exists to avoid or circumvent the obligation.[191] For example, if a liquidation is delayed (*e.g.*, by having a partnership carry on nominal business activities) to postpone payment of a partner's capital account deficit, the Service may conclude that no deficit-restoration obligation existed and disallow prior allocations.[192]

[b] Exceptions to Deficit-Restoration Requirement

[i] Alternate Economic-Effect Test

Under the alternate economic-effect test in the regulations, an allocation to a partner may have economic effect, even though the partner is not obligated to restore all or part of his deficit capital account balance. An allocation may be valid under this test only to the extent that it does not create or increase a deficit in a partner's capital account beyond any partial deficit-restoration obligation the partner has. The test is designed to validate special allocations to partners (particularly limited partners) who are not obligated by their partnership agreement or state law to restore a deficit capital account.[193] Thus, the alternate economic-effect test permits special allocations to partners who wish to avoid the

---

[189] Treas. Reg. § 1.704-1(b)(2)(ii)(b)(3).

[190] Treas. Reg. § 1.704-1(b)(2)(ii)(g).

[191] Treas. Reg. § 1.704-1(b)(2)(ii)(c). *See also* Treas. Reg. § 1.704-1(b)(5), *Examples (1)(ix), (x)*.

[192] Treas. Reg. § 1.704-1(b)(2)(ii)(c). *See* Treas. Reg. § 1.704-1(b)(4)(vi).

[193] Ordinarily, limited partners are not obligated to restore deficit capital accounts. A general partner's deficit restoration obligation can be limited by agreement to the amount needed to pay partnership creditors; in that case, they are not obligated to restore a deficit needed to repay another partner for his capital account balance. *See* U.P.A. §§ 15, 18, 40(a)-(d).

financial risk of the unlimited deficit-restoration obligation required under the general economic-effect test. The requirements of the alternate economic-effect test are:

(1) The partnership agreement must provide that capital accounts will be maintained in accordance with the rules in the regulations and that all liquidating distributions will be in accord with the partners' positive capital account balances (*i.e.*, the first two requirements of the general economic-effect test).

(2) The allocation must not create or increase a deficit in a partner's capital account after the account is reduced to reflect certain adjustments and distributions that are reasonably expected to occur in the future.

(3) The partnership agreement must include a qualified-income-offset provision, requiring an unexpected capital account deficit to be restored by an offsetting allocation of partnership income.[194]

Reasonably expected capital account adjustments. An allocation has economic effect under the alternate test only to the extent that it does not create or increase a deficit in the partner's capital account beyond any partial deficit-restoration obligation he may have at the end of each tax year.[195] In determining whether an allocation will cause or increase a deficit, the partner's capital account is first reduced to reflect a number of future adjustments that are reasonably expected at the end of the year. Capital account reductions are required for all reasonably expected

(1) future oil and gas depletion adjustments;[196]

(2) future losses and deductions allocated to the partner under

(a) the family partnership rules,[197]

(b) the rules governing retroactive allocations,[198] and

(c) the rules governing disproportionate distributions of unrealized receivables and substantially appreciated inventory;[199] and

(3) future distributions the partner will receive that exceed increases in his capital account which are reasonably expected to occur during or before the partnership tax year in which the distributions are expected to occur.[200]

When determining the amount of any expected distributions and capital account increases, the value of partnership property is presumed to equal its adjusted tax

---

[194] Treas. Reg. § 1.704-1(b)(2)(ii)(d)(1), (2), (3).

[195] Treas. Reg. § 1.704-1(b)(2)(ii)(d)(3) (flush language).

[196] Treas. Reg. § 1.704-1(b)(2)(iv)(k).

[197] I.R.C. § 704(e)(2).

[198] I.R.C. § 706(d).

[199] Treas. Reg. § 1.751-1(b)(2)(ii).

[200] Treas. Reg. § 1.704-1(b)(2)(ii)(d)(4), (5), (6).

basis.[201] Thus, partners cannot offset expected distributions with gain expected from sales of appreciated partnership assets.

Qualified Income Offset. A partnership agreement contains a qualified income offset only if it provides that a partner who unexpectedly receives any of the above adjustments, allocations, or distributions will be allocated partnership income and gain so as to eliminate any resulting deficit capital account "as quickly as possible."[202] The allocation must consist of a pro rata portion of each item of partnership income, including gross income and gain if needed to eliminate the deficit.

The alternate economic-effect test recognizes that a partner with a positive capital account bears the economic burden of partnership losses charged to his account by decreasing the dollar amount he will receive in a liquidation. Thus, an unlimited deficit-restoration obligation is not considered essential where a partner is not expected to have a deficit capital account. However, the test requires the partners' capital accounts to be reduced for certain deductions that are not otherwise subject to the substantial-economic-effect test and for reasonably anticipated distributions. This capital account reduction is designed to preclude a partner from receiving a loss allocation in one year, even though he can predict that later distributions or deductions will create a deficit capital account that he is not obligated to restore.

The regulations do not provide guidelines for determining when capital account adjustments are "reasonably expected." If a partner errs in determining whether his reasonably expected capital account adjustments will create a deficit at the end of a partnership tax year, his special allocations may be invalid because they lack economic effect. This may occur even if the allocation satisfied the alternate economic-effect test in all prior years.

It is important to note that the presence of a qualified-income-offset provision in the partnership agreement does not ensure that a special allocation satisfies the alternate economic-effect test. The qualified-income offset relates only to capital account deficits created by unexpected adjustments. The unexpected deficits do not invalidate the special allocation, but must be made up by an increased allocation of income. If the deficit is created by an adjustment that is reasonably expected by the end of the year, however, the special allocation lacks economic effect for that year.

Example (1): Lew and Mona are members of the LM Limited Liability Company. Lew contributes $10,000 for a 10-percent interest, and Mona contributes $90,000 for a 90-percent interest. The LLC uses its $100,000 of contributed capital plus $400,000 of borrowed funds to purchase a building. The LLC operating agreement provides that:

(1)   members' capital accounts will be maintained in accordance with the regulations;

---

[201]   Treas. Reg. § 1.704-1(b)(2)(ii)(d) (flush language).

[202]   Treas. Reg. § 1.704-1(b)(2)(ii)(d).

(2)   liquidating distributions will be made in accordance with members' positive capital account balances;

(3)   on liquidation, Lew must restore his deficit capital account balance, but Mona has no deficit-restoration obligation;

(4)   members will share profits and losses in proportion to their initial capital contributions; and

(5)   allocations will accord with the qualified income offset rules.

In its first two years, the LLC incurs total taxable losses of $90,000 and, pursuant to their agreement, $81,000 ($90,000 x 90%) is allocated to Mona. The allocation does not satisfy the general economic effect test because Mona is not obligated to restore any deficit capital account. However, the allocation satisfies the alternate economic-effect test because, assuming that no required capital account reductions are reasonably anticipated, the $81,000 loss does not create a deficit in Mona's capital account.

	Lew	Mona
Initial capital account	$10,000	$90,000
Losses in Years 1 and 2	(9,000)	(81,000)
Capital account, end of year 2	$1,000	$9,000

If partnership losses in Year 3 are $30,000, Mona's allocated share is $27,000 ($30,000 x 90%). However, only $9,000 meets the alternate economic-effect test. The balance, $18,000, does not satisfy this test because the allocation would create a deficit in Mona's capital account, and Mona is not obligated to restore a deficit balance. Therefore, the remaining $18,000 loss must be reallocated in accordance with the partners' interests in the partnership. It is likely that the entire $18,000 loss will be allocated to Lew because he bears the economic effect of these losses.

Example (2): Using the facts in Example (1), assume that in Year 3 the partners reasonably anticipate that: (1) Year 4's partnership income will equal partnership expenses, and (2) in Year 4 the partnership will distribute $500 to Lew and $4,500 to Mona. For purposes of the alternate economic-effect test, Mona's capital account at the end of Year 3 is reduced by the anticipated distribution ($9,000 – $4,500 = $4,500), thereby limiting the Year 3 loss allocable to her to $4,500.[203] Of the $27,000 loss allocated to Mona under the partnership agreement, $22,500 ($27,000 – $4,500) must be reallocated in accordance with the partners' interests in the partnership.

Example (3): Using the facts in Example (1), assume that the partners cannot reasonably anticipate that a distribution will occur in Year 4. Because Mona's capital account at the end of Year 3 is not reduced by Year 4's distribution, $9,000 of the allocated loss satisfies the alternate economic-effect test. Because the loss allocation reduces Mona's capital account to zero at the beginning of Year 4, the $4,500 distribution she receives during that year creates a corresponding deficit in her capital account. Therefore,

---

[203] Treas. Reg. § 1.704-1(b)(5), *Examples (1 evi), (ix). See* Elrod v. Comm'r, 87 T.C. 1046 (1986).

under the qualified-income-offset provision, $4,500 of partnership gross income must be allocated to Mona to eliminate that deficit. Because partnership income equals its expenses, the gross income allocation to Mona results in a net loss being allocated to Lew.

[ii]   Partial Obligation to Restore Deficit

An allocation may be valid even though a partner's deficit-restoration obligation is limited to a specific dollar amount. A partner is considered obligated to restore a partial capital account deficit to the extent of:

(1)   the outstanding balance of any promissory notes he makes and contributes to the partnership (if the note is not readily tradable on an established securities market); and

(2)   his unconditional obligation, imposed by the partnership agreement or by state or local law, to make subsequent contributions to the partnership.[204]

[iii]   Reduction of Deficit-Restoration Obligation

At the end of the partnership's tax year, a partner may eliminate or reduce his obligation to restore all or part of any future deficit in his capital account.[205] Eliminating or reducing a future deficit-restoration obligation does not invalidate any prior allocations, if the partner continues to be obligated to restore any existing deficit in his capital account. To determine the amount of his existing deficit, the partner reduces his capital account by the same reasonably expected adjustments, allocations, and distributions made under the alternate economic-effect test.

> **Example:** Bob and Carol each contribute $40,000 to form the BC Partnership. The partnership uses the contributed $80,000 to purchase depreciable equipment. Under the partnership agreement, the partners share income and loss equally, except that all cost-recovery deductions for the equipment are allocated to Bob. The agreement also provides that the partners' capital accounts will be maintained under the rules in the regulations, that liquidating distributions will agree with partners' positive capital account balances, and that both partners are obligated to restore any deficits in their capital accounts upon liquidation of their interests. Therefore, at the partnership's inception, the allocation of depreciation deductions to Bob satisfies the economic-effect test.
>
> In each of its first two tax years, partnership income equals expenses, except for a $16,000 cost-recovery deduction in Year 1 and a $25,000 cost-recovery deduction in Year 2. The allocation of cost-recovery deductions to Bob is reflected in the partner's capital accounts as follows:

---

[204] Treas. Reg. § 1.704-1(b)(2)(ii)(c). *See* Rev. Rul. 92-97, 1992-2 C.B. 124 (limited deficit restoration obligation exists if state law obligates partners to restore deficits needed to pay partnership creditors).

[205] Treas. Reg. § 1.704-1(b)(2)(ii)(f).

	Bob	Carol
Initial capital accounts	$40,000	$40,000
Year 1 cost-recovery deduction	(16,000)	0
Year 2 cost-recovery deduction	(25,000)	0
Capital accounts, end of Year 2	($1,000)	$40,000

Assuming that Bob cannot reasonably anticipate any capital account reductions at the end of Year 2, the partnership agreement can be amended to reduce Bob's obligation to restore a deficit capital account to $1,000 (his current deficit), without affecting the validity of the cost-recovery deductions previously allocated to him. If Bob makes a $1,000 capital contribution to BC and eliminates the $1,000 deficit balance in his capital account, the partnership can eliminate Bob's obligation to restore any capital account deficit.[206]

For purposes of the economic-effect test, a partner's interest is liquidated on the earlier of: (1) the date the partnership liquidates, or (2) the date the partner's entire interest in the partnership terminates.[207] A partnership liquidates on the earlier of:

(1)   the date it ceases to be a going concern (although it may continue to wind up its affairs, pay its debts, and distribute remaining assets to the partners), or

(2)   the date it terminates under the rules of I.R.C. Section 708(b)(1). This is generally the date that —

    (a)   it ceases business or financial operations as a partnership, or

    (b)   50 percent or more of the total interests in the partnership's capital and profits are sold or exchanged within a 12-month period.[208]

The date that a partner's interest in a partnership is liquidated is determined under Regulations Section 1.761-1(d). Generally, this occurs on the date the partner receives his final liquidating distribution from the partnership.

[4] Economic-Effect Equivalence

An allocation that fails the economic-effect test or the alternate economic-effect test may nevertheless be valid if the partners can demonstrate that its economic effect is equivalent to the results that would be obtained under those two tests. Economic-effect equivalence exists if a liquidation of the partnership at the end of the current, or any future, year would have the same economic results for the partners (regardless of the partnership's economic performance) as would occur if the economic-effect test had been satisfied.[209] The use of economic-effect equiva-

---

[206] Treas. Reg. § 1.704-1(b)(5), *Example (1)(viii)*.

[207] Treas. Reg. § 1.704-1(b)(2)(ii)(g).

[208] Treas. Reg. § 1.704-1(b)(2)(ii)(g); see I.R.C. § 708(b)(1).

[209] Treas. Reg. § 1.704-1(b)(2)(ii)(i). For application of this liquidation test, see Interhotel Co. v. Comm'r, 74 T.C.M. (CCH) 819 (1997). For criticism of the Tax Court's holding in that case, see Lipton, *Nonrecourse Deductions of Lower-Tier Partnerships: No Room at the Interhotel?*, 88 J. Tax'n 42 (1998).

lence requires the partners to show that the allocation has the same economic effect as if the partnership agreement provided for: (1) maintaining capital accounts under the rules in the regulations, (2) making liquidating distributions that agree with positive capital account balances, and (3) restoring deficit account balances.[210]

[5] Partial Economic Effect

If only part of an allocation satisfies the economic-effect test, the other, invalid part is reallocated among the partners in accordance with their interests in the partnership. Both the valid and the reallocated portions of the allocation consist of a proportionate share of all the items included in the allocation.[211]

[B] Substantiality Test

Allocations that satisfy the economic-effect test are not valid unless that economic effect is "substantial."[212] The economic effect of an allocation is generally substantial if a reasonable possibility exists that it will significantly change the dollar amounts the partners will receive from the partnership without regard to tax consequences.[213] However, if any of the following three special rules apply, the economic effect of an allocation is not considered substantial:

Rule (1) — The allocation enhances one partner's after-tax economic position, but is not likely to substantially diminish any other partner's after-tax economic position.[214]

Rule (2) — The allocation is likely to shift tax consequences for a year among the partners without substantially changing their economic consequences.[215]

Rule (3) — The allocation is transitory, because its effect is likely to be offset by a subsequent allocation.[216]

Whether the economic effect of an allocation is substantial is determined at the time it becomes part of the partnership agreement, taking into account all other allocations in the agreement at that time.[217] Also taken into account are subsequent amendments to the agreement, whose consequences are determined to be part of

---

The Service has conceded that its position in *Interhotel* regarding the minimum gain chargeback was wrong. Accordingly, the appeals court vacated and remanded the case in an unpublished opinion. Interhotel Co. v. Comm'r, 221 F.3d 1348 (9th Cir. 2000). On remand, the Tax Court reiterated its initial holding. Interhotel Co. v. Comm'r, 81 T.C.M. (CCH) 1804 (2001).

[210] Treas. Reg. § 1.704-1(b)(2)(ii)(i).

[211] Treas. Reg. § 1.704-1(b)(2)(ii)(e).

[212] Treas. Reg. § 1.704-1(b)(2)(i).

[213] Treas. Reg. § 1.704-1(b)(2)(iii)(a).

[214] *Id.*

[215] Treas. Reg. § 1.704-1(b)(2)(iii)(b).

[216] Treas. Reg. § 1.704-1(b)(2)(iii)(c).

[217] Treas. Reg. § 1.704-1(b)(2)(iii)(a), (b), (c).

the original agreement.[218]

For purposes of the substantiality test, the fair market value of partnership property is presumed equal to either its adjusted tax basis or, if the property is properly reflected on the partnership's records at a book value that differs from basis, its book value.[219] Any changes to the property's tax basis or book value are presumed to be matched by corresponding changes in its fair market value.[220] The effect of these presumptions is that it is unlikely that the economic effect of an allocation will be offset by an allocation of the gain or loss realized from a disposition of partnership property.[221]

[1]　After-Tax Economic Consequences Rule

The regulations state that the economic effect of an allocation is not substantial if, when it becomes part of the partnership agreement:

(1)　at least one partner's after-tax economic consequences, in present-value terms, may be enhanced, and

(2)　it is very unlikely that any partner's after-tax economic consequences, in present-value terms, will be substantially diminished.[222]

A partner's after-tax economic consequences are determined by taking into account tax attributes unrelated to the partnership (*e.g.*, his tax bracket, exemptions, or net-operating-loss carryovers).[223]

Virtually any allocation in a partnership agreement will enhance at least one partner's economic position while adversely affecting the other partners. Therefore, the substantiality of the allocation depends upon whether the adversely affected partners have nonpartnership tax attributes that are likely to negate the unfavorable economic consequences of the allocation. The regulations do not indicate how to compute the present value of a partner's after-tax consequences. Possibly the time-value-of-money rules apply.[224]

> **Example:** Exemptco (a corporation) and Dean (an individual taxpayer) contribute equal amounts to the ED Partnership, which they form to invest in taxable and tax-exempt securities. Exemptco is a tax-exempt organization; Dean expects to be in the 33 percent marginal tax bracket for the next several years. The partnership agreement satisfies the capital account

---

[218]　Treas. Reg. § 1.704-1(b)(4)(vi).

[219]　*But see* Rev. Rul. 99-43, 1999-42 I.R.B. 506, holding that the presumption that value equals basis does not apply where the partnership agreement provisions governing allocation of gain or loss from the disposition of property are changed after the property has been revalued on the partnership's books but apply to a period before the revaluation.

[220]　Treas. Reg. § 1.704-1(b)(2)(iii)(c).

[221]　*Id.*

[222]　Treas. Reg. § 1.704-1(b)(2)(iii)(a).

[223]　Treas. Reg. § 1.704-1(b)(2)(iii)(a). *See, e.g.*, Rev. Rul. 99-43, 1999-42 I.R.B. 506 (allocation of cancellation of debt income to insolvent partner).

[224]　*See, e.g.*, I.R.C. § 1272. *See also* preamble to T.D. 8065 (Mar. 31, 1986).

maintenance, liquidation, and deficit obligation requirements of the economic effect test. The agreement also:

(1) provides that partners share equally gains and losses from sales of all securities;

(2) allocates 100 percent of its taxable interest and dividend income from securities to Exemptco; and

(3) allocates 90 percent of its tax-exempt interest and dividends from securities to Dean and 10 percent to Exemptco.

A strong likelihood exists that the partnership will realize $1,000 of tax-exempt interest and $1,000 of taxable interest each year.

Although the allocation satisfies the economic-effect test, this effect is not substantial. Exemptco expects to receive $1,000 of taxable interest and $100 of tax-exempt interest. Because the corporation has no tax liability, its after-tax economic gain is $1,100. Dean expects $900 of tax-exempt interest, resulting in a $900 after-tax economic gain. Without the special allocation of income in the agreement, Exemptco and Dean would each receive $500 of taxable interest and $500 of tax-exempt interest. Exemptco would have a $1,000 after-tax economic gain. Dean's tax liability would be $167 ($500 * 33%); his after-tax economic gain would be $833 ($1,000 minus tax of $167). The allocation fails the substantiality test because, while it enhances Dean's after-tax consequences it does not diminish Exemptco's after-tax consequences (it enhances them), and the partners knew there was a strong likelihood that this imbalance would occur when the allocation was included in the partnership agreement.[225]

[2] Shifting Tax Consequences

The economic effect of an allocation is not substantial for any tax year in which it reduces the total tax liability of the partners without significantly changing their economic positions. This occurs if, at the time the allocation becomes part of the partnership agreement, a strong likelihood exists that:

(1) the net changes in the partners' capital accounts will not substantially differ from the net changes that would occur if the allocation were not made; and

(2) the partners' total tax liability is less than it would be if the allocation were not made.[226]

If both conditions exist at the end of a tax year in which the allocation applies, a presumption arises that there was a strong likelihood that this would occur when the allocation became part of the partnership agreement. The partners can rebut the presumption by showing facts and circumstances proving that a strong

---

[225] *See* Treas. Reg. § 1.704-1(b)(5), *Example (5)*. *See also* Treas. Reg. § 1.704-1(b)(5), *Example (9)*.

[226] Treas. Reg. § 1.704-1(b)(2)(iii)(b).

likelihood did not exist at that time.[227]

To apply the shifting-allocation test, the first step is to compare the partners' year-end capital accounts with how their capital accounts would appear if the allocation were not made. If no substantial difference exists, the partners' total tax liabilities with and without the allocation are then computed, taking into account each partner's nonpartnership tax attributes (*e.g.*, marginal tax rate, loss carryforwards, and credits).[228]

> **Example (1):** Vaughn and Wanda form a limited liability company to operate a travel agency. Wanda is a resident of a foreign country, and she will conduct LLC operations in that country. The partnership agreement requires capital accounts maintained in accordance with the regulations, distributions in accordance with capital account balances, and restoration of all deficit capital accounts. The agreement also provides that:
>
> - Vaughn and Wanda will share all LLC income equally, and
>
> - all income generated in Wanda's country will be allocated to her, up to the amount of her share of LLC income.

Although the allocation satisfies the economic-effect test, that effect is not substantial because a strong likelihood exists that (a) the net changes to both member's capital accounts will be the same with or without the allocation, and (b) the members' total tax liability will be lower with the allocation.[229]

> **Example (2):** Assume the same facts as in Example (1), except that the LLC operating agreement allocates 90 percent of the income generated in Wanda's country to her, the remaining 10 percent is allocated to Vaughn, and the members share equally any other LLC income. The amount of LLC income from any of the sources cannot be predicted with reasonable certainty. Because the economic effect of these allocations is substantial, they are deemed valid.

[3] Transitory Allocations

The economic effect of an allocation is not deemed substantial if it is "transitory," because it may be offset by an allocation in the future.[230] An allocation is transitory if, under the partnership agreement, it may be largely offset by an allocation in the future, and a strong likelihood exists that:

> (1) the net changes in the partners' capital accounts for the tax years to which the original and offsetting allocations relate will not substantially differ

---

[227] *Id.* The Service has ruled that a partnership's special allocation lacked substantiality where the partners amended their partnership agreement to specially allocate cancellation of debt income and book items from a related revaluation after the events creating these items occurred. Rev. Rul. 99-43, 1999-42 I.R.B. 506.

[228] Treas. Reg. § 1.704-1(b)(2)(iii)(b).

[229] Treas. Reg. § 1.704-1(b)(5), *Example (10)(ii). See also* Treas. Reg. § 1.704-1(b)(5), *Example (6).*

[230] Treas. Reg. § 1.704-1(b)(2)(iii)(c).

from the net changes that would occur if both allocations were not made; and

(2)   the partners' total tax liability for the tax years to which both allocations relate will be less than if the allocations are not made.[231]

The partners' total tax liabilities with and without the allocation are computed by taking into account each partner's nonpartnership tax attributes (*e.g.*, marginal tax rate, loss carryforwards, and credits).[232]

If both conditions exist at the end of a tax year to which an offsetting allocation applies, a presumption arises that there was a strong likelihood that this would occur when the allocation became part of the partnership agreement.[233] The partners can rebut the presumption by showing facts and circumstances proving that a strong likelihood did not exist at that time.[234] A safe-harbor rule provides that an allocation is not deemed transitory if it is not likely to be offset within five years.

> **Example:** Sheri and Todd are equal partners in the ST Partnership. Both partners expect to have the same marginal tax bracket for several years, but Sheri has a net-operating-loss carryforward that will expire at the end of ST's second tax year. The partners agree to allocate all of the partnership net taxable income to Sheri for the partnership's first two tax years. Beginning in the third year, partnership net taxable income is allocated to Todd, until the amount of income allocated to Sheri in the first two years is offset. The partnership agreement requires capital accounts maintained in accordance with the regulations, distributions in accordance with capital account balances, and restoration of deficit capital accounts. The partnership's income is primarily from highly rated corporate bonds, which are expected to produce enough income in the third through seventh partnership tax years to offset the allocation of income to Sheri in the first two years.
>
> Although the allocations have economic effect, the effect is transitory and, therefore, not substantial. The predictable income from the bonds creates a strong likelihood that the net increases and decreases to the partners' capital accounts will be the same at the end of ST's seventh year, with or without the allocations, and that the partners' total taxes will be reduced by the allocations.[235]

When determining whether an allocation will be offset by a future allocation, the value of partnership property is presumed equal to its adjusted tax basis or, if the property is properly reflected on the partnership's records at a book value that differs from basis, its book value.[236] Any changes to the property's tax basis or book

---

[231] *Id.*

[232] *Id.*

[233] *Id.*

[234] *Id.*

[235] Treas. Reg. § 1.704-1(b)(5), *Example (8)*.

[236] Treas. Reg. § 1.704-1(b)(2)(iii)(c).

value are presumed to be matched by corresponding changes in its fair market value. For example, reductions in the basis of partnership property reflecting depreciation deductions are presumed to correspond to actual decreases in the property's value.

The major effect of the basis-equals-value presumption is to permit loss allocations attributable to partnership property to be offset by subsequent allocations of gain realized on disposition of that property.[237] These allocations, or gain chargebacks, are not considered transitory. Because the value of the property is presumed to decline by the amount of the deducted losses, there cannot be a strong likelihood that any gain will be realized on its disposition.

> **Example:** Arnold and Betty each contribute $40,000 to form the AB Partnership. The partnership uses the contributed funds to purchase depreciable equipment. The partnership agreement requires capital accounts maintained in accordance with the regulations, distributions in accordance with capital account balances, and restoration of deficit capital accounts. The agreement also allocates all depreciation deductions for the equipment to Arnold, and provides that any gain on sale of the equipment be allocated to Arnold to the extent of his depreciation deductions. Gain exceeding the depreciation deductions is allocated to the partners equally.
>
> In Years 1 and 2, Arnold's depreciation deductions total $32,000; the partnership's basis in the equipment decreases to $48,000 ($80,000 minus $32,000). Although the value of the equipment has not, in fact, decreased, it is presumed that the property could be sold for $48,000 at the end of Year 2. Under this presumption, no gain would be realized on a disposition of the asset and the cost-recovery deductions allocated to Arnold would not be offset by his gain allocation. Therefore, the economic effect of the depreciation allocation is not transitory.[238]

Five-year safe-harbor rule. Under a safe-harbor rule, an allocation is not deemed transitory if a strong likelihood exists that it will not be largely offset within five years, determined on a first-in, first-out basis.[239]

§ 6.06 CAPITAL ACCOUNT REQUIREMENTS

As discussed above, allocations in a partnership agreement cannot satisfy the economic-effect test unless they are reflected in the partners' capital accounts in accordance with detailed rules provided in the regulations.[240]

This section describes the rules for maintaining partners' capital accounts, including the capital account adjustments required for contributions, distributions, partnership operations (income, loss, deductions), and the rules applicable to transfers of partnership interests.

---

[237] *Id.*

[238] Treas. Reg. § 1.704-1(b)(5), *Example (1)(vi).*

[239] Treas. Reg. § 1.704-1(b)(2)(iii)(c).

[240] Treas. Reg. § 1.704-1(b)(2)(iv)(a).

The general rule that tax allocations must follow book allocations cannot apply to allocations attributable to property with a book value that differs from its tax basis (*e.g.*, contributed or revalued property). This is true because the adjustments to the partners' capital accounts as determined from the book value of partnership property cannot match the corresponding tax allocations determined from the property's tax basis. To minimize capital account distortions created by book-value/tax-basis disparities, the regulations provide special capital account rules for allocations attributable to contributed and revalued property.

[A] General Rules

Allocations in a partnership agreement cannot satisfy the economic-effect test unless they are reflected in the partners' capital accounts in accordance with detailed rules provided in the regulations.[241] The capital accounts must be maintained under these rules during the full term of the partnership.[242] The rules provide that each partner has only one capital account that reflects all his interests in the partnership, regardless of when or how he acquires his interests or whether he owns more than one class of interest (*e.g.*, both general and limited interests).[243]

Under the basic rules set forth in the regulations, each partner's capital account must be increased by:

(1)   the amount of cash he contributes to the partnership;

(2)   the fair market value of any other property he contributes, decreased by any encumbering liabilities the partnership assumes or takes the property subject to; and

(3)   his distributive share of overall partnership income and gain and each separately stated item of income and gain, including tax-exempt income.[244]

A partner's capital account decreases by:

(1)   the amount of money the partnership distributes to him;

(2)   the fair market value of any property distributed to him, decreased by any encumbering liabilities he assumes or takes the property subject to;

(3)   his distributive share of overall partnership loss and each separately stated item of loss and deduction; and

(4)   his distributive share of partnership expenditures that cannot be deducted or capitalized.[245]

Example: George contributes $7,500 and Harriet contributes $2,500 to form the GH Partnership. George is allocated 75 percent of all partnership

---

[241] Treas. Reg. § 1.704-1(b)(2)(iv)(a).

[242] *Id.*

[243] Treas. Reg. § 1.704-1(b)(2)(iv)(b).

[244] *Id.*

[245] *Id.*

income and loss items; Harriet is allocated 25 percent of these items. In Year 1, the partnership has $1,000 of income, and incurs a capital loss of $200. At the end of Year 1, the partners' capital accounts are as follows:

	George	Harriet
Initial capital account	$7,500	$2,500
Year 1 income	$750	$250
Year 1 capital loss	(150)	(50)
Capital accounts, end of Year 2	$8,100	$2,700

The capital account adjustment for a partner's share of a partnership item is determined from its treatment at the partnership level, without regard to how the partner elects or is required to treat the item.[246] For example, a partner's election to amortize, rather than deduct, research and development expenditures is ignored in adjusting his capital account.[247] This rule does not apply, however, to mining exploration expenditures incurred by a partnership. For these expenditures, capital account adjustments must take into account each partner's elections, because the partnership's treatment of these items depends on the individual partner's elections.[248]

If the regulations do not specify how to make a particular capital account adjustment, the adjustment must be made in a manner that:

(1)   maintains equality between partners' capital accounts and the book value of the partnership's capital;

(2)   is consistent with the partners' economic arrangement; and

(3)   is based, when practicable, on federal tax accounting principles.[249]

[B] Adjustments for Contributions and Distributions

A partner's capital account increases by the fair market value of property he contributes to the partnership, less any encumbering liabilities the partnership assumes or takes the property subject to.[250] Conversely, the partner's capital account decreases by the value of property he receives in a current or liquidating distribution, less any encumbering liabilities he assumes or takes the property subject to.[251] If the contributed or distributed property is encumbered by a nonrecourse liability, the partners' capital accounts are adjusted to reflect the actual value of the property, even though it may be worth less than the liability. These adjustments are made on the date the property is contributed or distributed.

---

[246] Treas. Reg. § 1.704-1(b)(2)(iv)(n).

[247] I.R.C. §§ 174(a), 59(e).

[248] Treas. Reg. § 1.704-1(b)(2)(iv)(n).

[249] Treas. Reg. § 1.704-1(b)(2)(iv)(q).

[250] Treas. Reg. § 1.704-1(b)(2)(iv)(b), (d)(1).

[251] Treas. Reg. § 1.704-1(b)(2)(iv)(b), (e)(1).

Although capital accounts are credited with the value of contributed property (book value), the partnership's tax basis carries over from the contributing partner. Therefore, partnerships must keep two kinds of records: (1) records accounting for transactions by reference to the book value of contributed property (book income or loss) and (2) records showing the tax consequences of the transactions. Capital accounts are adjusted, under the rules of I.R.C. Section 704(b), to reflect each partner's share of partnership "book" income or loss (*i.e.*, income or loss computed by reference to the value of the property when contributed). However, tax consequences are determined under I.R.C. Section 704(c), which provides that allocations to partners must account for any differences between the value and basis of contributed property. Eventually, the interaction of I.R.C. Section 704(b) and 704(c) rules eliminates the disparities between the book value and tax basis of the partnership's property.

> **Example:** Assume that a partner contributes property worth $100 with a $50 tax basis. If the partnership later exchanges the property for securities worth $100, no book income or loss is realized, even though $50 of taxable gain is recognized. Under I.R.C. Section 704(b), the transaction does not result in any adjustments to the partners' capital accounts. Under I.R.C. Section 704(c), the entire taxable gain is allocated to the partner who contributed the property. The transaction eliminates the disparity between the book value and basis of partnership property — the partnership now owns securities with a $100 tax basis. These transactions affect the contributing partner's tax basis in his partnership interest and his capital account as follows:

	Tax Basis	Capital Account
Contribution of Property Beginning balance	$50	$100
Gain on exchange of property for securities	50	0
Ending balance	$100	$100

The fair market value assigned to contributed or distributed property is deemed correct if agreed to in arm's-length negotiations between partners with adverse interests. If the value is arrived at by a different process, and the property is significantly overvalued or undervalued, the partners' capital accounts are deemed invalid. Each contributed or distributed item must generally be valued separately.[252]

When property is distributed to a partner, the capital accounts of all partners (including the distributee(s), are adjusted for unrealized gains and losses inherent in property that were not previously reflected in their capital accounts.[253] These adjustments equal the amount of income, gain, loss, or deduction that would be allocated to each partner if the partnership sold the distributed property at its fair market value. For this purpose, the value of property subject to a nonrecourse debt

---

[252] Treas. Reg. § 1.704-1(b)(2)(iv)(e)(1).

[253] Treas. Reg. § 1.704-1(b)(2)(iv)(e)(1).

is deemed at least equal to the amount of the debt.

Adjustments are made only for unrealized gain or loss not previously reflected in the partners' capital accounts. Therefore, the unrealized amount is determined using book value, rather than the tax basis of the distributed property. Assume, for example, that a partner contributes property with a $20 basis that is worth $40. The value of the property on the partnership's books is $40, even though the $20 tax basis carries over from the contributing partner. If, at a later date, the property is distributed and at that time its value is $90, the partners' capital accounts increase by $50 of unrealized gain ($90 fair market value at distribution less $40 book value), not by $70 of unrealized taxable gain ($90 value less $20 basis).

> **Example:** Leo and Myra each contribute $10,000 to form the LM Limited Liability Company, which uses the $20,000 to purchase securities. When the securities have appreciated in value to $30,000, the LLC admits Elsa as a one-third member in exchange for her $15,000 cash contribution. Upon Elsa's admission, the LLC operating agreement is amended to allocate the first $10,000 of gain from the sale of the securities equally between Leo and Myra; future appreciation is allocated equally among the three members. When the securities appreciate in value to $36,000 they are distributed to the members.
>
> Each member's capital account is adjusted immediately before the distribution to reflect the amount of gain that would have been allocated to him if the LLC sold the securities at fair market value. These adjustments are as follows:[254]

	Leo	Myra	Elsa
Pre-distribution capital account	$10,000	$10,000	$15,000
Adjustment for deemed sale	7,000	7,000	2,000
Adjustment for distribution	(12,000)	(12,000)	(12,000)
Post-distribution capital account	$5,000	$5,000	$5,000

[C] Adjustments for Assumed Partnership Liabilities

A partner is deemed to contribute money to the partnership equal to the amount of partnership liabilities he actually assumes, and his capital account increases by that amount.[255] Conversely, a partner is deemed to receive a cash distribution from the partnership equal to the amount of his individual debts assumed by the partnership, and his capital account decreases by that amount.[256] A liability is considered assumed only if: (1) the assuming partner or partnership is personally and primarily liable for the obligation, and (2) the obligee is aware of the assumption and can enforce it directly against the assuming party.[257] Capital accounts are not adjusted to reflect any partner's share of a partnership liability

---

[254] *See* Treas. Reg. § 1.704-1(b)(5), *Example (14)(v)*.

[255] Treas. Reg. § 1.704-1(b)(2)(iv)(c).

[256] *Id.*

[257] *Id.*

not actually assumed.[258] Thus, capital accounts do not increase or decrease when a partnership incurs or pays debts. Similarly, capital accounts are not adjusted when property subject to an unassumed liability is contributed by or distributed to a partner. Instead, the value of the property credited or debited to the partner's capital account is reduced by the amount of the liability.[259]

[D] Promissory Notes

A partner's capital account is not increased by the value of a promissory note he makes and contributes to the partnership.[260] Instead, the partner's capital account increases when he makes principal payments or when the partnership disposes of the note in a taxable transaction. Similarly, a partner's capital account is not reduced by the value of a promissory note the partnership makes and distributes to him until the partnership makes principal payments or the partner disposes of the note in a taxable transaction.[261] However, these rules do not apply to contributed or distributed notes that are readily tradable on an established securities market. If a note is readily tradable, the partner's capital account is immediately credited or debited by the value of the note.[262]

[E] Revaluations of Partnership Property

Capital accounts may be increased or decreased to reflect revaluations of partnership property (including intangible property such as goodwill) on the partnership's books.[263] These adjustments are permitted only if they are made principally for substantial nontax business purposes in connection with the following events:[264]

(1)   A contribution of money or other property (other than a *de minimis* amount) by a new or existing partner as consideration for a partnership interest.

(2)   A distribution of money or property (other than a *de minimis* amount) in a partnership liquidation or as consideration for all or part of the interest of a retiring or continuing partner.

(3)   A revaluation of assets under generally accepted industry accounting practices, when substantially all the partnership's noncash property consists of securities or commodities that are readily tradable on an established securities market.

Revaluation is advantageous when partners acquire or relinquish partnership interests, because it adjusts all partners' capital accounts to reflect the current

---

[258] *Id.*

[259] Treas. Reg. § 1.704-1(b)(2)(iv)(b).

[260] Treas. Reg. § 1.704-1(b)(2)(iv)(d)(2).

[261] Treas. Reg. § 1.704-1(b)(2)(iv)(e)(2).

[262] Treas. Reg. § 1.704-1(b)(2)(iv)(d)(2), (e)(2).

[263] Treas. Reg. § 1.704-1(b)(2)(iv)(f).

[264] Treas. Reg. § 1.704-1(b)(2)(iv)(f)(5).

value of their interests in partnership property. Failure to revalue may result in an unintended transfer of value from an existing partner to a new partner, or it may burden the new partner with unrealized losses incurred before his admission to the partnership (*e.g.*, if partnership property is worth less than its book value when the partner acquires his interest).

Example: Arnold and Betty each contribute $9,000 to the AB Partnership, which uses the $18,000 of contributed funds to purchase land. When the land is worth $30,000, Carl makes a $15,000 contribution for a one-third interest in the partnership. If the property is not revalued when Carl joins the partnership, the partnership balance sheet appears as follows:

Assets	
Cash	$15,000
Land	18,000
Total	$33,000
Capital Accounts	
Arnold	$9,000
Betty	9,000
Carl	15,000
Total	$33,000

If the partnership later sells the land for $33,000, each partner's one-third share of the partnership's $15,000 gain is $5,000. The balance sheet appears as follows:

Assets	
Cash	$48,000
Total	$48,000
Capital Accounts	
Arnold	$14,000
Betty	14,000
Carl	20,000
Total	$48,000

If the partnership is liquidated, Carl receives $6,000 more than Arnold or Betty ($20,000 – $14,000) — an inequitable distribution — because the partnership's failure to revalue its land when Carl acquired his interest allowed him to share in appreciation occurring before his admission to the partnership.

However, if the partnership revalues its assets when Carl acquires his interest, the result is an equitable distribution of assets on liquidation. The balance sheet, after revaluation, appears as follows:

Assets
Cash $15,000
Land   30,000
Total $45,000
Capital Accounts
Arnold $15,000
Betty   15,000
Carl   15,000
Total $45,000

When the partnership later sells the land for $33,000, each partner's one-third share of the partnership's $15,000 gain is $5,000. The balance sheet appears as follows:

Assets
Cash $48,000
Total $48,000
Capital Accounts
Arnold $14,000
Betty   14,000
Carl   20,000
Total $48,000

If the partnership liquidates after revaluation, each of the equal partners receives an equal distribution from the partnership.

A revaluation of partnership assets and corresponding capital account adjustment is valid only if it is provided for in the partnership agreement and satisfies the following rules:[265]

(1)   The revaluation must be based on the fair market value of partnership property on the date of the adjustment.

   (a)   The value of property subject to a nonrecourse debt must be deemed at least equal to the amount of the debt.

   (b)   The fair market value assigned to partnership assets will be deemed correct if it is agreed to in arm's-length negotiations between partners with sufficiently adverse interests.[266] If value is determined in a different manner, the partners' capital accounts are invalid if the property is significantly over- or undervalued. Each contributed or distributed item must generally be valued separately.[267]

(2)   The adjustments must reflect any unrealized income, gain, loss, or deduction inherent in the property, determined by computing the

---

[265] Treas. Reg. § 1.704-1(b)(2)(iv)(f)(1)–(4).

[266] Treas. Reg. § 1.704-1(b)(2)(iv)(h).

[267] *Id.*

amount of each item that would be allocated to each partner if the partnership sold the property for its fair market value.

(3) The partnership agreement must require future capital account adjustments for depreciation, amortization, depletion, and gain or loss to be based upon the book value of the property after the revaluation.

(4) The partnership agreement must allocate tax depreciation, depletion, amortization, and gain or loss attributable to revalued property among partners in a manner that takes account of disparities between the fair market value and basis of the property created by the revaluation.[268] This allocation is made under the same rules (I.R.C. Section 704(c)) that apply when property is contributed with a tax basis that differs from its value.

Example: Roger and Sara each contribute $10,000 to form the RS Partnership. The partnership uses the $20,000 to purchase land. Two years later, when the land is worth $50,000, Tessa contributes $25,000 in cash for a one-third partnership interest. RS revalues its assets, which increases the book value of the land to $50,000, the fair market value of the property. Roger and Sara's capital accounts are each increased $15,000 (one-half of the $30,000 increase in book value), raising them to $25,000 ($10,000 plus $15,000).[269]

This revaluation complies with the capital account rules if the partnership agreement requires adjustments to capital accounts to reflect the unrealized appreciation inhernt in the land and also allocates the first $30,000 of taxable gain the partnership realizes on a disposition of the land to Roger and Sara.[270] After revaluation, the partners' capital accounts are as follows:

	Roger		Sara		Tessa	
	Tax	Book	Tax	Book	Tax	Book
Initial contribution:	$10,000	$10,000	$10,000	$10,000	$25,000	$25,000
Unrealized appreciation:	0	15,000	0	15,000	0	0
Adjusted for revaluation:	$10,000	$25,000	$10,000	$25,000	$25,000	$25,000

In Year 3, the partnership sells the land for $74,000. The $30,000 of gain attributable to appreciation that occurred before Tessa became a partner is allocated equally to Roger and Sara; the $24,000 of gain attributable to appreciation after Tessa joined the partnership is shared equally among Roger, Sara, and Tessa.[271] The partners' capital accounts are as follows:

---

[268] Treas. Reg. § 1.704-1(b)(2)(iv)(f)(1)–(4).

[269] Treas. Reg. § 1.704-1(b)(5), *Example (14)(i)*.

[270] *Id.*

[271] Treas. Reg. § 1.704-1(b)(5), *Example (14)(ii)*.

	Roger		Sara		Tessa	
	Tax	Book	Tax	Book	Tax	Book
After Tessa's admission:	$10,000	$25,000	$10,000	$25,000	$25,000	$25,000
Tax gain:	23,000	8,000	23,000	8,000	8,000	8,000
After sale:	$33,000	$33,000	$33,000	$33,000	$33,000	$33,000

[F] Adjustments for Disparities Between Book Value and Tax Basis of Contributed or Revalued Property

Special capital account rules apply when the book value of property reflected in the partners' capital accounts differs from the partnership's tax basis for the property. These rules are necessary because allocations for property with a book-value/tax-basis disparity cannot satisfy the basic principle of the economic-effect test, which requires allocations of tax items to follow the corresponding economic allocations to partner's capital accounts. When a book-value/tax-basis disparity exists, the adjustments to the partner's capital accounts computed from book value cannot match the tax allocations computed from the property's tax basis.

The special rules for computing capital account adjustments attributable to property with a book-value/tax-basis disparity apply in lieu of the economic-effect test.[272] Unless these requirements are satisfied, the partners' capital accounts are not considered properly maintained.[273] The capital account rules apply whenever the book value of property reflected in partners' capital accounts differs from the property's tax basis.[274] These differences arise when:

(1)   property is contributed with a value that differs from its basis;

(2)   accounts receivable, accounts payable, or other accrued but unpaid items are contributed; or

(3)   capital accounts are revalued to reflect the current value of partnership property.

When a disparity between book value and tax basis exists, capital account adjustments for depreciation, depletion, amortization, and gain or loss are computed from the book value of the property.[275] However, the partners' distributive shares of these items for tax-reporting purposes are determined from the property's tax basis. Eventually, the differences between the capital account and basis adjustments for these items will eliminate the disparities between book value and tax basis.

The book adjustments to capital accounts for depreciation, amortization, and depletion must bear the same ratio to the book value of partnership property as the

---

[272] Treas. Reg. § 1.704-1(b)(2)(iv)(d)(3), (g).

[273] Treas. Reg. § 1.704-1(b)(2)(iv)(d)(3), (f), (g).

[274] *Id.*

[275] Treas. Reg. § 1.704-1(b)(2)(iv)(g)(1), (b)(4)(i).

amounts computed for tax purposes bear to the property's adjusted tax basis.[276] Assume, for example, that a partnership asset has a $2,000 book value and an $800 tax basis. If a $50 tax depreciation deduction is allowable for the property, the capital account adjustment for book depreciation is $125 ($50/$800 = $125/$2,000). If the tax basis of the property is zero, depreciation, amortization, or depletion may be determined under any reasonable method.[277] Capital accounts are adjusted solely for the book items; no second adjustment is made for the corresponding tax items.[278]

The rules for making book and tax allocations for property with a book value/tax basis disparity are found in the regulations under I.R.C. Section 704(c). In general, the regulations provide that a partnership must use a reasonable method that prevents gain or loss from being shifted among the partners. Three reasonable allocation methods are described: the traditional method, the traditional method with curative allocations, and the remedial allocation method. Although the regulations focus on contributed property, tax items attributable to revaluation of partnership property (referred to as "reverse" I.R.C. Section 704(c) allocations) must be allocated "in the same manner" as under I.R.C. Section 704(c) to account for book/tax disparities.[279] For a complete discussion of allocations and capital account adjustments under I.R.C. Section 704(c), see § 6.02, *supra*.

In the following two examples, the "traditional" method for allocating for book value/tax basis disparities is used:

Example (1): Martha contributes $10,000 in cash, and Norm contributes stock worth $10,000, with a $3,000 basis, to form the MN Partnership. Each partner's capital account is credited with $10,000, the value of each partner's contribution. The partnership agreement provides that the partners will share equally in partnership income, gain, loss, deduction, and credits, except that the $7,000 of gain inherent in the contributed stock is allocated to Norm (as required by I.R.C. Section 704(c)). The partnership later sells the stock for $12,000, realizing a $2,000 book gain ($12,000 sale price minus $10,000 book value) and a $9,000 taxable gain ($12,000 amount realized minus $3,000 adjusted basis). The taxable gain is allocated $8,000 to Norm ($7,000 I.R.C. Section 704(c) allocation plus $1,000 equal share of post-contribution gain) and $1,000 to Martha.[280] The partners' capital accounts are as follows:

	Martha		Norm	
	Tax	Book	Tax	Book
Initial capital account	$10,000	$10,000	$3,000	$10,000
Plus: gain	1,000	1,000	8,000	1,000
Capital account, end of year	$11,000	$11,000	$11,000	$11,000

[276] Treas. Reg. § 1.704-1(b)(2)(iv)(g)(3).

[277] *Id.*

[278] Treas. Reg. § 1.704-1(b)(4)(i).

[279] *Id.*

[280] Treas. Reg. § 1.704-1(b)(5), *Example (13)(i)*.

Example (2): Lester and Miriam each contribute $30,000 to form the LM Partnership. The partnership uses the $60,000 to purchase depreciable property. The partnership agreement provides that the partners share all partnership items equally. In each of Years 1 and 2, the partnership's income equals its expenses, except for a $10,000 cost-recovery deduction. Capital accounts at the end of Year 2 are as follows:

	Lester	Miriam
Initial capital account	$30,000	$30,000
Less: net losses Yrs 1 & 2	(10,000)	(10,000)
Capital accounts, end of Year 2	$20,000	$20,000

In Year 3, Nora joins the partnership as an equal one-third partner, in exchange for a $30,000 cash contribution. When Nora is admitted, the partnership increases the book value of its property to $60,000 (the fair market value). Lester and Miriam's capital accounts increase to $30,000 ($20,000 plus $10,000 increase) to reflect the revaluation. Nora's capital account equals her $30,000 contribution.

The partnership agreement is amended to allocate book depreciation equally among the partners. Tax depreciation and gain or loss is allocated in a manner that takes into account the difference between the property's $40,000 tax basis and $60,000 book value. During Year 3, the partnership has a $10,000 cost-recovery deduction. Book depreciation is $15,000 ($10,000 tax depreciation/$40,000 tax basis of property = $15,000 book depreciation/$60,000 value of property). Each partner is allocated $5,000 of the book depreciation. The tax depreciation deduction is allocated to Nora, up to her book depreciation deduction ($5,000), and the remaining deduction is allocated equally between Lester and Miriam ($5,000/2 = $2,500).[281] Capital accounts at the end of Year 3 are as follows:

	Lester		Miriam		Nora	
	Tax	Book	Tax	Book	Tax	Book
Beginning, Year 3	$20,000	$30,000	$20,000	$30,000	$30,000	$30,000
Less Year 3 depreciation	(2,500)	(5,000)	(2,500)	(5,000)	(5,000)	(5,000)
End of year 3	$17,500	$25,000	$17,500	$25,000	$25,000	$25,000

Similar rules apply in determining adjustments for disparities between book value and tax basis of unrealized receivables and adjustments for deductions for accounts receivable, accounts payable, and other accrued but unpaid items.[282]

Example (3): Allen contributes $100 in cash for an interest in the AB Partnership. Betty contributes accounts receivable worth $125, in which her basis is zero, and also transfers $25 of payables to the partnership.

---

[281] Treas. Reg. § 1.704-1(b)(5), *Examples (18)(vii), (viii)*.

[282] Treas. Reg. § 1.704-1(b)(2)(iv)(g)(2).

Each partner's initial capital account is $100; the liability is recorded on the partnership's books. When the partnership collects the receivables, the entire $100 of income must be allocated to Betty. Similarly, when the partnership pays off the $25 payable balance, the entire deduction is allocated to Betty. However, neither the income nor the deduction is reflected in Betty's capital account; that balance remains at $100.

[G] Adjustments for Nondeductible, Noncapital Expenditures and Disallowed Losses

A partner's capital account is reduced by his share of any expenditure that the partnership cannot deduct or capitalize.[283] This adjustment is required because nondeductible expenditures reduce the amount of cash available to distribute to partners, even though they do not decrease partnership taxable income. If the adjustment were not made, the partners' capital accounts would not reflect the amount they would receive from the partnership upon a liquidation of their interests. Special allocations of nondeductible and noncapitalizable items are permitted if they satisfy the substantial-economic-effect test.

[H] Adjustments for Guaranteed Payments and Employee Benefit Plan Contributions

Under the capital account rules, a partner who receives a guaranteed payment from a partnership treats the payment as compensation income, and no adjustment to his capital account is made for the payment.[284] (See discussion of guaranteed payments in Chapter 7.) Because the guaranteed payment is deductible by the partnership, each partner (including the recipient) decreases his capital account by his distributive share of that deduction.

§ 6.07 PARTNERS' INTERESTS IN THE PARTNERSHIP

The general rule that a partner's distributive share of partnership income, gain, loss, deduction, or credit is determined by the partnership agreement does not apply if:

(1) the agreement fails to allocate overall or specific items of income, gain, loss, deduction, or credit; or

(2) an allocation in the agreement is invalid (*i.e.*, does not have substantial economic effect).[285]

If either of these conditions apply, each partner's distributive share of any unallocated amounts is determined from his "interest in the partnership" by taking into account all facts and circumstances.[286]

---

[283] Treas. Reg. § 1.704-1(b)(2)(iv)(i)(1). *See also* Treas. Reg. § 1.704-1(b)(5), *Example (11)*.

[284] Treas. Reg. § 1.704-1(b)(2)(iv)(o).

[285] I.R.C. § 704(b).

[286] *Id.*

[A]   General Rules

A partner's "interest in the partnership" refers to the manner in which he has agreed to share the economic benefit or burden associated with overall or specific items of partnership income, gain, loss, deduction, or credit.[287] This sharing agreement is ascertained from all the facts and circumstances that relate to the partners' economic arrangement. A partner's interest in specific partnership items generally need not correspond to his overall economic interest in the partnership. For example, a partner owning a 50 percent overall partnership interest may have a 90-percent interest in a particular item of income or deduction. However, this is not true for items "deemed" to accord with the partners' interests. These items must be allocated in accordance with the partners' overall interests in the partnership.

No objective test for determining a partner's "interest in the partnership" exists. Although the regulations indicate factors that the Service will consider in determining a partner's interest, the analysis remains vague and subjective. Therefore, the determination of a partner's interest is not practical or useful in tax planning. In effect, these rules merely provide the Service with guidelines for reallocating tax items that partners fail to allocate validly.

[B]   Factors Considered When Determining Partners' Interests in the Partnership

Partners are rebuttably presumed to have equal per capita interests in their partnership.[288] For example, each partner in a five-person partnership is presumed to have a 20-percent interest. In most situations, the taxpayer or the Service will be able to rebut this equal-interests presumption by showing facts and circumstances indicating that the partners have different interests. The regulations include these factors as considerations when determining partners' interests:

(1)   the partners' relative contributions to the partnership;

(2)   the partners' interests in economic profits and losses (if different from their interests in taxable income or loss);

(3)   the partners' interests in cash flow and other nonliquidating distributions; and

(4)   the partners' rights to distributions of capital upon liquidation.[289]

In most situations, the last two factors concerning the partner's rights to cash flow and distributions are of primary importance. This is in accord with the objective of I.R.C. Section 704(b): to ensure that tax allocations reflect the amount the partners actually will receive from the partnership.

> **Example (1):** Arthur and Betty form the AB Partnership by making cash contributions of $40,000 each. The partnership uses the $80,000 to purchase

---

[287] Treas. Reg. § 1.704-1(b)(3).

[288] *Id.*

[289] Treas. Reg. § 1.704-1(b)(3)(ii).

depreciable equipment. The partnership agreement provides that Arthur and Betty have equal shares of partnership income, loss, and cash flow, except that all depreciation deductions are allocated to Arthur. The agreement also provides that upon liquidation of the partnership, each partner is entitled to a distribution of one half of the partnership's capital.

The provision allowing the partners to receive equal distributions of partnership capital upon liquidation, regardless of their capital account balances, violates the requirements of the I.R.C. Section 704(b) regulations and causes the allocation to lack substantial economic effect. The special allocation of depreciation deductions to Arthur is disregarded and each partner's distributive share is determined in accordance with his interest in the partnership. The partners' equal capital contributions, equal shares in income, loss, and cash flow, and equal rights to liquidation proceeds, indicate that their economic arrangement is to share equally any potential decline in the value of the partnership's depreciable property. Therefore, depreciation deductions are allocated equally between Arthur and Betty.[290]

Example (2): Claire contributes $75,000 and Dell contributes $25,000 to form the CD Partnership. The partnership agreement provides that all income, gain, loss, and deductions are shared equally, but that all partnership distributions will be made 75 percent to Claire and 25 percent to Dell, regardless of capital accounts. Neither partner is obligated to restore deficit capital accounts.

Because the allocations in the agreement lack economic effect, partnership income, gain, loss, and deductions are reallocated in accordance with the partners' interests. The partners' 75/25 ratio for contributions, cash flow, and distributions indicates that the partners agreed to share the partnership's economic profits and losses in a 75/25 ratio. Accordingly, all partnership items are reallocated 75 percent to Claire and 25 percent to Dell.[291]

§ 6.08 ALLOCATIONS OF ITEMS ATTRIBUTABLE TO NONRECOURSE LIABILITIES

Allocations of deductions attributable to nonrecourse debt (nonrecourse deductions) lack economic effect because the creditor, rather than any partner, bears the economic loss if the partnership defaults when the property securing the debt is worth less than the unpaid principal. This fact is illustrated as follows:

Example (1): Anita and Brad contribute equal amounts of money for equal interests in the AB Partnership. The partnership purchases depreciable property for $100,000, financing the entire purchase price through a nonrecourse loan secured by the property. The full loan principal is due in five years. The partnership agreement allocates all depreciation on the property to Anita. In Year 1, Anita is allocated $10,000 of depreciation.

---

[290] *See* Treas. Reg. § 1.704-1(b)(5), *Example (1)*.

[291] Treas. Reg. § 1.704-1(b)(5), *Example (4)(i). See also* Treas. Reg. § 1.704-1(b)(5), *Examples (1)(i), (10)(ii), (19)(iii)*.

The allocation of all depreciation to Anita lacks economic effect because she will not bear any economic loss if the property declines in value by the amount of depreciation deductions she claims. If the value of the property actually depreciates to $90,000, the partnership may cease paying interest on a $100,000 loan for which it has no personal liability. The creditor would then foreclose on the securing property, incurring a $10,000 loss on the unpaid principal of his loan. Because the creditor bears the entire loss caused by the depreciation of the property, the allocation of depreciation to Anita lacks economic effect.

Despite this lack of economic effect, special allocations of nonrecourse deductions are permitted if they satisfy a four-part safe-harbor test in the regulations (described at § 6.09[B], *infra*). Allocations that satisfy the safe-harbor test are "deemed" to accord with the partners' interests in the partnership. Special allocations that do not meet the test are invalid, and the affected items are reallocated among the partners in accordance with their overall interests in the partnership.[292]

> **Example (2):** Continuing Example (1), if the safe-harbor tests are not met, the $10,000 depreciation deduction must be allocated in accordance with the partners' overall interests in the partnership. Because the partners have equal overall interests, each partner is allocated a $5,000 share of the depreciation.

Arguably, the fact that deductions attributable to nonrecourse liabilities lack economic effect should invalidate all allocations of these items, including allocations that accord with the partners' overall interests in the partnership. The regulations do not bar these allocations, however, because, under long-standing tax law principles, nonrecourse liabilities are treated in much the same manner as recourse debts.[293] This treatment requires the outstanding principal of the liability to be included in the partnership's amount realized when the securing property is sold or foreclosed, causing the partnership to recognize gain equal to the total amount of deductions claimed for the property.[294] The partners pay tax on their distributive shares of this gain, even though they do not actually receive any cash (for this reason the gain is referred to as "phantom gain").[295] Thus, the partners' advantage from the nonrecourse deduction is the tax deferral that arises when deductions are claimed before the corresponding income is taxed.

> **Example (3):** Continuing Example (1), the foreclosure by the creditor is treated as if the partnership sold the property to him for the $100,000 outstanding principal balance of the nonrecourse liability. Because the partnership's basis for the property is $90,000 ($100,000 cost basis less $10,000 depreciation), the partnership recognizes $10,000 of gain —

---

[292] Treas. Reg. § 1.704-2(b)(1).

[293] *See* Crane v. Comm'r, 331 U.S. 1 (1947).

[294] Comm'r v. Tufts, 461 U.S. 300 (1983); I.R.C. § 7701(g).

[295] The partners realize phantom gain even if the partnership pays the liability. Because the principal payments to the creditor are made with after-tax dollars (*i.e.*, partnership cannot deduct the payments), the partners must pay tax on income they never receive.

offsetting the entire depreciation deduction.

The fact that the tax benefit of nonrecourse deductions will be offset by the tax burden of the additional gain is central to the safe-harbor test in the regulations. That test is designed to ensure that a partner who receives a special allocation of nonrecourse deductions will be allocated an equal amount of additional gain when the partnership disposes of the assets securing its nonrecourse debts. The partner who obtains the tax benefit of the deduction also must bear the corresponding tax burden.

The rules and tests in the regulations use several terms having complex definitions. An overview of the basic terms is given below; these definitions are described in detail later in this section.

Partnership minimum gain. The regulations use the term "partnership minimum gain" to represent the total amount of gain that must be allocated to the partners to offset their nonrecourse deductions.[296] Essentially, partnership minimum gain is the amount of gain the partnership would realize if it sold all its property subject to nonrecourse liabilities solely for satisfaction of the debts.[297] Minimum gain for each partnership nonrecourse debt equals the amount by which the liability exceeds the basis of the property that secures it. Thus, minimum gain increases if the basis of partnership property securing a nonrecourse debt decreases (*e.g.*, to reflect depreciation deductions) and if the property is used to secure additional nonrecourse borrowing (*e.g.*, a second mortgage loan). Conversely, minimum gain decreases as the difference between a nonrecourse liability and the basis of the securing property decreases (*e.g.*, the partnership pays the liability or sells the securing property).

Nonrecourse deductions. Partnership losses and deductions attributable to nonrecourse liabilities in any year are referred to as nonrecourse deductions. A partnership's nonrecourse deductions equal the net increase in the amount of partnership minimum gain for the year, reduced by the amount of any nonrecourse loan proceeds distributed to partners during the year.[298] This relationship between nonrecourse deductions and minimum gain ensures that the nonrecourse deductions allocated to partners eventually will be offset by an equal amount of minimum gain.

A partnership's nonrecourse deductions for a year decrease by the amount of nonrecourse loan proceeds distributed to partners if the loan is allocable to a prior increase in minimum gain. This rule reflects the fact that a distribution of nonrecourse loan proceeds is equivalent to a distribution of the proceeds of a sale of the property securing the liability (*i.e.*, the distributee partners have the cash without any obligation to pay it back).[299]

---

[296] Treas. Reg. § 1.704-2(b)(2).

[297] Treas. Reg. § 1.704-2(d).

[298] Treas. Reg. § 1.704-2(c).

[299] A partner who receives a distribution of nonrecourse loan proceeds is allocated an additional share of minimum gain. Treas. Reg. § 1.704-2(g).

Minimum-gain chargeback. The regulations provide an enforcement mechanism called a "minimum-gain chargeback" to ensure that each partner is allocated the amount of gain required to offset his previous nonrecourse deductions. A minimum-gain chargeback requires a partnership to allocate additional income and gain to partners in any year that partnership minimum gain decreases. Generally, each partner must be allocated income and gain equal to his share of the net decrease in partnership minimum gain.[300] A partner's share of the net decrease in minimum gain is determined from his percentage share of total partnership minimum gain at the end of the prior year.[301] The safe harbor for special allocations of nonrecourse deductions cannot be satisfied unless the partnership agreement has a minimum-gain chargeback provision.

[A] Overview of Regulations

The following provisions are central to the regulations governing allocations attributable to a partnership's nonrecourse liabilities:

(1)   Partnership deductions and losses attributable to its nonrecourse debts (nonrecourse deductions) must be allocated in accordance with the partners' overall economic interests in the partnership unless the safe harbor test in the regulations is satisfied.[302]

(2)   A partner who is allocated nonrecourse deductions subsequently must be allocated an equal amount of income and gain from the property securing the partnership's nonrecourse liabilities. These allocations are made pursuant to the "minimum-gain chargeback" rules. A special allocation of nonrecourse deductions cannot satisfy the safe harbor in the regulations unless the partnership agreement contains a minimum-gain chargeback clause.

(3)   A minimum-gain chargeback triggers allocations of additional income and gain to partners in any year that a net decrease in partnership minimum gain occurs. Partnership minimum gain is the amount of gain the partnership would realize if each of its assets securing nonrecourse liabilities were sold for the principal amount of the debt. The amount of income and gain allocated to each partner is determined from his share of the net decrease in partnership minimum gain.

The specific rules and definitions set forth in the regulations are summarized as follows:

(1)   Nonrecourse deductions are losses, deductions, and nondeductible, noncapitalizable expenditures[303] attributable to a partnership's

---

[300] Treas. Reg. § 1.704-2(f).

[301] Treas. Reg. § 1.704-2(g)(2).

[302] Treas. Reg. § 1.704-2(b)(1). For discussion of how the partners' interests in the partnership are determined, see § 6.07, *supra*.

[303] These items are defined in I.R.C. § 705(a)(2)(B).

nonrecourse liabilities.[304] A partnership's nonrecourse deductions for a tax year equal the excess of:

(a) the net increase in "partnership minimum gain" for the year; over

(b) the aggregate proceeds of nonrecourse borrowings distributed to partners during the year.[305] The reduction for distributions of nonrecourse loan proceeds applies only if the distribution is allocable to an increase in partnership minimum gain.

(2) Partnership minimum gain equals the aggregate gain the partnership would realize if it sold each of its assets subject to a nonrecourse liability for the outstanding principal on the debt.[306] Partnership minimum gain

(a) increases when the basis of property securing a nonrecourse liability decreases and when the partnership incurs a nonrecourse debt that exceeds the basis of the property securing the liability; and

(b) decreases to the extent that the difference between a nonrecourse liability and the basis of the securing property decreases.[307] If a partnership asset is reflected on the partnership's books at a value that differs from its tax basis (*i.e.*, the property was contributed by a partner or revalued pursuant to the regulations),[308] changes in minimum gain are computed by reference to book value. Special rules apply in determining minimum gain changes in the year that partnership property is revalued.

(3) A partner who is allocated nonrecourse deductions or receives a distribution of the proceeds of a nonrecourse loan must be allocated an equal amount of income or gain pursuant to a "minimum-gain chargeback."[309] A minimum-gain chargeback is a provision requiring a partnership to allocate additional income and gain to partners for any year in which there is a net decrease in partnership minimum gain. The amount of income and gain allocated to each partner must equal his share of the net decrease in partnership minimum gain. A partner's share of the net decrease is determined by multiplying the total net decrease by his percentage share of the partnership's total minimum gain at the end of the prior year.[310]

(4) A partner who receives a distribution of the proceeds of a partnership nonrecourse loan also receives an additional share of minimum gain, which is subject to the minimum-gain chargeback requirement when partnership

---

[304] Treas. Reg. § 1.704-2(b)(1).

[305] Treas. Reg. § 1.704-2(c).

[306] Treas. Reg. § 1.704-2(d).

[307] *See* Treas. Reg. § 1.704-2(b)(2).

[308] *See* Treas. Reg. § 1.704-1(b)(2)(iv)(f).

[309] Treas. Reg. § 1.704-2(b)(2).

[310] Treas. Reg. § 1.704-2(g).

minimum gain decreases.[311] This is true only if the nonrecourse loan increased partnership minimum gain, and the distribution is allocable to the proceeds of that borrowing. Any reasonable method may be used to determine if a distribution is allocable to nonrecourse debt proceeds.

(5) Special rules apply to nonrecourse debts for which a partner bears the economic risk of loss, referred to as "partner nonrecourse debt."[312] This term generally refers to partnership nonrecourse loans made or guaranteed by partners or by persons related to partners. Deductions attributable to partner nonrecourse debt must be allocated to the lending or guaranteeing partner.

(6) Special rules apply in determining the effect of a subsidiary partnership's items on a parent partnership's minimum gain.[313] These rules generally permit the partners of the parent partnership to look through and directly account for the subsidiary's items.

[B] Safe Harbor for Allocations of Nonrecourse Deductions

Special allocations of nonrecourse deductions are deemed to accord with the partners' economic interests in the partnership and, thus, are valid if the partnership agreement satisfies each of the following four requirements:[314]

(1) For the duration of the partnership, the agreement will satisfy the basic requirements of the economic-effect test or the alternate economic-effect test in the regulations.[315] Specifically, the agreement must provide that:

(a) capital accounts will be maintained under the rules in the regulations;

(b) liquidating distributions will accord with the partners' positive capital account balances; and

(c) partners are either (i) obligated to restore any deficit capital in their capital accounts when their partnership interest is liquidated (satisfying the economic-effect test), or (ii) subject to income allocations pursuant to a qualified income offset provision (satisfying the alternate economic-effect test).

(2) Beginning in the year that nonrecourse deductions first arise, and thereafter for the duration of the partnership, allocations of nonrecourse deductions must be reasonably consistent with valid allocations (*i.e.*, allocations having substantial economic effect) of another significant partnership item that is attributable to property securing nonrecourse debts.

---

[311] Treas. Reg. § 1.704-2(h).

[312] Treas. Reg. § 1.704-2(i). Whether a partner bears the economic risk of loss for a liability is determined under the rules of I.R.C. § 752. See discussion in Chapter 5.

[313] Treas. Reg. § 1.704-2(k).

[314] Treas. Reg. § 1.704-2(e).

[315] These requirements are set forth in Treas. Reg. § 1.704-1(b)(2). *See* § 6.05[A], *supra*.

(3) Beginning in the first tax year that (a) nonrecourse deductions arise, or (b) the partnership distributes nonrecourse borrowings that are allocable to an increase in minimum gain, and thereafter for the partnership's duration, the agreement must contain a minimum-gain chargeback provision.

(4) All other material allocations and capital account adjustments in the agreement must be valid under the regulations.[316]

Example (1): Robert, the limited partner, contributes $180,000, and Steve, the general partner, contributes $20,000 to form the RS Limited Partnership. RS obtains an $800,000 nonrecourse loan and purchases a building for $1 million. The loan is secured by the building; no principal payments are due for five years.

The partnership agreement contains the following provisions:

(1) capital accounts will be maintained under the rules in the regulations;

(2) liquidating distributions will accord with partners' positive capital account balances;

(3) Steve must restore a deficit capital account balance when his interest is liquidated, but Robert does not have to restore any capital account deficit;

(4) a qualified income offset; and

(5) a minimum-gain chargeback.

The agreement allocates all partnership items, including nonrecourse deductions, 90 percent to Robert and 10 percent to Steve, until total partnership income and gain exceeds the partnership's total losses and deductions. When the income and gain exceed losses and deductions, all items are to be allocated equally between the partners.

The regulations indicate that the 90/10 allocation of nonrecourse deductions is consistent with allocations having substantial economic effect of other significant partnership items attributable to the building (*i.e.*, the initial allocations of gains and losses).

Example (2): Assume the facts in Example (1), except that the partnership agreement allocates all nonrecourse deductions equally between Robert and Steve. When the partnership agreement is entered into, a reasonable likelihood exists that, over the life of the partnership, income will significantly exceed losses.

The 50/50 allocation of nonrecourse deductions is valid because it corresponds to the partners' equal shares of partnership items after partnership income exceeds its losses. Because the amount of income is expected to be significant, the nonrecourse deduction allocation is deemed to be consistent with allocations of other significant partnership items

---

[316] The validity of these allocations is determined without regard to the validity of allocations of basis and amount realized for depletion properties under I.R.C. § 613A(c)(7)(D).

attributable to the building. The regulations indicate that nonrecourse deductions may be validly allocated between the partners in any ratio between 90 percent to Robert/10 percent to Steve and 50 percent to Robert/50 percent to Steve. For example, an allocation of 75 percent to Robert and 25 percent to Steve is valid.[317]

Example (3): Assume that nonrecourse deductions are allocated 99 percent to Robert and 1 percent to Steve. The allocation is invalid because it is not reasonably consistent with a valid allocation of any other significant partnership item attributable to the building. If the allocation is deemed invalid, nonrecourse deductions are reallocated in proportion to the partners' overall economic interests in the partnership.

[C] Partnership Minimum Gain

The regulations use the term "partnership minimum gain" to represent the total amount of gain that must be allocated to the partners to offset their prior deductions and distributions attributable to partnership nonrecourse liabilities. Partnership minimum gain is computed by aggregating the amount of ordinary and capital gain the partnership would realize if it sold each of its assets subject to a nonrecourse liability for an amount equal to the outstanding principal of the debt.[318] If the sale of an asset would generate a loss, that loss is not taken into account in computing minimum gain.

Example (1): Carlos and Donna contribute equal amounts of capital for equal interests in the AB Partnership. The partnership purchases depreciable Asset A for $50,000, and depreciable Asset B for $20,000, financing the entire purchase price of both assets through nonrecourse loans secured by the property. The full principal on each loan is due in five years. The partnership agreement allocates all depreciation on both properties to Donna. In Year 1, Donna is allocated $5,000 of depreciation for Asset A and $2,000 of depreciation for Asset B. Because the partnership's basis for Asset A is $45,000 ($50,000 cost basis less $5,000 depreciation), the partnership would recognize $5,000 of gain if it sold the property solely for satisfaction of the $50,000 nonrecourse liability. The partnership's basis for Asset B is $18,000 ($20,000 cost basis less $2,000 depreciation); thus, it would recognize $2,000 if it sold the property for satisfaction of the $20,000 debt. Partnership minimum gain is $7,000.

Example (2): Assume the same facts as Example (1), except that the partnership purchases Asset B by paying $10,000 in cash and financing the remaining $10,000 of the purchase price through a nonrecourse loan secured by the property. If the partnership sold the property (after deducting $2,000 of depreciation) solely in satisfaction of the debt, it would recognize an $8,000 loss ($10,000 amount realized less $18,000 basis). This loss is not taken into account in computing the partnership's minimum gain. Thus, minimum gain is $5,000 — all of which is attributable to Asset A.

---

[317] Treas. Reg. § 1.704-2(m), *Example (1)(i)*.

[318] Treas. Reg. § 1.704-2(d)(1).

Partnership minimum gain increases whenever the difference between (1) the amount of nonrecourse debt and (2) the basis of the property securing the liabilities increases. The increase may be attributable to:

(1)   additional nonrecourse borrowings (*e.g.*, second mortgages); or

(2)   losses, deductions, or nondeductible, noncapitalizable expenditures that decrease the basis of property; or

(3)   a refinancing, lapse of a guarantee, or other change to a debt instrument that causes a recourse debt or "partner nonrecourse liability" to become partially or wholly nonrecourse.

Minimum gain decreases if:

(1)   the amount of partnership nonrecourse liabilities decreases; or

(2)   the partnership disposes of property securing nonrecourse debts.

The net change in partnership minimum gain for any tax year is determined by comparing partnership minimum gain on the last day of the preceding year with the partnership minimum gain on the last day of the current year.[319]

> **Example (3):** [320] Robert, the limited partner, contributes $180,000, and Steve, the general partner, contributes $20,000 to form the RS Limited Partnership. RS obtains an $800,000 nonrecourse loan and purchases a building (on leased land) for $1 million. The loan is secured by the building; no principal payments are due for five years. The partnership's annual cost recovery deduction for the building is $90,000.
>
> No partnership minimum gain exists at the end of Years 1 or 2, because a sale of the building in satisfaction of the liability at the end of either year results in a net loss as follows:
>
> End of Year 1
> | | |
> |---|---|
> | $800,000 | outstanding principal |
> | - 910,000 | adjusted basis ($1,000,000 - $90,000) |
> | ($110,000) | loss |
>
> End of Year 2
> | | |
> |---|---|
> | $800,000 | outstanding principal |
> | - 820,000 | adjusted basis ($1,000,000 - $180,000) |
> | ($20,000) | loss |
>
> At the end of Year 3, there is partnership minimum gain of $70,000, the amount the partnership would realize on a sale of the building in satisfaction of the liability, as follows:

---

[319] *Id.*

[320] *See* Treas. Reg. § 1.704-2(m), *Example (1)(i).*

End of Year 3
  $800,000   outstanding principal
  - 730,000   adjusted basis ($1,000,000 - $270,000)
  $70,000   minimum gain

Example (4): Continuing Example (3), assume that in Year 4 Robert and Steve make additional cash contributions totaling $140,000, and the partnership applies the funds to reduce the principal of the nonrecourse liability to $660,000. At the end of Year 4, the partnership's basis for the building is $640,000 ($1 million cost less $360,000 cost recovery deductions). Because the partnership would realize a $20,000 gain on a sale of the building in satisfaction of the liability, minimum gain at the end of the year is $20,000. Thus, the partnership's minimum gain decreases by $50,000 in Year 4.

End of Year 4
  $660,000   outstanding principal
  - 640,000   adjusted basis ($1,000,000 - $360,000)
  $20,000   minimum gain

Minimum gain, end of Year 3	$70,000
Minimum gain, end of Year 4	20,000
Decrease in minimum gain	$50,000

This reduction in minimum gain does not trigger an income allocation under the minimum-gain chargeback rule. No minimum-gain chargeback is required to the extent that a partner's share of net decrease in partnership minimum gain is attributable to a capital contribution he makes to repay a nonrecourse liability. (*See* § 6.08[G], *supra.*)

[D]   Nonrecourse Deductions

Nonrecourse deductions consist of losses, deductions, and nondeductible, noncapitalizable expenditures[321] attributable to a partnership's nonrecourse liabilities.[322] Nonrecourse deductions generally must be allocated in accordance with the partners' overall economic interests in the partnership.[323] However, a special allocation of nonrecourse deductions is deemed to accord with the partners' economic interests if a four-part safe-harbor test is satisfied.

Total partnership nonrecourse deductions for a tax year equal the excess of (1) the net increase in partnership minimum gain for the year, over (2) the aggregate proceeds of nonrecourse borrowings distributed to partners during the year.[324]

---

[321] These items are defined in I.R.C. § 705(a)(2)(B).

[322] Treas. Reg. § 1.704-2(b)(1).

[323] *Id.*

[324] Treas. Reg. § 1.704-2(c). For discussion of when a distribution is allocable to proceeds of a nonrecourse debt, see § 6.08[F], *infra.*

The correlation between nonrecourse deductions and minimum gain ensures that partners who are allocated nonrecourse deductions eventually are allocated a corresponding amount of minimum gain. Distributions of nonrecourse debt proceeds reduce nonrecourse deductions because the effect of the distribution is equivalent to a sale of the property securing the liability (*i.e.*, the partners have the cash without any obligation to pay it back). Increases in partnership minimum gain from conversions, refinancings, or other changes to a debt instrument do not generate nonrecourse deductions.[325]

> **Example (1):** The LM Partnership purchases a depreciable asset for $60,000, financing the entire purchase price through a nonrecourse loan secured by the property. The loan principal is due in five years. In Year 1, the partnership claims a $10,000 cost recovery deduction, reducing the basis of the property to $50,000. Because the net increase in partnership minimum gain for the year is $10,000 (the amount the partnership would recognize if it sold the property in satisfaction of the $60,000 nonrecourse liability), the partnership has $10,000 of nonrecourse deductions for the year.

> **Example (2):** Continuing Example (1), assume that at the beginning of Year 2, the partnership uses the property to secure an additional $10,000 nonrecourse loan, also due in five years. Nonrecourse deductions for Year 2 total $20,000 — the net increase in partnership minimum gain for the year. This amount is computed as follows:

Minimum gain end of Year 2 =	$30,000	(amount partnership would realize if it sold property with a $40,000 basis [$60,000 cost less $20,000 cost recovery] to satisfy its $70,000 nonrecourse liability).
Minimum gain end of Year 1 =	$10,000	
	$20,000	net increase in minimum gain

> **Example (3):** Assume the same facts as Example (2), except that the partnership distributes $10,000 to its partners before the close of Year 2. The $20,000 increase in minimum gain is reduced by the $10,000 distribution attributable to nonrecourse borrowings, resulting in a $10,000 net increase in minimum gain during the year. Thus, nonrecourse deductions for the year are $10,000.

> If the partnership distributes only $5,000 of the loan proceeds, however, the increase in minimum gain is reduced by $5,000, resulting in a $15,000 increase in minimum gain. The partnership's nonrecourse deductions for the year equal $15,000.

Nonrecourse deductions consist first of depreciation and cost recovery deductions for property securing nonrecourse liabilities, up to the increase in minimum gain attributable to each property.[326] Remaining nonrecourse deductions consist of

---

[325] Treas. Reg. § 1.704-2(c).

[326] Treas. Reg. § 1.704-2(c), (j).

a pro rata portion of the partnership's other losses, deductions, and nondeductible, noncapitalizable expenditures.

Example (4): The AB Partnership owns properties W, X, Y, and Z, which are subject to nonrecourse liabilities. During Year 1, AB does the following:

(1) Generates a $10,000 cost recovery deduction for Property W and repays $5,000 of the nonrecourse liability secured by the property. Minimum gain increases by $5,000 ($10,000 - $5,000).

(2) Generates a $10,000 cost recovery deduction for Property X but does not repay any nonrecourse liability secured by that property. Minimum gain increases by $10,000.

(3) Generates a $2,000 cost recovery deduction for Property Y and repays $11,000 of the nonrecourse liability secured by the property. Minimum gain decreases by $9,000 ($2,000 - $11,000).

(4) Obtains a $5,000 nonrecourse loan secured by Property Z, undeveloped land with a $2,000 adjusted tax basis. Minimum gain increases by $3,000 ($5,000 - $2,000).

The increase in partnership minimum gain for the year is $9,000 ($5,000 + $10,000 + $3,000 - $9,000), and the amount of nonrecourse deductions is $9,000. The nonrecourse deductions consist of the following:[327]

Property W $3,000 cost recovery = $9,000 net minimum gain increase

$$\text{x}$$

$$\frac{\$5,000 \text{ cost recovery for W}}{\$15,000 \text{ total cost recovery}}$$

Property X $6,000 cost recovery = $9,000 net minimum gain increase

$$\text{x}$$

$$\frac{\$10,000 \text{ cost recovery for W}}{\$15,000 \text{ total cost recovery}}$$

Example (5): Assume the same facts as Example (4), except that the loan secured by Property Z is $15,000; thus, the net increase in partnership minimum gain is $19,000.

Nonrecourse deductions consist of the following:[328]

Property		Nonrecourse deduction
W	$5,000	cost recovery (the amount of minimum gain attributable to that asset)
X	$10,000	cost recovery (the amount of minimum gain attributable to that asset)
All	$4,000	pro rata share of other losses, deductions, and expenditures

If nonrecourse deductions for a tax year exceed the total amount of

---

[327] Treas. Reg. § 1.704-2(m), *Example (4)(i)*.

[328] Treas. Reg. § 1.704-2(m), *Example (4)(ii)*.

partnership deductions, losses, and nondeductible, noncapitalized expenditures, the excess is treated as an increase in partnership minimum gain for the next succeeding tax year (or years).[329] Consequently, a minimum gain increase that is not allocated to partners in the current year through nonrecourse deductions or distributions is carried forward and may be allocated in subsequent years.

Example (6): At the end of Year 1, the RS Partnership owns a building with a basis of $730,000 that is subject to an $800,000 nonrecourse debt. Annual cost recovery deductions for the building are $70,000, and the partnership has an additional $90,000 of operating and interest expenses each year. Partnership minimum gain at the end of Year 1 is $70,000. During Year 2, the partnership obtains an additional $200,000 nonrecourse loan secured by a second mortgage on the building.

The increase in partnership minimum gain in Year 2 is $270,000, computed as follows:

$340,000   minimum gain at end of Year 2 ($1 million amount realized if building is sold in satisfaction of first and second mortgages minus $660,000 basis after cost recovery deduction),
less

$70,000   partnership minimum gain at end of Year 1.

Because the $270,000 increase in minimum gain for Year 2 exceeds the partnership's actual deductions ($70,000 depreciation and $90,000 other expenses), all $160,000 of the deductions are nonrecourse deductions. The $110,000 excess nonrecourse deductions are carried over and increase partnership minimum gain in Year 3.

The increase in partnership minimum gain in Year 3 is $180,000:

$70,000   actual increase in partnership minimum gain ($410,000 minimum gain at year end [$1 million amount realized if building sold in satisfaction of first and second mortgages minus $590,000 basis after cost recovery deduction], less $340,000 minimum gain at end of Year 2),
plus

$110,000   deemed increase in minimum gain for carryover of prior year's nonrecourse deductions.

Because the $180,000 increase in minimum gain for Year 2 exceeds the partnership's actual deductions ($70,000 depreciation and $90,000 other expenses), all $160,000 of the deductions are nonrecourse deductions. The $20,000 excess nonrecourse deductions are carried over and increase partnership minimum gain in Year 4.

---

[329] Treas. Reg. § 1.704-2(j)(1)(iii).

[E] Partners' Shares of Partnership Minimum Gain

A partner's share of partnership minimum gain must be determined for two purposes:

(1) In applying the alternate economic-effect test in the regulations, a "partner's share of partnership minimum gain" is added to the dollar amount of any deficit capital account balance he is otherwise obligated to restore.[330]

(2) Under the alternate economic-effect test, a special allocation to a partner who is not obligated to restore a deficit capital account may be valid if additional income will be allocated to him pursuant to a "qualified income offset" in any year that his capital account becomes negative. Income allocations are required under a qualified income offset only to the extent that the partner is not otherwise obligated to restore the deficit. Because a partner is deemed obligated to restore a deficit capital account equal to his share of minimum gain, no qualified income offset allocation is required for deficits resulting from nonrecourse deductions or distributions of nonrecourse debt proceeds.

(3) Under the minimum-gain chargeback rules, each partner must be allocated income and gain equal to his share of any net decrease in partnership minimum gain for a year.

A partner's share of partnership minimum gain at the end of a partnership year equals:[331]

(1) the aggregate amount of nonrecourse deductions allocated to him (and to his predecessors in interest), plus aggregate distributions to him (and to his predecessors) of proceeds of nonrecourse borrowings that are allocable to increases in partnership minimum gain, less

(2) the partner's (and his predecessors') aggregate share of (a) net decreases in partnership minimum gain, and (b) decreases in partnership minimum gain resulting from revaluations of partnership property subject to nonrecourse liabilities. A partner's share of the decrease from a revaluation equals the increase in his capital account attributable to the revaluation.

Example: Steve contributes $10,000 for a general partnership interest in the ST Limited Partnership, and Tania contributes $90,000 for a limited partnership interest. The partnership acquires a building for $800,000, financing the entire purchase price through a nonrecourse debt secured by the property. Annual cost recovery deductions for the building are $40,000, and the partnership has an additional $20,000 of operating and interest expenses each year. All partnership items are allocated 90 percent to Tania and 10 percent to Steve. Steve must restore a deficit capital account balance when his interest is liquidated, but Tania does not have to restore any

---

[330] Treas. Reg. § 1.704-2(g).

[331] *Id.*

capital account deficit. The partnership agreement also contains qualified income offset and minimum-gain chargeback provisions.

The net increase in partnership minimum gain in Year 1 and Year 2 is $40,000 each year (fully attributable to cost recovery), and that is the amount of nonrecourse deductions each year. The nonrecourse deductions each year are allocated $36,000 to Tania and $4,000 to Steve, and other deductions are allocated $18,000 to Tania and $2,000 to Steve. At the end of Year 2, the partners' have the following capital accounts:

	Steve	Tania
Beginning capital account	$10,000	$90,000
Less Year 1 deductions other than nonrecourse deductions	(2,000)	(18,000)
Less Year 1 nonrecourse deductions	(4,000)	(36,000)
Capital account at end of Year 1	$4,000	$36,000
Less Year 2 deductions other than nonrecourse deductions	(2,000)	(18,000)
Less Year 2 nonrecourse deductions	(4,000)	(36,000)
Capital account at end of Year 2	($2,000)	($18,000)

At the end of Year 2, Tania's share of partnership minimum gain is $72,000, and Steve's share of partnership minimum gain is $8,000 — the aggregate amount of nonrecourse deductions allocated to each partner. Although Tania has an $18,000 deficit capital account in Year 2, income allocations are not required under the qualified income offset because she is deemed obligated to restore a $72,000 capital account deficit (her share of partnership minimum gain).[332]

In succeeding years, Tania may be allocated an additional $54,000 of partnership deductions or receive a $54,000 distribution ($72,000 total deficit restoration obligation less $18,000 current deficit) without triggering the qualified income offset. The $54,000 is Tania's 90 percent share of partnership assets that are not subject to nonrecourse liabilities ($90,000 contribution less her $36,000 total share of losses other than nonrecourse deductions).

[F]   Distributions Allocable to Nonrecourse Borrowings

A partner's share of partnership minimum gain increases to the extent that he receives distributions of proceeds of nonrecourse borrowings that are allocable to increases in partnership minimum gain.[333] Thus, the partner's share of minimum gain increases if (1) he receives a distribution allocable to the proceeds of a nonrecourse liability, and (2) that nonrecourse liability caused an increase in partnership minimum gain. The partner's additional share of minimum gain is subject to the minimum-gain chargeback requirement when the partnership's minimum gain decreases.

---

[332] Steve's deficit capital account does not affect his allocations because he has an unlimited deficit restoration obligation.

[333] Treas. Reg. § 1.704-2(g)(1).

A partnership may use any reasonable method to determine whether a distribution is derived from the proceeds of a nonrecourse liability.[334] The regulations state that it is reasonable to use the interest deduction rules governing allocations of debt to expenditures (applied as if the partnership was an individual) to determine (1) whether the proceeds of a nonrecourse liability have been distributed to partners, and (2) which partners received the distributions.[335]

A distribution is allocable to an increase in partnership minimum gain to the extent that the increase results from encumbering property with nonrecourse liabilities that exceed its basis.[336] If the net increase in partnership minimum gain arises from more than one nonrecourse liability, the increase is allocated among the liabilities in proportion to the amount each liability contributed to the increase in minimum gain.

A special rule applies if the proceeds of a nonrecourse loan are distributed in the year following the year in which the debt increased partnership minimum gain. This rule applies if:

(1)   the net increase in partnership minimum gain from the debt exceeds the distributions allocable to the loan (*i.e.*, there is an "excess allocable amount"), and

(2)   minimum gain is carried over to the succeeding year (*i.e.*, the partnership does not have enough other deductions to offset the increased minimum gain).

If these conditions are met, the excess allocable amount (or the minimum gain carried over, if less) is deemed to arise from a distribution of the nonrecourse debt proceeds in the succeeding tax year.[337]

> **Example:** The KL Partnership acquires a building for $800,000, financing the entire purchase price through a nonrecourse debt secured by the property. Annual cost recovery deductions for the building are $80,000, and the partnership has an additional $60,000 of operating and interest expenses each year. The partnership agreement allocates all partnership items 90 percent to Laura and 10 percent to Ken, and it provides that Ken must restore a deficit capital account balance when his interest is liquidated; Laura does not have to restore any capital account deficit. The agreement also contains qualified income offset and minimum-gain charge-back provisions.

At the end of Year 1, the partners have the following capital accounts:

---

[334] Treas. Reg. § 1.704-2(h)(2).

[335] *See* Temp. Treas. Reg. § 1.163-8T.

[336] Treas. Reg. § 1.704-2(h)(1).

[337] Treas. Reg. § 1.704-2(h)(4).

	Ken	Laura
Beginning capital account	$20,000	$180,000
Less Year 1 deductions other than nonrecourse deductions	(6,000)	(54,000)
Less Year 1 nonrecourse deductions	(8,000)	(72,000)
Capital account at end of Year 1	$6,000	$54,000

At the end of Year 1, Laura's share of partnership minimum gain is $72,000, and Ken's share of partnership minimum gain is $8,000.

During Year 2, the partnership obtains an additional $200,000 nonrecourse loan secured by a second mortgage on the building. The increase in partnership minimum gain in Year 2 is $280,000 ($360,000 minimum gain at end of Year 2 [$1 million amount realized if building sold in satisfaction of first and second mortgages minus $640,000 basis after cost recovery deduction], less $80,000 partnership minimum gain at end of Year 1). Because the $280,000 increase in minimum gain for Year 2 exceeds the partnership's actual deductions ($80,000 depreciation and $60,000 other expenses), all $140,000 of the deductions are nonrecourse deductions. Laura is allocated $126,000 (90 percent) of the nonrecourse deductions, and Ken is allocated $14,000. At the end of Year 2, Ken's share of partnership minimum gain is $22,000 ($8,000 in Year 1 plus $14,000 in Year 2), and Laura's share is $198,000 ($72,000 in Year 1 plus $126,000 in Year 2). The $140,000 excess nonrecourse deductions ($280,000 - $140,000) are carried over and increase partnership minimum gain in Year 3. Capital accounts at the end of Year 2 are as follows:

	Ken	Laura
Capital account at end of Year 1	$6,000	$54,000
Less Year 1 nonrecourse deductions	(14,000)	(126,000)
Capital account at end of Year 2	($8,000)	($72,000)

Although both partners have deficit capital accounts, no allocations are required under the qualified income offset provision. Ken is obligated to restore his entire capital account deficit, and Laura is deemed obligated to restore a deficit equal to her $198,000 share of partnership minimum gain.

The $140,000 minimum gain carryover is treated as an increase in partnership minimum gain in Year 3 arising from the nonrecourse loan in Year 2. Thus, the net increase in partnership minimum gain in Year 3 is $220,000 ($140,000 deemed increase plus $80,000 [excess of $440,000 minimum gain at the end of Year 3 over $360,000 minimum gain at end of Year 2]). At the beginning of Year 3, the partnership distributes $180,000 of the proceeds of the recourse loan obtained in the prior year ($162,000 to Laura and $18,000 to Ken). Because only $140,000 of the distribution is considered allocable to proceeds of a loan that increased partnership minimum gain, the distribution increases Laura's share of minimum gain by $126,000 (90 percent) and Ken's share by $14,000 (10 percent).

Nonrecourse deductions for the year are $80,000 ($220,000 increase in partnership minimum gain less $140,000 distribution allocable to nonrecourse loan proceeds). The nonrecourse deductions are allocated $8,000 to Ken and $72,000 to

Laura. Thus, at the end of Year 3, her share of partnership minimum gain is $396,000 ($270,000 total nonrecourse deductions plus $126,000 distribution of nonrecourse debt proceeds). Ken's share of minimum gain is $44,000 ($30,000 total nonrecourse deductions plus $14,000 distribution).

Capital accounts at the end of Year 3 are as follows:

	Ken	Laura
Capital account at end of Year 2	($8,000)	($72,000)
Less Year 3 deductions other than nonrecourse deductions	(6,000)	(54,000)
Less Year 3 nonrecourse deductions	(8,000)	(72,000)
Less distribution of loan proceeds	(18,000)	(162,000)
Capital account at end of Year 3	($40,000)	($360,000)

If a partner receiving a distribution of nonrecourse debt proceeds has a deficit restoration obligation, the partnership may elect to treat the distribution as not being allocable to an increase in minimum gain.[338] The election is permitted to the extent that the distribution does not create or increase the partner's deficit capital account beyond his restoration obligation at the end of the year the distribution occurs. The election prevents the distribution from increasing the partner's share of partnership minimum gain so that no additional minimum-gain chargeback to him will be required.

[G] Minimum-Gain Chargeback

The minimum-gain chargeback rules ensure that a partner who is allocated nonrecourse deductions also is allocated an equal amount of the income and gain from the property securing the partnership's nonrecourse debts. These offsetting income allocations are required in any year that a net decrease in partnership minimum gain occurs.[339] The amount allocated to each partner is determined from his percentage share of the net decrease in partnership minimum gain. Under the safe harbor in the regulations, special allocations of nonrecourse deductions are invalid unless the partnership agreement contains a minimum-gain chargeback clause.[340]

Pursuant to a minimum-gain chargeback, if a net decrease in partnership minimum gain occurs in a year, each partner must be allocated additional partnership income and gain equal to his share of the net decrease.

A partner's share of the net decrease is determined by multiplying the total net decrease by his percentage share of partnership minimum gain at the end of the preceding year.[341] For example, if a $500 net decrease in partnership minimum

---

[338] Treas. Reg. § 1.704-2(h)(3).

[339] No minimum-gain chargeback is required if a partnership terminates under I.R.C. § 708(b)(1)(B). Rev. Rul. 93-90, 1993-2 C.B. 238.

[340] Treas. Reg. § 1.704-2(e)(3).

[341] Treas. Reg. § 1.704-2(g)(2).

gain occurs, a partner with a 20 percent share of partnership minimum gain at the end of the prior year has a $100 share of the net decrease. A partner's share of partnership minimum gain equals the sum of (1) all nonrecourse deductions allocated to him, plus (2) all distributions of nonrecourse debt proceeds he received.

Example (1): Robert, the limited partner, contributes $180,000, and Steve, the general partner, contributes $20,000, to form the RS Limited Partnership. RS obtains an $800,000 nonrecourse loan and purchases a building for $1 million. The loan is secured by the building; no principal payments are due for five years.

The partnership agreement allocates all partnership items, other than nonrecourse deductions, 90 percent to Robert and 10 percent to Steve, until total partnership income and gain exceed its total losses and deductions. After the income and gain exceed the partnership's losses and deductions, all items are allocated equally between the partners. The partners share nonrecourse deductions equally. The agreement contains a minimum-gain chargeback clause and satisfies the other requirements of the safe harbor for allocating nonrecourse deductions.

In each of its first 3 years, RS has a $90,000 cost recovery deduction for the building. Partnership minimum gain at the end of Year 3 is $70,000 (the amount the partnership would realize on a sale of the building to satisfy the liability [$800,000 amount realized less $730,000 adjusted basis]). Pursuant to the partnership agreement, each partner is allocated $35,000 of the nonrecourse deductions in Year 3. At the end of Year 3, each partner's share of partnership minimum gain is $35,000 — the amount of nonrecourse deductions allocated to them.

At the beginning of Year 4, RS sells the building for $800,000, using the proceeds to pay the nonrecourse liability. The partnership realizes a $270,000 gain on the sale ($800,000 amount realized — $530,000 basis). Minimum gain at the end of Year 4 is zero so that the net decrease in partnership minimum gain is $70,000. Because each partner's share of that net decrease is $35,000 (50 percent share of partnership minimum gain * $70,000 net decrease in minimum gain), the minimum-gain chargeback requires the partnership to allocate $35,000 of its gain from the sale of the building to each partner before other allocations are made.

A minimum-gain chargeback consists of gains from dispositions of property that is subject to nonrecourse liabilities.[342] If these gains are not sufficient, then pro rata amounts of all other income and gain items are allocated. If the minimum-gain chargeback requirement exceeds the partnership's income and gains for the year, the excess carries over and is treated as a minimum-gain chargeback requirement in succeeding years until fully charged back.[343] The allocation of income and gain required by a minimum-gain chargeback is made before any other allocation of partnership items.

---

[342] Treas. Reg. § 1.704-2(f)(6), (j)(2).
[343] Treas. Reg. § 1.704-2(j)(2)(iii).

Exceptions to the minimum-gain chargeback rule.

(1)   No minimum-gain chargeback is required to the extent that a partner
      contributes capital used to repay a nonrecourse liability or increase the
      basis of property subject to a nonrecourse liability, and the partner's share
      of the net decrease in partnership minimum gain results from the
      repayment or basis increase.[344]

Example (2): Assume the facts in Example (1), except that instead of
selling the building in Year 4, Robert and Steve each contribute an
additional $80,000 to RS, and the partnership applies the funds to reduce
the principal of the nonrecourse liability to $640,000. At the end of Year 4,
the partnership's basis for the building also is $640,000. Because RS would
realize no gain if it sold the building to satisfy the liability, minimum gain
at the end of the year is zero. Thus, the net decrease in partnership
minimum gain is $70,000. Because each partners' share of the net decrease
in minimum gain results from his capital contribution used to pay the debt,
no minimum-gain chargeback is required.

(2)   No gain is allocated to a partner under a minimum-gain chargeback to
      the extent that his share of a net decrease in partnership minimum
      gain results from a guarantee, refinancing, or other change in a
      nonrecourse debt instrument that caused the partner to bear the
      economic risk of loss for the debt.[345] The regulations indicate that a
      chargeback is inappropriate because the partner has replaced his
      nonrecourse deductions with an obligation to contribute funds or pay a
      partnership creditor.

Example (3): [346] Carl and Donna each contribute $25 for equal profits and
loss interests in the CD Partnership. The partnership agreement contains
qualified income offset and minimum-gain chargeback provisions. Neither
partner is obligated to restore a deficit capital account. All other requirements of the safe harbor for allocations of nonrecourse deductions are
satisfied.

   The partnership obtains a $100 nonrecourse loan secured by depreciable
property purchased for $100. The partnership also purchases stock for $50.
In each of its first five years, the partnership's only tax item is a $20
depreciation deduction. The deductions are nonrecourse deductions that
are allocated to Carl and Donna equally. At the end of Year 5, both partners
have a $25 deficit capital account and a $50 share of partnership minimum
gain.

   In the beginning of Year 6, Carl guarantees the entire nonrecourse
liability, resulting in a $100 net decrease in partnership minimum gain.
Although each partner's share of the net decrease is $50, Carl is not subject
to a minimum-gain chargeback because the decrease in his share is caused

---

[344]   Treas. Reg. § 1.704-2(f)(3).

[345]   Treas. Reg. § 1.704-2(f)(2). Whether a partner bears the economic risk of loss for a debt is
determined under the rules of Treas. Reg. § 1.752-2.

[346]   Treas. Reg. § 1.704-2(f)(7), *Example (2)*.

by the guarantee of a debt for which he bears the economic risk of loss. (As discussed in § 6.08[H], *infra*, Carl's share of partner nonrecourse debt minimum gain is now $50).

Donna is subject to a $50 minimum-gain chargeback that cannot be satisfied in Year 6 because the partnership has no income. The $50 carries over as a minimum-gain chargeback requirement to Donna in each succeeding year until enough income is generated to cover the entire amount. Thus, if the partnership earns $100 in Year 7, the first $50 of that amount must be allocated to Donna as a minimum-gain chargeback.

(3)   The Service may waive a minimum-gain chargeback at the partnership's request if:

    (a)   the partnership has a net decrease in minimum gain for the year,

    (b)   the minimum-gain chargeback would create economic distortions, and

    (c)   the partnership does not expect to have sufficient other income to correct the distortions.[347]

A waiver is possible only if the partnership demonstrates that (1) the partners' previous nonrecourse deductions and distributions of nonrecourse debt proceeds have been restored by net income allocations or capital contributions, and (2) income allocations without the minimum-gain chargeback more accurately reflect the partners' economic arrangement, as evidenced by partnership allocations and distributions and partner contributions.

An example in the regulations indicates that the Service is likely to waive the minimum-gain chargeback requirement if the partners have restored their nonrecourse deductions through allocations of operating income before the year a net decrease in minimum gain occurs.[348]

[H]   Nonrecourse Debt for Which Partner Bears Risk of Loss

A "partner nonrecourse debt" is a partnership nonrecourse debt for which any partner bears the economic risk of loss.[349] Generally, this refers to nonrecourse loans made to the partnership by partners or by persons related to partners. Whether a person bears the economic risk of loss for a partnership liability is determined pursuant to the regulations under I.R.C. Section 752. (See discussion of economic risk of loss in Chapter 5.)

Losses, deductions, and expenditures attributable to a partner nonrecourse debt generally must be allocated to the partner who bears the risk of loss. Similarly, any decrease in minimum gain that is attributable to a partner nonrecourse debt triggers an allocation of income and gain similar to the allocation required by a

---

[347]   Treas. Reg. § 1.704-2(f)(4).

[348]   Treas. Reg. § 1.704-2(f)(7), *Example (1)*.

[349]   Treas. Reg. § 1.704-2(i)(1).

minimum-gain chargeback (the decrease is determined under rules analogous to the rules governing partnership minimum gain).

§ 6.09 LIMITATIONS ON PARTNER'S AND LLC MEMBER'S DEDUCTION FOR LOSSES — I.R.C. SECTION 704(d)

[A] General Rules

A partner's deduction for his distributive share of partnership loss (including capital loss) is limited to the basis in his partnership interest at the end of the partnership tax year in which the loss is incurred.[350] For this purpose, a partner's year-end basis is computed by taking into account all adjustments required under I.R.C. Section 705, except his share of partnership losses for the current year or any previously disallowed losses that have been carried forward to the current year.[351] A partner owning both limited and general partnership interests in the same partnership has a single basis in both interests.[352]

A partner may carry forward indefinitely any losses that are not currently deductible because of the I.R.C. Section 704(d) limitation, and he may deduct the losses at the end of the first succeeding partnership taxable year in which he has sufficient basis.[353] A partner may obtain sufficient basis at the end of a succeeding year through an increase in his share of partnership liabilities, an additional capital contribution, or an accumulation of his distributive share of partnership income.[354]

> **Example (1):** Allen contributes property worth $6,000 with a $1,000 tax basis for a one-third interest in the ABC Partnership. Barbara and Carl each contribute $6,000 in cash for their interests. The partnership and all partners use a calendar tax year.
>
> In Year 1, the partnership only tax item is a $6,000 taxable loss from operations. Although Allen's share of the loss is $2,000, he may deduct only $1,000 — the year-end basis of his partnership interest before deducting the loss — on his individual tax return for Year 1. Allen carries forward the $1,000 nondeductible portion of the loss and treats it as an operating loss arising in the subsequent year.
>
> Because Barbara and Carl each have a $6,000 year-end basis, they may each deduct their entire $2,000 share of the partnership loss.

---

[350] I.R.C. § 704(d); Treas. Reg. § 1.704-1(d)(1). *See, e.g.*, Goodman v. Comm'r, T.C. Memo. 1990-114; Hobson v. Comm'r, T.C. Memo. 1980-132.

[351] Treas. Reg. § 1.704-1(d)(2). *See* Rev. Rul. 66-94, 1966-1 C.B. 166. *See also* Scott v. Comm'r, T.C. Memo. 1997-507 (taxpayer's claim that his basis included value of his interest in partnership accounts receivable and his work in progress rejected because items had not been reflected in partnership income or partner's distributive share).

[352] Rev. Rul. 84-53, 1984-1 C.B. 159.

[353] Treas. Reg. § 1.704-1(d)(1).

[354] Apparently, a partner need not establish a business purpose for deducting his distributive share of losses. Corum v. U.S., 67-1 U.S.T.C. 9315, 268 F. Supp. 109.

To ensure that the character of the any deductible losses is preserved, the regulations provide special rules for allocating a partner's nondeductible loss among certain loss items specified in I.R.C. Section 702(a). These loss items are:

(1)   short-term gains and losses;

(2)   long-term gains and losses;

(3)   gains and losses from sales or exchanges of depreciable trade or business property (I.R.C. Section 1231 property);

(4)   income, gain, loss, deduction, or credit attributable to items listed in the regulations under I.R.C. Section 702(a)(7);[355] and

(5)   any other item of taxable income or loss that is not separately computed under I.R.C. Section 702.

The portion of the partner's share of each loss item that he may deduct currently is determined from the proportion that each loss item bears to the total of all such loss items for the year.[356] For this purpose, the partner's total losses for the year equal the sum of his share of losses for the current year plus any disallowed losses carried forward from prior years.[357] The disallowed portion of each loss item is carried forward and included in the partner's distributive share of loss in subsequent years.

> **Example (2):** Victor's basis in his limited liability company interest at the start of Year 1 is $10,000. Victor's distributive share of LLC tax items for Year 1 is as follows:
>
> (1) $40,000 long-term capital loss;
>
> (2) $20,000 short-term capital loss; and
>
> (3) $20,000 taxable income.
>
> Under I.R.C. Section 705(a)(1), Victor's basis is increased from $10,000 to $30,000 at the end of the year to reflect his $20,000 share of income. This basis increase is made before taking account of Victor's distributive share of losses. Victor's total share of LLC loss is $60,000 ($20,000 + $40,000 capital losses). Because Victor's year-end basis is only $30,000, he may deduct only one half of each loss ($30,000 / $60,000). Thus, Victor deducts $20,000 of his long-term capital loss and $10,000 of his short-term capital loss, and carries forward to succeeding taxable years $20,000 as a long-term capital loss and $10,000 as a short-term capital loss.[358]

---

[355] *See* Treas. Reg. § 1.702-1(a)(8).

[356] Treas. Reg. § 1.704-1(d)(2).

[357] *Id.*

[358] Treas. Reg. § 1.704-1(d)(4), *Example (3)*.

[B]   Effect of Sale, Death, Termination, or Gift

A partner who sells or exchanges his entire partnership interest may deduct any suspended losses up to the basis of his interest at the end of the short tax year closed by the transfer.[359] The partner's basis at the end of the year includes his share of income or loss for the year up to the date of sale but does not include any gain realized on the sale. Any suspended losses not deducted in the year of the transfer are lost; subsequently, the seller or the purchasing partner cannot deduct them.[360]

A partner who sells only a portion of his partnership interest determines the basis of his retained interest at the end of the partnership tax year, for determining his deduction limit under I.R.C. Section 704(d).[361] This rule applies even if the basis for his retained interest was reduced by the amount of basis allocated to the portion he sold.

Although no direct authority exists, it appears that losses suspended under I.R.C. Section 704(d) because of insufficient basis are eliminated when the partner dies.[362] The suspended losses do not carry over to the partner's successor and do not offset any gain realized upon a sale of the partner's interest at or after his death.[363] A partner's suspended losses are extinguished when the partnership terminates.[364]

It is unclear whether a donee of a partnership interest may use the donor's suspended losses. Because the donee's basis for the interest is generally the same as the donor's (which will be zero if the donor has suspended losses), it seems reasonable to allow the donee to use losses that have not been reflected in that basis. Thus, a donee may use the donor's suspended losses in a year that the donee's has sufficient basis in the interest.

---

[359]   Treas. Reg. § 1.704-1(d)(2).

[360]   Meinerz v. Comm'r, T.C. Memo. 1983-191.

[361]   *See* Richardson v. Comm'r, 76 T.C. 512 (1981), *aff'd*, 693 F.2d 1189 (5th Cir. 1982) (partner's basis for I.R.C. § 704(d) purposes determined at normal end of partnership year, even though his interest was reduced during the year by admission of new partners).

[362]   *See* Treas. Reg. § 1.704-1(d); Rev. Rul. 74-175, 1974-1 C.B. 52 (taxpayer's capital loss carryover terminates at death).

[363]   *See* Sennett v. Comm'r, 80 T.C. 825 (1983), *aff'd per curiam*, 752 F.2d 428 (9th Cir. 1985).

[364]   *Id.*

Chapter 7

TRANSACTIONS BETWEEN PARTNERS/MEMBERS AND PARTNERSHIP/LLC

§ 7.01 OVERVIEW OF PARTNERSHIP TRANSACTIONS

The tax treatment of a transaction between a partnership and one of its partners generally depends upon whether the partner is acting as a member of the partnership or in an individual, nonpartner capacity (*see* § 7.02, *infra*). If the partner does not act in his partner capacity, the transaction is treated as if it occurred between unrelated persons and is taxable under the general rules of the Code. Consider, for example, a partner's transfer of property to a partnership: if the partner is acting in a nonpartner capacity, the transaction is likely to be treated as a sale; however, if the partner is acting in a partner capacity, the transaction is subject to the special partnership tax rules of Subchapter K and is generally treated as a capital contribution. Whether the partner is acting in a partner or nonpartner capacity is determined from the facts surrounding the transaction.

If a partner, in his capacity as a partner, receives payments for services he performs for the partnership, or for capital he furnishes to the partnership, and the payments are determined without regard to the partnership's income, the payments are subject to special treatment as "guaranteed payments." Guaranteed payments include, for example, fixed salary payments a partner receives in addition to his share of partnership income and interest paid to a partner for the use of his contributed capital. However, if the amount of the payment the partner receives is based on a percentage of partnership income, the payments are considered part of, and included in, his distributive share of partnership income.

[A] Transactions in Which the Partner Acts in a Nonpartner Capacity

I.R.C. Section 707(a) governs the tax treatment of transactions between a partnership and a partner who is acting in his individual, nonpartner capacity. This kind of transaction is taxable as if it occurred between two unrelated parties; that is, each party determines and reports the tax consequences separately.[1]

When a partner acts in a nonpartner capacity, the partnership is considered to be a separate entity, distinct from its partners, rather than an aggregation of persons owning undivided interests in the partnership's assets. Because the partnership is treated as a separate entity in transactions governed by I.R.C.

---

[1] I.R.C. § 707(a)(1); Treas. Reg. § 1.707-1(a).

Section 707(a), resulting gains and losses are fully recognized, even though they are partially attributable to a partner's dealing with himself.

Example (1): Alice and Betty are equal partners in the AB Partnership. Alice owns land worth $100; her adjusted basis in the land is $50. Alice sells the land to the partnership for its $100 value. Under the entity treatment of I.R.C. Section 707(a), Alice recognizes a $50 gain on the sale ($100 realized less $50 basis).

Example (2): Assume that Betty (from Example (1)) performs services for the partnership. The services are unrelated to her capacity as a partner, and she is paid a $500 fee for her work. Under I.R.C. Section 707(a), Betty recognizes $500 of compensation income, and the partnership may deduct a $500 expense (if the payment is a business expense under I.R.C. Section 162).

[B] Transactions That May Be Recharacterized as Occurring Between the Partnership and a Partner Acting in a Nonpartner Capacity

Whether a partner is acting in a partner or nonpartner capacity is determined from the substance, rather than the form, of the transaction. However, in addition to this general substance-over-form rule, I.R.C. Section 707(a)(2) specifically authorizes the Service to recharacterize certain partner-partnership transactions as if they occurred between the partnership and a nonpartner. This recharacterized transaction is taxable, according to I.R.C. Section 707(a)(1), under the general rules of the Code. Recharacterization may occur in the following circumstances:

(1) A partner contributes property to a partnership and receives a related distribution from the partnership. The transaction is treated as if the partner sold the property to the partnership.[2]

(2) Partnership income is allocated to a partner in connection with services he performs or property he contributes to the partnership. The transaction is treated as a payment in compensation for services or for sale of the property.[3]

[C] Special Treatment of Losses and Capital Gains on Sales Between a Partnership and Persons With Controlling Interests

I.R.C. Section 707(b) is meant to prevent abusive transactions involving sales or exchanges of property between partners and the partnerships they directly or indirectly control, or between two partnerships controlled by the same persons. Under these rules:

---

[2] I.R.C. § 707(a)(2)(B).

[3] I.R.C. § 707(a)(2)(A).

(1)　A loss incurred on the sale or exchange is not recognized.[4] However, the disallowed loss may offset gain recognized on a later sale or exchange.[5]

(2)　Gain recognized on the sale or exchange is characterized as ordinary income if, in the transferee's hands, the property either (a) is not a capital asset, or (b) is depreciable.[6]

[D]　Accrual-Method Deductions Deferred Until Payment Occurs

Under I.R.C. Section 267(a), a partner or partnership using the accrual-method of accounting for tax purposes may not deduct expenses owed to a related partner or partnership until the payment is includible in the related partner's or partnership's gross income.[7] This rule prevents a deduction from being claimed before the related party reports the income.

[E]　Guaranteed Payments to a Partner Who Provides Services or Capital to the Partnership in a Partner Capacity

Under I.R.C. Section 707(c), salary or interest payments to a partner for services he renders or for capital he provides, while acting in a partner capacity, are subject to special treatment as "guaranteed payments," to the extent that the amount paid is determined without regard to the partnership's income (*see* § 7.03, *infra*). The partnership may deduct the payment from its ordinary income if it represents an ordinary and necessary trade or business expense. If the payment is for a capital expenditure, no current deduction is allowed, and the partnership depreciates or amortizes the payment under general tax rules.[8] The partner receiving the guaranteed payment includes the amount in his ordinary income for the year in which it is deducted by the partnership.[9] Even if the partnership capitalizes the payment, the partner reports it as ordinary income in the year he receives it.[10]

Guaranteed payments do not include compensation for a partner's services or capital if the amount is determined by reference to the partnership's income. These payments are included in the partner's distributive share and are treated as cash distributions to him when payment actually occurs.

---

[4]　I.R.C. § 707(b)(1).

[5]　*Id.*

[6]　I.R.C. §§ 707(b)(2), 1239.

[7]　I.R.C. § 267(a)(2), (e).

[8]　I.R.C. § 707(c).

[9]　Treas. Reg. § 1.707-1(c).

[10]　Jolin v. Comm'r, T.C. Memo. 1985-287; Gaines v. Comm'r, T.C. Memo. 1982-731; Rev. Rul. 80-234, 1980-2 C.B. 203.

[F] Partnership-Partner Transactions Treated as Contributions or Included in the Partner's Distributive Share

Transactions between a partnership and a person acting in his capacity as a partner are taxable under the special partnership rules of Subchapter K. Thus, a partner who transfers property to a partnership while acting in a partner capacity is deemed to contribute the property. Therefore, no gain or loss is recognized under I.R.C. Section 721, and the partner's and partnership's bases are determined under I.R.C. Sections 722 and 723. A payment to a person acting as a partner, other than a guaranteed payment for his services or capital, is treated as a distribution subject to I.R.C. Sections 731–736. Any increase in a partner's right to receive partnership income that is not a guaranteed payment is included in his distributive share subject to the rules of I.R.C. Section 704.

§ 7.02 DETERMINING WHETHER A PARTNER ACTS IN A PARTNER OR NONPARTNER CAPACITY

Whether a partner acts in a partner or nonpartner capacity in a transaction with his partnership is determined from the relevant facts and circumstances. Case law and rulings indicate that one important factor is whether the partner is acting as he would be expected to act in furthering the partnership's business or investment activities. In *Pratt v. Commissioner*,[11] for example, a partner who managed partnership real estate operations was considered to act in a partner capacity because his services were connected to the partnership's regular business activities. Similarly, the Service has ruled that a partner who receives a fee to manage partnership real estate activities acts in a partner capacity when the partnership agreement requires those services.[12]

In contrast, the Service ruled that a partner did not act in a partner capacity when he received payments that were not dependent upon the success of the partnership's business or upon the transaction in which the services were performed.[13] The partner managed the partnership's investment portfolio under the following circumstances:

(1) he performed similar services for clients other than the partnership;

(2) his services could be terminated upon 60 days' notice;

(3) he paid his own expenses;

(4) he was not liable for any losses the partnership incurred on its investments; and

(5) management decisions were controlled by other partners.

---

[11] 64 T.C. 203 (1975), *aff'd*, 550 F.2d 1023 (5th Cir. 1977).

[12] Rev. Rul. 81-300, 1981-2 C.B. 143.

[13] Rev. Rul. 81-301, 1981-2 C.B. 144.

In this factual setting, a question may arise as to whether a partner-partnership relationship exists.[14] Whether a partner acts in a partner or nonpartner capacity depends upon the substance, rather than the form, of the transaction, as determined from the surrounding facts.[15] Situations in which questions about the substance-over-form rule are likely to arise include the following:

(1) *Is a purported loan by a partner to his partnership, in substance, a capital contribution?* If the loan is, in fact, a capital contribution, any "interest" payments made to the partner are included in the partner's distributive share, and the partnership's corresponding interest deductions are disallowed.

(2) *Did the partner perform services for his partnership in a partner or nonpartner capacity?* The distinction is important in determining if payments for the services are treated as compensation to a nonpartner under I.R.C. Section 707(a) or as guaranteed payments subject to I.R.C. Section 707(c).

For example, in *Egolf v. Commissioner*,[16] a partnership required one partner to bear the partnership's organization and syndication expenses. The partnership reimbursed the partner by paying him a management fee. The Tax Court rejected the contention that the partner was acting in his nonpartner capacity as a broker, holding that the management fee was a guaranteed payment. The following facts supported the conclusion that the taxpayer acted in a partner capacity:

(a) the partner was the sole general partner;

(b) the partnership agreement did not distinguish between his partnership and purported nonpartnership duties; and

(c) the partner was not licensed to act as an independent broker.

(3) *Is a contribution of property that is related to a distribution from the partnership, in substance, a sale transaction?* If the partner who contributes property receives a related distribution, the transaction may be considered a sale of the property transferred to the partnership. If a partner, other than the one contributing the property, receives the distribution, the issue is whether the substance of that transaction is a sale of the distributee's partnership interest to the contributor. If the contribution and the distribution, when viewed together, are properly characterized as a sale, the transaction is taxable under I.R.C. Section 707(a) as occurring between the partnership and a nonpartner, or occurring between two nonpartners.[17]

(4) *Is an allocation of income, and a related distribution of cash to a*

---

[14] *See also* Priv. Ltr. Rul. 8642003 (partners who licensed property to their partnership acted in a nonpartner capacity when they retained ownership of the property).

[15] Treas. Reg. § 1.707-1(a).

[16] 87 T.C. 34 (1986).

[17] I.R.C. § 707(a)(2)(B).

partner, in substance, compensation for the partner's services or payment for property he transferred to the partnership? If the allocation and distribution, when viewed together, are properly characterized as payment for services or property, the transaction may be taxable under I.R.C. Section 707(a) as occurring between the partnership and a nonpartner.[18]

§ 7.03 GUARANTEED PAYMENTS FOR PARTNER'S SERVICES OR CAPITAL

[A] General Tax Consequences of Payments for Services or Use of Capital

The treatment of payments to a partner that are compensation for services or that are interest on capital the partner provides for the partnership depends upon whether the partner is acting in a partner or nonpartner capacity. The tax consequences of these transactions are summarized as follows:

(1) If the partner is not acting in his capacity as a partner, the transaction is treated as occurring between unrelated parties and is taxed according to the general rules of the Code.[19] The partner and partnership separately determine their tax consequences using their own tax years and tax accounting methods. However, an accrual-method partnership or partner may not deduct an expense for an amount owed to a cash-method partner or partnership until actual payment occurs.

(2) If the partner acts in a partner capacity when furnishing the services or capital, the amount he receives is either treated as a "guaranteed payment" or included in his distributive share of partnership income. Guaranteed-payment rules apply to the extent that the amount the partner receives is determined without regard to the partnership's income.[20] If the amount the partner receives is computed by reference to partnership income, the partner's right to receive it is considered part of his distributive share of partnership income.[21] When actual payment occurs, the transaction is treated as a distribution under I.R.C. Section 731.

Both guaranteed payments and distributive shares are taxable to the partner in his tax year in which (or with which) the partnership's tax year ends. The major differences between the tax treatment of a guaranteed payment and the treatment of a distributive share can be summarized as follows:

(1) A guaranteed payment is characterized as ordinary income to the partner; it is generally deductible against the partnership's ordinary income.

---

[18] I.R.C. § 707(a)(2)(A).

[19] I.R.C. § 707(a).

[20] I.R.C. § 707(c).

[21] I.R.C. §§ 704, 707(c).

(2)   The character of a partner's distributive share depends on the character of the income or loss earned by the partnership; the partnership cannot deduct a partner's distributive share against partnership income.

The following examples illustrate three situations involving partnership payments to a partner, each requiring a different tax treatment.

Example (1): Arthur and Barbara each contribute $10,000 for equal interests in the AB Partnership. Arthur also lends the partnership $90,000, represented by a bona fide note which is due in five years and bears interest at 10 percent per year. Because the facts indicate that Arthur made the loan in his individual, nonpartner capacity, Arthur and the partnership each determine the tax consequences of the transaction under I.R.C. Section 707(a), as if the loan were between unrelated parties.

Example (2): Assume the same facts as in Example (1), except that instead of making a loan, Arthur contributes $100,000 to the partnership. Barbara contributes $10,000 and agrees to provide services by managing future partnership operations. The partnership agreement states that:

(1)   Arthur will receive $10,000 each year, as a return on the capital he has invested in the partnership;

(2)   the partners will share any remaining partnership income equally; and

(3)   when Arthur's partnership interest is liquidated, he will receive the first $100,000 of partnership assets, and the partners will share any remaining assets equally.

Because each $10,000 payment to Arthur for the use of his capital is determined without regard to the partnership's income, it is a guaranteed payment subject to the rules of I.R.C. Section 707(c).

Example (3): Assume the same facts as in Example (2), except that the partnership agreement states that Arthur will receive the first $10,000 of the partnership's net income each year, if any, and that the partners will share any remaining income equally. If the partnership earns $100,000 of net income in its first year, Arthur's share is $55,000 and Betty's share is $45,000, as follows:

		Arthur	Betty
Net income	$100,000		
Less: Arthur's payment	(10,000)	$10,000	
Balance	$90,000		
Each partner's 50% share		45,000	$45,000
Total received		$55,000	$45,000

Because the amount Arthur receives depends on the partnership's income, the entire $55,000 is treated as an allocation of partnership income (under I.R.C. Section 704) and is included in his distributive share.

[B]   Guaranteed Payments

A partnership may agree to pay a specific amount to a partner as compensation for his services or as interest for capital he provides to the partnership. These amounts are subject to the guaranteed-payment rules of I.R.C. Section 707(c), if both of the following criteria are met:

(1)   The partner provides the services or loans in his capacity as a partner. If he is acting in a nonpartner capacity, the transaction is taxable under I.R.C. Section 707(a).

(2)   The amount of the payment is determined without regard to the partnership's income. Examples of guaranteed payments include a payment to a partner of a fixed annual salary of $10,000, and an annual payment of 10 percent of his invested capital. If the amount paid to the partner is determined as a portion of partnership income, the payment is not considered a guaranteed payment; it is considered an increase in the partner's distributive share (under I.R.C. Section 704), and the actual payment is treated as a distribution (under I.R.C. Section 731).

If a guaranteed payment by a partnership to a partner represents an ordinary and necessary trade or business expense under I.R.C. Section 162, the partnership may deduct the amount paid from its ordinary income. If the payment is a capital expenditure, no current deduction is allowed; the partnership depreciates or amortizes the payment under the general rules of the Code.[22] For purposes other than determining the partnership's deductions and capital expenditures, the partnership treats a guaranteed payment as part of the recipient partner's distributive share of ordinary income.[23]

NOTE:

Therefore, a guaranteed payment is not considered an interest in partnership profits when determining whether:

(1)   a partner is a principal partner for purposes of selecting a partnership taxable year under I.R.C. Section 706(b)(3);

(2)   a transaction is subject to the I.R.C. Section 707(b) rules governing sales between partnerships and controlling partners; or

(3)   a partnership is terminated under I.R.C. Section 708(b), because 50 percent or more of the total interest in partnership capital and profits have been sold or exchanged within a 12-month period.

A partner who receives a guaranteed payment includes it in his ordinary income for the tax year in which the partnership is permitted to deduct the payment under

---

[22] *See* I.R.C. § 263.

[23] I.R.C. § 707(c).

the partnership's method of accounting.[24] The timing of the partner's income is the same as if the payment were included in his distributive share (*i.e.*, he includes it in his tax year in which, or with which, the end of the relevant partnership tax year falls). If the partnership capitalizes the payment, the partner includes it in ordinary income when he receives it, not in the years that the partnership takes the related depreciation or amortization deductions.[25] The payment is characterized as compensation for services or as interest (*see* § 7.03[C], *infra*). It is taxed as ordinary income, even if the partnership has insufficient ordinary income to cover the payment.[26]

> **Example (1):** Richard and Steve are equal partners in the RS Partnership. Both partners and the partnership use a calendar tax year. In Year 1, Richard receives a $10,000 guaranteed payment for management services he performs for the partnership. Richard reports the $10,000 as ordinary compensation income. Partnership taxable income before taking the payment into account is $14,000. Assuming that RS is able to deduct the payment as a business expense, the partnership has $4,000 of taxable income after the payment is taken into account. The amounts are allocated between the partners as follows:

	Richard	Steve	Total
Guaranteed payment	$10,000	$0	$10,000
Distributive share	2,000	2,000	(4,000)
Total amount of partnership income	$12,000	$2,000	$14,000

> **Example (2):** Assume the facts in Example (1), except that taxable partnership income before taking the guaranteed payment into account is $6,000. Richard still reports the $10,000 payment as ordinary compensation income. However, because the payment is deductible as a trade or business expense, the partnership now has a $4,000 taxable loss after the payment is taken into account. The allocation of these amounts between the partners is as follows:

	Richard	Steve	Total
Guaranteed payment	$10,000	$0	$10,000
Distributive share	(2,000)	(2,000)	(4,000)
Total amount of partnership income	$8,000	$(2,000)	$6,000

> **Example (3):** Assume the facts in Example (1), except that the partnership's only taxable income is $10,000 of long-term capital gain. Richard reports his $10,000 guaranteed payment as ordinary compensation income;

---

[24] Treas. Reg. § 1.707-1(c).

[25] Jolin v. Comm'r, T.C. Memo. 1985-287; Gaines v. Comm'r, T.C. Memo. 1982-731; Rev. Rul. 80-234, 1980-2 C.B. 203.

[26] Treas. Reg. § 1.707-1(c), *Example (3)*. *See also* GCM 38133 (Oct. 10, 1979) (guaranteed payment for capital is interest income to partner).

the partnership deducts the payment with a resulting $10,000 ordinary loss. The guaranteed payment is deductible in the computation of partnership operating income or loss, but does not affect the computation of capital gain. Each partner reports his share of the partnership's ordinary loss and capital gain as follows:[27]

	Richard	Steve	Total
Guaranteed payment	$10,000	$0	$10,000
Distributive share of expense deduction	(5,000)	(5,000)	(10,000)
Total ordinary income (loss)	$5,000	$(5,000)	$-0-
Distributive share of Capital gain	$5,000	$5,000	$10,000

Example (4): Assume the facts in Example (1), except that partnership income is $14,000 and that the payment to Richard is a nondeductible, nonamortizable expenditure (*e.g.*, it is for his services in syndicating partnership interests). Richard is taxable on both the $10,000 guaranteed payment and his $7,000 ($14,000 * 50%) distributive share of partnership income. Steve reports only his $7,000 distributive share of partnership income. The guaranteed payment has the effect of creating current income for the partners, because Steve and Richard, together, must report $24,000 ($10,000 + $14,000), even though the partnership's income was only $14,000.

A partnership may guarantee that a partner will not receive less than a specified amount of income from the partnership for a year, even if his distributive share of partnership income is less than that amount (*e.g.*, the partner will receive 25 percent of partnership income, but not less than $10,000). If the partner's distributive share equals or exceeds the specified minimum, the partnership is not required to pay on its guarantee, and there is no guaranteed payment. However, if the partner's distributive share is less than the specified minimum, the difference between the distributive share and the minimum is treated as a guaranteed payment.[28]

Example (5): John, a partner with Ken in the JK Partnership, is to receive 30 percent of partnership income (before taking into account guaranteed payments), but not less than $10,000. He is also allocated 30 percent of partnership losses (after deduction of guaranteed payments). Partnership income for the year is $60,000, and John is entitled to $18,000 ($60,000 * 30%) as his distributive share. Because this amount is more than the specified minimum ($10,000), no part of the amount John receives is a guaranteed payment.

However, if partnership income is only $20,000, John's distributive share is $6,000 ($20,000 * 30%). Therefore, according to the agreement, John is entitled to an additional $4,000. This $4,000 is characterized as a guaranteed payment, and John includes it in his ordinary income. The partnership may deduct the $4,000 (because in this example, it qualifies as a business

---

[27] Treas. Reg. § 1.707-1(c), *Example (4)*.

[28] Treas. Reg. § 1.707-1(c), *Example (2)*; Rev. Rul. 66-95, 1966-1 C.B. 169.

expense). The deduction reduces partnership income and, therefore, both partners' distributive shares.

	John	Ken	Total
Guaranteed payment	$4,000	$0	$4,000
Distributive share	6,000	10,000	16,000
Total	$10,000	$10,000	$20,000

Computational difficulties arise if the partnership's deduction of the guaranteed payment reduces the receiving partner's share of partnership income below the amount used in determining the amount of his guaranteed payment. Although the regulations do not address this problem, a correct result can be obtained by treating the entire minimum as a guarantee and allocating the rest of partnership income (after deducting the guarantee) to the other partners.

Example (6): Assume the facts in Example (5), except that the JK Partnership has $8,000 of income, before taking the guaranteed payment into account. John's distributive share is $2,400 ($8,000 * 30%) and, therefore, his guarantee is $7,600 ($10,000 - $2,400). However, because the partnership's income after deducting the guaranteed payment is only $400 ($8,000 - $7,600), it is impossible to allocate the $2,400 distributive share computed for John. An appropriate result is obtained if the partnership characterizes the entire $10,000 minimum distribution as a guaranteed payment. After deducting the $10,000, JK has a $2,000 loss ($8,000 income - $10,000) that is allocated between the partners according to their loss-sharing ratio (30 percent to John, 70 percent to Ken), as follows:

	John	Ken	Total
Guaranteed payment	$10,000	$0	$10,000
Distributive share of loss	(600)	(1,400)	(2,000)
Total income	$9,400	$(1,400)	$8,000

When a partner's specified minimum payment exceeds his share of partnership ordinary income, and the partnership also has capital gain income, the partner receiving the guaranteed payment will receive a larger percentage of the capital gain than he would without the minimum payment. The allocation reduces the other partners' shares of the capital gain.

Example (7): Assume the facts in Example (5), except that the JK Partnership has a $20,000 profit for the year (before taking the guaranteed payment into account). The $20,000 is made up of $12,000 of ordinary income and $8,000 of capital gain. The allocations to the partners are as follows:

	John	Ken	Total
Guaranteed payment	$4,000	$0	$4,000
Ordinary income after guaranteed payment	3,000	5,000	8,000
Capital gain	3,000	5,000	8,000
Total allocations	$10,000	$10,000	$20,000

John's guaranteed payment is $4,000 [$10,000 minimum - $6,000 share of profits ($20,000 * 30%)]. After deducting the guarantee, partnership ordinary income is $8,000 ($12,000 - $4,000). John's $6,000 distributive share of the $16,000 total partnership income ($8,000 ordinary income + $8,000 capital gain) is a 6/16 share of profits for the year. Ken's $10,000 distributive share is a 10/16 share of profits. Because the partnership agreement does not specially allocate capital gains, the partners' share the capital in the same ratio as they share general profits. Thus, John reports $3,000 of capital gain (6/16 * $8,000) and Ken reports $5,000 of capital gain (10/16 * $8,000).[29]

The guaranteed payment increases John's share of capital gain from $2,400 (30% * $8,000) to $3,000 and reduces Ken's share accordingly. If this allocation is unsatisfactory to the partners, they can specify a different allocation of capital gain. The special allocation will be respected if it has substantial economic effect.

[C] Character of Guaranteed Payments for Use of Partner's Capital

A partner who makes a bona fide loan to his partnership generally is not considered to act in a partner capacity.[30] Therefore, under I.R.C. Section 707(a), the lending partner uses his normal accounting method in determining when his interest income must be reported. The partnership must also determine the extent and timing of any allowable interest expense deduction. For both partner and partnership, general tax rules governing interest income and deductions apply when determining the tax consequences of the loan.[31]

In contrast, interest payments made to a partner — in his partner capacity — for the use of capital he contributes (instead of lends) to the partnership are considered (under I.R.C. Section 707(c)) to be guaranteed payments. The partner includes the payment in his income for the year in which the partnership deducts (or capitalizes) the payment.

It is unclear whether guaranteed payments for capital constitute "interest" for determining the character of the partner's income and the nature and extent of the

---

[29] This example is derived from Rev. Rul. 69-180, 1969-1 C.B. 183.

[30] In Pratt v. Comm'r, 550 F.2d 1023 (5th Cir. 1977), the Commissioner conceded that interest payments on a bona fide loan are deductible under I.R.C. § 707(a) and are not guaranteed payments.

[31] Under I.R.C. § 267(a)(2), however, an accrual-method partner or partnership may not deduct expenses owed to a related cash-method partner or partnership until payment actually occurs.

partnership's deduction.[32] The regulations state that a guaranteed payment is included in the recipient partner's distributive share of partnership income for all purposes other than determining the partnership's deductions and capital expenditures.[33]

NOTE:

Therefore, a guaranteed payment is not considered an interest in partnership profits when determining:

(1)   whether a partner is a principal partner for purposes of selecting a partnership taxable year under I.R.C. Section 706(b)(3);

(2)   whether a transaction is subject to the I.R.C. Section 707(b) rules governing sales between partnerships and controlling partners; or

(3)   whether a partnership is terminated under I.R.C. Section 708(b), because 50 percent or more of the total interests in partnership capital and profits have been sold or exchanged within a 12-month period.

This rule suggests that the character of a guaranteed payment made for the use of capital depends on the character of the partnership's income, and that it is not treated as interest. Nevertheless, the Service appears to have concluded that all guaranteed payments a partner receives on his capital contribution constitute interest income.[34] The instructions to the partnership tax return (Form 1065) refer to guaranteed payments as interest. Although no persuasive authority exists, it is logical to treat the partnership's deduction as an interest expense when the corresponding income is reported as interest.

[D] Payments Computed from Gross Income

A payment to a partner that is computed by reference to partnership net income is included in the partner's distributive share. It is not treated as a guaranteed payment because it simply represents the partner's share of partnership profits — no amount is guaranteed, because no payment is made unless profits exist. However, if the payment is a percentage of the partnership's gross income, the amount the partner receives does not depend on the amount or existence of partnership profits. Thus, it is uncertain whether a payment based on partnership gross income is a guaranteed payment to the partner or an increase in his distributive share.

---

[32] *See* Banoff, *Determining the Character of Guaranteed Payments for Partner's Capital*, 67 J. Tax'n 284 (1987).

[33] Treas. Reg. § 1.707-1(c).

[34] GCM 36702 (Apr. 12, 1976); GCM 38133 (Oct. 10, 1979).

In *Pratt v. Commissioner*,[35] the Tax Court held that a payment a partner received for managing partnership real estate operations was not a guaranteed payment, even though it was computed as a percentage of the partnership's gross income from rentals. The Court concluded that the payments represented a portion of the partner's distributive share because the amount was computed by reference to the partnership's income. However, in Revenue Ruling 81-300,[36] the Service ruled that it would not follow *Pratt* on this issue. The ruling holds that a partner's fees for services rendered in his partner capacity are guaranteed payments, even though computed as a percentage of gross rental income.

[E]   Draws, Bonuses, and Payments Dependent on Profits

A payment to a partner is not a guaranteed payment if, in substance, it is a draw against his expected share of future partnership profits.[37] All draws a partner receives during the partnership's tax year ordinarily are treated as a distribution to him on the last day of the year.[38] However, a draw that is not chargeable against the partner's future profits is likely to be treated as a guaranteed payment.[39]

A payment is generally considered to be a draw if the partner is obligated to repay amounts that exceed his distributive share of partnership income. For this purpose, an actual repayment obligation must exist; a provision in the partnership agreement requiring repayment of an excess draw is not determinative on this issue if the conduct of the parties indicates otherwise.[40]

A bonus may be treated as a guaranteed payment even if it is attributable to a transaction between the partner and the partnership. For example, in *Kobernat v. Commissioner*,[41] a partner in a brokerage firm was taxable on compensation he received that was based on a percentage of sales commissions, including commissions he paid to the firm for trades he made for his own account. The partner was deemed to receive the commissions in his capacity as a member of the partnership.

Guaranteed payments generally do not include amounts that are payable to a partner only if the partnership has sufficient available cash.[42] Restrictions or conditions on a partner's right to receive a payment indicate that the payment is not guaranteed, because the risk of nonpayment makes the arrangement resemble

---

[35] 64 T.C. 203 (1975), *aff'd*, 550 F.2d 1023 (5th Cir. 1977).

[36] 1981-2 C.B. 143. *See also* GCM 38067 (Aug. 29, 1979); Egolf v. Comm'r, 87 T.C. 34 (1986); Priv. Ltr. Rul. 8034088.

[37] *See* Smith v. Comm'r, T.C. Memo. 1980-326. *See also* Fahey v. Comm'r, T.C. Memo. 1979-20.

[38] Treas. Reg. § 1.731-1(a)(1)(ii).

[39] Lynch v. Comm'r, T.C. Memo. 1982-305; Clark v. Comm'r, T.C. Memo. 1982-401.

[40] Mangham v. Comm'r, T.C. Memo. 1980-280.

[41] T.C. Memo. 1972-132. *Accord* Heggestad v. Comm'r, 91 T.C. 778 (1988).

[42] Investors Ins. Agency, Inc. v. Comm'r, 72 T.C. 1027 (1979), *aff'd*, 677 F.2d 1328 (9th Cir. 1982); GCM 38670 (Mar. 31, 1981) (conditioning payment on availability of cash is not determinative of whether it is a guaranteed payment).

a share of profits, rather than a fixed fee.[43]

§ 7.04   TRANSACTIONS IN WHICH PARTNER ACTS IN NONPARTNER CAPACITY

A transaction between a partnership and a partner acting as an individual, rather than as a partner, is taxable as if it occurred between unrelated persons under I.R.C. Section 707(a)(1). This general rule applies when determining the timing and character of any income, loss, or deduction the partnership and partner realize in the transaction. The partnership allocates its income, loss, or deductions among its partners, including the partner with whom the transaction occurs, in accordance with their distributive shares. The regulations provide the following examples of transactions in which a partner may be considered to act in a nonpartner capacity:[44]

(1)   lending money or property to the partnership, or borrowing money or property from the partnership;

(2)   selling or leasing property to the partnership, or buying or leasing property from the partnership; and

(3)   rendering services to, or receiving services from, the partnership.

Example: Arthur and Burt are equal partners in the AB Partnership. Both partners use a calendar tax year; the partnership uses a tax year ending on November 30. On December 31, Year 1, Arthur pays $12,000 to the partnership as rental for property he leased during the year for use in a different business enterprise. When Arthur computes his taxable income for Year 1, he deducts the entire $12,000 rental payment he made to the partnership. The partnership includes the $12,000 in its gross income for the year ending November 30, Year 2; Arthur and Burt each report a $6,000 distributive share of the rental income on their Year 2 tax returns.[45]

[A]   Loans and Leases

A loan of money or a lease of property between a partnership and one of its partners generally is taxable as if the transaction were between the partnership and a nonpartner.[46] The lender or lessor includes the interest or rent in gross income; the borrower either deducts or capitalizes the corresponding expense under general tax rules.[47]

---

[43] *See, e.g.,* Priv. Ltr. Rul. 7939005 (bonus paid to a partner based upon partnership's overall profitability not a guaranteed payment because based upon partnership income).

[44] Treas. Reg. § 1.707-1(a).

[45] *See* Rev. Rul. 72-504, 1972-2 C.B. 90.

[46] Treas. Reg. § 1.707-1(a).

[47] Rules that may affect the timing of the lender's interest income include the original-issue-discount rules (I.R.C. §§ 1271–1275), the step-rental rules (I.R.C. § 467), and the below-market-loan rules (I.R.C. § 7872). The borrower's interest deduction may be deferred or limited by the limitation on investment interest (I.R.C. § 163(d)), or by the rules relating to interest on debts used to carry tax-exempt securities

A partner is considered to act in a nonpartner capacity if he retains ownership of the property used by the partnership.[48] Therefore, a partner who leases property to the partnership, or pledges his own assets to secure a partnership debt, is taxable on any income or deductions the property generates.[49]

A purported loan by a partner to his partnership may be recharacterized as a capital contribution, if that is the substance of the transaction.[50] If the loan is recharacterized as a capital contribution, payments to the partner for the use of his capital are included in his distributive share of partnership income (or treated as guaranteed payments). An ostensible loan by a partnership to a partner may also be recharacterized as a distribution, if the substance of the transaction indicates that no repayment obligation is intended.

[1] Bad Debts

If a partner's loan to his partnership becomes uncollectible, the creditor-partner may deduct the unpaid amount as a bad debt under I.R.C. Section 166. Because the partnership is treated as a separate entity in the loan transaction, its business activities are not attributed to the lending partner when determining whether he may claim a business bad debt (deductible as an ordinary loss under I.R.C. Section 166(a)), or a nonbusiness bad debt (deductible as a short-term capital loss under I.R.C. Section 166(d)).[51] Therefore, a partner cannot claim a business-bad-debt deduction for a loan to his partnership unless he has a separate business purpose for making the loan, or he is in the business of making loans.[52] In other situations, worthless loans to a partnership by a partner should be treated as nonbusiness debts.[53]

[B] Services

Partner-partnership transactions involving compensation for services are taxable under the general rules of the Code if the partner is not acting in his capacity as a partner.[54] The partner and the partnership each determine their tax consequences using their own tax years and tax accounting methods (*see* Chapter 3). However, an accrual-method partnership or partner may not deduct an expense

---

(I.R.C. § 265(a)(2)), interest on consumer debts (I.R.C. § 163(h)), and interest prepayments (I.R.C. § 461(g)).

[48] Treas. Reg. § 1.707-1(a).

[49] *Id. See* Rev. Rul. 55-39, 1955-1 C.B. 403.

[50] *See* Hambuechen v. Comm'r, 43 T.C. 90 (1964).

[51] Authorities dealing with the law before the enactment of I.R.C. § 707(a) in 1954 concluded that the partner is engaged in the partnership's business and may deduct the unpaid amount as a business bad debt. *See* Butler v. Comm'r, 36 T.C. 1097 (1961); Priv. Ltr. Rul. 7907001.

[52] Oetting v. Comm'r, T.C. Memo. 1982-268. *Accord* Farrar v. Comm'r, T.C. Memo. 1988-385.

[53] *See* U.S. v. Generes, 405 U.S. 93 (1972); Whipple v. Comm'r, 373 U.S. 193 (1963). Although these cases relate to shareholder loans to corporations, the decisions were based on the rationale that the business or nonbusiness character of debt depends on the lender's motive for making the loan. That rationale should also apply to loans between partnerships and their partners.

[54] I.R.C. § 707(a).

for an amount owed to a cash-method partner cr partnership until actual payment occurs.

> **Example:** Carl and Donna are equal partners in the CD Partnership, which owns and operates a retail sales business. Both partners use a calendar tax year; the partnership uses a tax year ending on November 30. Both the partners and the partnership use the cash accounting method. On December 31, Year 1, CD pays Carl $5,000 as compensation for legal services he provided for a lawsuit in which the partnership is involved. Carl includes the $5,000 fee in his taxable income for Year 1. The partnership may deduct the expense under general tax rules, and the deduction is allowed for the partnership tax year ending November 30, Year 2. Carl and Donna each report their $2,500 distributive share of that expense on their Year 2 tax returns.[55]

[C] Sales

A partner may act in a nonpartner capacity in a purchase or sale transaction with his partnership. As a nonpartner transaction, the purchase or sale is subject to the general tax rules of realization, recognition, and characterization: the seller recognizes gain or loss; the sales price becomes the purchaser's cost basis in the property. Parties who structure their transaction as a sale are held to that form. They cannot argue, at a later date, that the transaction was partially a contribution to, or distribution from, the partnership.[56]

Special rules applicable to sales between a partnership and a controlling partner disallow any loss deductions and require any gain to be reported as ordinary income (*see* § 7.05, *infra*).

> **Example:** Edith is a one-third partner in the EFG Partnership. Acting in a nonpartner capacity, Edith sells equipment worth $1,000 to the partnership for its $1,000 fair market value. Edith's basis in the property is $500, and she recognizes a $500 gain. The partnership takes a $1,000 cost basis in the property. The character of Edith's gain depends on the nature of the asset in her hands and upon any applicable recapture rules.

[D] Contribution and Related Distribution Treated as Disguised Sale

A partner who contributes property to a partnership and receives a related distribution of cash or other property may be treated as if he sold his property to the partnership under I.R.C. Section 707(a)(2). Congress enacted that section in 1984 out of concern that property transfers between partners and partnerships were being structured as nontaxable contributions and distributions to "disguise"

---

[55] *See* Rev. Rul. 72-504, 1972-2 C.B. 90.

[56] Aladdin Industries, Inc. v. Comm'r, T.C. Memo. 1981-245; Spector v. Comm'r, 641 F.2d 376 (5th Cir. 1981).

transactions that were, in substance, taxable sales.[57] Although regulations existing in 1984 authorize the Service to recharacterize a purported contribution as a sale if that is the substance of the transaction,[58] Congress believed that the courts had not applied those regulations properly.[59] A number of court decisions allowed nontaxable property transfers between partners and partnerships in situations that Congress considered to be economically indistinguishable from a sale.[60]

The economic effect of a property contribution followed by a cash distribution to the contributing partner is similar to that of a sale; in both cases the partnership owns the property and the partner receives cash equal to its value.

The tax consequences of these transactions, however, are quite different. A partner who sells property to a partnership recognizes gain or loss as if the transaction were with an unrelated party. In contrast, a partner is not taxable on a contribution of property to a partnership, and he is taxable on a distribution from a partnership only to the extent that the amount of cash he receives exceeds the basis in his partnership interest.[61]

> **Example:** Alice, a 50-percent partner in the AB Partnership, transfers property worth $100 to the partnership. Alice's basis in the property is $10. After the transfer, the partnership obtains a recourse loan of $200 and distributes $100 in cash to Alice.

The effect of these transactions depends on whether the transfer of the property is considered a contribution or a sale, as follows:

	Contribution	Sale
Alice's taxable gain on transfer of property	0	$90
Partnership's basis in the property	$10	$100
Effect on Alice's basis in the partnership:		
(1) Transfer of property	$10	$0
(2) Share of nonrecourse loan	+100	+100
(3) Payment/distribution	- 100	0
Alice's basis after transactions	$10	$100

To ensure that a contribution and related distribution are treated as a sale, I.R.C. Section 707(a)(2) authorizes the Service to recharacterize the transfers as if occurring between the partnership and a nonpartner (or between two or more nonpartners). Because the nonrecognition rules of I.R.C. Section 721 do not apply to nonpartner transactions, the transfers between the partner and partnership constitute a taxable sale and gain or loss is recognized.

---

[57] *See* H.R. Rep. No. 432 (Pt. 2), 98th Cong., 2d Sess. 1218 (1984); S. Rep. No. 169 (Vol. I), 98th Cong., 2d Sess. 224–25 (1984).

[58] Treas. Reg. § 1.721-1(a); T.D. 6175 (May 23, 1956).

[59] H.R. Rep. No. 432 (Pt. 2) at 1218; S. Rep. No. 169 (Vol. I) at 225.

[60] *Id.* Committee reports indicate that Congress specifically disagreed with the holdings in Otey v. Comm'r, 70 T.C. 312 (1978), *aff'd per curiam*, 634 F.2d 1046 (6th Cir. 1980), Communications Satellite Corp. v. U.S., 625 F.2d 997, 223 Ct. Cl. 253 (1980), and Jupiter Corp. v. U.S., 2 Cl. Ct. 58 (1983).

[61] I.R.C. §§ 721, 731.

A transaction may be considered a sale under either of two rules:[62]

(1) I.R.C. Section 707(a)(2)(B) applies if a partner directly or indirectly transfers money or other property to a partnership, and the partnership makes a "related" direct or indirect distribution of money or other property to that partner (or to another partner). The transaction is treated as a sale if the two transfers "when viewed together, are properly characterized as a sale of property."

(2) I.R.C. Section 707(a)(2)(A) applies if a partner directly or indirectly transfers property to a partnership and receives a "related" direct or indirect allocation and distribution of partnership income.[63] The transaction is treated as a sale if the transfer, allocation and distribution, "when viewed together," are properly characterized as occurring between the partnership and a nonpartner.

Regulations provide that a disguised sale occurs when a partner transfers property to a partnership and receives a payment from the partnership that would not be made "but for" his property transfer.[64] If the payment to the partner will occur after he transfers property to the partnership, the transaction is considered a sale only if the subsequent payment does not depend on the entrepreneurial risks of partnership operations.[65] Whether a particular contribution and distribution is a disguised sale is determined from the relevant facts and circumstances.[66] Most importantly, the regulations create rebuttable presumptions that a contribution and distribution that occur within a two-year period constitute a sale and that transfers more than two years apart are not a sale.[67]

If a contribution and distribution is recharacterized under I.R.C. Section 707(a)(2), the transaction is treated as a sale or exchange between the partnership and a nonpartner for all tax purposes.[68] The sale is deemed to occur on the date that the partnership is considered the owner of the property.[69] Possible consequences of a recharacterization include:

(1) *The person who transfers the property recognizes gain or loss unless a specific nonrecognition provision applies.* For example, a disguised sale that meets the like-kind exchange requirements of I.R.C. Section 1031 is

---

[62] The final regulations issued in September, 1992, apply to both I.R.C. § 707(a)(2)(A) and (B). Treas. Reg. § 1.707-3(e).

[63] Under I.R.C. § 707(a)(2)(A), an allocation and distribution of partnership income to a partner that are related to services he performs for the partnership may be treated as a payment of compensation to a non-partner.

[64] Treas. Reg. § 1.707-3(b)(1)(i); T.D. 8439 (Sept. 30, 1992). These regulations finalize, with minor revisions, proposed regulations that were issued on April 25, 1991.

[65] Treas. Reg. § 1.707-3(b)(1)(ii).

[66] Treas. Reg. § 1.707-3(b)(2).

[67] Treas. Reg. § 1.707-3(c)(1). *See, e.g.,* Whitmire v. Comm'r, 178 F.3d 1050 (9th Cir. 1999) (taxpayer not at risk where shrouded by too much protection to leave a "realistic possibility" that he would suffer a loss).

[68] Treas. Reg. § 1.707-3(a)(2).

[69] *Id.*

treated as a tax-free exchange under that section.

(2)   *Any deferred payments on the sale may be reported under the installment-sale rules of I.R.C. Section 453, and interest imputed on the deferred amounts may be reported under I.R.C. Section 483.*

(3)   *If a debt instrument is received for the property, the original issue discount rules of I.R.C. Section 1274 may apply.*

(4)   *Recharacterization changes the transferring partner's basis in his partnership interest. Unlike a contribution, a partner's basis in property he sells to a partnership is not included in the basis of his partnership interest.* Similarly, the payment a partner receives in a sale does not decrease the basis in his interest.

(5)   *The partnership takes a cost basis in the property it receives in a sale,*[70] *rather than the carryover basis it would take for contributed property.* [71] The partnership can use its own cost-recovery method for property it is deemed to purchase, but must use the transferring partner's method for contributed property.[72]

(6)   *The partners' capital accounts are not adjusted to reflect the contributed property, and any allocations made for the property under I.R.C. Sections 704(b) or 704(c) are ineffective.*

(7)   *Anti-churning rules may apply.* These rules limit depreciation deductions if the transferring partner has an interest in the partnership greater than 10 percent.[73]

(8)   *The basis adjustment provisions of I.R.C. Sections 754 and 743 may apply if the transaction is considered a sale of a partnership interest.*

(9)   *The special rules of I.R.C. Section 732(d) for determining a partner's basis in distributed property do not apply.*

(10)   *The partnership may terminate for tax purposes under I.R.C. Section 708(b) if recharacterization of the transaction as a sale of a partnership interest results in a sale of 50 percent or more of the interests in partnership capital and profits within a 12-month period.*

(11)   *The family partnership rules of I.R.C. Section 704(e) may apply to a sale between family members.*

Case law in effect before the enactment of I.R.C. Section 707(a)(2) frequently allowed partners to obtain the economic benefit of a sale without recognizing gain through prearranged contribution/distribution transactions. Although the current statute overrides these cases, the facts involved illustrate the type of transactions the statute is designed to restrict.

---

[70] I.R.C. § 1012.

[71] I.R.C. § 723.

[72] *See* I.R.C. § 168(i)(7).

[73] *See* I.R.C. § 168(i)(7), (f)(5).

The following two cases involve a property contribution by a partner who subsequently received a prearranged cash distribution from the partnership. The Service unsuccessfully argued that the transactions were, in substance, a sale of the property to the partnership.

(1)   In *Otey v. Commissioner*,[74] the taxpayer contributed appreciated land worth $65,000 to a joint venture with a developer. The developer's only contribution was his ability to obtain financing for the construction of an apartment complex. Under the terms of the partnership agreement, the partnership immediately obtained an $870,000 construction loan (for which both partners were liable) and, shortly thereafter, distributed $65,000 to the contributing taxpayer. After the $65,000 distribution, the partners shared equally in future partnership distributions, profits, and losses. The Tax Court rejected the Service's argument that the substance of the transaction was a sale, holding that the contribution and distribution were separate, nontaxable transactions.

(2)   In *Park Realty Co. v. Commissioner*,[75] a partner who contributed land received payments from the partnership, ostensibly as reimbursement for development expenses the partner incurred before the contribution. According to provisions in the partnership agreement, the payments were made after the land had been developed into a shopping center and the partnership had made lease agreements with the anchor stores. The Service contended that the transaction was a sale because the amount of the reimbursement equaled the value of the land plus the development expenses. The court disagreed, holding that the transaction was not equivalent to a sale because the partner's payment was contingent on the success of the partnership's venture and involved a significant risk of nonpayment.[76]

The following two cases involve a contribution by one partner that is related to a distribution to another partner. The Service unsuccessfully argued that these related transactions were, in substance, a sale of the distributee partner's interest in the partnership to the contributor. The proposed regulations issued by the Service do not address disguised sales of partnership interests but reserve that issue for future regulations.

(1)   In *Communications Satellite Corporation v. United States*,[77] the partnership agreement provided that each new partner admitted to the partnership would pay an entry fee. The fee bore no relation to the actual value of the new partner's interest. The fees were distributed pro rata to the existing partners whose interests were diminished by the entry of new partners. The court disagreed with the Service's contention that, in substance, the contribution and distribution were a disguised sale of a

---

[74] 70 T.C. 312 (1978), *aff'd per curiam*, 634 F.2d 1046 (6th Cir. 1980).

[75] 77 T.C. 412 (1981).

[76] The Service later acquiesced in the decision, distinguishing it from *Otey v. Comm'r*, on the grounds that there was no significant risk of nonpayment in *Otey*. 1982-2 C.B. 2.

[77] 625 F.2d 997, 223 Ct. Cl. 253 (1980).

portion of the old partners' interests to the new partners.

(2)   In *Jupiter Corporation v. United States*,[78] new limited partners made cash contributions when they entered the partnership. These contributions were coupled with cash distributions to the general partners, whose interests in the partnership decreased. The court held that the transaction was not equivalent to a sale because the new partners acquired limited partnership interests, while the old partners relinquished general partnership interests.

The Service's arguments that a sale had occurred were not always fruitless. In *Colonnade Condominium, Inc. v. Commissioner*,[79] the shareholders of a corporate partner personally assumed the corporation's obligation to contribute funds to the partnership. In a related transaction, the shareholders were admitted to the partnership and received interests equal to the reduction in the corporation's interest. The Tax Court concluded that the transaction was a sale of the corporation's partnership interest to its shareholders, rather than a capital contribution to the partnership. The Court reasoned that a sale occurred because:

(1)   the admission of the new partners did not result in an infusion of new capital to the partnership (*i.e.*, the new partner merely assumed another partner's obligation to contribute funds); and

(2)   the admission of the new partners did not diminish the interests of any partners other than the partner whose obligation was assumed.[80]

[1] Overview of Regulations

The regulations governing disguised sales under I.R.C. Section 707(a)(2) are summarized in this section and fully analyzed in the succeeding sections.

Facts and circumstances test for disguised sale. The regulations provide that a contribution and distribution constitute a sale if the facts and circumstances show that the distribution would not have been made "but for" the contribution.[81] This test is likely to be met whenever the contribution and distribution occur simultaneously. If the contribution and distribution are not simultaneous, a sale is deemed to occur only if the facts show that the distribution to the partner does not depend on the entrepreneurial risks of partnership operations.[82] Rebuttable presumptions provide that a contribution and distribution that occur within two years constitute a sale, while transfers more than two years apart are not a sale.[83] (*See* § 7.04[D][2], *infra.*)

---

[78] 2 Cl. Ct. 58 (1983).

[79] 91 T.C. 793 (1988).

[80] The court relied on criteria established in Richardson v. Commissioner, 76 T.C. 512 (1981), *aff'd*, 693 F.2d 1189 (5th Cir. 1982).

[81] Treas. Reg. § 1.707-3(b)(1).

[82] *Id.*

[83] Treas. Reg. § 1.707-3(c)(1).

Partial sale and contribution. A transfer of property to a partnership may be treated as a partial sale and partial contribution if the amount the contributing partner receives from the partnership is less than the value of the transferred property.[84] The partner must prorate his basis in the property between the sale and contributed portions of the property.

> **Example (1):** On April 1, Year 1, Alma contributes realty worth $4 million with a tax basis of $1.2 million to the AB Partnership in exchange for a partnership interest. Immediately after the transfer, AB distributes $3 million in cash to Alma. The contribution and distribution are treated as a disguised sale under I.R.C. Section 707(a)(2)(B). Because the amount of cash Alma receives is less than the value of the realty, Alma is deemed to have sold a portion of realty worth $3 million to the partnership for cash. Alma recognizes $2.1 million of gain — $3 million amount realized less $900,000 tax basis in the portion sold [$1.2 million total basis * ($3 million / $4 million)]. Alma also is deemed to contribute to the partnership a portion of the realty worth $1 million with a $300,000 tax basis.[85]

Deferred payment sale. A contribution may be treated as part of a disguised sale even though the related distribution will not be received until a future time. In that case, the partner is deemed to receive a partnership obligation for the transferred property on the date the partnership acquires ownership.[86] Any deferred payments on the sale may be reported under the installment-sale rules of I.R.C. Section 453. The deferred amounts may be subject to the imputed-interest rules of I.R.C. Section 483 and the original-issue-discount rules of I.R.C. Section 1274.[87]

> **Example (2):** Assume the facts in Example (1), except that the partnership distributes $3 million to Alma on April 1, Year 2. Alma is treated as if she sold a portion of the realty to the partnership on April 1, Year 1, in exchange for AB's obligation to pay Alma $3 million one year later. I.R.C. Section 1274 applies to AB's obligation because it does not bear interest and is payable more than six months after the date of the sale. (In applying that statute, assume that the applicable Federal short-term rate for the month of the distribution is 10 percent, compounded semiannually.)
>
> Alma's amount realized when she receives the obligation is the imputed principal amount of the partnership's obligation to pay $3 million to Alma, which equals $2,721,088 (the present value on April 1, Year 1, of a $3 million payment due in one year, using the appropriate discount rate). Alma is deemed to have sold a portion of the realty to AB for $2,721,088 on April 1, Year 1. The remaining $278,912 Alma receives is reported as interest income under the rules of I.R.C. Section 1272.
>
> Alma recognizes $1,904,761 of gain — $2,721,088 amount realized less $816,327 tax basis [$1.2 million * ($2,721,088 / $4 million)] on the sale of realty to the partnership, and she may report that gain under the

---

[84] Treas. Reg. § 1.707-3(a)(1).

[85] Treas. Reg. § 1.707-3(f), (1).

[86] Treas. Reg. § 1.707-3(a)(2).

[87] *Id.*

installment method of I.R.C. Section 453. Alma also is deemed to contribute to the partnership a portion of the realty worth $1,278,912 with a $383,673 tax basis.[88]

Sale by nonpartner. A taxpayer who structures a property transfer as a contribution to a partnership may not avoid the disguised-sale rules by claiming that he is not a partner or that no partnership exists.[89] If it is determined that no partnership exists, the transferor of the property is deemed to have sold the property to the person who acquired ownership for tax purposes.[90]

Certain distributions not treated as disguised sale. The disguised sale rules do not apply when a partnership makes reasonable payments to a partner for the use of, rather than in exchange for, property he contributes. (*See* § 7.04[D][3], *infra.*) The regulations specify that the following payments for a partner's contributed capital are not treated as part of a sale:[91]

(1)   guaranteed payments to a partner for the use of his capital;

(2)   priority or preferential distributions to a partner for his capital contribution; and

(3)   distributions to a partner that do not exceed his interest in the partnership's operating cash flow for the year.

Transfers pursuant to constructive termination not treated as disguised sale. A partnership is deemed to terminate under I.R.C. Section 708(b)(1)(B) if 50 percent or more of the interests in its capital and profits are sold or exchanged within a 12-month period. (*See* § 13.04, *infra.*) On the termination date, the terminated partnership is deemed to contribute all its assets and liabilities to a new partnership and then make a liquidating distribution of its interest in the new partnership.[92] In applying the disguised sale rules, distributions and contributions resulting from a partnership termination under the 50-percent sale or exchange rule are disregarded.[93]

Transfer of encumbered property to partnership treated as sale. A contribution to a partnership is treated as a disguised sale if the property is encumbered with a debt in anticipation of the transfer, and the partnership assumes or takes the property subject to the debt.[94] A debt incurred within two years of a contribution is deemed to be incurred in anticipation of the transfer unless the facts and circumstances clearly establish otherwise.[95] No disguised sale occurs if the contributed property is encumbered by a "qualified liability," which includes:

---

[88]   Treas. Reg. § 1.707-3(f), *Example (2)*.

[89]   Treas. Reg. § 1.707-3(a)(3).

[90]   Treas. Reg. § 1.707-3(a)(3).

[91]   Treas. Reg. § 1.707-4.

[92]   Treas. Reg. § 1.708-1(b)(1)(iv).

[93]   Treas. Reg. § 1.707-3(a)(4).

[94]   Treas. Reg. § 1.707-5.

[95]   Treas. Reg. § 1.707-5(a)(7).

(1)   debts incurred more than two years before the contribution;

(2)   debts incurred within the two-year period but not in anticipation of the contribution;

(3)   debts incurred to acquire or improve the contributed property, and

(4)   debts that are trade payables of a contributed business.[96]

(*See* § 7.04[D][4], *infra.*)

Disguised sale by partnership to partner. A distribution of partnership property that is related to a contribution by the distributee partner may be treated as a disguised sale of the distributed property to the partner.[97] Whether a transaction is a disguised sale of partnership property is determined under rules similar to the rules governing disguised sales by a partner to a partnership. (*See* § 7.04[D][6], *infra.*)

Disclosure requirements. The regulations require certain transactions subject to the disguised sale rules to be disclosed to the Service. (*See* § 7.04[D][7], *infra.*)

[2]   Tests for Determining Whether Disguised Sale Occurs

A contribution and distribution are considered a disguised sale if the facts and circumstances show that:

(1)   the partnership would not have transferred money or other property to the partner but for the partner's transfer of property to the partnership; and

(2)   if the transfers do not occur simultaneously, the transfer the partnership makes to the partner is not dependent on the entrepreneurial risks of partnership operations.[98]

This determination is based on the facts and circumstances existing on the date of the earliest transfer.[99]

A contribution and distribution made within two years of each other (without regard to the order of the transfers) are presumed to be a sale,[100] *and transfers more than two years apart are presumed not to be a sale.* [101] These presumptions may be rebutted only by facts and circumstances that "clearly" establish the contrary.

Example: Ellen is an equal partner in the EF Partnership. The partnership owns two parcels of land, Parcel 1, worth $500,000, and Parcel 2, worth $1.5 million. Ellen contributes another parcel of land to the partnership, Parcel 3, worth $1 million, in exchange for an increased interest in partnership profits of 66 2/3 percent. Immediately after Ellen's contribu-

---

[96] Treas. Reg. § 1.707-5(a)(6).

[97] Treas. Reg. § 1.707-6.

[98] Treas. Reg. § 1.707-3(b)(1).

[99] Treas. Reg. § 1.707-3(b)(2).

[100] Treas. Reg. § 1.707-3(c)(1).

[101] Treas. Reg. § 1.707-3(d).

tion, the partnership sells Parcel 1 for $500,000 and distributes the $333,333 of the sale proceeds to Ellen and $166,667 of the proceeds to Frank, in accordance with their partnership interests.

Because the $333,333 payment to Ellen occurs within two years of her transfer of Parcel 3 to the partnership, the transaction is presumed to be a disguised sale. This presumption is rebutted, however, for $250,000 of the payment because Ellen would receive that amount (her 50-percent share of the Parcel 1 sale) even if she did not contribute Parcel 3. The regulations indicate that this fact is sufficient to clearly establish that $250,000 of the distribution to Ellen is not a disguised sale. Because Ellen is paid $83,333 more than she would have otherwise received ($333,333 - $250,000), that amount is presumed to be a payment in a disguised sale of a portion of Parcel 3 to the partnership.[102]

This example indicates that a contribution and distribution may be treated as a sale even though the distribution is made pro rata to all partners (*i.e.*, 2/3 to Ellen and 1/3 to Frank, according to their interests at the time of the distribution). The transaction is a sale to the extent that the distribution to the contributing partner exceeds the amount she would have received but for the contribution. Because the partnership sold other property and distributed the proceeds immediately after the contribution, the contributor had no entrepreneurial risk for the distribution.

The presumptions affect controversies involving disguised sales in two ways:

(1) The party against whom the presumption runs has the burden of "going forward" (*i.e.*, of showing that his position is correct) in litigation involving a disguised sale. For transfers less than two years apart, the taxpayer must show that no disguised sale occurred. For transfers more than two years apart, the Service must prove that a disguised sale occurred. Obviously, the Service also will consider the effect of the presumptions during audit and settlement procedures involving disguised sales.

(2) Requiring a party to "clearly" rebut a presumption imposes a burden of proof greater than ordinarily needed to prevail in litigation (the normal standard being a "preponderance" of evidence).[103]

Facts and circumstances indicating a disguised sale. The regulations list a number of specific facts and circumstances that tend to prove that a contribution and distribution are a disguised sale.[104] The weight given any of these factors depends on the particular case. Generally, the facts at the time of the earliest transfer are considered. The following factors may indicate a disguised sale:

(1) If, at the time the property contribution occurs, the timing and amount of the subsequent distribution can be determined with reasonable certainty.

---

[102] Treas. Reg. § 1.707-3(f), *Example (4)*.

[103] *See* Preamble to Final Regulations, T.D. 8439 (Sept. 30, 1992).

[104] Treas. Reg. § 1.707-3(b)(2).

(2)   If the contributor has a legally enforceable right to the subsequent transfer.

(3)   If the contributor's right to receive the distribution is secured in any manner. This factor is applied by taking into account the time period of the security arrangement.

(4)   If any person has made or is legally obligated to make contributions to the partnership to permit the partnership to make the distribution.

(5)   If any person has loaned or has agreed to loan the partnership the money or other consideration required to enable the partnership to make the distribution. This is taken into account when a lender's obligation to make the loan is subject to contingencies related to the success of partnership operations.

(6)   If the partnership has borrowed or is obligated to borrow the funds needed to make the distribution. This is applied by taking into account the likelihood that the partnership will be able to borrow the funds, considering whether anyone has agreed to guarantee or assume personal liability for the debt.

(7)   If the partnership holds money or liquid assets beyond the reasonable needs of its business. Any income that will be earned from these assets also is taken into account.

(8)   If partnership distributions, allocations, or control of partnership operations are designed to cause an exchange of the burdens and benefits of ownership of property.

(9)   If the distribution to the contributing partner is disproportionately large in relationship to his general and continuing interest in partnership profits.

(10)   If the contributing partner is not obligated to return or repay the amount distributed to him by the partnership. This is also considered if the partner has a repayment obligation that is likely to become due at such a distant point in the future that the obligation's present value is small in relation to the amount of the distribution.

The factors listed in the disguised sale regulations focus on two issues: (1) whether the contributing partner has an unconditional right to receive a distribution regardless of whether the partnership is successful, and (2) whether the partnership is likely to have sufficient funds to satisfy its distribution obligation without regard to its success. In determining the sufficiency of funds for the distribution, the commitments, guarantees, and credit of other partners or third parties are taken into account. Also considered are financial projections regarding future partnership income, the anticipated value of partnership assets, and the partnership's ability to borrow against its assets.

Although the regulations merely state that these factors tend to prove the existence of a disguised sale, the examples suggest that the absence of these factors may show that a sale has not occurred.[105]

The following examples, adapted from the regulations, illustrate the operation of the two-year presumptions and the type of facts and circumstances that may be considered in rebutting the presumptions:

(1) *Presumption for transfers within two-year period.*

Example: On May 10, Year 1, Carl contributes land worth $1 million, having a $500,000 tax basis to the CD partnership. The partnership intends to construct a building on the land. The partnership agreement provides that CD will distribute $900,000 to Carl when construction of the building is complete. On March 4, Year 3, the partnership distributes $900,000 to Carl. Because the distribution occurs within two years of Carl's contribution, the transfers are presumed to be a disguised sale of the land to the partnership. Carl may rebut the presumption by clearly establishing that (a) he would have received the distribution even if he had not transferred the land to the partnership, or (b) CD's obligation or ability to make the distribution depended on the entrepreneurial risks of partnership operations.

The regulations indicate that Carl could rebut the presumption by showing that CD can fund the cash distribution only to the extent that the proceeds of a permanent loan (*i.e.*, a loan that is not a construction loan) on the building exceed the cost of constructing the building, and that one of the following conditions exists:

> (a) permanent loan proceeds will not be available unless the construction cost is materially less than the amount projected by a reasonable budget; or
>
> (b) the amount of the permanent loan is likely to be limited to the cost of constructing the building.

The two-year presumption also may be rebutted by showing that, when the land is transferred to CD, no lender has committed to make a permanent loan to fund the cash distribution to Carl. This rebuttal factor may be offset, however, if the partnership is obligated to try to obtain a loan, and its ability to obtain the loan is not materially dependent on completion of the building. This factor also is offset if the partnership reasonably anticipates having an alternate source to fund the distribution to Carl.[106]

(2) *Presumption for transfers more than two years apart.*

Example: George contributes land worth $1 million that has a $500,000 tax basis to the GH Partnership. Heather contributes $1 million in cash in exchange for her partnership interest. The partnership agreement obligates the partnership to construct a building on the land. Projected construction costs are $5 million, which the partnership will fund with its $1

---

[105] *See, e.g.*, Treas. Reg. § 1.707-3(f), *Example (3)(iii)*.
[106] Treas. Reg. § 1.707-3(f), *Example (3)*.

million in cash and a $4 million construction loan.

Before George contributes the land the partnership secures a commitment from a lender for a permanent loan. The amount of that loan will be the lesser of $5 million or 80 percent of the value of the property when the loan closes. The partnership agreement obligates the partnership to use the permanent loan proceeds to satisfy the $4 million construction loan and then distribute any excess proceeds to George 25 months after he contributes the land. Accordingly, George will not receive any distribution unless the building is worth more than $5 million when the loan closes (and he cannot receive more than $1 million). The value of the property probably will not exceed $5 million at the closing unless the partnership leases a substantial portion of space by that time. A material risk exists that the partnership will not reach that occupancy level.

The value of the property at the closing is $7 million, allowing the partnership to borrow $5 million. The partnership pays the $4 million construction loan and distributes the remaining $1 million to George 25 months after he contributed the land.

Because George received the distribution more than two years after he contributed the land, the transfers are presumed not to be a disguised sale, unless the facts and circumstances clearly establish a sale. The following facts suggest that a disguised sale occurred:

(a)   the partnership would not have distributed the $1 million to George but for his contribution of the land; and

(b)   when George contributed the land, he had a legally enforceable right to receive a specified distribution (permanent loan proceeds over $4 million) from the partnership at a specified time (25 months after the contribution).

> However, a disguised sale is not deemed to occur in this situation because the uncertain occupancy level creates a significant risk that the value of the property may be insufficient to obtain a permanent loan over $4 million. Thus, when George contributed the land, his right to the subsequent distribution depended on the entrepreneurial risks of partnership operations.[107]

> George's distribution also depends on the entrepreneurial risks of partnership operations (*i.e.*, is not a disguised sale) if either of the following factors is present:

> (a)   A significant risk exists that the building will not be completed. In that event, the lender will not be required to make the permanent loan necessary to fund the distribution to George.

> (b)   A significant risk exists that the construction cost of the building will exceed $5 million. In that case, the $5 million permanent loan proceeds may be insufficient to satisfy the construction loan and

---

[107] Treas. Reg. § 1.707-3(f), *Example (5)*.

fund the distribution to George.[108]

(3) *Rebuttal of presumption for transfers more than two years apart.*

Example: Assume the facts in the preceding example, except that Heather guarantees completion of the building for $5 million and that the partnership obtains a commitment for a $5 million permanent loan without regard to the value of the property when the loan closes. Thus, the loan will be made when the building is completed. In this situation, George's right to the subsequent $1 million distribution does not depend on the entrepreneurial risks of partnership operations because:

(a) the lender's obligation to make the loan is not related to the risks of partnership operations, and

(b) the permanent loan proceeds will provide sufficient liquid assets for the partnership to make the distribution to George.

The regulations indicate that these facts and circumstances clearly establish that George's contribution of the land is part of a disguised sale, thereby rebutting the two-year presumption.

The following example involves a so-called "mixing bowl" transaction in which allocations in the partnership agreement are used to obtain the economic equivalent of a sale by shifting the economic benefits and burdens of property ownership between partners. Typically, the "selling" partner contributes property to a partnership that acquires low-risk financial assets (*e.g.*, government securities) approximately equal in value to the sale price of the contributed property. Through special allocations in the partnership agreement, the economic benefits, burdens, and control over the financial assets are allocated to the contributing partner, and the benefits, burdens, and control over the contributed property are allocated to the other partners. Upon liquidation of the partnership, each partner is entitled to receive a distribution of the assets in which he has the principal economic interest.

The example indicates that the Service will treat this kind of arrangement as if the contributing partner sold his equity in the contributed property in exchange for the partnership's commitment to distribute other assets to him in the future. Because the facts and circumstances are deemed clearly to establish a sale, the transaction is treated as a sale even though the distribution occurs more than two years after the contribution. A sale is deemed to occur even though the partnership was not obligated to distribute specific assets to the contributing partner; it is sufficient that the parties "contemplated" the distribution when the contribution occurred. Also note that the contributor is deemed to sell his entire interest in the contributed property even though only 90 percent of the cash flow from the financial assets is allocated to him, and he retains 10 percent of the allocations from the contributed property. Apparently, the Service considers the 10 percent minority interest insignificant when compared to the 90 percent ownership shift.

Example: On February 1, Year 1, Irma, Jane, and Ken form the IJK Partnership. Irma contributes a fully leased office building worth $50

---

[108] Treas. Reg. § 1.707-3(f), *Example (7)*.

million having a $20 million tax basis, and Jane and Ken each contribute U. S. government securities having a $25 million value and tax basis. When the partnership is formed, the partners contemplate liquidating Irma's interest after January 31, Year 3, by distributing the government securities and any necessary cash. The partnership agreement provides the following valid allocations:[109]

(1)   all tax items and all cash flow from the office building are allocated 45 percent to Jane, 45 percent to Ken, and 10 percent to Irma; and

(2)   all tax items and all cash flow from the government securities are allocated 90 percent to Irma, 5 percent to Jane, and 5 percent to Ken.

The partnership does not expect to need the government securities or the cash flow the securities generate to operate the office building.

On March 1, Year 4, the partnership liquidates Irma's interest for a distribution of the government securities and an amount of cash equal to the excess of her share of office building's appreciation in the partnership over Jane's and Ken's share of the appreciation in the government securities in the partnership.

Because Irma's contribution of the office building and the distribution of the securities and cash occur more than two years apart, the transfers are presumed not to be a disguised sale, unless the facts and circumstances clearly establish a sale.

The following facts and circumstances clearly establish that the contribution and distribution constitute a disguised sale of the office building to the partnership on February 1, Year 1, for the partnership's obligation to transfer the government securities and cash to Irma:

(1)   The partnership would not have made the distribution but for Irma's contribution of the building.

(2)   The amount and nature of partnership assets indicate that, when Irma contributed the building, the time of the transfer of the government securities to her was anticipated and did not depend on the entrepreneurial risks of partnership operations.

(3)   The partnership allocations were designed to cause, and actually resulted in, an exchange of the burdens and benefits of ownership of the government securities to Irma when the partnership was formed.[110]

---

[109] These allocations are presumed to be valid under the I.R.C. § 704(b) regulations governing special allocations.

[110] Treas. Reg. § 1.707-3(f), *Example (8)*.

CAUTION:

Recent cases illustrate the diverse and complex factual situations in which the Service may raise the disguised sale issue.[111]

*   *Virginia Historic Tax Credit Fund 2001 LP v. Commission- erginia Historic Tax Credit Fund 2001 LP v. Commissioner.*[112] This case involved individuals that formed partnerships to acquire interests in other entities engaged in projects eligible for Virginia's historic rehabilitation tax credit. Investors that contributed capital for limited partnership interests were allocated shares of the state tax credits.

    The Service asserted that, in substance, the investors were not truly partners and that the allocation of state tax credits to them are actually sales for federal tax purposes. Alternatively, the government maintained that the transactions between the investors and the partnerships were disguised sales under I.R.C. Section 707.

    The Tax Court disagreed, holding that the investors were partners for federal tax purposes, and that their contributions to the partnerships were not disguised sales under I.R.C. Section 707. The court concluded from the partnership documents and the conduct and testimony of the parties that the investors and organizers had joined together as partners in good faith. The evidence established that the parties intended to and did form a partnership.

    The court noted the facts that the nature of the state credit program required a partnership structure and the investors assumed a risk that the projects would not succeed or not qualify for the state credit. The court also determined that the partnership's purpose of pooling capital to invest in other entities and to earn state tax credits was a valid business purpose. Reduction of state taxes may be a valid business purpose. Since the investors and organizers joined together in good faith with a valid business purpose they were, in substance, partners in the venture.

    The Tax Court rejected the view that the allocation of credits to the investors was a disguised sale under I.R.C. Section 707(a)(2)(B). A disguised sale does not occur under that section if a subsequent transfer is subject to the entrepreneurial risks of partnership operations. The investors were not guaranteed that the venture would generate sufficient credits to allocate the promised amounts to the investors.

---

[111] See generally Lipton, Golub, McDonald, A Tale of Two Cases: G-I Holdings and Virginia Historic Tax Credit Fund — Can They Both Be Right?, 112 J. Tax'n 154 (Mar. 2010).

[112] T.C. Memo. 2009-295.

The Fourth Circuit Court of Appeals reversed the Tax Court, holding that the disguised sales rules apply where investors contribute money to partnerships engaged in rehabilitating historic buildings and are allocated state tax credits from the partnership.[113] The appellate court concluded that the tax credits were property for purposes of I.R.C. Section 707 — they were valuable and imbued with "some of the most essential property rights."[114] The following factors in the regulations showed that the transactions should be characterized as sales:

- The timing and amount of the subsequent transfer were determinable with reasonable certainty at the time of an earlier transfer. When the investors joined the partnership, they were promised a precise number of tax credits.

- The transferor had a legally enforceable right to the subsequent transfer. The partnership and subscriptions agreements explicitly promised delivery of tax credits in exchange for capital contributions.

- The partner's right to receive the transfer of money or other consideration was secured. Investors were promised that their capital would be refunded if sufficient credits could not be obtained or were revoked.

- The transfer of money or other consideration by the partnership to the partner was disproportionately large in relationship to the partner's general and continuing interest in partnership profits. The investors had essentially no interest in partnership profits and the transfer of tax credits to each investor was not correlated to the investors' interests in partnership profits.

- Partners were not obligated to return or repay money or other consideration to the partnership. The investors were not obligated to the partnership in any way and could use the credits for their personal tax benefit.

- *In re G-I Holdings, Inc.* [115] In this case, GAF formed a partnership with Rhone-Poulenc S.A. (RP) by transferring business assets to the partnership in exchange for a limited partnership interest, and used the partnership interest as collateral for a nonrecourse loan that RP was obligated to repay. The Service maintained that the transfer of GAF's assets to the limited partnership was not a capital contribution,

---

[113] 2011 U.S. App. LEXIS 6364 (4th Cir. Mar. 29, 2011). But see Historic Boardwalk Hall, LLC v. Comm'r, 136 T.C. 1 (2011) (rehabilitation tax credits under I.R.C. Section 47 allowed to corporate partners in partnership between a government agency and a private corporation).

[114] The court applied factors set forth in United States v. Craft, 535 U.S. 274 (2002).

[115] 105 A.F.T.R. 2d (RIA) 697 (D.N.J. 2009).

but rather a disguised sale of property under I.R.C. Section 707(a).

In determining that the transaction was a disguised sale, the court noted that:

○   At the time of the asset transfer, GAF received the proceeds of the loan and RP was fully responsible for repayment.

○   GAF received the loan proceeds free and clear.

○   RP was fully liable for the loan and the partnership agreement contained provisions that ensured its ability to pay.

○   The transfers, when viewed together, were properly characterized as a sale of assets because:

  •   The payment to GAF was not subject to an appreciable risk as to amount.

  •   GAF's partner status was transitory.

  •   GAF received the proceeds close in time to the transfer of the assets to the partnership.

  •   Facts and circumstances showed that GAF became a partner primarily to obtain tax benefits that would not have accrued if it transferred the assets as a non-partner.

Although the court reviewed the factors set forth in the regulations, these rules were issued after the transaction occurred and therefore were not specifically applicable. However, these factors showed that:

○   The context of the transaction suggested that the parties intended a sale.

○   The contribution and loan transactions were planned and structured together.

○   The asset transfer was designed to reduce taxation in an exchange of assets for cash.

○   The contribution and loan transactions were integrated.

○   The contribution and loan transactions occurred on the same date.

○   GAF ceded operational control of its assets.

○   The loan was, in substance, a payment.

[3]   Payments not Included in Disguised Sale

In accordance with the legislative history to I.R.C. Section 707(a)(2), the regulations exempt the following distributions from the disguised sale rules:[116]

(1)   *Payments for the use of a partner's capital.* The disguised-sale rules do not apply when a partnership makes reasonable payments to a partner for the use of, rather than in exchange for, property he contributes. The regulations specify that the following payments for a partner's contributed capital are not treated as part of a sale:

    (a)   guaranteed payments to a partner for the use of his capital; and

    (b)   priority or preferential distributions to a partner for his capital contribution.

(2)   *Distributions of operating cash flow.* A payment to a partner is not considered a disguised sale if it represents a distribution of the partner's interest in the partnership's operating cash flow for a year.

(3)   *Preformation expenditures.* A disguised sale does not occur when a partnership reimburses a partner for certain capital expenditures he incurred in anticipation of the formation of the partnership.

[4]   Contribution of Encumbered Property Treated as Disguised Sale

Whether a contribution of property encumbered by a liability is a disguised sale depends upon whether the debt is a "nonqualified" or "qualified" liability.[117] The regulations use these terms to distinguish between debts a contributing partner incurred in anticipation of the transfer to the partnership (nonqualified liabilities) and debts incurred without that expectation (qualified liabilities).[118] A contribution is considered a disguised sale only if the partnership assumes or takes the property subject to a nonqualified liability; no sale occurs if a qualified liability is transferred to the partnership.

A partner who contributes property encumbered by a nonqualified liability is deemed to receive a payment for the property from the partnership equal to the portion of the debt shifted to other partners. The amount shifted to other partners equals the difference between the total liability transferred to the partnership and the contributing partner's share of that liability after the contribution.[119]

If contributed property is encumbered by a qualified debt, the consequences of the shift in liabilities to the other partners are determined under the rules of I.R.C. Section 752. (*See* § 4.05, *supra.*) However, if the contribution is considered a disguised sale without regard to the qualified liability (*i.e.*, the partnership transfers other consideration to the partner), the qualified liability may be included

---

[116]   Treas. Reg. § 1.707-4. *See* H.R. Rep. No. 432 (Pt. 2) at 1221.

[117]   Treas. Reg. § 1.707-5(a).

[118]   *See* H.R. Rep. No. 432 (Pt. 2) at 1221; S. Rep. No. 169 (Vol. I) at 231.

[119]   Treas. Reg. § 1.707-5(a)(1), (a)(5).

in the payment the partner receives in the sale.[120]

When the proceeds of a partnership liability are used to satisfy another partnership debt (*i.e.*, the debt is refinanced), the new debt is treated as the old debt for the disguised-sale rules.[121] The same rule applies if a partner refinances a debt before transferring encumbered property to the partnership.[122] The extent to which the proceeds of the new liability are used to discharge the old debt are determined by applying interest-allocation rules of the I.R.C. Section 163 regulations.

A special "tacking" rule applies to liabilities shifted among members of a tiered partnership (*i.e.*, a parent partnership owns an interest in a subsidiary partnership). When a subsidiary partnership succeeds to a parent partnership's liability, the liability retains the same qualified or nonqualified character in the subsidiary that it had in the parent.[123]

[a]   Qualified Liabilities

A disguised sale does not occur when property encumbered by a qualified liability is contributed to a partnership. A "qualified liability" includes any of the following:[124]

(1)   A debt incurred more than two years before the contribution or before a written agreement to make the contribution.[125]

(2)   A debt incurred within the two-year precontribution period that was not incurred in anticipation of the contribution and has encumbered the transferred property since it was incurred.[126] A debt incurred within two years of being transferred to a partnership is presumed to be incurred in anticipation of the transfer unless rebutted by facts and circumstances that clearly show otherwise.[127]

(3)   A debt incurred in connection with a capital expenditure to acquire or improve the contributed property.[128]

(4)   A debt that is a trade payable the partnership assumes in connection with a contribution of all the assets of the business that generated the payables

---

[120] Treas. Reg. § 1.707-5(a)(5); Treas. Reg. § 1.707-5(c). The applicable allocation rules are found in Temp. Treas. Reg. § 1.163-8T.

[121] Treas. Reg. § 1.707-5(c). The applicable allocation rules are found in Temp. Treas. Reg. § 1.163-8T.

[122] The proposed regulations did not apply this rule to partner refinancing.

[123] Treas. Reg. § 1.707-5(e). The regulations indicate that the Service may issue similar rules for transactions between other related parties.

[124] Treas. Reg. § 1.707-5(a)(6)(i).

[125] Treas. Reg. § 1.707-5(a)(6)(i)(A).

[126] Treas. Reg. § 1.707-5(a)(6)(i)(B).

[127] Treas. Reg. § 1.707-5(a)(7).

[128] Treas. Reg. § 1.707-5(a)(6)(i)(C). The liability must be allocable to these capital expenditures for the property under the rules of Treas. Reg. § 1.163-8T.

other than assets that are not material to continuing the business;[129]

(5)   A recourse debt is not treated as a qualified liability to the extent that the debt exceeds the fair market value of the contributed property at the time of contribution (reduced by any encumbering liabilities that are senior, incurred to acquire or improve the property, or trade payables).[130]

Example (1): David contributes land worth $165,000 having a $75,000 basis to the DE Partnership. The land is encumbered by a $75,000 recourse liability which the partnership assumes. David incurred the liability more than two years ago and the liability has always been secured by the land. Immediately after the contribution, David's share of the transferred liability is $25,000. Because these facts show that the $75,000 liability is a qualified liability, the partnership's assumption of the debt is not treated as part of a disguised sale.[131]

Qualified liability associated with disguised sale. If a property transfer is otherwise treated as a disguised sale (*i.e.*, the partnership transfers other consideration to the partner in a sale), a qualified liability encumbering the property may be considered part of the sale. In that case, the amount of the qualified liability considered a payment to the partner for the property is the lesser of:

(1)   the amount of the debt that would be considered a payment for the property if the debt were not a qualified liability; or

(2)   the amount of the debt multiplied by the partner's "net equity percentage" in the property. A partner's net equity percentage is computed by dividing

(a)   the aggregate amount of money or other consideration the partner receives (other than qualified liabilities) in the disguised sale of the property, by

(b)   the fair market value of the property when contributed to the partnership reduced by qualified liabilities that are

(i)   secured by the property,

(ii)   incurred as capital expenditure to acquire or improve the property, or

(iii)   trade payables assumed in connection with the contribution of a business.[132]

Example (2): Assume the facts in the preceding example except that, in addition to assuming the $75,000 qualified liability, the partnership distributes $30,000 in cash to David and that payment is treated as a disguised sale. The assumption of the qualified liability requires $25,000 to be included in David's amount realized on the disguised sale. This amount is computed by multiplying the $75,000 qualified liability by David's 33

---

[129]   Treas. Reg. § 1.707-5(a)(6)(i)(D).

[130]   Treas. Reg. § 1.707-5(a)(6)(ii).

[131]   Treas. Reg. § 1.707-5(e), *Example (5)*.

[132]   Treas. Reg. § 1.707-5(a)(5).

percent net equity percentage in the land. David's net equity percentage is determined as follows:

$$\frac{\$30{,}000 \text{ consideration (other than qualified liabilities)}}{\$165{,}000 \text{ value of land} - \$75{,}000 \text{ qualified liability}}$$

The $25,000 amount is used because it is less than the $50,000 that would be included in David's amount realized if the liability were not a qualified liability ($75,000 total liability - David's $25,000 share of that liability).

David is deemed to sell a portion of the land worth $55,000 to the partnership in exchange for $30,000 in cash and the partnership's assumption of $25,000 of the qualified liability. David recognizes a $30,000 gain on the sale ($55,000 amount realized - $25,000 basis in one-third portion of land sold).[133]

[b]   Nonqualified Liabilities

A property contribution is considered a disguised sale if the partnership assumes or takes the property subject to a nonqualified liability.[134] If the partner contributes both money and encumbered property pursuant to a plan, the amount of liability the partnership is deemed to assume or take subject to is reduced (but not below zero) by the cash contribution.[135] The contributing partner is considered to receive a payment for the property from the partnership equal to the difference between the liability transferred to the partnership and the partner's share of that debt immediately after the transfer.[136] The rules for determining a partner's share of a liability are described below.

A liability is presumed to be nonqualified if it is incurred within two years of a property contribution or within two years of a written agreement to make the contribution.[137] The presumption may be rebutted by facts and circumstances clearly showing that the debt was not incurred in anticipation of the transfer. The two-year presumption does not apply to debts considered qualified liabilities under the regulations, including (1) debts incurred in connection with a capital expenditure to acquire or improve the contributed property,[138] and (2) trade payables the partnership assumes in connection with a contribution of the assets of the business that generated the payables.[139]

Partner's share of partnership liability. As noted above, the payment the contributing partner receives in the disguised sale equals the difference between the liability transferred to the partnership and his share of that debt immediately after the transfer.[140]

---

[133] Treas. Reg. § 1.707-5(e), *Example (6)*.

[134] Treas. Reg. § 1.707-5(a).

[135] Treas. Reg. § 1.707-5(d).

[136] Treas. Reg. § 1.707-5(a)(1).

[137] Prop. Treas. Reg. § 1.707-5(a)(7)(i).

[138] Treas. Reg. § 1.707-5(a)(6)(i)(C).

[139] Treas. Reg. § 1.707-5(a)(6)(i)(D).

[140] Treas. Reg. § 1.707-5(a)(1).

The following paragraphs describe the rules for determining a partner's share of a liability for the disguised sale rules.

Recourse liabilities. A partner's share of a partnership recourse liability is determined under the rules of I.R.C. Section 752.[141] That section generally provides that a partner's share of a recourse debt equals the economic risk of loss the partner bears for it. (For complete discussion of the I.R.C. Section 752 liability-sharing rules, *see* Chapter 5.)

> **Example:** Cathy contributes realty worth $10 million, having a $6 million tax basis, to the CD Partnership. The property is subject to an $8 million recourse liability which the partnership assumes. Cathy incurred the debt immediately before the contribution to finance other expenditures. Under the I.R.C. Section 752 regulations, Cathy's share of the liability after the partnership's assumption is $6 million.
>
> The $2 million of the liability shifted to the other partners is treated as payment in a disguised sale. Cathy is deemed to sell a portion of the realty worth $2 million to the partnership in exchange for the partnership's assuming the debt.[142]
>
> Because Cathy is deemed to sell one-fifth of the property ($2 million value of portion sold / $10 million total value), she determines her gain by subtracting one-fifth of her basis in the property, which is $1.2 million (1/5 * $6 million). Cathy's gain on the disguised sale is $800,000 ($2 million amount realized - $1.2 million basis).

[5] Debt-Financed Disguised Sales

A disguised sale may occur when a partnership borrows funds and distributes the proceeds to a partner who previously contributed property.[143] Under a special rule in the regulations, however, a distribution financed from the proceeds of a partnership liability may be considered a disguised sale only to the extent the distribution exceeds the distributee partner's allocable share of the partnership liability.[144]

If the distribution of money or other property to the partner is attributable to a liability the partnership incurs within 90 days of the distribution, the amount treated as a disguised sale is reduced by the partner's "allocable share" of that liability.[145] The portion of a distribution that is attributable to a liability incurred within 90 days is determined under the interest-allocation rules of the I.R.C. Section 163 regulations.[146]

---

[141] Treas. Reg. § 1.707-5(a)(2)(i). *See* Treas. Reg. § 1.752-1(a).

[142] Treas. Reg. § 1.707-5(e), *Example (2)*.

[143] Treas. Reg. § 1.707-5(b)(1).

[144] Treas. Reg. 1.707-5(b)(2)(i).

[145] *Id.*

[146] The applicable allocation rules are found in Temp. Treas. Reg. § 1.163-8T.

A partner's "allocable share" of a liability for this purpose is computed by multiplying his share of the liability by a fraction whose:

- numerator is the portion of the liability allocable to the distribution to the partner (determined under the I.R.C. Section 163 regulations); and

- denominator is the total amount of the liability.[147]

An anti-abuse rule provides that a partner's share of a liability does not include any anticipated reductions in his share of liabilities under a plan to minimize the distribution of debt proceeds treated as a disguised sale.[148]

Example: Gail contributes land for an interest in the GH Partnership on April 9, Year 1. On September 13, Year 1, the partnership incurs a recourse liability of $20,000 and Gail's share of that liability (under I.R.C. Section 752) is $10,000. On November 17, Year 1, the partnership distributes $20,000 to Gail; $10,000 of the distribution is allocable to the proceeds of the September 13 loan, and the remaining $10,000 is from other partnership funds (determined under the rules of I.R.C. Section 163).

The $10,000 portion of the distribution attributable to the September 13 loan is treated as part of a disguised sale only to the extent that it exceeds Gail's allocable share of that liability. Gail's allocable share of the $20,000 liability is $5,000:

$$\begin{array}{c} \$10,000 \\ \text{(Gail's share of the liability)} \end{array} \times \frac{\begin{array}{c} \$10,000 \\ \text{(portion of the liability allocable} \\ \text{to the distribution)} \end{array}}{\begin{array}{c} \$20,000 \text{ (total amount of the} \\ \text{liability)} \end{array}}$$

Although Gail received a $20,000 distribution from the partnership, her amount realized on the disguised sale of the land is limited to $15,000.[149]

Special rules apply if a partnership distributes the proceeds of one or more loans to more than one partner pursuant to a plan. In that situation, all liabilities incurred pursuant to the plan are considered one liability, and each partner's share of that liability is computed by multiplying the sum of the partner's shares of each liability by a fraction (1) whose numerator is the portion of the liabilities allocable to the distribution the partners receive under the plan (determined under the interest-allocation rules of I.R.C. Section 163), and (2) whose denominator is the total amount of liabilities.[150]

Example: In January, Year 1, Mary contributes receivables worth $100,000, having a zero tax basis for a 90 percent interest in the MN Partnership. Ned contributes $10,000 in cash for a 10-percent interest. In February, Year 1, the partnership applies the receivable to secure an $80,000 loan and

---

[147] Treas. Reg. § 1.707-5(b)(2)(i).

[148] Treas. Reg. § 1.707-5(b)(2)(iii).

[149] Treas. Reg. § 1.707-5(f), *Example (10)*.

[150] Treas. Reg. § 1.707-5(b)(1)(ii).

distributes \$72,000 to Mary and \$8,000 to Ned. Mary's share of the liability is \$72,000 (90 percent of \$80,000).

Because the debt-financed distribution occurred within 90 days of her contribution, Mary is deemed to sell the receivables to the partnership only to the extent that the amount she receives exceeds her allocable share of the partnership debt funding the transfer. Because her distribution was pursuant to a plan involving transfers to more than one partner, Mary's allocable share of the liability is computed as follows:

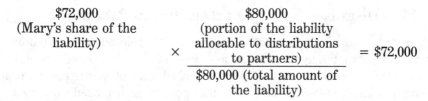

Because Mary's distribution does not exceed her share of the liability incurred to fund it, Mary is not deemed to sell any portion of the receivables to the partnership.[151]

PRACTICE NOTE:

In a recent case, the Tax Court ruled that purported contribution of assets to an LLC followed by a cash distribution to the contributing partner within 90 days was a disguised sale of the assets.[152] The court concluded that the debt-financed transfer exception did not apply because the transferee partner did not truly bear an economic risk of loss for the LLC debt that funded the distribution. The decision applies an anti-abuse rule which disregards a partner's obligation to make a payment if the facts and circumstances show:

- a principal purpose of the arrangement is to eliminate the partner's risk of loss or to create a facade that the partner's bears the risk of loss, or

- a plan to circumvent or avoid the obligation.[153]

The Tax Court disregarded the distributee's purported obligation under an indemnity agreement with the LLC because only a remote possibility of liability existed. The indemnity agreement did not create actual liability because:

- it covered only debt principal and not interest,

---

[151] Treas. Reg. § 1.707-5(f), *Example (11)*.

[152] Canal Corp. v. Comm'r, 135 T.C. 199 (2010).

[153] Treas. Reg. § 1.752-2(j)(1), 1.752-2(j)(3).

- the partners had to proceed against the LLC's assets before demanding indemnification,

- the distributee's interest in the LLC increased in proportion to any payments made under the indemnity, and

- the distribute was not required to maintain sufficient assets to cover its indemnity obligation.

[6] Disguised Sale by Partnership to Partner

A distribution of partnership property that is related a contribution by the distributee partner may be treated as a sale of the distributed property to the partner. Whether a transaction is a disguised sale of partnership property is determined under rules similar to the rules governing disguised sales by a partner to a partnership.[154]

> **Example:** The AB Partnership distributes Parcel 1, worth $1 million, to Allen. One year later, Allen contributes $1.1 million in cash to the partnership. On the date he receives Parcel 1, the imputed principal amount of Allen's obligation to transfer $1.1 million after one year is $1 million (determined under I.R.C. Section 1274).[155] Because Allen's contribution occurs within two years of the distribution, the transaction is presumed to be a disguised sale. Since no facts rebut the presumption, the partnership is deemed to sell Parcel 1 to Allen on the date of the distribution in exchange for Allen's obligation to transfer $1.1 million to the partnership one year later.

Distribution of encumbered property. A partnership may treat a property distribution as a disguised sale if the distributee partner assumes or takes the property subject to a nonqualified partnership liability. The partner is deemed to pay the partnership an amount equal to the difference between the amount of the liability transferred to the partner and the partner's share of that liability immediately before the transfer.[156]

Multiple distributions. If encumbered property is distributed to more than one partner pursuant to a plan, the amount each partner is deemed to pay the partnership for the property equals the difference between (1) all the liabilities (other than qualified liabilities) transferred to the partner under the plan, and (2) the partner's share of all of those liabilities immediately before the transfer.[157] This netting rule does not apply, however, if liabilities are transferred to the partner with a principal purpose to reduce the partnership's amount realized in a disguised

---

[154] Treas. Reg. § 1.707-6(a).

[155] Treas. Reg. § 1.707-6(d), *Example (1)*.

[156] Treas. Reg. § 1.707-6(b)(1). The partner's share of a liability is determined under the rules of Treas. Reg. § 1.707-5(a)(2), described above.

[157] Treas. Reg. § 1.707-6(b)(1). These rules are similar to the rules under Treas. Reg. § 1.707-5(a)(4), described above.

sale.[158]

Qualified liabilities. A disguised sale does not occur when property encumbered by a qualified liability is distributed to a partner who assumes or takes the property subject to the debt.[159] However, if the property transfer is otherwise treated as a disguised sale (*i.e.*, the partner transfers other consideration to the partnership in a sale), a qualified liability encumbering the property may be considered part of the sale.[160] In that case, the amount of the qualified liability included in the partnership's amount realized is the lesser of:

(1)   the amount of the debt that would be included in the partnership's amount realized if the debt were not a qualified liability; or

(2)   the amount of the debt multiplied by the partnership's "net equity percentage" in the property. A partnership's net equity percentage is computed by dividing

  (a)   the aggregate amount of money or other consideration the partnership receives (other than qualified liabilities) in the disguised sale of the property, by

  (b)   the fair market value of the property when distributed to the partner reduced by qualified liabilities secured by the property.[161]

Example: The BC Partnership distributes Parcel A, worth $1 million, to Barbara. Barbara takes the property subject to a $600,000 nonrecourse liability that the partnership incurred six months ago to obtain proceeds to purchase an unrelated asset. Barbara's share of the liability immediately before the distribution of Parcel A was $100,000.

Because the partnership incurred the liability within two years of the distribution, the liability is presumed to be incurred in anticipation of the transfer. Since no facts rebut the presumption, the partnership is deemed to receive $500,000 ($600,000 [liability transferred to Barbara] - $100,000 [Barbara's share of the liability before the transfer]) in a disguised sale of one-half of Parcel A ($500,000 / $1 million) to Barbara. The partnership is deemed to distribute the other half of Parcel A to Barbara.[162]

[7] Disguised Sale of Partnership Interest

Although final regulations relating to disguised sales of property to and by partnerships (described in the preceding sections) were promulgated in 1992, the rules for disguised sales of partnership interests were reserved for later issuance. Proposed regulations under I.R.C. Section 707(a)(2)(B), describing transactions that would be considered disguised sales of interests in a partnership were

---

[158] Treas. Reg. § 1.707-6(b)(1).

[159] Treas. Reg. § 1.707-6(b)(2)(i).

[160] Treas. Reg. § 1.707-6(b)(2).

[161] Treas. Reg. § 1.707-6(b)(2).

[162] Treas. Reg. § 1.707-6(d), *Example (2)*.

published in November, 2004.[163] However, the proposed rules were withdrawn in January, 2009 after the Treasury concluded its consideration of the public comments on their scope and substance.[164] The Service may issue new guidance in the future. Until such guidance is issued, determination of whether transfers between a partner (or partners) and a partnership is a transfer of a partnership interest will be based on statutory language, legislative history, and case law.

[8] Disclosure of Disguised Sale Transactions

The regulations require certain transactions subject to the disguised-sale rules to be disclosed to the Service. The disclosure rules ensure that partners taking aggressive or untested positions flag the relevant transactions on their tax returns.

[E] Contribution and Related Income Allocation Treated as Disguised Payment for Services or Property

The costs of acquiring partnership assets, including related services, generally must be capitalized and recovered over the life of the assets (through amortization or depreciation deductions) or deferred until a partner sells or liquidates his partnership interest. Before the Tax Reform Act of 1984, some partnerships obtained tax benefits when acquiring partnership assets that were equivalent to a current deduction by having the person performing services, or contributing property, join the partnership.[165] After joining the partnership, in lieu of a direct payment, the contributing partner received an allocation and distribution of partnership income equal to the value of the contributed services or property. The result of this allocation/distribution was the same as if these capital expenditures were directly deducted from partnership income: the partnership income that was taxable to the other partners was reduced.

To prevent partnerships from using allocations and distributions to avoid capitalizing expenses, Congress enacted I.R.C. Section 707(a)(2)(A) in 1984. The statute is directed at allocations used to pay for services that should be capitalized (e.g., architects' and brokers' fees). In particular, the legislation is aimed at allocations that are used to pay partnership organization or syndication expenses, because these expenses must be capitalized under I.R.C. Section 709.[166]

I.R.C. Section 707(a)(2)(A) also applies to allocations and distributions that are, in substance, payments for property the partnership purchased from the partner. These "disguised sales" are subject to the same proposed regulations that govern contributions and related distributions under I.R.C. Section 707(a)(2)(B). Thus, the same presumptions and tests apply under both sections in determining if a transfer

---

[163] 69 Fed. Reg. 68838 (Nov. 26, 2004), providing former Prop Treas. Reg. §§ 1.707-7 through 1.707-9. Notice 2001-64, 2001-2 C.B. 316, previously announced the Service's intent to issue these proposed regulations.

[164] 74 Fed. Reg. 3508 (Jan. 21, 2009).

[165] H.R. Rep. No. 432, 98th Cong., 2d Sess. 1219 (1984); S. Rep. No. 169, 98th Cong., 2d Sess. 224 (1984).

[166] S. Rep. No. 169, 98th Cong., 2d Sess. 232 (1984). *See also* Staff of Joint Committee on Taxation, General Explanation of the Revenue Provisions of the Deficit Reduction Act of 1984, p. 227.

of property to a partnership is a disguised sale. Because the rules governing disguised sales of property are described in detail in § 7.04[D], *supra*, the discussion is this section is limited to allocations that are disguised payments for services.

Under I.R.C. Section 707(a)(2)(A), an allocation and distribution to a partner that actually constitute a disguised payment for services is recharacterized and treated as a payment to a nonpartner. This recharacterization occurs if:

(1)   a partner performs services for a partnership;

(2)   the partner receives a related direct or indirect allocation and distribution; and

(3)   these two events, when viewed together, are properly characterized as a transaction between the partnership and a nonpartner.[167]

If the nature of this payment to the "nonpartner" requires it to be capitalized, the other partners' shares of partnership income increase.

On its face, the language of the statute is circular and nearly meaningless, because this is the treatment that a properly characterized transaction occurring between a partnership and a nonpartner should receive. The purpose of I.R.C. Section 707(a)(2) is to emphasize Congress's disagreement with recent case law and the aggressive positions taken by a number of partnerships, as well as to authorize the Treasury to issue new, more stringent regulations.

Example: The MN Partnership agreement provides that Mary will perform services in connection with syndicating interests in the partnership. The partnership agreement provides a special allocation to Mary of $20,000 a year from partnership gross income for two years after the partnership is organized. The agreement also states that Mary will receive a $20,000 preferential cash distribution for each of the first two years. Mary and Ned share all other partnership items equally. Partnership net income in each of the next two years is $100,000.

If the form of the transaction is respected, the special allocation has the tax effect of a partnership deduction, because Ned's distributive share is reduced by the payment to Mary. (Mary's distributive share is $60,000; Ned's distributive share is $40,000.) However, if the transaction is recharacterized as a payment to a nonpartner for syndication costs, the expenses are nondeductible for the partnership,[168] and Mary and Ned are each taxable on their $50,000 distributive shares. However, because of the preferential distribution to Mary, she actually receives $60,000, while Ned receives only $40,000.

The legislative history describes a number of factors that must be considered in determining whether an allocation should be respected or recharacterized as a payment to a nonpartner.[169]

---

[167]   I.R.C. § 707(a)(2)(A).

[168]   I.R.C. § 709(a).

[169]   S. Rep. No. 169, 98th Cong., 2d Sess. 232 (1984).

§ 7.05   SALES AND EXCHANGES INVOLVING CONTROLLED AND RELATED PARTNERSHIPS

[A]   Special Rules to Prevent Tax-Motivated Transactions Between a Partnership and Its Partners — An Overview

A number of special rules apply to prevent tax-motivated transactions between a partnership and its partners or persons related to its partners. These rules may be summarized as follows:

(1)   No loss may be recognized on a sale or exchange between a partnership and persons who control the partnership, or between two partnerships controlled by the same persons. However, a disallowed loss may offset gain recognized by the purchaser on a later sale or exchange of the same property.[170]

(2)   Any gain recognized on a sale or exchange between a partnership and persons who control the partnership, or between two partnerships controlled by the same persons, is characterized as ordinary income if the property is not a capital asset in the purchaser's hands.[171]

(3)   Any gain recognized on a sale or exchange between a partnership and certain related persons is characterized as ordinary income if the property is depreciable in the purchaser's hands.[172]

(4)   An accrual-method partner or partnership may not deduct expenses owed to a related cash-method partner or partnership until payment actually occurs.[173]

This rule prevents the mismatching of the time periods when income and related deductions are reported.

[B]   Definition of Control Under I.R.C. Section 707(b)

The loss disallowance and ordinary income rules of I.R.C. Section 707(b) apply to sales or exchanges between:

(1)   a partnership and a person who, directly or indirectly, owns more than 50 percent of the partnership's capital or profits interests; or

(2)   two partnerships in which the same persons own, directly or indirectly, more than 50 percent of the capital or profits interests.

A partner's direct percentage interest in capital or profits is determined from both the written partnership agreement and the partner's actual dealings with the partnership. Factors considered in making this determination include:

---

[170] I.R.C. § 707(b)(1).
[171] I.R.C. § 707(b)(2).
[172] I.R.C. § 1239.
[173] I.R.C. § 267(a)(2).

(1)   the partner's relative contribution to the partnership;

(2)   the partner's interest in profits and losses;

(3)   the partner's interest in cash flow and other nonliquidating distributions; and

(4)   the partner's rights to distributions of capital on liquidation.[174]

A partner's right to receive guaranteed payments is not considered an interest in partnership profits.[175]

> **Example (1):** Charles and Donald each own 30-percent interests in the profits and capital of the CDE Partnership (Edward owns the remaining 40 percent). They also each own 30 percent of the CDF Partnership (Freda owns the remaining 40 percent). Because the same persons (Charles and Donald) own more than 50 percent of the capital or profits of both partnerships, any loss on a property sale between CDE and CDF is disallowed.

> **Example (2):** Assume same facts as in Example (1), except that Charles owns a 48-percent interest in both Partnership CDE and Partnership CDF, and that Donald owns a 3-percent interest in each partnership. Because Charles and Donald together still own more than 50 percent of the interests in both partnerships, the loss-disallowance rules apply.

A person's ownership of an interest in partnership capital or profits includes any interests he is deemed to own under the constructive ownership rules of I.R.C. Section 267(c)(1), (2), (4), and (5). These are the rules that apply for attributing ownership of stock to a person when determining the ownership of a corporation.[176]

According to these rules:

(1)   A capital or profits interest directly or indirectly owned by, or for, a corporation, partnership, estate, or trust, is considered owned proportionally by its shareholders, partners, or beneficiaries.[177] However, a partnership interest owned by one partner is not constructively owned by the other partners.[178]

> **Example:** Mark is an 80-percent shareholder of Corporation X, which owns a 70-percent profits interest in the XYZ Partnership. Mark is deemed to own a 56 percent profits interest in XYZ (80% * 70%).

(2)   An individual constructively owns a capital or profits interest that is directly, or indirectly, owned by or for his family.[179] For this purpose, family includes only brothers and sisters (whether by whole or half

---

[174]   Treas. Reg. § 1.704-1(b)(3)(ii).

[175]   Treas. Reg. § 1.707-1(c).

[176]   I.R.C. §§ 707(b)(3), 1239(c)(2).

[177]   I.R.C. § 267(c)(1).

[178]   I.R.C. §§ 707(b)(3), 1239(c)(2).

[179]   I.R.C. § 267(c)(4).

blood), spouse, ancestors, and lineal descendants.[180]

Example: Quentin is a 55-percent partner in the QR Partnership. Quentin's wife Sara is a 55-percent partner in the ST Partnership. Because a husband and wife are related parties under the constructive-ownership rules,[181] Quentin and Sara each own the other's partnership interest for purposes of applying the loss-disallowance rules. Therefore, no loss is recognized on a sale or exchange of property between the QR and ST partnerships, even though there are no common partners in the two partnerships.

(3)   A partnership capital or profits interest constructively owned by one person or entity may be reattributed and constructively owned by another person or entity.[182] However, an interest constructively owned under the family-attribution rule is not reattributed to another family member.[183]

Example: Bob is an 80-percent shareholder in Corporation X, which owns 100 percent of the stock of Corporation Y. Y owns a 70-percent capital and profits interest in the XYZ Partnership. Therefore, Bob constructively owns 56 percent (80% * 70%) of XYZ. If Bob's brother, Charles, sells property to XYZ, the sale is subject to the loss-disallowance and gain-characterization rules, because Bob's ownership of XYZ is reattributed to his brother. However, if Charles's wife, Donna (*i.e.*, Bob's sister-in-law), sells property to XYZ, there is no reattribution, since Charles's interest is constructively owned by attribution from his brother.

[C]   Limitation on Loss Deductions

No deduction is allowed for a loss incurred on a direct or indirect sale or exchange of property between:

(1)   a partnership and a person who directly or indirectly owns more than 50 percent of partnership capital or profits interests; or

(2)   two partnerships in which the same persons directly or indirectly own more than 50 percent of partnership capital or profits interests.[184]

The seller's loss is disallowed but is not extinguished: it may be used by a purchaser who later sells the property at a gain. The gain on the subsequent sale is recognized only to the extent that it exceeds the previously disallowed loss.[185] The loss cannot be used, however, if the purchaser later sells the property for an

---

[180] *Id.*

[181] *See* I.R.C. § 267(c)(4).

[182] I.R.C. § 267(c)(5).

[183] *Id.*

[184] I.R.C. § 707(b)(1).

[185] If gain from the sale of partnership property is not recognized under I.R.C. §§ 707(b)(1) and 267(d), the basis of each partner's interest in the partnership increases (under I.R.C. § 705(a)(1)) by the partner's share of that gain. Rev. Rul. 96-10, 1996-1 C.B. 138.

amount equal to or less than the purchase price.[186]

> **Example:** Michael, a 55-percent partner in the MN Partnership, sells property with a basis of $400 to the partnership for $300. He may not recognize his $100 realized loss.
>
> If the partnership later sells the property for $600, MN recognizes only $200 of gain. Although a $300 gain is realized ($600 sales price - $300 basis), that gain is recognized only to the extent that it exceeds the $100 loss previously disallowed. Under the partners' profit-and-loss-sharing ratio, Michael's distributive share includes $110 of the gain recognized on the partnership's sale (55% * $200); the other partner's (Nora's) distributive share includes $90 of the gain (45% * $200).

Because Michael actually sustained the loss that offset the partnership's gain on the sale, the entire tax benefit of the loss should be allocated to him. The partnership agreement should contain a provision specifically allocating any gain from sale of the property to Nora, before taking the suspended loss into account.[187] If this provision is written into the MN Partnership's agreement, Nora is allocated $135 of the gain (45% * $300 realized before applying the suspended loss) and Michael is allocated the remaining $65 of gain. Reducing Michael's share of gain to $65 gives him the full tax benefit from his $100 suspended loss; without the suspended loss, Michael would have recognized gain of $165 (55% * $300).

If the MN Partnership sells the property for $300, it realizes no gain on the sale, and neither the partnership nor Michael can deduct the previously disallowed loss.

The loss-disallowance rule applies even though the transaction occurs indirectly. For example, the Tax Court applied I.R.C. Section 707(b)(1) in *Davis v. Commissioner*,[188] when a third party foreclosed on partnership property securing a debt, then resold the property to a related partnership. Other cases arising under I.R.C. Section 267 have been decided using principles that are similar to those applicable under I.R.C. Section 707(b).[189]

Loss limitation under I.R.C. Section 267. A slightly different loss-disallowance rule applies to losses incurred in a sale or exchange between a corporation and a related partnership.[190] The loss is disallowed if the same persons own more than 50 percent of the value of the corporation's outstanding stock and more than 50 percent of the interests in the partnership's capital or profits. Constructive-ownership rules apply in determining whether the requisite ownership of stock[191] and partnership interests[192] exist.

---

[186] I.R.C. § 267(d).

[187] I.R.C. § 704(b).

[188] 88 T.C. 122 (1987), *aff'd*, 866 F.2d 852 (6th Cir. 1989).

[189] *See* Hassen v. Comm'r, 63 T.C. 175 (1974), *aff'd*, 599 F.2d 305 (9th Cir. 1979). No indirect sale occurs if the foreclosure and subsequent sale are unrelated events. McCarty v. Cripe, 201 F.2d 679 (7th Cir. 1953).

[190] I.R.C. § 267(b)(10).

[191] I.R.C. § 267(c).

[192] I.R.C. § 267(c), (e)(3).

[D]   Gain Treated as Ordinary Income if Property Is Not a Capital Asset to Purchaser

Any gain from a sale or exchange of property must be reported as ordinary income if:

(1)   the transaction is between

(a)   a partnership and a person who directly or indirectly owns more than 50 percent of partnership capital or profits interests, or

(b)   two partnerships in which the same persons directly or indirectly own more than 50 percent of partnership capital or profits interests; and

(2)   the property is not a capital asset in the hands of the transferee.[193]

Example: Stan, a 55-percent partner in the ST Partnership, sells land with a basis of $100 to ST for $500. The partnership is in the real estate development business and intends to subdivide and sell the land. Stan's gain is ordinary income because the land is not a capital asset in the partnership's hands.[194]

[E]   Gain Treated as Ordinary Income if Property Is Depreciable by Purchaser

Any gain recognized on a sale or exchange of property between a partnership and certain related persons is characterized as ordinary income if the property is depreciable in the purchaser's hands.[195] For this purpose, a person is related to a partnership if he directly or indirectly owns more than 50 percent of the interests in its capital or profits.[196] A corporation and a partnership are deemed to be related if the same persons own more than 50 percent of the value of the corporation's outstanding stock and more than 50 percent of the partnership's capital or profits interests.[197]

Example: Arthur is a 55-percent partner in the AB Partnership; he also owns 60 percent of the value of the stock of X Corporation. Therefore, because Corporation X and Partnership AB are related entities, if X sells property to AB that is depreciable in the partnership's hands, X recognizes ordinary income.

I.R.C. Section 707(b)(2) does not apply in this situation because X does not control AB. If the property sold is not depreciable to AB, neither provision applies.

Installment-method reporting is not permitted if the seller's gain is treated

---

[193] I.R.C. § 707(b)(2).

[194] I.R.C. § 1221.

[195] I.R.C. § 1239(a).

[196] I.R.C. § 1239(b), (c).

[197] I.R.C. § 267(b)(10).

as ordinary income;[198] the seller must report all his gain in the year of the sale. However, this limitation does not apply if the seller establishes that the sale did not have tax avoidance as one of its principal purposes.[199]

[F] Deductions for Accrued Expenses

Under general tax rules, an accrual-method taxpayer may deduct an accrued but unpaid expense item even though the cash-method payee will not report income from the transaction until he actually receives payment. However, in transactions between a partnership and its partners, special rules preclude any tax advantage by prohibiting any mismatch in the reporting of income and deductions. An accrual-method partnership or partner is prohibited from deducting any expense or interest owed to a related cash-method partner or partnership until the underlying expense payment actually occurs.[200] This rule eliminates any tax advantage from a partner-partnership transaction in which the obligor deducts an expense in a tax year that precedes the year in which the payee reports the corresponding income. The limitation on deductions also applies to amounts owed by partners to other partners on behalf of the partnership (*e.g.*, payments partners are required to make under the partnership agreement).[201] In effect, the statute places the accrual-method taxpayer on the cash method for transactions with related persons.

---

[198] I.R.C. §§ 1239(a), 453(g).

[199] I.R.C. § 453(g)(2).

[200] I.R.C. § 267(a)(2).

[201] S. Rep. No. 98-169, 98th Cong., 2d Sess. 495 (1984).

Chapter 8

DISTRIBUTING PARTNERSHIP/LLC PROPERTY TO PARTNERS OR MEMBERS

§ 8.01 OVERVIEW OF DISTRIBUTION RULES

This chapter describes the rules governing distributions of partnership and limited liability company property to partners and members. The discussion focuses on the rules relating to the recognition of gain or loss; the basis, holding period, and character of distributed property; adjustments to the basis of undistributed partnership property; and the special I.R.C. Section 751 rules for distributions that change a partner's share of partnership ordinary-income property.

Although many of the distribution rules apply to current and liquidating distributions, some important differences exist. A distribution is current if the recipient partner or LLC member continues to own an interest in the partnership or LLC; a distribution is liquidating if the recipient's entire interest in the partnership or LLC is terminated.[1] Only a portion of a liquidating payment a partnership makes to a retiring partner or to a deceased partner's successor is considered a distribution. The amount of each liquidating payment that is treated as a distribution is determined under the rules of I.R.C. Section 736, which provide that a liquidating payment is a distribution only up to the value of the partner's share of partnership property; the remaining portion of the payment is treated as a guaranteed payment or is included in the partner's distributive share of partnership income.

The specific rules applicable to a distribution depend upon the context in which the distribution is made. Distributions typically occur in the following situations:

(1) Many partnerships and LLCs periodically distribute the cash they acquire from business or investment activities to partners and members in proportion to their interests in partnership or LLC capital. A pro rata cash distribution generally is treated as a nontaxable withdrawal of capital that reduces each partner's basis in his partnership interest. If the amount of cash distributed to a partner exceeds the basis of his partnership interest, however, that partner recognizes capital gain equal to the excess amount. Similar rules apply to distributions of marketable securities.

(2) Partnerships often make payments to liquidate the interests of retiring or deceased partners. Under the rules of I.R.C. Section 736, a liquidating payment is considered a distribution only up to the value of the partner's

---

[1] Treas. Reg. § 1.761-1(d).

share of partnership property. The portion of the payment that is treated as a distribution is further subdivided and taxed under the rules of I.R.C. Section 751, if the distribution changes the partner's share of partnership ordinary-income property.

(3)   A partnership may distribute cash or other property to partially liquidate (*i.e.*, reduce) a partner's percentage interest. If the distribution changes the partner's share of the partnership's unrealized receivables and appreciated inventory, the special rules of I.R.C. Section 751 apply.

(4)   A partner is deemed to receive a cash distribution when his share of partnership liabilities decreases. This "constructive" distribution is likely to occur if a partner's interest in a partnership that has liabilities is fully or partially liquidated, and if the amount of partnership liabilities decreases by satisfaction of the debts.

(5)   All partners are deemed to receive a liquidating distribution of interests in a "new" partnership if their "old" partnership terminates under the rules of I.R.C. Section 708(b). A partnership terminates if it stops conducting any business or investment activity, if it ceases to function as a partnership, or if 50 percent or more of its interests are sold or exchanged within a 12-month period. If a partnership terminates under the 50-percent sale or exchange rule, the terminated partnership is deemed to contribute all its assets to a new partnership and then make a liquidating distribution of its interests in the new partnership to its partners.

(6)   A number of special rules may apply if the partnership making the distribution previously received a property contribution from one of its partners. A partner who contributes property with a built-in gain or loss may recognize that gain or loss if the partnership makes a property distribution within seven years of the contribution. If the contributed property is distributed to another partner, the contributing partner recognizes the built-in gain or loss under I.R.C. Section 704(c)(1)(B). (*See* Chapter 4.) If the contributing partner receives a distribution of other partnership property, he may recognize gain under I.R.C. Section 737. (*See* Chapter 4.) According to the disguised sale rules of I.R.C. Section 707(a)(2)(B), a partner who receives a distribution within two years of a "related" property contribution may be presumed to have sold, rather than contributed, the property to the partnership. (*See* Chapter 7.)

[A]   General Rules Applicable to Distributions

The following sections summarize the basic rules governing current and liquidating distributions to partners and LLC members. Each of these rules is fully discussed later on in this chapter, as indicated by the cross-references.

[1]   Gain or Loss on Current or Liquidating Distribution

A partner does not recognize gain or loss when he receives a current or liquidating distribution of money or property, because most distributions are merely a recovery of the partner's capital contribution or a withdrawal of his previously taxed share of partnership income.[2] Two important exceptions to the nonrecognition rule may apply:

(1) A partner recognizes gain to the extent that the amount of money distributed to him in a current or liquidating distribution exceeds the basis in his partnership interest immediately before the distribution.[3] Generally, a distribution of marketable securities is treated as a distribution of money for this purpose.[4]

(2) A partner recognizes a loss on a liquidating distribution if

(a) the property he receives from the partnership consists only of money, unrealized receivables, and inventory items; and

(b) the basis in his partnership interest exceeds the sum of the money plus the partnership's basis in the receivables and inventory distributed to him.[5] Any gain or loss a partner recognizes on a distribution is deemed to arise from a sale or exchange of his partnership interest and is characterized under the rules of I.R.C. Section 741, resulting in a capital gain or loss unless the disproportionate-distribution rules of I.R.C. Section 751(b) apply (*see* § 8.06, *infra*).

A partnership does not recognize gain or loss when it distributes money or property to a partner.[6]

[2] Basis of Distributee Partner's Interest in the Partnership

Current distribution. A partner who receives a current distribution decreases the basis in his partnership interest by the sum of the amount of money he receives (see § 8.02, *infra*, for discussion of when marketable securities are treated as money), plus the partnership's basis in other distributed property.[7] In no event, however, may a partner reduce the basis in his interest below zero. (*See* § 8.03, *infra*.)

Liquidating distribution. A partner has no basis in his partnership interest after his interest is liquidated. If the liquidation is made through a series of installment distributions, the partner's interest is not liquidated until the final distribution occurs.[8] Consequently, the basis of his interest decreases as each distribution occurs. Two important consequences of this treatment are:

(1) A partner whose interest is liquidated through a series of cash distributions does not recognize gain under I.R.C. Section 731(a) until the amount

---

[2] I.R.C. § 731(a).

[3] I.R.C. § 731(a)(1).

[4] I.R.C. § 731(c).

[5] I.R.C. § 731(a)(2).

[6] I.R.C. § 731(b).

[7] I.R.C. § 733.

[8] Treas. Reg. § 1.761-1(d).

of money actually distributed to him exceeds the basis in his interest.[9] However, an election described in the regulations permits a partner who will receive a fixed total amount of liquidation distributions to report his gain, pro rata, as he receives the payments.[10]

(2)   A partner may not recognize a loss on the liquidation until he receives the final liquidating distribution. (*See* § 8.04, *infra*).[11]

[3] Basis of Distributed Property in the Distributee Partner's Hands

Current distribution. A partner's basis in property he receives in a current distribution equals the partnership's basis for the property immediately before the distribution.[12] However, the partner's total basis in all property he receives in a single distribution cannot exceed the basis in his partnership interest immediately before the distribution.[13] If money and other property are distributed in the same transaction, the partner reduces the basis in his partnership interest by the amount of money he receives before determining his basis in the distributed property.

Liquidating distribution. A partner's total basis in property he receives in a liquidating distribution equals the basis in his partnership interest reduced by the amount of money received in the same transaction.[14] (For rules governing allocation of basis to distributed properties, see § 8.04, *infra*.)

Partnership's basis for distributed property exceeds partner's basis. If the basis of the partner's interest is less than the partnership's total basis in the property distributed to him, the partner's basis is allocated among the distributed properties in accordance with the rules of I.R.C. Section 732(c). (See discussion in § 8.04, *infra*.)

Special basis rule under I.R.C. Section 732(d). A special rule determines the basis of partnership property distributed to a partner who acquired his partnership interest through a sale or exchange or as successor to a deceased partner. A partner may elect to use this basis-determination rule if the partnership did not have a basis-adjustment election in effect when the partner acquired his interest, and if the distribution occurs within two years of the acquisition. The I.R.C. Section 732(d) basis rule is mandatory for certain distributions regardless of when they occur (*see* Chapter 12).

---

[9] Treas. Reg. § 1.736-1(b)(6); Treas. Reg. § 1.736-1(b)(7), *Example (2)*.

[10] Treas. Reg. § 1.736-1(b)(6).

[11] I.R.C. § 732(a).

[12] *Id.*

[13] I.R.C. § 732(a)(2).

[14] I.R.C. § 732(b).

[4] Character and Holding Period of Distributed Property

The character of gain or loss a partner recognizes when he sells property received in a current or liquidating distribution ordinarily is determined from the character of the asset in his hands. Exceptions to this treatment apply:

(1) If a partner sells distributed property that was an unrealized receivable in the partnership, the partner recognizes ordinary income regardless of the character of the property in his hands.[15]

(2) If a partner sells property that was inventory in the partnership, the partner recognizes ordinary income or loss if he sells the inventory within five years of the distribution, regardless of the character of the property in his hands.[16]

(3) If a partner disposes of distributed property that was subject to ordinary income recapture in the partnership, any potential recapture income carries over from the partnership and is recaptured as ordinary income to the partner.[17] (*See* § 8.05, *infra.*)

The partnership's holding period for any distributed property "tacks" on and is included in the partner's holding period.[18] A partner who receives a distribution of partnership cost-recovery property (*i.e.*, property subject to I.R.C. Section 168) generally computes his cost-recovery deductions in the same manner as the partnership.[19]

[5] Distribution That Changes Partner's Share of I.R.C. Section 751 Property

A current or liquidating distribution that changes a partner's proportionate share of the partnership's unrealized receivables or substantially appreciated inventory is partially recharacterized as a sale under I.R.C. Section 751(b) (*see* § 8.07[E], *infra*; Chapter 12). This recharacterization occurs if the partner receives a disproportionate share of the partnership's I.R.C. Section 751 property in exchange for his interest in other partnership assets. The partner and the partnership may recognize gain or loss on this deemed sale, and the basis of any property deemed purchased in the transaction may increase or decrease.

[6] Partnership's Basis in Undistributed Property

A distribution of property to a partner generally does not affect the partnership's basis in its remaining, undistributed property.[20] However, if the partnership makes an election under I.R.C. Section 754 (*see* § 8.07, *infra*; Chapter 5), the following

---

[15] I.R.C. § 735(a)(1).

[16] I.R.C. § 735(a)(2).

[17] *See, e.g.*, I.R.C. §§ 617, 995, 1245, 1248, 1250, 1252, 1253.

[18] I.R.C. § 735(b).

[19] I.R.C. § 168(i)(7); Prop. Treas. Reg. § 1.168-5(b)(1).

[20] I.R.C. § 734(a).

adjustments to the bases of its undistributed assets are made pursuant to I.R.C. Section 734(b):

(1)   The basis of partnership assets increases by the amount of gain a partner recognizes as a result of receiving a current or liquidating distribution of money that exceeds the basis of his partnership interest.

(2)   The basis of partnership assets decreases by the amount of loss a partner recognizes on a liquidating distribution that consists only of money, receivables, and inventory.

(3)   The basis of partnership assets increases to the extent that the distributee-partner's basis in property received in a current or liquidating distribution is less than the partnership's basis.

(4)   The basis of partnership assets decreases to the extent that the distributee-partner's basis in property received in a liquidating distribution is greater than the partnership's basis.

These basis adjustments are allocated among the partnership's assets under rules provided in I.R.C. Section 755.

[7]   Payments to a Retiring Partner or Deceased Partner's Successor

Payments a continuing partnership makes to liquidate the interest of a retiring partner or a deceased partner's successor in interest are treated as liquidating distributions only to the extent that the payments are in exchange for the partner's share of partnership property under I.R.C. Section 736(b). Any other liquidating payments are not considered distributions but are treated as guaranteed payments or included in the partner's distributive share of partnership income according to I.R.C. Section 736(a). In a general partnership in which capital is not a material income producing factor (*e.g.*, services partnerships), unrealized receivables are not treated as partnership property, nor is goodwill unless the partnership agreement specifically requires payment for a withdrawing partner's share of goodwill. (*See* Chapter 10.)

[B]   Distinction Between Current and Liquidating Distributions

Although many of the rules governing distributions apply to current and liquidating distributions, two important differences exist:

(1)   A partner may not recognize a loss on a current distribution but may recognize a loss on a liquidating distribution if the only property he receives is cash, unrealized receivables, and inventory.[21]

(2)   A partner's basis in distributed property is computed differently for current and liquidating distributions. A partner's basis in property he receives in a current distribution equals the partnership's basis for the

---

[21] I.R.C. § 731(b).

property immediately before the distribution (limited to the basis in his partnership interest).[22] A partner's total basis in property he receives in a liquidating distribution equals the basis in his partnership interest reduced by the amount of money received in the same transaction.[23]

Current distribution. As previously mentioned, any distribution that does not terminate a partner's interest in the partnership is a current distribution.[24] Thus, the current-distribution rules may apply when a partner receives his previously taxed distributive share of partnership income or a return of all or part of his capital contribution. A partial liquidation of a partner's interest is a current distribution, even if the partner's interest in capital and profits is substantially reduced. The current-distribution rules do not apply, however, to a distribution that is part of a series of distributions intended to terminate a partner's entire interest.[25]

Example (1): Charles owns 50 percent of the capital and profits of the CDE Partnership; the basis for his partnership interest is $120,000. The partnership's assets consist of $100,000 in cash and a capital asset worth $100,000. CDE distributes $96,000 in cash to Charles and reduces his continuing interest in capital and profits to 2 percent. The payment to Charles is a current distribution, and he does not recognize any gain or loss on the transaction.

Liquidating distribution. A liquidating distribution is a distribution or part of a series of distributions that terminates a partner's interest in a partnership.[26] If a partner receives a series of liquidating distributions, his interest is not considered liquidated until he receives the final distribution,[27] even if the liquidating distributions are made over a number of years. Consequently, a partner does not recognize any gain until the year in which the aggregate amount of cash distributed to him exceeds the basis in his partnership interest. Similarly, a partner does not recognize any loss until the year in which he receives the final liquidating distribution.

Example (2): Assume the same facts as in Example (1), except Charles receives a $100,000 cash distribution that terminates his entire interest in the partnership. Because his basis in his partnership interest is $120,000, Charles recognizes a $20,000 loss on the liquidating distribution under I.R.C. Section 731(a)(2). If the distribution payments are made over two years in equal installments, Charles does not recognize any loss until he receives the final payment in Year 2.

---

[22] I.R.C. § 732(a).

[23] I.R.C. § 732(b).

[24] Treas. Reg. § 1.761-1(d).

[25] I.R.C. § 761(d).

[26] *Id.*

[27] Treas. Reg. § 1.761-1(d).

§ 8.02 SPECIAL RULES FOR CERTAIN DISTRIBUTIONS

[A] Distribution of Marketable Securities

As previously noted, a partner recognizes gain to the extent that the amount of money distributed to him exceeds the basis in his partnership interest immediately before the distribution.[28] Under I.R.C. Section 731(c), as amended in 1994, a distribution of marketable securities generally is treated as a money distribution equal to the value of the securities. Accordingly, a partner receiving a distribution of marketable securities recognizes gain to the extent that the value of the securities on the date of distribution[29] exceeds the basis in his partnership interest.[30] This rule only affects the distributee partner; neither the partnership nor any other partner recognize gain as a result of a distribution of marketable securities.[31]

[1] Marketable Securities Defined

Marketable securities are defined as financial instruments and foreign currencies that are actively traded[32] as of the distribution date.[33] Financial instruments include financial products such as stocks and other equity interests, evidences of indebtedness, options, futures and forward contracts, notional principal contracts, and derivatives. Also included are:[34]

(1) certain interests in a common trust fund or a regulated investment company (RIC);

(2) financial instruments readily convertible into, or exchangeable for, money or marketable securities (e.g., an in-the-money option to buy marketable securities);

(3) financial instruments whose value is determined substantially by reference to marketable securities;

(4) interests in precious metals that are actively traded (unless produced, used, or held in the partnership's active trade or business);

(5) interests in any entity if 90 percent or more of the entity's assets (by value) consist of marketable securities, money, or both;[35] and

(6) interests in an entity to the extent that the value of the interest is attributable to marketable securities, money, or both, if less than 90

---

[28] I.R.C. § 731(a).

[29] I.R.C. § 731(c)(1)(B).

[30] I.R.C. § 731(c)(1).

[31] Treas. Reg. § 1.731-2.

[32] Within the meaning of I.R.C. § 1092(d)(1).

[33] I.R.C. § 731(c)(2)(A).

[34] I.R.C. § 731(c)(2)(B).

[35] Treas. Reg. § 1.731-2(c)(3)(i).

percent but 20 percent or more of the entity's assets (by value) consist of such assets.[36]

All of a partnership's marketable securities are considered to be of the same class and issuer as the distributed securities.[37]

[2] Money Distribution Reduced by Partner's Share of Appreciation

The amount of distributed marketable securities treated as money is reduced by the distributee partner's share of the net appreciation of all the partnership's marketable securities.[38] The amount of the reduction equals the difference between the partner's share of the net gain the partnership would realize on a sale of all its marketable securities (1) before the distribution and (2) after the distribution.[39] The net gain in both sales is determined as if the securities are sold at the same fair market value. This provision allows a partner to withdraw his share of the partnership's appreciated marketable securities without recognizing gain. In effect, I.R.C. Section 731(c) only applies when a distribution of marketable securities is in exchange for a partner's share of other partnership appreciated assets.

> **Example (1):** [40] Alicia and Burton form equal partnership AB. Alicia contributes property with a fair market value of $1,000 and tax basis of $250. Burton contributes $1,000 cash. AB subsequently purchases Security X for $500 and immediately distributes the security to Alicia in a current distribution. The basis in Alicia's partnership interest at the time of distribution is $250.
>
> The distribution of Security X is treated as a distribution of money equal to the security's fair market value on the distribution date ($500). The amount of the distribution treated as money is not reduced because, if Security X were sold immediately before the distribution, no gain would be recognized by AB and Alicia's distributive share of the gain would be zero. Alicia recognizes $250 of gain ($500 distribution of money less $250 adjusted tax basis in Alicia's partnership interest).
>
> **Example (2):** [41] Chuck and Doris form the CD Limited Liability Company as equal members. The LLC subsequently distributes Security X to Chuck in a current distribution. Immediately before the distribution, the LLC held securities with the following fair market values, adjusted tax bases, and unrecognized gain or loss:

---

[36] Treas. Reg. § 1.731-2(c)(3)(ii).

[37] Treas. Reg. § 1.731-2(b)(1).

[38] Treas. Reg. § 1.731-2(b)(3).

[39] I.R.C. § 731(c)(3)(B); Treas. Reg. § 1.731-2(b)(2).

[40] Treas. Reg. § 1.731-2(j), *Example (1)*.

[41] Treas. Reg. 1.731-2(j), *Example (2)*.

	Value	Basis	Gain (Loss)
Security X	100	70	30
Security Y	100	80	20
Security Z	100	110	(10)

If the LLC sold the securities for fair market value immediately before the distribution to Chuck, it would have recognized $40 of net gain ($30 gain on Security X plus $20 gain on Security Y minus $10 loss on Security Z). Chuck's distributive share of this gain would have been $20 (one-half of $40 net gain). If the LLC sold the remaining securities immediately after the distribution, it would have $10 of net gain ($20 of gain on Security Y minus $10 loss on Security Z). Chuck's distributive share of this gain would have been $5 (one-half of $10 net gain). The decrease in Chuck's distributive share of the net gain in the LLC's securities is $15 ($20 net gain before distribution minus $5 net gain after distribution). Thus, the amount of the distribution of Security X treated as a distribution of money is reduced by $15. The distribution of Security X is treated as a distribution of $85 of money to Chuck ($100 fair market value of Security X minus $15 reduction).

Generally, gain recognized under I.R.C. Section 731(c) is capital gain.[42] However, if a distributed marketable security is an unrealized receivable or an inventory item, ordinary income is recognized.[43]

[3] Certain Distributions Not Subject to Gain Recognition Rule

Under the following exceptions to the general rule of I.R.C. Section 731(c), gain is not recognized on a distribution of marketable securities:

(1) I.R.C. Section 731(c) does not apply to a distribution of a marketable security that was contributed to the partnership by the distributee partner.[44] Under an "anti-stuffing" rule, this exception does not apply to the extent that 20 percent or more of the distributed security's value is attributable to marketable securities or money the partnership contributed to the entity to which the distributed security relates after it was contributed to the partnership. The anti-stuffing rule does not apply if the marketable securities the partnership contributes were originally contributed to the partnership by the distributee partner.[45]

(2) I.R.C. Section 731(c) does not apply to the extent that the partnership acquired the distributed security in a nonrecognition transaction if

(a) The value of any marketable securities and money the partnership exchanged in the nonrecognition transaction was less than 20

---

[42] I.R.C. § 741.

[43] I.R.C. § 731(c)(6).

[44] I.R.C. § 731(c)(3)(A)(i); Treas. Reg. § 1.731-2(d)(1)(i).

[45] Treas. Reg. § 1.731-2(d)(2).

percent of the value of all the assets the partnership exchanged in the transaction; and

(b)   The partnership distributes the security within five years of the later of the date the partnership acquired the security or the date the security became marketable.[46]

[4] Exception for Investment Partnerships

I.R.C. Section 731(c) does not apply to distribution of marketable securities by an "investment partnership" to an "eligible partner."[47] A partnership is an investment partnership if (1) it never engaged in a trade or business, and (2) substantially all its assets always consisted of the investment assets specified in the statute.[48] The specified assets include money, corporate stock, notes, bonds, debentures or other evidence of indebtedness, interest rate, currency, or equity notional principal contracts, foreign currencies, interests in or derivative financial instruments in any of these assets or in any traded commodity, other assets specified in the regulations, or any combination of these assets.[49]

A partner is an eligible partner if he contributed only these specified investment assets to the partnership before the distribution date.[50] Eligible partner status does not apply to a transferor or transferee of a partnership interest in a nonrecognition transaction if the transferor was not an eligible partner.[51] A partner who receives a partnership interest in exchange for services may be an eligible partner.[52] A "look through" rule applies to tiered partnerships where a partner contributes an interest in a lower tier partnership to another upper tier partnership.[53]

[5] Basis Adjustments

Basis in distributed securities. The distributee partner's basis in distributed marketable securities increases by the amount of gain the partner recognizes under I.R.C. Section 731(c).[54] That gain is allocated among the distributed marketable securities in proportion their relative amounts of unrealized appreciation.[55]

Basis of distributee's partnership interest. The basis of the partner's partnership interest and the partnership's basis in its undistributed assets are determined without regard to any gain recognized under I.R.C. Section 731(c).[56] Any basis

---

[46] I.R.C. § 731(c)(3)(A)(ii); Treas. Reg. § 1.731-2(d)(1)(ii).

[47] I.R.C. § 731(c)(3)(A)(iii).

[48] I.R.C. § 731(c)(3)(C).

[49] I.R.C. § 731(c)(3)(C)(i).

[50] I.R.C. § 731(c)(3)(C)(iii)(I).

[51] *Id.*

[52] Treas. Reg. § 1.731-2(e)(2)(i).

[53] Treas. Reg. § 1.731-2(e)(2)(ii).

[54] I.R.C. § 731(c)(4)(A).

[55] I.R.C. § 731(c)(4)(B); Treas. Reg. § 1.731-2(f)(1)(i).

[56] I.R.C. § 731(c)(5).

increase or decrease under I.R.C. Section 734 (if the partnership has an I.R.C. Section 754 election in effect) also is made as if no gain is recognized.

Example: [57] Martin and Nora form the MN Limited Liability Company as equal members. Martin contributes nondepreciable real property, with a fair market value of $100 and tax basis of $10. MN subsequently distributes Security X with a fair market value and tax basis of $40 to Martin in a current distribution and, as part of the same distribution, MN distributes Property Z to Martin with a tax basis and fair market value of $40. At the time of distribution, the basis in Martin's LLC interest is $10. Martin recognizes $30 of gain under I.R.C. Sections 731(a) and (c) on the distribution (excess of $40 distribution of money over $10 tax basis in Martin's LLC interest).

Martin's basis in Security X is $35 ($5 adjusted basis under I.R.C. Section 732(a)(2) plus $30 of gain recognized under I.R.C. Section 731(c)). Martin's basis in Property Z is $5, determined under I.R.C. Section 732(a)(2). The basis in Martin's LLC interest is $0, determined under I.R.C. Section 733 ($10 pre-distribution basis minus $10 basis allocated between Security X and Property Z under I.R.C. Section 732).

MN's basis in its remaining assets is unchanged unless an I.R.C. Section 754 election is in effect. If MN made an election, the aggregate basis of MN's assets increases by $70 (the difference between the $80 combined basis of Security X and Property Z in the LLC before the distribution and the $10 combined basis of the distributed property to Martin after the distribution). No basis adjustment is made to the LLC's property under I.R.C. Section 734 for the gain Martin recognized under I.R.C. Section 731(c) or for Martin's increased basis in the distributed marketable securities under I.R.C. Section 731(c).

[6] Anti-Abuse Rule

An anti-abuse rule in the regulations requires that rules of I.R.C. Section 731(c) and its regulations be applied in a manner consistent with I.R.C. Section 731(c)'s purpose and the transaction's substance.[58] The IRS may recast a transaction if its principal purpose is to achieve a tax result that is inconsistent with the purpose of I.R.C. Section 731(c) as appropriate to achieve appropriate tax results. Whether a tax result is inconsistent with the statute's is determined from all the facts and circumstances. Examples of transactions that may be subject to the anti-abuse rule include a change in partnership allocations or distribution rights for marketable securities if the change is, in substance, a distribution of the securities,[59] or, a distribution of multiple properties to one or more partners at different times that are part of a single distribution plan.[60]

---

[57] Treas. Reg. 1.731-2(j), *Example (6)*.

[58] Treas. Reg. § 1.731-2(h).

[59] Treas. Reg. § 1.731-2(h)(1).

[60] Treas. Reg. § 1.731-2(h)(3).

[B]   Constructive Distribution of Money Upon Decrease in Partner's Share of Partnership Liabilities

A partner is deemed to receive a constructive distribution of money from the partnership for any decrease in his share of the partnership's liabilities and for any of his individual liabilities that the partnership assumes,[61] according to I.R.C. Section 752(b). This constructive distribution is treated as an actual current or liquidating distribution of money for all tax purposes, even if the partner receives no cash in the transaction. For example, a retiring partner is deemed to receive a cash liquidating distribution when the continuing partners become liable for his share of partnership liabilities. If the amount of the constructive cash distribution exceeds the partner's basis in his partnership interest, he recognizes gain under I.R.C. Section 731(a)(1).

Each partner's share of a partnership liability generally depends on whether the debt is recourse or nonrecourse. Partners share recourse liabilities in proportion to the economic risk of loss that they bear for the debt. The economic risk of loss that a partner bears is usually the amount he would be required to pay to another partner or to contribute to the partnership if all of the partnership's assets became worthless and all of its debts became due. A partner's share of nonrecourse liabilities is determined in two steps:

Step 1. Each partner is allocated liabilities equal to the minimum gain he would be allocated under I.R.C. Sections 704(b) and 704(c) if the partnership exchanged the property securing the liabilities to cancel the debts.

Step 2. Any remaining nonrecourse debts are shared in the same ratio that the partners share partnership profits.

(The rules for determining a partner's share of partnership recourse and nonrecourse liabilities are discussed in depth in Chapter 5.)

Circumstances that may decrease a partner's share of partnership liabilities and result in a constructive money distribution include:

(1)   Partnership debts are paid off or the partnership disposes of property subject to a liability; the amount of partnership liabilities changes.

(2)   The partners agree to change their shares of partnership liabilities (*e.g.*, the partners adjust the ratio for sharing profits and losses).

(3)   The partnership adds partners; the new partners are allocated shares of existing partnership liabilities. Each partner's share of partnership liabilities generally decreases when a new partner is admitted and increases when an old one withdraws. Therefore, a change in a partnership's membership results in a constructive cash contribution or distribution.

Example: Sandra and Thelma are equal general partners in a partnership whose only liability is a $30,000 recourse debt owed to a bank. Richard joins the partnership and, after he is admitted, each of the partners has an equal

---

[61] The deemed distribution of money is treated as an advance or drawing to the extent of the partner's distributive share of income for the partnership tax year. Treas. Reg. § 1.731-1(a)(1)(ii).

one-third interest in the partnership, and each is equally liable for its debts. The effects of Richard's admission to the partnership are summarized below:

| | Basis and Share of Liabilities | | |
	Sandra	Thelma	Richard
Before Richard joins the Partnership	$15,000	$15,000	$0
After Richard joins the Partnership	10,000	10,000	10,000
Constructive cash Distribution	$5,000	$5,000	$0

(4)   A partner contributes encumbered property. The partnership is considered to assume the debt up to the value of the property at the time of contribution. At the same time, the partner assumes a share of the partnership's liabilities, including the liability he just transferred. The partner is deemed to receive a cash distribution from the partnership equal to the amount by which the decrease in his individual liabilities exceeds the increase in his share of partnership liabilities.

Example (1): Chris and Donna form the CD Partnership as equal partners. Chris contributes $5,000 in cash, and Donna contributes property worth $20,000, with a basis to her of $10,000. The property is subject to a $15,000 recourse debt. Although CD does not actually assume the liability, it is deemed to assume it for determining that Donna's individual liabilities decrease by $15,000 and that partnership liabilities increase by the same amount. Donna's share of the partnership liability is $15,000 because she is personally liable to the creditor and bears the economic risk of loss for the entire debt. Since no net change in her share of partnership liabilities and individual liabilities occurs, Donna is not deemed to make a cash contribution to, or receive a cash distribution from, the partnership.

Example (2): Assume the same facts as in Example (1), except that CD actually assumes Donna's liability to the creditor. If CD constructively liquidates (*i.e.*, liquidates when its assets are deemed worthless), both Chris and Donna must contribute $7,500 to satisfy CD's liability. Consequently, each partner bears the economic risk of loss for, and is deemed to contribute, that amount to the partnership. Because the $15,000 decrease in Donna's individual liabilities exceeds the $7,500 increase in her share of partnership liabilities, she receives a $7,500 constructive cash distribution. Donna's basis in her partnership interest before the distribution is $10,000 (her basis in the contributed property); therefore, the distribution decreases her basis to $2,500.

Example (3): Assume the same facts as in Example (2), except that Donna's basis for the contributed property is $5,000. Because the $7,500 constructive cash distribution Donna receives exceeds the $5,000 basis in her interest, Donna recognizes $2,500 of gain, and the basis in her partnership interest is zero.

(5)　The partnership distributes encumbered property to a partner. The partner who receives a distribution of encumbered property is considered to assume the liability up to the value of the property when the distribution occurs. At the same time, the partner's share of the partnership's liabilities decreases by his share of the liability transferred to him. The partner is deemed to contribute cash to the partnership equal to the amount by which the increase in his individual liabilities exceeds the decrease in his share of partnership liabilities. All other partners are deemed to receive a cash distribution from the partnership equal to the decrease in their shares of partnership liabilities.

Example (4): George, Harriet, and Ingrid are equal partners in the GHI Partnership. George's basis in his partnership interest is $40,000, Harriet's basis is $60,000, and Ingrid's basis is $20,000. The partnership distributes property with a basis of $100,000, subject to a $75,000 liability, to George. George assumes the debt. George is deemed to make a $50,000 net cash contribution to the partnership ($75,000 deemed cash contribution on assumption of partnership debt - $25,000 decrease in his share of partnership liabilities). Harriet and Ingrid are each deemed to receive a $25,000 cash distribution — their shares of the $75,000 decrease in partnership liabilities. The distribution reduces Harriet's basis in her partnership interest to $35,000. Because the distribution exceeds Ingrid's basis, she recognizes gain of $5,000, and the basis in her partnership interest is reduced to zero.

George's basis in the distributed property is $90,000 — the partnership's $100,000 carryover basis limited to George's $90,000 basis in his partnership interest ($40,000 initial basis + $50,000 constructive contribution). After he receives the property, George's basis in his partnership interest is also reduced to zero.

(6)　A partnership interest is abandoned or forfeited. A partner who abandons or forfeits a worthless interest in a partnership that has outstanding liabilities receives a constructive cash liquidating distribution equal to the decrease in his share of the partnership's liabilities. Under I.R.C. Section 731(a)(2), the partner recognizes a loss if the amount of cash deemed distributed to him is less than the basis of his partnership interest. The loss is generally an ordinary loss; however, if an actual or deemed distribution to the partner occurs, or if the transaction is otherwise a sale in substance, the loss is capital.[62]

[C]　Distributions Associated With Contribution of Property

The following special rules may apply if the partnership making the distribution previously received a property contribution from one of its partners:

(1)　*Distribution of contributed property to another partner.* A partner that

---

[62] Rev. Rul. 1993-2 C.B. 239. *But see* Miller v. U.S., 331 F.2d 854 (Ct. Cl. 1964); Pietz v. Comm'r, 59 T.C. 207 (1972).

contributes property to a partnership recognizes gain or loss if the property is distributed to another partner within seven years[63] of the contribution date.[64] The amount recognized equals the gain or loss that would have been allocated to the partner under I.R.C. Section 704(c) if the partnership sold the property to the distributee partner for its fair market value at the time of the distribution. The character of the gain or loss recognized by the contributing partner is determined in the same manner.[65] (For complete discussion, see § 4.02, *supra*.)

(2)   *Distribution of property to contributing partner.* Under I.R.C. Section 737, a partner recognizes the gain built into property he contributed if he receives a distribution of other partnership property within seven years of the contribution.[66] This provision is designed to prevent partnerships from avoiding the rules of I.R.C. Section 704(c) requiring allocation of built-in gain or loss to the contributing partner.[67] (For complete discussion, see § 4.02, *supra*.)

(3)   *Distribution related to contribution treated as disguised sale.* To ensure that a contribution and related distribution are treated as a sale, I.R.C. Section 707(a)(2) authorizes the Service to recharacterize the transfers as if occurring between the partnership and a nonpartner (or between two or more nonpartners). Because the I.R.C. Section 721 nonrecognition rules do not apply to nonpartner transactions, the transfers between the partner and partnership constitute a taxable sale and gain or loss is recognized. (*See* § 7.04, *supra*.)

[D]   Distribution of Stock to a Corporate Partner

I.R.C. Section 732(f) applies a special rule when a partnership distributes stock of a corporation to a corporate partner and, immediately after the distribution, the distributee corporation controls the corporation whose stock was distributed.[68] In that situation, the distributed corporation must reduce the basis of its assets by the amount of any reduction in the distributee corporate partner's basis in the stock. This rule was enacted in 1999 to prevent corporate partners from avoiding basis decreases to distributed assets under I.R.C. Section 732 by having the partnership

---

[63] The seven-year period applies to property contributed after June 8, 1997. Property contributed before that date is subject to a five-year period. Generally, the seven-year period begins on and includes the date of contribution. Treas. Reg. § 1.704-4(a)(4)(i).

[64] I.R.C. § 704(c)(1)(B); Treas. Reg. § 1.704-4(a). Generally, the seven-year period begins on and includes the date of contribution. Treas. Reg. § 1.704-4(a)(4)(i).

[65] Treas. Reg. § 1.704-4(b).

[66] I.R.C. Section 737 applies to distributions on or after June 25, 1992. The seven-year period applies to property contributed after June 8, 1997. Property contributed before that date is subject to a five-year period.

[67] *See* Senate Finance Committee, Technical Explanation of Revenue Act of 1992, p. 104.

[68] I.R.C. § 732(f) (enacted in the Tax Relief Extension Act of 1999). The statute generally applies to distributions after July 14, 1999. However, under a grandfather rule, it does not apply to a distribution before July 1, 2001, if the distributee partner owned an interest in the partnership as of July 14, 1999. H.R. Conf. Rep. No. 106-478 (1999).

distribute stock of a controlled corporation instead of the assets.

The statute applies if, after the distribution, the corporate partner owns 80% of the distributed corporation's stock.[69] Generally, the distributed corporation reduces the basis of its assets by the difference between

(1)   the partnership's basis in the distributed corporation's stock immediately before the distribution, and

(2)   the corporate partner's basis in that stock immediately after the distribution.[70]

However, the amount of the basis reduction cannot exceed either

(1)   the difference between the corporate partner's basis in the distributed stock and the distributed corporation's basis in its assets,[71] or

(2)   the adjusted basis of the distributed corporation's property.[72] The corporate partner recognizes gain to the extent that the basis reduction exceeds the distributed corporation's basis in its assets.[73]

Under an anti-abuse provision, the statute may apply if the corporate partner does not control the distributed corporation immediately after the distribution but later acquires such control.[74] This may occur, for example, if a partnership distributes stock to two non-controlling corporate partners and the two corporate partners subsequently merge. The Treasury Department is authorized to issue regulations to prevent the use of tiered partnerships to avoid the I.R.C. Section 732(f) rules.

§ 8.03   CURRENT (NONLIQUIDATING) DISTRIBUTIONS

A partner does not recognize gain or loss when a partnership distributes money or property to him unless the amount of money he receives exceeds the basis in his partnership interest according to I.R.C. Section 731(a)(1). The distribution is treated as a return of the partner's investment in the partnership which results in a decrease in the basis of his partnership interest that reflects the withdrawal.[75] The partner's basis is decreased by the amount of money distributed plus the partnership's basis in any other distributed property; however, a partner's basis cannot be reduced below zero.

---

[69] Whether a corporate partner has control of a distributed corporation for purposes of I.R.C. Section 732(f) is determined by applying the special aggregate stock ownership rules of Treas. Reg. § 1.1502-34. Treas. Reg. §§ 1.732-3, 1.1502-34. These rules apply on a nonelective basis to distributions after June 30, 2001, and on an elective basis to distributions after December 17, 1999.

[70] I.R.C. § 732(f)(1)(C).

[71] I.R.C. § 732(f)(3)(A).

[72] I.R.C. § 732(f)(3)(B).

[73] I.R.C. § 732(f)(4)(A).

[74] I.R.C. § 732(f)(6).

[75] I.R.C. § 733.

A partner's basis in property he receives in a distribution is the same as the partnership's basis for the property before the distribution according to I.R.C. Section 732. However, a partner's total basis in property received in a single distribution cannot exceed the basis of his partnership interest at that time. If cash and property are distributed at the same time, the partner first decreases his basis by the amount of money he receives. These rules ensure that any gain or loss the distributee partner does not recognize when he receives a property distribution is recognized when he later disposes of the property.

[A] Money Distribution

The only exception to the nonrecognition rule for current distributions applies if the amount of money (including marketable securities)[76] the partner receives exceeds the basis in his partnership interest immediately before the distribution.[77] The partner recognizes a gain equal to the excess cash he receives, even if the distribution creates a deficit in the partner's capital account which he is obligated to restore when his partnership interest is liquidated.[78] The partner's gain is considered to arise from a sale of his partnership interest, and it is characterized as a capital gain under I.R.C. Section 741. However, a distribution that changes the partner's share of unrealized receivables or inventory may be taxable as ordinary income under the partial-sale rules of I.R.C. Section 751(b).

> **Example:** Tom receives a $12,000 cash distribution when the basis in his interest in the ST Partnership is $10,000. The distribution does not change Tom's proportionate share of I.R.C. Section 751 property (*i.e.*, unrealized receivables or substantially appreciated inventory). Tom recognizes a $2,000 capital gain on the transaction, and the basis of his partnership interest is reduced to zero.
>
> If Tom's basis in his partnership interest was $13,000 before the distribution, he would recognize no gain, and the basis of his interest after the distribution would decrease to $1,000.

The source of the funds a partner receives from the partnership are irrelevant when applying the distribution rules. Thus, a partner may be taxable on a cash distribution that exceeds the basis of his partnership interest, even if the partnership's property consists solely of tax-exempt securities. Similarly, a distribution may be deemed to occur even if the distributed funds were not includable in the partnership's income before the distribution. In *Helmer v. Commissioner*,[79] for example, partners were taxable on a cash distribution attributable to a payment the partnership received for granting an option, even though the partnership was not taxable on the payment until the option was exercised at a later date. Similarly, in Revenue Ruling 81-241,[80] payments to partners were considered taxable distributions, even though the source of the partnership's funds were progress payments

---

[76] I.R.C. § 731(c). *See* § 8.02[A], *supra*.

[77] I.R.C. § 731(a)(1).

[78] Rev. Rul. 73-301, 1973-2 C.B. 215.

[79] T.C. Memo. 1975-160.

[80] 1981-2 C.B. 146 (*rev'g* Rev. Rul. 73-300, 1973-2 C.B. 215); TAM 8648076.

that were not taxable to the partnership until a later year.

[B]   Advances or Draws Against a Partner's Expected Distributive Share

It often is convenient for partners to receive funds from the partnership at intervals during the year as advances or draws against the distributive share of partnership income they expect at the end of the year. Under the general rule of I.R.C. Section 705(a), a partner's basis in his partnership interest does not increase as the partnership earns income; it only increases at the end of the year by the amount of the partner's distributive share of partnership income for the entire year.[81] The regulations indicate, similarly, that an advance or draw is not considered a distribution on the date it is received; it is treated as a current distribution on the last day of the partnership's tax year.[82] This rule increases the partner's basis in his partnership interest at the time of the distribution by his distributive share of partnership income for the year,[83] allowing the partner to receive cash advances or draws without being taxed on distributions, even if a withdrawal temporarily exceeds the basis in his partnership interest.

A payment to a partner is considered an advance or draw, however, only if the partner is unconditionally obligated to repay amounts that exceed his distributive share of income for the year. This repayment obligation generally should appear in the partnership agreement. However, including this provision in the agreement is not determinative if the actual conduct of the parties indicates that no bona fide obligation was intended.[84] Amounts received by a partner that are not chargeable against his share of expected profits are taxable as guaranteed payments rather than distributions, if they represent payments for services or capital the partner provides to the partnership.[85]

> **Example:** George's basis in his partnership interest at the beginning of the partnership taxable year is $3,000. George withdraws $3,000 each month during the year as an advance against his expected share of partnership income, and he is obligated to repay any excess withdrawals within 30 days of the year end. George's distributive share of partnership income for Year 1 is $40,000, which increases the year-end basis in his partnership interest to $43,000. Because the $3,000 monthly draw is deemed to be a $36,000 cash distribution on the last day of the year, George's year-end basis in his interest is $7,000:

---

[81] Treas. Reg. § 1.705-1(a)(1). The only exception is if the partner's entire interest has been sold or liquidated during the year, in which case his basis increases by his share of income up to the time of the sale or liquidation.

[82] *See* Treas. Reg. § 1.731-1(a)(1)(ii).

[83] I.R.C. § 705(a).

[84] Mangham v. Comm'r, T.C. Memo. 1980-280.

[85] Lynch v. Comm'r, T.C. Memo. 1982-305; Clark v. Comm'r, T.C. Memo. 1982-401.

George's basis in the partnership at the beginning of the year	$3,000
Add: Year 1 distributive share of income	40,000
Less: $3,000 monthly draw * 12 months	(36,000)
George's year-end basis in the Partnership	$7,000

If George has no repayment obligation, the withdrawals are treated as distributions rather than as advances. The basis in George's partnership interest is reduced to zero by the first $3,000 distribution he receives, and the remaining monthly distributions ($33,000) would be taxable under I.R.C. Section 731(a) as cash distributions in excess of his basis. At the end of Year 1, the basis of George's partnership interest increases to $40,000, his distributive share of the year's income.

If the payments George receives are interest on his capital contribution and are not charged against his capital account, they are characterized as guaranteed payments. George reports these payments as ordinary income, and the partnership may deduct them in computing its ordinary income.

[C]   Property Distribution

A partner does not recognize gain or loss when he receives a current distribution of partnership property, according to I.R.C. Section 731(a)(1), even if the value of the property exceeds the basis in his partnership interest.[86] Under I.R.C. Section 733, the partner's basis in his partnership interest decreases by the partnership's basis in the distributed property, but never decreases below zero.

I.R.C. Section 732 provides basis rules to ensure that any gain or loss the partner does not recognize when property is distributed is recognized when he subsequently disposes of the property. The general rule for a nonliquidating distribution is that a partner's basis in distributed property is the same as the partnership's basis for the asset immediately before the distribution.[87] If the partnership's basis in the distributed property exceeds the partner's basis in his partnership interest, an exception applies:[88] the partner's basis in the distributed property is limited to the basis in his interest before the distribution.

> **Example (1):** Dana's basis in his interest in the DE Partnership is $15,000. DE distributes property to Dana worth $20,000; the partnership's basis in the property is $12,000. Dana recognizes no gain on the distribution, and the basis in his partnership interest decreases to $3,000 (Dana's $15,000 basis in DE - $12,000 DE's basis in the property). Dana's basis for the distributed property is $12,000 — the same as the partnership's basis.

> **Example (2):** Assume the same facts as in Example (1), except that DE's basis in the property distributed to Dana is $16,000. Dana's basis in the property is limited to his $15,000 basis in his partnership interest. After the

---

[86] I.R.C. § 731(a).

[87] I.R.C. § 732(a).

[88] I.R.C. § 732(a)(2).

distribution, Dana's basis in his partnership interest is zero.

DE appears to lose $1,000 of basis in the transaction: DE's basis for the property was $16,000 before the distribution; Dana's basis is $15,000 after the distribution. The basis reduction means that Dana will recognize $1,000 more gain on a sale of the property than DE would. The effect of the basis reduction is mitigated, however, if the partnership has an I.R.C. Section 754 basis-adjustment election in effect when the distribution occurs. The election allows the partnership to increase the basis of its similar assets by the $1,000 basis "lost" as a result of the distribution.[89] (*See* § 8.07, *infra.*)

Allocation of basis among distributed properties. As noted above, a partner's basis in distributed property cannot exceed the basis in his partnership interest immediately before the distribution, reduced by the amount of cash distributed in the same transaction. If this basis limitation applies to a distribution in which a partner receives more than one asset, the partner must allocate his basis among the distributed properties. Under I.R.C. Section 732(c), the partner's basis must be allocated as follows:

(1)   ***Unrealized receivables and inventory.*** Basis first is allocated to distributed unrealized receivables and inventory up to the partnership's basis in these items.[90] If the partnership's basis in these items exceeds the partner's basis in his partnership interest, the difference results in a basis decrease. The method for allocating a basis decrease among assets distributed in the same transaction is described in paragraph (3) below.

(2)   ***Other distributed assets.*** Any remaining basis not allocated to unrealized receivables and inventory is then allocated among other distributed properties up to their basis in the partnership. If the partnership's basis in these items exceeds the partner's remaining basis in his partnership interest, the difference is a basis decrease that is allocated under the method described in the next paragraph.

(3)   ***Allocation of basis decrease.*** Any basis decrease (*i.e.*, excess of the partnership's basis in the distributed assets over the distributee partner's basis in his partnership interest) is allocated in proportion to the unrealized depreciation in each property (but only up to the amount of unrealized depreciation for each property).[91] Any remaining basis decrease is allocated to these properties in proportion to their adjusted bases (after determining the decreases to depreciated property).[92]

Example: Edward's basis for his interest in the DE Partnership is $4,000 at the time he receives a current distribution of the following items:

---

[89]   I.R.C. §§ 754, 734.

[90]   I.R.C. § 732(c)(1)(A); Treas. Reg. § 1.732-1(c)(1). Unrealized receivables and inventory are defined in I.R.C. Sections 751(c) and 751(d)(2), respectively.

[91]   I.R.C. § 732(c)(3)(A), as amended by the Taxpayer Relief Act of 1997; Treas. Reg. § 1.732-1(c)(2).

[92]   I.R.C. § 732(c)(3)(B); Treas. Reg. § 1.732-1(c)(2).

Asset	Partnership's Basis	Fair Market Value
Capital Asset A	3,000	3,000
Capital Asset B	3,000	1,000

Because the partnership's basis for the distributed properties totals $6,000 and Edward's basis is only $4,000, a $2,000 basis decrease must be allocated to these assets. Because only Capital Asset B has any unrealized depreciation, the entire $2,000 decrease is allocated to Capital Asset B, reducing Edward's basis for that asset to $1,000.

[D]   Money and Property Distribution

A partner who receives money and other property in a single distribution must reduce the basis in his partnership interest by the amount of money he receives before the basis of the other property is determined.[93] The remaining basis is then allocated among the other distributed properties. If the amount of money distributed exceeds the partner's basis, the partner's recognized gain is the excess amount. The distribution of money reduces the partner's basis in his interest to zero; therefore, his basis in the other distributed property also is zero.

Example (1): Sara's basis in her interest in the ST Partnership is $50,000 at the time she receives a current distribution of $40,000 cash and realty worth $15,000; ST's basis in the realty is $8,000. Sara recognizes no gain on the cash she receives because it does not exceed her basis in her partnership interest. Sara's basis in the realty is $8,000, the same as the partnership's basis in the property, and her basis in her partnership interest decreases to $2,000, calculated as follows:

Sara's basis in the partnership before the distribution	$50,000
Less cash distributed	(40,000)
Partnership's basis in distributed realty	(8,000)
Sara's basis in the partnership after the distribution	$2,000

Example (2): Assume the same facts as in Example (1), except that Sara's basis in her partnership interest before the distribution is $45,000. Sara still does not recognize gain. The cash distribution is deemed to decrease the basis in her partnership interest to $5,000 before she receives the realty. Therefore, Sara's basis in the realty is limited to $5,000, and the basis in her partnership interest decreases to zero, calculated as follows:

---

[93] Treas. Reg. § 1.731-1(a)(1)(i). *See also* Treas. Reg. § 1.732-1(a). Money may include marketable securities. I.R.C. § 731(c).

Sara's basis in the partnership before the distribution	$50,000
Less cash distributed	(45,000)
Balance available to allocate to the realty	$5,000
Less Sara's basis in the distributed realty	(5,000)
Sara's basis in the partnership after the distribution	$-0-

Example (3): Assume that Sara's basis in her partnership interest is $50,000 when she receives a current distribution of the following items:

Asset	Partnership's Basis
Cash	$35,000
Inventory	$25,000
Capital Asset A	10,000
Capital Asset B	20,000
Total distributed	$90,000

Sara recognizes no gain on the distribution because the $35,000 cash distribution does not exceed her $50,000 basis in her partnership interest. The distribution is allocated as follows:

Sara's basis in her partnership interest before the distribution	$50,000
Less cash distribution	(35,000)
Balance to be allocated	$15,000
Sara's basis for inventory	(15,000)
Sara's basis for:	
Capital Asset A	$-0-
Capital Asset B	$-0-

[E]   Special Basis in Distributed Property Under I.R.C. Section 732(d)

I.R.C. Section 732(d) provides special rules for determining the basis in property distributed to a partner who acquires his partnership interest by sale or exchange or as successor to a deceased partner when the partnership did not have an I.R.C. Section 754 election in effect. A distributee partner may elect under I.R.C. Section 732(d) to determine his basis in property the partnership distributes to him within two years of the date he acquired his interest as if the partnership had an I.R.C. Section 754 election in effect on the acquisition date.[94] (For discussion of tax consequences of an election under I.R.C. Section 754, see § 8.07, *infra.*)

A partner who acquires any part of his interest by transfer may be required to determine his basis in distributed property under the rules of I.R.C. Section 732(d), regardless of when the distribution is made (*i.e.*, the two-year limitation

---

[94] I.R.C. § 732(d).

does not apply), if at the time the partner acquires his partnership interest:

  (1)   the fair market value of all partnership property (other than money) exceeds 110 percent of its basis to the partnership;

  (2)   a hypothetical liquidation of the transferee-partner's interest immediately after the transfer would shift basis from property for which no depreciation, depletion, or amortization deduction is allowed to property for which these deductions are permitted; and

  (3)   a basis adjustment at the time of the transfer would change the basis of the property actually distributed to the transferee partner.[95] The mandatory basis-adjustment rules apply to current and liquidating distributions.[96]

A partnership is required to provide a transferee partner with any information necessary to compute the basis adjustments required under I.R.C. Section 732(d) if (1) the transferee partner notifies the partnership that it plans to make the Section 732(d) election or (2) if a partnership makes a distribution that triggers a mandatory basis adjustment under that section.[97]

[F] Partnership Tax Consequences

A partnership does not recognize gain or loss on a distribution of money or other property according to I.R.C. Section 731(b). However, a current distribution may result in tax consequences to the partnership:

  (1)   A distribution that changes a partner's proportionate share of partnership unrealized receivables or substantially appreciated inventory is subject to the partial-sale rules of I.R.C. Section 751(b). The transaction is treated as if the partner received a distribution of his proportionate share of these assets and then either sold a portion of them back to the partnership or purchased a portion of them from the partnership. This deemed sale or purchase will change the partnership's basis in its undistributed assets.

  (2)   A distribution may affect the basis of the partnership's undistributed assets if the partnership has an I.R.C. Section 754 basis-adjustment election in effect —

      (a)   If the distributee-partner recognizes gain on a distribution of money that exceeds the basis of his partnership interest,[98] the partnership increases the basis in its capital assets and I.R.C. Section 1231 trade or business property by the amount of gain the partner recognizes.[99]

---

[95] Treas. Reg. § 1.732-1(d)(4).

[96] Treas. Reg. § 1.732-1(d)(4), *Examples (1), (2)*.

[97] Treas. Reg. § 1.732-1(d)(5).

[98] I.R.C. § 734.

[99] I.R.C. § 734(b)(1)(A); Treas. Reg. § 1.755-1(c).

(b) If the partnership's basis in distributed property exceeds the distributee-partner's basis in his partnership interest,[100] the partner's total basis in all the property he receives will be less than the partnership's total basis in the distributed assets before the distribution. After the distribution, the partnership increases the basis of its undistributed assets by the amount that the basis of the distributed property decreased as a result of the distribution.

The increases to the bases of the undistributed property are allocated among the partnership's assets according to the rules of I.R.C. Section 755. (See discussion in § 8.07, *infra.*)

§ 8.04 LIQUIDATING DISTRIBUTIONS

A distribution — or one of a series of distributions — that terminates a partner's interest in a partnership is called a liquidating distribution.[101] When a partner receives a liquidating distribution of money or other property, under the general rule of I.R.C. Section 731(a)(1), he does not recognize gain or loss. This nonrecognition rule is subject to two important exceptions: (1) a partner recognizes gain if the amount of money distributed to him exceeds the basis in his partnership interest,[102] and (2) a partner may recognize a loss on a distribution that consists only of money, unrealized receivables, and inventory.[103]

Liquidating payments classified under I.R.C. Section 736. I.R.C. Section 736 provides special rules for classifying payments a partnership makes to liquidate the interest of a retiring partner or a deceased partner's successor in interest. These rules are fully discussed and illustrated in Chapter 10. The following summary of the I.R.C. Section 736 describes how the classification and distribution rules interact.

I.R.C. Section 736 divides each liquidating payment into two classes: (1) the portion that is a distribution for the partner's share of partnership property, and (2) the remaining amount of the payment. The statute only classifies the payments — it does not provide rules for determining the tax consequences of each class. Once the amount of the distribution portion is determined, that amount is taxable under the rules governing liquidating distributions.[104] The treatment of the remaining portion depends upon how the parties determine the amount the partner will receive: if the amount is computed as a percentage of partnership income, the payment is included in the partner's distributive share of partnership income;[105] if the amount is fixed, the payment is treated as a guaranteed payment.[106]

---

[100] I.R.C. § 734.

[101] I.R.C. § 761(d).

[102] I.R.C. § 731(a)(1). Money may include marketable securities under I.R.C. § 731(c).

[103] I.R.C. § 731(a)(2). Unrealized receivables are defined in I.R.C. § 751(c) and inventory is defined in I.R.C. § 751(d)(2).

[104] I.R.C. §§ 731, 732, 733, 751(b).

[105] I.R.C. § 702.

[106] I.R.C. § 707(c).

For a general partner in a partnership in which capital is not a material income producing factor (*e.g.*, services partnerships), unrealized receivables are not considered partnership property under I.R.C. Section 736 and thus, amounts paid to liquidate a partner's interest in partnership receivables are not treated as distributions. Payments for a general partner's share of partnership goodwill in such a partnership also are not treated as distributions unless the partnership agreement specifically requires payment for a withdrawing partner's share of goodwill.

I.R.C. Section 736 only applies to payments made by a continuing partnership to a withdrawing partner.[107] Thus, I.R.C. Section 736 does not apply to distributions related to the complete liquidation of a partnership nor to distributions that partially liquidate a partner's interest.[108]

> **Example:** The CDE services partnership pays retiring partner Dorothy $36,000 in cash to liquidate her one-third interest in the partnership. Immediately before the distribution, the partners agree on the following values for the partnership's assets:

	CDE's Basis	Dorothy's Basis
Unrealized accounts receivable	$30,000	$10,000
Capital assets	18,000	6,000
Cash	60,000	20,000
Total	$108,000	$36,000

> Because $26,000 of the payment to Dorothy is in exchange for her interest in partnership property (*i.e.*, the capital assets and cash), that amount is treated as a liquidating distribution. The remaining $10,000 of the payment for her share of unrealized receivables is not a distribution; it is a guaranteed payment because it is a fixed amount. For discussion of tax treatment of guaranteed payments (*see* Chapter 7).

[A] Recognizing Gain on Money Distribution

A partner recognizes gain to the extent that the amount of money distributed to him exceeds the basis in his partnership interest immediately before the distribution according to I.R.C. Section 731(a)(1).[109] If the liquidating distribution includes money and other property, the partner is deemed to receive the money first.[110] Any recognized gain is characterized as capital gain under I.R.C. Section 741, unless the distribution changes the partner's share of unrealized receivables or inventory, in which case it is subject to the partial-sale rules of I.R.C. Section 751(b).

> **Example:** The LMN Partnership distributes $60,000 in cash to Morris to liquidate his partnership interest. The payment does not exceed the value

---

[107] Treas. Reg. § 1.736-1(a)(2) refers to a retiring partner or the successor in interest to a deceased partner as the "withdrawing partner."

[108] Treas. Reg. § 1.736-1(a)(1)(i).

[109] Money may include marketable securities under I.R.C. § 731(c).

[110] Treas. Reg. § 1.731-1(a)(1).

of Morris's interest in partnership property, and it is not a disproportionate distribution for I.R.C. Section 751 property (*i.e.*, accounts receivable and substantially appreciated inventory). Immediately before the distribution, Morris's basis in his partnership interest is $50,000. Therefore, Morris recognizes a $10,000 capital gain, the amount that the distribution exceeds his basis in his partnership interest.

Assume the same facts except that in addition to the $60,000 in cash, Morris receives land worth $20,000 from the partnership. Because the money is deemed distributed first, Morris recognizes the same $10,000 capital gain he recognized in Example (1) — the amount that the $60,000 cash distribution exceeds his $50,000 basis in his partnership interest. Morris does not recognize a gain on the distribution of the land; his basis in the land is zero, and he will only have a gain when he sells or disposes of the property.

[B] Recognizing Loss on Liquidating Distributions

Under I.R.C. Section 731(a)(2), a partner recognizes a loss on a liquidating distribution if (1) the only assets he receives are money, unrealized receivables, and inventory, and (2) the basis in his partnership interest exceeds the amount of money he receives plus the partnership's basis in any distributed unrealized receivables.[111] The loss is characterized as a capital loss under I.R.C. Section 741, unless the distribution changes the partner's share of unrealized receivables or substantially appreciated inventory, and it is, therefore, subject to the partial-sale rules of I.R.C. Section 751(b).

The loss-recognition rule of I.R.C. Section 731(a)(2) applies when any inventory is distributed — not only when the distribution consists of "substantially appreciated" inventory subject to the I.R.C. Section 751(b) partial-sale rules.

Example (1): The MNO Partnership distributes $50,000 in cash to Nora to liquidate her partnership interest. The payment does not exceed the value of Nora's interest in partnership property, and it is not a disproportionate distribution of I.R.C. Section 751 property. Immediately before the distribution, Nora's basis in her partnership interest is $60,000. Because Nora receives only cash, she recognizes a $10,000 capital loss ($60,000 basis - $50,000 cash distribution).

Example (2): Assume the same facts as in Example (1), except that Nora receives the following distribution:

Asset	Value	MNO's Basis
Cash	$40,000	$40,000
Inventory	30,000	10,000
Total	$70,000	$50,000

Nora's basis in her partnership interest, $60,000, exceeds the $50,000

---

[111] Unrealized receivables are defined in I.R.C. § 751(c) to include unpaid amounts for goods or services as well as the ordinary income recapture potential in partnership property or inventory. Inventory is defined in I.R.C. § 751(d)(2).

sum of (1) the $40,000 in cash, and (2) the partnership's $10,000 basis in the inventory she receives. Therefore, Nora recognizes a $10,000 capital loss on the liquidation.

The previous example illustrates the purpose for the loss-recognition rule of I.R.C. Section 731(b): to ensure that a partner who receives a distribution of receivables and inventory recognizes the same amount of ordinary income that the partnership would recognize on a disposition of that property. Nora recognizes a tax loss on the distribution even though the $70,000 value of the distributed property exceeds her $60,000 investment in the partnership and she has not sustained an economic loss. However, Nora's basis in the inventory after the distribution is $10,000, the same as the partnership's basis. Therefore, if she later sells the inventory for its value, $30,000, she will recognize $20,000 of ordinary income. The net result to Nora, $20,000 of ordinary income and a $10,000 capital loss, appropriately reflects the $10,000 economic gain Nora realized in the liquidation and preserves the ordinary character of that gain for tax purposes.

[C] Determining and Reporting Gain or Loss on a Series of Liquidating Distributions

A partner's interest is frequently liquidated by a series of cash payments from the partnership paid over a period of time. A partner's interest is not considered liquidated until he receives the final distribution, even if the payment period spans more than one tax year.[112] Nevertheless, the tax consequences of each liquidating distribution generally must be determined when the distribution is made, rather than when the final distribution occurs. The time when a partner must report his gain or loss from a series of liquidating distributions depends on whether the total amount he will receive is fixed at the outset or contingent on the partnership's income during the period when the payments are made.

The rules for determining the treatment of a series of liquidating payments are fully discussed and illustrated in Chapter 10.

[D] Property Distribution

No gain is recognized when a partner receives a liquidating distribution of property other than money, even if the value of the property exceeds the basis of his partnership interest.[113] However, I.R.C. Section 732(b) provides basis rules that ensure that any gain the partner does not recognize when the distribution occurs is recognized when he subsequently disposes of the property. A partner recognizes a loss on a liquidating distribution only if the property he receives consists solely of cash, unrealized receivables, and inventory.

A partner's total basis in all the property he receives in a liquidating distribution equals the basis of his partnership interest immediately before the distribution, according to a general rule under I.R.C. Section 732(b). If the liquidating distribution consists of both money and other property, the partner decreases the

---

[112] Treas. Reg. § 1.761-1(d).

[113] I.R.C. § 731(a)(1).

basis of his interest by the amount of money he receives before determining his basis in the distributed property.

Under the I.R.C. Section 732(b) general rule, a partner's basis in distributed property can be more or less than the partnership's basis for the item before the distribution. However, an important exception may apply to this rule. Under I.R.C. Section 732(c)(1), a partner's basis in distributed unrealized receivables and inventory cannot exceed the partnership's basis in these items. Consequently, a partner who receives only cash, inventory, and receivables in a liquidating distribution may not be able to apply the entire basis of his partnership interest to these items. The partner is allowed a current loss deduction to the extent that the basis of his partnership interest exceeds the partnership's basis for the receivables and inventory plus the amount of distributed cash.

Examples:

(1) The STU Partnership distributes a parcel of realty to Terry to liquidate his partnership interest. The property is worth $50,000 and has a basis to STU of $10,000. Terry's basis in his partnership interest is $30,000. The transaction does not result in a disproportionate distribution of I.R.C. Section 751 property. If the realty is not partnership inventory, Terry recognizes no gain or loss on the distribution, and his basis in the realty is $30,000, the same as the basis in his partnership interest.

(2) Assume that the realty is considered partnership inventory. Terry's basis in the property is limited to $10,000, the partnership's basis in the inventory, but he recognizes a $20,000 capital loss — the amount by which the basis of his partnership interest ($30,000) exceeds the partnership's basis in the distributed inventory.

(3) Assume that the realty is not inventory and that Terry receives a $10,000 cash distribution in addition to the realty. The cash reduces the basis of Terry's partnership interest to $20,000 ($30,000 - $10,000), and therefore Terry's basis in the realty is also $20,000.

(4) Assume that Terry receives $40,000 in cash in addition to the realty. The cash distribution reduces Terry's basis in his interest to zero and he recognizes $10,000 of capital gain, i.e., the amount by which the cash distribution exceeds his $30,000 basis. Terry's basis in the realty is zero.

A distributee partner's holding period for distributed property includes the partnership's holding period.[114] The partnership's holding period for the property may include the holding period of the partner who contributed it to the partnership and, therefore, the distributee's holding period will also include the contributing partner's holding period.[115]

---

[114] I.R.C. § 735(b).

[115] Treas. Reg. § 1.735-1(b).

[E]   Allocating Basis to Distributed Property

A partner's total basis in all property he receives in a liquidating distribution is computed by reducing the basis of his partnership interest immediately before the distribution (or series of distributions) by any money he receives. The balance is allocated among the other distributed assets as follows:

(1)   The first basis allocation is to distributed unrealized receivables and inventory.[116] The amount allocated to each of these items, however, cannot exceed the partnership's basis for the asset before the distribution. If the amount the partner has available for allocation is less than the partnership's basis in the distributed unrealized receivables and inventory, the basis decrease is allocated among these items under the method described in paragraph (3) below.[117]

(2)   *Any basis remaining after the basis allocation for unrealized receivables and inventory is allocated among the other property distributed to the partner.* If the remaining basis is less than the partnership's total basis for the distributed properties, the basis decrease is allocated under the method described in paragraph (3) below.[118] If the remaining basis is greater than the partnership's total basis for the distributed properties, the basis increase is allocated under the method described in paragraph (4) below. The partner's basis in these assets can be more or less than the partnership's basis.

(3)   *Allocating basis decrease.* Any basis decrease is first allocated to distributed properties having unrealized depreciation (*i.e.*, a value lower than the partnership's basis) in proportion to their amounts of unrealized depreciation (but no more than the depreciation for any property). Any remaining basis decrease is allocated among the properties in proportion to their respective bases (taking into account any prior decrease).

(4)   *Allocating basis increase.* Any basis increase is first allocated to properties having unrealized appreciation (*i.e.*, a value higher than the partnership's basis) in proportion to their amounts of unrealized appreciation (but no more than the appreciation for any property). Any remaining basis increase is allocated among the properties in proportion to their fair market values.

Example (1): [119] Kevin is a member of the KLM Limited Liability Company. The basis for his LLC interest is $6,500. To liquidate Kevin's interest, the LLC distributes inventory items and Assets X and Y to him. Before the distribution the inventory has a value of $2,000 and a basis of $1,000; Asset X has value of $4,000 and a basis of $500; and Asset Y has a value and basis of $1,000.

---

[116]   I.R.C. § 732(b)(1).

[117]   Treas. Reg. § 1.732(c). Unrealized receivables are defined in I.R.C. Section 751(c) and inventory is defined in I.R.C. Section 751(d)(2).

[118]   I.R.C. § 732(c)(2), (3); Treas. Reg. § 1.732(c).

[119]   Treas. Reg. § 1.732-1(c)(4), *Example.*

Because the LLC's total basis for the distributed property is $2,500 and the basis for Kevin's interest is $6,500, Kevin obtains a basis increase of $4,000. This basis increase is applied to the distributed property as follows:

- Basis first is allocated to the inventory items in an amount equal to their basis to the LLC. Accordingly, Kevin's basis in the inventory items is $1,000.

- Each of the other assets then is allocated an amount of basis equal to its basis to the LLC. Asset X is allocated $500 and Asset Y is allocated $1,000.

- Each asset with unrealized appreciation then is allocated additional basis up to the amount of such appreciation. Accordingly, the basis of Asset X increases by $3,500 (to $4,000).

- The remaining $500 of basis is allocated to Assets X and Y in proportion to their fair market values: $400 to Asset X (400/500 x $500), and $100 to Asset Y (100/500 x $500). Therefore, after the distribution, Kevin's basis for Asset X is $4,400 and his basis for Asset Y is $1,100.

Example (2): Assume that Kevin's basis for his LLC interest is $2,000 and his liquidating distribution consists of Asset X having a value and basis of $1,500 and Asset Y having a value of $500 and a basis of $1,500 (neither asset is inventory or unrealized receivables). Because total basis of the distributed property is $3,000 and the basis for Kevin's interest is $2,000, a $1,000 decrease in the basis of the distributed property is required.

- Each asset is allocated an amount of basis equal to its basis to the LLC. Thus, Asset X and Asset Y each are allocated $1,500 of basis.

- Because Asset Y is the only property with unrealized depreciation ($500 value - $1,500 basis in the LLC), the entire $1,000 basis decrease is allocated to that asset. After the distribution, Kevin's basis for Asset X is $1,500 and his basis for Asset Y is $500.

The basis allocation rules also apply to property subject to potential depreciation recapture under a variety of Code sections.[120] A distribution of partnership recapture property is treated as if the amount of potential recapture (the amount that would be ordinary income if the property were sold at fair market value) is a separate, zero-basis, unrealized receivable (see discussion of I.R.C. Section 751(c) at § 8.05[A], [B], *infra*). The following example illustrates how basis allocations are made under I.R.C. Section 732(c) when recapture property is distributed:

Example (3): [121] Arthur, Carole and Dan are equal partners in the ACD Partnership. ACD owns three capital assets each with a basis and value of $20,000. The partnership also owns three items of depreciable equipment each with a basis of $5,000 and value of $30,000. Each item of equipment would have $25,000 of depreciation recapture if sold by the partnership for its $30,000 value.

---

[120] I.R.C. § 751(c)(2).

[121] This example is adapted from the Joint Committee on Taxation, General Explanation of Tax Legislation Enacted in 1998, p. 441. *See* Treas. Reg. § 1.732-1(c)(4).

One capital asset and one item of equipment is distributed to Arthur in liquidation of his interest. When the liquidation occurs, Arthur's basis in his partnership interest is $60,000. Arthur is deemed to receive a distribution of three assets:

(1)   depreciation recapture (an unrealized receivable) with a zero basis to the partnership and a $25,000 value;

(2)   an item of equipment with a $5,000 basis and value to the partnership ($30,000 value less $25,000 of depreciation recapture); and

(3)   a capital asset with a $20,000 basis and value to the partnership.

Arthur's $60,000 basis in his partnership interest is allocated as follows:

(1)   Zero basis (the partnership's basis) is allocated to the depreciation recapture.[122]

(2)   Basis is then allocated to each other distributed property up to its basis to the partnership:

    (a) $5,000 to the equipment (not including the depreciation recapture); and

    (b) $20,000 to the capital asset.

       (Note that $35,000 of remaining basis would be allocated among properties (other than inventory and unrealized receivables) with unrealized appreciation in proportion to their respective amounts of unrealized appreciation if either property had unrealized appreciation.)

(2)   Arthur's remaining $35,000 of basis is allocated in proportion to the values of the distributed properties ($5,000 for the equipment and $20,000 for the capital asset):

    (a) $7,000 is allocated to the equipment — resulting in a total basis to Arthur of $12,000; and

    (b) $28,000 is allocated to the capital asset — resulting in a total basis to Arthur of $48,000.

§ 8.05   CHARACTERIZING PARTNER'S GAIN OR LOSS ON DISPOSITION OF DISTRIBUTED PROPERTY

The character of the gain or loss a partner recognizes when he disposes of property received in a distribution generally depends on the nature of the property in his hands at the time of the disposition. Thus, a partner recognizes capital gain or loss on a sale of distributed property he holds as a capital asset even if it was not a capital asset for the partnership, and a partner recognizes ordinary income on a sale of distributed property that is inventory in his hands even if it was not inventory for the partnership.

---

[122]   I.R.C. § 732(c)(1)(A)(i); Treas. Reg. § 1.732-1(c)(4).

Example: The AB Partnership distributes a parcel of real estate to one of its partners, Albert. The partnership held the real estate as investment property. However, because Albert is a dealer in similar real property, immediately after the distribution, Albert holds the property as inventory and, on its sale, he will recognize ordinary income.

This general characterization rule is subject to three important exceptions:

(1)　Under I.R.C. Section 735(a), a partner recognizes ordinary income when he disposes of distributed property that was an unrealized receivable or inventory item in the partnership when the property was distributed. However, this ordinary-income rule applies to inventory only if the partner sells the property within five years of the distribution. I.R.C. Section 735(a) prevents a partnership from using a distribution of its assets to convert into capital gain the ordinary income it would recognize on a disposition of its receivables or inventory.

(2)　Under a variety of recapture rules (*i.e.*, depreciation recapture under I.R.C. Sections 1245 and 1250), a partner recognizes ordinary income when he disposes of distributed property that was subject to recapture in the partnership. The property retains its recapture potential after the distribution, and the partner reports that amount as ordinary income when he disposes of the property.

(3)　Under I.R.C. Section 168, a partner who receives a distribution of certain cost-recovery property must compute his ACRS deductions as if the property were still owned by the partnership.

[A]　Unrealized Receivables and Inventory

Under I.R.C. Section 735(a)(1), a partner recognizes ordinary income when he disposes of unrealized receivables distributed to him by a partnership, even if the receivables are capital assets in his hands. Unrealized receivables are defined by I.R.C. Section 751(c) to include the partnership's rights to payment for its goods (other than capital assets) and services. Other items defined as unrealized receivables under I.R.C. Section 751(c), such as the ordinary-income recapture potential in distributed property, are not considered unrealized receivables for purposes of the I.R.C. Section 735(a) characterization rule.

Under I.R.C. Section 735(a)(2), a partner recognizes ordinary income or loss when he sells an item that was partnership inventory immediately before the property was distributed to him.[123] Unlike the rule for distributed receivables, however, the ordinary-income taint for inventory applies only if the partner sells the property within five years of the date it is distributed to him. If the sale is within five years, the partner's entire gain or loss is ordinary — including amounts attributable to changes in value occurring after the distribution.

Example: The ST Partnership distributes an inventory item worth $10,000 to Steve. ST's $5,000 basis in the inventory carries over to Steve, but it is a capital asset in his hands. However, if Steve sells the property two years

---

[123] *See* Luckey v. Comm'r, 334 F.2d 719 (9th Cir. 1964).

later for $12,000, he must recognize the entire $7,000 gain as ordinary income.

Inventory includes items defined in I.R.C. Section 752(d)(2) and most property held for sale that is not a capital asset or an asset subject to the rules of I.R.C. Section 1231. When determining whether an item is I.R.C. Section 1231 property in the partnership (*i.e.*, property used in the trade of business and involuntary conversions), the holding-period requirements of I.R.C. Section 1231(b) are not considered.[124] Thus, distributed trade or business assets are not treated as inventory if the property otherwise would be an I.R.C. Section 1231 asset if held by the partnership for the requisite holding period.

The ordinary-income rules of I.R.C. Section 735(a) are not avoided if the partner transfers the distributed unrealized receivable or inventory to another person in a nonrecognition transaction. Under I.R.C. Section 735(c)(2)(A), any substituted-basis property[125] resulting from the nonrecognition transaction[126] is subject to the ordinary-income taint. This taint apparently attaches to the substituted-basis property received by both the transferee and transferor in the nonrecognition transaction.[127]

> **Example (1):** The MN Partnership distributes an inventory item to one of its partners, Mary, in whose hands the item is a capital asset. Mary exchanges this item for a capital asset held by Louis, who is not a partner, in a tax-free, like-kind exchange under I.R.C. Section 1031. Following the exchange, both the asset held by Mary and the asset held by Louis are substituted-basis property. Consequently, a sale of either item by Mary or by Louis within five years of the distribution generates ordinary income or loss.
>
> **Example (2):** Assume the same facts as in Example (1), except that Mary joins a new partnership, MT, and she contributes the distributed item to this new partnership. The transaction is subject to the nonrecognition rule of I.R.C. Section 721. Although the contributed item is a capital asset in MT, and Mary's partnership interest also is a capital asset, the ordinary-income rule applies if either asset is sold within five years of the initial distribution to Mary.

An exception to the substituted-basis property rule applies if the partner exchanges the distributed property for C corporation stock in a nonrecognition transaction under I.R.C. Section 351. The partner does not hold the stock subject to the ordinary-income taint, but the corporation holds the contributed property

---

[124] I.R.C. § 735(c)(1).

[125] Substituted basis property is defined in I.R.C. Section 7701(a)(42) to include property with a basis determined, in whole or part, by reference to the basis of (1) its basis in the hands of the person from whom it is acquired or (2) the basis of property transferred in exchange for it.

[126] I.R.C. Section 7701(a)(45) defines a nonrecognition transaction as any property disposition in which gain or loss is not fully recognized.

[127] Senate Finance Committee, Explanation of Provisions Approved by the Committee on March 21, 1984, S. Rep. No. 98-169 (Vol. I), 98th Cong., 2d Sess. 234 (1984).

subject to the taint.[128]

> **Example (3):** Assume the same facts as in Example (1), except that Mary contributes the item to the new X Corporation for stock as a nontaxable I.R.C. Section 351 exchange. X Corporation recognizes ordinary income if it sells the contributed item within five years of the date the partnership distributed it to Mary. However, Mary recognizes a capital gain whenever she sells her stock in X Corporation.

[B] Recapture Property

Under various provisions of the Code, capital gain realized on a sale of property is "recaptured" as ordinary income to the extent that ordinary deductions for depreciation, depletion, and similar items were previously allowable for the property. A distribution of partnership property with potential recapture income (*i.e.*, the ordinary income the partnership would recapture if it sold the property immediately before the distribution) may have the following tax consequences:

(1) *A distribution of partnership property generally is not considered a disposition that triggers the recapture rules.* Instead, the distributee-partner takes the property subject to the potential recapture in the property. When the partner subsequently sells the property, the gain he recognizes is characterized as ordinary income up to its potential recapture at the time of the distribution. The amount of the potential recapture depends on the specific recapture provisions that are applicable to the property.

(2) *The potential recapture in partnership property is an unrealized receivable under I.R.C. Section 751(b).* If the distribution changes the partner's share of I.R.C. Section 751 property, the distribution is recharacterized as a partial sale between the partner and the partnership and, therefore, ordinary income is recognized. To the extent that this constructive sale is deemed to occur, the transfer of money or property to the partner is not considered a distribution.

§ 8.06 DISPROPORTIONATE DISTRIBUTIONS OF UNREALIZED RECEIVABLES AND INVENTORY

I.R.C. Section 751(b) provides special rules for distributions by partnerships that own ordinary-income property consisting of unrealized receivables and substantially appreciated inventory (*i.e.*, I.R.C. Section 751 property). These rules ensure that a distribution does not convert any partner's share of the ordinary income inherent in these assets into capital gain.[129] The statute applies only if a distribution is "disproportionate," which means that it permanently changes a partner's proportionate share of the value of partnership I.R.C. Section 751 property. A disproportionate distribution occurs:

---

[128] I.R.C. § 735(c)(2)(B).

[129] H.R. Rep. No. 1137, 83d Cong., 2d Sess. 70 (1954); S. Rep. No. 1622, 83d Cong., 2d Sess. 88 (1954).

(1)   if a partner receives more than his share of I.R.C. Section 751 property in exchange for a reduction in his share of other partnership property; or

(2)   if a partner receives less than his share of I.R.C. Section 751 property in exchange for an increased share of other partnership property.[130]

To the extent that either of these hypothetical "exchanges" occurs, the distribution is recharacterized as a taxable sale or exchange between the partner and partnership. I.R.C. Section 751(b) treats the distribution as if it consists of two separate transactions:

(1)   In the first transaction, the partner is deemed to receive a current distribution of his proportionate share of two classes of partnership property: (a) I.R.C. Section 751 property, and (b) other property.

(2)   In the second transaction, the partner is considered to exchange property of one class that was deemed distributed to him for an increased portion of the property of the other class that he actually received.[131]

The exchange is considered to occur immediately after the deemed distribution, and all the tax consequences of that hypothetical transaction are determined at that time.[132]

Possible tax consequences of this hypothetical transaction include:

- Recognition of gain or loss to the extent that the partner or partnership is deemed to exchange appreciated or depreciated property. The character of the gain or loss is determined as if the partner actually received a distribution of the property he is deemed to exchange with the partnership. For example, a partner deemed to receive a distribution of partnership inventory or receivables recognizes ordinary income on a hypothetical sale of that property to the partnership, even if the property would not constitute inventory or receivables in the partner's hands under I.R.C. Section 735(a).

- Any property deemed acquired by the partner or partnership in the exchange obtains a tax basis equal to its hypothetical cost.

- The holding period of property deemed acquired in the exchange begins on the date that the I.R.C. Section 751(b) transaction occurs.[133]

The effect of I.R.C. Section 751(b) on a distribution is illustrated below:

Example: The CDE Partnership liquidates Carol's entire one-third partnership interest. When the partnership distributes Carol's liquidating share of the assets, her basis for her partnership interest is $10,000. Immediately before the distribution, CDE owns the following assets:

---

[130] I.R.C. § 751(b); Treas. Reg. § 1.751-1(b)(1)(i).

[131] Treas. Reg. § 1.751-1(b)(2), (3).

[132] Treas. Reg. § 1.751-1(b)(2)(iii), (b)(3)(iii). *See* Treas. Reg. § 1.751-1(g), *Example (3)(c)*. *See also* Treas. Reg. § 1.751-1(g), *Examples (2)(d)(1), (3)(d)(1)*.

[133] *See* Priv. Ltr. Rul. 7823013 (Mar. 7, 1978).

Assets	Basis	Value
Cash	$30,000	$30,000
Inventory	0	60,000
Total	$30,000	$90,000

If Carol's distribution consists of her pro rata share of each partnership asset, she receives $10,000 in cash and $20,000 worth of inventory. Carol recognizes no gain or loss on the distribution, her basis in the distributed receivables is zero and, under I.R.C. Section 735(a)(2), she will recognize ordinary income if she disposes of the inventory within five years of the distribution.

In contrast, the distribution has very different consequences if it consists of $30,000 in cash. Absent I.R.C. Section 751(b), the cash distribution would result in a $20,000 capital gain to Carol — $20,000 is the amount by which the cash distribution exceeds the basis of her partnership interest. To prevent recognition of capital gain when a pro rata distribution would result in ordinary income, I.R.C. Section 751(b) treats the transaction as if Carol exchanged her $20,000 share of partnership inventory for an additional $20,000 of partnership cash. Therefore, Carol recognizes $20,000 of ordinary income on this hypothetical sale, and the partnership increases its basis in the inventory by $20,000 to reflect the hypothetical purchase price.

A partnership's I.R.C. Section 751(b) property consists of its unrealized receivables and substantially appreciated inventory. Unrealized receivables include:

(1) *The partnership's rights to payment for goods (other than capital assets) delivered or to be delivered.* [134]

(2) *The partnership's rights to payment for services rendered or to be rendered.* Rights that exist when the distribution occurs are unrealized receivables, even if the partnership cannot enforce payment until a later time. These rights are unrealized receivables only to the extent that the partnership has not included them in its income. Thus, uncollected amounts for services rendered are not unrealized receivables if they were previously included in income by an accrual-method partnership.

(3) *The amount of gain subject to recapture as ordinary income, under a variety of Code sections, if the partnership sold all of its property immediately before the distribution.* [135] Unrealized receivables are not I.R.C. Section 751 property, however, if the distribution is made to liquidate the interest of a retiring or deceased general partner if capital is not a material income producing factor in the partnership (*e.g.*, a services partnership). Under I.R.C. Section 736, these payments are not considered distributions but are treated as guaranteed payments or are included in the partner's distributive share of partnership income.[136]

---

[134] Treas. Reg. § 1.751-1(c)(1)(i).

[135] I.R.C. § 751(c).

[136] I.R.C. § 736(b)(2).

In determining the amounts attributable to unrealized receivables in a distribution, full account must be taken not only of the estimated cost of completing performance of the contract or agreement, but also of the time between the distribution and the time of payment.[137]

Example (1): The JKLM services partnership, consisting of four equal partners, distributes $20,000 in cash to John. After the distribution, John's interest in the partnership decreases from 25 percent to 5 percent (an 80 percent reduction). Immediately before the distribution, the partnership's holds the following assets:

Assets	Basis	Value
Cash	$40,000	$40,000
Unrealized receivables	0	60,000
Total	$40,000	$100,000

In a pro rata distribution, John would receive $8,000 in cash (his $10,000 share of partnership cash x 80 percent) and receivables worth $12,000 (his $15,000 interest in partnership receivables x 80 percent). Because the distribution does not liquidate John's entire partnership interest, I.R.C. Section 736 does not apply, and, therefore, $12,000 of the cash he receives is deemed to be in exchange for 80 percent of his interest in the partnership's receivables. The hypothetical sale is taxable under I.R.C. Section 751(b) when the property is distributed, and John recognizes ordinary income on the transaction.

Example (2): Assume the same facts as in Example (1), except that JKLM distributes $25,000 in cash to John in complete liquidation of his interest ($100,000 value x 25 percent). Because any payments John receives for his share of the partnership's receivables are not distributions, no hypothetical sale is deemed to occur under I.R.C. Section 751. Under I.R.C. Section 736(a), however, John recognizes ordinary income on the liquidating payments ($15,000) he receives for the receivables.

Partnership inventory is substantially appreciated if its aggregate fair market value exceeds 120 percent of the partnership's aggregate basis in the property.[138] An anti-abuse rule excludes any inventory if a principal purpose for its acquisition was to avoid the 120 percent rule.[139]

Partnership inventory includes any property distributed or retained by a partnership that is:

(1)   its stock in trade and property held out for sale to customers, as defined in I.R.C. Section 1221;

(2)   property the partnership does not hold as a capital asset or I.R.C. Section 1231 asset;

---

[137] Treas. Reg. § 1.751-1(c)(3).

[138] I.R.C. § 751(d).

[139] I.R.C. § 751(d)(1)(B).

(3) foreign investment company stock that would result in gain taxable under I.R.C. Section 1246(a); and

(4) any property that would fall under one of the above three categories if held by the distributee partner.

The value and basis of the partnership's unrealized receivables are included in the value and basis of its inventory for the substantial appreciation tests, even in a liquidating distribution when the receivables are not treated as I.R.C. Section 751 property.

Example (3): The MNOP services partnership, consisting of four equal partners, distributes $37,500 in cash to Nora in liquidation of her entire partnership interest. Partnership assets — and Nora's share of them — immediately before the distribution are summarized below:

Assets	Basis	Value	Nora's 25% share
Cash	$40,000	$40,000	$10,000
Inventory	28,000	30,000	7,500
Accounts Receivable	0	80,000	20,000
Total	$68,000	$150,000	$37,500

Because Nora's entire interest is being liquidated, payments she receives for her $20,000 share of the partnership's receivables are not treated as distributions subject to I.R.C. Section 751(b), but they are taxable as ordinary income under I.R.C. Section 736(a). Only $17,500 of the cash Nora receives is a liquidating distribution for her share of partnership property. Of that amount, $10,000 is her proportionate share of the partnership's cash and the remaining $7,500 is for her share of its inventory. The value of the inventory is $110,000 ($30,000 inventory + $80,000 receivables) and its basis is $28,000 ($28,000 inventory + $0 for the receivables). The partnership's inventory is substantially appreciated because its value exceeds 120 percent of its basis. Consequently, the reduction in Nora's share of inventory for an increased share of cash is a taxable exchange under I.R.C. Section 751(b).

I.R.C. Section 751(b) may apply to any of the following distributions:

(1) a liquidating distribution that terminates an individual partner's entire interest;

(2) a current distribution that partially reduces a partner's interest;[140] or

(3) a distribution made in connection with the liquidation of the entire partnership.[141] The distribution may be an actual distribution or a constructive cash distribution deemed to occur when a partner's share of

---

[140] I.R.C. § 752(b); Treas. Reg. § 1.751-1(b)(1)(i).

[141] Rev. Rul. 77-412, 1977-2 C.B. 223 (termination of two-person partnership by liquidating distributions). *See* Wolcott v. Comm'r, 39 T.C. 538 (1962) (dissolution and division of partnership); Yourman v. U.S., 277 F. Supp. 818 (S.D. Cal. 1967) (dissolution of partnership).

partnership liabilities decreases or the partnership assumes a partner's individual liabilities.[142]

[A] Transactions Not Treated as Disproportionate Distributions

I.R.C. Section 751(b) cannot apply to a distribution unless (1) the partnership owns both I.R.C. Section 751 property and other property, and (2) the distribution of one class of property is in exchange for the partner's interest in another class of property. Thus, the statute does not apply to payments by a partnership that are not characterized as distributions or that do not permanently change a partner's proportionate share of I.R.C. Section 751 property.

Specific situations in which I.R.C. Section 751(b) does not apply include:

(1)   A distribution that consists of a partner's pro rata share of the partnership's I.R.C. Section 751 property and other property.[143]

(2)   Payments by a partnership to a partner that are draws, advances, loans, guaranteed payments, rent, compensation, or interest.

(3)   Liquidating payments made to a retiring partner or to a deceased partner's successor-in-interest that are subject to I.R.C. Section 736(a).[144]

(4)   A distribution of property to the partner who previously contributed the property to the partnership.[145]

[B] Computing Gain or Loss in a Disproportionate Distribution

[1] Computational Steps

Under I.R.C. Section 751(b), a distribution that changes a partner's relative share of the value of the partnership's I.R.C. Section 751 property is recharacterized as if a taxable exchange occurred between the partner and the partnership. The tax consequences of this hypothetical transaction are outlined and illustrated below.

(1)   The partnership divides its assets into two classes:

> ***Class (1)*** - I.R.C. Section 751 property consisting of unrealized receivables and substantially appreciated inventory, and
>
> ***Class (2)*** - all other property.

If the partnership owns only one class of property, I.R.C. Section 751(b) does not apply.

Example (1): Andy, Brenda, and Carl are equal general partners in the

---

[142]   *See* Treas. Reg. § 1.751-1(g), *Example (2)(c)*.

[143]   Treas. Reg. § 1.751-1(b)(1)(ii). *See* Rev. Rul. 57-68, 1957-1 C.B. 207.

[144]   I.R.C. § 751(b)(2)(A).

[145]   *Id.*; Treas. Reg. § 1.751-1(b)(4)(i).

ABC Partnership. The partnership and partners use the cash method of accounting and calendar taxable years. On January 1, the partnership distributes $40,000 in cash to completely liquidate Andy's interest in partnership property. Immediately before the distribution, the partnership balance sheet was as follows:

Assets	Basis	Value
Cash	$60,000	$60,000
Land	21,000	30,000
Inventory	18,000	30,000
Total Assets	$99,000	$120,000
Partner's Capital		
Andy	$33,000	$40,000
Brenda	33,000	40,000
Carl	33,000	40,000
Total Partners' Capital	$99,000	$120,000

The partnership's I.R.C. Section 751 property consists of its inventory. The inventory is substantially appreciated because its $30,000 value is more than 120 percent of ABC's basis in the inventory ($18,000 x 120% = $21,600).[146]

ABC Partnership's other class of property consists of cash and land.

(2)   *The distributee partner determines his proportionate share of the value of each class of partnership property immediately before the distribution.* [147] A partner's share of the assets in each class generally is determined from his overall percentage interest in the partnership. However, different sharing arrangements agreed on by the partners may be taken into account.

Example (2): Assume the same facts as in Example (1). Because Andy is an equal one-third partner for all partnership property, his proportionate share of partnership I.R.C. Section 751 property is worth $10,000, and his share of the other partnership property is worth $30,000 ($20,000 share of partnership cash + $10,000 share of the value of the land).

(3)   *In place of the assets actually distributed, the partner is deemed to receive a current distribution equal in value to the property actually received of both I.R.C. Section 751 property and other property.* [148] This hypothetical distribution is deemed to consist of I.R.C. Section 751 property and other property in proportion to the partner's share of the value of each class of property in the partnership.

Example (3): Assume the same facts as in Example (1). Although Andy actually received $40,000 in cash, for I.R.C. Section 751(b) he is deemed to have received a distribution of the following assets:

---

[146]   I.R.C. § 751(d).

[147]   Treas. Reg. § 1.751-1(b).

[148]   Treas. Reg. § 1.751-1(b)(2), (3).

(a)   I.R.C. Section 751 property consisting of inventory worth $10,000, and

(b)   other property worth $30,000, consisting of $20,000 in cash and an interest in land worth $10,000.

(4)   The partner determines his basis for the property deemed distributed to him under the I.R.C. Section 732(a) rules governing current distributions. The current-distribution rules apply even if the distribution liquidates the partner's interest in the partnership.[149]

Example (4): Assume the same facts as in Example (1). Under I.R.C. Section 732(a), Andy's basis for the distributed property is the same as the partnership's basis. This rule applies unless the total basis of all the distributed property exceeds the basis of his partnership interest, reduced by the amount of cash he receives in the same transaction. Andy's basis for the $10,000 worth of inventory is deemed to be $6,000 — the same as the partnership's basis before the distribution (one third of the partnership's $18,000 total basis in the inventory). His basis for the land is deemed to be $7,000 (one-third of the partnership's $21,000 basis).

(5)   The partner is considered to exchange the property of one class deemed distributed to him for an equal value of the property of the other class he actually received. [150]

This exchange is considered to occur immediately after the deemed distribution.[151]

Example (5): Assume the same facts as in Example (1). Andy is treated as if he exchanged the inventory he is deemed to have received with a $6,000 basis for $10,000 of the cash he actually received. Because this transaction involves an exchange of I.R.C. Section 751 property for other property, it is taxable under I.R.C. Section 751(b). The transaction appears to involve an exchange of the interest in land he is deemed to have received with a $7,000 basis for $10,000 of the cash he actually received. However, this transaction does not involve an exchange of I.R.C. Section 751 property for other property. Thus, it is not subject to the I.R.C. Section 751(b) rules. Consequently, no taxable exchange of the land for cash is deemed to occur. The remaining $20,000 of cash Andy receives is not an exchange because it represents his proportionate share of the partnership's $60,000 in cash.

(6)   The partner determines and reports the tax consequences of any hypothetical exchange subject to I.R.C. Section 751(b). Any ordinary income or loss resulting from the hypothetical exchange is recognized and the basis of any property acquired increases to reflect its

---

[149] Treas. Reg. § 1.751-1(b)(2)(iii), (3)(iii).

[150] Treas. Reg. § 1.751-1(b)(2), (3).

[151] Treas. Reg. § 1.751-1(b)(2)(iii), (b)(3)(iii). *See* Treas. Reg. § 1.751-1(g), *Example (3)(c). See also* Treas. Reg. § 1.751-1(g), *Examples (2)(d)(1), (3)(d)(1).*

hypothetical acquisition price.

The tax consequences of the exchange to the partner may include:

(a)   Recognition of gain or loss equal to the difference between the value of the property he receives and his basis in the property deemed distributed to him.[152] The character of the partner's gain or loss depends on the character of the deemed-distributed property in his hands.[153] If the property consists of I.R.C. Section 751 property, the partner recognizes ordinary income or loss. The partner's holding period in the deemed-distributed property includes the partnership's holding period.[154]

(b)   The partner's basis in the property he acquires from the partnership in the exchange is its fair market value when the exchange occurs.[155]

(c)   The partner's holding period in the property acquired in the exchange begins when the exchange occurs.[156]

Example (6): Assume the same facts as in Example (1). Because of the I.R.C. Section 751(b) exchange deemed to occur in connection with the distribution to Andy, the partnership is considered to have paid $10,000 in cash to Andy to purchase inventory. Because Andy's basis for the inventory is deemed to be $6,000, he recognizes $4,000 of gain. That gain is characterized as ordinary income under I.R.C. Section 735(a)(2), which provides that a partner recognizes ordinary income if he sells inventory distributed to him by a partnership within five years of the distribution date.

(7)   *The partner determines the tax consequences of the distribution of the portion of the assets that was not involved in the hypothetical exchange, applying the general rules governing current or liquidating distributions.* These assets are all the property actually distributed to the partner minus the property that was acquired in the hypothetical exchange.[157] These assets are considered to be distributed after the I.R.C. Section 751(b) exchange occurs. Thus, the consequences of the distribution are computed after reducing the basis of the partner's interest by the amount of cash and basis of the property he is deemed to receive in the hypothetical current distribution.

Example (7): Assume the same facts as in Example (1). Of the $40,000 in cash Andy actually received, he is considered to have acquired $10,000 in

---

[152]   *See* Treas. Reg. § 1.751-1(g), *Examples (2)(d)(1), (3)(d)(1)*.

[153]   *See* I.R.C. §§ 1221, 1231.

[154]   I.R.C. § 1223(1).

[155]   Treas. Reg. § 1.732-1(e).

[156]   I.R.C. § 1223(2).

[157]   Treas. Reg. § 1.751-1(g), *Example (2)(d)(2)*.

the I.R.C. Section 751(b) exchange. Consequently, the remainder of the distribution consists of $30,000 in cash. When Andy receives that distribution, his basis in his partnership interest is $27,000 ($33,000 initial basis - $6,000 basis of the inventory deemed distributed to him). Under I.R.C. Section 731, Andy recognizes $3,000 of capital gain on this distribution. This $3,000 is the excess of the cash he receives over the basis of his partnership interest.

(8)   *The partnership determines and reports the tax consequences of any hypothetical exchange subject to I.R.C. Section 751(b).* Any capital or ordinary income or loss resulting from the hypothetical exchange is recognized, and the basis of any property acquired increases to reflect its hypothetical acquisition price.

The tax consequences of these exchanges to the partnership may include:

(a)   Recognition of gain or loss equal to the difference between the value of the property the partnership reacquires from the partner and the partnership's basis in the property deemed transferred to reacquire it.[158] The character of the gain or loss depends on the character (in the partnership's hands) of the property used to reacquire the assets from the partner.[159] If the property used in the reacquisition is I.R.C. Section 751 property, the partnership recognizes ordinary income or loss.[160]

(b)   The partnership's basis in the property it reacquires from the partner is its fair market value at the time of the exchange.[161]

(c)   The partnership's holding period in the acquired property begins at the time of the exchange.[162]

Example (8): Assume the same facts as in Example (1). The partnership is treated as if it: (1) distributed inventory with a $6,000 basis to Andy, and (2) purchased new inventory for $10,000. The net result of these transactions is a $4,000 increase in the basis of the partnership's inventory. The partnership's balance sheet after the distribution appears as follows:

---

[158] Treas. Reg. § 1.751-1(b)(2)(ii), (b)(3)(ii). *See* I.R.C. § 1001(a). *See also* Treas. Reg. § 1.751-1(g), *Examples (2)(e)(1), (3)(e)(1).*

[159] Treas. Reg. § 1.751-1(b)(2)(ii), (b)(3)(ii). *See* I.R.C. §§ 1221, 1231.

[160] Treas. Reg. § 1.751-1(b)(2)(ii).

[161] I.R.C. § 1012.

[162] I.R.C. § 1223(2).

Assets	Basis	Value
Cash	$20,000	$20,000
Land	21,000	30,000
Inventory	22,000	30,000
Total Assets	$63,000	$80,000
Partner's Capital		
Brenda	33,000	40,000
Carl	33,000	40,000
Total Partners' Capital	$66,000	$80,000

The continuing partnership of Brenda and Carl now has an aggregate basis for its assets of $63,000 (inside basis), which is $3,000 less than the $66,000 aggregate basis that Brenda and Carl have for their partnership interests (outside basis) (*see* Chapter 5). This difference between the inside and the outside basis is attributable to the $3,000 gain that Andy recognized on the non-I.R.C. Section 751(b) portion of the distribution. The discrepancy is eliminated if the partnership has an I.R.C. Section 754 basis-adjustment election in effect.

[2] Noncash Distributions

I.R.C. Section 751(b) often applies when a partner receives a cash distribution in exchange for his interest in partnership receivables and inventory. The statute also applies if a partner receives other kinds of partnership property for his share of I.R.C. Section 751 property and, in that case, both the partner and partnership may recognize gain or loss. If the partnership distributes or is deemed to distribute more than one asset in each class of property, the portion of each asset deemed to be acquired in the I.R.C. Section 751(b) exchange is determined in proportion to the relative value of the assets.

> **Example:** Donna, Edgar, and Fran are equal general partners in the DEF Partnership. The partnership and partners use the cash method of accounting and calendar taxable years. On January 1, the partnership distributes land worth $30,000 and $15,000 in cash to liquidate Donna's interest in partnership property completely. No portion of the distribution is subject to special treatment under I.R.C. Section 736(a). Immediately before the distribution, the partnership balance sheet is as follows:

Assets	Basis	Value
Cash	$60,000	$60,000
Land	21,000	30,000
Stock	12,000	15,000
Inventory	18,000	30,000
Total Assets	$111,000	$135,000
Partner's Capital		
Donna	$37,000	$45,000
Edgar	37,000	45,000
Fran	37,000	45,000
Total Partners' Capital	$111,000	$135,000

The tax consequences of the distribution are determined as follows:

(1)   *The partnership categorizes its property according to class:*

    (a)   I.R.C. Section 751 property — substantially appreciated inventory; and

    (b)   other property — cash, land, and stock.

(2)   *Donna's proportionate share of the value of each item of partnership property is computed:*

Assets	Total Value	Donna's 1/3 Share
Cash	$60,000	$20,000
Land	30,000	10,000
Stock	15,000	5,000
Inventory	30,000	10,000
Total	$135,000	$45,000

(3)   *The assets distributed to Donna are categorized as either I.R.C. Section 751 property or other property.*

Although Donna actually received all the land and $15,000 of cash, for purposes of I.R.C. Section 751(b), she is deemed to have received a distribution of her one-third share of partnership assets as follows:

    (a)   I.R.C. Section 751 property — inventory worth $10,000; and

    (b)   other property — $20,000 in cash, an interest in land worth $10,000, and stock worth $5,000.

(4)   *Donna's basis in each of the distributed properties is computed:*

Assets	Partnership's Basis	Donna's Basis (1/3)
Cash	$60,000	$20,000
Land	21,000	7,000
Stock	12,000	4,000

Assets	Partnership's Basis	Donna's Basis (1/3)
Inventory	18,000	6,000
Total	$111,000	$37,000

(5)   *Determine whether there is a hypothetical exchange of I.R.C. Section 751 property. If there is a hypothetical exchange, compute the effect on Donna and on the partnership.*

The following table illustrates the distribution:

	Value of Donna's Share before Distribution	Value of Share Donna Received	Amount More than (less than) share
Section 751 Property			
Inventory	$10,000	$0	($10,000)
Other Property			
Cash	$20,000	$15,000	($5,000)
Land	10,000	30,000	20,000
Stock	5,000	0	(5,000)
Total Other Property	$35,000	$45,000	$10,000

(a)   *Is there a hypothetical exchange?*

Donna is treated as if she exchanged the inventory she is deemed to have received with the other property — land — that she actually received. Since this transaction involves an exchange of I.R.C. Section 751 property for other property, it is taxable under I.R.C. Section 751(b). No other portion of the transaction involves an exchange of I.R.C. Section 751 property for other property. None of the $15,000 of cash Donna receives is involved in this exchange because it does not exceed her $20,000 proportionate share of the partnership's cash. No taxable exchange of the land for cash or stock is deemed to occur under the I.R.C. Section 751(b) rules.

(b)   *What are the tax consequences for Donna?*

Under I.R.C. Section 751(b), the partnership is treated as if it transferred $10,000 worth of land to Donna in exchange for the inventory previously distributed to her. Since Donna's basis in the inventory is deemed to be $6,000, she recognizes $4,000 of gain. That gain is characterized as ordinary income under I.R.C. Section 735(a)(2). Because Donna is deemed to have acquired one-third of the land she received for $10,000, that amount becomes her basis for one-third of the land.

(c)   *What is Donna's basis in the property she receives?*

Of the total property actually distributed to Donna, she is deemed to have acquired $10,000 worth of the land in the I.R.C. Section 751(b) exchange. Consequently, the remainder of the distribution consists of two-thirds of the land she receives (worth $20,000), and $15,000 in cash. When she receives that distribution, Donna's basis in her partnership interest is $31,000 ($37,000 initial basis - $6,000 basis of inventory deemed distributed to her and sold to the partnership). Since this is a liquidating distribution, Donna first reduces the basis of her partnership interest by the $15,000 in cash she receives and the remaining $16,000 becomes her basis in the distributed two-thirds of the land. Donna's total basis in the land is $26,000 -$16,000 for the portion acquired in the distribution plus $10,000 for the portion acquired in the I.R.C. Section 751(b) exchange.

Summary: I.R.C. Section 751(b) ensures that a distribution does not change the character of a partner's gain or loss. Donna recognizes $4,000 of ordinary income when the property is distributed as a result of the hypothetical I.R.C. Section 751(b) transaction. Because Donna has a $26,000 basis in the land worth $30,000, she will recognize $4,000 of capital gain when she sells the property. Therefore, Donna realizes the same amount of ordinary income and the same amount of capital gain that she would recognize if the partnership sold all of its property and Donna was taxable on her distributive share of the gain from each sale.

[3]   Constructive Distribution When Partner's Share of Partnership Liabilities Decreases

I.R.C. Section 751(b) applies to constructive distributions as well as to actual partnership distributions that change a partner's share of the partnership's I.R.C. Section 751 property.[163] Under I.R.C. Section 752(b), a partner is deemed to receive a constructive cash distribution to the extent that his share of partnership liabilities decreases or the partnership assumes his individual liabilities.

Example: Frank is a one-third partner in the FGH Partnership, which uses the accrual method of tax accounting. Immediately before it makes a distribution to liquidate Frank's entire partnership interest, the partnership's balance sheet is as follows:

Assets	Basis	Value
Cash	$30,000	$30,000
Accounts receivable	18,000	18,000
Inventory	42,000	60,000
X Corp stock	78,000	90,000
Land	18,000	18,000
Total Assets	$186,000	$216,000
Liabilities		
Mortgage	$60,000	$60,000

	Basis	Value
Partner's Capital		
Frank	$42,000	$52,000
Greta	42,000	52,000
Harriet	42,000	52,000
	$126,000	$156,000
Total Liabilities and Partners' Capital	$186,000	$216,000

---

[163] *See* Rev. Rul. 84-102, 1984-2 C.B. 119.

The partnership distributes $20,000 in cash and $30,000 worth of X Corp stock to Frank to completely liquidate his interest in the partnership. Because Frank's share of the partnership's liabilities decreases from $22,000 (one-third of $66,000) to zero, he is deemed to receive a $22,000 cash distribution in addition to the cash he actually receives ($42,000 total cash). Because the entire liquidating payment is for Frank's interest in partnership property, no part of it is taxable under I.R.C. Section 736(a).

The consequences of these actual and constructive distributions are determined as follows:

(1)   The partnership categorizes its assets as I.R.C. Section 751 property or as other property.

    (a)   The partnership's I.R.C. Section 751 property consists of receivables and substantially appreciated inventory. For the substantial appreciation test, the inventory is worth $78,000 ($18,000 of unrealized receivables + $60,000 in inventory) and has a basis of $60,000 ($18,000 for the receivables + $42,000 for the inventory).

    (b)   The partnership's other class of property consists of its cash, X Corp stock, and land.

(2)   Frank determines his proportionate share of the value of each item of partnership property. Because Frank is a one-third partner for all partnership property, he is deemed to receive a distribution of his proportionate share of each partnership asset. Thus, for I.R.C. Section 751(b), Frank is deemed to have received a current distribution of assets with the following values and bases:

Section 751 Property	Basis	Value
Receivables	$6,000	$6,000
Inventory	14,000	20,000
Total	$20,000	26,000

Other Property	Basis	Value
Cash	$10,000	$10,000
X Corp stock	26,000	30,000
Land	6,000	6,000
Total	$42,000	$46,000

(3)   Frank is treated as if he transferred the receivables and inventory that he is deemed to have received to the partnership in exchange for $26,000 in cash. Because this transaction involves an exchange of I.R.C. Section 751 property for other property, it is taxable under I.R.C. Section 751(b). Therefore, Frank recognizes a $6,000 gain — the difference between his $20,000 basis in the receivables and the $26,000 cash he is deemed to have realized. The $6,000 is characterized as ordinary income under I.R.C. Section 735(a)(2). None of the X Corp stock Frank actually received is involved in this exchange because it does not exceed his $30,000 propor-

tionate share of the partnership's stock.

(4) Because the partnership treats the distribution as if it paid Frank $6,000 in cash for the receivables and $20,000 for the inventory, the partnership adjusts its bases in these assets to reflect the transaction. Therefore, the partnership increases its basis in the inventory by $6,000. The partnership's basis in the receivables was $6,000, the amount paid to Frank. Therefore, no basis adjustment is needed for the receivables.

(5) Of the total property actually distributed to Frank he is deemed to have acquired $26,000 in cash in the I.R.C. Section 751(b) exchange. Consequently, the remainder of the distribution consists of $16,000 in cash ($42,000 total cash - $26,000 in I.R.C. Section 751 exchange) and X Corp stock worth $30,000. When he receives the remainder of the distribution, Frank's basis in his partnership interest is $42,000 ($62,000 initial basis - $6,000 basis of receivables - $14,000 basis of inventory deemed distributed to Frank and sold to the partnership).

(5) Because this is a liquidating distribution, Frank reduces the basis of his partnership interest by the amount of cash received and determines his basis in the distributed stock:

Basis remaining after hypothetical I.R.C. Section 751 distribution	$42,000
Less: cash received	(16,000)
Basis in X Corp stock	$26,000

Summary: I.R.C. Section 751(b) ensures that a distribution does not change the character of a partner's gain. Because Frank has a $26,000 basis in the X Corp stock worth $30,000, he will recognize $4,000 of capital gain when he sells the property. These are the same amounts of ordinary income and capital gain that Frank would recognize if the partnership sold all of its property and Frank was taxable on his distributive share of the gain from each sale.

In Revenue Ruling 84-102,[164] the IRS held that members of a partnership that owns I.R.C. Section 751 property are taxable under I.R.C. Section 751(b) when a new partner is admitted and becomes responsible for a portion of the partnership's existing liabilities. The resulting decrease in the existing partners' shares of partnership liabilities is treated as a constructive cash distribution to them under I.R.C. Section 752(b). At the same time, the existing partner's proportionate shares of the partnership's I.R.C. Section 751 property decrease to the extent that the new partner acquires a share of these items. In the Service's view, the constructive cash distribution is subject to I.R.C. Section 751(b) because it results in a permanent change in the existing partners' shares of the partnership's I.R.C. Section 751 property.

---

[164] 1984-2 C.B. 119. The correctness of this ruling has been questioned. *See* Carmen, *Revenue Ruling 84-102 — An Erroneous Conclusion?*, 2 J. Partnership Tax'n 371 (1986).

[C] Distributions Involving Recapture Property

The gain that the partnership would recapture as ordinary income if the partnership sold all of its assets is included in the partnership's unrealized receivables.[165] Thus, in determining whether a distribution changes a partner's share of partnership unrealized receivables, the partner's share of potential recapture income are taken into account. The I.R.C. Section 751(c) definition of unrealized receivables includes amounts the partnership would recapture for depreciation and cost recovery under I.R.C. Sections 1245 and 1250.

Only the recapture gain inherent in each item of partnership recapture property is an unrealized receivable. Each recapture property is treated as if it consists of two separate assets:[166]

(1) *An unrealized receivable equal in value to the amount of gain the partnership would recapture as ordinary income if it sold the property for its current fair market value.* This asset is deemed to have a zero basis.

(2) *Other property equal in value to the value of the recapture property decreased by the amount treated as an unrealized receivable.* The basis of this asset is the same as the full basis of the recapture property.

Only assets that would generate gain are included in computing the partnership's unrealized receivables. Items that would generate losses are not taken into account.[167]

Example: The LMN Partnership owns Machine A worth $60,000. The partnership purchased the machine for $50,000, and its basis in the asset is $30,000 because it has taken depreciation deductions totaling $20,000. For I.R.C. Section 751(b), Machine A consists of two separate partnership assets:

Asset (1) *I.R.C. Section 751 property* — an unrealized receivable worth $20,000, the amount the partnership would recapture if it sold the property for its $50,000 current value. This asset has a zero basis.

Asset (2) *Other property* — worth $40,000 ($60,000 value of the machine - $20,000 potential recapture income). This asset has a $30,000 basis.

If the partnership also owns Machine B, worth $30,000, with a $40,000 basis, the potential loss on Machine B does not offset the potential recapture income from Machine A.

---

[165] I.R.C. § 751(c).

[166] Treas. Reg. § 1.751-1(c)(4), (5).

[167] Treas. Reg. § 1.751-1(c)(4)(i).

[D]   Distributions in Liquidation of Entire Partnership

When a partnership liquidates, the constructive-sale rules of I.R.C. Section 751(b) apply if the partnership's I.R.C. Section 751 property is not distributed among its partners pro rata.[168] In computing the income or loss on the hypothetical exchanges between the partner and the partnership, the partnership is deemed to continue after the liquidating distribution.[169]

> **Example:** Sandra and Theo are equal partners in the ST Partnership. Sandra, Theo, and the partnership use the cash method of accounting and have calendar taxable years. The partnership balance sheet appears as follows:
>
> | Assets | Basis | Value |
> | --- | --- | --- |
> | Receivables | $0 | $10,000 |
> | Land (capital Asset) | 5,000 | 10,000 |
> | Total Assets | $5,000 | $20,000 |
> | Partners' Capital | | |
> | Sandra | $2,500 | $10,000 |
> | Theo | 2,500 | 10,000 |
> | Total Partners' Capital | $5,000 | $20,000 |

The partners liquidate the partnership, transferring the receivables to Sandra and the land to Theo. Under I.R.C. Section 751(b), each partner is treated as if he received one-half of the receivables and a one-half interest in the land. Sandra, therefore, is deemed to sell her interest in the land to the partnership — which now consists of Theo — in exchange for the additional amount of receivables that Theo actually obtained.

Sandra recognizes $2,500 of capital gain on the sale ($5,000 value of receivables - $2,500 basis in a one-half interest in the land). Sandra's basis in the receivables is the same as her cost, $5,000.

Theo is deemed to sell his receivables to the partnership — which now consists of Sandra — for an additional interest in the land he actually received. Theo recognizes $5,000 of ordinary income on the sale ($5,000 value of land - zero basis in one-half of the receivables). Theo's basis in the one-half of the land he is deemed to purchase equals his $5,000 purchase price. His total basis in the land is $7,500: $5,000 basis in the portion purchased from the partnership and $2,500 basis in the portion distributed to him.

---

[168] Rev. Rul. 77-412, 1977-2 C.B. 223 (termination of two-person partnership by liquidating distributions). *See* Wolcott v. Comm'r, 39 T.C. 538 (1962) (dissolution and division of partnership); Yourman v. U.S., 277 F. Supp. 818 (S.D. Cal. 1967) (dissolution of partnership).

[169] Yourman v. U.S., 277 F. Supp. 818, 819 (S.D. Cal. 1967). Each partner's income or loss apparently is determined as if his distribution occurs before the liquidation of the other partners' interests. Rev. Rul. 77-412, 1977-2 C.B. 223.

§ 8.07 BASIS ADJUSTMENTS RELATED TO DISTRIBUTIONS

A distribution of some partnership assets to a partner generally does not affect the partnership's basis in its undistributed property.[170] Under I.R.C. Section 754, however, a partnership may elect to adjust the basis of its retained assets after certain distributions. The election applies to all distributions and transfers of partnership interests during the year of the election and subsequent years until it is revoked with the Service's permission.[171] If the election is in effect when a distribution is made, the total adjustment to the basis of partnership property is determined under I.R.C. Section 734(b), and that amount is allocated among partnership assets under the rules of I.R.C. Section 755.

Mandatory Basis Reduction. IRC Section 734(d) makes a basis adjustment mandatory whenever a distribution occurs that creates a *substantial basis reduction* to the basis of partnership assets.[172] A substantial basis reduction is defined as a gross reduction of more than $250,000 that would be made to the common basis of all partnership assets if an IRC Section 754 election were in effect.[173] This new provision is likely to affect cases where a partnership redeems a partner's interest when its assets have declined in value and a basis reduction of more than $250,000 is required. Similarly, under IRC Section 743, a partnership must reduce the basis of its property if a partnership interest is transferred by reason of sale, exchange, or death and the partnership has a *substantial built-in loss* immediately after the transfer.[174] A substantial built-in loss exists if the aggregate tax basis of partnership property exceeds the fair market value of the property by more than $250,000.

A *securitization partnership* is exempt from the mandatory downward basis adjustment rule for distributions.[175] A securitization partnership is a partnership whose sole business activity is issuing securities with fixed principal that are primarily serviced by the cash flows of a discrete pool of receivables or other financial assets.

A partnership makes an I.R.C. Section 754 election to eliminate changes in the timing and character of the nondistributee partners' gains and losses caused by a distribution. These changes occur in three situations summarized below.

Situation (1): When the distributee partner recognizes gain on the distribution.

Under I.R.C. Section 731(a)(1), a partner recognizes gain if he receives a cash distribution that exceeds the basis of his partnership interest. Because the distributee's gain is attributable to appreciation of assets retained by the partnership, the other partners recognize that gain when the partnership sells those assets,

---

[170] I.R.C. § 734.

[171] Treas. Reg. § 1.754-1(a).

[172] I.R.C. § 734(d), as amended by the American Jobs Creation Act (AJCA), Pub. L. No. 108-357 (2004). These rules apply to distributions after October 22, 2004.

[173] I.R.C. § 734(d)(1).

[174] I.R.C. § 734(d)(1).

[175] I.R.C. §§ 734(e), 743(f).

and they recognize an offsetting loss when they dispose of their partnership interests. Although the partners' increased gain is offset, the time value and consequences of capital-loss treatment cannot be recovered.

Example: John's interest in the JKL Partnership is liquidated in exchange for a $120,000 cash distribution. Immediately before the distribution, the partnership has the following balance sheet:

Assets	Basis	Value
Cash	$120,000	$120,000
Capital asset	86,000	140,000
Inventory	94,000	100,000
Total Assets	$300,000	$360,000
Partner's Capital		
John	$100,000	$120,000
Karen	100,000	120,000
Larry	100,000	120,000
Total Partners' Capital	$300,000	$360,000

Because the $120,000 cash distribution exceeds the basis of John's partnership interest, he recognizes a $20,000 gain. He reports the entire amount as capital gain, even though $2,000 of the gain is attributable to his share of the appreciation in partnership inventory, and $18,000 is attributable to his share of the appreciation of the capital asset. I.R.C. Section 751(b) does not apply because the inventory is not substantially appreciated.

After the distribution, the partnership's balance sheet appears as follows:

Assets	Basis	Value	Potential Gain
Capital Asset	$86,000	$140,000	$54,000
Inventory	94,000	100,000	6,000
Total Assets	$180,000	$240,000	
Partners' Capital			
Karen	$100,000	$120,000	
Larry	100,000	120,000	
Total Partners' Capital	$200,000	$240,000	

If the partnership sells its remaining assets for value, it recognizes a $54,000 capital gain on the sale of the capital asset and $6,000 of ordinary income on the sale of the inventory. Karen and Larry each report a $27,000 capital gain and $3,000 of ordinary income. Thus, the gain realized by all three partners from partnership property totals $80,000, even though the total appreciation in partnership property is only $60,000. The partnership's balance sheet now appears as follows:

Assets	Basis	Value
Cash	$240,000	$240,000
Partner's Capital		
Karen	$130,000	$120,000
Larry	$130,000	$120,000
Total Partners' Capital	$260,000	$240,000

Upon liquidation of the partnership, Karen and Larry each recognize a $10,000 capital loss. Although the net amount of gain each partner recognizes is $20,000 ($27,000 capital gain + $3,000 ordinary income - $10,000 capital loss), the timing and character of their gain is greatly distorted by the previous cash distribution to John.

An I.R.C. Section 754 election eliminates this distortion. When the property is distributed to John, the partnership increases the basis of its assets by the $20,000 gain John recognizes, and this basis adjustment reduces the amount of gain the partnership recognizes when it sells its assets.

Situation (2): When the distributee partner recognizes a loss on the distribution.

Under I.R.C. Section 731(a)(2), a partner recognizes loss if he receives a liquidating distribution consisting solely of cash, unrealized receivables, and inventory, and the total basis of the distributed property exceeds the basis in his partnership interest. Because the distributee's loss is attributable to depreciation of assets retained by the partnership, the other partners recognize that same loss when the partnership sells those assets, and the partners recognize an offsetting gain when they dispose of their partnership interests.

Situation (3): When the distributee partner takes the distributed property with a basis that differs from the partnership's basis for the asset before the distribution.

This basis difference occurs in the following situations:

(1)   In a current distribution, the partner's basis in distributed property cannot exceed the basis in his partnership interest.[176] This limitation decreases the basis of distributed property when the partner's basis in his interest is less than the partnership's basis in the property.

(2)   In a liquidating distribution, the partner's total basis in the assets he receives equals the basis in his partnership interest.[177] This rule increases or decreases the basis of distributed property, depending on whether the partner's basis in his interest is more or less than the partnership's basis in the distributed property.

Example: The DEF Partnership distributes land worth $46,000 to Dave in complete liquidation of his partnership interest. Immediately before the distribution, DEF's balance sheet is as follows:

---

[176] I.R.C. § 732(a)(2).
[177] I.R.C. § 732(b).

Assets	Basis	Value
Stock	$48,000	$92,000
Land	42,000	46,000
Total Assets	$90,000	$138,000
Partners' Capital		
Dave	$30,000	$46,000
Edward	30,000	46,000
Fran	30,000	46,000
Total Partners' Capital	$90,000	$138,000

Dave's basis in the land is $30,000 — the basis in his partnership interest when the liquidating distribution is made. Because the partnership's basis in the land was $42,000, the distribution decreases the basis of the land by $12,000. Dave recognizes a $16,000 gain when he sells the land, and the partnership recognizes a $44,000 gain when it sells the stock. Consequently, the total amount of gain recognized on these sales is $60,000, even though the amount of gain inherent in these assets before the distribution was only $48,000. This discrepancy occurs because $12,000 of the basis for the land was "lost" in the distribution. DEF's balance sheet appears as follows after it distributes the land to Dave and sells the stock:

Assets	Basis	Value
Cash	$92,000	$92,000
Partners' Capital		
Edward	$52,000	$46,000
Fran	$52,000	$46,000
Total Partners' Capital	$104,000	$92,000

Upon liquidation of the partnership, Edward and Fran each recognize a $6,000 capital loss. Although the net amount of gain each partner recognizes is $16,000 ($22,000 capital gain - $6,000 capital loss), the timing is distorted by the previous distribution to Dave.

If DEF has a basis-adjustment election in effect, however, the basis of its undistributed property increases by $12,000 when the land is distributed to Dave. Thus the partnership recognizes $12,000 less gain when it sells the stock.

[A] Computing and Allocating Basis Adjustments Under I.R.C. Section 754 Election

The effect of an I.R.C. Section 754 election is that the partnership is treated as an aggregate of individuals who own undivided interests in the partnership's assets. Each partner has a separate basis in his share of each partnership asset that he uses to compute his share of the partnership's gain, loss, depreciation, or depletion. Once made, the election applies to all transfers and distributions, and it cannot be revoked without the Service's permission.[178] If the I.R.C. Section 754 election is in effect when a distribution is made, the bases of the partnership's undistributed properties are adjusted as follows:

(1)   The total amount of increase or decrease in the bases of partnership assets that is allowable under I.R.C. Section 734(b) must be determined. The bases of partnership properties

(a)   increase by the amount of gain the distributee partner recognizes under I.R.C. Section 731(a)(1) for a cash distribution that exceeds the basis in his partnership interest;

(b)   decrease by the amount of any loss the distributee partner recognizes under I.R.C. Section 731(a)(2) for a liquidating distribution consisting solely of cash, unrealized receivables, and inventory;

(c)   increase by the amount that the distributee partner's basis in property he receives in a current or liquidating distribution is less than the partnership's basis before the distribution; or

(d)   decrease by the amount that the distributee partner's basis in property he receives in a liquidating distribution is greater than the partnership's basis in the property.

(2)   The total basis adjustment determined under I.R.C. Section 734(b) is then allocated among the partnership's assets under the rules of I.R.C. Section 755. The allocation is made as follows:

(a)   All partnership property is divided into two classes:

(i)   capital assets and I.R.C. Section 1231 property (*i.e.*, capital gain property), and

(ii)   all other property (*i.e.*, ordinary income property).[179] This class includes all unrealized receivables as defined in I.R.C. Section 751(c). For this purpose, any potential gain subject to recapture as ordinary income is considered a separate unrealized receivable.[180] *See* § 8.05, *supra.*

(b)   Any increase or decrease arising from gain or loss a distributee partner recognizes under I.R.C. Section 731(a)(1) (gain on cash distribution) or 731(a)(2) (loss on certain liquidating distributions) is fully allocated to the class of partnership capital gain property.[181]

(c)   Any increase or decrease arising from a change in the basis of distributed property is allocated to the class of partnership assets

---

[178]   I.R.C. § 732(b).

[179]   I.R.C. § 755(b); Treas. Reg. § 1.755-1(c).

[180]   Treas. Reg. § 1.755-1(a).

[181]   Treas. Reg. § 1.755-1(c)(1)(ii).

that the distributed property belonged to before the distribution.[182] Thus, (i) adjustments attributable to distributions of capital gain property are allocated to the partnership capital-gain assets, and (ii) adjustments attributable to distributions of other kinds of property are allocated to the partnership ordinary-income assets.

(d) The total basis increase or decrease allocated to a class is allocated among the assets in the class as follows:[183]

    (i) The total basis increase or decrease allocated to each class of partnership property is allocated among the assets in the class, so that it reduces the difference between the value and basis of each asset. Consequently

        • Basis increases are allocated only among assets with values that exceed their bases. The total basis increase is allocated among those assets in proportion to the differences between the value and basis of each asset. The basis of an asset cannot increase above its fair market value.

        • Basis decreases are allocated only among assets with values that are less than their bases. The total basis decrease is allocated among those assets in proportion to the differences between the basis and value of each asset. The basis of an asset cannot decrease below zero.

    (ii) A basis increase is first allocated to properties with unrealized appreciation in proportion to the amount of the appreciation. Any remaining increase is allocated among the properties within the class in proportion to their fair market values.

    (iii) A basis decrease is first allocated to properties with unrealized depreciation in proportion to the amount of the depreciation.[184] Any remaining decrease is allocated among the properties within the class in proportion to their adjusted bases.

In applying the basis allocation rules to a distribution in liquidation of a partner's interest, a partnership may not decrease the basis of corporate stock of a partner or a related person. The effect of this rule is to deny basis reductions to the stock of a corporate partner.[185] Any basis that would have been allocated to the stock must be allocated to other partnership assets. If a basis decrease exceeds the basis of other partnership assets, the partnership recognizes gain in the amount of the excess.

---

[182] Treas. Reg. § 1.755-1(c)(1)(i).

[183] Treas. Reg. § 1.755-1(c)(2). These allocation rules apply to distributions on or after December 15, 1999.

[184] The basis of partnership property cannot be reduced below zero. Treas. Reg. § 1.755-1(c)(3).

[185] I.R.C. § 755(c), as amended by the American Jobs Creation Act (AJCA), Pub. L. No. 108-357 (2004). These rules apply to distributions after October 22, 2004.

Adjustments to basis of cost recovery property. In computing cost recovery adjustments arising from an adjustment to the basis of partnership property:[186]

(1)   If the basis of partnership recovery property increases because of a property distribution, the increased portion of basis is accounted for as newly purchased recovery property placed in service when the distribution occurs. Thus, any applicable recovery period and method may be used for the increased portion of the basis.

(2)   If the basis of a partnership recovery property decreases because of a property distribution, the basis decrease is accounted for over the property's remaining recovery period beginning with the period in which the basis is decreased.

[B]   Illustrating Basis Adjustments

[1]   Distributee Partner Recognizes Gain on Cash Distribution

Example (1): Tony's interest in the RST Partnership is liquidated in exchange for a $90,000 cash distribution. Immediately before the distribution is made, the partnership has an I.R.C. Section 754 election, in effect and its balance sheet is as follows:

Assets	Basis	Value
Cash	$90,000	$90,000
Capital Asset 1	30,000	60,000
Capital Asset 2	25,000	20,000
Capital Asset 3	15,000	30,000
Inventory	65,000	70,000
Total Assets	$225,000	$270,000

Partners' Capital	Basis	Value
Rhea	$75,000	$90,000
Tony	75,000	90,000
Sara	75,000	90,000
Total Partners' Capital	$225,000	$270,000

Because the cash distribution exceeds the basis of Tony's partnership interest, he recognizes a $15,000 capital gain, (I.R.C. Section 751(b) does not apply because the inventory is not substantially appreciated.) The distribution results in a $15,000 basis increase to partnership assets, all of which is allocated to the class of capital assets. The basis increase is first allocated among the appreciated assets in that class properties in proportion to the amount of unrealized appreciation. Capital Asset 1 has $30,000 of unrealized appreciation and Capital Asset 3 has $15,000 of unrealized appreciation. Consequently, the basis of Capital Asset 1 increases by

---

[186] Treas. Reg. § 1.734-1(e).

$10,000 [$15,000 x ($30,000 / $45,000)], and the basis of Capital Asset 3 increases by $5,000 [$15,000 x ($15,000 / $45,000)].

The partnership's balance sheet after the basis adjustments appears as follows:

Assets	Basis	Value
Capital Asset 1	40,000	60,000
Capital Asset 2	25,000	20,000
Capital Asset 3	20,000	30,000
Inventory	65,000	70,000
Total Assets	$150,000	$180,000
Partners' Capital		
Rhea	$75,000	$90,000
Sara	75,000	90,000
Total Partners' Capital	$150,000	$180,000

Example (2): Moira's one-fourth interest in the MNOP Partnership is liquidated in exchange for a $110,000 cash distribution. Immediately before the distribution is made, the partnership has an I.R.C. Section 754 election, in effect and its balance sheet is as follows:

Assets	Basis	Value
Cash	$110,000	$110,000
Capital Asset 1	48,000	50,000
Capital Asset 2	24,000	30,000
Inventory	222,000	250,000
Total Assets	$404,000	$440,000

Partners' Capital	Basis	Value
Moira	$101,000	$110,000
Nathan	101,000	110,000
Oliver	101,000	110,000
Penny	101,000	110,000
Total Partners' Capital	$404,000	$440,000

Moira recognizes a $9,000 capital gain, resulting in a $9,000 basis increase to partnership capital assets. (I.R.C. Section 751 does not apply because the inventory is not substantially appreciated.) First, $2,000 of basis increase for unrealized appreciation is allocated to Capital Asset 1 and $6,000 of basis increase is allocated to Capital Asset 2. The remaining $1,000 of basis increase is allocated among all the capital assets in proportion to their fair market values. Thus $625 of basis is allocated to Capital Asset 1 (50,000/80,000 x 1,000) and $375 is allocated to Capital Asset 2 (30,000/80,000 x 1,000). The partnership's balance sheet now appears as follows:

Assets	Basis	Value
Capital Asset 1	50,625	50,000
Capital Asset 2	30,375	30,000
Inventory	222,000	250,000
Total Assets	$303,000	$330,000
Partners' Capital		
Nathan	101,000	110,000
Oliver	101,000	110,000
Penny	101,000	110,000
Total Partners' Capital	$303,000	$330,000

[2] Distributee Partner Recognizes Loss on Liquidating Distribution

The KLM Partnership distributes $50,000 in cash to Marsha in complete liquidation of her partnership interest. Immediately before the distribution, KLM's balance sheet is as follows:

Assets	Basis	Value
Cash	$50,000	$50,000
Capital Asset 1	70,000	55,000
Capital Asset 2	60,000	45,000
Total Assets	$180,000	$150,000
Partners' Capital		
Ken	$60,000	$50,000
Lewis	60,000	50,000
Marsha	60,000	50,000
Total Partners' Capital	$180,000	$150,000

Because the amount of cash Marsha receives in the liquidating distribution is less than the basis of her partnership interest, she recognizes a $10,000 loss under I.R.C. Section 731(a)(2). If KLM has an I.R.C. Section 754 election in effect, the basis in its class of capital assets decreases by $10,000. Since both Capital Asset 1 and Capital Asset 2 have equal amounts of unrealized depreciation ($15,000), $5,000 of basis decrease is allocated to each asset. After the I.R.C. Section 754 adjustment, the partnership's balance sheet appears as follows:

Assets	Basis	Value
Capital Asset 1	$65,000	$55,000
Capital Asset 2	55,000	45,000
Total Assets	$120,000	$100,000
Partners' Capital		
Ken	$60,000	$50,000
Lewis	60,000	50,000
Total Partners' Capital	$120,000	$100,000

[3]   Basis of Distributed Property Changes

Situation (1). The ABC Partnership makes a current distribution of Capital Asset A to Arthur. The partnership has an I.R.C. Section 754 election in effect immediately before the distribution is made, and its balance sheet is as follows:

Assets	Basis	Value
Capital Asset A	$60,000	$60,000
Capital Asset B	10,000	50,000
Inventory Item 1	10,000	30,000
Inventory Item 2	70,000	70,000
Total Assets	$150,000	$210,000
Partners' Capital		
Arthur	$50,000	$70,000
Barry	50,000	70,000
Carol	50,000	70,000
Total Partners' Capital	$150,000	$210,000

Although the partnership's basis for Capital Asset A is $60,000, Arthur's basis for the property is limited to the $50,000 basis of his partnership interest. Because the distributed property is a capital asset, the partnership increases the basis of its undistributed capital assets by the $10,000 in basis "lost" in the distribution.

After the basis adjustment, the balance sheet appears as follows:

Assets	Basis	Value
Capital Asset B	20,000	50,000
Inventory Item 1	10,000	30,000
Inventory Item 2	70,000	70,000
Total Assets	$100,000	$150,000
Partners' Capital		
Arthur	$0	$10,000
Barry	50,000	70,000
Carol	50,000	70,000
Total Partners' Capital	$100,000	$150,000

Situation (2). Assume the same facts as in Situation (1), except that the partnership distributes Inventory Item 2 to Arthur. Although the partnership's basis for the inventory is $70,000, Arthur's basis for the property is limited to the $50,000 basis of his partnership interest. Because the distributed property is not a capital asset, the partnership increases the basis of its undistributed ordinary-income property by the $20,000 in basis "lost" in the distribution. After the adjustment, ABC's balance sheet appears as follows:

Assets	Basis	Value
Capital Asset A	$60,000	$60,000
Capital Asset B	10,000	50,000
Inventory Item 1	30,000	30,000
Total Assets	$100,000	$140,000
Partners' Capital		
Arthur	$0	$0
Barry	50,000	70,000
Carol	50,000	70,000
Total Partners' Capital	$100,000	$140,000

Situation (3). The CDE Partnership distributes Capital Asset A to Charles in complete liquidation of his partnership interest. When the property is distributed, the partnership has an I.R.C. Section 754 election in effect, and its balance sheet is as follows:

Assets	Basis	Value
Capital Asset A	$50,000	$70,000
Capital Asset B	10,000	30,000
Capital Asset C	10,000	6,000
Capital Asset D	10,000	4,000
Inventory	100,000	100,000
Total Assets	$180,000	$210,000

Partners' Capital	Basis	Value
Charles	$60,000	$70,000
Dana	60,000	70,000
Errol	60,000	70,000
Total Partners' Capital	$180,000	$210,000

Although the partnership's basis for Capital Asset A is only $50,000, Charles's basis for the property is $60,000 — the basis of his partnership interest at the time he receives the liquidating distribution. Because the distributed property is a capital asset, the partnership decreases the basis of its capital-gain property by the $10,000 of basis Charles "gained" in the distribution. The basis decrease is allocated to the assets with unrealized depreciation — $4,000 to Asset C and $6,000 to Asset D. After the adjustment, ABC's balance sheet appears as follows:

Assets	Basis	Value
Capital Asset B	$10,000	$30,000
Capital Asset C	6,000	6,000
Capital Asset D	4,000	4,000
Inventory	100,000	100,000
Total Assets	$120,000	$140,000

Partners' Capital	Basis	Value
Dana	$60,000	$70,000
Errol	60,000	70,000
Total Partners' Capital	$120,000	$140,000

[4]   Elective Adjustment Under I.R.C. Section 732(d)

I.R.C. Section 732(d) provides special rules for determining the basis in property distributed to a partner who acquires his partnership interest by sale or exchange or as successor to a deceased partner when the partnership did not have an I.R.C. Section 754 election in effect. A distributee partner may elect under I.R.C. Section 732(d) to determine his basis in property the partnership distributes to him within two years of the date he acquired his interest as if the partnership had an I.R.C. Section 754 election in effect on the acquisition date. In some situations, a partner may be required to determine his basis in distributed property under the rules of I.R.C. Section 732(d), regardless of when the distribution is made (*i.e.*, the two-year limitation does not apply). For complete discussion of I.R.C. Section 732(d), see § 12.08, *infra*.

> **Example:** [187] Toni purchased a one-fourth interest in the PRS Partnership for $17,000 when no election under I.R.C. Section 754 was in effect. On the purchase date, the partnership owned inventory with a basis of $14,000 and a fair market value of $16,000. Thus, $4,000 of the amount Toni paid for her interest was attributable to her share of inventory with a basis to the partnership of $3,500. One year later, Toni retired from the partnership and made an election under I.R.C. Section 732(d) with respect to her liquidating distribution of the following property (which includes her one-fourth share of partnership inventory):[188]

Assets	Basis to PRS	Fair market value
Cash	$1,500	$1,500
Inventory	3,500	4,000
Asset X	2,000	4,000
Asset Y	4,000	5,000
Total Assets	$11,000	$14,500

Toni's basis for the inventory increases by $500 (one-fourth of the $2,000 difference between the $16,000 fair market value of the inventory and its $14,000 basis to the partnership when Toni purchased her interest). This adjustment applies only to Toni's distribution and not for purposes of partnership depreciation, depletion, or gain or loss on disposition. The total basis allocated among the properties Toni received in the liquidating distribution is $15,500 ($17,000 basis for Toni's partnership interest less

---

[187]   Treas. Reg. § 1.732-1(d)(1)(vi).

[188]   The Regulations indicate that it is immaterial whether the inventory Toni received was on hand when she acquired the interest. Treas. Reg. § 1.732-1(d)(1)(vi), *Example*.

$1,500 of cash she received). Of this amount, $4,000 of basis is allocated to the inventory ($3,500 common partnership basis plus the $500 basis adjustment). The remaining $11,500 of basis is allocated among the two capital assets as follows:

(1) $5,111 basis to Asset X ($2,000 partnership basis, plus $2,000 of unrealized appreciation, plus $1,111 [$4,000/$9,000 x $2,500]).

(2) $6,389 basis to Asset Y ($4,000 partnership basis of Asset Y plus $1,000 of unrealized appreciation plus $1,389 [$5,000/$9,000 x $2,500]).

[C] Unusable Basis Adjustments Carried Forward

A partnership may be unable to apply all or a part of the basis increase or decrease triggered by a distribution because the partnership owns no property in the class to which the adjustment applies, or because the basis of all the property in that class has been reduced to zero. In these situations, the adjustment is suspended and subsequently applied when the partnership acquires property to which the adjustment can be made.[189]

(1) *Basis adjustment cannot be used currently because the partnership does not retain any property in the class to which the basis adjustment must be allocated.* The unused adjustment is carried forward indefinitely, and it is applied when the partnership subsequently acquires property to which the adjustment can be made.

Example: The MNO Partnership has an I.R.C. Section 754 election in effect when it distributes stock valued at $60,000 to Mary in liquidation of her partnership interest. Before MNO distributes the stock, MNO's balance sheet is as follows:

Assets	Basis	Value
Cash	$30,000	$30,000
Stock	60,000	60,000
Inventory	84,000	90,000
Total Assets	$174,000	$180,000

Partners' Capital	Basis	Value
Mary	$58,000	$60,000
Ned	58,000	60,000
Oliver	58,000	60,000
Total Partners' Capital	$174,000	$180,000

Because this is a liquidating distribution, Mary's basis in the stock equals the $58,000 basis of her partnership interest. I.R.C. Section 751(b) does not apply because the inventory is not substantially appreciated. The distribution decreases the basis of the stock by $2,000, and therefore, MNO may increase the basis of its capital gain property by $2,000. Because the

---

[189] I.R.C. § 755(b); Treas. Reg. § 1.755-1(c)(4).

partnership has no remaining capital gain property, the basis adjustment is carried forward. When the partnership acquires capital gain property, the suspended basis adjustment may be applied to increase the basis of that asset.

(2)   *Basis adjustment cannot be used currently to the extent that the basis decrease allocated to an asset would result in a basis that is less than zero.* [190]

Example: The CDE Partnership distributes Capital Asset A to Charles in complete liquidation of his partnership interest. When the distribution is made, the partnership has an I.R.C. Section 754 election in effect, and its balance sheet is as follows:

Assets	Basis	Value
Capital Asset A	$50,000	$70,000
Capital Asset B	10,000	5,000
Inventory	135,000	135,000
Total Assets	$195,000	$210,000
Partners' Capital		
Charles	$65,000	$70,000
Dana	65,000	7 0,000
Errol	65,000	70,000
Total Partners' Capital	$195,000	$210,000

Although the partnership's basis for Capital Asset A is only $50,000, Charles's basis for the property is $65,000 — the basis of his partnership interest at the time he receives the liquidating distribution. Because the distributed property is a capital asset, the $15,000 basis decrease resulting from the distribution is allocated to the class of partnership capital gain property. Because the basis of Capital Asset B cannot be reduced to less than zero, its basis decreases by $10,000. The remaining $5,000 of basis decrease is suspended until the partnership acquires property in the capital asset class to which the basis adjustment can be applied.

[D]   Distributions By Tiered Partnerships

Distribution of interest in another partnership. When the property distributed to a partner consists of an interest in another partnership, the last sentence of I.R.C. Section 734(b)(2)(B) provides a special rule: a distributing partnership (parent) with a basis-adjustment election in effect cannot increase the basis of its retained property, unless the partnership whose interest is distributed (subsidiary) also has an election in effect. This rule was enacted to prevent parent-subsidiary partnerships from being used to defer recognition of gain.[191]

---

[190]   Treas. Reg. § 1.755-1(a)(1)(iii).

[191]   H.R. Rep. No. 98-861, 98th Cong., 2d Sess. 21 (1984).

The basis adjustment limitation of I.R.C. Section 734(b)(2)(B) applies only if the subsidiary partnership does not have an I.R.C. Section 754 election in effect when the parent distributes its interest in the subsidiary. If both parent and subsidiary partnerships have elections in effect when the distribution occurs, the parent adjusts the basis of its undistributed property under the general rules of I.R.C. Section 734(b)(1)(B).[192]

Revenue Ruling 92-15[193] indicates that certain distributions will reduce the basis of property held by both parent and subsidiary partnerships if both have I.R.C. Section 754 elections in effect. For example, a liquidating distribution by a parent partnership to a partner having a higher basis in his partnership interest than in the distributed property may trigger decreases in the basis of both parent's and subsidiary's assets.

[E]   Basis Adjustment on Distributions Subject to I.R.C. Section 751(b)

A partnership that makes a distribution subject to I.R.C. Section 751(b) must determine the assets to which an I.R.C. Section 754 basis adjustment may apply. A disproportionate distribution of I.R.C. Section 751 property is treated as if:

(1)   the distributee partner received a current distribution of his proportionate share of the partnership's I.R.C. Section 751 property and other property; and

(2)   the distributee partner exchanged a portion of one class of property for an extra amount of the other class of property that he actually received.

To determine the effect of an I.R.C. Section 754 election on a distribution subject to I.R.C. Section 751(b), the distribution must be divided into two parts:

Part (1) - The property deemed to have been distributed to the partner and transferred back to the partnership in exchange for the property he actually received.

Although no direct authority exists, statutory language indicates that the basis-adjustment rules do not apply to this deemed distribution. I.R.C. Section 734(b) indicates that adjustments are made to reflect:

(1)   gain or loss recognized under I.R.C. Section 731(a); and

(2)   changes in the basis of distributed property that occur pursuant to I.R.C. Section 732.

Neither I.R.C. Section 731(a) nor I.R.C. Section 732 apply to the extent that a distribution is subject to I.R.C. Section 751(b).[194]

Part (2) - The property actually distributed to the partner that is not subject to the hypothetical sale treatment under I.R.C. Section 751(b).

---

[192] Rev. Rul. 92-15, 1992-1 C.B. 215, Situation (2).

[193] 1992-1 C.B. 215.

[194] I.R.C. §§ 731(c), 732(e).

The basis-adjustment rules of I.R.C. Section 734(b) clearly apply to this part of the distribution. Thus, the partnership increases or decreases the basis of its undistributed assets if the partner recognizes gain or loss on the distribution or if the distribution changes the basis of the property.

[F] Making a Basis-Adjustment Election

A partnership makes a basis-adjustment election by filing a statement, signed by a partner, with its income tax return, filed in a timely manner, for the year the distribution or transfer was made.[195] The election applies to distributions and transfers of partnership interests in that tax year[196] and in all subsequent years, unless it is revoked with the permission of the Service.

---

[195] Treas. Reg. § 1.754-1(b)(1).

[196] Jones v. U.S., 553 F.2d 667 (Ct. Cl. 1977).

Chapter 9

FAMILY PARTNERSHIPS AND LIMITED LIABILITY COMPANIES

§ 9.01 OVERVIEW OF FAMILY PARTNERSHIP RULES

The family partnership rules are designed to prevent partnerships and limited liability companies from being used to shift income from higher-bracket family members to lower-bracket family members. The rules reflect the assignment-of-income doctrine, which requires the income from property to be taxed to the person who owns the property, and the income from services to be taxed to the person who performs the services. I.R.C. Section 704(e)(1) applies the assignment-of-income doctrine to partnerships that derive most of their income from invested capital, and the courts have developed similar rules for partnerships that derive most of their income from services. The family partnership rules may be summarized as follows:

(1) I.R.C. Section 704(e)(1) provides rules for determining when a person is recognized as a partner for tax purposes. Although the statute is not specifically limited to family partnerships, it usually applies in establishing whether a relative who receives a partnership interest by gift or purchase is considered a partner. I.R.C. Section 704(e)(1) applies only to partnerships in which capital is a material income-producing factor; it does not affect partnerships that derive most of their income from services. A donee of a partnership interest is recognized as a partner if he is given genuine ownership of an interest in the partnership's capital. Thus, a purported gift of a partnership interest is ignored for tax purposes if, in substance, the donor continues to own the interest through his power to control or influence the donee's business decisions. Because a person who is not recognized as a partner cannot share in partnership income, his purported share is reallocated to the other partners.

(2) I.R.C. Section 704(e)(2) governs the amount of partnership income that may be allocated to a partner who receives a partnership interest by gift. The statute prevents excessive income shifting among family members by reallocating income from the donee to the donor if

(a) the donee's share of income is determined without accounting for the value of the donor's services to the partnership, or

(b) the donee's share of partnership income is disproportionately greater than the interest in partnership capital he receives.

The allocation rules apply to all gifts of partnership interests, regardless of whether the partnership generates its income from invested capital or by rendering services.

(3)   Under I.R.C. Section 704(e)(3), a partnership interest purchased from certain family members is treated as a gift. Thus, rules specifically applicable to gifts of partnership interests also may apply to purchased interests.

(4)   Because I.R.C. Section 704(e)(1) is specifically limited to partnerships in which capital is a material income-producing factor, it does not apply to partnerships that derive income primarily from services. Whether a family partnership in a services business is recognized for tax purposes is determined under a test established by the Supreme Court in *Commissioner v. Culbertson.* [1] The Court held that a partnership is recognized for tax purposes if the facts show that the parties, acting in good faith and with a business purpose, intended to join together in a partnership.[2] Subsequent cases that have applied the *Culbertson* test to service partnerships indicate that the basic issue is whether the family members seeking recognition as partners will contribute substantial services to the business.[3] For example, a parent-daughter partnership was disregarded when the daughter did nothing to benefit or further the partnership's business.[4]

§ 9.02   KEY ISSUES IN ESTABLISHING PARTNER STATUS IN A FAMILY PARTNERSHIP

The current rules governing family partnerships are best understood in the context of their historical development. In *Commissioner v. Tower*,[5] the Supreme Court attempted to limit the use of family partnerships as income-shifting devices by holding that a partnership is not recognized for tax purposes unless the parties "really and truly" intend to jointly conduct a business and share its profits and losses. The Court indicated that a person may establish his intention to become a partner by providing either "original capital" or "vital services" to the partnership. Lower courts subsequently misapplied the Supreme Court's opinion by requiring family members to contribute original capital or vital services in order to be recognized as partners.[6] In effect, the original capital requirement precluded a family member who received a partnership interest by gift from being recognized as a partner, unless he performed significant services for the partnership.

---

[1]   337 U.S. 733 (1949).

[2]   *See, e.g.*, Poggetto v. U.S., 306 F.2d 76, 79 (9th Cir. 1962).

[3]   Payton v. U.S., 425 F.2d 1324 (5th Cir.), *cert. denied*, 400 U.S. 957 (1970); Manuel v. Comm'r, T.C. Memo. 1983-138.

[4]   Poggetto v. U.S., 306 F.2d 76 (9th Cir. 1962). *But see* Ketter v. Comm'r, 70 T.C. 637, 644 (1978), *aff'd without published opinion*, 605 F.2d 1209 (8th Cir. 1979).

[5]   327 U.S. 280 (1946). *See also* Lusthaus v. Comm'r, 327 U.S. 293 (1946).

[6]   *See, e.g.*, Akers v. Comm'r, 6 T.C. 693 (1946); Lang v. Comm'r, 7 T.C. 6 (1946); Simons v. Comm'r, 7 T.C. 114 (1946); Friedman v. Comm'r, 10 T.C. 1145 (1948); Greenberg v. Comm'r, 158 F.2d 800 (6th Cir. 1946); Dawson v. Comm'r, 163 F.2d 664 (6th Cir. 1947).

[A]   Subjective Test of Partner Status: *Commissioner v. Culbertson*

In *Commissioner v. Culbertson*,[7] the Supreme Court rejected the view that the original-capital and vital-services requirements were the only tests for recognizing family partnerships. The Court held that all the facts must be considered in determining whether the parties, in good faith and with a business purpose, intended to join together to conduct the enterprise.[8] Consequently, the trier of fact in each case must analyze objective factors such as contributions of capital and of services, the partnership agreement, the conduct and relationships of the parties, and the control over income, to determine the subjective intentions of the parties.[9]

The *Culbertson* decision did not end the confusion in the lower courts regarding the appropriate tests for recognizing family partnerships.[10] To clarify the situation, Congress enacted the statutory family partnerships rules in 1951, currently found in I.R.C. Section 704(e)(1).[11] Legislative history indicates that these rules are intended to ensure that a partnership interest is treated in the same manner as other property or business interests.[12] Thus, the owner of a partnership interest is taxable on his share of partnership income even though he obtains the interest by gift. The only issue to be resolved in each case is whether the donee actually owns the partnership interest purportedly given to him.[13]

Enactment of the I.R.C. Section 704(e) rules did not completely eliminate the subjective test for partner status set forth in *Culbertson*. I.R.C. Section 704(e)(1) is specifically limited to situations in which a person receives a capital interest in a partnership in which capital is a material income-producing factor. Thus, the *Culbertson* facts and circumstances analysis is still applied to determine whether a donee is recognized as a partner when the donee does not own an interest in partnership capital or the partnership derives most of its income from services.[14]

---

[7]   337 U.S. 733 (1949).

[8]   *Id.* at 742–43.

[9]   *Id.* at 743.

[10]   *See, e.g.*, Barrett v. Comm'r, 13 T.C. 539 (1949), *aff'd*, 185 F.2d 150 (1st Cir. 1950) (original capital rule applied); Harkness v. Comm'r, 193 F.2d 655 (9th Cir. 1951) (same); Feldman v. Comm'r, 14 T.C. 17, *aff'd*, 186 F.2d 87 (4th Cir. 1950) (same); Giffen v. Comm'r, 14 T.C. 1272 (1950), *aff'd*, 190 F.2d 188 (9th Cir. 1951) (business purpose required for recognition of family partnership).

[11]   § 3797(a)(2), 191 of the 1939 I.R.C., enacted in the Revenue Act of 1951.

[12]   H.R. Rep. No. 586, 82d Cong., 1st Sess. 32 (1951), and S. Rep. No. 781, 82d Cong., 1st Sess. 485 (1951).

[13]   S. Rep. No. 781, 82d Cong., 1st Sess. 32, 33 (1951).

[14]   *See, e.g.*, Poggetto v. U.S., 306 F.2d 76 (9th Cir. 1962); Carriage Square, Inc. v. Comm'r, 69 T.C. 119 (1977); Cirelli v. Comm'r, 82 T.C. 335 (1984). The Service will not issue private letter rulings regarding the validity of partnerships in which capital is not a material income-producing factor. Rev. Proc. 93-1, 1993-1 C.B. 313.

[B]   Partner Status When Capital Is Material in Producing Income: I.R.C. Section 704(e)(1)

A person is recognized as a partner if he obtains actual ownership of a capital interest in a partnership in which capital is a material income-producing factor, regardless of whether the partner purchases the capital interest, acquires it by gift, or is given funds to contribute to the partnership for the interest.[15] In effect, I.R.C. Section 704(e)(1) provides a safe harbor test for ensuring that a person is considered a partner for tax purposes. A person seeking to establish partner status under the safe harbor must satisfy two tests:

(1)   The partnership must be one in which capital is a material income-producing factor.

(2)   The partner must have actual ownership of an interest in the partnership's capital.

If these tests are not satisfied, partner status must be established under the facts and circumstances test set forth by the Supreme Court in *Commissioner v. Culbertson.* [16]

The safe harbor of I.R.C. Section 704(e)(1) regarding recognition of a person as a partner is limited to partnerships in which capital is a material income-producing factor. This limitation is designed to preclude the use of a family partnership to shift the income of a personal services business among family members. In each case, reference to all the facts and circumstances determines whether capital is a material income-producing factor in a partnership.[17]

Although no precise formula exists, the regulations provide general guidelines:

Capital is a material income-producing factor if a substantial portion of the gross income of the business is attributable to the employment of capital in the business conducted by the partnership. In general, capital is not a material income-producing factor where the income of the business consists principally of fees, commissions, or other compensation for personal services performed by members or employees of the partnership. On the other hand, capital is ordinarily a material income-producing factor if the operation of the business requires substantial inventories or a substantial investment in plant, machinery, or other equipment.[18]

The question to be addressed in each case is whether a substantial portion of the partnership's gross income is generated by its use of capital.[19] In some situations

---

[15]   An assignee of a partnership interest may be considered a partner under I.R.C. § 704(e)(1). Evans v. Comm'r, 447 F.2d 547 (7th Cir. 1971) (corporation that received assignment of partnership interest recognized as partner even though other partner refused to consent to assignment).

[16]   337 U.S. 733 (1949).

[17]   Treas. Reg. § 1.704-1(e)(1)(iv).

[18]   Treas. Reg. § 1.704-1(e)(1)(iv).

[19]   Evans v. Comm'r, 54 T.C. 40 (1970), *aff'd*, 447 F.2d 547 (7th Cir. 1971), *acq.* 1978-2 C.B. 2 (significant investments in plant, machinery or equipment required to produce partnership products); Reddig v. Comm'r, 30 T.C. 1382 (1958) (same); U.S. v. Levasseur, 80-1 U.S.T.C. ¶ 9349, 45 A.F.T.R.2d 1507 (D. Vt.

the answer is fairly obvious — law practices usually do not generate substantial income from capital, most retail shops do. In many cases, however, the diverse sources of partnership income make it more difficult to determine whether a substantial portion of the income is attributable to capital. The following factors derived from case law should be considered when making this determination:

(1) An investment of capital in a business does not satisfy the income-production requirement if the capital is merely incidental to the performance of services that produce income.[20] For example, the income of a law firm or an accounting practice is not substantially derived from capital even though the attorneys and accountants have expended large amounts for libraries, office equipment, and other capital items.[21]

(2) Partnership capital is not considered incidental to a services business if it is used to finance inventory, accounts receivable, or other contractual business expenses.[22]

(3) Capital is not producing income even if large amounts of cash are needed to pay the salaries of employees who perform services for a professional partnership.[23] Rather, the income is generated by the professional judgment, reputation, experience, and managerial know-how of the partners, and not by the employees they supervise.

(4) Partnership goodwill can be a material income-producing factor if it generates a substantial portion of partnership income,[24] even if the goodwill does not appear on the partnership's balance sheet.[25] Many family partnerships may find it difficult to establish the value of goodwill because, in order for it to be considered, the goodwill must belong to the partnership

1980) (same); Garcia v. Comm'r, T.C. Memo. 1984-340 (same); Woodbury v. Comm'r, 49 T.C. 180 (1967), *acq.* 1969-2 C.B. xxv (use of land needed in farming or ranching operations); Speelman v. Comm'r, T.C. Memo. 1981-115 (same).

[20] Treas. Reg. § 1.704-1(e)(1)(iv). *See, e.g.,* Poggetto v. U.S., 193 F. Supp. 688 (N.D. Cal. 1961), *aff'd,* 306 F.2d 76 (9th Cir. 1962) (income derived from canning operation not substantial in brokerage business that operated for many years with minimal capital); Ketter v. Comm'r, 70 T.C. 637 (1978), *aff'd without published opinion,* 605 F.2d 1209 (8th Cir. 1979) (value of partnership equipment small in comparison to salaries paid to employees and partnership's gross income); Payton v. U.S., 425 F.2d 1324 (5th Cir.), *cert. denied,* 400 U.S. 957 (1970) (same).

[21] *See, e.g.,* Payton v. U.S., 425 F.2d 1324 (5th Cir. 1970) (capital not material income-producing factor in optical sales business operated in conjunction with ophthalmology practice).

[22] Garcia v. Comm'r, T.C. Memo. 1984-340 (large inventories needed); Hartman v. Comm'r, 43 T.C. 105 (1964), *acq.* 1965-2 C.B. 5 (reserves needed to extend customer credit and to pay advance sales commissions and other continuing expenses); Bennett v. Comm'r, T.C. Memo. 1962-163 (substantial capital reserves required to carry accounts receivable); O'Donnell v. Comm'r, T.C. Memo. 1964-38 (funds needed for investment where substantial income derived from securities investments). *See also* Krause v. Comm'r, 57 T.C. 890 (1972), *aff'd,* 497 F.2d 1109 (6th Cir. 1974), *cert. denied,* 419 U.S. 1108 (1975).

[23] Ketter v. Comm'r, 70 T.C. 637 (1978), *aff'd without published opinion,* 605 F.2d 1209 (8th Cir. 1979) (capital not material income-producing factor in partnership CPA in sole proprietorship formed by transferring employees and work-in-progress to partnership of family trusts).

[24] Bateman v. U.S., 490 F.2d 549 (9th Cir. 1973) (capital was material in a food brokerage business that had unbooked goodwill worth $400,000, many non-partner employees, and substantial accounts receivable).

[25] *Id.*

and not to the partners as individuals.[26] Goodwill is generally deemed personal to a partner who can withdraw it from the partnership.[27] A partnership can prove its ownership of goodwill if the goodwill's value is reflected in the price that new partners pay for partnership interests.

(5)   A partnership can operate at a net loss and still satisfy the capital income-production requirement[28] because gross income is gross receipts less cost of goods sold and is determined before other expenses are deducted.[29]

Are borrowed funds considered capital? In *Carriage Square, Inc. v. Commissioner*,[30] the Tax Court held that a loan to a family partnership that was guaranteed by a nonpartner was not partnership capital for the material income-production test of I.R.C. Section 704(e)(1). This decision indicates that whether borrowed funds are considered capital depends on the circumstances surrounding the loan. Although the correctness of *Carriage Square* is doubtful, particularly in light of earlier cases that included borrowed capital to satisfy the material income-production test,[31] this case has created considerable uncertainty.

[C]   Partner Status When Capital Interest Is Acquired by Gift

As previously mentioned, the safe harbor of I.R.C. Section 704(e)(1) applies only to persons who have a capital interest in the partnership. The regulations state that a partner has a capital interest to the extent that partnership assets will be distributed to him if he withdraws from the partnership or if the partnership liquidates.[32] Consequently, an interest in the partnership's earnings or profits is not sufficient for purposes of the statute.[33]

A donee-partner may own a capital interest even though nothing is credited to his capital account on the partnership's books. For example, if the donee receives an interest that entitles him to share in the unrealized appreciation in partnership assets, the value of the capital interest given to the donee equals the amount that would have been credited to his capital account if the partnership revalued its assets on the date of the gift (*i.e.*, the amount that would be distributed to him if the partnership liquidated immediately after the gift). Actual revaluation of the

---

[26] Bennett v. Comm'r, T.C. Memo. 1962-163 (goodwill belonged to taxpayer individually and not the partnership).

[27] *See* Treas. Reg. § 1.704-1(e)(2)(ii)*(c)*.

[28] Treas. Reg. § 1.61-3.

[29] *See, e.g.*, Edward P. Allison Co. v. Comm'r, 63 F.2d 553 (8th Cir. 1933); Brewster v. Comm'r, 55 T.C. 251 (1970), *aff'd*, 473 F.2d 160 (D.C. Cir. 1972).

[30] 69 T.C. 119 (1977).

[31] Hartman v. Comm'r, 43 T.C. 105 (1964); Bennett v. Comm'r, T.C. Memo. 1962-163; Walberg v. Smyth, 142 F. Supp. 293 (N.D. Cal. 1956) (decided under predecessor to I.R.C. § 704(e)). *See generally* Banoff, Long, Steele & Smith, *Family Partnerships: Capital as a Material Income-Producing Factor*, 37 Tax Law. 2 (1984).

[32] Treas. Reg. § 1.704-1(e)(1)(v).

[33] *Id.*

partnership's assets usually is not possible because the regulations governing special allocations bar revaluations when a partnership interest is transferred by gift or sale.[34]

Once a person receives a capital interest, he should continue to be recognized as a partner even if the value of his share of partnership assets decreases to the point at which he will not receive any distribution on liquidation of the partnership. To hold otherwise would necessitate continual appraisals of partnership property to determine whether a person is still a partner.

A person is not recognized as a partner under I.R.C. Section 704(e)(1) unless he obtains real ownership of a capital interest in the partnership.[35] Although this real-ownership test is not limited to family partnerships, the ownership issue does not arise for nonfamily members because of their presumed self-interest. Consequently, the rules for determining actual ownership of a partnership interest focus on interests transferred by gift. However, under I.R.C. Section 704(e)(3), even a person who purchases a partnership interest from a family member is generally deemed to acquire the interest by gift.

A donee is not recognized as a partner under I.R.C. Section 704(e)(1) unless he acquires his partnership interest in a bona fide transaction, not a mere sham transaction for tax purposes, and he must have real ownership of the interest.[36] Whether the transaction is bona fide is determined by examining all the facts and circumstances with particular emphasis on the actual conduct of the parties.[37] A gift of a partnership interest may be ignored if the state law formalities required to evidence the transfer are not satisfied.[38]

The regulations describe the factors deemed important in establishing whether the donor actually owns the interest.[39] Most of these factors concern various controls over partnership operations that the owner of a partnership interest normally exercises.

A gift of an interest in a partnership or LLC may not qualify for the annual gift tax exclusion if it is considered a future, rather than a present interest. Under IRC Section 2503(b), up to $13,000 (in 2010) per donee may be transferred each year without gift tax reporting. Future interests that do not qualify for this exclusion include reversions, remainders, and other interests that are limited to begin in use, possession, or enjoyment at a future date.[40]

---

[34] Treas. Reg. § 1.704-1(b)(2)(iv)(f). See Chapter 4.

[35] Treas. Reg. § 1.704-1(e)(2)(i).

[36] Treas. Reg. § 1.704-1(e)(1)(iii).

[37] Treas. Reg. § 1.704-1(e)(1)(iii).

[38] Treas. Reg. § 1.704-1(e)(1)(iii). See Woodbury v. Comm'r, 49 T.C. 180 (1967), acq. 1969-2 C.B. xxv; Ramos v. U.S., 260 F. Supp. 479 (N.D. Cal. 1966), rev'd and remanded, 393 F.2d 618 (9th Cir. 1968); Driscoll v. U.S., 69-2 U.S.T.C. ¶ 9536 (C.D. Cal. 1969). However, the fact that legally sufficient transfer documents are executed does not, by itself, conclusively establish ownership for tax purposes. Treas. Reg. § 1.704-1(e)(2)(i).

[39] Treas. Reg. § 1.704-1(e)(2)(i)–(x).

[40] Treas. Reg. 25.2503-3(a).

[1]   Donor Is the Real Owner

The regulations cite four controls over a partnership interest that are important in determining that the donor is the real owner of the partnership interest:

(1)   control over income distributions;

(2)   control over the right to liquidate or sell the interest;

(3)   control over essential business assets; and

(4)   control over partnership management.[41]

If the donor, rather than the donee, exercises these controls directly or indirectly, the purported transfer may be disregarded and the donor may be treated as the owner of the partnership interest, but only if the donor exercises these controls for his own benefit and not when the donor acts as a fiduciary on the donee's behalf.[42]

Control over distribution of income. A donee's ownership of a partnership interest may be questioned if the donor retains the right to control distributions of partnership income to the donee.[43] The control over distributions may arise because the donor is empowered to manage partnership affairs (*e.g.*, when the donor is the managing partner or is the general partner in a limited partnership) or because the donor places limitations on distributions in the partnership agreement (*e.g.*, the partnership agreement requires accumulation of a substantial percentage of partnership income).[44] Case law indicates that a donee will not be treated as the owner of a partnership interest if he cannot receive or use income distributions without the donor's approval,[45] or if he is required to apply his share of partnership income against his preexisting indebtedness to the donor.[46]

A donor's control over distributions of amounts the partnership retains each year to meet its reasonable business needs does not indicate lack of ownership by the donee; the donor may retain these amounts in the partnership with the consent of all the partners, including the donee.[47] If the partnership agreement provides for one or more managing partners, the partnership may accumulate income for the reasonable needs of its business without the consent of all the partners.[48] Although no direct authority exists,[49] a partnership should be able to determine the reasonable needs of its business by applying the same analysis used for determining the accumulated earnings tax on corporations.

---

[41]   Treas. Reg. § 1.704-1(e)(2)(ii).

[42]   H.R. Rep. No. 586, 82d Cong., 1st Sess. 33 (1951); S. Rep. No. 781, 82d Cong., 1st Sess. 40 (1951).

[43]   Treas. Reg. § 1.704-1(e)(2)(ii)*(a)*.

[44]   Kuney v. Frank, 308 F.2d 719 (9th Cir. 1962).

[45]   Sellers v. Comm'r, 218 F.2d 380 (9th Cir. 1955); Lieber v. U.S., 119 F. Supp. 951 (Ct. Cl. 1954); Fiore v. Comm'r, T.C. Memo. 1979-360, *aff'd in unpublished opinion*, 636 F.2d 1208 (3d Cir. 1980).

[46]   Manuel v. Comm'r, T.C. Memo. 1983-138.

[47]   Treas. Reg. § 1.704-1(e)(2)(ii)*(a)*.

[48]   Treas. Reg. § 1.704-1(e)(2)(ii)*(a)*.

[49]   *See* Tiberti v. Comm'r, T.C. Memo. 1962-174; Bennett v. Comm'r, T.C. Memo. 1962-163 (retention of earnings allowed without discussion of that issue).

Appropriate provisions in the partnership agreement may evidence the donor's lack of control over income distributions, *e.g.*, the agreement can state that all income will be distributed except for amounts that all partners agree to retain in the partnership to meet its reasonable business needs. If there is a managing partner, the partnership agreement should authorize him to determine the amount required to be retained to meet these needs.

The fact that a donee actually receives distributions of all or most of his distributive share of partnership income for his sole benefit and use is substantial evidence that he truly owns a partnership interest.[50] Distributed amounts are not considered to be for the donee's sole benefit and use if they are deposited, loaned, or invested so that the donor controls their use and enjoyment.[51]

Control over disposition of partnership interest. A donor who limits the donee's right to liquidate or sell his interest in the partnership at his discretion without financial detriment is considered to retain a significant control over that interest.[52] This control may be considered to exist if the donor or partnership can purchase the donee's interest for substantially less than its actual value[53] or can absolutely prohibit the donee from selling or liquidating the interest.[54] A limitation on the donee's right to liquidate his interest is particularly significant when the donor has managerial or voting control over the partnership.[55]

Certain restrictions on a donee's right to transfer or liquidate his interest are not considered retained control by the donor. If the donee must first offer to sell his partnership interest to the partnership or other partners at the same price offered by a third party, that restriction is not considered a retained control.[56] Limitations on a donee's right to dispose of his partnership interests are less significant when all the partners' interests are subject to similar limitations.[57]

Control over essential partnership assets. A donor may be treated as the owner of an interest purportedly given away if he retains control over assets that are essential to the partnership's business.[58] This provision is directed at situations in which the donor leases essential assets to the partnership on an at-will or short-term basis.[59] The donor's control of property needed to conduct the partner-

---

[50]　Treas. Reg. § 1.704-1(e)(2)(v).

[51]　Treas. Reg. § 1.704-1(e)(2)(v).

[52]　Treas. Reg. § 1.704-1(e)(2)(ii)*(b)*.

[53]　Ginsberg v. Comm'r, 502 F.2d 965 (6th Cir. 1974); Toor v. Westover, 200 F.2d 713 (9th Cir. 1952), *cert. denied*, 345 U.S. 975 (1953); Offord v. Comm'r. T.C. Memo. 1961-159.

[54]　Krause v. Comm'r, 57 T.C. 890 (1972), *aff'd*, 497 F.2d 1109 (6th Cir. 1974).

[55]　Treas. Reg. § 1.704-1(e)(2)(ii)*(d)*.

[56]　Middlebrook v. Comm'r, 13 T.C. 385 (1949). The donor's right of first refusal is not a financial detriment to the donee, and it should not indicate that he is not the real owner of his partnership interest. Garcia v. Comm'r, T.C. Memo. 1984-340.

[57]　Middlebrook v. Comm'r, 13 T.C. 385 (1949); Bellamy v. Comm'r, 14 T.C. 867 (1950).

[58]　Treas. Reg. § 1.704-1(e)(2)(ii)*(c)*.

[59]　The dissenting opinion in Bateman v. U.S., 490 F.2d 549 (9th Cir. 1973) would have treated goodwill personal to donor as a control over an essential asset.

ship's business permits him to end the partnership's operations and make the donee's interest worthless.

The essential asset provision was a factor considered in *United States v. Ramos*,[60] a case that invalidated a family ranching partnership when the donor retained complete ownership of all the land and equipment needed to operate the ranch. In *Ketter v. Commissioner*,[61] a CPA assigned his work in progress and employment contracts with his employees to a partnership whose partners were trusts for his children. The CPA gave the partnership the rights to perform services for which he had contracts, but he retained complete control over his client lists. The court held that the CPA had retained control of the partnership's essential business assets through his control over the client list, the source of its work.

A donor should not be deemed to control essential assets that he leases to the partnership on commercially reasonable terms for a reasonable period or essential assets that the partnership can purchase if the lease is terminated for any reason. The purchase price should not exceed the value of the assets at the time of the purchase, the donor should not be able to control whether the option is exercised, and the partnership should be able to pay for the property.

Control over partnership management. A donor may be considered to retain significant control over a partnership interest if he retains management powers that are inconsistent with the normal relationship among partners.[62] The retention of voting rights or managerial control common in ordinary business relationships is not, by itself, inconsistent with the donee's ownership if the donee is free to liquidate his partnership interest at his discretion without financial detriment.[63] Thus, a donee who is free to liquidate his interest may be recognized as a partner even though the donor is the managing partner.

A donee is not considered free to liquidate his interest unless he is independent of the donor and has sufficient maturity and understanding to exercise his right to withdraw his capital from the partnership.[64]

Indirect controls. The question of whether a donee is the owner of a partnership interest arises whether the donor's control over the donee's partnership interest is direct or indirect.[65] Indirect controls may be exercised through a separate business organization, estate, trust, individual, or other partnership.[66] If indirect control exists, the reality of the donee's ownership is determined as if the donor can exercise the controls directly.

---

[60] 393 F.2d 618 (9th Cir.), *cert. denied*, 393 U.S. 983 (1968).

[61] 70 T.C. 637 (1978), *aff'd without published opinion*, 605 F.2d 1209 (8th Cir. 1979).

[62] Treas. Reg. § 1.704-1(e)(2)(ii)*(d)*.

[63] Treas. Reg. § 1.704-1(e)(2)(ii)*(d)*.

[64] Treas. Reg. § 1.704-1(e)(2)(ii)*(d)*.

[65] Treas. Reg. § 1.704-1(e)(2)(iii).

[66] Treas. Reg. § 1.704-1(e)(2)(iii).

The indirect control issue is illustrated in *Krause v. Commissioner*,[67] when a donor was treated as owner of an interest in a partnership that derived most of its income from dividends on stock of a corporation the donor controlled. The donor's control over the corporation's dividend payments was deemed an indirect control over the partnership's income.

[2] Donee Is the Real Owner

Factors indicative of a donee's ownership of a partnership interest concern the donee's participation in management, the distributions he receives, and whether he actually is treated as a partner in partnership operations. The following sections describe these factors in detail.

Participation in management. The regulations state that a donee's substantial participation in the control and management of the partnership's business, including participation in major policy decisions, is strong evidence that he owns his partnership interest.[68] This evidentiary factor assumes that the donee is sufficiently mature and experienced to deal with the partnership's business problems.[69] Thus, the donee's ownership cannot be inferred when he performs ministerial or low-level duties.

Activities that constitute substantial participation are illustrated in *Hartman v. Commissioner*,[70] where the Tax Court held that a trustee's active participation in management evidenced a valid partnership between a father and the trusts he created for his children. The Court found that the trustee, who was the father's brother-in-law, exercised independent judgment and contributed important services to the partnership's business.

Actual income distributions. The regulations state that substantial evidence that a donee owns his interest exists when the donee actually receives distributions of all or most of his distributive share of the partnership's business income.[71] However, the distributions must be for the sole benefit and use of the donee, and the donor must not retain controls inconsistent with the donee's ownership.

Conduct of partnership business. The fact that a donee actually is treated as a partner in the operation of the partnership's business is considered an indication of partnership status.[72] The most important issue is whether the donee has been held out publicly as a partner to customers, creditors, or other sources of financing.[73]

Other factors cited in the regulations as indications of partner status are:

---

[67] 57 T.C. 890 (1972), *aff'd*, 497 F.2d 1109 (6th Cir. 1974), *cert. denied*, 419 U.S. 1108 (1975). *See also* Ketter v. Comm'r, 70 T.C. 637 (1978) (donor had indirect control where partnership depended on his CPA proprietorship for income).

[68] Treas. Reg. § 1.704-1(e)(2)(iv).

[69] Treas. Reg. § 1.704-1(e)(2)(iv).

[70] 43 T.C. 105 (1964), *acq.* 1965-2 C.B. 5. *See also* Nichols v. Comm'r, 32 T.C. 1322 (1959); Tiberti v. Comm'r, T.C. Memo. 1962-174.

[71] Treas. Reg. § 1.704-1(e)(2)(v).

[72] Treas. Reg. § 1.704-1(e)(2)(vi).

[73] *Id.*

(1)   compliance with local partnership, fictitious name, and business registration statutes in a manner that acknowledges or reveals the donee's partnership interest;

(2)   control of business bank accounts in a manner consistent with the donee's status as a partner;

(3)   recognition of the donee's rights in distributions of partnership property and profits;

(4)   recognition of the donee's interest in insurance policies, leases, other business contracts, and in litigation affecting the business;

(5)   existence of written agreements, records, or memoranda, contemporaneous with the taxable year involved, that establish the nature of the partnership agreement and the rights and liabilities of the partners, including the donee; and

(6)   filing partnership tax returns that acknowledge the donee's interest.[74]

The fact that a partnership observes these formalities does not ensure that a donee will be recognized as a partner. Other circumstances may indicate that the donor retained substantial ownership of the interest purportedly transferred.[75]

It is unlikely that a partnership will be held invalid merely because it did not comply with these formalities if most other factors indicate that the donee actually owns his partnership interest.[76] In a borderline case, however, failure to satisfy these formalities can be decisive. In *Ketter v. Commissioner*,[77] for example, a purported partnership's failure to hold itself out as a separate entity and to register its name under the state's fictitious name statute were significant factors leading to nonrecognition of the partnership.

These formalities are likely to be examined quite early in an audit of the donor's or donee's tax returns. Noncompliance may foster closer examination. To observe the formalities, a family partnership should follow local laws concerning business form, list the donee as a partner on partnership documents, and authorize the donee to sign partnership documents. A written partnership agreement should be executed, and partnership tax returns should be filed.

---

[74] *Id.*

[75] *Id.*

[76] *See, e.g.,* Liebesman v. Comm'r, T.C. Memo. 1966-88 (husband and wife partnership recognized even though no partnership tax returns filed, lease renewals and employer withholding tax returns were in husband's name only, and all business profit was allocated to husband for self-employment tax reporting). *See also* Elrod v. Comm'r, 87 T.C. 1046 (1986).

[77] 70 T.C. 637 (1978), *aff'd without published opinion*, 605 F.2d 1209 (8th Cir. 1979). *See also* Cirelli v. Comm'r, 82 T.C. 335 (1984).

[3]　Limited Partnership Interest Acquired by Gift

The basic rule for gifts of limited partnership interests is the same as the rule applicable to gifts of general partnership interests: a donee is recognized as a limited partner if he obtains real ownership of a capital interest.[78] The tests for actual ownership are modified, however, because of the restricted nature of a limited partner's participation in partnership affairs. Under state law, a partner loses his limited partner status if he participates in managing the partnership's business.[79] Therefore, the criteria for ownership of a limited partnership interest focus on whether the donee fully enjoys the benefits of his capital interest rather than on his participation in partnership affairs.

A donee limited partner's failure to provide services for the partnership or to participate in its management is immaterial if the other requirements in the regulations are met, including qualification as a limited partnership under state law.[80] In addition, the regulations state that a donee's inability to liquidate his interest without substantial restrictions is strong evidence that he lacks real ownership.[81] Substantial restrictions apply if the donee's interest is not assignable in a real sense, or if the interest must be left in the business for many years.[82] The donee's ownership also may be questioned if the general partner retains controls beyond those normally retained in limited partnerships between unrelated persons.[83]

As is the case for general partnership interests, the reality of the donee's interest is determined from all the facts and circumstances. Therefore, failure to comply with any particular formality, such as filing a certificate of limited partnership, does not cause nonrecognition if other factors prove that the donee owns the interest.[84] The fact that restrictions are placed on a donee limited partner's right to receive distributions or to sell or liquidate his interest do not, by themselves, establish that the donee's ownership is not real if these restrictions apply to all partners and are reasonably related to the partnership's business needs.[85]

[4]　Tax-Avoidance Motive in Gift of Partnership Interest

A taxpayer's motive for forming a family partnership generally is immaterial in determining if he satisfactorily establishes that a partnership interest was actually transferred.[86] Thus, a family member may be recognized as a partner regardless of whether any business purpose for making him a partner exists.[87] The presence or

---

[78] Treas. Reg. § 1.704-1(e)(2)(ix).

[79] See R.U.L.P.A. § 303.

[80] Treas. Reg. § 1.704-1(e)(2)(ix).

[81] Id.

[82] Id.

[83] Id.

[84] Buehner v. Comm'r, 65 T.C. 723, 745–46 (1976).

[85] Garcia v. Comm'r, T.C. Memo. 1984-340.

[86] Treas. Reg. § 1.704-1(e)(2)(x).

[87] But see Hornback v. U.S., 298 F. Supp. 977 (W.D. Mo. 1969) (husband-wife partnership disregarded

absence of a tax avoidance motive, however, is one of the factors considered in determining whether a donee has been given a real ownership interest.[88]

§ 9.03   DETERMINING PARTNER STATUS OF TRUSTEES

When a partnership interest is transferred to a trust for the benefit of a family member, the trustee becomes the legal owner of the interest. In that situation, the trustee's status as a partner for tax purposes is determined under the same principles used to determine if a family member is a partner.[89] Thus, a trustee is recognized as a partner if the facts show that he obtained actual ownership of a capital interest in a partnership in which capital is a material income-producing factor.

In determining actual ownership, the regulations distinguish between a trustee who is unrelated to and independent of the grantor, and a trustee who is the grantor or who is amenable to the grantor's will.[90] An unrelated and independent trustee ordinarily is considered the owner of a partnership interest if he participates as a partner and receives distributions of partnership income on behalf of the trust, unless the donor retains direct or indirect controls inconsistent with the trustee's status as partner.[91] If the trustee is the grantor or is someone amenable to the grantor's will, however, his status as a partner is subject to increased scrutiny. Additional factors considered in this situation are:

(1)   the provisions of the trust instrument (particularly whether the trustee has fiduciary responsibilities);

(2)   the provisions of the partnership agreement; and

(3)   the actual conduct of the parties.[92]

The trustee must actively represent and protect the interests of the trust beneficiaries in accordance with fiduciary obligations, and must not subordinate the beneficiaries interests to the grantor's interests.[93] Of particular importance is whether the trust is recognized as a partner in business dealings and whether income that exceeds the reasonable needs of the business is distributed to the trust and either paid to the beneficiary or reinvested for his benefit.[94]

It is unclear when a trustee is considered related to the grantor for the family partnership rules. Presumably a trustee is related if there is any relationship by blood or marriage. It is also unclear when a trustee is deemed amenable to the grantor's will. Some assistance is found in I.R.C. Section 672(c), which defines the analogous term "related or subordinate party" for purposes of the grantor trust

---

partially on basis of wife's testimony that she never intended to be partner).

[88]   Hornback v. U.S., 298 F. Supp. 977 (W.D. Mo. 1969).

[89]   Treas. Reg. § 1.704-1(e)(2)(vii).

[90]   *Id.*

[91]   *Id.*

[92]   *Id.*

[93]   *Id.*

[94]   *Id.*

rules. That term includes the grantor, his spouse, parents, issue, siblings, employees, corporations or employees of a corporation in which the grantor and the trust have significant voting control, and subordinate employees of a corporation in which the grantor is an executive.

It cannot be assumed that I.R.C. Section 672 covers all parties who may be considered amenable to the grantor's will for the family partnership rules. The Service has ruled privately that a clause in a trust instrument exculpating the trustee from fiduciary liability to the beneficiary is evidence that the trustee lacks real ownership of the partnership interest.

The many cases that have considered the partner status of trustees who are grantors or who are amenable to a grantor's will have focused on whether the trustee actively represented the beneficiaries' interests or have administered the trust on the donor's behalf. These cases suggest that a trustee who actually conducts himself as a fiduciary is likely to be treated as a partner despite the absence of other factors indicative of ownership.[95]

A trustee who does not act in a fiduciary manner usually is not recognized as a partner.[96] The fact that trust assets will revert to the donor at the end of the trust does not preclude recognition of the trust as a partner,[97] although this arrangement is likely to receive careful scrutiny by the courts and the Service.

Trusts are often used when a partnership interest is transferred to minor children. A trustee who is an unrelated, independent party is likely to be recognized as a partner if he acts in a fiduciary manner. Recognition is less likely, however, when the donor or a related person is the trustee. When the trustee is a related person, questions may arise as to whether he acted on his own behalf or for the beneficiary when making decisions about partnership affairs and distributions. Therefore, if possible, it is advisable to use an independent person as trustee, although a trustee need not be hostile to the grantor in order to be independent.

Even if a trustee satisfies the partner-status requirements of I.R.C. Section 704(e)(1), the grantor of the trust may be treated as the owner-in-fact of the partnership interest under the grantor trust rules of I.R.C. Sections 671-678,[98] and

---

[95] See, e.g., Smith v. Comm'r, 32 T.C. 1261 (1959), acq. 1960-2 C.B. 7 (grantor-trustees recognized as partners where trusts received substantial partnership income distributions that were invested in income-producing properties unrelated to the partnership's business and later received stock in corporation formed to acquire the partnership); Hartman v. Comm'r, 43 T.C. 105 (1964), acq. 1965-2 C.B. 5 (donor's brother-in-law serving as trustee recognized as partner where he contributed services to partnership, prevailed over the donor in business disagreements, and trusts received substantial cash distributions).

[96] Kuney v. Frank, 308 F.2d 719 (9th Cir. 1962) (trustees who leased partnership property to their corporation not considered partners where lease payments very low and partnership income not distributed to trusts); Reddig v. Comm'r, 30 T.C. 1382 (1958) (attorney trustee not partner where trust instruments required trustee to follow the grantors' decisions on partnership business and distributions and trustee could not sell interest at fair market value on withdrawal from partnership).

[97] Bateman v. U.S., 490 F.2d 549 (9th Cir. 1973). See also Flitcroft v. Comm'r, 328 F.2d 449 (9th Cir. 1964).

[98] See Rev. Rul. 68-196, 1968-1 C.B. 307.

the grantor, rather than the trustee, may be considered the partner.[99] Treating the grantor as the partner means that the trust's share of partnership income, gains, deductions, and losses are taxable to the grantor rather than to the trust or its beneficiaries even if they own the trust's assets or income under state law.

Trusts that were created before March 6, 1986, are grantor trusts if the grantor can control or reacquire trust income or corpus within a period of 10 years or less. Trusts created on or after March 6, 1986, are grantor trusts if the value of the donor's reversionary interest equals or exceeds 5 percent of the value of the interest given to the trust. Based on current actuarial tables, a trust must continue for 32 years for the value of the reversion to be less than 5 percent.

§ 9.04 DETERMINING PARTNER STATUS OF MINOR CHILDREN

A minor child generally is not recognized as a partner unless a fiduciary who manages the property for the minor's sole benefit legally controls the child's partnership interest.[100] The fiduciary must comply with relevant state laws concerning judicial supervision, including the filing of accountings and reports.[101] The use of a child's share of partnership capital or income to provide support for which a parent is legally responsible, is considered a use for the parent's benefit, and the child's interest may not be recognized.[102]

A gift of a partnership interest usually satisfies the fiduciary requirement if it is made to a custodian or guardian under the Uniform Gifts to Minors Act or Uniform Transfers to Minors Act, which have been adopted in many states.[103] Because the guardianship or custodianship terminates when the minor reaches adulthood, the child must receive outright ownership of the partnership interest by age 18 or age 21 in some states. When direct ownership is undesirable, the gift should be made in trust.

No fiduciary is required in the exceptional case when the minor is competent to manage his own property and participate in partnership activities commensurate with his interest.[104] The minor must have sufficient maturity and experience for disinterested parties to treat him as competent to enter business dealings and to

---

[99] Madorin v. Comm'r, 84 T.C. 667 (1985). *Cf.* Bennett v. Comm'r, 79 T.C. 470 (1982).

[100] Treas. Reg. § 1.704-1(e)(2)(viii). *See* Pflugradt v. U.S., 310 F.2d 412 (7th Cir. 1962) (very young children not recognized as limited partners where no trustee or fiduciary subject to judicial supervision appointed for them). *See also* Virgil v. Comm'r, T.C. Memo. 1983-757.

[101] Spiesman v. Comm'r, 28 T.C. 567 (1957), *aff'd*, 260 F.2d 940 (9th Cir. 1958) (minor not treated as partner even though court appointed parent as guardian because guardian did not file inventory and accounting required by law and guardianship was not supervised by court). *But see* Garcia v. Comm'r, T.C. Memo. 1984-340 (minor child recognized as limited partner even though state law did not require judicial supervision of custodian or filing of accountings or reports — custodian demonstrated that she fulfilled requirements of fiduciary by revising children's capital accounts to include their shares of partnership profits).

[102] Treas. Reg. § 1.704-1(e)(2)(viii). *See* Pflugradt v. U.S., 310 F.2d 412 (7th Cir. 1962).

[103] *See, e.g.*, Illinois Uniform Transfers to Minors Act, Ill. Rev. Stat. Chapter 110 1/2, ¶¶ 251–274.

[104] Treas. Reg. § 1.704-1(e)(2)(viii).

conduct his affairs as an adult, notwithstanding his legal disabilities under state law.[105]

A minor is not likely to be recognized as a general partner unless he actually provides important services and participates in partnership management. If this is not the case, the general partnership interests should be given to the minor in trust, or a court-supervised guardian should be appointed. It is somewhat easier to give the minor a limited partnership interest. Although a limited partner must obtain actual ownership of his interest to be considered a partner, the limited partner is not required to participate in management. The restrictions on a limited partner's managerial function make it easier to prove that he participates in accordance with his interest in the partnership.

§ 9.05   SELLING A PARTNERSHIP INTEREST TO A FAMILY MEMBER: SALE OR GIFT?

A person who purchases a partnership interest from a family member may not be considered a partner if the transaction is a disguised gift rather than a bona fide sale.[106]

The purported purchaser is recognized as a partner only if he satisfies the same tests that apply to interests acquired by gift.[107]

The regulations provide guidelines for determining whether a transaction is a bona fide purchase or a disguised gift. These rules apply to partnership interests purchased directly from family members and to indirect purchases financed with a family member's loan or credit. A purchase is considered bona fide if it meets either of two tests:

(1)   The relevant facts show that the sale has the usual characteristics of an arm's-length transaction.[108] The relevant facts include the terms of the purchase agreement (*e.g.*, price, due date of payment, rate of interest, security), any collateral loan or credit arrangement, the credit standing of the purchaser (apart from his relationship to the seller), and the purchaser's capacity to incur a legally binding obligation.[109]

(2)   The purchase is genuinely intended to promote the success of the business by obtaining the purchaser's participation or credit, even if the purchase is not an arm's-length transaction.[110]

These tests are inconclusive, however, if the buyer has not actually paid the purchase price or has not satisfied any loan or obligation to a family member. These

---

[105] *Id.*

[106] Krause v. Comm'r, 57 T.C. 890 (1972), *aff'd*, 497 F.2d 1109 (6th Cir. 1974), *cert. denied*, 419 U.S. 1108 (1975) (trust for children not recognized as partner where it purchased limited partnership interests from father by agreeing to pay him 80 percent of its share of partnership income for 16 years).

[107] Treas. Reg. § 1.704-1(e)(4)(i).

[108] Treas. Reg. § 1.704-1(e)(4)(ii)(*a*).

[109] *Id.*

[110] Treas. Reg. § 1.704-1(e)(4)(ii)(*b*).

tests are considered only factors in determining if a bona fide purchase or loan obligation exist.[111]

A person who purchases a partnership interest from family members is treated as if he received the interest as a gift, and the fair market value of the transferred interest is considered to be donated capital.[112] This rule applies to purchases from a spouse, ancestor, lineal descendant, or trust for any of these persons.[113] The rule governs allocations of partnership income between the donor and donee, and it applies to purchases that are bona fide, arm's-length transactions.[114]

§ 9.06   ALLOCATING PARTNERSHIP INCOME AMONG FAMILY MEMBERS

When a partnership interest is transferred by gift, I.R.C. Section 704(e)(2) provides two rules that limit the amount of partnership income that may be allocated to the donee:[115]

(1) The donee's distributive share of income must be determined after taking into account an allowance for reasonable compensation to the donor for services he renders to the partnership. The purpose of this rule is to prevent a gift of a partnership interest from being used to shift income derived from the donor's services to the donee.

(2) The share of income allocated to the donee's capital interest cannot be proportionately greater than the share allocated to the capital interest the donor retains. This rule precludes shifting income by means of a disproportionately large allocation of partnership income to the donee.

If the partnership agreement does not allocate partnership income in accordance with these rules, a portion of the donee's share of income is reallocated to the donor as follows:

(1) The donor is allocated an amount equal to the reasonable value of his services to the partnership.[116]

(2) The remaining income attributable to partnership capital is allocated between donor and donee in proportion to their respective interests in partnership capital.[117]

---

[111]   Treas. Reg. § 1.704-1(e)(4)(ii).

[112]   I.R.C. § 704(e)(3).

[113]   *Id. See* Paul v. Comm'r, T.C. Memo. 1957-170 (son-in-law not family).

[114]   I.R.C. § 704(e)(2).

[115]   The specific family partnership allocation rules of I.R.C. § 704(e) override the more general allocation rules of I.R.C. § 704(b). Treas. Reg. § 1.704-1(b)(1)(iii). Thus, an allocation arrangement permitted between unrelated partners may be disallowed if the partners are related.

[116]   Treas. Reg. § 1.704-1(e)(3)(i)*(b)*.

[117]   *Id. See* H.R. Rep. No. 586, 82d Cong., 1st Sess. 32 (1951); S. Rep. No. 781, 82d Cong., 1st Sess. 38 (1951).

This reallocation does not affect partners other than the donor and donee, and the validity of their allocations is determined under the normal allocation rules of I.R.C. Section 704(b).

The value of a partnership capital interest given to a family member need not equal the amount credited to his capital account on the partnership's books. A disparity will arise, for example, if the donee receives an interest that entitles him to share in the unrealized appreciation in partnership assets. In that situation, the value of the donee's capital interest equals the amount that would be assigned to his capital account if the partnership revalued its assets immediately after the gift (*i.e.*, the amount that would be distributed to him if the partnership liquidated immediately after the gift).[118]

An actual revaluation of partnership assets usually is not feasible because the regulations governing special allocations do not permit revaluations when a partnership interest is transferred by gift or sale.[119] Instead, the partners may compute the allocations required under the family partnership rules by establishing hypothetical capital accounts for the donor and the donee based on the value of the capital shifted between these parties. The hypothetical capital accounts may be used to determine the relative allocations of partnership income between the donor and donee partners, but they do not affect the amounts allocated to other partners.

Example: Some years ago, Allen and Barrie, who are unrelated, each contributed $50,000 for equal interests in the AB Partnership. The partnership purchased a building for $100,000 and has been allowed cost recovery deductions totalling $40,000. Although the value of the building on the partnership's books is $60,000 ($100,000 cost - $40,000 cost recovery), its actual value is $80,000. Allen gives one half of his partnership interest to his son Chester. Immediately before the gift, the partnership's balance sheet is as follows:

Assets	Basis	Value
Building	$60,000	$60,000
Partners' Capital		
Allen	$30,000	$30,000
Barrie	30,000	30,000
Total	$60,000	$60,000

Because the building actually is worth $80,000, the 25-percent capital interest Allen gives Chester is worth $20,000, and the 25-percent interest he retains also is worth $20,000. In determining the allocations required under the family partnership rules, both Allen and Chester may be deemed to have a $20,000 capital account in the partnership. For all other purposes (*e.g.*, in determining the allocations to Barrie), Allen and Chester each have a $15,000 capital account.

---

[118] *See* Treas. Reg. § 1.704-1(e)(1)(v).

[119] Treas. Reg. § 1.704-1(b)(2)(iv)(*f*). *See* Chapter 4.

Forming a partnership of family members does not automatically trigger application of the I.R.C. Section 704(e)(2) allocation rules. These rules apply only if a person acquires a partnership interest by a direct or indirect gift. A gift is deemed to occur when a partnership interest is purchased from certain family members. Thus, the allocations are not required when a child contributes his own assets, *i.e.*, assets not acquired by gift or purchase from a family member, for an interest in a partnership with his parent.[120] Similarly, the allocation rules do not apply when a person inherits an interest in a partnership that includes family members.[121]

[A]   Intrafamily Sales Considered Indirect Gifts

The I.R.C. Section 704(e)(2) allocation rules apply whenever a gift of a partnership interest occurs, regardless of the relationship between the donor and donee.[122]

I.R.C. Section 704(e)(3) expands the scope of these rules to provide that a purchase of a partnership interest from a spouse, ancestor, lineal descendant, or trust that primarily benefits any of these persons is considered a gift. The fair market value of the purchased interest is considered donated capital in determining whether income allocations to the donor and donee are disproportionate to their capital accounts. Gift treatment applies even if the donee can establish that he acquired the interest from the family member in a bona fide sale.

The regulations provide guidelines for determining whether a partnership interest was acquired by gift or pursuant to a bona fide sale.[123] These regulations apply only for determining whether a person is recognized as a partner under I.R.C. Section 704(e)(1). The specific language of I.R.C. Section 704(e)(3) regarding purchases from family members appears to require application of the income allocation rules regardless of whether the sale is bona fide.

> **Example:** Barbara owns a 60-percent capital and profits interest in the AB Partnership. The interest is valued at $300,000. Barbara sells one-third of her interest to her daughter, Carrie, for its $100,000 value. The transaction is treated as a gift for the allocation rules of I.R.C. Section 704(e)(2).
>
> Partnership income for the current year is $100,000. Carrie's share of partnership income must be determined after taking into account the reasonable value of Barbara's services to the partnership; and her share cannot be proportionately greater than the share allocated to Barbara's capital. If Barbara performs no services for the partnership, the amount of income that may be allocated to Carrie is computed as follows:
>
> (1)   Barbara's proportionate interest in AB's capital is 40 percent ($200,000

---

[120] *See, e.g.*, Priv. Ltr. Rul. 8024013.

[121] Marcus v. Comm'r, 22 T.C. 824 (1954), *acq.* 1955-2 C.B. 7 (where children inherited father's interest in partnership, value of mother's services not taken into account in determining children's share of partnership income).

[122] Marcus v. Comm'r, 22 T.C. 824 (1954), *acq.* 1955-2 C.B. 7.

[123] Treas. Reg. § 1.704-1(e)(4).

/ $500,000 = 40%); therefore, Barbara's share of the current year's income is $40,000 ($100,000 * 40%).

(2)   Carrie's proportionate interest in the partnership's capital is 20 percent ($100,000 / $500,000 = 20%); therefore, Carrie cannot be allocated more than $20,000 of the current year's income ($100,000 * 20%).

[B]   Indirect Gifts

The allocation rules of I.R.C. Section 704(e)(2) apply to direct or indirect gifts of partnership interests.[124] When a gift is indirect, the person considered the donor may be someone other than the nominal transferor of the interest. The regulations provide three illustrations of indirect gifts. In these three examples, a father is considered the donor of a child's partnership interest when

(1)   The father gives property to the child, and the child transfers the property to a partnership consisting of the father and child.

(2)   The father gives an interest in his sole proprietorship to his wife, the wife transfers the interest to their child, and the child contributes it to a partnership consisting of the father and child.

(3)   The father gives stock in the family corporation to the child, the father liquidates the corporation, and the child contributes the property received in the liquidation to a partnership of the father and child.[125]

[C]   Reallocation for Reasonable Value of Donor's Services

A portion of the donee's share of partnership income is reallocated to the donor if the share was determined without taking into account the reasonable value of the donor's services to the partnership.[126] The regulations indicate that the partners also may allow for the reasonable value of the donee's services in determining his share of income.[127]

Example: Herb and his daughter, Irene, join together as equal partners in the HI investment partnership. Irene receives her entire capital interest in the partnership as a gift from Herb. Herb contributes $400,000 to the partnership, and each partner's opening capital account is stated as $200,000. In Year 1, partnership income is $40,000. During the year, Herb provided services worth $10,000 to the partnership, and Irene provided services worth $5,000. Herb is allocated $10,000 of partnership income for his services, and Irene is allocated $5,000 for her services. The remaining $25,000 of partnership income is divided equally between the partners in accordance with their equal interests in partnership capital.

---

[124] Treas. Reg. § 1.704-1(e)(3)(ii).

[125] Treas. Reg. § 1.704-1(e)(3)(ii)(a), Examples (1), (2), (3).

[126] I.R.C. § 704(e)(2).

[127] Treas. Reg. § 1.704-1(e)(3)(i)(b).

A reallocation of income to reflect the value of the donor's services does not affect partners other than the donor and donee, and the validity of their allocations is determined under the normal allocation rules of I.R.C. Section 704(b). The allocations to the other partners should be determined before determining the effect of the family partnership rules on the donor and donee.

> **Example (1):** Fran owns a 20-percent interest in the FG Partnership, and Gilbert, an unrelated person, owns the remaining 80 percent. Fran gives one-half of her partnership interest to her son, Irwin. In Year 1 following the gift, partnership income is $100,000, and Fran provides services to the partnership worth $10,000. Gilbert is allocated $80,000 — his 80-percent share of partnership income. The remaining $20,000 of partnership income is allocated between Fran and Irwin pursuant to the family partnership rules. Fran is allocated $10,000 of income for the value of her services. The remaining $10,000 of income is allocated equally between Fran and Irwin in accordance with their proportionate shares of partnership capital.

The amount of income reallocated to the donor for his services does not represent actual compensation income subject to the various rules governing compensation (*e.g.*, no withholding or W-2 form is required). Rather, the donor's Schedule K-1 should reflect his increased distributive share of partnership income. The amount reallocated to the donor cannot exceed the aggregate amount allocated to both donor and donee.

> **Example (2):** Assume the facts in the preceding example, except that the value of Fran's services to the partnership in Year 1 is $30,000. Because the total amount allocated to Fran and Irwin is only $20,000, the entire $20,000 is allocated to Fran.

The reasonable value of the donor's services is determined by considering the facts and circumstances of the partnership's business.[128] The regulations refer to two factors that usually are significant in valuing services in the context of a family business:

(1)   some partners have greater managerial responsibilities than others;[129] and

(2)   consideration should be given to the amount that ordinarily would be paid to obtain comparable services from a nonpartner.[130]

The language of I.R.C. Section 704(e)(2) indicates that reallocation is required only if the donor of the partnership interest is a partner. In a parent-child partnership, for example, income should not be reallocated to a parent who provides services if the child received his partnership interest from a grandparent. Similarly,

---

[128]   Treas. Reg. § 1.704-1(e)(3)(i)*(c)*. *See* Peterson v. Gray, 59-2 U.S.T.C. ¶ 9692 (W.D. Ky. 1959). *See also* Weller v. Brownell, 240 F. Supp. 201 (M.D. Pa. 1965); Ramos v. U.S., 260 F. Supp. 479 (N.D. Cal. 1966), *rev'd and remanded*, 393 F.2d 618 (9th Cir.), *cert. denied*, 393 U.S. 983 (1968); Payton v. U.S., 69-2 U.S.T.C. ¶ 9444 (E.D. Tex. 1969), *rev'd and remanded on other issues*, 425 F.2d 1324 (5th Cir.), *cert. denied*, 400 U.S. 957 (1970); Stanback v. Comm'r, 271 F.2d 514 (4th Cir. 1959).

[129]   Treas. Reg. § 1.704-1(e)(3)(i)*(c)*.

[130]   *Id. See, e.g.*, Woodbury v. Comm'r, 49 T.C. 180 (1967), *acq.* 1969-2 C.B. xxv; Gorrill v. Comm'r, T.C. Memo. 1963-168; Weller v. Brownell, 240 F. Supp. 201 (M.D. Pa. 1965); Ramos v. U.S., 260 F. Supp. 479 (N.D. Cal. 1966), *rev'd*, 393 F.2d 618 (9th Cir.), *cert. denied*, 393 U.S. 983 (1968).

the statute provides that partnership income should not be allocated to a nonpartner donor even if he provides services to the partnership. For example, a parent who gives a business to a child who forms a partnership with other persons is not allocated partnership income even though he manages the business as an employee of the partnership.

Although income is allocated only to a partner under I.R.C. Section 704(e)(2), a nonpartner donor may be taxable under other rules. Under the related trade or business rules of I.R.C. Section 482, the Service has broad authority to reallocate income or deductions among any related businesses if that reallocation is necessary to reflect income clearly or to prevent tax avoidance. The Service has used this power to reallocate income between members of a partnership.[131] If an arrangement purported to be a partnership is disregarded as a sham, the venture's income is fully taxable to the actual owner.[132]

[D] Reallocation for Disproportionate Allocation

I.R.C. Section 704(e)(2) requires reallocation of partnership income to a donor partner to the extent that the share of income allocated to the donee's capital interest is proportionately greater than the share allocated to the capital interest the donor retains.

Allocations required by the family partnership rules override inconsistent allocations in the partnership agreement.[133] Thus, the amount of income reallocated to the donor under these rules must be credited to his capital account.[134] If the donor wishes to transfer the reallocated amount to the donee, the partnership agreement should provide that these amounts are to be subtracted from the donor's capital account and added to the donee's capital account. The amount shifted from the donor's capital account to the donee's account constitutes an additional gift.

> **Example:** Mark creates the MN Partnership with his daughter, Nora. Mark gives Nora a capital interest with an initial capital account worth $250,000, and he retains an interest with a capital account initially worth $750,000. Although the partnership derives most of its income from invested capital, Mark provides managerial services worth $10,000 per year. The partnership agreement allocates net partnership income equally between Mark and Nora.
>
> Partnership net income for the current year is $130,000. MN's income allocation is as follows:
>
> (1) Mark is allocated $10,000 of income for the reasonable value of his services.
>
> (2) Of the remaining $120,000 of income, Mark is allocated $90,000

---

[131] Rodebaugh v. Comm'r, T.C. Memo. 1974-36, *aff'd per curiam*, 518 F.2d 73 (6th Cir. 1975).

[132] Cirelli v. Comm'r, 82 T.C. 335 (1984).

[133] *See* Treas. Reg. § 1.704-1(b)(1)(iii).

[134] *See* Treas. Reg. § 1.704-1(b)(2)(iv)*(b)*.

($120,000 * 75%, in accordance with his interest in partnership capital).

(3)   Nora is allocated $30,000 ($120,000 * 25%, for her interest in partnership capital).

Under the partnership agreement, Nora is entitled to receive $65,000 of partnership income ($130,000 * 50%), which is greater than the $30,000 allocated to her under I.R.C. Section 704(e)(2). If the additional $35,000 actually is distributed or credited to Nora's capital account, it is considered a further gift from Mark.

In a limited partnership, the relative capital interests of the donor and donee are determined by taking into account the fact that a general partner risks his personal assets in the business.[135] Thus, if the donor is a general partner and the donee a limited partner, it may be necessary to allocate additional income to the donor in consideration of his increased risk.

Although I.R.C. Section 704(e)(2) does not specifically refer to losses, the rationale for the statute suggests that it should apply to prevent a disproportionate allocation of losses or deductions to the donor. This rationale is apparent when a loss allocation to the donor has the effect of increasing the donee's share of income above the share attributable to his capital interest. Moreover, the donor's control over loss allocations raises the issue of whether the donee has actual ownership of his interest. Regardless of whether the family partnership rules of I.R.C. Section 704(e) apply, a disproportionate loss allocation is not valid unless it satisfies the substantial economic effect test of I.R.C. Section 704(b) or accords with the donee's actual interest in the partnership.

[E]   Allocation in Year of Gift

The partnership's taxable year does not close for a partner who makes a gift of all or part of his partnership interest.[136] Under I.R.C. Section 706(d), however, partnership income or loss for the year of the gift must be allocated between the donor and donee in accordance with their varying interests during the year.[137]

§ 9.07   ESTATE AND GIFT TAX CONSIDERATIONS: EFFECT OF I.R.C. SECTIONS 2701–2704 ON TRANSFERS TO FAMILY MEMBERS[138]

Partnership interests often are given to family members to remove the value of that asset from the donor's estate. This technique can be useful in minimizing estate taxes when partnership assets are expected to appreciate greatly before the donor's

---

[135] Treas. Reg. § 1.704-1(e)(3)(ii)*(c)*.

[136] I.R.C. § 706(c).

[137] Treas. Reg. § 1.706-1(c)(5) provides that income up to the date of the gift is allocated to the donor under I.R.C. § 704(e)(2). That regulation appears to be superseded by the amendments to I.R.C. § 706(c), (d) in 1976 and 1984. Consequently, the varying interest rules of I.R.C. § 706(d) apply to the allocations for the entire year of the gift, regardless of whether the donor gives away all or part of his interest.

[138] See § 9.07, *infra*, for the final regulations under I.R.C. §§ 2701–2704.

death. Although the donor incurs a current gift tax on the transfer,[139] the future income and appreciation attributable to the interest are excluded from his estate.

PLANNING NOTE:

Family Limited Partnerships (FLP) and Family Limited Liability Companies (FLLC) often are used to limit the gift and estate tax consequences of transferring assets such as real estate or stocks and securities to younger family members. The gift is minimized by applying valuation discounts to interests in an FLP or FLLC that is controlled by parents or grandparents through provisions in the partnership agreement. In determining whether to use a FLP or FLLC, practitioners should carefully consider whether the valuation applied will be respected by the IRS and courts.

Many valuation issues arise under IRC Section 2036(a), which provides that a decedent's gross estate includes the value of property he transferred during his life if he retained possession or enjoyment of, or the right to income from, the property. The right need not be legally enforceable so long as it is expressed or implied that the decedent retains the benefit. The rule does not apply to a bona fide sale for adequate consideration.

Practitioners should carefully consider recent IRS positions and court decisions in which property transferred to a FLP or FLLC has been revalued as a retained interest under IRC Section 2036(a). Of particular note is the recent decision in Estate of *Strangi v. Commisioner*,[140] where the decedent was determined to have retained enjoyment of the partnership's assets because he, in conjunction with others, could designate the managing partner and dissolve the FLP.[141]

Many gifts of partnership interests, however, are subject to special valuation rules under Chapter 14 of the Code (I.R.C. Sections 2701–2704).[142] These rules are designed to preclude abusive transactions used to "freeze" the value of assets included in the estate of an older family member. In a partnership estate "freeze," the donor of a partnership interest attempts to decrease the value of his taxable gift

---

[139] If the donor's share of partnership liabilities exceeds his basis in the interest he gives away, he recognizes gain on a partial sale of the interest. Rev. Rul. 75-194, 1975-1 C.B. 80.

[140] 417 F.3d 468 (5th Cir. 2005).

[141] See also Estate of Thompson v. Comm'r, 382 F.3d 367 (3d Cir. 2004), aff'g T.C. Memo. 2002-246; Kimbell v. U.S., 371 F.3d 257 (5th Cir. 2004), rev'g 244 F. Supp. 2d 700 (N.D. Tex. 2003).

[142] Chapter 14 was enacted in Section 11602(a) of the Revenue Reconciliation Act of 1990, Pub. L. No. 101-508, 101st Cong., 2d Sess. (Nov. 5, 1990). These rules govern the valuation of transferred interests in closely held corporations, partnerships, and trusts to family members. I.R.C. §§ 2701–2704 replace I.R.C. § 2036(c), which was enacted in 1987 to inhibit estate freeze transactions by including the transferred property in the transferor's gross estate for estate tax purposes. Congress retroactively repealed I.R.C. § 2036(c) in 1990 because it affected too many non-abusive transactions between family members. The new valuation rules of I.R.C. §§ 2701–2704 apply to transfers made after October 8, 1990.

by retaining, and assigning considerable value to, a right to receive preferred income distributions through a special allocation of partnership income.

Chapter 14 of the Code consists of the following sections:

(1)   I.R.C. Section 2701 provides rules for determining the estate or gift tax value of certain interests in partnerships or corporations transferred to family members.

(2)   I.R.C. Section 2702 provides rules for determining the estate or gift tax value of property interests transferred to a trust for a family member where the transferor retains an interest in the trust.

(3)   I.R.C. Section 2703 provides rules for determining the effect of buy-sell agreements and similar arrangements on the estate or gift tax value of property.

(4)   I.R.C. Section 2704 provides rules for determining the estate or gift tax consequences of the lapse of a voting or liquidation right in a partnership or corporation.

Although Chapter 14 of the Code applies transfers of interests in corporations and trusts as well as to partnerships, the discussion in this section focuses on the partnership aspect of these rules. A typical partnership "freeze" involves a partnership between a parent, who contributes most of the assets, and children, who contribute either a small amount of property or who receive their partnership interests as gifts. The transaction usually is structured so that the parent retains control of the partnership until death, at which time control shifts to the children. The partnership agreement allocates most partnership current income to the parent (the parent retains a "senior" interest) and most future appreciation in partnership assets to the children (the children are given "junior" interests). To minimize the gift tax value of the junior interests, the parents may retain discretionary liquidation, put, call, or conversion rights. These retained rights, it is argued, substantially diminish the value of the junior interests transferred to the children because the parents can "undo" the transaction at their discretion. At the parent's death, the parent's estate claims that the allocation of future appreciation to the children "froze" the value of the parent's partnership interest at its value when the partnership was formed.

Chapter 14 of the Code provides the following rules to deter partnership freeze transactions:

(1)   The gift tax value of a transferred partnership interest is computed by assigning a minimal value (often zero) to the transferor's retained income interest unless stringent payment requirements are satisfied. Similarly, a liquidation, put, call, or conversion right retained by the transferor is deemed to have no value. Reducing the value of the retained interest increases the gift tax value of the transferred interest.

(2)   If subsequent payments on the retained interest do not accord with the assumptions used in valuing the interest when the transfer occurred, the transferor's later taxable gifts or taxable estate are increased to reflect the value of the unpaid amounts.

(3)   For estate and gift tax valuation purposes, a buy-sell agreement, option, right, or restriction that reduces the sale price of a partnership interest below its fair market value ordinarily is disregarded.[143]

(4)   A lapse of any voting or liquidation right in a family-controlled partnership is treated as a transfer from the person holding the right to other partners.[144] If the lapse occurs during the transferor's life, the value of the transfer is taxable as a gift; if the lapse occurs at death, the value of the transfer is subject to estate tax

To ensure compliance with these valuation rules, I.R.C. Section 6501(c)(9) extends the statute of limitations for assessing tax on gifts subject to the Chapter 14 valuation rules. The Service may assess the gift tax at any time if the proper valuation is not adequately shown on an estate or gift tax return.

---

[143] I.R.C. § 2703(a), (b).
[144] I.R.C. § 2704.

Chapter 10

LIQUIDATING PAYMENTS TO A RETIRING PARTNER/MEMBER OR A DECEDENT'S SUCCESSOR

§ 10.01 OVERVIEW OF LIQUIDATING PAYMENTS — I.R.C. SECTION 736

I.R.C. Section 736 provides rules for classifying payments a partnership or LLC makes to liquidate the interest of a retiring or deceased partner or member. Congress enacted these rules in 1954 to ensure proper characterization of the portion of the payments attributable to the partner's share of partnership capital assets and the portion attributable to partnership ordinary income.[1]

Under I.R.C. Section 736, each liquidating payment is divided into two classes: (1) the portion that is a distribution for the partner's share of partnership property, and (2) the remaining amount of the payment. The statute only classifies the payments — it does not provide rules for determining the tax consequences of each class. Once the amount of the payment in each category is computed, the tax consequences are determined under the appropriate Code sections. The distribution portion is taxable under the rules governing liquidating distributions.[2] The treatment of the remaining portion depends on how the parties determine the amount the partner will receive: if the amount is computed as a percentage of partnership income, the payment is included in the partner's distributive share of partnership income;[3] if the amount is fixed, the payment is treated as a guaranteed payment.[4] (*See* Chapter 7.)

I.R.C. Section 736 pertains only to payments made by a continuing partnership to a withdrawing partner.[5] Thus, I.R.C. Section 736 does not apply to distributions related to a partnership's complete liquidation, distributions that partially liquidate

---

[1] *See* H.R. Rep. No. 1337, 83d Cong., 2d Sess. 71 (1954). Case law prior to the enactment of I.R.C. § 736 in 1954 ordinarily did not divide liquidating payments into distribution and current income components. Instead, the courts tended to treat the payments as entirely distributions (*see, e.g.,* Brown v. Comm'r, 1 T.C. 760 (1943), *aff'd,* 141 F.2d 307 (2d Cir. 1944)) or as entirely income payments (*see, e.g.,* Coates v. Comm'r, 7 T.C. 125 (1946)).

[2] I.R.C. §§ 731, 732, 733, 751(b).

[3] I.R.C. § 702.

[4] I.R.C. § 707(c).

[5] Treas. Reg. § 1.736-1(a)(2) refers to a retiring partner or the successor in interest to a deceased partner as the "withdrawing partner."

a partner's interest, or payments a partner receives when he sells his interest to other partners or third parties.[6]

[A] Payments Governed by I.R.C. Section 736

The I.R.C. Section 736 classification rules apply only to payments a continuing partnership makes to liquidate the entire partnership interest of a retiring partner or a deceased partner's successor. Thus, four conditions must exist:

(1) the partnership must continue to exist;

(2) the payment must be from the partnership and not from another partner or a third party;

(3) the payment must be made to a person who is completely withdrawing from the partnership; and

(4) the payments must be made to liquidate that partner's entire interest.

The following rules and definitions pertain to determining the applicability of I.R.C. Section 736:

(1) A partner is deemed to retire when he ceases to be a partner under local law.[7] The retirement may result from a voluntary withdrawal or an expulsion from the partnership.[8]

(2) A partner's interest is liquidated when it is terminated by a distribution or series of distributions by the partnership.[9] The distribution may be in the form of an actual payment, or it may be a constructive distribution (under I.R.C. Section 752(b)) resulting from a reduction in the withdrawing partner's share of partnership liabilities.[10] (*See* Chapter 8.)

(3) A withdrawing partner who receives a series of liquidating payments continues to be treated as a partner until he receives the final payment.[11]

---

[6] Treas. Reg. § 1.736-1(a)(1)(i).

[7] Treas. Reg. § 1.736-1(a)(1)(ii).

[8] Estate of Quirk v. Comm'r, 928 F.2d 751 (6th Cir. 1991), *aff'g and remanding on other issues* T.C. Memo. 1988-286 (partner ceases being partner under local law when he stops sharing in ongoing partnership business even if he institutes lawsuit against partnership relating to value of his interest); Holman v. Comm'r, 66 T.C. 809 (1976), *aff'd*, 564 F.2d 283 (9th Cir. 1977) (same); Milliken v. Comm'r, 72 T.C. 256 (1979), *aff'd in unpublished opinion* (1st Cir. 1979) (partner ceases being partner when he is expelled). Although a deceased partner's successor is not considered a partner under local law, he is treated as a partner for tax purposes. Treas. Reg. § 1.736-1(a)(1)(ii).

[9] Treas. Reg. §§ 1.736-1(a)(1)(ii), 1.761-1(d).

[10] Treas. Reg. § 1.736-1(a)(1)(ii). *See* Pietz v. Comm'r, 59 T.C. 207 (1972); Stilwell v. Comm'r, 46 T.C. 247 (1966).

[11] *See* Fuchs v. Comm'r, 80 T.C. 506 (1983). *See also* Findley v. Comm'r, T.C. Memo. 1991-339 (retired partners who assigned partnership interest to wholly owned corporation are taxable on liquidating payments under assignment of income doctrine). The partnership's tax year does not close for a withdrawing partner until his interest is fully liquidated by the partnership. I.R.C. § 706(c).

The classification rules of I.R.C. Section 736 apply to each payment in a series of liquidating payments.[12]

(4)   Although a two-person partnership terminates under local law when one partner retires or dies, the partnership continues for tax purposes until the withdrawing partner's interest is entirely liquidated by a distribution or series of distributions.[13] (See discussion of partnership terminations in Chapter 13.) Thus, I.R.C. Section 736 applies to payments a withdrawing partner receives from a two-person partnership until his interest is completely liquidated.

(5)   I.R.C. Section 736 does not apply to payments made in connection with a partial liquidation of a partner's interest. These payments are taxable under the rules governing current distributions.

(6)   I.R.C. Section 736 applies only to payments made by a partnership and not to payments partners make to each other.[14] Thus, the statute does not apply when a withdrawing partner sells his interest to the continuing partners, even though the transaction is economically equivalent to a liquidation.

[B]   Classification of Liquidating Payments

Under I.R.C. Section 736, each liquidating payment is divided into the following two categories:

(1)   The portion of the payment that is attributable to the partner's share of partnership property — which is treated as a distribution. This amount, called the I.R.C. Section 736(b) payment, is taxable under the rules governing liquidating distributions (I.R.C. Sections 731 through 735). The following items are excluded from the I.R.C. Section 736(b) payment if the retiring partner is a general partner and capital is not a material income producing factor in the partnership (e.g., it is a services partnership) —

   (a)   Amounts a withdrawing partner receives in exchange for his share of partnership unrealized receivables. For this purpose, unrealized receivables are limited to cash method accounts receivable for goods and services and do not include recapture items.[15]

   (b)   Amounts a withdrawing partner receives for his share of partnership goodwill unless the partnership agreement specifically provides for goodwill payments.

(2)   The remaining portion of the payment — which is included in the partner's distributive share or is treated as a guaranteed payment. (See Chapter 7.) This portion consists of all amounts that are not considered to

---

[12]   Treas. Reg. § 1.736-1(b)(5).

[13]   Treas. Reg. § 1.736-1(a)(6).

[14]   Treas. Reg. § 1.736-1(a)(1).

[15]   I.R.C. § 751(c).

be for the partner's share of partnership property and includes amounts paid for partnership unrealized receivables and goodwill that are excluded from the I.R.C. Section 736(b) payment. This amount, called the I.R.C. Section 736(a) payment, is taxable in one of two ways —

(a)   To the extent that the amount the partner receives is determined by reference to the partnership's income (*i.e.*, as a percentage of its income), the payment is treated as the partner's distributive share of partnership income (under I.R.C. Section 702).

(b)   To the extent that the amount the partner receives is not determined by reference to partnership income (*i.e.*, it is a fixed amount), the payment is treated as a guaranteed payment — subject to I.R.C. Section 707(c).

[C]   Payments for Partner's/Member's Interest in Partnership/LLC Property — I.R.C. Section 736(b) Payments

The tax consequences of the portion of a liquidating payment classified as an I.R.C. Section 736(b) payment (*i.e.*, the payment for the partner's share of partnership property) are determined in two steps:

(1)   the amount of the I.R.C. Section 736(b) payment is determined by establishing the value of the partner's share of partnership property; and

(2)   that amount is treated as a distribution to the partner that is taxable under the rules governing liquidating distributions.

[1]   Valuing Partner's/Member's Share of Partnership/LLC Property

The regulations state that the value the partners place on a withdrawing partner's share of property is generally deemed correct if it is the result of an arm's-length agreement.[16] Presumably, this means that the partners' valuation should be accepted unless the parties do not have adverse interests because of their relationship to each other (*e.g.*, father and son), or because of their individual tax situations.[17] The partners must determine the gross value, rather than net value, of the withdrawing partner's share of partnership property (*i.e.*, the value undiminished by the partner's share of partnership liabilities).[18] This valuation is necessary because the withdrawing partner is deemed to receive a cash distribution equal to the decrease in his share of partnership liabilities resulting from the liquidation. Therefore, if the partners determine the net value of the partner's share of property

---

[16]   Treas. Reg. § 1.736-1(b)(1).

[17]   A partner must determine the value of his interest when he withdraws from the partnership even if he institutes a lawsuit against the partnership relating to the value of his interest. Estate of Quirk v. Comm'r, 928 F.2d 751 (6th Cir. 1991), *aff'g and remanding on other issues* T.C. Memo. 1988-286; Holman v. Comm'r, 66 T.C. 809 (1976), *aff'd*, 564 F.2d 283 (9th Cir. 1977) (same).

[18]   Treas. Reg. § 1.736-1(b)(1).

(*i.e.*, gross value less liabilities), the value must be adjusted to take into account the retiring partner's share of partnership liabilities.

[2]   Limited Exclusion for Unrealized Receivables and Goodwill

Generally, the amount paid for a partner's share of any partnership asset is an I.R.C. Section 736(b) payment, including payments for the partner's share of unrealized receivables and goodwill. A limited exception applies to payments for certain partnership unrealized receivables and goodwill if:

(1)   the withdrawing partner is a general partner; and

(2)   capital is not a material income producing factor in the partnership (*e.g.*, it is a services partnership).[19] Whether capital is a material income producing factor is determined under principals derived from other Code sections that use that term.[20] Generally, capital is not a material factor if substantially all business income is attributable to personal services provided by individuals (*e.g.*, professional and other services partnerships).[21]

If these tests are met, payments for the partner's share of the following items are excluded from the I.R.C. Section 736(b) payment (and included under I.R.C. Section 736(a)):

(1)   *Unrealized receivables*. For purposes of the exclusion, unrealized receivables include accounts receivable and other rights to receive payments for services rendered or to be rendered, or for non-capital assets delivered or to be delivered, that have not yet been included in income under the partnership's method of accounting.[22] An item is an unrealized receivable only to the extent that its value exceeds its basis in the partnership.[23] Thus, amounts a partner receives for his share of unrealized receivables are I.R.C. Section 736(b) payments up to that partner's share of the basis of the receivables; the rest of the payment is taxable under I.R.C. Section 736(a). The partnership's basis for its unrealized receivables includes any basis adjustments previously made to the withdrawing partner's interest in partnership property under I.R.C. Section 743(b) (*i.e.*, adjustments made when a partnership interest is sold, exchanged, or transferred at a partner's death).[24] (For discussion of basis-adjustment elections, see Chapters 5 and 8.) Basis also includes any costs or expenses attributable to generating the receivables that have not been taken into account under the

---

[19]   I.R.C. § 736(b)(2), (3). Before 1993, the exclusions for unrealized receivables and goodwill applied to any partner of any partnership.

[20]   *See* I.R.C. §§ 401(c)(2), 911(d); former I.R.C § 1348(b).

[21]   H.R. Rep. No. 213, 103rd Cong., 1st Sess. 241 (1993).

[22]   Defined in I.R.C. § 751(c).

[23]   Treas. Reg. § 1.736-1(b)(2).

[24]   Treas. Reg. § 1.736-1(b)(2) refers to special basis adjustments to which the distributee is entitled. Because basis adjustments under I.R.C. § 734(b) apply to all partners, these adjustments are not taken into account.

partnership's accounting method (*e.g.*, unpaid expenses of a cash-method partnership).[25]

Because the payment for the withdrawing partner's share of unrealized receivables under I.R.C. Section 736(a) is a fixed amount, it is treated as a guaranteed payment and taxed as ordinary income. If the payment is not excluded from I.R.C. Section 736(b) (*i.e.*, the partner is a limited partner or capital is a material income producing factor), amounts received for the unrealized receivables also will be taxed as ordinary income under the distribution rules of I.R.C. Section 751. Accordingly, the exclusion of unrealized receivables from I.R.C. Section 736(b) does not provide any tax benefits.

(2) *Goodwill.* Payments to a withdrawing general partner in a services partnership are excluded from the I.R.C. Section 736(b) payment only if the partnership agreement does not specifically provide that the partner is to be paid for his share of goodwill. In that case, the partner's I.R.C. Section 736(b) payment includes only his share of any basis the partnership has in the goodwill (including any basis adjustments previously made for that partner under I.R.C. Section 743(b)).[26] If the partnership agreement does not contain such a provision, amounts the partner receives for his share of partnership goodwill are treated as I.R.C. Section 736(b) payments (*i.e.*, as payments for partnership property).

Partners of a services partnership have some flexibility in determining the tax treatment of liquidating payments for a withdrawing partner's share of partnership goodwill. The partners may decide among themselves whether the payment will be an I.R.C. Section 736(b) distribution for the partner's share of partnership property or a distributive share or guaranteed payment under I.R.C. Section 736(a). If the amount is computed by reference to partnership income, the payment is treated as a distributive share. If the amount is fixed, the payment is treated as a guaranteed payment.

Treating the goodwill payment as a distribution generally results in a capital gain for the withdrawing partner and, therefore, no deduction for the partnership. In contrast, treating a fixed payment for goodwill as a guaranteed payment results in ordinary income to the withdrawing partner with a corresponding deduction for the partnership.

Example: Tom receives an $80,000 cash payment to liquidate his one-third interest in the STV Legal Partnership. When the payment is made, the partners agree, after arm's-length negotiations, that the following balance sheet reflects the value of partnership assets:

---

[25] Treas. Reg. §§ 1.736-1(b)(2), 1.751-1(c)(2).

[26] Treas. Reg. § 1.736-1(b)(3). Ordinarily, a partnership has no basis in its goodwill. The goodwill can have basis, however, if the partnership acquired a business with pre-existing goodwill or if a basis increase previously occurred pursuant to an election under I.R.C. § 754.

Assets	Basis	Value
Cash	$90,000	$90,000
Accounts receivable	0	120,000
Goodwill	0	30,000
	$90,000	$240,000
Partners' Capital		
Steve	$30,000	$80,000
Tom	30,000	80,000
Veronica	30,000	80,000
	$90,000	$240,000

If the partnership agreement does not provide for payments for Tom's share of goodwill, only $30,000 (his share of partnership cash) is classified as a distribution under I.R.C. Section 736(b). Because the cash distribution equals Tom's basis in his partnership interest, he recognizes no gain or loss. The remaining $50,000 Tom receives is classified as a guaranteed payment under I.R.C. Section 736(a). Tom recognizes $50,000 of ordinary income and the partnership is allowed a $50,000 ordinary business expense deduction under I.R.C. Section 162. If the partnership agreement requires payments for Tom's share of goodwill ($10,000), his cash distribution under I.R.C. Section 736(b) is $40,000. Because the basis in his partnership interest is $30,000, Tom recognizes a $10,000 capital gain pursuant to I.R.C. Section 731(a) and the partnership may not deduct that amount. The remaining $40,000 Tom receives is classified as a guaranteed payment under I.R.C. Section 736(a). He reports that amount as ordinary income and the partnership is allowed a corresponding deduction.

Value of goodwill. The partners may determine the value of partnership goodwill either by specifying an amount or by providing a formula for computing the value.[27] The value the partners place on goodwill in an arm's-length agreement is generally considered correct.[28] However, a payment for a withdrawing partner's share of goodwill is treated as a distribution under I.R.C. Section 736(b) only to the extent that it is "reasonable."[29]

Provision in partnership agreement required. A payment for goodwill is classified as a distribution under I.R.C. Section 736(b) only if the partnership agreement specifically provides that the partnership will pay for the withdrawing partner's share of goodwill. In the absence of a provision, or if the partnership agreement specifically states that no value is assigned to goodwill, the payments are classified under I.R.C. Section 736(a).[30] The courts will not look beyond an unambiguous, written agreement to determine the actual intention of the parties.[31]

---

[27] Treas. Reg. § 1.736-1(b)(3).

[28] *Id.*

[29] *Id.*

[30] *See* Smith v. Comm'r, 37 T.C. 1033, *aff'd*, 313 F.2d 16 (10th Cir. 1962); Spector v. Comm'r, T.C. Memo. 1982-433; Miller v. U.S., 181 Ct. Cl. 331 (1967).

[31] I.R.C. § 736(b)(2)(B); Treas. Reg. § 1.736-1(b)(3). *See* Smith v. Comm'r, 37 T.C. 1033, *aff'd*, 313 F.2d 16 (10th Cir. 1962).

However, if the partnership agreement is unclear about goodwill payments, the courts will consider other factors to discern the parties' intent.[32]

The provision on partnership goodwill may be in the initial partnership agreement or it may be added as an amendment before the partner withdraws.[33] The partnership agreement for a year is generally deemed to include any amendments adopted on or before the date the partnership return must be filed for that year (not including extensions).[34] Presumably, an amendment adopted after the filing date cannot change the treatment of payments to a partner who withdrew in the previous year.

The provision regarding payments for goodwill should be incorporated into the overall written partnership agreement and not relegated to a separate withdrawal agreement affecting one partner. The Tax Court refused to treat a withdrawal agreement as part of the partnership agreement because it dealt with only one partner and did not concern partnership operations.[35]

[3]   Taxation of I.R.C. Section 736(b) Payments

I.R.C. Section 736(b) provides that the portion of a liquidating payment that a withdrawing partner receives in exchange for his share of partnership property is taxable under the rules governing liquidating distributions. These rules are summarized as follows:

(1)   *Under I.R.C. Section 731(a)(1), a partner recognizes capital gain on a liquidating distribution to the extent that the amount of cash he receives exceeds the basis in his partnership interest.* The amount of cash the partner receives includes a deemed cash distribution equal to any decrease in his share of partnership liabilities resulting from the liquidation. A distribution of marketable securities may be treated as cash.[36]

A partner who receives a series of cash liquidating distributions over more than one year does not recognize gain until the amount of cash he receives (including amounts he is deemed to receive) exceeds the basis in his partnership interest.[37]

However, if the partner will receive a fixed total amount for his interest, he may elect to report his gain pro rata as he receives payments.[38]

(2)   *Under I.R.C. Section 731(a)(2), a partner recognizes a capital loss on a*

---

[32] Comm'r v. Jackson Inv. Co., 346 F.2d 187 (9th Cir. 1965), *rev'g and remanding* 41 T.C. 675 (1964); Jacobs v. Comm'r, T.C. Memo. 1974-196.

[33] *See* Comm'r v. Jackson Inv. Co., 346 F.2d 187 (9th Cir. 1965), *rev'g and remanding* 41 T.C. 675 (1964).

[34] I.R.C. § 761(c).

[35] Jackson Investment Co. v. Comm'r, 41 T.C. 675 (1964), *rev'd and remanded*, 346 F.2d 187 (9th Cir. 1965). However, the Ninth Circuit Court reversed that decision, noting that I.R.C. Section 736 is designed to permit the partners to allocate tax burdens as they choose.

[36] I.R.C. § 731(c). *See* § 8.02, *supra.*

[37] Treas. Reg. § 1.736-1(b)(6), (7).

[38] Treas. Reg. § 1.736-1(b)(6).

liquidating distribution if the distribution consists solely of cash, unrealized receivables, and inventory, and the basis of his interest exceeds the amount of cash and the partnership's basis in the other property he receives. A partner may report his entire loss when he receives his final liquidating distribution.[39] or may elect to report the loss ratably as he receives payments.[40]

(3)   *Under I.R.C. Section 751(b), a portion of the distribution may be recharacterized as a sale between the partner and partnership, resulting in recognition of income or loss.* This recharacterization occurs to the extent that the payment the partner receives is in exchange for his share of the partnership's I.R.C. Section 751 property (*see* Chapter 12). I.R.C. Section 751 property ordinarily includes a partnership's unrealized receivables and substantially appreciated inventory. However, payments for a general partner's share of accounts receivable from sales of goods and services (to the extent that their value exceeds basis) are not treated as distributions under I.R.C. Section 736(b) in a partnership where capital is not a material income producing factor (*e.g.*, a services partnership).

Although unrealized receivables are not characterized as partnership property for I.R.C. Section 736(b), they are included in the partnership's inventory in determining whether the partnership's inventory is substantially appreciated under I.R.C. Section 751.[41]

A withdrawing partner who receives cash in exchange for an actual distribution of his share of substantially appreciated inventory is treated as if he received a distribution of the inventory and then sold it back to the partnership.[42] The partner recognizes ordinary income or loss on the deemed sale, and the partnership increases its basis in the inventory it is deemed to purchase from the partner.

Example (1): Donna receives a $110,000 cash payment to liquidate her one-third interest in the DEF Medical Partnership. Capital is not a material income producing factor in the partnership. The partnership agreement does not provide for a payment for a partner's share of partnership goodwill. When the payment is made, the partners agree, after arm's-length negotiations, that the following balance sheet reflects the value of partnership assets:

---

[39] *See* Treas. Reg. § 1.736-1(b)(6).

[40] *Id.*

[41] Treas. Reg. § 1.751-1(d)(2)(ii). But see S. Rep. No. 1622, 83d Cong., 2d Sess. 404 (1954), suggesting that Congress did not intend to include unrealized receivables in determining the value of inventory.

[42] I.R.C. § 751(b).

Assets	Basis	Value
Cash	$120,000	$120,000
Accounts receivable for service	0	120,000
Inventory	30,000	60,000
Goodwill	0	30,000
	$150,000	$330,000
Partners' Capital		
Donna	$50,000	$110,000
Edgar	50,000	110,000
Frank	50,000	110,000
	$150,000	$330,000

The liquidating payment is classified under I.R.C. Section 736 as follows:

	I.R.C.§ 736(b)	I.R.C. § 736(a)
Cash	$40,000	$0
Accounts receivable	0	40,000
Inventory	20,000	0
Goodwill	0	10,000
	$60,000	$50,000

This classification is the sole function of I.R.C. Section 736. Once the amount of the I.R.C. Section 736(a) and I.R.C. Section 736(b) payments are determined, the tax consequences of each category are determined under other applicable Code sections as follows:

(1)   *The consequences of the I.R.C. Section 736(b) payment (i.e., the payment for Donna's share of partnership property) are determined under the rules governing distributions.* The amount of Donna's I.R.C. Section 736(b) payment is $60,000—$80,000 share of cash plus $20,000 for her share of the inventory. Because the inventory is substantially appreciated, the constructive sale rules of I.R.C. Section 751(b) apply (*see* Chapter 12). Under these rules, Donna is treated as if she received a distribution of her share of the inventory worth $20,000 with a $10,000 basis, and then sold the inventory back to the partnership for the $20,000 in cash she actually received. Donna recognizes $10,000 of ordinary income on this constructive sale, and the partnership increases the basis in its inventory by $10,000 to reflect the deemed purchase price. The rest of the distribution consists of $40,000 in cash and the remaining basis in Donna's partnership interest is $40,000 ($50,000 total basis less $10,000 basis of inventory deemed distributed to her). Because the cash distribution does not exceed the basis in Donna's interest, she does not recognize gain or loss on this part of the distribution.

(2)   *The consequences of the I.R.C. Section 736(a) payment are determined under the rules governing partners' distributive shares and guaranteed payments to partners.* The amount of Donna's I.R.C. Section 736(a) payment is $50,000 (attributable to the value of her share of accounts

receivable and goodwill). This amount is treated as a guaranteed payment because the amount is fixed rather than computed as a percentage of partnership income. (See discussion of I.R.C. Section 736(a) payments at § 10.01[D], *infra.*)

Example (2): Assume the same facts except that capital is a material income producing factor in the partnership and that the receivables are for sales of goods (hypothetically not yet realized). In that case, the entire $110,000 payment is an I.R.C. Section 736(b) payment. The unrealized receivables are included in the constructive sale under I.R.C. Section 751, resulting in $50,000 of ordinary income ($10,000 from deemed sale of inventory and $40,000 from deemed sale of zero basis receivables). The rest of the distribution consists of $50,000 in cash ($110,000 total — $60,000 attributed to the I.R.C. Section 751 assets). Because Donna's remaining basis in her interest is $40,000 ($50,000 initial basis — $10,000 attributable to her share of the basis for the inventory), she also recognizes a $10,000 capital gain.

A withdrawing partner recognizes ordinary income or loss under I.R.C. Section 751(b) only to the extent that the amount of money or other property he receives exceeds his share of the partnership's basis for the inventory. If the withdrawing partner is a successor to a deceased partner, the successor's share of the partnership's basis increases to its value on the date of the partner's death (or alternate valuation date) if the partnership had an I.R.C. Section 754 election in effect at that time.[43] Thus, the successor's ordinary income or loss under I.R.C. Section 751(b) is limited to changes in value occurring since that date. No basis increase occurs, however, for partnership items that are income in respect of a decedent under I.R.C. Section 691.[44] This precludes a basis increase for the deceased partner's share of accounts receivable. (See discussion of income in respect of a decedent in Chapter 11.)

If no I.R.C. Section 754 election was in effect when the successor acquired his interest from the deceased partner, similar treatment may be obtained through an election under I.R.C. **Section 732 (d).** An I.R.C. Section 732 (d) election applies only to distributions made within two years of the date a partner receives his partnership interest by transfer (*i.e.*, by purchase or as successor to a deceased partner). This election permits a partner to determine his basis in any property actually or constructively distributed to him within that two-year period as if the partnership had an I.R.C. Section 754 election in effect when he acquired the interest. Because the election would increase the basis of the successor's share of partnership inventory to its value on the date of the deceased partner's death (or alternate valuation date), the successor's ordinary income or loss under I.R.C. Section 751(b) is limited to changes in value occurring

[43]   Treas. Reg. § 1.736-1(b)(4).

[44]   Treas. Reg. §§ 1.743-1(b), 1.755-1(b)(4).

since that date. (See discussion of I.R.C. Section 732(d) in Chapter 11.)

(3)   The partnership may not deduct any portion of the payment that is treated as a liquidating distribution to the withdrawing partner.

(4)   If the partnership has an I.R.C. Section 754 election in effect, the partnership adjusts the basis in its undistributed property by the amount of gain or loss the partner recognizes on the distribution. [45] (*See* Chapter 8.)

[D]   Payments Exceeding Partner's/Member's Interest in Partnership/LLC Property — I.R.C. Section 736(a) Payment

The tax consequences of the portion of a liquidating payment classified as an I.R.C. Section 736(a) payment are determined in two steps:

(1)   The portion of the payment classified as an I.R.C. Section 736(a) payment is determined. This is the portion of the payment that is not an I.R.C. Section 736(b) payment (*i.e,* the amount that exceeds the payment for the partner's share of partnership property).

(2)   To the extent that the amount of the I.R.C. Section 736(a) payment is computed as a percentage of partnership income, it is treated as the partner's distributive share under I.R.C. Section 702. If the amount is fixed, the payment is treated as a guaranteed payment under I.R.C. Section 707(c). The partnership may not deduct an I.R.C. Section 736(a) payment treated as a distributive share (although the continuing partners' distributive shares decrease by the amount allocated to the withdrawing partner). Amounts treated as guaranteed payments are deductible by the partnership as business expenses. (*See* Chapters 3, 7.)

PRACTICE NOTE:

   Payments in liquidation of a partnership interest may be taxable as ordinary income where the partnership agreement provides that the partner will receive amounts upon reaching a specific age or withdrawal from the partnership. In a recent case, the partnership agreement awarded each partner 50 "Schedule C" units per year valued at $300 per unit (a total of $15,000) to be paid quarterly each year after a partner died, became disabled, was expelled, or turned 68 years old.[46] Although the partnership deducted its payment for the Schedule C units on the partnership return, the taxpayer did not report the amount received as income. The Eleventh Circuit upheld the Tax Court holding that the

---

[45] I.R.C. § 754.

[46] Wallis v. Comm'r, 106 A.F.T.R. 2d (RIA) 5755 (11th Cir. 2010) (unpub. op.).

payments were essentially a retirement benefit classified as a guaranteed payment under I.R.C. Section 736(a) and taxable as ordinary income. The appellate court also upheld imposition of an accuracy-related penalty under I.R.C. Section 6662(a).

[1]   Determining the Amount of I.R.C. Section 736(a) Payments

Under I.R.C. Section 736(a), the portion of a liquidating payment that is not in exchange for a withdrawing partner's share of partnership property is included in the partner's distributive share or is treated as a guaranteed payment. The amount taxable under I.R.C. Section 736(a) includes:

(1)   Payments a withdrawing general partner receives for his share of the partnership's unrealized receivables if capital is not a material income producing factor in the partnership (*e.g.*, a services partnership). This is true only to the extent that the value of the partner's share of the receivables exceeds his share of the partnership's basis for these items. Amounts a partner receives for his share of unrealized receivables are I.R.C. Section 736(b) payments up to his share of the partnership's basis in the receivables.

(2)   Payments a withdrawing general partner receives for his share of the partnership's goodwill. This is true only —

    (a)   if capital is not a material income producing factor in the partnership;

    (b)   to the extent that the value of the partner's share of the goodwill exceeds his share of the partnership's basis for it; and

    (c)   to the extent that the partnership agreement does not provide that the partner is entitled to a reasonable payment for his share of partnership goodwill.

(3)   All other liquidating payments in excess of the value of the withdrawing partner's share of the partnership's property. Presumably, these additional amounts that do not relate to goodwill represent some form of mutual insurance or retirement benefit payable out of partnership income.[47]

[2]   Taxation of I.R.C. Section 736(a) Payments

Liquidating payments classified under I.R.C. Section 736(a) are taxable as though the withdrawing partner continues to own an interest in the partnership's income. The precise treatment depends upon how the amount of these payments is computed:

(1)   If the amount the withdrawing partner receives is computed by reference to the amount of partnership income (*i.e.*, as a percentage of partnership

---

[47] Treas. Reg. § 1.736-1(a)(2).

income), the payment is treated as the partner's distributive share of partnership income.[48] Under I.R.C. Sections 702 and 704, the character of amounts included in a partner's distributive share is determined from the partner's share of each item of partnership income or gain. For example, the withdrawing partner recognizes ordinary income to the extent of his share of partnership ordinary income items, and he recognizes capital gain to the extent of his share of partnership capital gain. Although the partnership cannot deduct these payments, they do reduce the amount of income and gain allocable to the continuing partners.

The withdrawing partner is taxable on amounts treated as a distributive share in his taxable year in which (or with which) the partnership's taxable year ends.[49] (*See* Chapter 3.) The partnership's tax year ends for a partner on the date that his interest is completely liquidated. (For discussion of rules when a partner receives a series of payments over more than one year, see § 10.02, *infra*.)

Example: Dave retires from the CDE Partnership on January 1, Year 1. (All parties use a calendar tax year.) At that time, the partnership pays Dave an amount of cash equal to his share of the value of the partnership's property (as determined under I.R.C. Section 736(b)) and agrees to pay him one-third of the net amounts the partnership earns during the year. For Year 1, the partnership earns $300,000 of ordinary income and has a $120,000 capital gain. Dave receives a $140,000 cash payment for his share of these amounts in January, Year 1.

The consequences of these payments are as follows:

(a)   The payment Dave receives on January 1, Year 1 for his share of partnership property is classified as a distribution under I.R.C. Section 736(b). As discussed above, the tax consequences of this payment are determined under the rules governing liquidating distributions.

(b)   All additional payments to Dave are classified as I.R.C. Section 736(a) payments. This includes the entire one-third net amount of partnership income for Year 1. Because that amount is computed as a percentage of partnership income, it is taxable as Dave's distributive share of partnership income for Year 1.

(c)   Under the rules governing taxation of distributive shares (I.R.C. Sections 702, 706(a)), Dave reports $100,000 as ordinary income and $40,000 as capital gain on his tax return for Year 1. Under I.R.C. Section 705(a)(1), Dave's basis in his partnership interest increases by $140,000 at the end of Year 1.

(d)   The $140,000 payment to Dave in Year 2 is treated as a final liquidating distribution. Because the amount of cash he receives equals the basis in his partnership interest, he recognizes no

---

[48] I.R.C. § 736(a); Treas. Reg. § 1.736-1(a)(3).

[49] Treas. Reg. § 1.736-1(a)(5).

gain or loss on receipt of the payment in that year.

A partner who desires assurance that his continued interest in partnership income will not diminish may ask for an allocation based on partnership gross, rather than net, income. For example, a partner retiring from a partnership that owns rental property may agree to receive a percentage of gross rental income for a period of years following his retirement. Although uncertainty about the treatment of this arrangement exists, it appears that the Service will treat payments based on gross income as guaranteed payments rather than as a distributive share.[50]

(2)   If the amount the withdrawing partner receives is computed without reference to partnership income (*i.e.*, a fixed amount), the payment is treated as a guaranteed payment.[51] Under I.R.C. Section 707(c), guaranteed payments are characterized as ordinary income to the recipient partner. The partnership may deduct the entire amount of the withdrawing partner's guaranteed payment from its ordinary income. This deduction decreases the amount of ordinary income allocated to the continuing partners. The partnership's deduction is permitted as a business expense under I.R.C. Section 162 and need not be capitalized.[52] The withdrawing partner is taxable on the guaranteed payment at the end of the partnership tax year in which the payment is deductible by the partnership.[53]

Example (1): On December 1, Year 1 the LMN Partnership agrees to pay Marie $70,000 in cash as a liquidating payment for her entire partnership interest. The amount of the payment that is for Marie's share of partnership property (the I.R.C. Section 736(b) payment) is $50,000, and the amount classified as an I.R.C. Section 736(a) payment is $20,000. The payment is made on March 1, Year 2. All parties use a calendar tax year.

Because the amount of the Section 736(a) payment is fixed, the entire $20,000 is a guaranteed payment. Under the guaranteed payment rules of I.R.C. Section 707(c), the partnership deducts the $20,000 in computing its ordinary income for Year 1. Marie reports the $20,000 guaranteed payment as ordinary income for Year 1 — the year that the partnership deducts the payment — even though she receives it in Year 2.

Example (2): The RST Limited Liability Company operating agreement provides that when Richard retires, the LLC will pay him the value of his interest in LLC property (as determined under I.R.C. Section 736(b)), plus

---

[50] Rev. Rul. 81-300, 1981-2 C.B. 143; Rev. Rul. 81-301, 1981-2 C.B. 144. *But see* Pratt v. Comm'r, 64 T.C. 203 (1975), *aff'd*, 550 F.2d 1023 (5th Cir. 1977).

[51] I.R.C. § 736(a); Treas. Reg. § 1.736-1(a)(3). *See* I.R.C. § 707(c). *See, e.g.*, Estate of Quirk v. Comm'r, 928 F.2d 751 (6th Cir. 1991), *aff'g and remanding on other issues* T.C. Memo. 1988-286 (amount of payment fixed if calculated as percentage of partnership assets).

[52] Treas. Reg. § 1.707-1(c). *But see* Banoff, *Determining the Character of Guaranteed Payments for Partners' Capital*, 67 J. Tax'n 284 (Nov. 1987).

[53] Treas. Reg. § 1.736-1(a)(5).

an amount equal to his share of LLC income for the two years preceding his retirement. Since the amount of the payment in excess of the value of Richard's share of LLC property (I.R.C. Section 736(a) payment) is determined without reference to the LLC's income for the year it is paid, it is a guaranteed payment. Richard includes the entire amount in his ordinary income, and the LLC deducts that amount in computing its ordinary income.

[3]   Summary — Steps in Determining Taxation Of Lump-Sum Liquidating Payment

Step 1. Divide total payment into I.R.C. Section 736(a) payment and I.R.C. Section 736(b) payment portions.

Step 2. Determine tax consequences of I.R.C. Section 736(b) payment as follows:

(a)   If partnership owns substantially appreciated inventory, compute amount recognized under I.R.C. Section 751(b). Partner is deemed to receive distribution of his share of the inventory and sell it back to the partnership for cash. Partner recognizes ordinary income on the sale and partnership increases basis in inventory to reflect deemed purchase.

(b)   Compute consequences of cash distribution under I.R.C. Section 731. Amount of distribution equals amount of I.R.C. Section 736(b) payment not considered amount realized for substantially appreciated inventory.

    (i)   If distribution equals basis, no gain or loss is recognized.

    (ii)   If distribution exceeds basis, partner recognizes excess amount as capital gain.

    (iii)   If basis exceeds distribution, partner recognizes difference as capital loss.

Step 3. Determine tax consequences of I.R.C. Section 736(a) payment as follows:

(a)   If amount partner will receive is computed as percentage of partnership income, payment is treated as partner's distributive share of partnership income. Character of payment is determined at partnership level.

(b)   If amount partner will receive is fixed, payment is treated as guaranteed payment. Partner reports ordinary income and partnership may deduct same amount as trade or business expense.

§ 10.02   SERIES OF CASH LIQUIDATING PAYMENTS

Frequently, a withdrawing partner's interest is liquidated through a series of payments over a period of years. The tax consequences of these payments are determined as follows:

(1)   The I.R.C. Section 736(b) payment and I.R.C. Section 736(a) payment portions of the amount received each year is determined.[54] The I.R.C.

---

[54] Treas. Reg. § 1.736-1(b)(5).

Section 736(b) payment is treated as a distribution and the I.R.C. Section 736(a) payment is included in the partner's distributive share or treated as a guaranteed payment.

(2) The tax consequences of the distribution (I.R.C. Section 736(b) payment), distributive share, or guaranteed payment (I.R.C. Section 736(a) payment) are determined under the appropriate Code sections. The regulations provide elections that allow partners to accelerate or defer recognition of gain or loss on the liquidating payments in a number of circumstances.

[A] Determining the I.R.C. Section 736(a) and I.R.C. Section 736(b) Portions of Each Payment

When a withdrawing partner's interest is liquidated through a series of payments over a period of years, part of the amount received each year is classified as a liquidating distribution under I.R.C. Section 736(b), and the remainder is treated as a guaranteed payment or distributive share under I.R.C. Section 736(a).[55] The following rules apply in determining the amount of the payment that is allocated to each class:

(1) If the total amount the withdrawing partner will receive is fixed, the amount treated as a liquidating distribution under I.R.C. Section 736(b) each year is computed by multiplying

   (a) the total amount the partnership agreed to pay during the current year (not the amount he actually receives); by

   (b) a fraction, with a numerator that is the total amount the partner will receive for his share of partnership property (total I.R.C. Section 736(b) payments), and a denominator that is the total amount of all payments he will receive (total I.R.C. Section 736(a) and I.R.C. Section 736(b) payments).[56] he amount paid during the year that exceeds the amount classified as an I.R.C. Section 736(b) payment is a guaranteed payment under I.R.C. Section 736(a).[57] If the amount the partner actually receives during the year is less than the amount computed as I.R.C. Section 736(b) payments under this formula, the entire amount received is treated as a distribution under I.R.C. Section 736(b). The amount of I.R.C. Section 736(b) payments not actually received is added to the amount treated as an I.R.C. Section 736(b) payment in the next year.

Example: Upon his retirement from the ABC Partnership, Allen is entitled to receive $60,000 in cash as a liquidating payment each year for five years. Of the total $300,000 ($60,000 * 5) Allen will receive, $200,000 is for his share of partnership property as determined under I.R.C. Section 736(b). When he retires, Allen's basis for his partnership interest is $100,000. The partnership does not own I.R.C. Section 751 property.

---

[55] *Id.*

[56] Treas. Reg. § 1.736-1(b)(5)(i), (ii).

[57] Treas. Reg. § 1.736-1(b)(5)(i).

In Year 1–ABC pays Allen $60,000:

(a) $40,000 is classified under I.R.C. Section 736(b) as a distribution for Allen's share of partnership property ($60,000 * $200,000 Allen's share of partnership property/$300,000 total fixed payments). The distribution reduces Allen's basis in his partnership interest to $60,000 and he does not recognize any gain in Year 1 (I.R.C. Section 731(a)).

(b) The remaining $20,000 of the payment is classified as a guaranteed payment under I.R.C. Section 736(a). Allen includes that amount in his ordinary income, and the partnership is allowed a corresponding deduction.

In Year 2–ABC is able to pay Allen only $30,000:

The entire amount is classified under I.R.C. Section 736(b) as a distribution for Allen's share of partnership property. The distribution decreases Allen's basis in his partnership interest to $30,000 and he recognizes no gain or loss in Year 2.

In Year 3–Allen receives a $90,000 payment from the partnership:

$50,000 is classified under I.R.C. Section 736(b) as a distribution ($40,000 for the current year + $10,000 deficit from Year 2). Because the $50,000 cash distribution exceeds Allen's $30,000 basis in his partnership interest, Allen recognizes $20,000 of capital gain under I.R.C. Section 731(a).

$40,000 is classified under I.R.C. Section 736(a) as a guaranteed payment. Allen reports that amount as ordinary income and the partnership is allowed a corresponding deduction.

In Years 4 and 5–ABC pays Allen $60,000 each year:

The entire amount Allen receives each year is classified under I.R.C. Section 736(a) as a guaranteed payment. Allen reports these amounts as ordinary income, and the partnership is allowed corresponding deductions.

The following chart summarizes the allocation and taxation of ABC's payments to Allen:

Year	Total Payment	I.R.C. § 736(b) Payment	I.R.C. § 736(a) Payment	Amount Taxable	Character
1	$60,000	$40,000	$20,000	$20,000	ordinary income
2	$30,000	$30,000	$0	$0	
3	$90,000	$50,000	$40,000	$60,000	$20,000 capital gain, $40,000 ordinary income
4	$60,000	0	$60,000	$60,000	ordinary income
5	$60,000	0	$60,000	$60,000	ordinary income

(2)   If the total amount the withdrawing partner will receive is contingent rather than fixed (*e.g.*, the payments are based on a percentage of partnership income), all payments are classified as distributions under I.R.C. Section 736(b) until the total amount the partner receives equals the value of his share of partnership property.[58] All additional payments are classified as the partner's distributive share of partnership income under I.R.C. Section 736(a).

Example: Upon her retirement from the DEF Partnership, Dora is entitled to receive liquidating payments equal to 20 percent of partnership income each year for four years. When she retires, the agreed value of Dora's share of partnership property, determined under I.R.C. Section 736(b), is $100,000, and the basis of her partnership interest is $60,000. The partnership does not own I.R.C. Section 751 property.

In Year 1, Dora's share of partnership income is $50,000 and she receives a payment of that amount. The entire payment is classified under I.R.C. Section 736(b) as a distribution, which reduces Dora's basis for her partnership interest to $10,000 ($60,000 - $50,000). Dora recognizes no gain or loss.

In Year 2, Dora receives a $60,000 payment from the partnership. The first $50,000 is classified as a distribution under I.R.C. Section 736(b). Dora recognizes a $40,000 capital gain under I.R.C. Section 731(a) — the excess of the cash distribution over Dora's basis for her partnership interest ($50,000 distribution - $10,000 basis). The remaining $10,000 of the payment is classified under I.R.C. Section 736(a) as Dora's distributive share of partnership income.

Dora receives a $70,000 payment from the partnership in each of Years 3 and 4. These payments are classified under I.R.C. Section 736(a) as Dora's distributive share of partnership income.

Under I.R.C. Section 702(b), the character of a distributive share depends upon the source of the partnership's income during the year.

---

[58] *Id.*

Year	Total Payment	I.R.C. § 736(b) Payment	I.R.C. § 736(a) Payment	Amount Taxable	Character
1	$50,000	$50,000	0	0	
2	$60,000	$50,000	$10,000	$50,000	$40,000 Capital gain, Remainder under I.R.C. § 702
3	$70,000	0	$70,000	$70,000	Determined under I.R.C. § 702
4	$70,000	0	$70,000	$70,000	Determined under I.R.C. § 702

(3) If the withdrawing partner is to receive a fixed amount plus additional contingent amounts, the payments each year are allocated under the rules governing fixed payments until the partner receives the fixed amount the partnership agreed to pay in the current year.[59] This amount is treated as a distribution under I.R.C. Section 736(b) and a guaranteed payment under I.R.C. Section 736(a). Payments that exceed the fixed amount are classified as the partner's distributive share under I.R.C. Section 736(a).[60]

Example: Upon his retirement from the GHI Partnership, George is entitled to receive liquidating payments of $40,000 each year for five years ($200,000 total fixed amount) plus 20 percent of the partnership's net income above $80,000 in each of those years. When he retires, the agreed value of George's share of partnership property, determined under I.R.C. Section 736(b), is $120,000 and the basis for his partnership interest is $60,000. The partnership does not own I.R.C. Section 751 property.

In Year 1, the partnership pays George $50,000. Of this amount, $40,000 is George's fixed payment and $10,000 is for his share of partnership profits above $80,000. The payment is subject to the following treatment:

(a) $24,000 of the payment is classified under I.R.C. Section 736(b) as a distribution ($40,000 agreed payment for the year * $120,000 total fixed amount for property/$200,000 total fixed payments). George recognizes no gain on that portion of the payment, and the basis for his partnership interest decreases to $36,000.

(b) $16,000 is classified under I.R.C. Section 736(a) as a guaranteed payment (the amount by which the $40,000 fixed payment exceeds the amount classified under I.R.C. Section 736(b)). This portion of the payment is treated as a guaranteed payment because the amount is determined without reference to the partnership's income.

(c) $10,000 is classified under I.R.C. Section 736(a) as George's distributive share of partnership income because the amount was determined as a percentage of partnership income.

---

[59] *See* Treas. Reg. § 1.736-1(b)(5)(ii).

[60] *See Id.*

The withdrawing and continuing partners may agree to use a different method for allocating annual payments between I.R.C. Sections 736(a) and 736(b).[61] The agreement is respected if the total amount to be treated as a distribution under I.R.C. Section 736(b) does not exceed the fair market value of the withdrawing partner's share of partnership property on the date he retires or dies.[62] Apparently, the agreement may be evidenced by consistency in the manner the partners report the transaction. It is prudent, however, for the partners to reduce their agreement to writing.

[B] Computing Gain or Loss Recognized on the I.R.C. Section 736(b) Portion

The following rules govern the recognition of gain or loss on the portion of each liquidating payment classified as a distribution under I.R.C. Section 736(b):

(1) A withdrawing partner recognizes gain (under I.R.C. Section 731(a)(1)) only if the amount of cash he receives as an I.R.C. Section 736(b) distribution exceeds the basis of his partnership interest. The partner decreases the basis of his interest as he receives each distribution. Thus, the partner recognizes gain only after the basis of his partnership interest is reduced to zero.[63]

Example: The LMO Limited Liability Company agrees to pay Leon $50,000 a year for three years in liquidation of his LLC interest: $40,000 of each payment is classified as a distribution under I.R.C. Section 736(b); the remaining $10,000 is a guaranteed payment under I.R.C. Section 736(a). The LLC does not own substantially appreciated inventory.[64] When Leon receives the first payment, the basis of his LLC interest is $60,000.

In Year 1, Leon recognizes no gain under I.R.C. Section 731 (although he is taxable on the guaranteed payment), and the $40,000 distribution reduces the basis of his LLC interest to $20,000. The distribution in Year 2 exceeds Leon's remaining basis by $20,000, and he recognizes that amount as capital gain. In Year 3 Leon's basis in his LLC interest is zero; therefore, he recognizes $40,000 of capital gain on the distribution that year.

The allocation and taxation of these distributions is summarized as follows:

---

[61] Treas. Reg. § 1.736-1(b)(5)(iii).

[62] *Id.*

[63] Treas. Reg. § 1.736-1(b)(6); I.R.C. § 731(a).

[64] If the partnership owns substantially appreciated inventory, a portion of the distribution may be recharacterized as a sale under I.R.C. § 751(b). (*See* Chapter 8.) Although unrealized receivables are also subject to I.R.C. § 751(b), the receivables are not considered property under I.R.C. § 736(b). Thus, liquidating payments a partner receives for his share of unrealized receivables are classified as I.R.C. Section 736(a) payments.

Year	Total Payment	Leon's Basic	I.R.C. § 736(b) Payment	I.R.C. § 736(a) Payment	Amount Taxable	Character
1	$50,000	$40,000	$20,000	$10,000	$10,000	$10,000 ordinary income
2	$50,000	$40,000	0	$10,000	$30,000	$20,000 capital gain, $10,000 ordinary income
3	$50,000	$40,000	0	$10,000	$50,000	$40,000 capital gain, $10,000 ordinary income

If the partnership liquidates a partner's interest through a series of cash payments that are treated as distributions under I.R.C. Section 736(b)(1), any I.R.C. Section 734(b) basis adjustments to partnership property correspond in timing and amount with the gain or loss the retiring partner recognizes for those payments.[65]

(2)   A withdrawing partner recognizes a loss under I.R.C. Section 731(a)(2) if the total amount of cash he receives as a distribution under I.R.C. Section 736(b) is less than the basis of his partnership interest. The partner recognizes the entire loss in the year in which he receives the final payment classified as a liquidating distribution.[66]

Example: The STU Partnership agrees to pay Sandra $40,000 a year for three years in liquidation of her partnership interest: $30,000 of each payment is classified as a distribution under I.R.C. Section 736(b) and the remaining $10,000 is a guaranteed payment under I.R.C. Section 736(a). The partnership does not own substantially appreciated inventory. The basis of Sandra's partnership interest is $100,000.

Sandra does not recognize any gain or loss on the distributions in Year 1 or Year 2 (although she is taxable on the guaranteed payment). When Sandra receives the $30,000 final distribution in Year 3, the basis of her partnership interest is $40,000 ($100,000 beginning basis — $60,000 total distributions). Therefore, Sandra recognizes a $10,000 capital loss in Year 3.

(3)   A withdrawing partner who will receive a fixed amount for his interest in partnership property (I.R.C. Section 736(b) payments) over a period of years may elect to report the total gain or loss he will recognize ratably as he receives each distribution.[67]

The amount of gain or loss recognized each year equals the difference between:

---

[65]   Rev. Rul. 93-13, 1993-1 C.B. 126.

[66]   Treas. Reg. § 1.736-1(b)(6); I.R.C. § 731(a).

[67]   Treas. Reg. § 1.736-1(b)(6). Any I.R.C. § 734(b) basis adjustments to partnership property correspond in timing and amount with the gain or loss the retiring partner recognizes for I.R.C. Section 736(b) payments. Rev. Rul. 93-13, 1993-1 C.B. 126.

(a)   the amount treated as a distribution under I.R.C. Section 736(b) that year; and

(b)   the portion of the partner's basis in his partnership interest attributable to the distribution he receives that year. This portion is computed by multiplying the partner's total basis by a fraction whose numerator is the distribution received during the year and whose denominator is the total I.R.C. Section 736(b) distributions he will receive.

The withdrawing partner makes the election by attaching a statement to his tax return for the year in which he receives the first liquidating payment.[68] The statement must indicate that an election is being made and show the computation of the partner's gain or loss.

Example: The RST Limited Liability company agrees to pay Richard a total of $300,000 over a three-year period for his interest in LLC property (*i.e.*, I.R.C. Section 736(b) payments). In Year 1, Richard will receive $100,000; in Year 2, $150,000, and in Year 3, $50,000. The LLC does not own substantially appreciated inventory. The basis of Richard's LLC interest is $180,000.

Richard may elect to report his gain on the distributions by attaching a statement, in the following form, to his tax return for Year 1:

ELECTION TO RECOGNIZE GAIN RATABLY UNDER REGULATIONS SECTION 1.736-1(b)(6)

Taxpayer Richard Simes retired from the RST Limited Liability Company on January 1, Year 1. Taxpayer elects to recognize gain each year under Regulations Section 1.736-1(b)(6). Taxpayer will receive total distributions of $300,000 and the basis of his LLC interest is $180,000.

The amount of gain the taxpayer will recognize each year is computed as follows:

60 percent ($180,000/$300,000) of the total cash distributed represents recovery of taxpayer's basis. Thus, 60 percent of each payment is treated as a return of capital and 40 percent is capital gain:

Year	Total Received	Return of Basis	Capital Gain
1	$100,000	$60,000	$40,000
2	150,000	90,000	60,000
3	50,000	30,000	20,000
	$300,000	$180,000	$120,000

Ordinarily, it is advantageous for a partner to elect to prorate a loss he will recognize on a distribution because it accelerates the time when the loss is reported. However, an election by the withdrawing partner also affects the partnership if an I.R.C. Section 754 basis-adjustment election is in effect. Under that election, the loss a partner recognizes on a distribution results

---

[68] Treas. Reg. § 1.736-1(b)(6).

in a corresponding decrease to the bases of undistributed partnership property.[69] Proration of the loss accelerates the time when the partnership's basis decrease occurs. This may be disadvantageous to the continuing partners because it may decrease allowable deductions or increase gain recognized on disposition of the property.

(4)　Different timing rules apply if the partnership owns property subject to the rules of I.R.C. Section 751 (I.R.C. Section 751 property). If the withdrawing partner receives a cash liquidating distribution, a portion of the distribution is taxable under the disproportionate distribution rules of I.R.C. Section 751(b). The partner is treated as if he received a distribution of his proportionate share of the I.R.C. Section 751 property and then sold it back to the partnership for cash. The partner must determine the portion of each distribution that is treated as a sale under I.R.C. Section 751(b) and report the amount of ordinary income or loss he recognizes.

A withdrawing partner recognizes ordinary income (or loss) under I.R.C. Section 751(b) only to the extent that the amount of money or other property he receives exceeds (or is less than) his share of the partnership's basis for the I.R.C. Section 751 property. If the withdrawing partner is a successor to a deceased partner, the successor's share of the partnership's basis increases (or decreases) to its value at the date of the partner's death if the partnership had an I.R.C. Section 754 election in effect at that time.[70] The basis increase does not apply to the extent that the I.R.C. Section 751 property, such as unrealized receivables, represents income in respect of a decedent under I.R.C. 691.[71]

[C]　Computing Gain or Loss Recognized on the I.R.C. Section 736(a) Portion

When a partner receives a series of liquidating payments, the portion of each payment that is classified under I.R.C. Section 736(a) is taxable as follows:

(1)　*To the extent that the amount the partner receives is determined by reference to the partnership's income (i.e., a percentage of its income), the payment is treated as the partner's distributive share of partnership income (under I.R.C. Section 702).* The partner reports his share of each item of partnership income with the same character that it has to the partnership.[72] Although the partnership is not allowed a deduction, the amount included in the retiring partner's distributive share reduces the continuing partners' distributive shares.[73]

Example: Don retires from the CDE Partnership on January 1, Year 1. (All parties use a calendar tax year.) At that time, the partnership pays Don an

---

[69]　I.R.C. §§ 734, 743.

[70]　Treas. Reg. § 1.736-1(b)(4).

[71]　Treas. Reg. §§ 1.743-1(b), 1.755-1(b)(4).

[72]　I.R.C. § 702. He includes the distributive share in his income for his taxable year in which (or with which) the partnership's year ends. Treas. Reg. § 1.736-1(a)(5).

[73]　Treas. Reg. § 1.736-1(a)(4).

amount of cash equal to his share of the value of the partnership's property (as determined under I.R.C. Section 736(b)), and agrees to pay him one third of the net amounts the partnership earns during Year 1 and Year 2. In Year 1, the partnership earns $300,000 of ordinary income and has a $120,000 capital gain. In Year 2, the partnership has only a $150,000 capital gain. Don receives a $140,000 cash payment in January, Year 2 and a $50,000 cash payment in January, Year 3.

The consequences of these payments are as follows:

(a) ***I.R.C. Section 736(b) payment for Don's share of partnership property.*** The payment Don receives in Year 1 for his share of partnership property is classified as a distribution under I.R.C. Section 736(b). The tax consequences of this payment are determined under the rules governing liquidating distributions.

(b) ***I.R.C. Section 736(a) payment for Don's share of partnership income (Year 1).*** Don's total share of partnership income for Year 1 is $140,000 (1/3 of $420,000). He reports $100,000 ($300,000 * 1/3) as ordinary income and $40,000 ($120,000 * 1/3) as capital gain on his tax return for Year 1 as his distributive share. Under I.R.C. Section 705(a)(1), Don's basis in his partnership interest increases by $140,000 at the end of Year 1, and it decreases by that amount when he receives the actual $140,000 distribution in Year 2.

(c) ***I.R.C. Section 736(a) payment for Don's share of partnership income (Year 2).*** Don reports a $50,000 ($150,000 * 1/3) capital gain on his tax return for Year 2 as a distributive share of partnership income. Don's basis in his partnership interest increases by $50,000 at the end of Year 2. Don's basis is reduced to zero when he receives the payment in Year 3.

(2) ***To the extent that the amount the partner receives is not determined by reference to partnership income (i.e., a fixed amount), the payment is treated as a guaranteed payment (subject to I.R.C. Section 707(c)).*** The partnership may deduct the entire guaranteed payment made to the withdrawing partner from partnership ordinary income. This deduction decreases the amount of ordinary income allocated to the continuing partners.[74] The withdrawing partner is taxable on the guaranteed payment at the end of the partnership tax year in which the payment is deductible,[75] even if the partner does not receive the payment until a later year.

Example: Ina retires from the GHI Partnership in December, Year 1. All parties use a calendar tax year. Ina is a cash-method taxpayer, and the partnership uses the accrual method. In December, Year 1, the partnership pays Ina cash equal to her share of the value of the partnership's property (as determined under I.R.C. Section 736(b)) and agrees to pay her an

---

[74] I.R.C. § 707(c).

[75] Treas. Reg. § 1.736-1(a)(5).

additional $50,000 in March, Year 2. The $50,000 amount is fixed and is treated as a guaranteed payment. Because the partnership can deduct the payment in Year 1, Ina reports that amount as ordinary income on her Year 1 tax return, even though she does not receive the payment until Year 2.

(3) *If a partnership terminates before it has made all the guaranteed payments that are required to liquidate a retired partner's interest, other partners who individually assume liability for these payments may deduct them as business expenses.* [76] This deduction is permitted in situations when the partnership could have deducted the payments if it had continued.[77] Similarly, a corporate successor to a partnership may claim business expense deductions for payments to a retired partner if the corporation assumes the obligation for these payments.[78]

§ 10.03   NONCASH LIQUIDATING PAYMENTS

A partnership may liquidate all or a portion of a partner's interest by transferring property other than cash to him. However, I.R.C. Section 736 does not specifically address the treatment of noncash liquidating payments. Indeed, all the issues covered and examples provided in the regulations and administrative rulings focus on the treatment of cash payments. Nevertheless, noncash liquidating payments to a withdrawing partner are not excluded from I.R.C. Section 736 and are subject to the same rules as cash payments. The application of the rules to in-kind payments, however, raises a number of confusing and unresolved issues.

In describing the tax consequences of noncash liquidating payments, the discussion below assumes that rules analogous to those governing cash payments apply. For the discussion, it is necessary to bear in mind the special treatment afforded payments to a withdrawing general partner for his share of unrealized receivables and goodwill under I.R.C. Section 736 if capital is not a material income producing factor in the partnership. As discussed above, amounts paid for the partner's share of certain unrealized accounts receivable (in excess of his share of the partnership's basis for the receivables) are not treated as distributions for his share of partnership property under I.R.C. Section 736(b) but are classified as I.R.C. Section 736(a) payments. Payments for goodwill (in excess of the partner's share of the partnership's basis for the goodwill) are not I.R.C. Section 736(b) payments unless specifically required by the partnership agreement.[79]

Noncash payments to a withdrawing partner that are treated as guaranteed payments under I.R.C. Section 736(a) (*i.e.*, fixed amounts) may cause the partnership to recognize gain or loss. Because the partnership is obligated to pay a fixed value to the withdrawing partner, the partnership recognizes gain or loss when it

---

[76] Rev. Rul. 75-154, 1975-1 C.B. 186; Priv. Ltr. Ruls. 8332031, 8304078, 8213051, 7930089, 7748032.

[77] Rev. Rul. 75-154, 1975-1 C.B. 186. *See* Sloan v. Comm'r, T.C. Memo. 1981-641; Flood v. U.S., 133 F.2d 173 (1st Cir. 1943).

[78] Rev. Rul. 83-155, 1983-2 C.B. 38.

[79] I.R.C. § 736(b).

transfers property to satisfy that obligation. The partnership's gain or loss equals the difference between the amount of its guaranteed payment obligation and the basis of the transferred property.[80] Under I.R.C. Section 736, noncash liquidating payments are treated as follows:

(1) ***The assets the withdrawing partner receives are allocated between the portion that is a distribution under I.R.C. Section 736(b) and the portion taxable under I.R.C. Section 736(a).*** The assets are treated as a distribution under I.R.C. Section 736(b) up to the value of the partner's share of partnership property. As noted above, amounts paid for the partner's share of the partnership's goodwill (unless provided in the partnership agreement) and payments for the partnership's unrealized receivables may be excluded from the I.R.C. Section 736(b) payments. No direct authority exists regarding the method for allocating noncash liquidating payments between I.R.C. Sections 736(a) and (b). Possible allocation methods include:

(a) ***Allocating a ratable portion of each asset the withdrawing partner receives, including cash, to each category of payment.***

Example (1): Charles and the CDE Partnership agree that Charles will receive cash and property worth $100,000 to liquidate his one-third partnership interest. The partnership agreement does not provide that withdrawing partners will receive payment for partnership goodwill. The partnership has the following balance sheet:

Assets	Basis	Fair Market Value
Cash	$60,000	$60,000
Stock X	10,000	50,000
Stock Y	50,000	40,000
	$120,000	$150,000
Partners' Capital		
Charles	$40,000	$50,000
Dana	40,000	50,000
Edward	40,000	50,000
	$120,000	$150,000

The parties agree that the partnership will pay Charles $50,000 in cash and will also transfer Stock X to him. Because the value of Charles's share of partnership property is $50,000, $50,000 of the value of any assets he receives will be classified as a distribution under I.R.C. Section 736(b), and the remaining $50,000 value will be treated as a guaranteed payment under I.R.C. Section 736(a).

If the cash and property are allocated ratably as I.R.C. Section 736(a) and I.R.C. Section 736(b) payments, each category of payment consists of $25,000 worth of stock and $25,000 in cash. This allocation method has the following consequences:

---

[80] *See* Rev. Rul. 75-498, 1975-2 C.B. 29; Treas. Reg. § 1.83-6(b).

(i)   The partnership deducts the $50,000 guaranteed payment and Charles recognizes that amount as ordinary income. The partnership also recognizes a $20,000 capital gain when it discharges a portion of its guaranteed payment obligation with appreciated property ($25,000 value of Stock X — $5,000 basis in the stock). Because Charles acquired $25,000 of the Stock X in a taxable exchange for his right to a guaranteed payment, his basis in that portion of the stock is $25,000.

(ii) Because the $25,000 in cash Charles receives as an I.R.C. Section 736(b) distribution does not exceed the $40,000 basis in his partnership interest, he recognizes no gain on the distribution. The cash distribution reduces Charles's basis to $15,000 immediately before the stock is deemed distributed to him. Under I.R.C. Section 732(b), Charles's $15,000 basis in his partnership interest becomes his basis in the distributed stock.

(iii) Charles's total basis in Stock X is $40,000. This is the sum of:

      -$25,000 "cost" basis he obtains in the portion of the stock he is deemed to receive in exchange for his right to the guaranteed payment; plus

      -$15,000 attributable to his basis in the portion of the stock he received as a liquidating distribution for his share of partnership property.

(iv) If the partnership has an I.R.C. Section 754 basis-adjustment election in effect, its basis in the retained Stock Y decreases by $10,000 — the amount by which the distribution increased the basis of Stock X in Charles's hands.

(b) *Treating noncash assets as distributions under I.R.C. Section 736(b), up to the value of the partner's share of partnership property before allocating any cash payments to that category.* If the value of the noncash assets exceeds the value of the partner's share of partnership property, the additional value is classified under I.R.C. Section 736(a).

Example (2): Assume the facts in Example (1) except that the stock payment is first allocated to the I.R.C. Section 736(b) distribution portion of the transaction and the entire $50,000 cash distribution is allocated to the I.R.C. Section 736(a) guaranteed payment portion. In that case:

(i)   Charles reports $50,000 of ordinary income and the partnership is allowed a corresponding deduction. Because the guaranteed payment is in cash, the partnership recognizes no gain or loss when it discharges this obligation.

(ii)   The distribution under I.R.C. Section 736(b) consists solely of Stock X. Neither Charles nor the partnership recognize gain or loss, and Charles's basis in the stock is $40,000 — the basis in his partnership interest (I.R.C. Section 732(b)). Note that the distribution increases the basis of the stock from $10,000 in the partnership to $40,000 in Charles's hands.

(iii) If the partnership has an I.R.C. Section 754 basis-adjustment election in effect, its basis in the retained Stock Y decreases by $30,000 — the amount by which the distribution increases the basis of Stock X in Charles's hands.

(c) *Treating all cash payments as distributions under I.R.C. Section 736(b), up to the value of the partner's share of partnership property before allocating any other assets to that category.* To the extent that the value of the cash and noncash assets paid to the withdrawing partner exceed the value of his share of partnership property, the payments are classified under I.R.C. Section 736(a).

Example (3): Assume the facts in Example (1) except that the entire $50,000 cash payment is allocated to the I.R.C. Section 736(b) payment for Charles's share of partnership property.

(i)   Because the $50,000 cash distribution Charles receives as an I.R.C. Section 736(b) payment exceeds the $40,000 basis in his partnership interest, Charles recognizes a $10,000 capital gain under I.R.C. Section 731(a).

(ii) The I.R.C. Section 736(a) payment consists solely of the X Stock. The partnership recognizes $40,000 of capital gain on its transfer of the stock to satisfy its guaranteed payment obligation to Charles ($50,000 amount realized less $10,000 basis). Charles reports the $50,000 guaranteed payment as ordinary income and the partnership is allowed a corresponding deduction. Charles obtains a $50,000 "cost" basis in stock he is deemed to receive in exchange for his right to the guaranteed payment.

(2) *The tax consequences of the portion of the payment treated as a liquidating distribution under I.R.C. Section 736(b) are determined.* If no cash is included in this portion, the withdrawing partner does not recognize any gain, and his basis in the distributed property equals the basis in his partnership interest immediately before the distribution.[81] If the partner receives both cash and property, he first reduces the basis in his partnership interest by the amount of cash he receives (but not below zero) and recognizes gain to the extent that the cash received exceeds his basis.[82] In appropriate circumstances, the withdrawing

[81] I.R.C. §§ 731, 732.
[82] I.R.C. § 731(a).

partner may recognize a loss under I.R.C. Section 731(a)(2).

If the partnership owns substantially appreciated inventory, the disproportionate distribution rules of I.R.C. Section 751(b) may apply to the I.R.C. Section 736(b) payment. These rules apply if the partnership owns substantially appreciated inventory and the withdrawing partner receives more or less than his share of the inventory. In that case, a portion of the distribution is recharacterized as a sale.[83] (For discussion of I.R.C. Section 751(b), see Chapter 8.)

(a) *If the withdrawing partner receives less than his proportionate share of the inventory, he is treated as if he received his share of the inventory and then exchanged a portion of it for the other partnership property actually distributed to him.* The partner realizes ordinary income on the exchange, and the partnership obtains a basis in the inventory equal to its deemed purchase price.

(b) *If the partner receives more than his share of the inventory, he is deemed to have received his share of other partnership property and exchanged it for the excess amount of partnership inventory actually distributed to him.* The partnership realizes gain or loss on the exchange, and the partner obtains a basis equal to his deemed purchase price.

(3) *The tax consequences of the portion treated as an I.R.C. Section 736(a) payment are determined. If the amount the partner receives is fixed, the payment is treated as a guaranteed payment.* If it is measured by partnership income, it is treated as the partner's distributive share of partnership income.

A property transfer classified as a guaranteed payment may cause the partnership to recognize gain or loss. Because the partnership is obligated to pay a fixed value to the withdrawing partner, the partnership may recognize gain or loss when it transfers property to satisfy its guaranteed payment obligation. The partnership's gain or loss equals the difference between the amount of its obligation and the basis of the transferred property.[84] The recipient partner realizes ordinary income on the guaranteed payment and the partnership is allowed a corresponding deduction.[85]

(4) *If a services partnership owns unrealized receivables, the tax consequences depend upon whether a withdrawing general partner receives more or less than his proportionate share of the receivables.* A withdrawing general partner who receives less than his share is deemed to obtain other partnership property in exchange for his interest in the receivables. Property or cash a partner receives in

---

[83] I.R.C. § 751(b).

[84] *See* Rev. Rul. 75-498, 1975-2 C.B. 29; Treas. Reg. § 1.83-6(b).

[85] Treas. Reg. § 1.736-1(a)(4).

exchange for his share of receivables is not treated as a distribution under I.R.C. Section 736(b); the property or cash is classified as an I.R.C. Section 736(a) payment.[86]

Example: Martha receives Stock X worth $50,000 and receivables worth $10,000 as a liquidating payment for her one-third interest in the MNO Services Partnership. The partnership's balance sheet is as follows:

Assets	Basis	Fair Market Value
Stock X	$30,000	$60,000
Receivables	0	120,000
	$30,000	$180,000
Partners' Capital		
Martha	$10,000	$60,000
Nathan	10,000	60,000
Olivia	10,000	60,000
	$30,000	$180,000

Martha's share of partnership receivables is worth $40,000, and she receives $40,000 worth of Stock X in exchange for that share. Because the amount paid for the receivables is fixed at $40,000, this portion of the transaction is treated as a guaranteed payment under I.R.C. Section 736(a). Martha includes $40,000 in her ordinary income, and the partnership deducts that amount. The partnership satisfies its $40,000 guaranteed payment obligation with the distribution of two-thirds of its Stock X, which has a $20,000 basis (two-thirds of the basis for all the stock) and, therefore, the partnership recognizes a $20,000 capital gain. The remainder of the transaction, consisting of Stock X worth $10,000 and receivables worth $10,000 are treated as a liquidating distribution under I.R.C. Section 736(b). These transactions are summarized as follows:

	Martha's 1/3 share	§ 736(b)	§ 736(a)
Stock X	$20,000	$10,000	$0
Receivables	40,000	10,000	40,000
(2/3 Stock X)	$60,000	$20,000	$40,000

If the withdrawing partner receives more than his share of the partnership's unrealized receivables, the payment is divided into two parts:

(a) *An amount of receivables equal to the withdrawing partner's proportionate share of the partnership's receivables.* The partner is considered to receive this amount under I.R.C. Section 736(b) as a liquidating distribution for his share of partnership property. The partner's basis for the receivables is determined under I.R.C. Section 732(c), which provides that

---

[86] I.R.C. § 736(b)(2)(A).

(i)   basis is first allocated to distributed unrealized receivables and inventory, and

(ii)   the partner's basis in the receivables cannot exceed the partnership's basis immediately before the distribution.

The basis of unrealized receivables generally is zero, and the withdrawing partner recognizes ordinary income when he collects or sells the receivables.[87] (*See* Chapter 8.)

Arguably, the withdrawing partner may be considered to receive this portion of the receivables as a "payment" for his share of the partnership's unrealized receivables. Under that view, the transfer of the receivables would be treated as a guaranteed payment under I.R.C. Section 736(a). Because the partnership transfers the receivables to satisfy its guaranteed payment obligation, it recognizes gain or loss equal to the difference between the amount of its obligation and its basis for the transferred receivables.[88] The withdrawing partner realizes ordinary income on the guaranteed payment, and the partnership is allowed a corresponding deduction.[89] This approach appears inappropriate because it requires an implausible interpretation of I.R.C. Section 736(b)(2) — that is, distribution of a partner's share of unrealized receivables is equivalent to a payment in exchange for the receivables.

(b)   *An amount of receivables in excess of the partner's share of the partnership's receivables.* To the extent that this portion of the receivables is in exchange for the partner's interest in partnership property (*i.e.*, a distribution under I.R.C. Section 736(b)), the transfer is subject to the disproportionate distribution rules of I.R.C. Section 751(b). (*See* Chapter 8.) The partner is treated as if he received a distribution of his proportionate share of the receivables and other property, and then he exchanged the other property for the excess amount of partnership receivables he actually received. This hypothetical exchange is a taxable transaction with the following consequences:

(i)   The partnership recognizes ordinary income on the exchange of receivables for the withdrawing partner's other property.

(ii)   The partnership increases or decreases the basis in the assets it is deemed to have received in the exchange — to reflect the value of the receivables transferred to the withdrawing partner.

(iii)   The withdrawing partner's basis in the receivables

---

[87]   I.R.C. § 735.

[88]   Rev. Rul. 75-498, 1975-2 C.B. 29; Treas. Reg. § 1.83-6(b).

[89]   Treas. Reg. § 1.736-1(a)(4).

increases-to reflect the value of the property he transferred to the partnership in the exchange.

Example: Jared receives partnership receivables worth $50,000 as a liquidating payment for his one-third interest in the JKL Partnership. The partnership's balance sheet is as follows:

Assets	Basis	Fair Market Value
Cash	$60,000	$60,000
Receivables	0	90,000
	$60,000	$150,000
Partners' Capital		
Jared	$20,000	$50,000
Karen	20,000	50,000
Lauren	20,000	50,000
	$60,000	$150,000

Because the value of the property Jared receives equals the value of his share of partnership property, the entire payment is classified as a distribution under I.R.C. Section 736(b). (Because Jared does not receive any payment "in exchange for" his interest in partnership receivables, the distribution of the receivables is not an I.R.C. Section 736(a) payment.) Under I.R.C. Section 751(b), Jared is deemed to receive his share of receivables worth $30,000 and his $20,000 share of partnership cash. He is then deemed to pay the $20,000 in cash to the partnership for the $20,000 excess value of the receivables actually transferred to him. The partnership recognizes $20,000 of ordinary income on this sale, and Jared's basis in the receivables he purchased is $20,000.

Chapter 11

WHEN A PARTNER OR LLC MEMBER DIES

§ 11.01 OVERVIEW OF STATE LAW AND TAX CONSIDERATIONS

[A] State Law Considerations

[1] General Partnership

When a partner in a general partnership dies, there is a change in the relationship between the remaining partners called "dissolution."[1] Upon dissolution, the remaining partners cease acting as agents for the partnership and each other, except for purposes of winding up the partnership's affairs. Dissolution does not "terminate" the partnership for state law purposes, since termination occurs only after the partnership winds up business and liquidates.[2]

Unless the partners have agreed otherwise, the successor to a deceased partner's interest may require the partnership to liquidate its assets, pay partnership creditors, and distribute the remaining proceeds.[3] Alternatively, the successor may permit the partnership to continue its operations in exchange for the partnership's obligation to pay him the value of the interest. In that case, the successor becomes a partnership creditor and he may claim either (1) interest on the unpaid balance of the partnership's obligation, or (2) the profits attributable to the use of the deceased partner's share of partnership property. As discussed below, the successor may not demand a liquidation of the partnership if the partners previously agreed to continue the partnership following a dissolution.[4]

Although the successor to a deceased general partner may require the partnership to wind up its business and liquidate, many partnerships have business continuation agreements that allow the remaining partners to reconstitute and continue the partnership.[5] Continuation agreements usually specify the obligations of the partnership or continuing partners to the deceased partner's successor, the method for determining the amount, if any, to be paid for the partner's interest, and the manner of any payments. Although continuation agreements are usually in effect before a partner dies, they can also be made after the death.

---

[1] Uniform Partnership Act (U.P.A.) §§ 29, 31(c) (1969).

[2] U.P.A. § 30.

[3] U.P.A. § 38(1).

[4] *Id.*

[5] *See* U.P.A. § 41.

There are two kinds of business continuation agreements:

(1)   Redemption agreement — if the partnership is required to purchase the deceased partner's interest through liquidation payments; and

(2)   Cross-purchase agreement — if the continuing partners must purchase the interest.

(See Chapter 8 for discussion of tax consequences of liquidation payments and Chapter 12 for discussion of consequences of sale of partnership interest.)

[2] Limited Partnership

The death of a general partner in a limited partnership does not cause a dissolution if (1) the partnership agreement authorizes another general partner to conduct the partnership, or (2) the remaining partners agree to appoint a new general partner.[6] The limited partners may enter a continuation agreement that prevents dissolution before or after the general partner's death. In many limited partnerships, however, the issue of continuation after a general partner's death does not arise because the general partner is a corporation.

A limited partnership does not dissolve when a limited partner dies, and the successor to the deceased partner's interest cannot require the partnership to wind up business and liquidate.[7] Instead, the successor may withdraw from the partnership and receive a liquidating distribution of the amount stated in the partnership agreement, or if the agreement is silent on that matter, he may receive a distribution equal to the value of his interest.[8]

[3] Limited Liability Company

The death of any member of a limited liability company causes the LLC's dissolution unless the remaining members continue the venture as provided under the specific state statute.[9] In this respect, LLCs are similar to general partnerships, but differ from limited partnerships, which dissolve only if a general partner withdraws. State statutes permitting an LLC to continue fall into the following categories:

(1)   continuation requires unanimous consent of the remaining members;[10] (2) continuation requires unanimous consent of the remaining members under a right stated in the LLC's articles of organization or operating agreement;[11]

(3)   continuation requires majority members' consent under a right stated in

---

[6] Revised Uniform Limited Partnership Act (R.U.L.P.A.) § 801 (1976).

[7] *Id.* The partnership agreement may provide otherwise.

[8] R.U.L.P.A. §§ 603, 604.

[9] *See, e.g.*, Uniform Limited Liability Company Act (U.L.L.C.A.) § 601; Illinois Limited Liability Company Act (Illinois LLC Act) § 35-1.

[10] *See, e.g.*, Illinois LLC Act § 15.23.

[11] *See, e.g.*, Colorado LLC Act § 15.16.

the articles of organization or the operating agreement;[12] and

(4)   continuation is permitted without consent under the articles of organization or the operating agreement.[13]

Ordinarily, a successor to a deceased member's limited liability company interest is not admitted as a substitute member with full management participation rights unless all current members consent.[14] However, the operating agreement may provide that a lower percentage of members' consent is sufficient to admit a substitute member.

[B]   Tax Considerations — In General

A partner's death usually generates both income tax and estate tax consequences which affect the successor to his partnership interest, the partnership itself, and the remaining partners. Some of these consequences occur whenever a partner dies, while others depend upon whether the deceased partner's successor sells or liquidates the partnership interest or whether the successor becomes a member of the partnership in his own right.

The following sections describe factors and alternative courses of action that may affect the tax consequences of a partner's death.

[1]   Tax Year Closes for Deceased Partner or Member

When a partner or LLC member dies, the partnership tax year closes for the decedent and his share of all partnership or LLC income or loss up to the date of death is included on his final tax return.[15] If the partner and partnership use different tax years, the partner's death may cause a "bunching" of partnership income for more than 12 months on the decedent's final return. However, because most partnerships having individuals as partners are required to use a calendar year, the possibility of such bunching is reduced.[16] (See § 3.04, *supra*, for discussion of allowable partnership tax years.)

> **Example:** Dorothy and Filo Corporation are equal partners in the DF Limited Liability Company. Dorothy is a calendar year taxpayer, but DF uses a fiscal year ending on March 31. Dorothy dies on October 31, 1999. Her final tax return includes her share of LLC income for the LLC tax year April 1, 1998 through March 31, 1999 plus her share of LLC income for the period April 1, 1999 through October 31, 1999 — a period of 19 months. If DF used a calendar tax year, however, Dorothy's final return would include only 10 months of partnership income for the period January 1, 1999 through October 31, 1999.

---

[12] *See, e.g.,* Texas LLC Act § 15.53.

[13] *See, e.g.,* Delaware LLC Act § 15.18.

[14] *See, e.g.,* U.L.L.C.A. § 503; Illinois LLC Act § 10-1.

[15] I.R.C. § 706(c)(2).

[16] *See* § 1246 House Report Accompanying the Taxpayer Relief Act of 1997, H.R. 2014.

A partner's distributive share of partnership income for the periods before and after his death is determined under rules analogous to those governing income allocations following a sale of a partnership interest.[17] These rules permit allocations to be based on an interim closing of the partnership's books, a daily proration of partnership income, or another reasonable method (*see* Chapter 6).

[2] Death of Partner or Member May Terminate Partnership or LLC

The partnership's tax year closes for all partners, as well as the deceased partner, if events triggered by the partner's death or if a subsequent transaction terminates the partnership. (For a complete discussion of tax consequences of a partnership termination, see Chapter 14.) A partnership terminates when (1) aggregate sales and exchanges of interests in partnership profits and capital during a 12-month period are 50 percent or more of the total interests, or (2) the partnership ceases conducting any business or financial operations in the form of a partnership.[18]

(1) *Aggregate sales and exchanges of interests in partnership profits and capital during a 12-month period are 50 percent or more of the total interests.* This rule may cause a termination when a partner dies if another person is obligated to purchase his interest at death, and the sale, together with other sales during the preceding 12 months, results in transfers of 50 percent or more of the total interests in the partnership. Similarly, a subsequent sale of the deceased partner's interest by his successor may result in termination of the partnership on the date of sale. (*See* § 11.01[B][7], [8], *infra.*)

Under I.R.C. Section 761(e), a distribution of a partnership interest (*e.g.*, by a corporation or another partnership) is considered an exchange of the interest in determining if the partnership terminates under the 50-percent sale or exchange rule. However, an exchange is not deemed to occur when an estate distributes a partnership interest to a beneficiary.[19] It is unclear whether a distribution from a testamentary trust to a beneficiary constitutes an exchange. Although the Service has ruled that a distribution by a trust to a beneficiary closes the partnership tax year for the trust,[20] no rationale exists for treating a distribution by a trust differently from a distribution by an estate. (Legislative history, however, calls for the Treasury to adopt a different position in forthcoming regulations.)[21]

(2) *The partnership ceases conducting any business or financial opera-*

---

[17] I.R.C. § 706(c)(2)(A) and regulations thereunder. *See* Baumann & McBryde, *Ownership of a Partnership Interest by an Estate or Trust: Tax and Other Considerations*, 38 Tax Law. 33 (Fall 1984).

[18] I.R.C. § 708(b)(1).

[19] *See* Treas. Reg. §§ 1.706-1(c)(3)(iv), 1.706-1(c)(3)(vi), *Example (3)* (distribution by estate to beneficiary does not close partnership tax year); S. Rep. No. 313, 99th Cong., 2d Sess. 924 (1986) (distributions by estate or testamentary trust should not be treated as exchanges).

[20] Rev. Rul. 72-352, 1972-2 C.B. 395.

[21] S. Rep. No. 313, 99th Cong., 2d Sess. 924 (1986).

tions in the form of a partnership. Because this situation may arise when a partner in a two-member partnership dies (because the partnership may be viewed as a sole proprietorship), the regulations provide these two rules to prevent termination. Termination does not occur as long as:

(a) the partner's successor continues to share in partnership profits; or

(b) the partnership makes installment payments to liquidate the decedent's partnership interest.[22] (*See* § 11.01[B][6], *infra.*)

[3] Basis of Successor's Partnership/LLC Interest

The basis of a partnership interest acquired from a deceased partner is its fair market value on the date of death (or alternate valuation date, if elected).[23] No basis change occurs, however, for the portion of the partnership interest attributable to partnership property that would be income in respect of a decedent under I.R.C. Section 691 if owned directly by the partner (*see* § 11.03, *infra*). For example, no basis increase is permitted to reflect the value of a deceased partner's share of partnership accounts receivable.

[4] Basis of Partnership/LLC Property

Generally, a partner's death does not affect the basis of the partnership's assets. This is true even though the successor's basis in the partnership interest he acquires increases or decreases to its value on the partner's date of death.[24] (*See* § 11.04, *infra.*) Therefore, a partner's death often creates a disparity between the successor's basis for his partnership interest — outside basis — and his share of the basis of partnership assets — inside basis (*see* Chapter 5). This disparity affects the timing and character of the gain, loss, and income the successor realizes from the partnership.

Ordinarily, the disparity between outside and inside basis is disadvantageous if the successor's basis in his partnership interest is greater than his share of the basis of partnership assets. The successor is allocated more gain and lower deductions for items such as depreciation than he would be if the basis of partnership assets increased to their value on the date of the partner's death. Many of these adverse tax consequences can be mitigated, however, by one of the following elections:

(1) I.R.C. Section 754 Election. If the partnership has an I.R.C. Section 754 election in effect for the year in which the partner dies, the basis of partnership assets is adjusted under the rules of I.R.C. Section 743(b) and I.R.C. Section 755. These rules increase or decrease the basis of partnership property in order to eliminate the difference between the successor's basis for his partnership interest and his share of the basis of partnership assets. These basis adjustments apply only in determining the successor's income, gain, or loss, and they do not affect the other partners. A partnership election after the partner's death may be retroactive to the

---

[22] Treas. Reg. § 1.708-1(b)(1)(i)(a), (b).

[23] I.R.C. § 1014.

[24] I.R.C. §§ 742, 1014.

beginning of the partnership tax year. (*See* Chapter 12.)

(2)   I.R.C. Section 732(d) Election. If the partnership does not have an I.R.C. Section 754 election in effect for the year of the partner's death, the decedent's successor may obtain similar tax treatment through an election under I.R.C. Section 732(d). The election permits the successor to determine his basis in property the partnership distributes to him within two years of the partner's death, as though an I.R.C. Section 754 election was in effect at the time of death.[25] (*See* Chapter 8.)

[5]   Value of Decedent's Interest Subject to Estate Tax

The value of a deceased partner's partnership interest is included in his gross estate for estate tax purposes.[26] This value may be determined from the price set in an existing buy-sell agreement between the deceased partner and the partnership or remaining partners. Special valuation and estate tax payment rules may apply to certain family-operated partnerships (*see* Chapter 9). A successor to a deceased partner who is taxed on the portion of the partnership interest attributable to partnership property treated as income in respect of a decedent (IRD), is allowed an income tax deduction for any estate taxes attributable to inclusion of the IRD items in the decedent's estate (*see* § 11.05, *infra*).

[6]   Liquidation of Interest of Deceased Partner or Member

The partnership may liquidate the deceased partner's interest through a payment or through a series of payments to his successor. Frequently, the amount and timing of the payments are determined in advance through buy-sell agreements with the partnership (*i.e.*, redemption agreements). Without a buy-sell agreement, the successor and partnership must negotiate the terms of the liquidation after the partner's death. Partners often ensure that adequate funds will be available to liquidate their interests by requiring the partnership to purchase insurance on their lives.

For tax purposes, the deceased partner's successor should be treated as a partner until his interest is completely liquidated. The partner's successor is taxable on the decedent's share of partnership income or loss for the period beginning on the date of death. Income or loss for the period up to the date of death is reported on the decedent's final tax return. The partnership tax year does close for the successor on the date that his partnership interest is completely liquidated.[27] The successor's distributive share of partnership income or loss is computed up to the liquidation date, and it is included in his return for that year.

---

[25] I.R.C. § 732(d); Treas. Reg. § 1.732-1(d).

[26] *See, e.g.*, Estate of Nowell v. Comm'r, T.C. Memo. 1999-15 (Tax Court applied state law to find that, without general partners' consent to make him a substitute limited partner, successor was an assignee of limited partnership interests for valuation purposes).

[27] I.R.C. § 706(c)(2)(A).

The taxation of liquidating payments to the successor is determined under I.R.C. Section 736, which divides the payments into two classes:

(1) *The portion of the payment that is in exchange for the deceased partner's interest in partnership property* (I.R.C. *Section 736(b) payment*). This portion is taxable under the rules governing partnership distributions, including the rules of I.R.C. Section 751(b) governing disproportionate distributions of receivables and inventory. In determining the consequences of a distribution to a deceased partner's successor, basis adjustments to partnership assets resulting from an I.R.C. Section 754 election must be taken into account. If no I.R.C. Section 754 election is in effect, the mandatory and elective basis-adjustment provisions of I.R.C. Section 732(d) should be considered. (*See* Chapters 8, 12.)

(2) *The portion derived from partnership income* (I.R.C. *Section 736(a) payment*). This portion is taxable as a guaranteed payment if the amount the partner receives is fixed, or it is taxable as a distributive share if the amount is measured by reference to partnership income. A partner's successor who receives I.R.C. Section 736(a) liquidating payments must report these amounts as income in respect of a decedent (*see* Chapter 10).

(For complete discussion of the treatment of liquidating payments to a deceased partner's successor, see Chapter 10.)

[7] Sale of Decedent's Interest to Remaining Partners or Members

The remaining partners may purchase a deceased partner's interest by a payment or a series of payments to his successor. The amount and timing of the purchase price may be determined in advance through buy-sell agreements between the partners (*i.e.*, cross-purchase agreements). A partner can ensure that adequate funds will be available by requiring the partners obligated to purchase his interest to obtain insurance on his life. Without a buy-sell agreement, the successor and remaining partners must negotiate the terms of the sale after the partner's death.

The seller generally realizes capital gain or loss on the sale, except to the extent that the purchase price is attributable to his interest in the partnership's unrealized receivables and inventory (I.R.C. Section 751 property).[28] (*See* Chapter 12.) In computing the gain or loss on a sale, the basis of a partnership interest received from a deceased partner generally equals its value on the date of death. No basis increase occurs, however, for partnership items that represent income in respect of a decedent (IRD). (For discussion of IRD, see § 11.03, *infra*.) The basis of partnership assets may also change if the partnership has an I.R.C. Section 754 basis-adjustment election in effect for the year in which the partner died. (*See* Chapter 8; § 11.04, *infra*.)

---

[28] I.R.C. §§ 741, 751.

The partnership's tax year closes for the seller on the date he transfers his entire partnership interest.[29] Therefore, the seller must report his share of partnership income up to that date on his tax return for the year in which the sale date falls.

Although a partner's death, by itself, does not terminate a partnership, a subsequent sale of his partnership interest by his successor may cause a termination. Termination occurs if the interest the successor sells, alone or together with other sales during the preceding 12-month period, is 50 percent or more of the total interests in partnership capital and profits (see Chapter 14).

A purchasing partner's basis for the interest he acquires equals the amount paid for the interest, including any increase in his share of partnership liabilities resulting from the purchase (see Chapter 5). If the partnership has an I.R.C. Section 754 basis-adjustment election in effect, the purchaser's share of the basis of partnership assets may change.

[8] Sale of Decedent's Interest to Third Party

A third party may purchase a deceased partner's or member's interest from the successor. A sale of a partnership interest to a third party has the same tax consequences as a sale of an interest to current partners.

A person who buys a general partnership interest does not ordinarily become a partner, unless all the other partners consent to admit him to the partnership. Without their consent, the buyer is considered an assignee who is entitled to receive the seller's share of partnership profits, as well as repayment of the seller's share of capital, when the partnership dissolves.[30]

An assignee of an interest in a limited partnership may become a limited partner if all the partners consent, or if the partnership agreement permits the seller to confer limited partnership status on an assignee.[31]

Ordinarily, a transferee of a limited liability company interest is not admitted as a substitute member with full management participation rights unless all current members consent.[32] However, the operating agreement may provide that a lower percentage of members' consent (e.g., two-thirds) is sufficient to admit a substitute member. A transferee who does not become a member is entitled to receive distributions and liquidating payments that the decedent member was entitled to.[33]

[9] Liquidation of Partnership or LLC

Upon a partner's death, all the partners' interests may be liquidated and the partnership terminated. This is most likely to occur upon the death of one partner or member in a two-member partnership or LLC. (For discussion of partnership termination, see Chapter 13.) However, the death of a partner in a two-person

---

29 I.R.C. § 706(c)(2)(A).

30 U.P.A. § 27.

31 R.U.L.P.A. §§ 702, 704.

32 See, e.g., U.L.L.C.A. § 503; Illinois LLC Act § 10-1.

33 See U.L.L.C.A. § 503(e).

partnership does not necessarily terminate the partnership. The partnership continues during its winding-up period and during the period that the decedent's estate or successor continues to share in the profits or losses of the business.[34]

[10] Successor Joins Partnership or LLC

A deceased partner's or LLC member's successor may continue as a partner or member and may share in partnership or LLC profits and losses on an ongoing basis. This continuation requires the remaining partners or members to admit the successor according to the existing terms of the partnership or LLC agreement or by mutual agreement following the partner's or member's death.

Upon joining the partnership, the successor's basis in his partnership interest generally equals its date-of-death value (*see* § 11.04[A], *infra*). If the partnership has an I.R.C. Section 754 election in effect, the bases of partnership assets are adjusted to eliminate the difference between the successor's basis for his partnership interest and his share of the basis of partnership property.

§ 11.02 PRE-1998 RULES FOR ALLOCATING INCOME FOR YEAR OF PARTNER'S DEATH

For partnership tax years beginning before January 1, 1998, the partnership tax year did not close for a partner on the date of his death, but continued to its normal end. Consequently, the partner's share of income for the year of death, including amounts earned before the date of death, were excluded from his final tax return, even if he actually received the income in the form of a cash draw.[35] The deceased partner's share of partnership income for the year of his death was reported on his successor's tax return.[36] The successor reported the amount of income attributable to the period before the partner's death as income in respect of a decedent under I.R.C. Section 691.[37]

If the successor retained the partnership interest, he reported the deceased partner's share of partnership income for the entire partnership tax year ending in or with his own tax year. The successor continued to be taxable on the deceased partner's distributive share as long as he continued to share in partnership profits and losses or continued to receive liquidating payments from the partnership.[38] If the successor sold or liquidated the entire interest, the partnership tax year ended on the date of the sale or liquidation, and the successor included in his return for the year in which the sale or liquidation occurred, the deceased partner's share of income up to that date.[39]

---

[34] Treas. Reg. § 1.708-1(b)(1)(i).

[35] *See* Treas. Reg. § 1.706-1(c)(3)(ii), (vi), *Example (4)*; Estate of Freund v. Comm'r, 303 F.2d 30 (2d Cir. 1962).

[36] Treas. Reg. § 1.706-1(c)(3)(ii).

[37] Treas. Reg. § 1.706-1(c)(3)(v).

[38] I.R.C. § 736; Treas. Reg. § 1.736-1(a)(6).

[39] Treas. Reg. § 1.706-1(c)(3)(i).

The rule excluding a partner's pre-death share of income from his final return was enacted in 1954 to prevent "bunching§§ more than 12 months of income in a single year.[40] This bunching occurs, for example, when a calendar-year partner owning an interest in a partnership with a tax year ending on March 31, dies on November 30, Year 2. If the partnership's tax year closes on his death, the partner's final tax return includes 20 months of partnership income (income from the 12-month partnership year April 1, Year 1, to March 31, Year 2, plus eight months of income from April 1, Year 2, to November 30, Year 2). However, this bunching of income occurs only if the partnership and deceased partner use different tax years. Since 1954, the rules governing selection of a partnership's tax year have changed significantly, making it unlikely that a partnership's tax year will differ from the tax year used by its partners. Consequently, the statute was rarely advantageous and often created significant tax problems.

§ 11.03   EFFECTS OF INCOME-IN-RESPECT-OF-A-DECEDENT (IRD) RULES

[A]   General Explanation of IRD Rules

The term "income in respect of a decedent" (IRD) applies generally to amounts the decedent was entitled to at, or before, his death and that were not previously includible in income under his method of accounting.[41] Examples of IRD for a cash-method decedent include compensation or receivables that were earned but not received before his death and unpaid proceeds of property sales.[43] I.R.C. Section 691 ensures that the amounts do not escape income taxation, by requiring the decedent's successor to report the IRD when it is received. To prevent any of the income from being eliminated by a basis increase at death, I.R.C. Section 1014(c) provides that no basis increase occurs for any property that constitutes IRD.

The following general rules apply to IRD:

(1) *A decedent's estate or other successor is taxable on IRD in the year it is received.*[42] For example, if a decedent were entitled to receive a cash payment in each of the five years following his death, these amounts would be reported as IRD in each of the succeeding years.[43]

(2) *The character of each IRD item is the same as it would be if received by the decedent during his life.*[44] However, the character of the IRD portion of a deceased partner's share of partnership income is determined at the partnership level.[45]

---

40 *See* H.R. Rep. No. 1337, 83d Cong., 2d Sess. 67 (1954); S. Rep. No. 1622, 83d Cong., 2d Sess. 91 (1954). Under the steeply graduated tax brackets in effect at that time, bunching income often resulted in a significantly higher tax rate. This is less likely to be a problem under the current tax structure.

41 Treas. Reg. § 1.691(a)-1(b).

42 I.R.C. § 691(a)(1).

43 Treas. Reg. § 1.691(a)-2(b), *Example (1)*.

44 I.R.C. § 691(a)(3).

45 *See* Treas. Reg. § 1.702-1(b).

(3) ***The person who is taxable on the IRD is allowed an income tax deduction for any estate taxes attributable to inclusion of the IRD items in the decedent's estate.*** [46] The amount deductible is the difference between the actual estate tax and the estate tax that would be incurred if the IRD item were excluded from the estate.[47] The deduction is allowed in the same year that the successor is taxable on the IRD.[48]

(4) ***The basis for an IRD item does not increase or decrease to its value on the date of death (or alternate valuation date).*** [49] Therefore, the successor's basis in IRD property is the basis of the property in the hands of the decedent. The basis of a deceased partner's partnership interest does not increase to the extent that the value of the interest is attributable to his share of partnership items that would be IRD if held directly by the partner. The partnership's basis for the items does not change, even though the partnership has an I.R.C. Section 754 election in effect when the partner dies. After the successor reports the partnership income as IRD, the basis of his partnership interest increases by the amount of income recognized.[50]

[B]   IRD Attributable to a Partnership or LLC Interest

The applicability of the IRD rules to a deceased partner is determined under I.R.C. Section 753.[51] Although I.R.C. Section 753 appears to limit IRD to liquidation payments that are treated as a distributive share or as guaranteed payments under I.R.C. Section 736(a), regulations and case law have greatly expanded the scope of IRD attributable to a partnership interest.[52] The following sections discuss specific items that the successor to a deceased partner must treat as IRD.

[1]   Liquidating Payments

Liquidating payments a successor receives from the partnership that are classified as a distributive share or as guaranteed payments under I.R.C. Section 736(a) must be treated as IRD.[53] These payments include:

(1)   payments on a liquidation triggered by a partner's death;

---

[46]   I.R.C. § 691(c)(2). Although the early Supreme Court decision in Bull v. U.S., 295 U.S. 247 (1935), holds that payments of partnership profits to a decedent's estate are not subject to estate tax, this is no longer valid. I.R.C. § 691(c). *See* Estate of Riegelman v. Comm'r, 27 T.C. 833, *aff'd*, 253 F.2d 315 (2d Cir. 1958).

[47]   Treas. Reg. § 1.691(c)-1(a)(2).

[48]   Treas. Reg. § 1.691(c)-1(a).

[49]   I.R.C. § 1014(c).

[50]   I.R.C. § 705(a)(1)(A).

[51]   I.R.C. § 691(e).

[52]   *See* Treas. Reg. § 1.753-1(b); Quick Trust v. Comm'r, 54 T.C. 1336 (1970), *aff'd*, 444 F.2d 90 (8th Cir. 1971); Woodhall v. Comm'r, T.C. Memo. 1969-279, *aff'd*, 454 F.2d 226 (9th Cir. 1972).

[53]   I.R.C. § 753.

(2) continuing payments related to a liquidation begun before the partner's death; and

(3) payments from a third party in exchange for the successor's rights to receive I.R.C. Section 736(a) liquidating payments from the partnership.[54]

Presumably, only payments made pursuant to a state law or liquidation agreement in effect when a partner dies are considered IRD. If the partner's successor negotiates a liquidation agreement after the partner's death, the I.R.C. Section 736(a) payments he receives should not be considered IRD.[55]

I.R.C. Section 736(a) generally covers liquidating payments that exceed the value of a partner's interest in partnership property and, in a services partnership, payments for the partner's share of partnership goodwill (if payment is not required by the partnership agreement) and payments for unrealized accounts receivable from sales of goods and services (see Chapter 10).

[2] Assets That Would Be IRD if Held by Decedent

Income in respect of a decedent includes a deceased partner's share of partnership assets that would be treated as IRD if held by the partner directly.[56] This category of IRD is not described in the Code or regulations, but has been created judicially. Although the scope of the judicial rule is uncertain, it applies to a partner's share of accounts receivable in a cash-method partnership and probably covers his share of deferred installment income.[57]

Treating these partnership items as IRD has the following consequences:

(1) The successor's basis in his partnership interest does not increase to reflect the date-of-death, or alternate-date, value of the deceased partner's share of partnership IRD items.[58]

(2) The partnership's basis for these items does not increase for the successor, even though an I.R.C. Section 754 basis adjustment election is in effect when the partner dies.

(3) The successor must report the IRD when the partnership collects or otherwise realizes income from these items.

Items excluded from this judicially created class of IRD items include the recapture potential in partnership property treated as an unrealized receivable under I.R.C. Section 751(c) and the unrealized appreciation in partnership inventory. These items are excluded because they would be permitted a basis adjustment to reflect date-of-death values if held directly by the partner.

---

[54] Treas. Reg. § 1.753-1(a).

[55] See Baumann & McBryde, *Ownership of a Partnership Interest by an Estate or Trust: Tax and Other Considerations*, 38 Tax Law. 33 (Fall 1984).

[56] See Quick Trust v. Comm'r, 54 T.C. 1336 (1970), aff'd, 444 F.2d 90 (8th Cir. 1971); Woodhall v. Comm'r, T.C. Memo. 1969-279, aff'd, 454 F.2d 226 (9th Cir. 1972).

[57] See I.R.C. § 691(a).

[58] I.R.C. § 1014(c).

Example: When Louis died, his interest in the LMN Partnership passed to his estate. At his death, Louis's interest was worth $100,000: $60,000 attributable to Louis's share of partnership accounts receivable; $40,000 attributable to his share of partnership inventory. The estate's initial basis for the partnership interest is $40,000. When the partnership collects the $60,000 of receivables, that amount is included in the estate's distributive share of income, and the basis for its partnership interest increases by $60,000.[59] If the partnership had an I.R.C. Section 754 election in effect for the year of Louis's death, the partnership would not increase its basis for the estate's share of its accounts receivable.

§ 11.04   EFFECT OF PARTNER'S OR MEMBER'S DEATH ON BASIS

[A]   Successor's Basis for Partnership or LLC Interest

I.R.C. Section 742 specifies that the basis of a partnership interest acquired by any means other than a property contribution is determined under the general basis rules of the Code. Under I.R.C. Section 1014, the basis of property acquired from a decedent is the fair market value of the property on the date of death (or alternate valuation date, if used).[60] For community property, the date-of-death basis rule applies to the entire asset and not only to the half that the surviving spouse acquires from the decedent.[61]

When a partnership interest is acquired from a deceased partner, two adjustments to the initial basis determined under I.R.C. Section 1014 are required:[62]

(1)   The basis increases by the successor's share of partnership liabilities, as determined under I.R.C. Section 752. This basis increase reflects the rule of I.R.C. Section 752(b); that is, a partner is deemed to make a cash contribution equal to his share of the partnership's liabilities.

(2)   The basis decreases to the extent that the value of the interest is attributable to items constituting income in respect of a decedent (IRD) under I.R.C. Section 691. The basis decrease for IRD items prevents a basis increase for items that represent income that was earned but not realized at the time of the deceased partner's death. This ensures that the partner's successor is taxable on the income from the items when it is eventually realized.

Example: When Peter dies, his interest in the PQR partnership passes to his daughter, Marie. On the date of death, the partnership has the following balance sheet:

---

[59] I.R.C. § 705(a).

[60] The alternate valuation date is provided under I.R.C. § 2032.

[61] I.R.C. § 1014(b)(6).

[62] Treas. Reg. § 1.742-1.

Assets	Basis	Value
Cash	$10,000	$10,000
Accounts receivable	0	15,000
Investments	20,000	35,000
Land & building	60,000	120,000
	$90,000	$180,000
Liabilities		
Mortgage	$30,000	$30,000
Capital		
Peter	20,000	50,000
Quentin	20,000	50,000
Roger	20,000	50,000
Total Partner's Capital	$60,000	$150,000
Total Capital plus Liabilities	$120,000	$180,000

Marie's basis for the partnership interest is $55,000 [$50,000 date-of-death value, less $5,000 share of IRD items (accounts receivable), plus $10,000 share of partnership liabilities].

[B]   Basis of Partnership or LLC Property

I.R.C. Section 743(a) contains a general rule that a partnership's basis for its property does not change when a partnership interest is transferred to a deceased partner's successor. This rule applies even though the successor's basis in the partnership interest he acquires increases or decreases to its value on the partner's date of death.[63] Therefore, a partner's death often creates a disparity between the successor's basis for his partnership interest (outside basis) and his share of the basis of partnership assets (inside basis). This disparity affects the timing and character of the gain, loss, and income the successor realizes from the partnership.

[1]   I.R.C. Section 754 Election

The disparity between the partnership's inside basis and the successor's outside basis may be reduced or eliminated if the partnership has an I.R.C. Section 754 election in effect for the year in which the partner dies.[64] If the election is made, I.R.C. Section 743(b) requires that the basis of partnership property increases or decreases by the difference between the successor's basis in his partnership interest and his proportionate share of the basis of partnership assets. The total basis increase or decrease is then allocated among the partnership's assets under the rules of I.R.C. Section 755.[65] The I.R.C. Section 743(b) basis adjustment applies only to the successor's share of the partnership's basis and only affects his tax situation.

---

[63] I.R.C. §§ 742, 1014.

[64] The partnership may file the election before the date of death on its return for its tax year that includes the date of death.

[65] No basis adjustment is allocated to assets that represent income in respect of a decedent under I.R.C. § 691. Treas. Reg. § 1.755-1(b)(4). See Treas. Reg. § 1.743-1(b).

No adjustment to the basis of partnership property occurs under I.R.C. Section 743(b), unless the partnership has an I.R.C. Section 754 election in effect for the partnership tax year in which the partner dies. An election in a prior year continues in effect, and no new election is required for the year of death. If no prior-year election was made, an election in the year of death is retroactively effective to the beginning of the year, if the election is filed no later than the due date for the partnership's tax return (with extensions).[66] Once made, the election cannot be revoked without IRS permission.[67]

A partnership that makes an I.R.C. Section 754 election must adjust the basis of partnership property (1) under I.R.C. Section 743(b)) whenever a partnership interest is transferred by sale or exchange or at a partner's death, and (2) under I.R.C. Section 734(b) whenever certain distributions occur. A partnership makes an I.R.C. Section 754 election by filing a written statement with the partnership return.[68] (For complete discussion of the effect of an I.R.C. Section 754 election when an interest is transferred, see § 12.08, *infra*.)

An I.R.C. Section 754 election may be undesirable for the following reasons:

(1) *If the successor's share of the basis of partnership property exceeds the basis of his partnership interest, the election results in a decreased basis for partnership property.* The lower basis for partnership assets will increase the amount of gain and decrease the cost recovery deductions included in the successor's distributive share.

(2) *If the value of partnership property declines, the election will decrease the basis of partnership assets when the other partners transfer their interests.* This decrease may adversely affect the partners' ability to sell their interests and reduce the value of the interests to their successors.

(3) *The election creates bookkeeping complications for partnerships with many partners or with a high turnover of partners, because the partnership must maintain separate basis records for every partner who transfers his interest by sale, exchange, or death.*

(4) *The partnership must appraise the value of each of its assets whenever a basis adjustment is required.* The appraisal is necessary to allocate properly the basis adjustment among partnership assets.

[2] I.R.C. Section 732(d) Election for Distributed Property

If the partnership does not have an I.R.C. Section 754 election in effect for the year of a partner's death, the partner's successor may obtain similar tax benefits through an election under I.R.C. Section 732(d). An I.R.C. Section 732(d) election permits a successor to determine his basis in property the partnership distributes to him within two years of the partner's death, as though an I.R.C. Section 754

---

[66] Treas. Reg. § 1.754-1(b).

[67] Treas. Reg. § 1.754-1(c).

[68] Treas. Reg. § 1.754-1(b)(1).

election was in effect at the time of death.[69] (For more discussion of the I.R.C. Section 732(d) election, see Chapter 8.)

The basis adjustment is made only for property (other than cash) actually distributed to the successor. The adjustment occurs immediately before the distribution and the new basis carries over to the successor.[70] The amount of the adjustment is not affected by depletion or depreciation that would have been allowed if an adjustment under I.R.C. Section 743(b) occurred when the successor received his partnership interest.[71] The adjustment generally applies only to distributed property that the partnership owned when the partner died. The adjustment may apply to other distributed property, however, if the successor relinquishes his interest in property of the same class (*e.g.*, stock in trade, trade or business assets, capital assets)[72] that is retained in the partnership.[73]

If the distribution includes depreciable, depletable, or amortizable property, the successor makes the election with his tax return for the year in which distribution occurs. For other kinds of distributions, the election is made with the successor's return for the first tax year in which the basis of the distributed property must be known in order to compute the successor's income tax.[74]

Example: Upon Charles's death last month, Dawn succeeded to his one-third interest in the ABC Partnership. When Charles died, his partnership interest was worth $30,000. The partnership did not have an I.R.C. Section 754 election in effect for the year of Charles's death. The partnership's balance sheet appeared as follows at the time of Charles's death:

Assets	Basis	Fair Market Value
Cash	$30,000	$30,000
Inventory	30,000	60,000
	$60,000	$90,000
Partners' Capital		
Arnold	$20,000	$30,000
Bill	20,000	30,000
Charles	20,000	30,000
	$60,000	$90,000

The partnership distributes $10,000 in cash and inventory worth $20,000 to Dawn in complete liquidation of her partnership interest. (Because Dawn receives her proportionate share of I.R.C. Section 751 property, the constructive-sale rules of I.R.C. Section 751 do not apply.) If Dawn does not make an I.R.C. Section 732(d) election, her basis in the distributed

---

[69] I.R.C. § 732(d); Treas. Reg. § 1.732-1(d).

[70] Treas. Reg. § 1.732-1(d)(1)(iii).

[71] Treas. Reg. § 1.732-1(d)(1)(iv).

[72] Treas. Reg. § 1.743-1(b)(2)(ii).

[73] Treas. Reg. § 1.732-1(d)(1)(v).

[74] Treas. Reg. § 1.732-1(d)(2).

inventory is $10,000 — the same as the partnership's basis before the distribution. Dawn recognizes a $10,000 capital loss on the liquidation,[75] and upon a sale of the inventory, she recognizes $10,000 of ordinary income.[76]

If Dawn makes the I.R.C. Section 732(d) election, her basis in the inventory is determined as if the partnership had an I.R.C. Section 754 election in effect when Charles died. Under I.R.C. Section 743(b), the basis of partnership property increases for Dawn by the $10,000 difference between the $30,000 basis of her partnership interest (its date-of-death value) and her $20,000 proportionate share of the basis of partnership property. Under the rules of I.R.C. Section 755, the entire increase is allocated to the inventory. Therefore, the I.R.C. Section 732(d) election increases Dawn's basis in the distributed inventory to $20,000. As a result, Dawn would not realize income upon either the liquidation or the sale of the inventory.

An I.R.C. Section 732(d) election does not reduce or eliminate increases attributable to the difference between the value and basis of unrealized accounts receivable for goods and services owned by a partnership. Because the receivables represent IRD items, no basis increase is permitted under I.R.C. Section 1014. Thus, the receivables continue to have a zero basis for a successor whether or not they are distributed to him. Therefore, a successor is taxable on all the ordinary income attributable to receivables when they are collected.

[3] Summary of Effect of Partner's or Member's Death on Basis of Partnership/LLC Interests and Partnership/ LLC Property

Partnership Interest:

Successor's basis in partnership interest *equals*

Fair market value of interest on date of death (or alternate valuation date if elected)

plus

Successor's share of partnership liabilities (determined under I.R.C. Section 752)

minus

Deceased partner's share of partnership items taxable as income in respect of a decedent

Basis of Partnership's Property:

(i) *General Rule* — Partnership's basis unaffected by partner's death.

(ii) If I.R.C. Section 754 election is in effect — Successor's share of basis of partnership assets increases or decreases to equal successor's basis in

---

[75] I.R.C. §§ 731(a)(2), 741.

[76] I.R.C. § 735.

partnership interest. The total basis adjustment allocated among partnership assets under rules of I.R.C. Section 755. No portion of the basis adjustment is allocated to IRD items.[77]

(iii) No I.R.C. Section 754 election, but property distributed to successor within two years of partner's death[78] -Basis of distributed property may increase or decrease under I.R.C. Section 732(d) to basis it would have had if I.R.C. Section 754 election was in effect when successor acquired partnership interest from deceased partner.

Example (1): The ABCD Partnership consists of four partners: Allen and Barbara each own 30 percent interests, while Carol and Donald each own 20 percent interests. The partnership and all its partners use a calendar tax year. Allen dies on June 30, Year 1, and his partnership interest passes to his wife, Enid. The tax basis and fair market value of the partnership's assets and the partners' interests are as follows when Allen dies:

Assets	Basis	Value
Cash	$120,000	$120,000
Accounts receivable	0	180,000
Real estate	180,000	240,000
	$300,000	$540,000
Capital		
Allen	$90,000	$162,000
Barbara	90,000	162,000
Carol	60,000	108,000
Donald	60,000	108,000
	$300,000	$540,000

Enid's basis for the partnership interest she inherits is $108,000 [$162,000 date-of-death value less $54,000 share of IRD items (accounts receivable)].

The tax basis and fair market value of the partnership's assets and the partners' interests now appear as follows:

---

[77] Treas. Reg. § 1.755-1(b)(4).

[78] In certain cases, the Service can require the I.R.C. Section 732(d) adjustments to be made to distributed property.

Assets	Basis	Value
Cash	$120,000	$120,000
Accounts receivable	0	180,000
Real estate	180,000	240,000
	$300,000	$540,000
Capital		
Enid (as successor)	$108,000	$162,000
Barbara	90,000	162,000
Carol	60,000	108,000
Donald	60,000	108,000
	$318,000	$540,000

Example (2): Assume that the partnership has an I.R.C. Section 754 election in effect for the year of Allen's death. The partnership increases the basis of Enid's share of partnership assets by $18,000 (difference between $108,000 basis for her interest under I.R.C. Section 1014 and her $90,000 share of the basis of partnership assets). Because no basis adjustment is attributable to the accounts receivable (since they represent amounts taxable as income in respect of a decedent), the entire basis increase is allocated to the real estate. The tax basis and fair market value of the partnership's assets and the partners' interests now appear as follows:

Assets	Basis	Value
Cash	$120,000	$120,000
Accounts receivable	0	180,000
Real estate	198,000	240,000
	$318,000	$540,000
Capital		
Enid (as successor)	$108,000	$162,000
Barbara	90,000	162,000
Carol	60,000	108,000
Donald	60,000	108,000
	$318,000	$540,000

Example (3): Assume that the partnership does not have an I.R.C. Section 754 election in effect for the year of Allen's death. Six months following his death, the partnership distributes a 30-percent interest in its real estate to Enid. Under the general rule of I.R.C. Section 732(a), Enid's basis in the distributed property would be $54,000 (30 percent of the partnership's $180,000 basis in the property). If Enid makes the election under I.R.C. Section 732(d), however, her basis is determined as if the partnership had an I.R.C. Section 754 election in effect when she succeeded to Allen's interest. Because the I.R.C. Section 754 adjustment would have increased Enid's share of the basis for the real estate by $18,000, her basis in the distributed property is $72,000.

After the distribution of 30 percent of the real estate is accounted for, the partnership's records appear as follows:

Assets	Basis	Value
Cash	$120,000	$120,000
Accounts receivable	0	180,000
Real estate	126,000	168,000
	$246,000	$468,000
Capital		
Enid (as successor)	$36,000	$90,000
Barbara	90,000	162,000
Carol	60,000	108,000
Donald	60,000	108,000
	$246,000	$468,000

§ 11.05   ESTATE TAXATION: DETERMINING THE VALUE OF A PARTNERSHIP/LLC INTEREST

The value of a deceased partner's partnership interest is included in his gross estate for estate tax purposes. The fair market value of the partnership interest is generally the net amount a willing purchaser would pay a willing seller for the interest, if neither is under any compulsion to buy or sell the interest and both have reasonable knowledge of the relevant facts.[79] The following factors must be considered in determining the value of a partnership interest:[80]

(1)   *The value of the partnership's tangible assets, such as its productive facilities and inventory.*

(2)   *The value of the partner's share of partnership goodwill.* [81] Goodwill generally represents the value of earnings expected to exceed a fair return on the capital invested in the partnership's tangible assets and other means of production.[82] The excess earnings may be attributable to—

(a)   the earning capacity of the business, based upon its performance in prior years;

(b)   the economic outlook, generally, and the outlook for the specific partnership business;

(c)   the competence, reputation, skill, and experience of management; and

(d)   the availability of trained and experienced personnel.

Goodwill does not include the value of earnings attributable to the personal

---

[79]   Treas. Reg. §§ 20.2031-3, 25.2512-3.

[80]   Rev. Rul. 59-60, 1959-1 C.B. 237. *See also* Rev. Rul. 65-193, 1965-2 C.B. 370; Rev. Rul. 68-609, 1968-2 C.B. 327.

[81]   Estate of Trammell v. Comm'r, 18 T.C. 662 (1952).

[82]   Rev. Rul. 65-193, 1965-2 C.B. 370; Rev. Rul. 68-609, 1968-2 C.B. 327.

services or attributes of individual partners.[83] Therefore, little value is assigned to goodwill of service partnerships.[84] Partnership goodwill is not included in the value of a partnership interest if the surviving partners are not required to pay the deceased partner's successor for it.[85]

(3) *The value of a partnership interest includes the present value of the deceased partner's right to receive future liquidating payments from the partnership* including the present value of-

   (a) future installment payments to be paid for the partner's share of partnership property; and

   (b) any rights to share in future partnership income.

These amounts are included even if the total amount of the liquidating payments is not fixed but is contingent on future partnership income. For example, a partner's estate includes the present value of his successor's right to receive a percentage of partnership income for a period following the partner's death.[86] The amount of partnership income for the period must be reasonably approximated and its present value determined.

[A] Effects of Partnership/LLC Agreements

The value of a partnership interest is frequently determined from the price set by the parties in a binding agreement between a partner and partnership or in an agreement between partners.[87]

This value is respected for estate tax purposes if the agreement:

(1) is reached at arm's length;

(2) binds all parties; and

(3) significantly restricts lifetime transfers by the deceased partner.[88]

If no restriction on lifetime transfers exists, the price set in the agreement may be disregarded.[89] The price is also disregarded if the agreement is not a bona fide business arrangement that attempts to pass a partner's interest to his successor

---

[83] Wilmont Fleming Engineering Co. v. Comm'r, 65 T.C. 847 (1976).

[84] *See, e.g.*, Coates v. Comm'r, 7 T.C. 125 (1946); Gannon v. Comm'r, 21 T.C. 1073 (1954); Maddock v. Comm'r, 16 T.C. 324 (1951), *acq.* 1951-2 C.B. 3; Kaffie v. Comm'r, 44 B.T.A. 843 (1941), *nonacq.* 1941-2 C.B. 20; Brandt v. Comm'r, 8 T.C.M. 820 (1949).

[85] Treas. Reg. § 20.2031-3 (agreement transferring goodwill to surviving partners supported by consideration); Blodget v. Comm'r, 18 B.T.A. 1050 (1930).

[86] Estate of Riegelman v. Comm'r, 253 F.2d 315 (2d Cir. 1958). The Second Circuit indicated that the early Supreme Court decision in Bull v. U.S., 295 U.S. 247 (1935), holding that payments of partnership profits to a decedent's estate are not subject estate tax is no longer valid.

[87] *See, e.g.*, Estate of Bischoff v. Comm'r, 69 T.C. 32 (1977).

[88] Treas. Reg. § 20.2031-2(h). *See* Weil v. Comm'r, 22 T.C. 1267 (1954); Fiorito v. Comm'r, 33 T.C. 440 (1959), *acq.* 1960-2 C.B. 4.

[89] Treas. Reg. § 20.2031-2(h) (little weight accorded price contained in option or contract under which the decedent is free to dispose assets at any price during his lifetime). *See, e.g.*, Gannon v. Comm'r, 21 T.C. 1073 (1954); Trammell v. Comm'r, 18 T.C. 662 (1952); Hoffman v. Comm'r, 2 T.C. 1160 (1943).

for less than its actual value.[90] If income interests are retained, the anti-estate freeze provisions of I.R.C. Sections 2701-2704 may apply. (See discussion at § 9.07, *supra*.)

An agreement that obligates the partnership to purchase a deceased partner's interest is referred to as a redemption agreement. The tax consequences of the redemption are determined under the rules governing liquidating payments to a deceased partner's successor. An agreement obligating continuing partners to purchase the interest of a deceased partner is called a cross-purchase agreement. The tax consequences of this kind of arrangement are determined under the rules governing sales and exchanges of partnership interests (*see* Chapter 12).

Redemption and cross-purchase agreements often require the parties to obtain insurance policies on the lives of the partners whose interests they must purchase at death. The policies ensure that the partnership or continuing partners have sufficient cash to meet their obligations to purchase the deceased partner's interest. The income and estate tax consequences of insurance-funded buy-sell agreements depend upon which parties are the owners of the policies and which parties are the beneficiaries.

[1] Insurance-Funded Cross-Purchase Agreements

A cross-purchase agreement funded by insurance typically requires the partners to own or pay for an insurance policy on the life of each other partner. Following is a listing of some of the arrangements possible under these insurance agreements:

(1) *Each partner owns, and is the beneficiary of, a policy on the life of each other partner. The policyowner is not taxable when he receives the insurance proceeds and uses them to purchase the deceased partner's interest.* [91] Because the continuing partners are the policies' beneficiaries, the proceeds are not included in the deceased partner's estate.[92] However, the value of any policies the deceased partner owns on the other partners' lives is included in his estate. This arrangement may not adequately ensure that the insurance proceeds are used to purchase the decedent's partnership interest.

(2) *Each partner owns a policy on each other partner, and each of these policies designates the insured partner's estate as beneficiary.* The amount that the continuing partner must pay for the decedent's partnership interest is reduced by the amount of insurance the estate receives. For estate tax purposes, the value of a partnership interest is not includible in the partner's gross estate to the extent that the insurance payment decreases the amount that the continuing partners' must pay for the interest.[93] The continuing partners' cost basis for the interest they

---

[90] Treas. Reg. § 20.2031-2(h). *See* Davis v. U.S., 60-1 U.S.T.C. ¶ 11,943 (D. Utah 1960).

[91] I.R.C. § 101(a).

[92] Rev. Rul. 56-397, 1956-2 C.B. 599. *See* Weil v. Comm'r, 22 T.C. 1267 (1954).

[93] Dobrzensky v. Comm'r, 34 B.T.A. 305 (1936); Estate of Mitchell v. Comm'r, 37 B.T.A. 1 (1938); Tompkins v. Comm'r, 13 T.C. 1054 (1949). *See also* Mushro v. Comm'r, 50 T.C. 43 (1968), *nonacq.* 1970-2

purchase includes the amount of insurance paid to the estate.[94]

The two arrangements described above may be impractical for a partnership with many partners or with a high turnover of partners. The number of policies and frequent change in owners, beneficiaries, and premiums can be inordinately complex and expensive.

(3) *Each partner owns a policy on his own life which designates the other partners as beneficiaries, subject to their agreement to pay the premiums.* This arrangement is undesirable because the Service may contend that the value of the decedent's gross estate includes the insurance proceeds as well as the full value of his partnership interest. Under I.R.C. Section 2042(2), insurance proceeds are included in the estate of a decedent who possesses the "incidents of ownership" of the policy at his death. Although the few courts who have considered this issue concluded that a decedent lacks the incidents of ownership in these circumstances, substantial litigation risks exist.[95]

[2] Insurance-Funded Redemption Agreements

A redemption agreement funded by insurance requires the partnership to insure its partners' lives and use the insurance proceeds to liquidate a deceased partner's interest. The value of the decedent's gross estate under this kind of arrangement should not include both the insurance proceeds and the full value of the partnership interest. Insurance proceeds are included in the estate of a decedent who possesses the "incidents of ownership" of the policy at his death under I.R.C. Section 2042(2) and, therefore, the policy proceeds should not be included in the deceased partner's estate if:

(1) The partnership has a binding obligation to apply the proceeds to liquidate the deceased partner's interest.[96]

(2) The partner does not have incidents of ownership (*e.g.*, the right to change beneficiaries) over the policy. The Service has ruled that a partner possesses the incidents of ownership if the insurance proceeds may be paid to or for the benefit of someone other than the partnership.[97] However, incidents of ownership held by a partnership are not attributed to its partners.[98]

C.B. xxii (continuing partner deemed to receive insurance proceeds and apply them to purchase of deceased partner's interest).

[94] Mushro v. Comm'r, 50 T.C. 43 (1968), *nonacq.* 1970-2 C.B. xxii.

[95] First Nat'l Bank v. U.S., 358 F.2d 625 (5th Cir. 1966); Fuchs v. Comm'r, 47 T.C. 199 (1966), *acq.* 1967-2 C.B. 2.

[96] *See* Knipp v. Comm'r, 25 T.C. 153 (1955); First Nat'l Bank v. U.S., 358 F.2d 625 (5th Cir. 1966).

[97] Rev. Rul. 83-148, 1983-2 C.B. 157.

[98] Rev. Rul. 83-147, 1983-2 C.B. 158.

[B]   Special Valuation Rules — I.R.C. Section 2032A

In limited circumstances, the special valuation rules of I.R.C. Section 2032A may decrease the estate tax valuation of an interest in a partnership that passes to members of the deceased partner's family. The lower valuation promotes the continuation of certain family businesses (especially farms), because it reduces the estate tax and, in that way, it helps to avoid the need to sell the business in order to raise the cash for estate taxes. If the statutory requirements are met, the estate tax value of real estate used in the family business is determined by reference to its current use rather than its actual market value. The reduction from actual market value, however, cannot exceed $770,000.

Chapter 12

SELLING OR EXCHANGING A PARTNERSHIP OR LLC INTEREST

§ 12.01   OVERVIEW

A sale or exchange of a partnership or LLC interest generally is taxable in the same manner as a sale or exchange of other kinds of property. The seller realizes gain or loss for the difference between his amount realized on the sale and the adjusted basis of his partnership or LLC interest.[1] The buyer obtains a cost basis for the interest he acquires.[2] A partner who sells only a portion of his partnership interest allocates the basis of his entire interest between the portion he sells and the portion he retains in determining his gain or loss.[3]

Seller's amount realized and basis. The amount realized by a partner on a sale or exchange of a partnership interest equals the amount of money and the fair market value of any property the partner receives,[4] plus his share of the partnership's recourse and nonrecourse liabilities.[5] A partner determines the basis in his partnership interest at the time of the sale (under I.R.C. Section 705), adjusted to reflect his distributive share of partnership tax items for the portion of the partnership tax year up to the sale date.[6]

Character of selling partner's gain or loss. A partner recognizes capital gain or loss on a sale of a partnership interest, unless the partnership owns unrealized receivables or inventory (Section 751 property) when the sale occurs (*see* § 12.03[A], *infra; see also* Chapter 8).[7] If the partnership owns I.R.C. Section 751 property, the seller computes and characterizes his gain or loss in the sale in two steps:

(1)   The seller realizes ordinary income or loss equal to the amount of gain or loss from Section 751 property (including any remedial allocations for

---

[1]   I.R.C. § 1001(b). A selling partner may not deduct a loss he incurs on a sale or exchange of his partnership interest directly or indirectly to a person who is related to him under the rules of I.R.C. § 267.

[2]   I.R.C. § 742.

[3]   Rev. Rul. 84-53, 1984-1 C.B. 159. *See* Treas. Reg. § 1.61-6(a).

[4]   I.R.C. § 1001(b). This includes the amount of the partner's individual liabilities the purchaser assumes or discharges. Treas. Reg. § 1.1001-2(a)(1).

[5]   I.R.C. § 752(d); Treas. Reg. §§ 1.752-1(d), 1.1001-2(a)(4)(v); Rev. Rul. 75-194, 1975-1 C.B. 80; Rev. Rul. 74-40, 1974-1 C.B. 159.

[6]   Treas. Reg. § 1.705-1(a)(1).

[7]   I.R.C. §§ 741, 751.

contributed property)[8] that would be allocated to him if the partnership sold all of its property at fair market value[9] immediately before the sale of his interest.

(2)   The seller realizes capital gain or loss equal to the difference between the total gain or loss from the sale of his interest and amount of ordinary income or loss computed in paragraph (1).[10]

Tax rate applicable to seller's capital gain or loss. The rate of capital gain tax the seller pays may vary depending upon the nature of the partnership's assets and its holding period for each asset. The selling partner computes the portion of capital gain taxable at each capital gain rate by "looking through" the partnership to determine his share of each category of partnership capital asset.[11]

Seller's share of income or loss for year of sale. A partnership's taxable year closes for a partner on the date he sells, exchanges, or liquidates his entire interest in the partnership (*see* § 12.04, *infra*).[12] A partner who sells or exchanges his interest reports his distributive share of partnership income or loss and any guaranteed payments through the date of the sale or exchange on his tax return for the year in which the transaction occurs.[13] The seller may deduct any losses suspended under I.R.C. Section 704(d) up to the basis of his interest at the end of the short tax year closed by the transfer (*see* § 12.05[A], *infra*).[14] Any suspended losses not deducted in the year of the sale are lost.

Purchaser's basis. The purchaser's basis in his partnership interest is determined under the general tax rules applicable to property acquisitions.[15] Thus, the basis of a purchased interest is its cost, which includes the share of partnership liabilities the buyer incurs as a result of the acquisition (*see* Chapter 5).[16]

Effect of I.R.C. Section 754 election. Because a partnership interest is an asset that is separate and distinct from the partnership's property, a purchase of a partnership interest does not ordinarily affect the basis of partnership property.[17] The bases of partnership assets are adjusted, however, if the partnership has an I.R.C. Section 754 election in effect when the sale or exchange occurs. The I.R.C. Section 754 election requires the partnership to increase or decrease the basis of its assets to reflect the difference between the new partner's basis for his partnership

---

[8]   This amount is determined under Treas. Reg. § 1.704-3(d).

[9]   Taking into account the rule of I.R.C. § 7701(g) holding that the value of property subject to a nonrecourse debt is not less than the principal amount of the debt.

[10]   Treas. Reg. § 1.751-1(a)(2). These rules apply to transfers of partnership interests on or after December 15, 1999. Treas. Reg. § 1.751-1(f).

[11]   Prop. Treas. Reg. § 1.1(h)-1. Generally, the maximum capital gains rate is 20 percent with respect to property held for more than one year. I.R.C. § 1(h).

[12]   I.R.C. § 706(c)(2)(A)(i).

[13]   I.R.C. § 706(a).

[14]   Treas. Reg. § 1.704-1(d)(2).

[15]   I.R.C. § 743(a).

[16]   I.R.C. § 1012.

[17]   I.R.C. § 743(a).

interest and his share of the basis of the partnership's property. This basis adjustment applies only in determining the transferee partner's tax consequences (*see* § 12.08, *infra*).

Effect of I.R.C. Section 732(d) election. A partner who purchases a partnership interest when the partnership does not have an I.R.C. Section 754 election in effect may elect to adjust the bases of property the partnership distributes to him within two years of the acquisition date under I.R.C. Section 732(d). The election permits the partner to determine his basis in the distributed property as if the partnership had an I.R.C. Section 754 election in effect when he acquired his partnership interest.

§ 12.02 COMPUTING SELLING PARTNER'S OR MEMBER'S GAIN OR LOSS

A partner who sells his partnership interest realizes gain or loss equal to the difference between his amount realized on the sale and the adjusted basis of his partnership interest.[18] The selling partner's amount realized equals the amount of money and the fair market value of any property the partner receives,[19] plus his share of the partnership's recourse and nonrecourse liabilities.[20] A partner determines the basis in his partnership interest at the time of the sale, adjusted to reflect his distributive share of partnership tax items for the portion of the partnership tax year up to the sale date.[21]

[A] Seller's Amount Realized

The total amount realized by a partner on a sale or exchange of a partnership interest is the sum of:

(1) the money the partner receives;[22]

(2) the fair market value of any other property the partner receives;[23]

(3) the partner's individual liabilities that the purchaser assumes or discharges;[24] and

(4) the decrease in the partner's share of the partnership's liabilities.[25]

---

[18] I.R.C. § 1001(b).

[19] *Id.* This includes the amount of the partner's individual liabilities the purchaser assumes or discharges. Treas. Reg. § 1.1001-2(a)(1).

[20] I.R.C. § 752(d); Treas. Reg. §§ 1.752-1(d), 1.1001-2(a)(4)(v); Rev. Rul. 75-194, 1975-1 C.B. 80; Rev. Rul. 74-40, 1974-1 C.B. 159.

[21] Treas. Reg. § 1.705-1(a)(1).

[22] I.R.C. § 1001(b).

[23] *Id.*

[24] Treas. Reg. § 1.1001-2(a)(1).

[25] I.R.C. § 752(d); Treas. Reg. §§ 1.752-1(d), 1.1001-2(a)(4)(v); Rev. Rul. 75-194, 1975-1 C.B. 80; Rev. Rul. 74-40, 1974-1 C.B. 159.

Liabilities transferred to buyer. Shifts in partnership liabilities occurring when a partner sells or exchanges a partnership interest are accounted for according to I.R.C. Section 752(d), in the same way as liabilities related to sales of other kinds of property. Under general tax principles, the selling partner's amount realized includes his share of partnership liabilities transferred to the purchaser by the sale.[26] Because a partner's basis for his partnership interest increases to reflect his share of the partnership's liabilities, including the discharged liabilities, a selling partner's amount realized does not increase his gain or loss on a sale or exchange.[27]

> **Example:** June contributes $20,000 to the JKLM Partnership for a one-fourth general partnership interest. The partnership is indebted for a $60,000 recourse note at the time that June acquires her interest. Therefore, under I.R.C. Section 752, June's share of that debt is $15,000 ($60,000 × 25%), and June is deemed to contribute an additional $15,000. This constructive cash contribution increases the basis of her partnership interest to $35,000 ($20,000 actual cash contribution + $15,000 constructive contribution). If June sells her interest for $30,000 in cash, her amount realized is $45,000 ($30,000 cash payment + $15,000 transfer of liability).

The seller's amount realized includes the principal of his share of any recourse and nonrecourse liabilities that are transferred to the buyer. The amount realized includes partnership debts that the buyer assumes personally, as well as obligations that only encumber partnership property.[28] The seller includes his entire share of the principal of a partnership nonrecourse liability in his amount realized, even if the obligation exceeds the value of the property it encumbers.[29]

Under I.R.C. Section 752(c), the amount of nonrecourse liabilities deemed transferred with encumbered property that is contributed to, or distributed by, a partnership cannot exceed the value of the property. This value-limitation rule applies only in computing a partner's constructive cash contribution or distribution under I.R.C. Sections 752(a) or (b), and it does not affect his amount realized on a transfer of his partnership interest.[30] Thus, a selling partner's amount realized includes the full principal of nonrecourse liabilities transferred to the buyer regardless of the value of encumbered property.

> **Example:** Mary contributes $100,000 for a 25-percent interest in the LMN Limited Liability Company. The LLC obtains a $4 million nonrecourse loan to finance construction of a building to secure the debt. The LLC liability increases the basis of Mary's LLC interest to $1.1 million ($100,000 cash contribution + $1 million constructive cash contribution attributable to her 25 percent share of the LLC's liabilities). In Year 2, Mary's distributive share of LLC losses is $200,000, reducing the basis of her interest to $900,000. During this period, the value of the building declines to $1.6 million, and the LLC does not make any principal payments on the loan. In

---

[26] I.R.C. § 1001(b); Treas. Reg. § 1.1001-2(a).

[27] I.R.C. § 752(b).

[28] Crane v. Comm'r, 331 U.S. 1 (1947).

[29] Comm'r v. Tufts, 461 U.S. 300 (1983). I.R.C. § 7701(g) codifies the result in *Tufts*.

[30] Comm'r v. Tufts, 461 U.S. 300 (1983).

Year 3, Mary sells her LLC interest to Olivia for $1,000 in cash.

Mary's amount realized on the sale of her interest is $1,001,000:

$1,000	cash payment
1,000,000	25% of the LLC liability transferred to Olivia
$1,001,000	amount realized

Mary realizes her entire share of the principal of the transferred debt, even though the securing property is worth less than the liability, and neither she nor Olivia is liable for any deficiency. Since Mary's basis for her LLC interest is $900,000, she recognizes a $101,000 gain on the sale of her interest.

[B] Seller's Basis

A partner may compute his basis in the partnership interest at the time of the sale by determining the initial basis for his interest and adjusting that amount. A partner has one basis for his partnership interest, even if he acquired portions of the interest at different times or if he owns both general and limited interests in the partnership.[31] A partner's initial basis in his partnership interest depends on how he acquires it:

(1)   The basis of an interest acquired in exchange for a contribution of money or property is the amount of money or the adjusted basis of the property contributed.[32] A partner is deemed to contribute an amount of money equal to his share of partnership liabilities.[33]

(2)   The basis of a purchased interest is its cost, including any share of partnership liabilities the purchaser incurs.[34]

(3)   The basis for an interest acquired at a partner's death is its net fair market value on the date of death or the alternate valuation date, less the value of income-in-respect-of-a-decedent items, under I.R.C. Section 691, plus the successor's share of partnership liabilities (see Chapter 11).[35]

(4)   The basis of an interest acquired by gift is the donor's basis limited to the value of the interest on the date of the gift, plus any gift tax the donor paid.[36]

The partner's initial basis is adjusted to reflect subsequent events that change his after-tax investment in the partnership. His basis increases by the amount of money and by the basis of any property he later contributes, including cash contributions he is deemed to make when his share of partnership liabilities

---

[31] Rev. Rul. 84-52, 1984-1 C.B. 157.

[32] I.R.C. §§ 705(a), 722.

[33] I.R.C. § 752(a).

[34] I.R.C. §§ 752(d), 1012; Treas. Reg. § 1.742-1.

[35] I.R.C. § 1014; Treas. Reg. § 1.742-1.

[36] I.R.C. § 1015.

increases.[37] The partner's basis decreases — not below zero — by the amount of money and by the basis of property the partnership distributed to him, including cash distributions he is deemed to receive when his share of partnership liabilities decreases.[38] Each partnership tax year, the partner's basis increases or decreases by his distributive share of partnership tax items described in I.R.C. Section 705(a).

The partnership's tax year closes for a partner on the date that he sells or exchanges his entire partnership interest.[39] Consequently, a partner who transfers his entire interest must adjust the basis of that interest to reflect his distributive share of partnership tax items described in I.R.C. Section 705(a) for the portion of the current partnership tax year up to the sale date.[40]

> **Example:** Dora's basis for her interest in the BCD Partnership at the beginning of Year 1 is $15,000, including her $5,000 share of the partnership's liabilities. Both Dora and the partnership use a calendar tax year. On June 30, Year 1, Dora sells her interest to Edgar for an $18,000 cash payment. Dora's share of partnership income from January 1 to June 30 is $4,000, and she has not received any distributions from the partnership. Assuming there are no other basis adjustments, the basis of Dora's partnership interest at the time of the sale is $19,000 (initial basis of $15,000 + her $4,000 Year 1 distributive share). Dora's amount realized on the sale is $23,000 ($18,000 cash payment + $5,000 transfer of her share of partnership liabilities). If the partnership does not own I.R.C. Section 751 property, Dora recognizes a $4,000 capital gain ($23,000 amount realized - $19,000 adjusted basis).

[C]   Sale of Portion of Partner's Interest

A partner who transfers less than his entire partnership interest computes his gain or loss by allocating part of the basis of his interest to the transferred portion.[41] A partner has only one basis for his partnership interest, even if he acquired portions of the interest for different amounts at different times. A partner who is both a general partner and a limited partner also has only one basis for all of his interests in the partnership.[42]

When a partner transfers only part of his partnership interest, the method of allocating the partner's basis to the transferred portion depends on whether his basis includes any share of partnership liabilities:

(1)   If no liabilities are included, the partner's basis is allocated to the transferred portion in the same ratio that the value of the transferred

---

[37] I.R.C. §§ 705, 752(a), 722; Treas. Reg. § 1.705-1(a)(2).

[38] I.R.C. §§ 705, 752(b), 733.

[39] I.R.C. § 706(c)(2)(B).

[40] Treas. Reg. § 1.705-1(a)(1).

[41] Rev. Rul. 84-53, 1984-1 C.B. 159. *See* Treas. Reg. § 1.61-6(a).

[42] Rev. Rul. 84-52, 1984-2 C.B. 157.

interest bears to the value of his entire interest.[43] Thus, a partner who sells a partnership interest worth one-half of the value of his entire interest allocates one half of his total basis to the transferred portion.

(2) If the partner's basis includes a share of partnership liabilities, the partner determines the basis for his entire interest without taking into account his share of these liabilities, and

   (a) if that amount is positive (*i.e.*, his share of liabilities does not exceed his basis), the partner (i) allocates basis to the transferred interest in the same ratio that the value of the transferred interest bears to the value of his entire interest, and (ii) increases the basis of the transferred interest by the amount that his partnership liabilities are discharged in the transfer;[44] or

   (b) if that amount is negative (*i.e.*, the partner's share of liabilities exceeds the basis of his entire interest), the partner's basis is allocated to the transferred interest in the ratio that his liabilities discharged in the transaction bear to his total share of partnership liabilities.

[D] Abandoned or Worthless Interest: Character of Loss

The character of the loss a partner incurs when his partnership interest is abandoned[45] or becomes worthless[46] depends upon whether he is relieved of a share of partnership liabilities as a result of the abandonment or worthlessness.[47] A partner who withdraws from a partnership is deemed to receive a cash liquidating distribution equal to any decrease in his share of partnership liabilities.[48] This deemed cash distribution is considered to be in exchange for the withdrawing partner's interest, resulting in a capital gain or loss for the partner. If the withdrawing partner is not relieved of any liabilities, no cash distribution is deemed to occur, resulting in an ordinary loss equal to the basis of his partnership interest.[49] The loss is ordinary because there is no sale or exchange to trigger the capital loss provisions.[50] Thus, partners have been allowed ordinary loss deductions when they abandoned interests in bankrupt[51] and worthless partnerships.[52]

---

[43] Rev. Rul. 84-53, 1984-1 C.B. 159.

[44] *Id.*

[45] A partnership interest is abandoned when a partner manifests an intent to abandon the interest by an overt act. The focus is on the partner's action concerning his interest, not on the partnership's actions concerning its property. Echols v. Comm'r, 935 F.2d 703 (5th Cir. 1991), *rev'g* 93 T.C. 553 (1989).

[46] An asset is worthless when it in fact has no value. Laport v. Comm'r, 671 F.2d 1028 (7th Cir. 1982); Boehm v. Comm'r, 326 U.S. 287 (1945).

[47] *See* Rieser, Hitt & Aromatorio, *Obtaining an Abandonment or Worthlessness Deduction for a Partnership Interest*, 15 J. Partnership Tax'n 42 (Spring 1998).

[48] I.R.C. § 752(b). *See* Chapter 5.

[49] Rev. Rul. 93-80, 1993-2 C.B. 239.

[50] Citron v. Comm'r, 97 T.C. 200 (1991).

[51] *See* Rev. Rul. 70-355, 1970-2 C.B. 51, *clarified and superseded by* Rev. Rul. 93-80, 1993-2 C.B. 239.

[52] Tejon Ranch Co. v. Comm'r, T.C. Memo. 1985-207. *See* Hutcheson v. Comm'r, 17 T.C. 14 (1951), *acq.*

A partner may dispose of an interest in an unsuccessful partnership, or in a partnership whose tax advantages have ceased, by abandoning the interest or declaring it worthless. If the partner shares in any partnership liabilities, his tax consequences are equivalent to a sale of the interest for release of the liabilities; the partner realizes capital gain or loss equal to the difference between his share of the liabilities and the basis for his partnership interest. If the partner does not share in any partnership liabilities, the abandonment or worthlessness generates an ordinary loss equal to the partner's basis for his interest.[53]

Ordinarily, recourse partnership debts are fully allocated to the general partners who bear the economic risk of loss for payment if the partnership fails. (*See* Chapter 5.) A general partner who abandons his interest or declares it worthless, may be allowed an ordinary loss if he continues to be liable for partnership debts.[54] If the partner is relieved of the obligations, however, he realizes capital gain or loss.[55]

Limited partners typically do not share in recourse partnership liabilities because they bear no risk of loss for the debts. Thus, a limited partner should realize an ordinary loss upon the abandonment or worthlessness of an interest in a partnership whose debts are all recourse.[56]

Both general and limited partners may share in nonrecourse partnership liabilities. Consequently, the abandonment or worthlessness of either kind of interest in a partnership having nonrecourse debts may result in a capital gain or loss.

A partner claiming an abandonment loss must be able to prove that he intended to abandon the interest by showing an overt act such as a declaration to other parties that his interest is abandoned.[57] A partner who decides that his partnership interest is worthless should be able to identify objective factors that support his determination.[58]

> **Example:** Judy is a limited partner in the Investo Limited Partnership. Investo became insolvent and Judy took the necessary steps to abandon her limited partnership interest, without receiving any money or property from the partnership. Judy's basis when she abandoned her interest was $200,000. She did not bear the economic risk of loss for any partnership liabilities and did not include a share of these liabilities in the basis of her interest.

Because Judy did not receive any actual or deemed distribution from the

---

1951-2 C.B. 2 (1939 Code); Gannon v. Comm'r, 16 T.C. 1134 (1951), *acq.* 1951-2 C.B. 2 (1939 Code).

[53] *See, e.g.*, Citron v. Comm'r, 97 T.C. 200 (1991).

[54] Tejon Ranch Co. v. Comm'r, T.C. Memo. 1985-207. *See* Kreidle v. Department of Treasury, IRS, 91-2 U.S.T.C. ¶ 50,371 (Bankr. D. Colo. 1991). *See also* Weiss v. Comm'r, 956 F.2d 242 (11th Cir. 1992), *vacating and remanding* T.C. Memo. 1990-492 (partner did not realize capital gain upon expulsion from partnership because, under state law, he remained liable to partnership creditors).

[55] *See, e.g.*, Pietz v. Comm'r, 59 T.C. 207 (1972); La Rue v. Comm'r, 90 T.C. 465 (1988).

[56] *See, e.g.*, Zeeman v. U.S., 275 F. Supp. 235 (S.D.N.Y. 1967).

[57] Echols v. Comm'r, 935 F.2d 703 (5th Cir.), *reh'g denied*, 950 F.2d 209 (5th Cir. 1991).

[58] *Id.*

partnership, she realizes an ordinary loss of $200,000 dollars upon the abandonment. The results are the same if Judy's interest became worthless.

A partner generally recognizes capital gain or loss if, as a result of the abandonment or forfeiture, he is relieved of a share of partnership liabilities.[59] When the withdrawing partner's share of liabilities decreases, he is deemed to receive a cash liquidating distribution from the partnership equal to the share of his liabilities shifted to the other partners, according to I.R.C. Section 752(b).[60] Under I.R.C. Section 731, the withdrawing partner realizes a capital loss if the basis of his partnership interest exceeds the deemed cash distribution, and he recognizes capital gain to the extent that the deemed distribution exceeds his basis.[61] If the partnership owns unrealized receivables and inventory, the deemed cash distribution may result in ordinary income under I.R.C. Section 751. (For discussion of treatment of distributions under I.R.C. Section 751, see Chapter 8.)

> **Example:** [62] Kurt, Lois and Matt or equal general partners in the KLM Partnership. The partnership becomes insolvent, and Lois's interest becomes worthless. When the interest becomes worthless, Lois's basis in her partnership interest is $180,000 and her share of the partnership's nonrecourse liabilities is $40,000. Because the interest is worthless, Lois's share of partnership liabilities decreases to zero, and she is deemed to receive a $40,000 cash distribution. The distribution reduces the basis in her interest to $140,000 and Lois realizes a capital loss of that amount.

If a partnership interest is sold in a foreclosure to satisfy the partner's debts, if the interest is transferred to another partner for nominal consideration, or if it is transferred to a creditor in lieu of foreclosure, the transaction is treated as though the partner sold the interest to the creditor.[63]

[E] Deficit-Capital-Account Effect on Amount Realized

Many partnership agreements require partners to restore deficit capital accounts when their interests are liquidated. This provision often is necessary to validate special allocations of partnership income or loss under the substantial-economic-effect test of I.R.C. Section 704(b). (*See* Chapter 6.) A deficit capital account may be attributable to distributions a partner receives or to his share of partnership losses.

---

[59] Rev. Rul. 93-80, 1993-2 C.B. 239.

[60] I.R.C. § 752(b). *See* Stilwell v. Comm'r, 46 T.C. 247 (1966); O'Brien v. Comm'r, 77 T.C. 113 (1981); Middleton v. Comm'r, 77 T.C. 310 (1981), *aff'd per curiam*, 693 F.2d 124 (11th Cir. 1982); Yarbro v. Comm'r, 737 F.2d 479 (5th Cir. 1984); Pietz v. Comm'r, 59 T.C. 207 (1972); La Rue v. Comm'r, 90 T.C. 465 (1988); Rev. Rul. 74-40, 1974-1 C.B. 159. *But see* Rudd v. Comm'r, 79 T.C. 225 (1982) (I.R.C. § 731 inapplicable because abandonment of interest deemed to occur after dissolution of partnership).

[61] I.R.C. §§ 731(a), 741.

[62] *See* Rev. Rul. 93-80, 1993-2 C.B. 239, *Situation 1*.

[63] I.R.C. §§ 752(d), 741; Treas. Reg. § 1.1001-2. *See also* Stilwell v. Comm'r, 46 T.C. 247 (1966); Austin v. U.S., 461 F.2d 733 (10th Cir. 1972); Pietz v. Comm'r, 59 T.C. 207 (1972). The partner's amount realized on the sale equals his share of the partnership's liabilities. I.R.C. § 752(d).

A partner's deficit capital account is considered a loan to the partner by the partnership if he is unconditionally obligated to repay the deficit.[64] If the partnership releases a partner from his repayment obligation when he transfers his interest, the partner is deemed to receive a cash distribution for the amount of the deficit immediately before the transfer.[65] The partner recognizes gain under I.R.C. Section 731(a) if the amount of the deemed distribution exceeds the basis in his partnership interest.[66] A selling partner must include his deficit capital account in his amount realized if the purchaser assumes his obligation to repay the deficit.[67]

[F] Tax Rate and Holding Period Applied to Seller's Capital Gain or Loss

The rate of capital gain tax imposed a partner who sells his partnership interest depends upon the nature of the partnership's assets and its holding period for each asset. The selling partner computes the portion of capital gain taxable at each capital gain rate by "looking through" the partnership to determine his share of each category of partnership capital asset.[68] Generally, the maximum capital gains rate is 20 percent with respect to property held for more than one year.[69] This rate applies to the residual capital gain determined after computing the amount of gain subject to higher capital gain rates. The maximum rate is 25 percent for unrecaptured section 1250 gain.[70] Generally, a 28 percent rate applies to capital gains and losses from the sale or exchange of "collectibles"[71] held for more than one year and a portion of the gain attributable to the sale of Section 1202 stock.[72]

The long- or short-term nature of the selling partner's capital gain or loss generally depends on how long the partner held his partnership interest.[73] A selling partner's holding period is governed by the following rules:

(1)   A partner's holding period for a purchased partnership interest begins on the purchase date.[74]

---

[64] Rev. Rul. 73-301, 1973-2 C.B. 215. If no repayment obligation exists, the initial transaction is not a loan for tax purposes.

[65] Rev. Rul. 57-318, 1957-2 C.B. 362.

[66] See McDaniel v. Comm'r, T.C. Memo. 1999-133 (partner realized capital gain equal to negative capital account balance when discharged from guaranty of partnership liabilities).

[67] I.R.C. § 752(d). But see Hirsch v. Comm'r, T.C. Memo. 1984-52 (deficit capital account not included in amount realized where selling partner remained liable to repay it after sale).

[68] Prop. Treas. Reg. § 1.1(h)-1.

[69] I.R.C. § 1(h).

[70] This is the amount of long-term capital gain that would be ordinary income if I.R.C. § 1250(b)(1) included all depreciation and the applicable percentage under I.R.C. § 1250(a) were 100 percent, reduced by any net loss in the 28-percent rate gain category.

[71] As defined in I.R.C. § 408(m) without regard to I.R.C. § 408(m)(3).

[72] I.R.C. § 1(h)(13).

[73] I.R.C. § 1222.

[74] I.R.C. § 1223(1).

(2) The holding period for an interest acquired for a contribution of capital assets or I.R.C. Section 1231 assets includes the contributing partner's holding period for the property.[75]

(3) The holding period for an interest acquired for a contribution of other property (*e.g.*, inventory or receivables) begins on the acquisition date.

Subsequent changes in a partner's percentage interest in the partnership normally do not affect his holding period.[76] However, a partner may have a separate holding period for an additional interest he acquires from another partner or in exchange for a capital contribution to the partnership.

§ 12.03   CHARACTERIZING SELLER'S GAIN OR LOSS: ORDINARY INCOME RECOGNIZED ON I.R.C. SECTION 751 PROPERTY

Gain or loss recognized on a sale or exchange of a partnership interest is considered gain or loss from the sale or exchange of a capital asset under the general rule of I.R.C. Section 741. A partnership interest is considered a capital asset regardless of the partner's motive for acquiring the interest.[77]

I.R.C. Section 751(a), however, provides an important exception to the general treatment of a partnership interest as a single capital asset. I.R.C. Section 751(a) requires a partner who sells or exchanges his partnership interest to divide the transaction into two parts:

(1) the selling partner realizes ordinary income or loss equal to the amount of gain or loss that would be allocated to him from partnership unrealized receivables and inventory (Section 751 property) if the partnership sold all of its property at fair market value immediately before the sale of his interest.

(2) The seller realizes capital gain or loss equal to the difference between the total gain or loss from the sale of his interest and amount of ordinary income or loss realized under I.R.C. Section 751.[78]

Example: [79] Sheldon and Trish are equal partners in personal service partnership ST. Trish transfers her interest to Vaughn for $15,000 when ST's balance sheet is as follows:

---

[75] *Id.*

[76] *See* Thornley v. Comm'r, 147 F.2d 416 (3d Cir. 1945); Lehman v. Comm'r, 7 T.C. 1088 (1946), *aff'd*, 165 F.2d 383 (2d Cir.), *cert. denied*, 334 U.S. 819 (1948), *acq.* 1950-2 C.B. 3.

[77] *See* Arkansas Best Corp. v. Comm'r, 485 U.S. 212 (1988).

[78] Treas. Reg. § 1.751-1(a)(2). These rules apply to transfers of partnership interests that occur on or after December 15, 1999.

[79] Treas. Reg. § 1.751-1(g).

Assets	Basis	Value
Cash	$3,000	$3,000
Loans Receivable	10,000	10,000
Capital Assets	7,000	5,000
Unrealized Receivables	0	14,000
Total	20,000	32,000
Liabilities	$2,000	$2,000
Partner's Capital		
Sheldon	9,000	15,000
Trish	9,000	15,000
Total Liabilities & Capital	20,000	32,000

Trish's amount realized on the sale is $16,000 ($15,000 cash plus $1,000 share of partnership liabilities assumed by Vaughn) and the basis for her partnership interest is $10,000 ($9,000 per books plus $1,000 share of liabilities). Thus, her total gain from the sale of her interest is $6,000.

Trish realizes $7,000 of ordinary income — the amount of ordinary income she would be allocated from unrealized receivables if RST sold all its assets before the sale of her interest. Trish also realizes a $1,000 capital loss — the difference between her total gain ($6,000) and the amount of ordinary income she realizes under I.R.C. Section 751.

[A] Defining I.R.C. Section 751 Property

A partner who sells or exchanges his partnership interest realizes ordinary income under I.R.C. Section 751(a) on the portion of the transaction attributable to his share of the partnership's I.R.C. Section 751 property. I.R.C. Section 751 property consists of:

(1)   unrealized receivables, as defined in I.R.C. Section 751(c), and

(2)   inventory, as defined in I.R.C. Section 751(d).[80]

The portion of the sale or exchange that is not attributable to the partner's share of I.R.C. Section 751 property results in capital gain or loss, even if the other partnership assets would be ordinary income property if owned directly by the partner.

[1] Unrealized Receivables

A partnership's unrealized receivables consist of three categories of items that were not previously includable in partnership income under its accounting method.[81] These three categories are:

---

[80] For sales and exchanges before August 5, 1997, this treatment only applied to "substantially appreciated inventory" having a value exceeding 120 percent of its basis. The substantial appreciation requirement continues to apply to distributions subject to I.R.C. § 751.

[81] I.R.C. § 751(c).

Category (1) — the partnership's contractual or other rights to payment for its goods.

Category (2) — similar partnership rights to be paid for its services.[82] The payment rights in these two categories are unrealized receivables when a partnership interest is sold, even if they cannot be enforced until a later time.[83] Examples include the accounts receivable of a cash-method partnership, amounts receivable for income reported on the completed-contract method, and payment rights related to work in progress when the sale occurs.

Category (3) — expands the definition of unrealized receivables to cover the potential gain in partnership assets subject to recapture as ordinary income under a variety of recapture provisions.

The following specific rules apply in identifying partnership assets that are unrealized receivables:

(1) *Contractual or other rights to payment for goods delivered, or to be delivered in the future, are unrealized receivables if receipt of the payment would be treated as a sale of property that is not a capital asset.* [84] A right to payment for a capital asset is not an unrealized receivable regardless of the partnership's holding period.[85]

(2) *All contractual or other rights to payment for services rendered or to be rendered are unrealized receivables.* [86] An uncompleted service contract is an unrealized receivable for the value of the work performed, even if the partnership cannot enforce any right to payment until the entire contract is fulfilled.[87]

An unrealized receivable does not exist merely because a service partnership has a relationship with a client.[88] A contractual right to payment should be an unrealized receivable if it is cancellable only upon conditions that are unlikely to occur — however, the conditional nature of the contract may reduce the value of the receivable.

---

[82] *See, e.g.*, Ware v. Comm'r, 906 F.2d 62 (2d Cir. 1990) (unpaid fee for legal services is unrealized receivable).

[83] Treas. Reg. § 1.751-1(c)(1); *see* Hale v. Comm'r, T.C. Memo. 1965-274; Rev. Rul. 79-51, 1979-1 C.B. 225; Rev. Rul. 73-301, 1973-2 C.B. 215.

[84] I.R.C. § 751(c); Treas. Reg. § 1.751-1(c)(1)(i).

[85] I.R.C. § 1221.

[86] *See, e.g.*, Frankfort v. Comm'r, 52 T.C. 163 (1969), *acq.* 1969-2 C.B. xxiv (rights to brokerage commissions earned at the time of real estate sale but not payable until closing are unrealized receivables); Blacketor v. U.S., 204 Ct. Cl. 897 (1974) (sales commission agreement); U.S. v. Woolsey, 326 F.2d 287 (5th Cir. 1963) (long-term contract to manage insurance company is unrealized receivable); Ledoux v. Comm'r, 77 T.C. 293 (1981), *aff'd per curiam*, 695 F.2d 1320 (11th Cir. 1983) (management agreement is unrealized receivable); Wolcott v. Comm'r, 39 T.C. 538 (1962) (amount due under uncompleted contract for architectural services is unrealized receivable).

[87] Logan v. Comm'r, 51 T.C. 482 (1968).

[88] Miller v. U.S., 181 Ct. Cl. 331 (1967). A contractual relationship with a client who has discretion to cancel on short notice also is not an unrealized receivable. Phillips v. Comm'r, 40 T.C. 157 (1963), *nonacq.* 1968-1 C.B. 3. *Cf.* Baxter v. Comm'r, T.C. Memo. 1969-87, *aff'd*, 433 F.2d 757 (9th Cir. 1970).

(3)   ***The potential gain in partnership assets that would be recaptured as ordinary income under a variety of recapture provisions in the Code are unrealized receivables.*** The selling partner's share of this potential recapture income is the amount that would be allocated to him if the partnership sold all of its recapture property for its value on the date the partner sells his interest.[89] The rules for determining a partner's distributive share of recapture income are described in Chapter 6.

The seller's allocable share of gain from each recapture asset is computed by taking into account any special basis adjustments that occurred when he acquired his partnership interest.[90] For contributed property, all of the potential recapture income inherent in the property at the time of contribution must be allocated to the contributing partner under I.R.C. Section 704(c).[91]

Specific items of potential recapture income treated as unrealized receivables include:[92]

(1)   depreciation recapture;[93]

(2)   recapture of mining exploration expenditures;[94]

(3)   recapture of farmland deductions;[95]

(4)   income that would be treated as a dividend on the sale of stock in a domestic international sales corporation (DISC);[96]

(5)   income that would be treated as a dividend on the sale of stock in a controlled foreign corporation;[97]

(6)   amounts that would be ordinary income on the sale of a franchise, trademark, or trade name;[98]

(7)   recapture on oil, gas, geothermal, and other mineral properties;

(8)   amounts that would be ordinary income on the sale of market discount bonds;[99]

---

[89]   Treas. Reg. §§ 1.751-1(c)(4), 1.1245-1(e)(2).

[90]   Treas. Reg. § 1.751-1(c)(6)(ii).

[91]   This rule applies to property contributed after March 31, 1984.

[92]   I.R.C. § 751(c).

[93]   I.R.C. §§ 1245, 1250. Additional depreciation recapture may be required for corporate partners under I.R.C. § 291.

[94]   I.R.C. § 617.

[95]   I.R.C. § 1252.

[96]   I.R.C. §§ 995(c), 996(f)(1). The amount of ordinary income equals the accumulated untaxed DISC income attributable to the partnership's DISC stock.

[97]   I.R.C. § 1248(d)(1).

[98]   I.R.C. § 1253.

[99]   I.R.C. § 1278. Gain on the sale of a market discount bond is treated as ordinary income to the extent of the accrued market discount.

(9)   gain on the sale of a short-term obligation;[100] and

(10)   recapture of accrued but unpaid rent.[101]

[2]   Inventory

A partner's share of partnership inventory is subject to the ordinary-income rules of I.R.C. Section 751(a).[102] For I.R.C. Section 751(a), inventory includes:

(1)   The partnership's stock in trade or other property properly includable in its inventory at the end of its tax year and property held primarily for sale to customers in the ordinary course of the partnership's trade or business.[103] The factual issue is whether the partnership holds the property for investment or primarily for sale to customers.[104]

(2)   Other partnership property that would not be considered a capital asset or I.R.C. Section 1231 property if sold by the partnership.[105] This includes all realized and unrealized accounts and notes receivable the partnership acquired from the sale of stock in trade or for its services.[106] These items are treated as inventory regardless of whether the partnership uses the cash or the accrual method of tax accounting. Unrealized receivables are included in inventory when determining whether the partnership's inventory is substantially appreciated.

(3)   Appreciated foreign investment company stock. Foreign corporation stock is included:

     (a)   If the corporation was a foreign investment company at any time during the period that the partnership held the stock; and

     (b)   If gain on the sale of the stock would be ordinary income to the extent of the partnership's ratable share of the corporation's post-1962 accumulated earnings and profits.[107]

(4)   Other property that would be included in categories (1), (2), or (3) above, if held by the selling partner.[108] A partnership capital asset is treated as inventory if it would be inventory in the hands of the selling partner. For example, securities held by a partnership for investment purposes would

---

[100] I.R.C. § 1271(a)(4), (d).

[101] I.R.C. § 467(c)(2).

[102] For sales and exchanges before August 5, 1997, this treatment only applied to "substantially appreciated inventory" having a value exceeding 120 percent of its basis. The substantial appreciation requirement continues to apply to distributions subject to I.R.C. § 751.

[103] I.R.C. §§ 751(d)(2)(A), 1221; Treas. Reg. § 1.751-1(d)(2)(i). *See* Treas. Reg. § 1.471-1.

[104] *See* Martin v. U.S., 330 F. Supp. 681 (M.D. Ga. 1971); Requard v. Comm'r, T.C. Memo. 1966-141. *See also* Freeland v. Comm'r, T.C. Memo. 1966-283; Morse v. U.S., 371 F.2d 474 (Ct. Cl. 1967); Ginsburg v. U.S., 396 F.2d 983 (Ct. Cl. 1968).

[105] I.R.C. § 751(d)(2)(B).

[106] Treas. Reg. § 1.751-1(d)(2)(ii).

[107] I.R.C. §§ 1246(a), 751(d)(2)(C).

[108] I.R.C. § 751(d)(2)(D).

be considered inventory if the selling partner is a securities dealer.

[B]   Reporting Requirements

A partner who sells or exchanges an interest in a partnership that owns I.R.C. Section 751 property must file a statement with his tax return for the year of the transaction stating:

(1)   the date of transfer;

(2)   the amount of gain or loss attributable to the section 751 property; and

(3)   the amount of capital gain or loss on the sale of the partnership interest.[109]

§ 12.04   DETERMINING EFFECTS OF SALE OR EXCHANGE ON PARTNERSHIP TAX YEAR

A partnership's tax year closes for a partner on the date he sells, exchanges, or liquidates his entire interest in the partnership.[110] When a partner sells or exchanges his interest, he reports his distributive share of partnership income or loss through the date of the sale or exchange on his tax return for the year in which the transaction occurs.[111] Under I.R.C. Section 707(c), the partner also reports his guaranteed payments from the partnership at that time.

The seller is allocated his share of the partnership's income or loss and other tax items for the portion of the partnership tax year through the date of transfer, and the purchaser is allocated his share of those items for the remainder of the tax year.[112] The selling partner increases or decreases the basis in his partnership interest by the amount of partnership income or loss that is allocated to him for the short partnership year.[113] Because the basis change occurs before the partner transfers the interest, his gain or loss on the transfer increases or decreases correspondingly.[114]

If the partnership and the withdrawing partner use the same tax year, the closing of the partnership year does not change the time when the partner reports his pre-sale share of partnership income. If the withdrawing partner and the partnership use different tax years, however, the partner's share of income for the short, pre-sale tax year may be included in the same year as his income from the prior partnership year, and the partner will recognize more than 12 months of partnership income in one tax year.[115]

---

[109]   Treas. Reg. § 1.751-1(a)(3).

[110]   I.R.C. § 706(c)(2)(A)(i).

[111]   I.R.C. § 706(a).

[112]   Treas. Reg. § 1.706-1(c)(2)(ii).

[113]   I.R.C. § 705(a).

[114]   Treas. Reg. § 1.705-1(a).

[115]   See I.R.C. § 706(a).

§ 12.05   DETERMINING EFFECTS OF SALE OR EXCHANGE ON PARTNER'S LOSS DEDUCTIONS

A partner may not deduct the share of his partnership losses that exceed the basis in his partnership interest at the end of the partnership year, according to I.R.C. Section 704(d). The partner may carry forward any losses that are not currently deductible because of this rule, and he may deduct them when he has sufficient basis.[116] A partner who sells or exchanges his entire partnership interest may deduct any suspended losses up to the basis of his interest at the end of the short tax year closed by the transfer.[117] The partner's basis at the end of the year includes his share of income or loss for the year up to the date of sale, but does not include any gain realized on the sale. Any suspended losses not deducted in the year of the transfer are lost; the seller or the purchasing partner cannot deduct them subsequently.[118]

A partner who expects to sell his partnership interest should satisfy his obligations to restore a deficit capital account balance before the sale occurs. In *Sennett v. Commissioner*,[119] the Tax Court held that a former partner may not deduct suspended losses that were extinguished when he sold or exchanged his partnership interest, even if he repaid the partnership for these amounts in the subsequent tax year. The court maintained that a suspended loss can be deducted only if the partner has sufficient basis at the end of the partnership tax year. Because the partnership year ended for the former partner on the date he sold his interest, the subsequent repayment did not satisfy that requirement. Although the ordinary deduction was denied, the court allowed the former partner to apply his repayment of the loss to reduce the amount of capital gain he realized on the sale of his interest.

A partner's deduction for his share of partnership losses may be limited under other Code sections:

(1)   I.R.C. Section 465 limits a partner's deduction for losses from a partnership activity to his amount "at risk" in that activity. A partner who sells or exchanges his entire partnership interest in a taxable transaction may increase his amount at risk in each partnership activity to the extent that his gain in the transaction is attributable to that activity.[120] The increased amount at risk allows the partner to deduct his suspended losses in the year of the sale or exchange.[121]

(2)   I.R.C. Section 469 limits a partner's deduction for losses incurred in a partnership passive activity (*i.e.*, an activity in which the partner does not materially participate) to the partner's income from passive activity sources. Generally, a partner who sells or exchanges his entire partnership

---

[116]   Treas. Reg. § 1.704-1(d)(1).

[117]   Treas. Reg. § 1.704-1(d)(2).

[118]   Meinerz v. Comm'r, T.C. Memo. 1983-191.

[119]   80 T.C. 825 (1983), *aff'd per curiam*, 752 F.2d 428 (9th Cir. 1985).

[120]   Prop. Treas. Reg. §§ 1.465-12, 1.465-66.

[121]   Prop. Treas. Reg. §§ 1.465-66(a), 1.465-12.

interest in a taxable transaction may deduct his suspended losses from all of the partnership's activities in the year of sale.

§ 12.06   EXCHANGE OF PARTNERSHIP INTERESTS IN NONRECOGNITION TRANSACTION

Read literally, I.R.C. Section 741 appears to preclude application of the Code's nonrecognition provisions on a sale or exchange of a partnership interest, by stating that gain or loss "shall be recognized to the transferor partner." Although the Service once took that position,[122] such a narrow interpretation is not supported by the regulations, and it has been consistently rejected by the courts.[123] It now appears to be well-established that the general nonrecognition provisions of the Code apply to transfers of partnership interests.

[A]   Exchanging Interests in the Same Partnership

A conversion of a general partnership interest into a limited partnership interest in the same partnership, or vice versa, is not treated as a taxable sale or exchange of the partnership interest.[124] The Service regards the conversion as if the partner contributed his original interest to the partnership in exchange for his new interest. Under I.R.C. Section 721, this exchange of contributed property for a partnership interest is not taxable. To the extent that the conversion decreases a partner's share of partnership liabilities, the contributing partner is deemed to receive a cash distribution from the partnership.[125] The partner recognizes gain on the constructive distribution if it exceeds the basis of his partnership interest.[126]

The partner takes the same basis and holding period in his new partnership interest that he had in his old interest.[127] However, his basis increases to the extent that the conversion increases his share of partnership liabilities, or his basis decreases (not below zero) to the extent that his share of liabilities decreases.

> **Example:** Marion and Nate are equal general partners in the MN Partnership. Each partner has a $50,000 basis in his partnership interest, including his $40,000 share of an $80,000 recourse partnership liability. Marion converts her general partnership interest into a limited interest, and she no longer bears any economic risk of loss for the partnership liability. Because Marion's share of partnership liabilities decreases by $40,000, she is deemed to receive a cash distribution of that amount.

---

[122] Rev. Rul. 78-135, 1978-1 C.B. 256 (I.R.C. § 741 overrides nonrecognition provisions of I.R.C. § 1031).

[123] *See* Treas. Reg. § 1.741-1(c); Pappas v. Comm'r, 78 T.C. 1078 (1982); Long v. Comm'r, 77 T.C. 1045 (1981); Gulfstream Land and Development Corp. v. Comm'r, 71 T.C. 587 (1979). *See also* Estate of Meyer v. Comm'r, 58 T.C. 311 (1972), *aff'd per curiam*, 503 F.2d 556 (9th Cir. 1974), *nonacq.* 1975-2 C.B. 3.

[124] Rev. Rul. 84-52, 1984-1 C.B. 157. *See also* Priv. Ltr. Ruls. 9841030, 8609021, 8542044, 8150134, 7948063.

[125] I.R.C. § 752(b). *See* Priv. Ltr. Rul. 9007045.

[126] I.R.C. § 731(a).

[127] I.R.C. § 722.

Therefore, the distribution reduces the basis of Marion's limited partnership interest to $10,000.

Because the conversion is not treated as a sale or exchange, the old partnership does not terminate under the 50-percent transfer rule of I.R.C. Section 708(b). However, the old partnership may terminate if its business is not continued by the new partnership. The conversion does not cause the partnership tax year to close for the partnership or any partner.

[B] Converting Partnership's Interests to LLC Interests and Vice-Versa

In Revenue Ruling 95-37,[128] the Service holds that the conversion of a domestic partnership to a domestic limited liability company (and vice-versa) is not a taxable exchange of partnership or LLC interests if the business of the old partnership or LLC continues.[129] The ruling concludes that the conversion is treated in the same manner as an exchange of interests in the same partnership (described in the previous section).[130] Of course, this is true only if the LLC is classified as a partnership for federal tax purposes; if the LLC is classified as a corporation, the transaction is treated as an incorporation of a partnership (see § 12.06, infra).

If the conversion of the partnership to an LLC (or vice-versa) does not change the partners' shares of partnership liabilities, each LLC member's basis in his LLC interest is the same as his basis in the old partnership. However, a decrease in a member's share of the old partnership's liabilities is treated as a constructive cash distribution that reduces the basis of his LLC interest.[131] If the cash distribution exceeds the member's basis, he recognizes gain and his basis decreases to zero.[132] An increase in a member's share of the old partnership's liabilities causes a corresponding increase in the basis of his LLC interest. Each member's holding period for his LLC interest is the same as the holding period for the converted partnership interest.

As noted above, a partner recognizes gain on a conversion of a partnership to an LLC only if his share of partnership liabilities decreases by an amount that exceeds the basis in his partnership interest. A general partner of a limited partnership may experience such a decrease if the conversion changes recourse partnership debts into nonrecourse liabilities. Before the conversion, the general partner bears all the economic risk of loss for recourse debts and no limited partners share in these liabilities. If the conversion terminates the general partners' personal liability, the debts become nonrecourse liabilities shared among

---

[128] 1995-1 C.B. 130. This ruling reiterates the Service's position in a number of private letter rulings. See Priv. Ltr. Ruls. 9633021, 9525065, 9525058, 9422034 (general partnership converts to LLC), 9417009 (limited partnership converts to LLC). See also Priv. Ltr. Rul. 9412020 (limited liability partnership merges into LLC).

[129] This treatment also applies to a conversion of a partnership to limited liability partnership. See Rev. Rul. 95-55, 1995-2 C.B. 313.

[130] These tax consequences are set forth in Rev. Rul. 84-52, 1984-1 C.B. 157.

[131] I.R.C. §§ 752, 722.

[132] I.R.C. § 731(a).

all LLC members. The shift in liabilities from the general to the limited partners results in gain to the general partner if the cash distribution he is deemed to receive exceeds the basis in his interest. A similar shift in liabilities may occur if the conversion changes the partners' shares of profits or losses.

The conversions of a partnership to an LLC ordinarily will not shift the partners' shares of liabilities. This is true because the general partners of the old partnership generally remain personally liable for debts incurred before the conversion to the LLC form. The continued personal liability may arise from state law or pursuant to a personal guarantee required by the creditors.

[C]   Exchanging Interests in Different Partnerships

An exchange of an interest in one partnership for an interest in another partnership is specifically excluded from the nonrecognition provisions applicable to like-kind property exchanges under I.R.C. Section 1031.[133] Thus, a partner recognizes gain or loss on the exchange to the extent of the difference between the value of the interest received and the basis of the interest transferred.

Nonrecognition treatment under I.R.C. Section 1031 ordinarily does not apply if two partnerships distribute property to partners who then exchange the distributed assets. I.R.C. Section 1031 applies only to exchanges of property a taxpayer holds for trade or business or investment purposes.[134] Because the partners hold the distributed property only to exchange it, I.R.C. Section 1031 is unlikely to apply to the transaction.

[D]   Contributing a Partnership or LLC Interest to a Corporation

A contribution of a partnership interest to a corporation in exchange for stock is governed by the rules applicable to other property contributions[135] — that is, the exchange is currently taxable unless it satisfies the requirements for nonrecognition under I.R.C. Section 351. I.R.C. Section 351 provides that an exchange of property for stock is not taxable if the parties transferring the property own at least 80 percent of all classes of voting and nonvoting stock immediately after the exchange. A contributor recognizes gain, however, to the extent that the sum of the liabilities he transfers to the corporation exceeds his aggregate basis in the contributed property. This rule applies to liabilities the corporation assumes, as well as to liabilities to which the contributed property is subject.[136]

---

[133]   I.R.C. § 1031(a)(2)(D); Treas. Reg. § 1.1031(a)-1(a)(1) (effective for transfers on or after April 25, 1991).

[134]   I.R.C. § 1031(a)(1).

[135]   Rev. Rul. 84-111, 1984-2 C.B. 88.

[136]   I.R.C. § 357(c). A contributor who transfers any liabilities to the corporation with a tax-avoidance purpose or without a bona fide business purpose is deemed to receive a cash distribution from the corporation equal to the total amount of liabilities transferred. I.R.C. § 356(b).

A partner who contributes his partnership interest in exchange for stock is treated as if the transferred interest is encumbered by his share of the partnership liabilities.[137] If the partner's basis exceeds his share of partnership liabilities, no gain is recognized, and his basis for the stock he receives equals his basis for the contributed interest less the amount of the transferred liabilities.[138] If the partner's share of partnership liabilities exceeds his basis for the contributed interest, he recognizes gain equal to the difference.[139]

Although a partner does not recognize gain or loss on a transfer of a partnership interest to a controlled corporation, the transaction may be treated as an exchange of the interest for other tax purposes such as basis adjustments under I.R.C. Section 743(b) or terminations under I.R.C. Section 708.[140]

[E] Conversion of a Corporation to a Partnership or LLC

The conversion of a corporation into a partnership or LLC results in the corporation's taxable liquidation. If the corporation owns appreciated assets, that appreciation is taxed twice, at both the corporate and shareholder levels. The double taxation may be avoided if the corporation has net operative loss carryovers or if corporate assets have not appreciated. If the liquidation results in a substantial tax liability, alternatives to LLC conversion should be considered. These alternatives include using a parallel or "mirror" LLC to conduct future business operations and expansions; selling corporate assets to a new LLC on the installment method; engaging in a joint venture with a new LLC; and leasing or licensing corporate assets to a new LLC. These transactions must be carefully structured to avoid reallocation of the LLC's income to the corporation under assignment of income principles.

[F] Contributing a Partnership or LLC Interest to Another Partnership

A contribution of a partnership interest to another partnership in exchange for an interest in the transferee partnership is governed by the rules applicable to other property contributions. The exchange generally is nontaxable under I.R.C. Section 721, and the contributing partner's basis in the new partnership interest is the same as his basis in the contributed interest under I.R.C. Section 722. Since the transaction is a contribution rather than a distribution, the rules of I.R.C. Section 751(b) do not apply. Thus, the contributing partner does not recognize income, even if his share of the I.R.C. Section 751 property of the contributed partnership

---

[137] Treas. Reg. § 1.741-1(c); Rev. Rul. 80-323, 1980-2 C.B. 124.

[138] I.R.C. § 358(d).

[139] *See, e.g.*, Jackson v. Comm'r, T.C. Memo. 1981-594, holding that a joint venturer was taxable under I.R.C. § 357(c) when he transferred his interest in the venture to a wholly owned corporation. The Tax Court was reversed on this issue by the Ninth Circuit (708 F.2d 1402 (9th Cir. 1983)). The appeals court concluded that no gain was recognized under I.R.C. § 357(c) because state law precluded the corporation from assuming the taxpayer's liabilities.

[140] *See* Rev. Rul. 81-40, 1981-1 C.B. 508; Rev. Rul. 64-155, 1964-1 C.B. 138.

changes in the transfer.[141]

Additional tax consequences occur if a net change in the contributing partner's share of partnership liabilities results from the contribution. Under I.R.C. Section 752(b), the contributing partner is deemed to receive a cash distribution of his share of the liabilities attributable to the contributed partnership interest, and, under I.R.C. Section 752(a), he is deemed to make a cash contribution of his share of the new partnership's liabilities. The partner's basis in the new interest increases or decreases by the net change in his share of liabilities.[142] If the net decrease in his share of liabilities exceeds the basis of his new partnership interest, the partner recognizes the excess amount as gain.[143] A portion of this gain may be ordinary income if the partner's share of I.R.C. Section 751 property changes in the transaction.[144]

> **Example:** Nelson owns a 30-percent general partnership interest in the MNO Partnership. His basis for his interest is $10,000, including his $10,000 share of partnership liabilities. Nelson contributes his interest in MNO in exchange for a 25-percent general partnership interest in the RST Partnership. Nelson's share of RST's existing liabilities is $30,000. Nelson recognizes no gain in the transaction, and the basis for his interest in the RST Partnership is $32,500, computed as follows:
>
> $10,000   the initial basis for his interest in RST, the same as his basis in MNO,
>
> plus
>
> $32,500   deemed cash contribution to RST for the increase in his share of RST's liabilities ($30,000 share of existing liabilities plus $2,500 share [25% x $10,000] of MNO's liabilities transferred to RST),
>
> less
>
> ($10,000)   basis decrease for deemed distribution from RST for Nelson's individual liabilities (his share of MNO's liabilities) transferred to RST.
>
> $32,500   Resulting basis.

Assume that Nelson's share of MNO's liabilities is $60,000 when he contributes his interest to RST. Nelson recognizes a $5,000 gain on the exchange, and his basis for his interest in RST is zero:

---

[141] Rev. Rul. 84-115, 1984-2 C.B. 118.

[142] Rev. Rul. 79-205, 1979-2 C.B. 255.

[143] I.R.C. § 731(a).

[144] The contributing partner would eventually recognize ordinary income on the contributed I.R.C. Section 751 property even if no deemed distribution occurs. Under I.R.C. § 704(c), gain or loss inherent in contributed property is allocated to the contributing partner. Thus, the partner would recognize ordinary income when the partnership disposes of the contributed I.R.C. Section 751 property.

$10,000	the initial basis for his interest in RST,
	plus
$45,000	deemed cash contribution to RST for the increase in his share of RST's liabilities ($30,000 share of existing liabilities plus $15,000 share [25 % x $60,000] of MNO's liabilities transferred to RST),
	less
$60,000	basis decrease (not below zero) for deemed distribution from RST for Nelson's individual liabilities (his share of MNO's liabilities) transferred to RST.
0	Resulting basis
$5,000	Gain Recognized under I.R.C. Section 731(a).

[G] Distribution of a Partnership or LLC Interest by a Corporation

A corporation that distributes a partnership interest to its shareholders recognizes gain to the extent that the value of the interest exceeds its basis.[145] The gain is characterized in the same manner as if the corporation sold the interest to the shareholder.[146] The corporation's gain on this deemed sale is computed by taking into account the share of partnership liabilities transferred to the shareholders in the distribution. For this purpose, the deemed value of a distributed partnership interest cannot be less than the corporation's share of its liabilities.[147]

A corporate distribution of a partnership interest is treated as an exchange of the interest for other tax purposes under I.R.C. Section 761(e); therefore, the distribution may trigger tax consequences such as basis adjustments under I.R.C. Section 743(b) or terminations under I.R.C. Section 708.

[H] Distribution of a Partnership or LLC Interest by a Partnership

A partnership distribution of an interest in another partnership generally is subject to the rules applicable to other partnership distributions. The distribution is not taxable unless it changes the distributee's share of I.R.C. Section 751 property or results in a cash distribution that exceeds the distributee's basis in his partnership interest.[148]

A partnership's distribution of a partnership interest is treated as an exchange of the interest for other tax purposes under I.R.C. Section 761(e); therefore, the distribution may trigger tax consequences such as basis adjustments under I.R.C. Section 743(b) or terminations under I.R.C. Section 708.

---

[145] I.R.C. §§ 311(b), 336(b).

[146] I.R.C. § 311(b)(1).

[147] I.R.C. §§ 311(b), 336(b).

[148] I.R.C. § 731(a).

[I]   Distribution of a Partnership or LLC Interest by a Trust or Estate

A trust or an estate generally does not recognize gain or loss when it distributes a partnership interest to a beneficiary.[149] If the partnership interest is distributed at the trust's termination, the Service may treat the transfer as one that closes the partnership tax year for the trust under I.R.C. Section 706(c)(2)(A).[150] The distribution is treated as an exchange that triggers other tax consequences such as basis adjustments under I.R.C. Section 743(b) or terminations under I.R.C. Section 708.

[J]   Transferring a Partnership Interest at Partner's Death

The transfer of a partnership interest to a deceased partner's successor in interest is not a sale or exchange, and no gain or loss is recognized,[151] even if the deceased partner's share of partnership liabilities exceeds the basis in his interest at the time of death (*see* Chapter 11). The partnership tax year closes at the partner's death, and his distributive share of income or loss for the portion of the partnership tax year up to the date of death is reported on his final tax return.[152]

A transfer at death is not a sale or exchange for determining whether the partnership terminates under the 50-percent sale or exchange rule of I.R.C. Section 708(b).[153] The death of one member of a two-member partnership similarly does not result in termination as long as the successor in interest shares in the profits and losses of the partnership's business.[154] If the partnership interest is subject to a prearranged sale agreement, however, the sale closes the tax year for the deceased partner, and it may terminate the partnership under I.R.C. Section 708(b). A prearranged agreement to convert a deceased general partner's interest into a limited partnership interest is not a sale or exchange for termination purposes.[155]

[K]   Gifting a Partnership or LLC Interest

A partner generally is not taxable when he makes a gift of all or part of his interest in a partnership. Because the donor's basis carries over to the donee,[156] the donee recognizes any gain or loss inherent in the interest. Although the partnership tax year does not close for the donor when the gift is made,

---

[149] *See* Treas. Reg. § 1.661(a)-2(f)(1).

[150] Rev. Rul. 72-352, 1972-2 C.B. 395.

[151] *See* I.R.C. §§ 761(e), 706(c)(2).

[152] Treas. Reg. § 1.706-1(c)(1)(3). This rule applies to partnership tax years beginning after 1997. For prior years, the partnership tax year did not close at a partner's death and his share of partnership income for the entire year was reported on his successor's tax return.

[153] Treas. Reg. § 1.708-1(b)(1)(ii).

[154] Treas. Reg. § 1.708-1(b)(1)(i)(*a*).

[155] Rev. Rul. 86-101, 1986-2 C.B. 94.

[156] I.R.C. § 1015.

partnership income for the year is allocated between the donor and the donee.[157] The gift is not considered a sale or exchange that terminates the partnership under the 50-percent sale or exchange rule of I.R.C. Section 708(b).[158]

Although no direct authority exists, case law[159] and regulations[160] indicate that a donor partner recognizes gain on a gift of a partnership interest if his share of partnership liabilities transferred to the donee exceeds the basis in his interest. The transfer apparently is treated as a sale of the interest for the amount of the transferred liabilities.[161] Similar treatment should apply if the donee becomes obligated to restore the donor's existing capital account deficit.

[L]　Making a Charitable Contribution

A partner who makes a charitable contribution of a partnership interest may recognize gain if he transfers his share of partnership liabilities to the charity. Under the bargain-sale rules of I.R.C. Section 1011(b), the portion of the contribution attributable to partnership liabilities is treated as a sale to the charity.[162] The donor partner determines the tax consequences of the sale by allocating the basis of his interest between the sale and nonsale portions of the transfer in proportion to the value of the interest attributable to the liabilities.[163] He recognizes gain to the extent that his relief of liabilities exceeds the basis allocated to the sale, and he is allowed a contribution deduction to the extent that the value of the donated interest exceeds the liabilities allocated to it.[164]

> **Example:** Mona contributes her interest in the MN Partnership to a charity. The value of Mona's share of partnership assets is $10,000; her share of partnership liabilities is $8,000; and her basis for the transferred interest is $4,000. Mona is allowed a charitable contribution deduction of $2,000: the $10,000 value of her share of partnership assets less her $8,000 share of partnership liabilities. Since 80 percent of the value of the gifted interest is allocable to liabilities ($8,000 / $10,000), $3,200 of Mona's basis ($4,000 × 80%) is allocated to the liabilities. This allocation results in a gain of $4,800 ($8,000 liabilities - $3,200 basis) for Mona on the partial sale.

---

[157] Treas. Reg. § 1.706-1(c)(5). *See* I.R.C. § 706(e)(2)(B).

[158] Treas. Reg. § 1.708-1(b)(1)(ii).

[159] *See* Diedrich v. Comm'r, 457 U.S. 191 (1982); Evangelista v. Comm'r, 71 T.C. 1057 (1979), *aff'd on other grounds*, 629 F.2d 1218 (7th Cir. 1980); Estate of Levine v. Comm'r, 72 T.C. 780 (1979), *aff'd*, 634 F.2d 12 (2d Cir. 1980); Guest v. Comm'r, 77 T.C. 9 (1981). *See also* Malone v. U.S., 326 F. Supp. 106 (N.D. Miss. 1971), *aff'd per curiam*, 455 F.2d 502 (5th Cir. 1972).

[160] *See* Treas. Reg. § 1.1001-2(a)(1), (4), (c), *Examples (3), (4)*.

[161] *See* I.R.C. § 752(d).

[162] *See* Treas. Reg. § 1.1011-2.

[163] Rev. Rul. 75-1, 1975-1 C.B. 80.

[164] *Id.*

§ 12.07   RECHARACTERIZING SALE OR EXCHANGE OF A PARTNERSHIP INTEREST

The form of the transaction that a partner uses to transfer his interest in a partnership generally is respected for tax purposes even though the economic effect of the transaction is similar to another form of transfer. For example, a liquidation of a partner's interest is taxable under the liquidation rules even if the transaction is economically identical to a pro rata sale of his interest to the other partners. If the form of the transfer does not reflect its economic substance, however, the transaction may be recharacterized for tax purposes. This recharacterization may occur in several situations:

(1)   *A purported sale of a partnership interest may be ignored for tax purposes if the transaction does not materially change the selling partner's economic interest in the partnership's assets.* [165] A sale is likely to be disregarded if the purchase price of the partnership interest is computed and payable only by reference to gains and earnings generated by partnership assets, because the purported seller bears the same economic risk for the assets before and after the transaction.

Example: Allen owns a 5-percent interest in the ABC Partnership, which was organized to produce and distribute a movie. After the picture was completed, ABC granted Distro Company exclusive rights to market the movie for five years and, in exchange, Distro received a percentage of the gross receipts for its services. At that time, Allen sold his partnership interest to Donna in exchange for Donna's promise to pay him 5 percent of all amounts ABC received from Distro under the distribution contract and 5 percent of the film's residual value at the end of the five-year period. Given this arrangement, the IRS and the courts are likely to agree that, in substance, Allen did not sell his partnership interest.

The facts in this example are similar to those in *Roth v. Commissioner*,[166] in which the Ninth Circuit concluded that no sale occurred, because the transaction did not change the amount and timing of the payments that the purported seller received or his economic risk. Because the seller's payments depended on the movie's box-office success, his economic position was the same as if the purported sale did not take place. The court's holding might have been different had the selling partner shown that significant risk existed of the purchaser not making the payments called for in the sales contract.

(2)   *A partnership interest owned by a grantor trust may be considered sold when the grantor's powers to revoke or control the trust lapse, expire, or are relinquished.* [167] The grantor is deemed to sell the interest to the trust for the amount of the partnership's liabilities of

---

[165]   *See, e.g.*, Blacketor v. U.S., 204 Ct. Cl. 897 (1974); Grinnell Corp. v. U.S., 390 F.2d 932 (Ct. Cl. 1968); Roth v. Comm'r, 321 F.2d 607 (9th Cir. 1963); Ashlock v. Comm'r, 18 T.C. 405 (1952); Collins v. Comm'r, 14 T.C. 301 (1950), *acq.* 1950-2 C.B. 1.

[166]   321 F.2d 607 (9th Cir. 1963).

[167]   Under I.R.C. §§ 671-679, the grantor of a grantor trust is treated as the owner of the trust assets

which he is relieved, and he recognizes gain to the extent that the liabilities exceed the basis of his partnership interest.

Example: Lester contributes $20,000 to an irrevocable trust for his children. The trust is a grantor trust because Lester retains administrative powers. The trust uses the cash contribution to purchase a 10-percent interest in the RST Real Estate Partnership. The partnership liabilities allocable to the trust's interest total $80,000. Consequently, the trust's basis for the interest is $100,000. In Years 1 to 6, the trust generates a total of $60,000 in losses, and Lester deducts these losses on his individual tax return. The deductions reduce the basis for the trust's partnership interest to $40,000 ($100,000 basis - $60,000 losses). After Year 6, when Lester renounces his administrative powers and the trust ceases being a grantor trust:

(a) ownership of trust assets is deemed to shift from Lester to the trust;

(b) the $80,000 share of liabilities allocated to the partnership interest is deemed to shift from Lester to the trust; and

(c) Lester recognizes a $40,000 gain on this sale of the partnership interest ($80,000 transferred liabilities - $40,000 basis).

(3) *A purported sale of a partnership interest may be disregarded to the extent that it represents an assignment of a partner's right to receive future income.* [168] For example, a partner may be deemed to assign his right to a share of partnership income if he sells his partnership interest after the partnership substantially completes developing its sole property.[169] The major effect of recharacterizing this kind of transaction is to require the partner to report ordinary income on the assignment rather than capital gain on the sale.

Assignment-of-income principles also may apply to transfers of partnership interests other than sales or exchanges. Thus, a partner who contributes his partnership interest to a charity may be taxable on partnership income that the charity collects after the transfer.[170] A partner also may be deemed to dispose of his share of a partnership-owned installment obligation when he makes a gift of his partnership interest.[171]

(4) *A partnership's sale of all its operating business assets may be*

---

if he retains certain powers to revoke, control, or administer the trust. Treas. Reg. § 1.1001-2(c), *Example (5).*

[168] Hale v. Comm'r, T.C. Memo. 1965-274. Pre-1954 Code cases applying the assignment of income doctrine to sales of partnership interests include Tunnell v. U.S., 259 F.2d 916 (3d Cir. 1958); Spicker v. Comm'r, 26 T.C. 91 (1956). *But see* U.S. v. Donoho, 275 F.2d 489 (8th Cir. 1960); Swiren v. Comm'r, 183 F.2d 656 (7th Cir. 1950), *cert. denied,* 340 U.S. 912 (1951).

[169] Hale v. Comm'r, T.C. Memo. 1965-274.

[170] Seyburn v. Comm'r, 51 T.C. 578 (1969).

[171] *See* Rev. Rul. 60-352, 1960-2C.B. 208; Tennyson v. U.S., 76-1 U.S.T.C. ¶ 13,128 (W.D. Ark. 1976).

regarded in some cases as if all the partners sold their partnership interests. [172] The courts apparently reasoned that, in effect, the partnership disappears after the sale because the purchaser has acquired the partnership's entire business. In *Barran v. Commissioner*,[173] for example, the court recharacterized a partnership's sale of its dairy and milk processing business as a sale of the partners' interests in the partnership. This conclusion was important because the partnership's holding period for some assets was less than was required for long-term capital gain treatment, but all of the partners held their partnership interests for the required period.

Courts have not applied this "sale of a business doctrine" in cases when the partnership sells assets that are not part of an operating business. For example, a partnership's sale of a hospital was not treated as a sale of the partners' interests when the hospital had been closed before the sale.[174]

The sale-of-business doctrine may apply to the purchaser as well as to the seller of a partnership interest. Thus, a taxpayer who buys all of the partnership interests from the partners may be treated as if he made a direct purchase of the partnership's business assets. In *McCauslen v. Commissioner*,[175] for example, a partner in a two-member partnership purchased the other partner's entire interest. The purchasing partner considered the sale a termination of the partnership under I.R.C. Section 708(b) with a resulting constructive liquidating distribution of the partnership's assets. The purchaser reported a long-term capital gain when he subsequently sold all of the partnership assets, asserting that the partnership's holding period "tacked on" to the distributed property under I.R.C. Section 735(b). The court rejected the "tacked on" holding period for half of the property, reasoning that the taxpayer purchased half of the partnership's assets from the other partner, rather than his partnership interest.[176]

---

[172] Barran v. Comm'r, 334 F.2d 58 (5th Cir. 1964); Hatch's Estate v. Comm'r, 198 F.2d 26 (9th Cir. 1952); Kaiser v. Glenn, 216 F.2d 551 (6th Cir. 1954); Dahlen v. Comm'r, 24 T.C. 159 (1955), *acq.* 1955-2 C.B. 5.

[173] 334 F.2d 58 (5th Cir. 1964).

[174] Baker Commodities, Inc. v. Comm'r, 415 F.2d 519 (9th Cir. 1969), *cert. denied*, 397 U.S. 988 (1970). *See also* Rev. Rul. 67-188, 1967-1 C.B. 216. Service rulings suggest that the IRS has not adopted the sale of business doctrine. Rev. Rul. 72-172, 1972-1 C.B. 265 (sales of partnership interests by a husband and wife to their controlled corporation treated as a transfer of the partnership's assets); Rev. Rul. 68-289, 1968-1 C.B. 314 (merger of three partnerships treated as contribution of assets of terminating partnerships to continuing partnership).

[175] 45 T.C. 588 (1966).

[176] *See* Rev. Rul. 99-6, 1999-6 I.R.B. 6, concerning the consequences when one person purchases all the interests in a limited liability company causing the LLC's partnership status to terminate under I.R.C. § 708(b)(1).

§ 12.08   ADJUSTING BASIS OF PARTNERSHIP OR LLC PROPERTY

[A]   General Rule: Sale or Exchange of Interest Does Not Affect Basis of Partnership or LLC Property

For most tax purposes, a partnership or LLC interest is considered a separate and distinct asset from the assets owned by the partnership or LLC. This treatment of a partnership as a separate entity is reflected in the general rule of I.R.C. Section 743(a), which provides that a transfer of a partnership interest in a sale or exchange, or at a partner's death, does not affect the basis of partnership property. The basis of partnership property is not affected even if the basis of the transferred partnership interest increases or decreases to reflect its purchase price or the date-of-death value.

A sale or exchange that results in a large discrepancy between the purchaser's basis for his partnership interest and his share of the basis of the partnership's assets may significantly affect the timing and character of his income or loss from the partnership. If the partnership owns appreciated assets, for example, the purchasing partner's share of depreciation deductions is lower, and he recognizes more gain when the assets are sold than if he purchased a direct, undivided interest in the assets. Although a corresponding loss offsets the partner's increased gain and income when he sells or liquidates his partnership interest, he never recovers the time value of his tax payments. Also, he may be limited to a capital loss on a sale or liquidation of the interest, even if he realized ordinary income when the partnership sold the asset.

> **Example:** Carla purchases a 25-percent interest in the BCD Limited Liability Company from Alice for $30,000. Immediately before the sale, the LLC has the following assets:

	Basis	Value
Inventory	$20,000	$60,000
Depreciable Fixtures	$40,000	$60,000

If the LLC does not have an I.R.C. Section 754 election in effect:

(1)   Carla will recognize $10,000 of ordinary income when the LLC subsequently sells its inventory ($40,000 gain × 25%), even though Carla's purchase price reflected the current value of the inventory.

(2)   Carla's depreciation deductions will be determined based on a $10,000 share of the basis of the depreciable fixtures, even though $15,000 of her purchase price is attributable to that property.

After the inventory is sold and the fixture is fully depreciated, assuming no other transactions, the LLC's only asset is $60,000, cash, and Carla's basis in her LLC interest is $30,000:

$30,000	Carla's initial basis
10,000	increase from sale of inventory
(10,000)	decrease for depreciation deductions
$30,000	Carla's adjusted basis

If Carla sells her 25-percent interest for its $15,000 value ($60,000 × 25%), she realizes a $15,000 capital loss, which is equal to the additional income she reported because the basis of LLC assets did not reflect the amount she paid for her interest. Although Carla's loss is the same amount as the additional income reported, two disadvantages to this treatment are:

(1)   Carla never recovers the time value of the tax payments; and

(2)   the loss on the sale of the LLC interest is a capital loss — the income from the inventory and the depreciation deductions were ordinary.

[B]   Electing to Adjust Basis of Partnership or LLC Property

An election under I.R.C. Section 754 allows the purchaser of a partnership interest to be taxed almost as if he acquired a direct interest in partnership property. A partnership that makes an I.R.C. Section 754 election must adjust the basis of partnership assets under I.R.C. Section 743(b) whenever a partnership interest is transferred by sale or exchange or at a partner's death. The adjustment increases or decreases the purchaser's share of the basis of the partnership's assets to equal the amount he paid for his partnership interest.[177] These adjustments apply only in determining the purchasing partner's tax consequences; they do not affect the other partners.

Mandatory Basis Adjustment: An amendment to IRC Section 743 in 2004 makes a basis adjustment mandatory whenever a partnership interest is transferred for which a substantial built-in loss (defined as more than $250,000) exists.[178] Thus, a partnership that does not have an IRC Section 754 election in effect generally *must* adjust the basis of partnership property under IRC Section 743 if a substantial built-in loss will be shifted to the transferee.[179]

If the amount the purchaser pays for his interest exceeds his share of the basis of partnership property, the partnership increases the basis of its assets to reflect the difference. If the amount the purchaser pays is less than his share of the basis of partnership property, the partnership decreases the basis of its assets by that difference. The increase or decrease in the partner's share of basis is reflected in corresponding changes in his allocable share of partnership tax items, including

---

[177]   Treas. Reg. § 1.743-1(b). The election also applies when a partnership interest is transferred at a partner's death. In that case the purchase price is deemed to be the fair market value of the decedent's interest at the time of death.

[178]   I.R.C. § 743(d), as amended by the American Jobs Creation Act (AJCA), Pub. L. No. 108-357 (2004). These rules apply to transfers after October 22, 2004.

[179]   An exception to this mandatory basis adjustment rule applies to electing investment partnerships that satisfy the statutory requirements set forth in I.R.C. § 743(e).

depreciation, depletion, amortization, income, and gain or loss from the sale of partnership assets.

Example: Assume the same facts as in the Example above, except that the LLC has an I.R.C. Section 754 election in effect when Carla acquires her LLC interest. Under I.R.C. Section 743(b), the basis of the LLC's assets increases by $15,000-the difference between Carla's $30,000 cost basis for her LLC interest and her $15,000 share of the total basis of LLC property. The effect of this basis adjustment is illustrated below:

	LLC's Basis Before Section Adjustment	Basis After 754 Adjustment	Carla's Share of Basis
Inventory	$20,000	$30,000	$15,000
Depreciable fixtures	40,000	45,000	15,000
	$60,000	$75,000	$30,000

Because Carla has a special basis in each of the partnership's assets, no partnership income is allocated to her if the partnership sells the inventory for its current value, and her allocation of depreciation is computed based on her purchase price.

[C] Determining Whether Basis Adjustment Rules Apply

The basis-adjustment rules of I.R.C. Section 743(b) apply only to partnerships that have an election under I.R.C. Section 754 in effect when a partnership interest is transferred by sale or exchange, or at the death of a partner.[180] In determining whether a transfer of a partnership interest triggers an I.R.C. Section 743(b) basis adjustment, the following rules apply:

(1) *If a partnership has an I.R.C. Section 754 election in effect when a partner dies, an I.R.C. Section 743(b) basis adjustment is made for the deceased partner's successor in interest.* Under I.R.C. Section 1014, the successor's basis in his partnership interest increases or decreases to its value on the date of death or on the alternate valuation date. The amount of the basis adjustment is the difference between the successor's basis for his partnership interest and his share of the basis of the partnership's assets.[181] These adjustments are made in the same manner as they are made when a partnership interest is sold or exchanged.

(2) *A partnership interest held in a grantor trust that becomes irrevocable at the grantor's death is not transferred under I.R.C. Section 743(b)*

---

[180] An I.R.C. § 754 election does not result in any basis adjustment when a partner contributes money or other property to a partnership. Treas. Reg. § 1.743-1(a).

[181] If the partnership holds assets representing income in respect of a decedent under I.R.C. § 691, no part of the basis adjustment is allocated to these assets. Treas. Reg. § 1.755-1(b)(4). For discussion of income in respect of a decedent, see § 11.03, *supra*.

until the grantor dies. [182] If the partnership has an I.R.C. Section 754 election in effect for the year in which the grantor dies, a basis adjustment is made for the trust beneficiary at that time.

(3)   *In community property states, both spouses are deemed to own one-half of a partnership interest owned by either spouse.* Consequently:

    (a)   the death of either the partner or the nonpartner spouse triggers a basis adjustment; and

    (b)   the adjustment at the death of either spouse applies to the entire partnership interest, even if he or she owns only one-half of the partnership interest under state law.[183]

(4)   *A distribution of a partnership interest is treated as an exchange under I.R.C. Section 743(b).* [184] This rule applies when a corporate partner distributes its partnership interest to its shareholders and when a partnership that owns an interest in another partnership distributes the interest to its partners.[185]

This rule prevents taxpayers from avoiding ordinary income recapture by contributing recapture property to a partnership or corporation and following the contribution with a distribution of the partnership interest.[186] This strategy was of particular importance for corporate distributions before 1987, because a corporation did not recognize gain on most distributions of nonrecapture property. Since 1987, however, the importance of the rule is diminished because corporations must recognize gain on property distributions when the value of the property exceeds the corporation's basis.[187]

(5)   *No basis adjustment ordinarily occurs when a partnership interest is transferred by gift or by charitable contribution.* If the gift or contribution is treated as a partial sale because liabilities are transferred to the donee, a basis adjustment should be allowed to reflect any gain recognized.

(6)   *A transfer of partnership property to a foreign corporation triggers an I.R.C. Section 743(b) basis adjustment if gain is recognized under I.R.C. Section 367.* [188] The adjustment applies only in determining the partnership's basis in the foreign corporation's stock.

---

[182] Rev. Rul. 79-84, 1979-1 C.B. 223.

[183] Rev. Rul. 79-124, 1979-1 C.B. 224.

[184] I.R.C. § 761(e).

[185] Staff of Joint Committee on Taxation, General Explanation of the Revenue Provisions of the Deficit Reduction Act of 1984, 98th Cong., 2d Sess. 237 (1984).

[186] *Id.*

[187] I.R.C. § 336.

[188] Temp. Treas. Reg. § 1.367(a)-1T(c). *See, e.g.,* F.S.A. 199938007 (U.S. corporation's transfer of interest in a U.S. partnership to foreign partnerships treated as transfer of corporation's pro rata share U.S. partnership's assets under I.R.C. § 367).

[D] Computing the I.R.C. Section 743(b) Basis Adjustment

Under I.R.C. Section 743(b), the total adjustment to the basis of partnership assets resulting from a sale or exchange of a partnership interest is the difference between the purchaser's initial basis in his partnership interest and his proportionate share of the basis of the partnership assets. A purchaser's initial basis for his partnership interest is its cost, which includes any partnership liabilities transferred to him in the transaction.[189] The total adjustment is allocated among partnership assets under the rules of I.R.C. Section 755.[190]

The procedure for computing the I.R.C. Section 743(b) special basis adjustment for a purchaser of partnership interest is summarized as follows:

Step 1 — Determine the purchaser's initial basis for the acquired interest, including the share of partnership liabilities transferred to the purchaser in the sale.

Step 2 — Determine the purchaser's share of the partnership's basis in its property. This share of basis equals:

(1)   The purchaser's share of partnership *previously taxed capital* (defined below); plus

(2)   The share of partnership liabilities transferred to the purchaser in the sale.

Step 3 — Determine the total I.R.C. Section 743(b) basis adjustment. The adjustment equals the difference between the purchaser's initial basis computed in Step 1 and his share of partnership basis computed in Step 2.

Step 4 — Divide the partnership's assets into two classes: (1)capital gain and I.R.C. Section 1231 property, and (2) other property.

Step 5 — Allocate total basis adjustment computed in Step 3 to each class of property in Step 4 under the rules of I.R.C. Section 755 described below.

Step 6 — Allocate basis adjustment among assets in each class of property under the rules of I.R.C. Section 755 described below.

In computing the purchasing partner's share of the basis of partnership property under I.R.C. Section 743(b) and the related regulations, the following rules apply:

(1)   *A transferee partner's share of the basis of partnership property equals the sum of:* [191]

(a)   the partner's interest in the partnership's *previously taxed capital*, plus

(b)   the partner's share of partnership liabilities.[192]

---

[189] I.R.C. §§ 1012, 742, 752(d). A successor's initial basis in an interest acquired at the death of a partner is the fair market value of the interest on the date of the death or on the alternate valuation date. I.R.C. § 1014.

[190] Treas. Reg. § 1.743-1(e).

[191] Treas. Reg. § 1.743-1(d). These computation rules are effective as of December 15, 1999. T.D. 8847 (Dec. 15, 1999), *corrected* 2000-11 C.B. 771.

[192] A partner's share of liabilities is determined pursuant to the regulations under I.R.C. § 752. *See* § 5.05, *supra*.

The partnership's *previously taxed capital* is determined by assuming that, immediately after the partner receives his interest, the partnership sells all of its assets at fair market value[193] in a hypothetical taxable transaction. The new partner's share of partnership previously taxed capital equals:

(i)   the amount of cash he would receive if the partnership liquidated immediately after the hypothetical sale; plus

(ii)   any tax loss allocable to him from the hypothetical sale, minus

(iii)   any tax gain allocable to him from the hypothetical sale.[194]

In determining the amount of gain or loss that would be allocated to the partner, any remedial allocations for contributed property under I.R.C. Section 704(c) are taken into account.[195]

Generally, a transferee partner's interest in the partnership's previously taxed capital equals his capital account immediately after the transfer, adjusted for the hypothetical sale.[196] A transferee's capital account is the same as the transferor's before the transfer.[197]

Example (1): [198] Paul, an equal partner in the PRS Partnership, sells his interest to Terry for $21,000. PRS has an I.R.C. Section 754 election in effect when the sale occurs. On the sale date, the partnership's balance sheet is as follows:

---

[193] The preamble to the regulations states that the IRS intends to issue rules for determining the fair market value of partnership assets and that these rules are likely to provide that I.R.C. § 7701(g) will apply in allocating basis adjustments under I.R.C. § 743(b). I.R.C. § 7701(g) states that the value of property securing a nonrecourse debt is presumed to be no less than the principle amount of the debt.

[194] Treas. Reg. § 1.743-1(d)(1), (2). These allocations are limited to the amounts that are attributable to the acquired partnership interest.

[195] Remedial allocations are described in Treas. Reg. § 1.704-3(d). For complete discussion of remedial allocations under I.R.C. § 704(c), see § 4.02, *supra.*

[196] The proposed regulations expressly stated that a new partner's interest in previously taxed capital generally will equal his capital account, adjusted for the hypothetical sale. The final regulations deleted this sentence as redundant but notes in the preamble that no substantive change is intended by the deletion.

[197] Treas. Reg. § 1.704-1(b)(2)(iv)*(l)*. If a partner transfers only part of his interest, a portion of his capital account corresponding to the transferred interest carries over to the transferee. *See* § 4.06, *supra.*

[198] *See* Treas. Reg. § 1.743-1(d)(3).

Assets	Basis	Value
Cash	$1,000	$1,000
Accounts receivable	10,000	10,000
Inventory	20,000	21,000
Depreciable assets	17,000	40,000
Total	$48,000	$72,000
Liabilities and Capital		
Liabilities	$9,000	$9,000
Capital		
Paul	13,000	21,000
Rachel	13,000	21,000
Sandy	13,000	21,000
Total	$48,000	$72,000

The basis of Terry's interest is $24,000 ($21,000 cash paid for Paul's interest plus Terry's $3,000 share of partnership liabilities). On a hypothetical sale of all its assets, the partnership would realize a $24,000 gain and Terry's one-third share would be $8,000. Thus, Terry's interest in the partnership's previously taxed capital is $13,000 ($21,000, cash she would receive if PRS liquidated immediately after a hypothetical sale of all its assets, minus the $8,000 of tax gain that would be allocable to her from that sale). Terry's share of the basis of partnership property is $16,000 ($13,000 share of previously taxed capital, plus $3,000 share of the partnership's liabilities). The basis adjustment to partnership property for Terry is $8,000 ($24,000 basis for her partnership interest minus her $16,000 share of the basis of partnership property).

(2) ***A partner's share of the basis of partnership property is determined by taking into account any allocations required under I.R.C. Section 704(c) regarding property contributed to the partnership.*** [199] Under I.R.C. Section 704(c), gain, loss, depreciation, depletion, and other tax items attributable to the difference between the value and basis of property when contributed to a partnership must be allocated to the contributing partner. When a partner who contributed property with built-in gain or loss transfers his partnership interest, the built-in gain or loss is allocated to the transferee partner as it would have been to the transferor.[200]

Example (2): Lew, Mary, and Neil form the LMN Partnership as equal partners. In exchange for their partnership interests, Lew and Mary each contribute $12,000 in cash, and Neil contributes land valued at $12,000, in which he has an adjusted basis of $6,000. As a result of these contributions, $6,000 of built-in gain is allocable to Neil under I.R.C. Section 704(c). The partnership's balance sheet is as follows:

---

[199] I.R.C. § 743(b). *See* Treas. Reg. § 1.743-1(d)(3), *Example (2)*.

[200] Treas. Reg. § 1.704-3(a)(7). If a portion of the interest is transferred, a proportionate share of built-in gain or loss is allocated to the transferee.

Assets	Basis	Value
Cash	$24,000	$24,000
Land	6,000	12,000
Total Assets	$30,000	$36,000
Partners' Capital		
Lew	$12,000	$12,000
Mary	12,000	12,000
Neil	6,000	12,000
Total Partners' Capital	$30,000	$36,000

The land increases in value to $15,000, and Neil sells his interest to Olivia for $13,000 at a time when the partnership has an I.R.C. Section 754 election in effect. Olivia's basis for her partnership interest is its cost of $13,000.

If the partnership sold all its assets (only land and cash at this time) at fair market value, it would realize a $9,000 gain ($15,000 value of land minus $6,000 basis).

The amount of tax gain allocable to Olivia from the hypothetical sale is $7,000 ($6,000 built-in gain transferred from Neil under I.R.C. Section 704(c), plus one-third of the $3,000 additional gain). Olivia's interest in the partnership's previously taxed capital is $6,000 ($13,000 in cash she would receive if the partnership liquidated after the hypothetical sale minus her $7,000 share of gain from that sale). The basis adjustment to partnership property for Olivia is $7,000 ($13,000 cost basis for Olivia's interest minus her $6,000 share of the basis of partnership property).

Under the rules described below, the entire adjustment is allocated to the land, so that Olivia's special basis in the land is $13,000.

Sometime later, LMN sells the land for $18,000, realizing a $12,000 gain. The first $6,000 of that gain is allocated to Olivia under I.R.C. Section 704(c). The remaining $6,000 gain is allocated $2,000 to Lew, $2,000 to Mary, and $2,000 to Olivia. Although the total gain allocated to Olivia is $8,000, that amount is reduced by her $7,000 basis adjustment on the land. Therefore, Olivia's taxable gain is $1,000 — one-third of the land's appreciation after her purchase of Neil's partnership interest.

Example (3): Assume that Olivia purchases Lew's interest for $13,000. In that case, Olivia's basis adjustment is $1,000. The total adjustment is allocated to the land. If the partnership sells the land for $18,000 and realizes a $12,000 gain on the sale, the first $6,000 of gain is allocated to Neil, and the remaining $6,000 of gain is allocated $2,000 to Mary, $2,000 to Neil, and $2,000 to Olivia. The $2,000 of gain allocated to Olivia is reduced by her $1,000 basis adjustment, and her taxable gain is $1,000.

(3)   *If the same partnership interest is transferred more than once, the last transferee's special basis in partnership property is determined from his share of the partnership's common basis in its assets, without regard to any basis adjustments that occurred in*

previous transfers. [201]

Example (4): Charles, David, and Edward form the CDE Limited Liability Company. Charles and David each contribute $10,000 in cash, and Edward contributes land with basis and value of $10,000. Assume the following facts:

(1)   The land appreciates in value to $13,000. Charles sells his interest to Fred for $11,000; the LLC has an I.R.C. Section 754 election in effect at that time. Fred's I.R.C. Section 743(b) basis adjustment is $1,000: the difference between the $11,000 cost basis in his LLC interest and his $10,000 share of the basis of partnership property. The total adjustment is allocated to the land, increasing its basis to $11,000.

(2)   The land appreciates in value to $16,000, and Fred sells his LLC interest to Greta for $12,000. Greta's I.R.C. Section 743(b) basis adjustment is $2,000: the difference between the $12,000 cost basis in her LLC interest and her $10,000 share of the basis of partnership property, which is determined without regard to Fred's special basis adjustment. The total $2,000 adjustment is allocated to the land.

For a gift of a partnership interest, the donor is deemed to transfer, and the donee to receive, the portion of the basis adjustment attributable to the gifted interest.[202]

Example (5): Assume the facts of the previous example and that during the following year, Greta makes a gift to Hal of fifty percent of her partnership interest. Because Greta has a $2,000 basis adjustment under I.R.C. Section 743(b) when the gift is made, she is deemed to transfer $1,000 of that basis adjustment to Hal with the gift of the partnership interest.

[E]   Transferring an Interest in a Tiered Partnership

A sale or exchange of an interest in a partnership (parent) that owns an interest in a second partnership (subsidiary) results in basis adjustments under I.R.C. Section 743(b) for both partnerships if both have I.R.C. Section 754 elections in effect.[203] The basis adjustment occurs in two steps:

Step (1) — The purchaser of the interest in the parent partnership obtains an I.R.C. Section 743(b) adjustment for his share of the parent's assets. A portion of this basis adjustment is allocated to the parent's interest in the subsidiary partnership under the I.R.C. Section 755 allocation rules.

Step (2) — The bases of the subsidiary partnership's assets are adjusted by the amount allocated to the parent partnership's interest in the subsidiary. This basis adjustment applies only to the parent partnership and to the partner who purchased the interest in the parent.

---

[201]   Treas. Reg. § 1.743-1(f).

[202]   *Id.*

[203]   Rev. Rul. 87-115, 1987-2 C.B. 163. *See also* Rev. Rul. 78-2, 1978-1 C.B. 202 (purchaser or interest in parent partnership treated as partner of subsidiary); Priv. Ltr. Rul. 7726014. *Cf.* Rev. Rul. 77-309, 1977-2 C.B. 216 (pass through of liabilities in two-tier partnership); Rev. Rul. 77-311, 1977-2 C.B. 218 (pass through of retroactive loss adjustment in two-tier partnership).

If the parent partnership has an I.R.C. Section 754 election in effect but the subsidiary does not, a sale of an interest in the parent does not result in an adjustment to the basis of the subsidiary's assets, and an adjustment is made only for the bases of the parent partnership's assets.[204]

[F] Allocating Basis Adjustments Among Partnership Assets

The rules for allocating the basis increase or decrease computed under I.R.C. Section 743(b) among partnership assets are set forth in the regulations under I.R.C. Section 755. Generally, these rules require the following steps:

Step 1 — Divide partnership property into two classes:

> ***Class (1)*** *Capital gain property* consisting of the partnership's capital gain assets and I.R.C. Section 1231(b) property, and

> ***Class (2)*** *Ordinary income property* consisting of all other partnership property. Any property and potential recapture gain treated as unrealized receivables under I.R.C. Section 751(c) are treated as separate items of ordinary income property.[205]

Step 2 — Determine the amount of income, gain or loss that would be allocated to the transferee partner from each item of partnership property if all partnership assets were sold in a hypothetical sale at fair market value immediately after he acquired his interest. [206] The income or loss allocation must include remedial allocations for contributed property under I.R.C. Section 704(c).[207]

Step 3 — Allocate basis adjustment to class of ordinary income property. The amount of basis adjustment allocated to the class of ordinary income property equals the total amount of income, gain, or loss that would be allocated to the transferee from a sale of all partnership ordinary income property.

Step 4 — Allocate basis adjustment to class of capital gain property. The amount of basis adjustment allocated to the class of capital gain property equals:

(a)   the total I.R.C. Section 743 basis adjustment; minus

(b)   the basis adjustment allocated to ordinary income property.

> If the amount of basis decrease allocable to capital gain property exceeds the partnership's basis for such property, the excess is applied to reduce the basis of ordinary income property.[208]

Step 5 — Allocate basis adjustment among items of ordinary income property. [209] The basis adjustment allocated to each item of ordinary income property equals:

---

[204] Rev. Rul. 87-115, 1987-2 C.B. 163.

[205] The rules described in the text apply to transfers of partnership interests that occur on or after December 15, 1999.

[206] Treas. Reg. § 1.755-1(b)(1)(ii).

[207] *See* Treas. Reg. § 1.704-3(d).

[208] Treas. Reg. § 1.755-1(b)(2)(i).

[209] Treas. Reg. § 1.755-1(b)(3)(i).

(a)   the amount of income, gain, or loss allocable to the transferee from the hypothetical sale of the item; minus

(b)   the product of:

(i)   any decrease to the basis adjustment to ordinary income property required because the partnership did not have enough basis in capital gain property to reduce, multiplied by

(ii)   a fraction, having a numerator that is the fair market value of the item and a denominator that is the total fair market value of all ordinary income property.

Step 6 — Allocate *basis adjustment among items of capital gain property.* [210] The basis adjustment allocated to each item of capital gain property equals:

(a)   the amount of income, gain, or loss allocable to the transferee from the hypothetical sale of the item; minus

(b)   the product of:

(i)   the total gain or loss allocable from the hypothetical sale of all items of capital gain property, minus the positive basis adjustment to all capital gain property or plus the negative basis adjustment to all capital gain property, multiplied by

(ii)   a fraction, having a numerator that is the fair market value of the item and a denominator that is the total fair market value of all capital gain property.

Example (1): For equal interests in the AB partnership, Anne contributes $50,000 and Asset 1, a nondepreciable capital asset with a fair market value of $50,000 and a basis of $25,000, while Ben contributes $100,000 in cash. The partnership uses the cash to purchase Assets 2, 3, and 4. In year 2, Anne sells her entire partnership interest to Carla for $120,000. At the time of the transfer, Anne's share of the basis of partnership assets is $75,000. Since the partnership has an I.R.C. Section 754 election in effect, Carla receives a $45,000 positive basis adjustment under I.R.C. Section 743(b)- $120,000 cost basis minus $75,000 share of basis of partnership assets.

When the sale occurs, the partnership books are as follows:

Assets	Basis	Fair market value
Capital Gain Property:		
Asset 1	$25,000	$75,000
Asset 2	100,000	117,500
Ordinary Income Property:		
Asset 3	40,000	45,000
Asset 4	10,000	2,500
Total	$175,000	$240,000

---

[210] Treas. Reg. § 1.755-1(b)(3)(ii).

In a hypothetical sale of the partnership's assets immediately after the transfer, $46,250 of capital gain would be allocated to Carla ($25,000 built-in gain under I.R.C. Section 704(c) from Asset 1, plus fifty percent of the additional $42,500 appreciation in capital gain property). Carla would be allocated a $1,250 ordinary loss on a hypothetical sale of partnership ordinary income property.

(a)   The basis adjustment allocated to ordinary income property is a $1,250 basis decrease.

(b)   The basis adjustment allocated to capital gain property is a $46,250 basis increase ($45,000 total I.R.C. Section 743(b) adjustment, increased by the $1,250 negative basis adjustment to the ordinary income property).

These adjustments are allocated among the assets in each class as follows (in accordance with the amount of gain or loss Carla would be allocated on a hypothetical sale):

Ordinary Income property

    Asset 3 - basis increase of $2,500

    Asset 4 - basis decrease of $3,750

Capital Assets:

    Asset 1 - basis increase of $37,500

    Asset 2 - basis increase of $8,750

Example (2): Assume the same facts except that Anne sold her interest to Carla for $110,000. Carla's total I.R.C. Section 743(b) basis adjustment is $35,000. Of this amount, a $1,250 basis decrease is allocated to ordinary income property, and a $36,250 basis increase is allocated to capital gain property.

These adjustments are allocated among the assets in each class as follows (in accordance with the amount of gain or loss Carla would be allocated on a hypothetical sale):

Ordinary Income property

    Asset 3 - basis increase of $2,500

    Asset 4 - basis decrease of $3,750

Capital Assets:

In a hypothetical sale, Carla would be allocated $37,500 from the sale of Asset 1, and $8,750 from the sale of Asset 2, for a total of $46,250. This total amount of gain exceeds the $36,250 basis increase allocated to capital gain property by $10,000. Consequently, the basis adjustments to capital assets are computed as follows:

Asset 1 - basis increase of $33,604 ($37,500 minus $3,896 [$10,000 × $75,000/192,500]).

Asset 2 - basis increase of $2,646 ($8,750 minus $6,104 [$10,000 × $117,500/192,500]).

The basis adjustment allocated to one class of property may be an increase while the portion allocated to the other class is a decrease. This may occur even if the total amount of the basis adjustment is zero. Similarly, the basis adjustment allocated to an item of property within a class may be an increase while the portion allocated to another is a decrease, even if the basis adjustment allocated to the class is zero.[211]

Example (3): For equal interests in the DE LLC, Dell and Edna each contribute $1,000 in cash which the partnership uses to purchase Assets 1, 2, 3, and 4. In year 2, Dell sells his LLC interest to Frank for $1,000. The LLC has an I.R.C. Section 754 election in effect. Frank's basis adjustment under section 743(b) is zero ($1,000 cost basis minus $1,000 share of basis of partnership assets).

When the sale occurs, the partnership books are as follows:

Assets	Basis	Fair market value
Capital Gain Property:		
Asset 1	$500	$750
Asset 2	500	500
Ordinary Income Property:		
Asset 3	500	250
Asset 4	500	500
Total	$2,000	$2,000

In a hypothetical sale of the LLC's assets immediately after the transfer, Frank would be allocated a loss of $125 from the sale of the ordinary income property. Thus, the amount of the basis adjustment to ordinary income property is negative $125. The amount of the basis adjustment to capital gain property is $125 (zero total I.R.C. Section 743(b) adjustment increased by the $125 negative basis adjustment to ordinary income property.

[1] Income in Respect of a Decedent

If a partnership interest is transferred as a result of a partner's death, the transferee's basis in the interest is not adjusted for any portion of the interest that is attributable to items representing income in respect of a decedent (IRD) under I.R.C. Section 691.[212] Similarly, no part of an I.R.C. Section 743(b) basis adjustment 743(b) is allocated to the IRD assets.[213]

Example: Vera inherited a 50 percent interest in the ST Partnership from her aunt Sheila when the interest was worth $10,000. At Sheila's death, ST's

---

[211] Treas. Reg. § 1.755-1(b)(1)(i).

[212] I.R.C. § 1014(c). *See* Treas. Reg. § 1.742-1.

[213] Treas. Reg. § 1.755-1(b)(4).

balance sheet (reflecting the cash method of tax accounting) appeared as follows:

Assets	Basis	Fair market value
Capital Assets	$2,000	$5,000
Unrealized Receivables	0	15,000
Total	$2,000	$20,000
Partner's Capital:		
Sheila	1,000	10,000
Todd	1,000	10,000
Total	$2,000	$20,000

Although the value of the interest Vera inherits is $10,000, $7,500 of that amount is attributable to partnership receivables that are IRD items. Because no basis increase is made to the IRD items, Vera's basis in the interest she receives is $2,500. Vera's I.R.C. Section 743(b) basis adjustment is $1,500 ($2,500 basis minus her 1,000 share of the basis of partnership's assets). The entire adjustment is allocated to the capital asset.

[2] Carryover Basis Transaction

Special rules apply to I.R.C. Section 743(b) basis adjustments that result from exchanges in which the transferee's basis is determined in whole or in part by reference to the transferor's basis in the transferred interest.[214] Examples of such basis transfer situations include contributions of a partnership interest to a corporation under I.R.C. Section 351 and a contribution of interests to another partnership under I.R.C. Section 721.

These rules are summarized as follows:

(1)   If the amount of the I.R.C. Section 743(b) basis adjustment is zero, no adjustment to the basis of partnership property in any class is made.

(2)   A positive I.R.C. Section 743(b) basis adjustment is made only if a hypothetical sale of partnership property would result in an allocation of *net* gain or income to the transferee. The increase is allocated to each class of partnership property in proportion to the net gain or income that would be allocated to the transferee from a sale of the assets in each class.

(3)   A negative I.R.C. Section 743(b) basis adjustment is made only if a hypothetical sale of partnership property would result in an allocation of *net* loss to the transferee. If decrease is allocated to each class of partnership property in proportion to the net loss that would be allocated to the transferee from a sale of the assets in each class.

(4)   A basis increase allocated to a class of partnership property is first applied to assets with unrealized appreciation in proportion to the transferee's share of the unrealized appreciation. Any remaining increase is allocated among assets in the class in proportion to the transferee's share of the

---

[214] Treas. Reg. § 1.755-1(b)(5).

amount the partnership would realize on a hypothetical sale of each asset in the class.

(5)   A basis decrease allocated to a class of partnership property is first applied to assets with unrealized depreciation in proportion to the transferee's share of the unrealized depreciation. Any remaining decrease is allocated among the assets in the class in proportion to the transferee's share of their adjusted bases (as adjusted under the preceding sentence).

(6)   A basis decrease allocated to a class of partnership property can be applied to property in the class only up to the transferee's share of the partnership's basis for depreciated assets in the class. A basis decrease that cannot be currently allocated to any asset because of this limitation is suspended until the partnership subsequently acquires property of a like character to which an adjustment can be made.

Ordinarily, the transfer of a partnership interest in a carryover basis transaction does not create an I.R.C. Section 743(b) adjustment because the transferor's basis for the interest equals his share of the basis of partnership property. When this is not true (*e.g.*, if the transferor partner acquired his interest when the partnership did not have an I.R.C. Section 754 election in effect), the regulations are intended to prevent partners from using a carryover basis exchange to shift basis from capital gain assets to ordinary income assets, or vice versa. The effect of these regulations is to require a net positive adjustment to be allocated only to appreciated assets and a net negative adjustment to be allocated only to depreciated assets.

The following examples derived from the regulations illustrate the operation of these special rules:

Example (1): Martha, Noreen and Owen own equal interests in the MNO Partnership, which has an I.R.C. Section 754 election in effect. Martha contributes her interest in MNO (in a nontaxable I.R.C. Section 721 transaction) to the Upco LLC in exchange for an interest in that limited liability company. At the time of the transfer:

(a)   Martha's basis for her interest in MNO is $5,000, which also is her share of the basis of MNO's assets.

(b)   LTP's assets are inventory worth $7,500 with a basis of $5,000, and a nondepreciable capital asset worth $7,500 with a basis of $10,000.

Under I.R.C. Section 723, Upco's basis for its interest in MNO is $5,000. The I.R.C. Section 743(b) basis adjustment to partnership property is $0 ($5,000, Upco's basis for its interest in MNO, minus $5,000, Upco's share of MNO's basis in partnership assets).

UTP does not receive an I.R.C. Section 743(b) basis adjustment for its share of MNO property because:

(a)   Upco acquired its interest in MNO in a transferred basis exchange under I.R.C. Section 721, and

(b)   the total amount of the basis adjustment is zero.

Example (2): Quentin purchased an equal interest in the QRS partnership when an I.R.C. Section 754 election was *not* in effect. As a result, Quentin's cost basis for his interest exceeds his share of the basis of partnership assets (and exceeds the basis of his interest shown on the partnership books). In a later year, when an I.R.C. Section 754 election was in effect, Quentin contributed his interest in QRS to the Inco LLC (in an nontaxable I.R.C. Section 721 transaction) in exchange for an interest in that limited liability company.

At the time of the transfer:

(a)   Quentin's basis for his interest in QRS is $20,433.

(b)   Inco's balance shows:

Assets	Basis	Fair market value
Cash	$5,000	$5,000
Accounts receivable	10,000	10,000
Inventory	20,000	21,000
Nondepreciable capital asset	20,000	40,000
Total	$55,000	$76,000
Liabilities and Capital	(As per partner-ship books)	
Liabilities	$10,000	$10,000
Capital		
Apco	15,000	22,000
Bilco	15,000	22,000
Catco	15,000	22,000
Total	$55,000	$76,000

Following the transfer, Inco's basis for its interest in QRS is $20,433 (the same as Quentin's basis for the interest pursuant to I.R.C. Section 723). (Quentin's basis for his interest in Inco also is $20,433 pursuant to I.R.C. Section 722).

Inco's share of the basis of QRS's property is $18,333 — ($15,000 share of QRS's previously taxed capital [$22,000 cash Inco would receive if QRS sold all its assets and liquidated, minus $7,000 of tax gain that would be allocated to Inco from the hypothetical sale] plus $3,333 share of QRS's liabilities). Accordingly, the I.R.C. Section 743(b) basis adjustment to QRS's property for Inco is $2,100-$20,433 basis for Inco's interest in QRS minus Inco's $18,333 share of the basis of QRS's property.

The gain that would be allocated to Inco from a hypothetical sale of QRS's capital gain property is $6,666.67 (one-third of $20,000 gain). The gain that would be allocated to Inco from a sale of QRS's ordinary income property is $333.33 (one-third of $1,000 gain).

QRS must allocate $2,000 ($6,666.67 divided by $7,000 times $2,100) of Inco's total basis increase to the capital asset and $100 ($333.33 divided by $7,000 times $2,100) of the basis increase to its inventory.

[G]   Contribution of Basis Adjusted Property to a Partnership or Corporation

Contribution to a partnership. Special rules apply when a partnership (upper tier) contributes property subject to a basis adjustment for a partner to another partnership (lower tier).[215] These rules are summarized as follows:

(1)   The lower tier's basis in the contributed property and the upper tier's basis in the partnership interest it receives must include the basis adjustment regardless of whether the lower-tier makes an I.R.C. Section 754 election.

(2)   The portion of the upper tier's basis for its interest in the lower tier attributable to the basis adjustment is segregated and allocated solely to the partner for whom the basis adjustment was made.

(3)   The portion of the lower tier's basis in its assets attributable to the basis adjustment is segregated and allocated solely to the upper tier and the relevant partner.

(4)   If a partnership termination occurs under I.R.C. Section 708(b)(1)(B) (sale of 50 percent of partnership interests within 12 months), a partner with a basis adjustment in the terminating partnership's property has the same basis adjustment for property deemed contributed to by the resulting new partnership, regardless of whether the new partnership makes an I.R.C. Section 754 election.[216]

Contribution to a corporation. If a partnership contributes property to a corporation in a transaction under I.R.C. Section 351, the corporation's basis includes any I.R.C. Section 743(b) basis adjustments to the property.[217] However, in determining the amount of any gain the partnership recognizes on the transfer, the basis adjustments are not taken into account. The basis adjustments are taken into account in determining the amount of partnership gain allocated to a partner with a basis adjustment in the transferred property.

The partnership's basis in the stock received from the corporation is determined without reference to basis adjustments for the contributed property. However, a partner with a basis adjustment for property transferred to the corporation has a basis adjustment for the stock received by the partnership equal to the partner's basis adjustment in the transferred property, reduced by any basis adjustment that reduced the partner's gain (as described in the preceding paragraph).

Example: [218] Kevin, Laura, and Mary are equal partners in the KLM Partnership. KLM's sole asset (Asset 1) is a nondepreciable capital asset worth $120, with a basis of $60. Kevin's basis in his partnership interest is $40, and he has a positive I.R.C. Section 743(b) adjustment of $20 in Asset

---

[215] Treas. Reg. § 1.743-1(h)(1). These rules apply to contributions in which gain or loss is not recognized under I.R.C. Section 721(a).

[216] The termination rules are found in Treas. Reg. § 1.708-1(b)(1)(iv).

[217] Treas. Reg. § 1.743-1(h)(2).

[218] Treas. Reg. § 1.743-1(h)(2)(iv).

1. KLM contributes Asset 1 to Xyco Corporation in exchange for $15 in cash and Xyco stock worth $105.

Although KLM realizes $60 of gain on the transfer of Asset 1 to Xyco ($120 amount realized, minus $60 basis), only $15 of gain is recognized under I.R.C. Section 351(b)(1). Each partner is allocated $5 of the gain. Kevin must use $5 of his basis adjustment in Asset 1 to offset his share of KLM's gain.

KLM's basis in the Xyco stock received $60. However, Kevin's basis adjustment for the stock is $15 (his $20 basis adjustment in Asset 1, reduced by the $5 portion of the adjustment that reduced his gain). Xyco's basis in Asset 1 is $75 (KLM's $60 basis, plus Kevin's $20 I.R.C. Section 743(b) basis adjustment minus the $5 portion of the adjustment that reduced Kevin's gain).

[H] Allocations to Goodwill

I.R.C. Section 1060 provides rules governing the portion of the purchase price for an interest in a business that must be allocated to goodwill and going concern value. These rules apply to any "applicable asset acquisition" which occurs:

(1)   if the sale involves a transfer of assets constituting a trade or business;[219] and

(2)   if the purchaser determines his basis in the assets wholly from the consideration paid for them. The basis requirement is satisfied if the purchaser's basis in his proportionate share of partnership's assets is adjusted under I.R.C. Sections 743(b) or 732(d) to reflect the purchase price. Consequently, the purchaser of an interest in a partnership that has goodwill or going-concern value must allocate a portion of his I.R.C. Section 743(b) basis adjustment to those items, even if these assets are not recorded on the partnership's books.

The allocation is made pursuant to the "residual method" under which the amount of the purchase price that exceeds the value of specified business assets in allocated to goodwill and similar items subject to amortization under I.R.C. Section 197.[220] The allocation is made only to determine the value of the "Section 197 intangibles" for purposes of applying the basis adjustment pursuant to I.R.C. Section 755.[221]

Temporary regulations have been issued to coordinate I.R.C. Section 1060 with the basis-allocation rules of I.R.C. Section 755.[222] The effect of the regulations is to

---

[219] In the preamble to proposed regulations issued in April, 2000, the Treasury Department states that it anticipates that the final regulations under Treas. Reg. § 1.755-2 will apply to *all* transfers of partnership interests and partnership distributions, not just transactions relating to partnerships conducting a trade or business. 65 Fed. Reg. 17829 (Apr. 5, 2000).

[220] I.R.C. § 1060(a).

[221] I.R.C. § 1060(d)(1). If I.R.C. § 755 applies, the purchase is subject to reporting requirements under I.R.C. § 1060(b). I.R.C. § 1060(d)(2).

[222] Temp. Treas. Reg. § 1.755-2T(d). These rules also should apply to § 197 intangibles. See *infra*.

ensure that the basis allocated to any asset under I.R.C. Section 755 does not exceed the difference between the value and basis of the property. The regulations provide the following "residual method" for determining the value of partnership goodwill:[223]

(1) *The value of all partnership property other than goodwill or going-concern value is determined from all the facts and circumstances.* [224]

(2) *The value of partnership goodwill or going-concern value is deemed to be the amount which, if added to the net value of all other partnership property (i.e., after payment of all partnership liabilities), would equal the amount needed to liquidate the purchaser's partnership interest.* [225] In computing this amount, the partnership is deemed to sell all of its assets at current value, pay all of its liabilities, and completely liquidate all of its partners' interests. This class includes goodwill and similar items subject to amortization under I.R.C. Section 197.[226]

Example: Leo purchases Karen's one-third interest in the IJK partnership for $1.2 million. Immediately before the sale, the partnership's books reflect the following assets:

Assets	Basis	value
Section 1231(b) Asset	$1,200,000	$1,800,000
Inventory	600,000	1,200,000
Total Assets	$1,800,000	$3,000,000

The value of the partnership's goodwill is deemed to be the amount needed, in addition to the partnership's other assets, for the partnership to distribute $1.2 million to Leo in a complete liquidation of all the partner's interests immediately after Leo acquires his interest. Leo is a one-third partner, and he can receive a $1.2 million liquidating distribution only if the partnership could sell all of its property, including goodwill, for $3.6 million. Because the other partnership property is worth $3 million, partnership goodwill is assigned a $600,000 value. Consequently, $200,000 of the amount that Leo paid for his partnership interest is deemed to be for his share of goodwill.

CAUTION:

Proposed regulations issued in April, 2000, would replace the temporary regulations described above and provide new rules to coordinate the application of the residual method for valuing goodwill under I.R.C. Section 1060 with the rules for allocating basis adjustments to items of partnership

---

[223] Temp. Treas. Reg. § 1.755-2T(a)(2).

[224] Temp. Treas. Reg. § 1.755-2T(b)(1).

[225] *See* Temp. Treas. Reg. § 1.755-2T(b)(2). *See* Prop. Treas. Reg. § 1.755-1(c)(5).

[226] Temp. Treas. Reg. § 1.1060-1T; T.D. 8711 (Jan. 16, 1997), *corrected* 1997-20 I.R.B. 8.

property under I.R.C. Section 755.[227] These rules would apply to basis adjustments under I.R.C. Section 743(b) (relating to purchased partnership interests) and I.R.C. Section 732(d) (relating to distributions following the purchase of a partnership interest).[228]

Under the proposed regulations, allocating basis adjustments among partnership assets requires two steps:

1. *Partnership gross value* is determined.

2. *Partnership gross value* is allocated among partnership property.

Generally, partnership gross value equals the amount that, if assigned to all partnership property, would result in a liquidating distribution to the purchasing partner equal to the basis for his partnership interest immediately following the purchase (reduced by any basis that is attributable to partnership liabilities).[229] In effect, the value of the interest is determined by reference to the purchase price.[230]

After partnership gross value is determined,[231] that amount is allocated among five classes of property in the following order:[232]

(1)   To cash;[233]

(2)   To partnership ordinary income property (*i.e.*, noncash partnership assets other than capital assets, I.R.C. Section 1231(b) property, and Section 197 intangibles);

(3)   To capital assets and I.R.C. Section 1231(b) property other than Section 197 intangibles;

(4)   To Section 197 intangibles other than goodwill and going concern value;

---

[227] Prop. Treas. Reg. § 1.755-2(a)(1). The proposed regulations would apply to any basis adjustment occurring on or after the date final regulations are published in the Federal Register. Prop. Treas. Reg. § 1.755-2(f).

[228] Prop. Treas. Reg. § 1.755-2(a)(2). For discussion of I.R.C. § 732(d), see § 12.09, *infra*.

[229] Prop. Treas. Reg. § 1.755-2(c). If a partnership interest is transferred because of a partner's death, the transferee's basis is determined without regard to I.R.C. § 1014(c) (relating to income in respect of a decedent), and is deemed to be adjusted for any portion of the interest attributable income in respect of a decedent's items under I.R.C. § 691.

[230] The proposed regulations do not provide any guidance about valuation when the transferee partner's basis is determined in whole or part from the transferor's basis (a transferred basis exchange).

[231] The proposed regulations provide a special rule for determining partnership gross value where book income or loss from particular partnership assets is allocated differently among partners. Prop. Treas. Reg. § 1.755-2(b)(2).

[232] If partnership gross value exceeds the aggregate value of the partnership's individual assets, the excess must be allocated entirely to goodwill. If, however, goodwill could not possibly attach to the assets (*e.g.*, the partnership's only asset is vacant real estate that does not produce current income), the excess partnership gross value is allocated among all partnership assets other than cash in proportion to their fair market values. Prop. Treas. Reg. § 1.755-2(b)(2).

[233] This includes general deposit accounts (including savings and checking accounts) other than certificates of deposit held in banks, savings and loan associations, and other depository institutions. Prop. Treas. Reg. § 1.755-2(b).

(5)   To goodwill and going concern value.

Recapture income treated as unrealized receivables. Potential recapture (considered an unrealized receivable under I.R.C. Section 751(c)) that is included in the value of assets in classes (3), (4) and (5) is not counted as ordinary income property in class (2). For example, goodwill that would result in ordinary income under I.R.C. Section 1245 if sold would be included in the residual class for goodwill. The recapture amounts are treated as separate items of ordinary income property for purposes of allocating basis adjustments.[234] If the value assigned to a class is less than the total values of the assets in that class, the assigned value is allocated among the individual assets in proportion to their fair market values. Values assigned to classes (3), (4), and (5) are first allocated to properties or potential gain treated as unrealized receivables under I.R.C. Section 751(c) in proportion to the income that would be recognized if the assets were sold at their fair market values. Any remaining value in each class is allocated among the remaining assets in that class in proportion to their fair market values.

[I]   Computing Tax Consequences of I.R.C. Section 743(b) Basis Adjustment

A basis adjustment under I.R.C. Section 743(b) affects only the tax consequences of the transferee partner who acquired his partnership interest by sale or exchange or as successor to a deceased partner.[235] The transferee obtains a special basis for the partnership assets to which adjustments have been allocated and his distributive share of partnership income, deduction, gain, and loss is determined by reference to the special basis. An I.R.C. Section 743(b) adjustment does not change the common basis of partnership property and does not affect the partnership's computation of any tax item or any other partner's distributive share of partnership income or loss.

The effect of the special basis adjustment on the transferee partner's distributive share is determined as follows:[236]

(1)   The partnership computes its tax items of income, deduction, gain, or loss.

(2)   Each partner, including the transferee, is allocated his distributive share of these items in accordance with the rules of I.R.C. Sections 704 and the partners' capital accounts are adjusted accordingly.

(3)   The partnership adjusts the transferee's distributive share of partnership tax items to reflect the effects of the special basis adjustment (as described below).

(4)   The adjustments to the transferee's distributive share are reflected on the partnership's Schedules K and K-1.

---

[234]   Prop. Treas. Reg. § 1.755-2(b)(i)(1)(B).

[235]   Treas. Reg. § 1.743-1(j)(1).

[236]   Treas. Reg. § 1.743-1(j)(2).

(5)   The adjustments to the transferee's distributive share do not affect his capital account.

[1]   Effect of Basis Adjustment on Partner's Income, Gain, or Loss

A partner's income, gain, or loss from the sale or exchange of a partnership asset in which he has a basis adjustment equals the partner's distributive share of the partnership's gain or loss from the sale[237]

(1)   minus, the partner's positive basis adjustment for the asset, or

(2)   plus, the partner's negative basis adjustment for the asset.[238]

Example (1): For equal interests in the BC Partnership, Bill contributes nondepreciable property worth $50 with a basis of $100 and Carla contributes $50 in cash. Bill sells his interest to Don for $50 when the partnership has an I.R.C. Section 754 election in effect. Don's $50 negative basis adjustment under I.R.C. Section 743(b) is allocated to the nondepreciable property.

If BC sells the property for $60, the partnership recognizes a book gain of $10 (allocated equally between Don and Carla) and a $40 tax loss. Don is allocated the entire $40 tax loss (under I.R.C. Section 704(c))[239] which is increased by Don's negative $50 basis adjustment for the asset that was sold. The net result is that Don recognizes a $10 tax gain ([- $40] + $50) from the partnership's sale of the property.

Example (2): Assume that the land was worth $100 and had a $50 basis when contributed and Bill sells his interest to Don for $100.

Don's positive $50 basis adjustment is allocated to the nondepreciable property. If BC sells the property for $90, the partnership recognizes a book loss of $10 (allocated equally between Don and Carla) and a $40 tax gain. Don is allocated the entire $40 tax gain (under I.R.C. Section 704(c)), which is decreased by his positive $50 basis adjustment for the asset that was sold. Don recognizes a $10 loss ($40 - $50) from the partnership's sale of the property.

[2]   Effect of Basis Adjustment on Partner's Cost Recovery, Amortization and Depletion Deductions

Cost recovery of positive basis adjustmentst. In computing the effect of a partner's positive I.R.C. Section 743(b) adjustment on his cost recovery deductions, the following rules apply:

(1)   The portion of a positive basis adjustment recovered in a year is added to

---

[237] This includes any remedial allocations under Treas. Reg. § 1.704-3(d).

[238] Treas. Reg. § 1.743-1(j)(3).

[239] When a partner who contributed property with built-in gain or loss transfers his partnership interest, the built-in gain or loss is allocated to the transferee partner as it would have been to the transferor. Treas. Reg. § 1.704-3(a)(7).

the transferee partner's distributive share of the partnership's depreciation or amortization deductions for the year.

(2) The partner's I.R.C. Section 743(b) basis adjustment decreases by the amount of basis adjustment recovered each year.[240]

(3) Generally, cost recovery and similar deductions attributable to a positive I.R.C. Section 743(b) basis adjustment are recovered as if the adjustment is an item of newly-purchased recovery property placed in service when the transferee partner acquired his partnership interest.[241] Any recovery period and method may be used to determine the cost recovery deduction for the increased portion of the basis. The recovery period and method for the remaining basis does not change.

(4) Special rules apply to deductions from contributed property subject I.R.C. Section 704(c) for which the partnership uses the remedial allocation method.[242] For such property, positive basis adjustments attributable to built-in gain are recovered over the remaining recovery period for the partnership's "excess book basis" in the property.[243] Any remaining basis adjustment is recovered as newly purchased property described in paragraph (3).

A partnership may use the remedial allocation method for contributed property if the "ceiling rule" causes the book allocations to a noncontributing partner from the property to differ from the partner's corresponding tax allocation.[244] The ceiling rule provides that the amount of any tax item allocated to a partner cannot exceed the amount of that item the partnership realizes for tax purposes. This limitation may cause the amount of income, gain, loss, or deduction allocated to a partner for tax purposes to differ from the amount reflected in the partner's capital account. In that case, the partnership can eliminate the disparity between book and tax items through (1) a remedial allocation to the noncontributing partner of the appropriate amount and kind of income, deduction, loss, or gain and (2) a simultaneous offsetting remedial allocation to the contributing partner. In effect, the remedial allocation method eliminates ceiling rule distortions by creating "notional" tax items that are allocated among the partners. Although these notional items shift tax items among the partners, they do not affect their book capital accounts, or change partnership taxable income, or the basis of partnership property.

To apply the remedial allocation method, depreciation for a contributed property is computed as if two separate assets are involved:

(1) A portion of the property's book value equal to its tax basis is recovered in the same manner and amount as allowed for tax purposes (*i.e.*, over the property's remaining depreciation period). This depreciation is allocated among the partners using the traditional method.

---

[240] Treas. Reg. § 1.743-1(j)(4). *See* I.R.C. § 1013(a)(2).

[241] Treas. Reg. § 1.743-1(j)(4)(i)(B)(1).

[242] The rules for applying the remedial method are set forth in Treas. Reg. § 1.704-3(d)(1).

[243] Treas. Reg. § 1.743-1(j)(4)(i)(B)(2).

[244] *See* Treas. Reg. § 1.704-3(d).

(2)   The remaining book value (the excess of the property's book over tax basis — "excess book value") is recovered using any depreciation method and recovery period that would be allowed if the partnership purchased the property on the contribution date.

For complete discussion and examples, see Chapter 6.

Example: For equal interests in the LM Partnership, Lew contributes Asset X worth $500,000 with a basis of $100,000, and Mary contributes $500,000 cash. When contributed, Asset X had five years remaining in its recovery period, allowing the LM to recover its $100,000 basis over that five year period. If LM had purchased Asset X, its recovery period would have been 10 years.

As a result of the contribution, $400,000 of built-in gain must be allocated under the rules of I.R.C. Section 704(c). LM elects to use the remedial allocation method for Asset X. Under that method, the $400,000 of built-in gain is treated as a separate asset amortized over a 10-year period beginning at the time of the contribution.

Book depreciation is $60,000 ($30,000 to each partner) in each of the first five years ($100,000/5 plus $400,000/10) and $40,000 for the next five years ($400,000/10). To allow Mary's tax depreciation to equal her book depreciation, the remedial method creates and allocates a $10,000 deduction for Mary each year that is offset by a $10,000 income item created and allocated to Lew.

If LM's income and expenses other than depreciation are equal, the partner's capital accounts (and shares of the basis of partnership property) after two years will be:

| | | Capital accounts | | |
| | | Lew | | Mary |
	Tax	Book	Tax	Book
Initial Contribution	$500,000	$100,000	$500,000	$500,000
Depreciation Year 1	(30,000)		(30,000)	(20,000)
Remedial		10,000		(10,000)
	470,000	110,000	470,000	470,000
Depreciation Year 2	(30,000)		(30,000)	(20,000)
Remedial		10,000		(10,000)
	440,000	120,000	440,000	440,000

At this time, Lew sells his interest to Nate for $440,000, when an I.R.C. Section 754 election is in effect. The resulting positive I.R.C. Section 743(b) adjustment for Nate is $320,000 ($440,000 cost basis minus $120,000 share of basis of partnership property). Under I.R.C. Section 755, the entire basis adjustment is allocated to the property contributed by Lew.

The amount of remaining "excess book value" to be amortized is $320,000 ($400,000 minus $80,000 recovered over prior two years). Since Nate's entire basis adjustment is attributable to that excess book value, he will recover the basis adjustment over the remaining 8 years of its initial 10 year recovery period.

Cost recovery of negative basis adjustments. In computing the effect of a partner's negative I.R.C. Section 743(b) adjustment on his cost recovery deductions, the following rules apply:

(1)   The portion of a negative basis adjustment for an asset that is recovered in a year first decreases the transferee partner's distributive share of partnership depreciation or amortization deductions from that asset for the year.[245]

(2)   If the negative basis adjustment recovered in a year exceeds the transferee partner's share of partnership deductions from the asset, the transferee partner reduces his share of recovery deductions from other partnership property. If the recovered negative basis adjustment exceeds the partner's share of all other partnership cost recovery deductions, the partner recognizes ordinary income equal to the excess amount.

(3)   A negative I.R.C. Section 743(b) basis adjustment is recovered over the remaining useful life of the partnership property to which the adjustment applies.[246] The portion of the decrease recovered in any year equals the product of:

(a)   The decrease to the asset's basis, multiplied by

(b)   A fraction, having a numerator equal to the portion of the asset's basis the partnership recovers that year, and a denominator equal to the partnership's basis for the asset on the date the partner acquired his interest (before any basis adjustments).

Example: For equal interests in the NO Partnership, Nigel contributes Asset Y worth $50,000 with a basis of $100,000 and Oliver contributes $50,000 cash. When contributed, Asset Y has five years remaining in its recovery period, allowing the partnership to recover its $100,000 over that five year period. As a result of the contribution, $50,000 of built-in loss must be allocated under the rules of I.R.C. Section 704(c). NO uses the traditional allocation method for the property. Under that method, Oliver is allocated $5,000 of depreciation deductions from the property in each of years 1-5, and Nigel, as contributing partner, is allocated $15,000 of depreciation deductions in each of these years.

In each of the next two years, NO's income and expenses, other than depreciation, are equal. At the end of the second year, Nigel's share of the basis of partnership property is $70,000 ($110,000 - $30,000) and Oliver's is $40,000 ($50,000 - $10,000). At this time, Nigel sells his interest to Paula for $40,000, when an I.R.C. Section 754 election is in effect; this results in a $30,000 negative I.R.C. Section 743(b) basis adjustment ($40,000 cost basis

---

[245]   Treas. Reg. § 1.743-1(j)(4)(ii)(A).
[246]   Treas. Reg. § 1.743-1(j)(4)(ii)(B).

minus $70,000 share of basis of partnership property), which is allocated to Asset Y.

When Paula acquires her interest, the partnership's basis in Asset Y is $60,000 ($100,000 initial basis minus $40,000 cost recovery). Because the partnership will recover its remaining basis over the next three years ($20,000 each year), Paula's $30,000 negative basis adjustment also is recovered over the next three years ($10,000 each year). Consequently, Paula's depreciation deduction from the partnership each year is $15,000 (the same as Nigel(s), and she will recover $10,000 of her negative basis adjustment each year. Thus, Paula's net depreciation deduction from the partnership is $5,000 in each of the next three years.

Depletion. If an I.R.C. Section 743(b) basis adjustment is made to depletable property, depletion allowances are determined separately for each partner, including the transferee, based on the each partner's interest in the property.[247] If the partnership's oil and gas properties are depleted at the partner level under I.R.C. Section 613A(c)(7)(D), the transferee partner (not the partnership) makes the I.R.C. Section 743(b) adjustment to the properties.[248]

[J]   Distributing Property for Which I.R.C. Section 743(b) Adjustment Has Been Made

A partner may receive a distribution of partnership property for which an I.R.C. Section 743(b) basis adjustment has been made. The following rules apply in determining the distributee partner's basis in the distributed property:

(1) *If the basis adjustment was made for the same partner who receives the distribution, the adjustment is taken into account in determining his basis in the property.* [249]

(2) *When property for which one partner has a special basis adjustment is distributed to other partners, the distributees do not take the adjustment into account in determining their basis in the property.* [250] Instead, the partner entitled to the special basis adjustment reallocates it to other partnership property of the same class.[251] The reallocation is subject to the same I.R.C. Section 755 rules as an original allocation.

(3) *The basis of property a partner receives in a liquidating distribution includes any basis adjustments for other partnership property in which the partner relinquished an interest (either because it remained in the partnership or was distributed to another partner).* [252] The basis adjustment attributable to the relinquished property is

---

[247]   Treas. Reg. § 1.743-1(j)(5). *See* Treas. Reg. § 1.702-1(a)(8).

[248]   *See* Treas. Reg. § 1.613A-3(e)(6)(iv).

[249]   Treas. Reg. §§ 1.732-2(b), 1.743-1(g)(1).

[250]   Treas. Reg. §§ 1.732-2(b), 1.743-1(g)(2)(i).

[251]   Treas. Reg. §§ 1.732-2(b), 1.743-1(g)(2)(ii).

[252]   Treas. Reg. § 1.743-1(g)(3).

reallocated among the properties distributed to the partner under the regulations governing basis adjustments for distributions.[253] *See* § 8.07, *supra.* Generally, these regulations (under I.R.C. Section 734(b)) require such adjustments to be allocated to property of similar character to the property for which the adjustment arose.

Example: [254] For equal interests in the Parco Limited Liability Company, Paul, Rachel, and Steve each contributed $10,000 in cash, and Parco used the contributions to purchase five nondepreciable capital assets. Parco has no liabilities. After five years, Parco's balance sheet appears as follows:

Assets	Basis	Fair market value
Asset 1	$10,000(	$10,000
Asset 2	4,000	6,000
Asset 3	6,000	6,000
Asset 4	7,000	4,000
Asset 5	3,000	13,000
Total	30,000	39,000

Partner's Capital	Basis	Fair market value
Paul	$10,000	$13,000
Rachel	10,000	13,000
Steve	10,000	13,000
Total	30,000	39,000

Paul sells his interest to Toni for $13,000 when Parco has an I.R.C. Section 754 election in effect. Toni's basis adjustment to LLC property under I.R.C. Section 743(b) is $3,000 ($13,000 basis for Toni's LLC interest minus her $10,000 share of the basis of partnership property). After allocating the adjustment to LLC property (under the rules of I.R.C. Section 755), Parco's balance sheet appears as follows:

---

[253] These allocation rules are set forth in Treas. Reg. § 1.755-1(c).
[254] Treas. Reg. § 1.743(g)(5).

Assets	Basis	Fair market value	Basis adjustment
Asset 1	$10,000	$10,000	$0.00
Asset 2	4,000	6,000	666.67
Asset 3	6,000	6,000	0.00
Asset 4	7,000	4,000	(1,000.00)
Asset 5	3,000	13,000	3,333.33
Total	30,000	39,000	3,000.00

Partner's Capital			Special basis
Toni	$10,000	$13,000	$3,000
Rachel	10,000	13,000	0
Steve	10,000	13,000	0
Total	30,000	39,000	3,000

(a)   If Parco distributes Asset 2 to Toni, she takes her $666.67 basis adjustment into account in determining her basis in the distributed asset. Therefore, Toni's basis in Asset 2 is $4,666.67.

(b)   If Parco distributes Asset 5 to Steve in complete liquidation of his LLC interest, Steve does not take Toni's basis adjustment into account in determining his basis for the distributed asset. Instead, Toni's $3,333.33 basis adjustment for Asset 5 is reallocated among the remaining partnership assets.

(c)   If Parco distributes Asset 5 to Toni in complete liquidation of her LLC interest, Parco's basis for Asset 5 immediately before the distribution is adjusted to take into account Toni's basis adjustments for property she is relinquishing (i.e., Assets 1,2,3, and 4). Thus, Parco's basis in Asset 5 is deemed to be $6,000 — the sum of:

$3,000.00	Parco's common basis in Asset 5, plus
$3,333.33	Toni's basis adjustment to Asset 5, plus
($333.33)	Toni's net basis adjustments in Assets 2 and 4.

[K]   Sale of Partnership Interests Between Members of Affiliated Group of Corporations

An affiliated group of corporations that files a consolidated tax return generally does not recognize gain or loss on a sale of property between group members (i.e., a "deferred intercompany sale"). Instead, the group recognizes the gain or loss when it subsequently disposes of the property.[255] If the intercompany sale increases the basis of depreciable, depletable, or amortizable property, however, the selling group member recognizes gain to the extent that the buying group

---

[255] Treas. Reg. § 1.1502-13(c)(1)(i).

member claims increased deductions for the assets.[256] This rule is designed to preclude the group from obtaining the double tax benefits of deferred gain and increased depreciation deductions.

The Service applies a similar approach when a deferred intercompany sale of a partnership interest results in an increased basis for the partnership's assets pursuant to an I.R.C. Section 743(b) basis adjustment. The Service has ruled that the intercompany sale has the following consequences:[257]

(1)   The selling group member recognizes the deferred gain or loss from the intercompany sale when the purchasing group member claims cost-recovery deductions attributable to the basis adjustment.

(2)   The selling group member also recognizes deferred gain or loss for the partnership's installment obligations and property subject to amortization or depletion.

(3)   If the partnership sells appreciated assets after the deferred intercompany sale, the selling group member recognizes the balance of the deferred gain to the extent of the purchasing group member's I.R.C. Section 743(b) adjustment.

(4)   If the purchasing group member disposes of the partnership interest, the selling group member recognizes the balance of the deferred gain.

[L]   Transfer Terminating a Partnership

A partnership terminates for tax purposes if 50 percent or more of the interests in its capital and profits are sold or exchanged within a 12-month period, according to I.R.C. Section 708(b). If a partnership terminates by a sale or exchange of an interest, the following is deemed to occur:[258]

(1)   the partnership contributes all of its assets and liabilities to a new partnership in exchange for an interest in the new partnership; and

(2)   immediately thereafter, the terminated partnership makes a liquidating distribution of interests in the new partnership to the purchasing partner and other remaining partners in proportion to their interests in the terminated partnership.

(See Chapter 13 for discussion of partnership terminations.)

If the terminated partnership has an I.R.C. Section 754 election in effect (including an election made on the terminated partnership's final return), the bases of partnership assets are adjusted under I.R.C. Sections 743 and 755 before their

---

[256] *Id.*

[257] Rev. Rul. 89-85, 1989-2 C.B. 218.

[258] Treas. Reg. § 1.708-1(b)(1)(iv). This rule applies to terminations occurring on or after May 9, 1997. Before that date, the following was deemed to occur: (1) the old partnership distributes all of its assets to the purchasing and continuing partners, and (2) these partners are deemed to contribute the same assets to a new partnership.

deemed contribution to the new partnership.[259]

PRACTICE NOTE:

If the old partnership has an I.R.C. Section 754 election in effect for the termination year, the basis of its assets are adjusted under I.R.C. Section 743(b) when the old partnership interests are deemed to be transferred. This adjustment is made before the old partnership is deemed to contribute its property to the new partnership. Consequently, the new adjusted basis carries over to the new partnership. The basis adjustment occurs before the old partnership terminates, but after the incoming partner acquires his partnership interest. Thus, the basis adjustment applies to the incoming partner and carries over for the assets he is deemed to contribute to the new partnership.

A partner having a special basis adjustment for partnership property continues to have that basis adjustment if the partnership terminates under I.R.C. Section 708(b)(1)(B); the adjustment carries over to the new partnership regardless of whether the new partnership makes an I.R.C. Section 754 election.[260]

A termination under I.R.C. Section 708(b) extinguishes the I.R.C. Section 754 election of the terminated partnership. If the new partnership wants an election to apply to future transfers and distributions, it must file a new election.

If the partnership does not have an I.R.C. Section 754 election in effect when it terminates, the purchaser's basis in the new partnership's property is determined under the general rules for partnership distributions. A partner who acquired his partnership interest within two years of the distribution, however, may elect under I.R.C. Section 732(d) to adjust the basis in the assets he receives as if the partnership had an I.R.C. Section 754 election in effect when he acquired his interest.[261] In some situations, the Service may require this treatment even if the partner does not make the election.[262]

Tiered partnerships. If the sale of an interest in an upper tier partnership terminates that partnership, the upper tier partnership is deemed to exchange its entire interest in the capital and profits of the lower tier partnership.[263] A sale or exchange of an interest in an upper tier partnership that does not terminate that partnership is not considered a sale of a proportionate share of the upper tier partnership's interest in the capital and profits of the lower tier partnership.[264]

---

[259] Treas. Reg. § 1.708-1(b)(1)(v). This rule applies to terminations on or after May 9, 1997.

[260] Treas. Reg. § 1.743-1(h). *See* Treas. Reg. § 1.708-1(b)(1)(iv).

[261] *See* G.C.M. 39502 (May 2, 1986).

[262] I.R.C. § 732(d).

[263] Treas. Reg. § 1.708-1(b)(1)(ii). Effective on or after May 9, 1997.

[264] *Id.*

[M]   Making and Reporting the I.R.C. Section 754 Election

A partnership makes an I.R.C. Section 754 election by filing a statement, signed by a partner, with its income tax return, filed in a timely manner, for the first year to which it wishes the election to apply.[265] Once made, the election applies to all transfers of partnership interests (subject to I.R.C. Section 743(b)) and all distributions (subject to I.R.C. Section 734(b)) in that tax year[266] and in all subsequent years, unless it is revoked with the permission of the Service.[267]

The regulations provide rules for reporting I.R.C. Section 743(b) basis adjustments and the related tax consequences. Generally, a partnership that makes an I.R.C. Section 743(b) basis adjustment must attach a statement to its return for the year of the transfer providing the transferee's name and taxpayer identification and showing how the adjustment was computed and allocated among partnership properties.[268] To ensure that the partnership has the sufficient information, the transferee partner must provide a written notice to the partnership that includes information about the acquisition transaction.[269]

§ 12.09   ADJUSTING BASIS OF PROPERTY DISTRIBUTED TO PURCHASING PARTNER: I.R.C. SECTION 732(d) ELECTION

A partner who acquires his partnership interest by sale or exchange, or as successor to a deceased partner when the partnership does not have an I.R.C. Section 754 election in effect, may elect to adjust the basis of property the partnership distributed to him within two years of the acquisition date under I.R.C. Section 732(d). The election permits the partner to determine his basis in the distributed property as if the partnership had an I.R.C. Section 754 election in effect when he acquired his partnership interest.[270] The adjustment is made under the rules of I.R.C. Section 743(b), but applies only at the time of the distribution and only to the property actually distributed. The distributee partner's basis is not reduced by depletion or depreciation that would have been allowed if the adjustment had been made when he actually acquired the interest.[271]

Differences between the I.R.C. Section 754 and I.R.C. Section 732(d) elections are:

    (1)   The I.R.C. Section 732(d) election applies only if a distribution occurs. The I.R.C. Section 754 election applies to any transfer or distribution.

    (2)   The I.R.C. Section 732(d) adjustment has tax consequences only after a

---

[265]   Treas. Reg. § 1.754-1(b)(1).

[266]   Jones v. U.S., 553 F.2d 667 (Ct. Cl. 1977).

[267]   Treas. Reg. § 1.754-1(a).

[268]   Treas. Reg. § 1.743-1(k)(1)(i).

[269]   Treas. Reg. § 1.743-1(k)(2)(i).

[270]   I.R.C. § 732(d).

[271]   Treas. Reg. § 1.732-1(d)(1)(iv).

distribution; the adjustment does not affect the depreciation allowed or allowable to a partner for the period before the distribution. The I.R.C. Section 754 election applies as soon as a partner purchases his interest.

(3)   The Section 732(d) election is allowed only for distributions within two years of a transfer. The Section 754 election applies to any distribution made when the election is in effect.

(4)   The purchasing partner alone makes the I.R.C. Section 732(d). The Section 754 election requires consent of the unaffected partners.

(5)   The Section 732(d) election is made separately for each distribution. The I.R.C. Section 754 election applies to all partnership property for all present or future partners.

Example: Maynard purchases a one-third interest in the KLM Partnership for $90,000. KLM, which does not have an I.R.C. Section 754 election in effect, has the following balance sheet:

Assets	Basis	value
Stock	$90,000	$120,000
Land	60,000	90,000
Inventory	30,000	60,000
Total Assets	$180,000	$270,000
Partners' Capital		
Maynard	$90,000	$90,000
Nora	60,000	90,000
Olive	60,000	90,000
Total Partners' Capital	$210,000	$270,000

One year later, MNO distributes stock worth $40,000 to Maynard. If Maynard does not elect under I.R.C. Section 732(d) to adjust the basis of the distributed property, his basis in the stock is $30,000, and he will realize a $10,000 capital gain if he sells the property for its current value. If Maynard makes the I.R.C. Section 732(d) election, his basis in the stock is determined as if the partnership had an I.R.C. Section 754 election in effect when he acquired his interest. Maynard would have had a $30,000 total special basis adjustment at that time, $10,000 of which would have been allocated to the stock. Therefore, the election increases his basis in the distributed property to $40,000, and he recognizes no gain or loss if he sells the stock for its current value.

The partner's basis adjustment is allocated, under I.R.C. Section 743(b), to property the partnership owned at the time he received his interest. If different property is distributed, the partner may apply the basis adjustments to property he receives of the same class (*e.g.*, stock in trade, trade or business assets, capital assets),[272] but in exchange for the distributed property, he must relinquish his

---

[272] Treas. Reg. § 1.743-1(b)(2)(ii). *See* Treas. Reg. § 1.743-1(g).

interest in property for which he would have a basis adjustment.[273] The like property may be property the partnership acquired after the partner acquired his interest,[274] or it may be partnership property that was not eligible for the adjustment at the time it was acquired.[275] A partner relinquishes his interest in partnership property when his partnership interest is liquidated or when the property is distributed to other partners.[276]

Example: Stan purchases a one-fourth interest in the QRST Partnership for $17,000. Immediately before the purchase, the partnership owns the following assets:

Assets	Basis	Fair market value
Cash	$10,000	$10,000
Capital Assets	40,000	42,000
Inventory	14,000	16,000
Total Assets	$64,000	$68,000

If an election were in effect, Stan would be allowed a $500 basis increase for his share of the inventory under I.R.C. Section 743(b). One year later, Stan withdraws from the partnership, receiving a liquidating distribution of:

(1) $1,500 in cash;

(2)   inventory the partnership acquired after Stan acquired his interest, with a basis to the partnership of $3,500; and

(3)   a capital asset with a basis to the partnership of $6,000.

If Stan elects under I.R.C. Section 732(d):

(1)   the $17,000 basis in his partnership interest decreases by the $1,500 cash he receives;

(2)   his basis in the inventory he receives is $4,000 ($3,500 partnership basis plus $500 special basis adjustment that would have occurred if I.R.C. Section 754 election was in effect); and

(3)   his basis in the capital asset is $11,500 (the remaining basis in his partnership interest).

[A]   Effect of Election on Disproportionate Distributions of I.R.C. Section 751 Property

A partner's I.R.C. Section 732(d) election applies in determining the tax consequences of a disproportionate distribution of I.R.C. Section 751 property.[277] Under I.R.C. Section 751, partnership property is divided into two classes: (1)

---

[273] Treas. Reg. § 1.732-1(d)(1)(v).

[274] Treas. Reg. § 1.732-1(d)(1)(vi).

[275] *See* Treas. Reg. § 1.743-1(b)(2)(ii). *See* Treas. Reg. § 1.743-1(g).

[276] *Id.*

[277] Treas. Reg. § 1.732-1(e).

unrealized receivables and substantially appreciated inventory, and (2) other property.

A distribution that increases a partner's proportionate share of one class of property in exchange for his interest in the other class is treated as if the partner:

(1)   received a current distribution of his proportionate share of both classes of property; and

(2)   sold or exchanged a portion of one class of property for the extra amount of the other class of property he actually received.

If the partner makes an I.R.C. Section 732(d) election for a disproportionate distribution, he may apply the adjustment in determining his basis in the property he is deemed to sell to or exchange with the partnership.[278] No basis adjustment is made, however, for the property actually distributed to him that he is deemed to acquire by purchase or exchange.[279]

[B]   Making the Election

If the distribution includes depreciable, depletable, or amortizable property, the partner must make the election with his tax return for the year in which the distribution is made.[280] If the distribution does not include depreciable, depletable, or amortizable property, the election must be made with the partner's return for the first tax year in which the basis of the distributed property must be known to compute his income tax.[281]

The election is made on a schedule attached to the return that states:[282]

(1)   that the partner elects to adjust the basis of property received in a distribution;

(2)   the properties to which the adjustment has been allocated; and

(3)   the computation of the basis adjustment for the distributed property.

[C]   Mandatory I.R.C. Section 732(d) Adjustments

Under specific circumstances, a partner who acquires any part of his interest by transfer may be required to determine his basis in distributed property under the rules of I.R.C. Section 732(d), regardless of when the distribution is made (i.e., the two-year limitation does not apply), if at the time the partner acquires his partnership interest:

(1)   the fair market value of all partnership property (other than money) exceeds 110 percent of its basis to the partnership;

---

[278] Id.

[279] Id.

[280] Treas. Reg. § 1.732-2(d)(2).

[281] Id.

[282] Treas. Reg. § 1.732-2(d)(3).

(2)　a hypothetical liquidation of the transferee-partner's interest immediately after the transfer would shift basis from property for which no depreciation, depletion, or amortization deduction is allowed to property for which these deductions are permitted; and

(3)　a basis adjustment at the time of the transfer would change the basis of the property actually distributed to the transferee partner.[283]

The mandatory basis-adjustment rules apply to current and liquidating distributions.[284]

NOTE:

Although the regulations suggest that the partner's basis adjustment is determined from a hypothetical liquidation of his interest immediately after he acquires it,[285] the example in the regulations computes the basis adjustments by reference to the value and basis of partnership property when the distribution occurs (*i.e.*, four years later in the example).[286] Under the facts of the example, however, the time at which the computation is made does not change the result.

Example: David purchases an interest in the ABC Partnership for $105,000. The partnership does not have an I.R.C. Section 754 election in effect at the time, and the fair market value of partnership assets exceeds 110 percent of their bases. At the time of purchase, ABC owns the following assets:

Assets	Basis	value
Land Parcel #1	$5,000	$55,000
Land Parcel #2	5,000	55,000
Land Parcel #3	5,000	55,000
Depreciable Equipment	150,000	150,000
Total Assets	$165,000	$315,000

Four years later, David receives a liquidating distribution of Land Parcel #1 and one-third of the depreciable equipment. At the time of the distribution, the partnership has taken $15,000 in depreciation deductions for the equipment, $5,000 of which has been allocated to David. The depreciation deductions reduce David's share of ABC's basis in the

---

[283] Treas. Reg. § 1.732-1(d)(4). Because the 1997 amendments to I.R.C. § 732(c) make the distortions targeted by the mandatory basis adjustment rule of I.R.C. § 732(d) less likely to occur, the Treasury is contemplating changing the scope of these rules. *See* Summary of Proposed Regulations, 63 Fed. Reg. 4408-01 (Jan. 28, 1998).

[284] Treas. Reg. § 1.732-1(d)(4), *Examples (1), (2)*.

[285] Treas. Reg. § 1.732-1(d)(4)(ii).

[286] Treas. Reg. § 1.732-1(d)(4), *Example (1)*.

equipment to $45,000 and reduce the basis of his partnership interest to $100,000.

If the mandatory basis adjustment did not apply, David's $100,000 basis in his partnership interest would be allocated among the distributed property as follows:

(1) $10,000 to Land Parcel #1: $100,000 × [$5,000 / ($5,000 + $45,000)]; and

(2) $90,000 to the depreciable equipment: $100,000 × [$45,000 / ($5,000 + $45,000)].

The distribution shifts part of the basis in David's partnership interest attributable to the appreciation in nondepreciable land to the depreciable equipment he receives.

Applying David's mandatory special basis adjustment, however, increases his basis in partnership land to $50,000 ($55,000 value when he acquired his interest - $5,000 share of partnership basis). Thus, his basis in the property distributed to him in the liquidation is allocated as follows:

(1) $55,000 to Land Parcel #1: $100,000 × ($55,000 / $100,000); and

(2) $45,000 to the depreciable equipment: $100,000 × ($45,000 / $100,000).

Chapter 13

TERMINATING A PARTNERSHIP OR LLC

§ 13.01 OVERVIEW OF EVENTS TERMINATING A PARTNERSHIP OR LLC

The date that a partnership or LLC terminates for tax purposes is governed solely by I.R.C. Section 708.[1] State laws concerning the dissolution or liquidation of a partnership do not control the tax consequences of related events or transactions.[2] For example, a partnership does not terminate for tax purposes when a general partner withdraws, even if the withdrawal dissolves the partnership under state law.[3] However, a partnership is terminated for tax purposes if 50 percent of its interests are sold within a 12-month period, even if the sale does not affect the partnership's status under state law.

I.R.C. Section 708(a) provides a general rule that a partnership is deemed to continue for tax purposes unless it is terminated by one of the events specified in I.R.C. Section 708(b), as follows:

(1) The partnership ceases carrying on any business, financial operation, or venture.[4]

(2) The partnership stops operating in the partnership form (*e.g.*, one partner of a two-member partnership purchases the other partner's interest and the partnership becomes a sole proprietorship).[5]

(3) Within a 12-month period, 50 percent or more of the total interests in partnership capital and profits are sold or exchanged.[6]

---

[1] [1] I.R.C. § 708(a).

[2] *See, e.g.*, Fensel v. U.S., 617 F. Supp. 22 (W.D. Pa. 1985), *aff'd*, 791 F.2d 916 (3d Cir. 1986) (two-member partnership continued even though one partner ceased acting as a partner and received no income from partnership); Fuchs v. Comm'r, 80 T.C. 506 (1983); Evans v. Comm'r, 54 T.C. 40 (1970), *aff'd*, 447 F.2d 547 (7th Cir. 1971) (partnership terminated for tax purposes even though not dissolved under state law).

[3] *See, e.g.*, Maxcy v. Comm'r, 59 T.C. 716 (1973), *nonacq.* 1975-2 C.B. 3 (partnership does not terminate when a partner dies); Rev. Rul. 66-325, 1966-2 C.B. 249 (same even if the deceased partner was member of two-member partnership).

[4] I.R.C. § 708(b)(1)(A).

[5] *Id.*

[6] I.R.C. § 708(b)(1)(B).

Any termination closes the partnership's taxable year for all partners on the termination date.[7]

When a termination is the result of the cessation of business or investment activity, it usually coincides with the actual liquidating distribution of partnership assets that occurs on the date the partnership winds up its affairs.[8] A partnership that converts to another business form generally terminates when it ceases all operations as a partnership. In both situations, the rules governing liquidations of partnership interests determine the main tax consequences for the partners. Ordinarily, a termination does not occur when a partnership converts to a limited liability company or vice versa because both entities are considered partnerships for tax purposes.[9]

A termination that results from a sale or exchange is deemed to occur on the date within a 12-month period that sales or exchanges of interests in partnership capital and profits total more than 50 percent.[10] On that date, the following events are deemed to occur:[11]

(1)   the partnership contributes all of its assets and liabilities to a new partnership in exchange for an interest in the new partnership; and,

(2)   the terminated partnership immediately distributes interests in the new partnership to the purchasing partner and the other remaining partners in proportion to their respective interests in the terminated partnership in liquidation of the terminated partnership.

The liquidation distribution may result in either the continuation of the terminated partnership's business by the new partnership or for its dissolution and winding up.

I.R.C. Section 708(b)(2) provides special rules governing the termination of partnerships that merge, consolidate, or divide. If two or more partnerships merge or consolidate, the resulting partnership is treated as a continuation of any merging or consolidating partnership whose members own more than 50 percent of the resulting partnership's capital and profits.[12] If a partnership divides into two or more partnerships, any resulting partnership is treated as a continuation of the original partnership if its members owned more than 50 percent of the capital and profits of the original partnership.[13]

---

[7] I.R.C. § 706(c)(1); Treas. Reg. § 1.708-1(b)(1)(iii), (iv).

[8] *See* Treas. Reg. § 1.708-1(b)(1)(iii), (iv).

[9] Rev. Rul. 95-37, 1995-1 C.B. 130. *See* Rev. Rul. 95-55, 1995-2 C.B. 313 (no termination when New York general partnership registers as a New York registered limited liability partnership).

[10] Treas. Reg. § 1.708-1(b)(1)(iii)(b).

[11] Treas. Reg. § 1.708-1(b)(1)(iv).

[12] I.R.C. § 708(b)(2)(A).

[13] I.R.C. § 708(b)(2)(B).

§ 13.02 CEASING PARTNERSHIP BUSINESS OR FINANCIAL ACTIVITIES

A partnership terminates for tax purposes when it ceases carrying on any business, financial operation, or venture.[14] If partners have agreed to discontinue the partnership's business, termination is deemed to occur on the date on which the partnership winds up its affairs and distributes all of its assets to its partners.[15] Thus, the partnership does not terminate when it stops its business operations; it continues until it completes its administrative activities (*e.g.*, converting property to cash, collecting receivables, and paying bills).

> **Example:** On April 30, DEF Partnership's three partners, Donna, Edward, and Fred, agree to dissolve the partnership and to carry on business through a winding-up period ending on September 30, at which time all partnership assets will be distributed. The partnership terminates on September 30.

Case law indicates that a partnership that stops operating its principal business does not terminate if it continues to carry on even minimal business or financial activities. For example, a partnership engaged in land development did not terminate when it ceased that activity but continued to hold land as investment property.[16] Similarly, a partnership that sold all of its assets did not terminate when it continued to hold promissory notes from the sale, collect interest, and make minor investments.[17]

§ 13.03 CHANGING BUSINESS FORM

A partnership terminates if it no longer carries on any activities in the form of a partnership,[18] such as when it converts into a corporation or into a sole proprietorship.[19] A termination does not occur when a partnership converts to a limited liability company or vice versa if both entities are considered partnerships for tax purposes.[20]

> **Example:** Arthur and Barbara are each 20 percent partners in the ABC Partnership, and Charles owns the remaining 60 percent. If Arthur and Barbara sell their interests to Charles on November 20, Year 1, the

---

[14] I.R.C. § 708(b)(1)(A); Treas. Reg. § 1.708-1(b)(1)(i).

[15] Treas. Reg. § 1.708-1(b)(1)(i). *See, e.g.,* Sargent v. Comm'r, T.C. Memo. 1970-214 (father-son partnership not terminated at end of year even though partners agreed to liquidate business at that time because winding up not completed until two months later).

[16] Ginsburg v. U.S., 396 F.2d 983 (Ct. Cl. 1968).

[17] Foxman v. Comm'r, 41 T.C. 535 (1964), *acq.* 1966-2 C.B. 4, *aff'd,* 352 F.2d 466 (3d Cir. 1965). *See* Baker Commodities, Inc. v. Comm'r, 48 T.C. 374 (1967), *aff'd,* 415 F.2d 519 (9th Cir. 1969), *cert. denied,* 397 U.S. 988 (1970) (partnership not terminated even though sole activity was holding promissory note from sale of its assets).

[18] I.R.C. § 708(b)(1)(A).

[19] Treas. Reg. § 1.708-1(b)(1)(i).

[20] Rev. Rul. 95-37, 1995-1 C.B. 130. *See* Rev. Rul. 95-55, 1995-2 C.B. 313 (no termination when New York general partnership registers as a New York registered limited liability partnership).

partnership terminates on that date,[21] because the partnership's business is no longer carried on by any of its partners in partnership form.

The partnership also terminates if Arthur's and Barbara's interests are liquidated in exchange for distributions from the partnership. However, unlike the immediate termination caused by a sale, Arthur and Barbara are considered partners until their final liquidating distribution occurs, and the partnership will not terminate until their interests are completely liquidated. A partnership's termination can be delayed if a withdrawing partner's interests are liquidated by a series of installment payments spanning a number of years.

The termination described in this example also will occur if ABC is a limited liability company rather than a partnership. Under the entity classification regulations, a one member LLC cannot be considered a partnership for tax purposes. Charles's one member LLC will be treated as a sole proprietorship unless it elects to be taxable as a corporation. (See Chapter 2 for discussion of classification rules.)

A partnership does not terminate if any of its members continue to carry on a portion of its business in partnership form.[22] In *Neubecker v. Commissioner*,[23] for example, a partnership formed by two attorneys who withdrew from a three-member law partnership was treated as a continuation of the initial partnership. Similarly, the Service ruled that a partnership with five equal members did not terminate when three of the members purchased all of the partnership's assets and continued its business as a new three-member partnership.[24]

[A] Changing to a Sole Proprietorship

A partnership terminates when it is converted into a sole proprietorship. This conversion is most likely to occur in a two-member partnership when one partner's entire partnership interest is sold to the other partner or the partnership completely liquidates one partner's interest.[25] A two-member partnership does not terminate, however, because one member stops engaging in partnership affairs.[26] In *Fensel v. United States*,[27] for example, a two-person partnership did not terminate even though one of the partners ceased acting as a partner and stopped receiving income from the partnership. The court concluded that the partner had not withdrawn from the partnership, even though he stopped functioning as a partner.

---

[21] Treas. Reg. § 1.708-1(b)(1)(i).

[22] I.R.C. § 708(b)(1(A).

[23] 65 T.C. 577 (1975).

[24] Rev. Rul. 66-264, 1966-2 C.B. 248. *See also* Priv. Ltr. Rul. 8302108.

[25] Treas. Reg. § 1.708-1(b)(1)(i).

[26] *See, e.g.*, Fuchs v. Comm'r, 80 T.C. 506 (1983) (partnership not terminated when one partner gave written notice of termination and moved out of state because the remaining partners continued partnership business and the withdrawing partner continued to report his receipts, as a partner, on his tax returns).

[27] 791 F.2d 916 (3d Cir. 1986), *aff'g* 617 F. Supp. 22 (W.D. Pa. 1985).

The general rule that a partnership terminates when only one partner remains is subject to two important exceptions that apply for tax purposes, even if the partnership ceases to exist under state law:[28]

(1) *A partnership does not terminate when a partner dies if the deceased partner's estate or other successor in interest continues to share in partnership profits and losses.*[29] This rule applies even if the estate or successor is not considered a partner under state law.[30] If the remaining partner purchases the deceased partner's interest, however, the partnership terminates on the date of the sale.[31] The date of sale is deemed to be the date of the partner's death, if a preexisting partnership agreement provides that the successor must sell the interest to the surviving partner (*see* Chapter 11).

(2) *A partnership does not terminate during the liquidation of a deceased or retired partner's interest.*[32] The partnership continues until the deceased or retired partner's entire interest is fully liquidated, even if it is operated by only one person.[33] This rule applies even if the existence of a one-person partnership is not recognized under state law.[34] (For discussion of I.R.C. Section 736 rules governing liquidating payments, see Chapter 10.)

PLANNING NOTE:

A two-member partnership can avoid termination when one partner withdraws by following relatively simple procedures:

(1) *The partnership can liquidate the withdrawing partner's interest rather than have the continuing member purchase the*

---

[28] Uniform Partnership Act § 6 defines a partnership as an association of two or more persons. Consequently, an entity with only one member cannot be a partnership under state law.

[29] Treas. Reg. § 1.708-1(b)(1)(i)(a).

[30] *See, e.g.,* Maxcy v. Comm'r, 59 T.C. 716 (1973), *nonacq.* 1975-2 C.B. 3 (partnership does not terminate when a partner dies); Rev. Rul. 66-325, 1966-2 C.B. 249 (same even if the deceased partner was member of two-member partnership); Panero v. Comm'r, 48 T.C. 147 (1967) (same, for death of sole general partner of a limited partnership); Requard v. Comm'r, T.C. Memo. 1966-141 (partnership does not terminate when it is formally dissolved in state court proceeding); Estate of Smith v. Comm'r, T.C. Memo. 1963-312 (no termination when a partner is adjudged incompetent by a state court). *See* U.P.A § 31; U.L.P.A. § 20; R.U.L.P.A. § 801.

[31] McCauslen v. Comm'r, 45 T.C. 588 (1966); Rev. Rul. 67-65, 1967-1 C.B. 168. *See also* Treas. Reg. § 1.706-1(c)(3)(iv).

[32] Treas. Reg. §§ 1.708-1(b)(1)(i)(b), 1.736-1(a).

[33] Treas. Reg. § 1.736-1(a).

[34] *See, e.g.,* Fensel v. U.S., 617 F. Supp. 22 (W.D. Pa. 1985), *aff'd,* 791 F.2d 916 (3d Cir. 1986) (two-member partnership continued even though one partner ceased acting as a partner and received no income from partnership); Fuchs v. Comm'r, 80 T.C. 506 (1983); Evans v. Comm'r, 54 T.C. 40 (1970), *aff'd,* 447 F.2d 547 (7th Cir. 1971) (partnership terminated for tax purposes even though not dissolved under state law.)

interest. To avoid a claim by the Service that he is purchasing the interest in his individual capacity, the continuing member should be able to establish that the payments to the retiring partner are liquidating payments made by the partnership. The partnership agreement should clearly provide for the liquidation of the withdrawing partner's interest, and it should describe the payments that are to be made. If possible, payments should be made from the partnership's bank account, and partnership books and records should be maintained. Partnership tax returns should continue to be filed. (See Chapter 10 for discussion of sale versus liquidation.)

(2) *The withdrawing partner can maintain a small interest in partnership profits or losses*. If only nominal amounts of money or property are distributed to the partner over an extended period of time, however, the Service may assert that the continuing interest is a sham and that the partnership terminated when the withdrawing partner's interest was substantially reduced.

[B]   Changing to a Corporation

A partnership terminates when it is converted into a corporation. In Revenue Ruling 84-11,[35] the Service ruled that the termination date depends on the form of the transaction used in the incorporation. The ruling describes methods for incorporating a partnership and the time of termination under each method:

(1) *Each partner contributes his partnership interest to the corporation in exchange for corporate stock.* The partnership terminates on the date the partners contribute their interests to the corporation, because at that time only one partner, the corporation, remains.

(2) *The partnership distributes all of its assets to liquidate the interests of all of its partners; the partners contribute the assets to the corporation in exchange for stock.* The partnership terminates on the date the liquidation of all of the interests occurs because, at that time, no partners remain.

(3) *The partnership contributes all of its assets to the corporation in exchange for stock; the partnership distributes the stock to the partners in liquidation of their interests.* The partnership terminates on the date the partnership makes the liquidating distribution of the stock. A partnership that converts to (or elects to be taxed as) a corporation is treated as if it contributed all its property to a newly formed corporation in a transaction that is nontaxable under I.R.C. Section 351. Generally, the corporate transferee's basis in the property deemed transferred to it by the partnership is the same as the partnership's basis in the property. Under the regulations, a corporate transferee's basis in property

---

[35] 1984-2 C.B. 88, *rev'g* Rev. Rul. 70-239, 1970-1 C.B. 74.

transferred by a partnership in an I.R.C. Section 351 transfer includes any special basis adjustment under I.R.C. Section 743.[36] Any gain the partnership may recognize as a result of the deemed transfer of its property to the association is determined without reference to any special basis adjustment. However, the partner with the special basis adjustment can use the special basis adjustment to reduce its share of gain the partnership recognizes.[37] The special basis adjustment is also taken into account in determining the partner's basis in the stock received in the exchange.[38] (For discussion about contributing a partnership interest to a corporation, see §§ 12.06, 13.03, *supra*.)

NOTE:

Under method (3), above, partners can control the date of the termination by distributing the stock when it is most advantageous to them. Because the partnership can hold the corporate stock as an investment, the partnership should not terminate under the cessation-of-operations rule of I.R.C. Section 708(b)(1)(A).

Revenue Ruling 2004-59[39] describes the tax consequences when a partnership converts into a corporation under a state statute that does not require an actual transfer of the unincorporated entity's assets or interests. The ruling holds that a conversion under this type of formless conversion statute is treated as if the partnership elected to be taxed as an association under the rules governing classification of entities for tax purposes.[40] Under these rules, the following steps are deemed to occur at the time of the conversion:

1. the partnership contributes all of its assets and liabilities to the new corporation in exchange for stock, and

2. immediately after, the partnership liquidates and distributes the new corporate stock to its partners.

[C] Converting Interests in the Same Partnership

A conversion of a general partnership interest into a limited partnership interest in the same partnership, or vice versa, is not treated as a taxable sale or exchange of the partnership interest.[41] The Service regards the conversion as if the

---

[36] Treas. Reg. § 1.743-1(h).

[37] *Id.*

[38] *Id.*

[39] 2004-1 C.B. 1050.

[40] Treas. Reg. § 301.7701-3(c)(1). *See* § 2.02.

[41] Treas. Reg. § 1.708-1(b)(1)(ii); Rev. Rul. 84-52, 1984-1 C.B. 157. *See also* Priv. Ltr. Ruls. 8609021, 8542044, 8150134, 7948063. *See generally* Banoff, In New Revenue Ruling 84-52, the IRS Uses an

partner contributed his original interest to the partnership in exchange for his new interest. The converted interests are not taken into account in determining the percentage of partnership interests sold or exchanged within a 12-month period. (For complete discussion, see Chapter 12.)

[D] Converting a Partnership to an LLC and Vice Versa

The conversion of a domestic partnership to a domestic limited liability company (and vice-versa) is not a taxable exchange of partnership or LLC interests if the business of the old partnership or LLC continues.[42] The conversion is treated in the same manner as an exchange of interests in the same partnership.[43] Of course, this is true only if the LLC is classified as a partnership for federal tax purposes; if the LLC is classified as a corporation, the transaction is treated as an incorporation of a partnership.

Because the conversion is not treated as a sale or exchange, the old partnership or LLC does not terminate under the 50 percent transfer rule of I.R.C. Section 708(b). However, the old partnership or LLC may terminate if its business is not continued by the new entity. The conversion does not cause the tax year to close for the old partnership or LLC or for any partner or member. (For complete discussion and illustrating examples of partnership-LLC conversions, see § 12.06, *supra*.)

§ 13.04 SELLING OR EXCHANGING 50 PERCENT OR MORE OF INTERESTS IN PARTNERSHIP OR LLC PROFITS AND CAPITAL

Under I.R.C. Section 708(b)(1)(B), a partnership terminates if 50 percent or more of the interests in its capital and profits are sold or exchanged within a 12-month period. The termination may be caused by one transaction or by a series of transactions that result in aggregate sales or exchanges of 50 percent or more of the interests in partnership capital and profits.[44] Partnership profits and capital must be transferred in the sales or exchanges. Thus, a sale of a 40 percent interest in partnership capital and a 60 percent interest in partnership profits does not terminate the partnership.[45]

"*Exchange*" *Approach to Conversions*, 61 J. Tax'n 98 (1984).

[42] Rev. Rul. 95-37, 1995-1 C.B. 130. This ruling reiterates the Service's position in a number of private letter rulings. *See* Priv. Ltr. Ruls. 9633021, 9525065, 9525058, 9422034 (general partnership converts to LLC), 9417009 (limited partnership converts to LLC). *See also* Priv. Ltr. Rul. 9412020 (limited liability partnership merges into LLC). This treatment also applies to a conversion of a partnership to limited liability partnership. *See* Rev. Rul. 95-55, 1995-2 C.B. 313.

[43] These tax consequences are set forth in Rev. Rul. 84-52, 1984-1 C.B. 157.

[44] Treas. Reg. § 1.708-1(b)(1)(ii).

[45] *Id. See* Priv. Ltr. Rul. 8851004 (sale of majority partnership interest did not terminate partnership where interest was transferred in installments of less than 50 percent each year).

NOTE:

I.R.C. Section 708(b)(1)(B) is based on the premise that a sudden, major change in partnership ownership makes it inappropriate for continuing partners to enjoy or to bear the partnership's pre-sale tax attributes. Because the termination rule is limited to sales or exchanges within a 12-month period, however, it is relatively easy to prevent or to induce a termination. For example, a new partner can obtain more than 50 percent of a partnership's interests in exchange for a capital contribution without causing a termination. If the contribution is related to a distribution to another partner, however, the transaction may be recharacterized as a disguised sale of a partnership interest under I.R.C. Section 707(b)(1)(B). If sales of the partners' interests are extended over a longer period of time than 12 months, the partnership will not terminate. A provision in the partnership agreement barring sales or exchanges that will terminate the partnership can compel partners to structure sales of their interests in this way.

The 12-month period referred to in the statute is not limited to a calendar year or to the partnership's tax year — it is any period of 12 consecutive months. Whenever a sale or exchange occurs, it is aggregated with all the sales or exchanges that took place in the preceding 12 months to determine whether 50 percent of the interests in the partnership were sold during that period. Termination occurs on the date that cumulative sales and exchanges equal or exceed 50 percent of the partnership's interests in capital and profits.

Example (1): Kevin, Laura, and Martin are members in the KLM Limited Liability Company, a calendar-year LLC. On May 12, Year 1, Kevin sells a 30 percent interest in LLC capital and profits to Oliver, and on March 27, Year 2, Martin sells a 30 percent interest in capital and profits to Perry. The LLC terminates on March 27, Year 2.

Multiple sales of the same partnership interest during the same 12-month period are not aggregated for purposes of the 50 percent rule.[46]

Example (2): In Example (1), above, if Kevin sells a 30 percent interest to Oliver on May 12, Year 1, and Oliver sells the same interest to Perry on March 27, Year 2, the LLC does not terminate, because only 30 percent of the interests in the LLC are transferred.

NOTE:

To avoid termination under I.R.C. Section 708(b)(1)(B), a sale of a

---

[46] Treas. Reg. § 1.708-1(b)(1)(ii).

partnership interest that would otherwise terminate the partnership can be divided into two sales that are more than 12 months apart. For example, a partner owning a 50 percent partnership interest can sell 49 percent of the interest on one date, and he can sell the remaining 1 percent interest to the same purchaser on a date more than 12 months later.[47] To protect the purchaser and to ensure that the transaction will be completed, the purchaser can be given an option to acquire the remaining partnership interest on a date more than 12 months later. This arrangement should not be recharacterized under the step-transaction doctrine if neither the title nor the burdens and benefits of ownership of the remaining interest are transferred before 12 months from the initial sale.

[A] Sale or Exchange Requirement

The termination rule of I.R.C. Section 708(b)(1)(B) applies only if the requisite percentage of interests in partnership capital and profits is sold or exchanged. These sales or exchanges may be made to other members of the partnership or to outside parties.[48] For this purpose, a sale or exchange is taken into account even if the purchaser is not, or cannot be, formally admitted as a partner under the partnership agreement or under state law.[49] Thus, an assignment of a limited partner's right to share in partnership capital and profits is a sale even if, under the partnership agreement, an assignee cannot become a substituted limited partner.[50]

A partner may be considered to sell his partnership interest if he abandons the interest and is relieved of a share of partnership liabilities. However, if there are no partnership debts, the abandonment should not be a treated as a sale (*see* Chapter 12).

[1] Transfers Not Causing Termination

Certain transactions are not considered sales or exchanges of partnership interests for the termination rules. These include the following transfers:

(1) *The acquisition of a partnership interest for a contribution of property to the partnership.*[51] For example, the Service ruled that a partnership did not terminate when newly admitted partners received 60 percent of partnership profits and losses in exchange for cash capital contributions.[52]

---

[47] Priv. Ltr. Ruls. 881004, 8517022, 8404027, 8252023, 8217028, 7952057.

[48] Treas. Reg. § 1.708-1(b)(1)(ii). *See, e.g.*, Weiss v. Comm'r, T.C. Memo. 1990-492, *vacated and remanded*, 956 F.2d 242 (11th Cir. 1992) (partnership terminated when 50 percent partner expelled and his interest acquired by other partners).

[49] *See* Evans v. Comm'r, 447 F.2d 547 (7th Cir. 1971), *aff'g* 54 T.C. 40 (1970), *acq.* 1978-2 C.B. 2 (transfer of 50 percent interest without knowledge or consent of other partner to a corporation owned by transferor is treated as exchange for I.R.C. § 708(b) purposes even though transfer not recognized under state law). *See also* U.S. v. Atkins, 191 F.2d 146 (5th Cir. 1951), *cert. denied*, 343 U.S. 941 (1952).

[50] Rev. Rul. 77-137, 1977-1 C.B. 178.

[51] Treas. Reg. § 1.708-1(b)(1)(ii).

[52] Rev. Rul. 75-423, 1975-2 C.B. 260. *See* Priv. Ltr. Rul. 8015088 (partnership did not terminate when

Thus, a partnership can avoid termination when a new partner is admitted by having the partner acquire his interest from the partnership for a contribution rather than having him purchase the interest from another partner, even though both of these transactions have similar economic effects.[53] However, if an entering partner's contribution is related to a distribution to a retiring partner, the Service may recharacterize the transaction under I.R.C. Section 707(a)(2)(B) as a disguised sale of the interest by the retiring partner to the contributor (*see* Chapter 7).

(2)   *A liquidation of a partner's interest by a partnership.*[54] If the interests of retiring partners are liquidated by the partnership rather than purchased by the other partners, termination can be avoided.

(3)   *Transfers of partnership or LLC interests by gift, bequest, or inheritance.*[55] However, a gift of a partnership interest may be treated as a partial sale to the extent that the transfer relieves the donor of liabilities that exceed his basis in the donated partnership interest.[56] In *Madorin v. Commissioner*,[57] for example, a partnership interest previously given to a grantor trust was deemed to be sold by the transferor when the trust became irrevocable, because the transferor was relieved of partnership liabilities that exceeded his basis in the interest. A partial sale is taken into account in determining whether 50 percent or more of the interests in the partnership have been sold or exchanged.

(4)   *A transfer of a partnership or LLC interest to a spouse "incident" to a marital dissolution.* Under I.R.C. Section 1041, the treatment of such transfers is similar to gifts.[58]

(5)   *A charitable contribution of a partnership interest generally is not a sale or exchange under the termination rules.*[59] However, a charitable contribution is regarded as a partial sale of the interest, to the extent that the donee partner is relieved of partnership liabilities,[60] even if the liabilities do not exceed the donor's basis in the transferred interest (*see*

---

99 percent of interests in its profits and losses were exchanged for cash contributions in private placement of limited partnership).

[53] An important difference between these transactions is that a contribution expands the partnership and increases its assets, while a sale does not.

[54] Treas. Reg. § 1.731-1(c)(3).

[55] *Id.* A transfer of a partnership interest pursuant to a divorce is treated as a gift pursuant to I.R.C. § 1041 and should be treated as a gift for purposes of the termination rules. *See* I.R.C. § 1041(b)(1).

[56] *See* I.R.C. §§ 731, 741, 752(b).

[57] 84 T.C. 667 (1985).

[58] I.R.C. § 1041(b)(1).

[59] *See, e.g.,* Priv. Ltr. Rul. 8228094 (charitable contribution of one percent interest in partnership profits did not terminate partnership when 50 percent capital and 49 percent profits interest were exchanged during same 12-month period).

[60] I.R.C. § 1011(b).

Chapters 5, 12).[61] The portion of the interest deemed sold is taken into account in determining whether the partnership terminates under I.R.C. Section 708(b).

[2] Nontaxable Transfers Considered Exchanges Under Termination Rules

A transfer of a partnership interest may be considered an exchange for I.R.C. Section 708(b)(1)(B), even if the transaction is not taxable under a specific nonrecognition provision of the Code.[62] These nonrecognition transfers relate to contributions to, or distributions from, corporations, partnerships, estates, and trusts. Nontaxable transfers that are considered sales or exchanges under the partnership termination rules include:

(1) *Contributions of partnership interests.* A contribution of a partnership interest to a corporation for stock,[63] or to another partnership for a partnership interest,[64] is an exchange of the interest, even if the transaction is not taxable under I.R.C. Section 351 or 721. Thus, a partnership terminates if its partners contribute 50 percent or more of the interests in its capital and profits to a corporation or another partnership.

(2) *Distributions of partnership interests by a corporation.* A distribution of a partnership interest by a corporation is an exchange for determining whether a partnership terminates under the 50 percent sale or exchange rule of I.R.C. Section 708.[65] According to this rule, an exchange is deemed to occur when a corporation distributes a partnership interest to a shareholder.[66] This applies when a partnership interest is distributed as a dividend or in a stock redemption or corporate liquidation.[67] Thus, a corporate partner's distribution of its partnership interest terminates the partnership if the distribution, together with other sales or exchanges during a 12-month period, total 50 percent or more of the interests in capital and profits.[68] An exchange should not be deemed to occur in a

---

[61] *See* Rev. Rul. 75-194, 1975-1 C.B. 80; Rev. Rul. 81-163, 1981-1 C.B. 433. See Chapter 9 for discussion of gifts of partnership interests.

[62] *See, e.g.,* Long v. Comm'r, 77 T.C. 1045 (1981) (like-kind exchange of partnership interests not taxable under I.R.C. § 1031 may terminate partnership). I.R.C. § 1031(a) was subsequently amended to exclude exchanges of partnership interests from qualifying as like-kind exchanges.

[63] Evans v. Comm'r, 447 F.2d 547 (7th Cir. 1971), *aff'g* 54 T.C. 40 (1970); *see also* Jackson v. Comm'r, T.C. Memo. 1981-594, *rev'd in part, aff'd in part, and remanded in part,* 708 F.2d 1402 (9th Cir. 1983); Owen v. Comm'r, 881 F.2d 832 (9th Cir. 1989); Rev. Rul. 87-110, 1987-2 C.B. 159; Rev. Rul. 81-38, 1981-1 C.B. 386. *See* Rev. Rul. 81-40, 1981-1 C.B. 508; Rev. Rul. 64-155, 1964-1 C.B. 138.

[64] *See* Rev. Rul. 84-115, 1984-2 C.B. 118; Rev. Rul. 81-38, 1981-1 C.B. 386. *See* Priv. Ltr. Rul. 8229034; Priv. Ltr. Rul. 8116041. *See generally* Rev. Rul. 84-115, 1984-2 C.B. 118.

[65] I.R.C. § 761(e).

[66] *See* H.R. Rep. No. 98-861, 98th Cong., 2d Sess. 864 (1984).

[67] *See* I.R.C. §§ 301 (dividend), 302 (redemption), 303 (redemption to pay death taxes), 331 or 332 (liquidations).

[68] A private letter ruling suggests that the Service interprets I.R.C. Section 761(e) to mean that a sale or exchange occurs when a corporation owning a partnership interest merges with another corporation.

reorganization that does not involve a transfer of assets. This applies to reorganizations involving voting stock for voting stock;[69] and recapitalizations.[70] For reorganizations that are merely a change in identity, form, or place of incorporation,[71] Revenue Ruling 87-51 suggests that an exchange occurs only if the corporation would be taxable if the nonrecognition provisions of I.R.C. Section 361 did not apply.[72]

(3) *Distribution by a partnership.* A distribution of a partnership interest by another partnership is an exchange for the termination rules.[73] An exchange is deemed to occur when a parent partnership distributes its interest in a subsidiary partnership to a partner.[74] A distribution of a partnership interest by a parent partnership terminates the partnership if the distribution, together with other sales or exchanges during a 12-month period, total 50 percent or more of the interests in capital and profits.

(4) *Distribution by trusts and estates.* It is unclear whether an exchange is deemed to occur when an estate or trust distributes a partnership interest to a beneficiary. Although I.R.C. Section 761(e) indicates that any distribution is an exchange, legislative history suggests that distributions by an estate or testamentary trust by reason of a partner's death should not be subject to this rule.[75] Logically these distributions should not be considered sales or exchanges in accordance with the treatment afforded gifted and inherited partnership interests. The Service has not yet used its specific authority to issue regulations on this point.[76]

[3] Tiered Partnerships

A parent partnership that terminates because of the 50 percent sale or exchange rule is deemed to sell or exchange all the interests it owns in any subsidiary partnerships. Consequently, a subsidiary partnership may terminate if sales or exchanges of interests in the parent (together with other sales or exchanges) cause the parent to terminate under I.R.C. Section 708(b).[77]

Example: Sara sells an 80 percent interest in the RS Partnership. The sale terminates the partnership. If RS owns a 60 percent interest in the XY Partnership, that 60 percent interest also is deemed sold, and XY also terminates. However, if RS owns only 40 percent of XY, the 40 percent interest is deemed sold on the date RS terminates. The deemed sale of the 40 percent interest in XY does not, by itself, terminate the XY Partnership,

---

Priv. Ltr. Rul. 8643062, withdrawing Priv. Ltr. Rul. 8444069.

[69] I.R.C. § 368(a)(1)(B).

[70] I.R.C. § 368(a)(1)(E).

[71] I.R.C. § 368(a)(1)(F).

[72] 1987-1 C.B. 158. *See also* GCM 39673.

[73] I.R.C. § 761(e).

[74] *Id. See* Rev. Rul. 92-15, 1992-1 C.B. 215.

[75] *See* S. Rep. No. 99-313, 99th Cong., 2d Sess. 924 (1986).

[76] I.R.C. § 761(e)(3).

[77] Treas. Reg. § 1.708-1(b)(ii). *See* Rev. Rul. 87-50, 1987-1 C.B. 157. *See also* GCM 39643.

but it is aggregated with other sales and exchanges of interests in XY within a 12-month period to determine if the termination rules apply.

A sale of an interest in a parent partnership that does not cause it to terminate is not considered a sale or exchange of a corresponding interest in the subsidiary.[78]

Example: Allen owns 40 percent of the AB Partnership which, in turn, owns 50 percent of the KLM Partnership. Karen owns 30 percent of KLM. KLM does not terminate if Allen sells his interest in AB and Karen sells her interest in KLM within a 12-month period. Although Allen's interest in KLM is indirectly a 20 percent interest (40% x 50%), the sale of his interest in AB is not considered a sale of his proportionate share of AB's interest in KLM.

[B]   Determining Whether 50 Percent of Profits and Capital Are Transferred

A termination occurs under I.R.C. Section 708(b)(1)(B) if 50 percent or more of the total interests in both partnership capital and profits are sold or exchanged within a 12-month period. To determine the percent of interests a partner transfers, his interest in capital and profits is determined on the date that the sale or exchange occurs.[79] This rule may be significant if the partners' interests in capital or profits change during the year. Partners' interests are likely to change when a new partner is admitted for a capital contribution or when the partnership liquidates an existing partner's interest.

[1]   Determining Capital Interest

No statutory or regulatory rule specifies how to determine a partner's interest in partnership capital. A partner's interest in partnership capital presumably is the value of the partnership assets that would be distributed to him if the partnership were liquidated on the date that he sells or exchanges his interest. In computing this liquidation value, the partner's distribution rights under the partnership agreement, as well as changes in partnership liabilities and changes in the value of partnership assets up to the date of sale, must be taken into account.

Example: Lester and Marie each contribute $5,000 for interests in the LM partnership. The partnership uses the $10,000 to acquire depreciable property. The LM Partnership agreement provides that:

(1)   Lester and Marie share profits equally, except that Lester is allocated the first $5,000 of partnership depreciation;

(2)   on a sale of partnership property, Lester is allocated a gain equal to the depreciation previously allocated to him (*i.e.*, a gain chargeback); and

(3)   each partner is entitled to a liquidating distribution for the value of their capital account.

---

[78]   Rev. Rul. 87-51, 1987-1 C.B. 158. *See also* GCM 39643.
[79]   Treas. Reg. § 1.708-1(b)(1)(ii).

Lester sells his partnership interest to Neil after he has been allocated $1,000 of partnership depreciation. When the sale occurs, Lester's capital account is $4,000 ($5,000 initial capital account less $1,000 share of losses), and the value of the partnership's sole asset is $9,000. Because Lester would receive a $4,000 distribution if his interest were liquidated on the date of the sale, his interest in partnership capital on that date is less than 50 percent ($4,000 / $9,000 = 44.4%). Thus, the sale of his interest does not terminate the partnership.

However, if the value of the partnership's asset on the sale date is $10,000, Lester would receive a $5,000 distribution if his interest were liquidated on the sale date, since the partnership would recognize a gain of $1,000 on a sale of the asset and, under the chargeback provision, this amount would be allocated to Lester. Consequently, the sale of Lester's interest would be a sale of a 50 percent interest in partnership capital ($5,000 / $10,000). If Lester also sells a 50 percent profits interest at that time, the partnership terminates under I.R.C. Section 708(b)(1)(B).

[2] Determining Profits Interest

A partner's interest in partnership profits may be determined from the partnership agreement if the agreement allocates profits among the partners in fixed percentages that do not vary during the partnership's existence. The determination is more complex, however, if the partner's interest in profits varies during the year, or if the partner has different interests in different categories of partnership profits. For example, a variation occurs when income from partnership operations is allocated in a different ratio than gain from dispositions of partnership assets. The determination is also complex when the partners' shares of profits are computed at the close of the year, based on each partner's performance during the year. If that is the method used, the selling partner's share of partnership profits on the date of the sale cannot be determined until the end of the year.

A partner's right to receive guaranteed payments is not an interest in partnership profits for the 50 percent rule.[80] Thus, a partnership's payments of a partner's salary or interest on his capital contribution are not included in his share of profits. (See discussion of guaranteed payments in Chapter 7.)

§ 13.05 MERGING, CONSOLIDATING, DIVIDING, AND CONVERTING PARTNERSHIPS OR LLCS

[A] Continuing or Terminating Partnership or LLC in Merger or Consolidation

I.R.C. Section 708(b)(2)(A) provides that if two or more partnerships merge or consolidate into one, the resulting entity is considered a continuation of the partnership that has members owning more than 50 percent of its capital and profits. The other partnerships involved in the merger or consolidation are

---

[80] Treas. Reg. § 1.707-1(c).

terminated.[81] If none of the partnerships involved in the merger or consolidation own more than 50 percent of the resulting partnership's capital and profits, all of the partnerships terminate and a new partnership results.[82] These rules apply to any consolidation or merger of the operations of general or limited partnerships,[83] regardless of the form of the transaction.[84]

> **Example (1):** Allen, Betty, and Charles are equal one-third partners in the ABC Partnership; Don and Elspeth are equal one-half partners in the DE Partnership. The ABC and DE partnerships merge, and each partner receives a 20 percent interest in the new ABCDE Partnership. The ABCDE Partnership is considered a continuation of the ABC Partnership because its partners own 60 percent of ABCDE's capital and profits. The DE Partnership terminates on the merger date.

> **Example (2):** Gary and Harriet are equal partners in the GH Partnership; Irma and James are equal partners in the IJ Partnership. The GH and IJ Partnerships merge, and each partner receives a 25 percent interest in the new GHIJ Partnership. Both GH and IJ terminate on the date of the merger because neither partnership satisfies the more-than-50 percent ownership test.

When members of more than one of the merging or consolidating partnerships own more than 50 percent of the capital and profits of the resulting partnership, the regulations state that the new entity is considered a continuation of the partnership that contributes the greatest dollar value of assets.[85] This situation can arise, for example, if the same parties are partners in more than one of the merging or consolidating partnerships.

> **Example (1):** Partnerships ABC and ADE merge into the ABCDE Partnership. The capital and profits interests of the merging partnerships are owned as follows:

---

[81] Treas. Reg. § 1.708-1(b)(2)(i).

[82] *Id.*

[83] *See* Priv. Ltr. Rul. 8407029 (merger of limited partnerships and general partnerships into limited partnership); Priv. Ltr. Rul. 9809003 (conversion of two-partner general partnership into limited liability company to limit partners' liability under state law did not result in gain or loss recognition).

[84] *See* Rev. Rul. 77-458, 1977-2 C.B. 220 (all assets and liabilities of nine partnerships transferred to one other existing partnership).

[85] Treas. Reg. § 1.708-1(b)(2). *See* Rev. Rul. 77-458, 1977-2 C.B. 220; Priv. Ltr. Ruls. 7705028, 8246095, 8407029, 8619015. The regulations indicate that the Commissioner may grant permission for different treatment. The circumstances when permission will be granted are unclear. Perhaps more than one partnership may be deemed to continue if more than one partnership owns more than 50 percent of capital and profits of the new partnership and the partnerships have assets with equal dollar values.

Partnership ABC	Capital and Profits Interest
Andrew	55%
Bob	25%
Carla	20%
Partnership ADE	
Andrew	55%
David	35%
Edgar	10%

Because Andrew owns more than 50 percent of the capital and profits interests of both of the merging partnerships, both ABC and ADE meet the more-than-50 percent test. Therefore, the partnership that contributed the greatest dollar value to the merger is considered the continuing partnership. The dollar value of Partnership ABC's assets is $120,000, and the value of Partnership ADE's assets is $100,000. Partnership ABC is considered to continue because it contributed the greatest dollar value of assets, and Partnership ADE terminates on the date of the merger.

Example (2): Mary and Nolan are equal 50 percent partners in five separate partnerships that operate retail stores. The first four partnerships own assets worth $100,000 and the fifth partnership owns assets worth $150,000. To lower operating costs, the assets and liabilities of the five partnerships are consolidated into one partnership. The four smaller partnerships terminate on the consolidation date, and the larger partnership is considered to continue.[86]

Tax returns. A partnership that is considered a continuation of a preexisting partnership under I.R.C. Section 708(b)(2)(A) files its tax return for the full taxable year of the continuing partnership.[87] The return must state that the partnership is a continuation of a merging or consolidating partnership, and it must identify all of the partnerships that were terminated in the merger or consolidation.[88] The return must also show the distributive shares of the partners for the periods before and after the date of the merger, as determined under the rules of I.R.C. Section 706(c).[89] The allocation of the distributive shares can be made by prorating income or loss for the termination year on a daily basis.[90] The tax years of any terminated partnerships close on the date of the merger, and these partnerships must file tax returns for a tax year ending on that date.[91]

Example: Roger and Sara each own 50 percent capital and profits interests in Partnership RS, and Carol and Don each own 50 percent interests in

---

[86] *See* Rev. Rul. 77-458, 1977-2 C.B. 220.

[87] Treas. Reg. § 1.708-1(c)(2).

[88] *Id.*

[89] *Id.*

[90] Treas. Reg. § 1.706-1(c)(2)(ii). Although the regulations provide for allocations based on an interim closing of the partnership's books, the application of this rule appears limited to situations in which a partner sells his entire partnership interest.

[91] Treas. Reg. § 1.708-1(c)(2); I.R.C. § 706(c)(1).

Partnership CD. Both partnerships use a calendar tax year. On September 30, 2001, the partnerships merge and form Partnership RSCD. The partners' capital and profits interests in new RSCD are

Roger	30%
Sara	30%
Carol	20%
Don	20%

Because Roger and Sara together own more than 50 percent of its capital and profits, RSCD is considered a continuation of Partnership RS which continues to file returns on a calendar year basis. Because Carol and Don own less than 50 percent of Partnership RSCD, Partnership CD terminates on September 30, 2001 and its tax year closes on that date. Partnership RSCD must file a return for the tax year January 1 to December 31, 2001, indicating that it was partnership RS until September 30, 2001. Partnership CD must file a return for its final tax year, January 1 through September 30, 2001.

[B] Tax Consequences of Merger or Consolidation

Partnership Mergers. When two or more partnerships merge, the resulting partnership is considered a continuation of any merging partnership whose members own more than 50 percent of its capital and profits.[92] Generally, a merger of partnerships under local law is treated as an "assets-over" transaction in which any terminated partnership is (1) deemed to contribute its assets and liabilities in exchange for interests in the resulting partnership, and (2) immediately distribute interests in the resulting partnership to its partners in liquidation of the terminated partnership.[93]

The tax consequences of a partnership consolidation or merger depend upon which one of the following two forms prescribed in the regulations are used in the transaction:[94]

Assets-over form. The merging or consolidating partnerships transfer all their assets and liabilities in exchange for interests in a resulting partnership. The terminating partnerships then liquidate by distributing the interests in the resulting partnership to their partners.[95]

---

[92] I.R.C. § 708(b)(2)(A).

[93] Treas. Reg. § 1.708-1(c)(3)(i). A partnership may choose, however, to structure the merger in the "assets-up" form, in which the terminating partnership is deemed to distribute its assets and liabilities to its partners who then contribute these assets and liabilities to the resulting partnership. Treas. Reg. § 1.708-1(c)(3)(ii).

[94] Treas. Reg. § 1.708-1(c)(3). Final regulations governing partnership mergers and divisions were published on January 4, 2001 to apply to mergers and divisions occurring on or after that date. T.D. 8925 (Jan. 4, 2001). However, a partnership may apply the rules in the final regulations to mergers and divisions occurring on or after January 11, 2000.

[95] Treas. Reg. § 1.708-1(c)(3)(i).

Assets-up form. The merging or consolidating partnerships distribute their assets and liabilities to their partners in complete liquidation of all partnership interests. The partners then contribute the distributed assets and liabilities in exchange for interests in the resulting partnership.[96] This form is respected only if the partners of the terminated partnership are considered to own the distributed assets under local law, even though such ownership immediately ends when the assets are reconveyed to the resulting partnership.[97] It is not necessary, however, for the partners to actually assume partnership liabilities.[98] A partnership may use the assets-up form even though the partners cannot otherwise hold assets such as undivided interests in goodwill outside of a partnership.[99] The assets-over form is the default rule — if partnerships merge under local law without implementing the assets-up method, the merger is treated as an assets-over transaction regardless of the form actually used.[100]

> **Example (1):** LLC X and LLC Y merge when the members of LLC X transfer their interests to LLC Y in exchange for LLC Y interests. LLC X immediately liquidates into LLC Y. The resulting partnership is considered a continuation of LLC Y, and LLC X is terminated.
>
> Because this is not the assets-up form, the transaction is treated as occurring under the assets-over default rule. Thus, for tax purposes, LLC X is-
>
> * deemed to contribute its assets and liabilities to LLC Y for interests in LLC Y, and
>
> * immediately distribute the interests in LLC Y to its partners in liquidation of their LLC X interests.
>
> **Example (2):** Alex owns a 40 percent interest and Brenda owns a 60 percent interest in the AB LLC. Brenda owns a 60 percent interest and Charles owns a 40 percent interest in the BC LLC. Both limited liability companies merge on September 30, 2001 to form the ABC LLC. The net fair market value of AB's assets is $100,000, and the net fair market value of the BC's assets is $200,000. The merger is accomplished under state law by BC contributing its assets and liabilities to AB in exchange for interests in AB, with BC then liquidating by distributing its interests in AB to Brenda and Charles.
>
> The resulting ABC LLC is considered a continuation of the BC LLC because the net fair market value of BC's assets exceeded AB's. AB terminates in the merger.

---

[96] Treas. Reg. § 1.708-1(c)(3)(ii).

[97] *See* Treas. Reg. § 1.708-1(c)(5), *Example (3)*. The preamble to the regulations indicates that a partnership must actually undertake the steps necessary under local law to convey ownership of the distributed assets to the partners. This does not necessarily require an actual transfer and recording of a deed or certificate of title.

[98] This rule prevents the momentary assumption of a partner's share of debt from causing recognition of gain under I.R.C. §§ 752(b) and 731(a). *See* § 5.03, *supra.*

[99] *See* Treas. Reg. § 1.708-1(c)(5), *Example (3)*.

[100] Treas. Reg. § 1.708-1(c)(3)(i).

Although a different transactional form is actually used, for tax purposes, this merger is treated as if an assets-over form was used. Under that form, the merging partnerships transfer all their assets and liabilities for interests in the resulting partnership and the terminating partnership then liquidates by distributing the interests in the resulting partnership to its partners. In this case, the tax consequences are determined as if AB contributed its assets to BC in exchange for interests in BC and then liquidated, distributing interests in partnership BC to Alex and Brenda.

Example (3): Use the facts in Example (1) above, except that one of AB's assets is goodwill from its business and that the merger occurs under state law by having AB convey an undivided 40 percent interest in each of its assets to Alex and an undivided 60 percent interest in each of its assets to Brenda. Alex and Brenda then contribute their interests in these assets to BC, with BC assuming all of AB's liabilities. Since the transaction follows the requirements of the assets-up form, the tax consequences are determined under that form.

NOTE:

The regulations are designed to provide administrable rules that taxpayers and the Service can apply in characterizing partnership mergers and divisions. Although these transactions can be structured in many ways under local law, the tax consequences are determined under the assets-over or assets-up form only.

A merging partnership cannot use different forms for different assets. Each partner is deemed to participate in the partnership merger in the same manner. Therefore, a partnership that wants its merger to be characterized under the assets-up form, must actually use the assets-up form for all of its assets distributed to its partners or the transaction will be treated as an assets-over form. However, if more than two partnerships merge, each combination is considered a separate merger. Consequently, structuring the merger of one partnership into the resulting partnership under the assets-over form does not prevent a simultaneous merger of another partnership into the resulting partnership using the assets-up form.[101]

CAUTION:

Generally, the assets-over form is a simpler method for partnership mergers because actual distribution and changing title to assets is not required. However, the assets-up form may be preferable where disparities

---

[101] Preamble to Final Regulations, T.D. 8925 (Jan. 4, 2000).

exist between the basis of partnership assets and the basis of the partners' interests in the partnership ("inside-outside" basis disparities). If the assets-up form is desired, it is important that the surviving partnership (under the partnership tax regulations) also is the surviving partnership under state law. If not, the IRS may treat the transaction as an assets-over merger of the terminating partnership into the surviving partnership.

Sale of an interest in a merging or consolidating partnership. The regulations provide a "buyout" rule that allows the resulting partnership in an assets-over form merger to fund a purchase of interests in the terminating partnership from partners who are exiting. This special rule is necessary to prevent the buyout from being treated as a "disguised sale" of assets to the resulting partnership. Under the regulations, a buyout will be treated as a sale of the exiting partner's interest, rather than a disguised sale of assets, if the merger agreement specifies (i) that the resulting partnership is purchasing the exiting partner's interest and (ii) the amount paid for the interest.[102] The exiting partner need not be a party to the merger agreement to benefit from the buyout rule. However, prior to or contemporaneous with the transfer, the exiting partner must consent to the sale treatment of the rule. After the buyout, the resulting partnership inherits the exiting partner's capital account and his allocation obligations for contributed property under I.R.C. Section 704(c). If exiting partners sell 50 percent or more of the interests in the terminating partnership's capital and profits, the partnership terminates under I.R.C. Section 708(b)(1)(B) immediately before the merger.[103]

Under the buyout rule, the resulting partnership is deemed to acquire an interest in the terminating partnership in exchange for the amount used to fund the buyout. The regulations indicate that the terminating partnership, as part of the merger, is deemed to distribute assets to the resulting partnership to liquidate that interest. If the terminating partnership has an I.R.C. Section 754 election in effect, the resulting partnership obtains a special basis adjustment for the terminating partnership's property under I.R.C. Section 732(b).[104]

NOTE:

A basis adjustment under I.R.C. Section 732(b) arising from a distribution applies to the common basis of partnership property and benefits all the partners of the resulting partnership, including those from the terminated partnership. By contrast, if the adjustment were deemed to arise under I.R.C. Section 743 from a purchase of the exiting partner's interest, the adjustment would be allocated solely to those who were partners in the resulting partnership before the merger.

---

[102] Treas. Reg. § 1.708-1(c)(4).

[103] Preamble to Regulations, T.D. 8925 (Jan. 4, 2000).

[104] Treas. Reg. § 1.708-1(c)(5), *Example (5)*.

Example: Lewis, Marni, and Nan are partners in Partnership LMN. Dawn, Edgar, and Frank are partners in Partnership DEF. LMN and DEF merge, using the assets-over form. The resulting partnership is considered a continuation of DEF and LMN is terminated. Because Nan does not want to become a partner in DEF, Nan, LMN, and DEF enter into an agreement specifying that DEF will purchase Nan's interest in LMN for $15,000 before the merger. In the agreement, Nan consents to treat the transaction consistent with the agreement. In the merger, LMN receives $15,000 from DEF to distribute to Nan immediately before the merger, as well as interests in DEF in exchange for partnership LMN's assets and liabilities.

Nan is treated as selling her interest in LMN to DEF for $15,000 before the merger and her tax consequences are determined accordingly.[105]

DEF is treated as purchasing Nan's interest in LMN for $15,000 immediately before the merger and its tax consequences are determined accordingly.[106] Any built-in gain or loss from I.R.C. Section 704(c) property in LMN that would have been allocated to Nan (including allocations for revalued property)[107] are apportioned to DEF. After the merger, the built-in gain or loss (and allocations for revalued property) attributable to Nan's interest are apportioned to Dawn, Edgar, and Frank.

Following the purchase of Nan's interest, LMN is considered to:

- contribute its assets and liabilities attributable to the interests of Lewis and Marni to DEF in exchange for interests in DEF;

- immediately distribute the DEF interests to Lewis and Marni in liquidation of their interests in LMN; and

- distribute assets to DEF in liquidation of DEF's interest in LMN. DEF's bases in these distributed assets are determined under I.R.C. Section 732(b).

The regulations provide an anti-abuse rule providing that the IRS may disregard or recharacterize a merger or buyout transaction that is part of a larger series of transactions if, in substance, the larger series is inconsistent with the forms prescribed in the regulations.[108]

Treatment of partnership liabilities in a merger. Increases and decreases in liabilities associated with a merger or consolidation of two or more partnerships are netted by the partners of the terminating and resulting partnerships to determine the effect of the merger under I.R.C. Section 752.[109] That section provides that increases in a partner's share of partnership liabilities are treated as cash

---

[105] See Chapter 12 for discussion of the sale of a partnership interest.

[106] *See* Chapter 12 and Treas. Reg. § 1.704-1(b)(2)(iv)(l) for determining DEF's capital account in LMN. *See* I.R.C. § 742 and Treas. Reg. § 1.742 1 for determining DEF's basis for its interest in LMN.

[107] *See* I.R.C. § 704(b); Treas. Reg. § 1.704-3(a)(7).

[108] Treas. Reg. § 1.708-1(c)(6).

[109] Treas. Reg. § 1.752-1(f). This rule for treating liabilities in a merger was added to the regulations in T.D. 8925 (Jan. 4, 2001). Although the rule does not apply to a liability incurred or assumed by a partnership prior to January 4, 2001, the regulations indicate that taxpayers may rely on the treatment

contributions to the partnership and decreases in a partner's share of liabilities are treated as cash distributions. See § 5.03, *supra*, for complete discussion of partnership liabilities.

> **Example:**[110] Barry owns 70 percent of Partnership BC. BC's sole asset is Property X, which is worth $1,000, has a basis of $600 in BC and is encumbered by a $900 liability. Barry's basis for his interest in BC is $420. Barry also owns 20 percent of Partnership DB. DB's sole asset is Property Y, which is worth $1,000, has a basis of $200 to DB and is encumbered by a $100 liability. Barry's basis for his interest in DB is $40.
>
> Partnerships BC and DB merge. BC is considered terminated and the resulting partnership is a continuation of DB. The merger uses the assets-over form, so that BC contributes Property X and its $900 liability to DB for an interest in DB. BC immediately distributes the DB interests to its partners to liquidate their interests in BC. Barry now owns a 25 percent interest in DB.
>
> Barry nets the increases and decreases in his share of partnership liabilities associated with the merger of BC and DB. Before the merger, Barry's share of partnership liabilities was $650 ($630 share of BC's liabilities and a $20 share of DB's pre-merger liabilities). After the merger, Barry's share of DB's liabilities is $250 (25 percent of DB's total $1,000 liabilities). Thus, Barry has a $400 net decrease in his share of DB's liabilities and he is deemed to receive a $400 cash distribution from DB under I.R.C. Section 752(b). Since Barry's basis for his interest in DB before the deemed distribution is $460 ($420 + $40), Barry does not recognize gain under I.R.C. Section 731. After the merger, Barry's basis for his interest in DB is $60.

PRACTICE NOTE:

A partnership that wishes to acquire a controlling interest in another partnership can do so by either (1) merging the two partnerships or (2) acquiring a majority interest in the target partnership. Although these transactions may have similar economic results, the tax effect can be quite different, particularly under the proposed regulations described above. Practitioners should carefully consider the tax of these alternative acquisition transactions under the following Code sections:

- Under IRC Section 704(c)(1)(B)(i), when a partnership distributes property contributed by one partner to a different partner within seven years of the contribution, the contributing partner recognizes gain or loss equal to amount that would have been allocated to him if the property were sold at its fair market value at the time of the distribution.

---

afforded by the rule for other liabilities. Treas. Reg. § 1.752-5.

[110] *See* Treas. Reg. § 1.752-1(g), *Example (2)*.

- Under IRC Section 737(a), a partner receiving a distribution of property recognizes gain equal to the lesser of

  o   the excess of

    - the value of the property (other than money) received in the distribution over

    - the basis of the partner's interest in the partnership immediately before the distribution reduced (but not below zero) by the amount of money received in the distribution, or

  o   (2) the partner's net precontribution gain. Net precontribution gain is the net gain the distributee would have recognized under IRC Section 704(c)(1)(B) if all property that partner contributed to the partnership within seven years of the distribution was distributed to another partner.[111]

Acquisition of Majority Interest: A partnership is deemed to terminate if there is a sale or exchange of 50 percent or more of the total interest in partnership capital and profits within a 12-month period.[112] A partnership that terminates under this rule is deemed to contribute all its assets and liabilities to a new partnership in exchange for an interest in the new partnership and then immediately liquidate by distributing interests in the new partnership to the purchasing and continuing partners. Essentially, the transaction deemed to occur on a partnership termination under is the "assets-over" form described above.

The tax treatment of a partnership termination is coordinated with the rules of I.R.C. Sections 704(c)(1)B) and 737 governing allocations of gain or loss built-in to property contributed by partners to the partnership.[113] No gain or loss is recognized under these sections as a result of the deemed distribution on termination and that distribution does not affect the allocation requirements of I.R.C. Section 704(c) for the gain or loss built-in to property contributed to the partnership before the termination.

Under the regulations, property deemed transferred to the new partnership is not considered I.R.C. Section 704(c) property, except to the extent that it was such property in the hands of the terminating partnership.[114] Also, a partnership termination does not begin a new seven-year period for partners for built-in gain or loss in property the terminated partnership is deemed to contribute to the new partnership.[115] A distribution of property by the new partnership to a former partner of the terminated partnership is subject to I.R.C. Section 737 to the same

---

[111] I.R.C. § 737(b).

[112] I.R.C. § 708(b)(1)(B).

[113] H. Rep. No. 101-247, 101st Cong., 1st Sess. 1355 (1989); H. Rep. No. 102-1018, 102d Cong., 2d Sess. 428 (1992).

[114] Treas. Reg. § 1.704-3(a)(3)(i).

[115] Notice of Proposed Rulemaking, 61 Fed. Reg. 21985 (5/13/96).

extent as a distribution from the terminated partnership.[116]

[C]   Dividing a Partnership or LLC

When a partnership divides into two or more partnerships, I.R.C. Section 708(b)(2)(B) provides that any resulting partnerships whose partners owned more than 50 percent of the original partnership's capital and profits is considered a continuation of that partnership.[117] Any resulting partnership that does not meet this 50 percent continuity-of-ownership requirement is not a continuation of the original partnership, and it is considered to be a new partnership.[118] If none of the resulting partnerships have partners who owned more than 50 percent of the previous partnership's capital and profits, the original partnership terminates.[119] If a member of the original partnership does not join any partnership that is a continuation of the partnership, his interest in the original partnership is deemed liquidated on the date of the division.[120]

The tax consequences of a partnership division depend upon which one of the two forms prescribed in the regulations are used in the transaction.[121]

In determining the consequences of these forms, the following definitions apply:[122]

- **Prior partnership** - The partnership existing before the division.

- **Resulting partnership(s)** - The partnership or partnerships existing after the division. At least two members of the prior partnership must be members of each resulting partnership.

- **Recipient partnership** - A partnership that, for tax purposes, is considered to receive assets and liabilities in a division.

- **Divided partnership** - Generally, the divided partnership is the continuing partnership that, in form, actually transferred assets and liabilities in the division. If only one continuing partnership exists, it is treated as the divided partnership. If there is more than one continuing partnership and the partnership that actually transferred assets cannot be determined, the divided partnership is the continuing partnership with assets having the greatest net fair market value.

---

[116] Treas. Reg. § 1.737-2(a).

[117] *See* Treas. Reg. § 1.708-1(b)(2)(ii); Priv. Ltr. Rul. 9108015 (investment limited partnership not terminated where limited partners owning less than 50 percent surrendered interests for interests in new partnership). *See also* Priv. Ltr. Rul. 8605047.

[118] Treas. Reg. § 1.708-1(b)(2)(ii).

[119] *Id.*

[120] *Id.*

[121] Treas. Reg. § 1.708-1(d). Final regulations governing partnership mergers and divisions were published on January 4, 2001 to apply to mergers and divisions occurring on or after that date. T.D. 8925 (Jan. 4, 2001). However, a partnership may apply the rules in the final regulations to mergers and divisions occurring on or after January 11, 2000.

[122] Treas. Reg. § 1.708-1(d)(4).

The tax consequences of a partnership division are determined by reference to which of the following two forms is (or deemed) used in the transaction:

Assets-over form — if at least one resulting partnership is a continuation of the prior partnership. The divided partnership transfers certain assets and liabilities for interests in one or more recipient partnerships. The divided partnership immediately distributes the interests in the recipient partnership interests to designated partners in partial or complete liquidation their interests.[123]

> **Example (1):** Quentin and Roberta each own a 40 percent interest in Partnership QRST, and Susan and Ted each own a 10 percent interest. QRST owns the following assets:
>
> (1)   Property X, worth $500;
>
> (2)   Property Y, worth $300; and
>
> (3)   Property Z, worth $200.
>
> On November 1, 2002, QRST divides into three partnerships, QR1, QR2, and ST, as follows:
>
> •   by contributing Property X to QR1 and distributing all interests in that partnership to Quentin and Roberta as equal partners, and
>
> •   by contributing Property Z to ST and distributing all interests in that partnership to Susan and Ted as equal partners in liquidation of their interests in QRST.
>
> QRST, which holds onto Property X, is now referred to as QR2. Susan and Ted have ceased being partners.
>
> QR1 and QR2 are both continuations of QRST and ST is a new partnership formed on November 2, 2002. The division is treated as an assets-over form, so that QRST is deemed to contribute Property X to QR1 and Property Z to ST, and distribute the interests in these partnerships to the designated partners. Because QR1 is the resulting partnership that transferred assets, it is the divided partnership.
>
> **Example (2):** Use the same facts as Example (1) above, except that QRST divides into three partnerships under state law, without using a specific form. Because it holds assets having the greatest net fair market value, QR1 is considered the divided partnership. QRST is treated as using the assets-over form — contributing Property Y to partnership QR2 and Property Z to partnership ST, and distributing the interests in these partnerships to the designated partners.
>
> **Example (3):** Use the same facts as Example (1) above, except that QRST divides into three partnerships by:
>
> •   contributing Property X to newly formed partnership QR1, and
>
> •   contributing Property Y to newly formed partnership QR2, and

---

[123]   Treas. Reg. § 1.708-1(d)(3)(i)(A).

- distributing all interests in each partnership to Quentin and Roberta in liquidation of their interests in QRST.

Because ST is not a continuing partnership, it cannot be considered the divided partnership. Because it holds assets having the greatest net fair market value, QR1 is considered the divided partnership. QRST is treated as using the assets-over form-contributing Property Y to QR2 and Property Z to ST, and distributing the interests in these partnerships to the designated partners.

Assets-over form — if no resulting partnership is a continuation of the prior partnership. The prior partnership contributes all of its assets and liabilities in exchange for interests in new resulting partnerships. The prior partnership immediately liquidates by distributing to its partners the interests in the new resulting partnerships.[124]

Assets-up form — if the partnership distributing assets is a continuation of the prior partnership. The divided partnership distributes certain assets to some or all of its partners in partial or complete liquidation of the partners' interests in the divided partnership. (The partners must be considered to own the distributed assets under local law even though such ownership immediately ends when the assets are reconveyed to the recipient partnership.) The distributee partners immediately contribute the distributed assets for interests in a recipient partnership (or partnerships). All assets of the prior partnership transferred to a particular recipient partnership must be distributed to, and then contributed by, the partners of the recipient partnership.[125]

Assets-up form — if none of the resulting partnerships is a continuation of the prior partnership. The prior partnership distributes certain assets to some or all of its partners in partial or complete liquidation of the partners' interests in the prior partnership. (The partners must be considered to own the distributed assets under local law.) The distributee partners immediately contribute the distributed assets for interests in one or more resulting partnerships. All assets of the prior partnership transferred to the resulting partnership must be distributed to, and then contributed by, the partners of the resulting partnership. If the prior partnership does not liquidate under local law, any assets and liabilities of the prior partnership not transferred to a new resulting partnership are considered transferred to a new resulting partnership under the assets-over form.[126]

Example: Partnership ABCDE owns Blackacre, Whiteacre, and Redacre, and divides into partnerships AB, CD, and DE. No resulting partnership is a continuation of ABCDE because no members of the new partnerships owned more than 50 percent of ABCDE. The division occurs as follows:

- ABCDE distributes and transfers title in Blackacre to partners Alice and Barney. Alice and Barney then contribute Blackacre in exchange for their interests in Partnership AB.

---

[124] Treas. Reg. § 1.708-1(d)(3)(i)(B).

[125] Treas. Reg. § 1.708-1(d)(3)(ii)(A).

[126] Treas. Reg. § 1.708-1(d)(3)(ii)(B).

- ABCDE distributes and transfers title in Whiteacre to partners Cary and Dan. Cary and Dan then contribute Whiteacre in exchange for their interests in Partnership CD.

- ABCDE does not liquidate under state law and becomes DE. The assets of DE are not considered to have been transferred under state law.

ABCDE is treated as following the assets-up form with respect to the assets transferred to Partnerships AB and CD. However, ABCDE is treated as using the assets-over form with respect to the assets of DE.

ABCDE is deemed to contribute Redacre in exchange for interests in DE and immediately distributes the interests in DE to Dan and Elwin in liquidation of their interests in ABCDE. ABCDE then terminates.

A partnership that divides other than by the two specified forms is deemed to use the assets-over form.[127] A division that involves an actual or deemed transfer of assets to multiple partnerships, the transfer to each resulting partnership is characterized separately. Thus, a transfer to one resulting partnership may be treated as an assets-over form while the transfer to another resulting partnership is treated as an assets-up form.[128]

Example (1): Partnership EFGH owns properties W, X, Y, and Z, and divides into partnership EF and partnership GH. EF is considered a continuation of EFGH and GH is considered a new partnership. EFGH distributes property Y to Garth and property Z to Hal. Each property is titled in the distributee's name. Garth and Hal then contribute properties Y and Z to GH in exchange for interests in GH. Properties W and X remain in partnership EF. EFGH is treated as following the assets-up form of division.

Example (2): Assume instead that EFGH distributes and titles property Y to Garth and Garth then contributes the asset to GH. Simultaneously, EFGH contributes property Z to GH for a partnership interest. EFGH immediately distributes the interest in GH to Hal in liquidation of his interest in EFGH.

Because EFGH did not use the assets up form for all the assets transferred to GH, it is treated as using the assets-over form. Accordingly, EFGH is treated as contributing properties Y and Z for interests in GH and immediately distributing the interests in GH to Garth and Hal to liquidate their interests in EFGH.

Tax returns. The reporting consequences of a partnership division depend upon how many continuing and "resulting partnerships" exist after the division. These requirements are summarized as follows:[129]

- The resulting partnership treated as the divided partnership must file a return for the tax year of the partnership that has been divided and retain

---

[127] Treas. Reg. § 1.708-1(d)(3)(i).

[128] *See* Treas. Reg. § 1.708-1(d)(5), *Example 7.*

[129] Treas. Reg. § 1.708-1(d)(2)(i).

that partnership's employer identification number (EIN). The return must include the names, addresses, and EINs of all continuing resulting partnerships, state that the partnership is a continuation of the prior partnership and provide the distributive shares its partners up to and after the date of the division.

- All other continuing resulting partnerships and all new partnerships must file separate returns for the tax year beginning on the day after the division date with new EINs for each partnership.

- return for a continuing resulting partnership that is not the divided partnership must include the name, address, and EIN of the prior partnership.

All continuing resulting partnerships are subject to preexisting elections made by the prior partnership. However, subsequent elections by a resulting partnership do not affect other resulting partnerships.[130]

> **Example:** Arthur owns a 40 percent interest, and Burt, Carol, and Dave each own 20 percent interests in the ABCD Partnership, which operates real estate and insurance businesses. Partnership and partners report their income on a calendar year. On November 1, 2001, they separate the real estate and insurance businesses, forming Partnership AB to take over the real estate business, and Partnership CD to take over the insurance business.
>
> Because members of resulting partnership AB own more than 50 percent of ABCD (Arthur, 40 percent, and Burt, 20 percent), AB is considered a continuation of ABCD. Partnership AB must file a return for the tax year January 1 to December 31, 2001, indicating that until November 1, 2001, it was partnership ABCD.
>
> CD is considered a new partnership formed on November 2, 2001, and must file a return for the tax year it adopts.

§ 13.06   TAX CONSEQUENCES OF PARTNERSHIP TERMINATION

[A]   Partnership Tax Year Closes

The partnership's taxable year closes for all partners on the date the partnership terminates.[131] Each partner reports his distributive share of partnership income, gain, or loss up to the termination date on his return for the taxable year in which termination occurs.[132]

> **Example (1):** Ellen and Fred each own 50 percent interests in the EF Partnership. Both partners and the partnership use a calendar tax year.

---

[130] Treas. Reg. § 1.708-1(d)(2)(ii).

[131] Treas. Reg. § 1.708-1(b)(1)(iii). *See* I.R.C. § 706(c).

[132] Treas. Reg. § 1.706-1(c).

Ellen sells her interest to George on November 30, Year 1, causing the partnership to terminate on that date under I.R.C. Section 708(b)(1)(B). Ellen and Fred must include their distributive shares of EF's income, gain, or loss for the period January 1 to November 30, Year 1, on their tax returns for Year 1. Following EF's termination, a new FG Partnership is deemed to arise. Assuming that the new partnership uses a calendar tax year, Fred and George report their shares of FG's income for the short tax year December 1 to December 31, Year 1, on their tax returns for Year 1.

The closing of the partnership year does not have adverse tax consequences for partners who use the same tax year as the partnership. However, if a partner uses a different tax year than the partnership, the closing of the tax year may require that partner to report more than 12 months of partnership income on his tax return for the year of termination. (For discussion of partnership taxable year, see Chapter 3.)

Example (2): Assume the same facts as in Example (1), except that the EF Partnership uses a fiscal tax year ending June 30. If the partnership terminates on November 30, Year 1, Ellen and Fred must include their distributive shares of partnership income, gain, or loss for a 17-month period on their tax returns for Year 1. They must include income for the 12-month period from July 1, Year 0, to June 30, Year 1, plus the five-month period from July 1, Year 1, to November 30, Year 1.

NOTE:

It is unclear how income, gain, or loss is allocated between the old and new partnerships. Because two entities are deemed to be involved, it is appropriate to close the old partnership's books on the termination date and to open the new partnership's books at that time.

[B]   Elections

If a partnership terminates under the 50 percent sale or exchange rule of I.R.C. Section 708(b)(1)(B), the new partnership resulting from the termination does not acquire the original partnership's elections.[133] The new partnership must make all the elections that affect the computation of its taxable income, except those that I.R.C. Section 703(b) specifically requires to be made by the partners individually.[134] The partnership must:

(1)   elect the partnership's accounting method under I.R.C. Section 446;

(2)   elect the partnership's taxable year under I.R.C. Section 706(b);

---

[133] *See* I.R.C. § 703(b).

[134] Elections required to be made by partners individually are: (1) I.R.C. § 108(b)(5) (income from cancellation of indebtedness); (2) I.R.C. § 617 (mining exploration expenditures, deductions, and recapture); and (3) I.R.C. § 901 (foreign tax credit). (*See* Chapter 3.)

(3)   elect the I.R.C. Section 754 basis adjustment;

(4)   elect the partnership's inventory method under I.R.C. Sections 471 and 472;

(5)   elect to expense depreciable business assets under I.R.C. Section 179; and

(6)   elect to expense intangible drilling and development costs of oil and gas wells under I.R.C. Section 263(c).

NOTE:

A partnership that has made an election to adjust the basis of partnership property may wish to terminate under the 50 percent sale or exchange rule in order to eliminate that election. This strategy may be desirable if the partnership expects its assets to decline in value. If a partnership has an I.R.C. Section 754 election in effect when it terminates, the basis-adjustment rules apply to the new partner whose purchase caused the termination.[135]

[C]   Cessation of Business — Assets Deemed Distributed

When a partnership terminates because it ceases conducting any business or financial operations, it is deemed to distribute all of its assets to its partners in complete liquidation of their interests. The termination usually occurs on the same date that the partnership actually makes a final liquidating distribution. If a partnership terminates because it converts to a nonpartnership form, a constructive distribution is deemed to occur on the conversion date. The partners determine their bases in the distributed property of the liquidation distribution rules of I.R.C. Section 732(b) or 732(d) (see Chapter 10).

[D]   Termination by Sale or Exchange — Assets Deemed Contributed to New Partnership

On the date that a partnership terminates under the 50 percent sale or exchange rule of I.R.C. Section 708(b)(1)(B), the following events are deemed to occur:[136]

(1)   *The terminating partnership contributes all of its assets and liabilities to a new partnership in exchange for an interest in the new partnership.* The new partnership's basis for the property deemed received as a contribution is the same as the terminating partnership's basis.

(2)   *If the terminating partnership has an I.R.C. Section 754 election in effect, the basis for its assets is adjusted under I.R.C. Section 743(b)*

---

[135]   Treas. Reg. § 1.708-1(b)(v); Rev. Rul. 86-73, 1986-1 C.B. 282. *See* Treas. Reg. § 1.743-1(h).

[136]   Treas. Reg. § 1.708-1(b)(1)(iv).

immediately before the termination occurs.[137] These adjustments, which apply to the purchasing partner only, carry over to the new partnership. A partner having a special basis adjustment for partnership property continues to have that basis adjustment if the partnership terminates; the adjustment carries over to the new partnership regardless of whether the new partnership makes a an I.R.C. Section 754 election.[138]

Before purchasing an interest in a partnership that will terminate under the sale or exchange rule, the purchaser should be sure that the partnership has an I.R.C. Section 754 election in effect. If not, the purchaser can condition the transaction on having the election made on the terminating partnership's final tax return.

An election under I.R.C. Section 732(d) is not available to the purchasing partner because the property deemed distributed to him is an interest in the new partnership rather than the assets held by the new partnership. (For discussion of the effect of the elections under I.R.C. Sections 754 and 732(d) on the purchaser of a partnership interest, see § 12.08, *supra*.)

(3)   *The terminating partnership immediately makes a liquidating distribution of interests in the new partnership to the purchasing partner and the other partners in proportion to their interests in the terminating partnership.* The partners' bases in the new partnership interests are the same as the bases in their interests in the terminating partnership.

(4)   *The capital accounts of the purchasing and continuing partners of the terminating partnership carry over to the new partnership.*[139] For capital account purposes, the deemed contribution of the terminated partnership's assets and liabilities to the new partnership and the deemed liquidation of the terminated partnership are disregarded.

(5)   *The property deemed contributed to the new partnership is not considered I.R.C. Section 704(c) property unless it was such property in the hands of the terminated partnership immediately before the termination.*[140]

I.R.C. Section 704(c) requires allocations for contributed property to take account of any difference between the basis and value of the property when contributed. Property deemed contributed following a termination is not subject to this rule. (For discussion of I.R.C. Section 704(c) property, see Chapter 6.)

(6)   *Because the new partnership's property does not become I.R.C. Section 704(c) property as a result of the deemed contribution, no gain is*

---

[137] Treas. Reg. § 1.708-1(b)(v). *See* Rev. Rul. 86-73, 1986-1 C.B. 282.

[138] Treas. Reg. § 1.743-1(h). *See* Treas. Reg. § 1.708-1(b)(1)(iv).

[139] Treas. Reg. § 1.704-1(b)(2)(iv)(l) as amended by T.D. 8717, 62 Fed. Reg. 25498. The effective date is May 9, 1997. However, the provision may be applied to terminations occurring after May 9, 1996, if the partnership and its partners apply the provision in a consistent manner.

[140] Treas. Reg. § 1.704-3(a).

recognized under I.R.C. Section 704(c)(1)(B) if the new partnership distributes the property to any partner within seven years.[141] Thus, a subsequent distribution of I.R.C. Section 704(c) property by the new partnership is subject to I.R.C. Section 704(c)(1)(B) to the same extent as a distribution by the terminated partnership.[142] A new seven-year period does not begin for each partner for the I.R.C. Section 704(c) property the terminated partnership is deemed to contribute to the new partnership.[143] The new partnership is not required to use the same allocation method as the terminated partnership for I.R.C. Section 704(c) property deemed contributed to it by the terminated partnership.[144] (See discussion of I.R.C. Section 704(c)(1)(B) in § 4.02, *supra*.)

(7)   *Because the new partnership's property does not become I.R.C. Section 704(c) property as a result of the deemed contribution, no gain is recognized under I.R.C. Section 737 if any property acquired after the new partnership arises is distributed.*[145] A subsequent property distribution by the new partnership is subject to I.R.C. Section 737 to the same extent as a distribution from the terminated partnership[146] (*see* § 4.02, *supra*).

(8)   *The deemed distribution of the new partnership interest by the terminating partnership is not a sale or exchange of the interest for other tax purposes.*[147] However, the deemed distribution is considered an exchange of the interest in the new partnership for purposes of making any basis adjustments under I.R.C. Section 743.

(9)   *The new partnership retains the terminated partnership's taxpayer identification number.*[148]

Example (1):[149] Allen and Bea each contribute $10,000 for equal interests in the AB General Partnership. AB purchases depreciable Property X for $20,000. Property X increases in value to $30,000, at which time Allen sells his entire 50 percent interest to Cleo for $15,000. The sale terminates the AB Partnership under I.R.C. Section 708(b)(1)(B).

At the time of the sale, Property X had tax basis and book value of $16,000 ($20,000 initial basis and book value - $4,000 depreciation). Both Allen and Bea had capital account balances of $8,000 ($10,000 initial capital account - $2,000 depreciation allocations for Property X).

---

[141]   Treas. Reg. § 1.704-4(c)(3).

[142]   *Id.* The property deemed contributed to a new partnership is treated as I.R.C. Section 704(c) property in the new partnership only to the extent that the property was I.R.C. Section 704(c) property in the terminated partnership immediately prior to the termination.

[143]   Treas. Reg. § 1.704-4(a)(4).

[144]   Treas. Reg. § 1.704-3(a)(2).

[145]   Treas. Reg. § 1.737-2(a).

[146]   *Id.*

[147]   Treas. Reg. § 1.761-1(e).

[148]   Treas. Reg. § 301.6109-1(d)(2)(iii).

[149]   Treas. Reg. § 1.708-1(b)(iv), *Example.*

Terminated Partnership AB is deemed to contribute all its assets to new Partnership BC in exchange for all the interests in BC. AB is then deemed to make a liquidating distribution of equal interests in BC to Bea and Cleo. Under I.R.C. section 723, new BC's tax basis for the property deemed contributed by AB is the same as AB's basis before the contribution. Thus, BC's basis in Property X is $16,000. The book value of Property X in the new BC also is $16,000 (the book value of that property immediately before the termination). Bea and Cleo each have a capital account of $8,000 in new BC (the same as their capital accounts in AB prior to the termination). New BC retains the taxpayer identification number of the terminated AB partnership.

Because Property X was not I.R.C. Section 704(c) in the hands of terminated AB, it is not subject to the allocation rules of I.R.C. Section 704(c) in new BC, even though it is deemed contributed when its value ($30,000) differed from its tax basis ($16,000).

Example (2): If the AB Partnership has an I.R.C. Section 754 election in effect for the termination year (or makes the election on its final tax return), the partnership's basis in Property X increases by $7,000 (the difference between the $15,000 cost basis for Cleo's interest and her $8,000 share of the basis for partnership assets). All tax consequences of that basis increase are allocated to Cleo. The basis adjustment carries over to the new BC Partnership in the deemed contribution by AB. BC's basis in Property X is $23,000 ($15,000 with respect to Cleo and $8,000 with respect to Bea). Cleo's capital account and tax basis in BC is $15,000. Bea's capital account and tax basis are unaffected by the election and remain at $8,000.

[E]   Holding Period for Partnership Assets Following Termination

When a partnership terminates upon cessation of business, a partner's holding period for assets distributed includes the partnership's holding period.[150] The Tax Court[151] and the Service[152] have held that the holding period does not carry over from a two-member partnership that terminates when one member purchases the other member's interest. The purchaser's holding period starts anew in this situation, because he purchased the partnership's assets rather than a partnership interest.

The decisions regarding two-member partnerships do not apply to terminations under the 50 percent sale or exchange rule because the purchaser is considered a member of the terminated partnership immediately before the termination — he is not deemed to purchase partnership assets.[153] When a partnership terminates under that rule, its assets are constructively contributed to a new partnership. The

---

[150] I.R.C. § 735(b).

[151] McCauslen v. Comm'r, 45 T.C. 588 (1966).

[152] Rev. Rul. 67-65, 1967-1 C.B. 168.

[153] *See* Rev. Rul. 86-73, 1986-1 C.B. 282 (purchaser treated as pre-termination partner for purposes of basis adjustment rules of I.R.C. § 754).

terminated partnership's holding period for the distributed assets carries over to the new partnership when the property is constructively contributed.[154]

Presumably, the terminating partnership's holding period in the new partnership interest is bifurcated between the portion of the interest deemed received for the terminating partnership's capital assets and the portion deemed received for other assets.[155] This bifurcated holding period carries over to the partners who receive the new partnership interest in the constructive liquidating distribution.[156]

[F]   Character of Partnership Property Following Termination

The character of the property a partnership is deemed to contribute to the new partnership when it terminates under I.R.C. Section 708(b)(1)(B) carries to the new partnership. I.R.C. Section 702(b) generally governs the characterization of most assets; it provides that the character of partnership property is determined at the partnership rather than at the partner level. Under I.R.C. Section 724, a partnership recognizes ordinary income on any disposition of contributed unrealized receivables and on a disposition of contributed inventory within five years of the contribution. The partnership recognizes capital loss on a disposition of a capital asset with a built-in loss within five years of its contribution.

[G]   Suspended Losses

Under I.R.C. Section 704(d), a partner's deduction for his share of partnership losses in any year may not exceed the basis of his partnership interest at the end of the partnership year in which the loss occurs. Losses disallowed under I.R.C. Section 704(d) are carried over to subsequent years and may be deducted when the partner has sufficient basis in his partnership interest to offset the loss. A partner's suspended losses are extinguished when the partnership terminates.[157] The suspended losses do not carry over to the new partnership that arises after a termination under I.R.C. Section 708(b)(1)(B).

---

[154] I.R.C. § 1223(2) (tacked holding period for assets constructively contributed to new partnership).

[155] *See* I.R.C. § 1223(1).

[156] *See* I.R.C. § 735(b).

[157] *See* Sennett v. Comm'r, 80 T.C. 825 (1983), *aff'd per curiam*, 752 F.2d 428 (9th Cir. 1985).

TABLE OF CASES

[References are to pages]

A

ACM Pshp. v. Commissioner. 169; 174; 177
Active Lipid Dev. Partners, Ltd. v. Comm'r 75
Agro Science Co. v. Commissioner 173
Akers v. Commissioner 410
Aladdin Industries, Inc. v. Comm'r 305
Ambrose v. Commissioner. 104
Arkansas Best Corp. v. Comm'r. 505
Arundel Corp. v. U.S. 80
Ashlock v. Commissioner 520
Atkins; U.S. v. 568
Au v. Commissioner. 109
Austin v. U.S. 503

B

Baker Commodities, Inc. v. Comm'r 522; 561
Baron, Estate of v. Comm'r 175
Barran v. Commissioner. 522
Barrett v. Commissioner. 411
Basye; U.S. v. 1; 59; 199
Bateman v. U.S. 413; 417; 423
Baxter v. Commissioner 507
Beilke v. Commissioner. 75
Bellamy v. Commissioner 417
Bennett v. Commissioner 413, 414; 416; 424
Bischoff, Estate of v. Comm'r. 491
Blacketor v. United States 507; 520
Blodget v. Commissioner 491
Boehm v. Commissioner. 501
Bolger v. Commissioner. 175
Brandt v. Commissioner. 491
Brewster v. Commissioner. 414
Brountas v. Commissioner. 175
Brown v. Commissioner. 21
Brown v. Commissioner. 437
Brown Group v. Commissioner. 65; 70
Bryant v. Commissioner. 52
Buehner v. Commissioner 421
Bull v. U.S. 481; 491
Bussing v. Commissioner 106
Butler v. Commissioner 304

C

Cagle v. Commissioner 135
Campbell v. Commissioner 117, 118; 127–130
Campbell v. U.S. 68
Canal Corp. v. Comm'r 329

Carriage Square, Inc. v. Comm'r 411; 414
Cemco Investors, LLC v. U.S. 176
Cirelli v. Commissioner. 411; 420; 431
Citron v. Commissioner 501, 502
Clapp v. Commissioner 89
Clark v. Commissioner. 302
Coates v. Commissioner 437; 491
Cohan v. Comm'r 168
Cokes v. Commissioner. 52
Cole v. Commissioner. 68
Collins v. Commissioner. 520
COLM Producer, Inc. v. U.S. 176
Coloman v. Commissioner. 168
Colonnade Condominium, Inc. v. Commissioner . 310
Coltec Indus. v. U.S. 174
Comm'r v. Culbertson 410–412
Comm'r v. North American Bond Trust 30
Commissioner v. (see name of defendant) . . . . . .
Communications Satellite Corp. v. U.S. . . .306; 309
Cooper v. Commissioner. 173
Corum v. U.S. 286
Craft; United States v. 321
Crane v. Commissioner. 197; 266; 498

D

Dahlen v. Commissioner. 522
Davis v. Commissioner 67, 68
Davis v. Commissioner 337
Davis v. U.S. 492
Davis; U.S. v. 126
Dawson v. Commissioner 410
Demirjian v. Commissioner. 76
Diamond v. Commissioner . . 75; 117, 118; 127, 128
Diedrich v. Commissioner 519
Dillingham v. U.S. 175
Dillon v. U.S. 104; 106
Dobrzensky v. Commissioner 492
Donoho; U.S. v. 521
Driscoll v. U.S. 415

E

E. I. du Pont de Nemours & Co. v. U.S. 105
Echols v. Commissioner 501, 502
Edward P. Allison Co. v. Comm'r 414
Egolf v. Commissioner. 293; 302

[References are to pages]

Elrod v. Commissioner. 243; 420

Estate of (see name of party) . . . .

Evangelista v. Comm'r. 519

Evans v. Comm'r 412; 559; 563; 568; 570

F

Fahey v. Commissioner 302

Falsetti v. Commissioner. 173

Farrar v. Commissioner 304

Feldman v. Commissioner. 411

Fensel v. U.S.. . . . . .559; 562, 563

Findley v. Commissioner. 438

Fiore v. Commissioner. 416

Fiorito v. Commissioner. 491

First Nat'l Bank v. U.S.. 493

Flitcroft v. Commissioner 423

Flood v. U.S.. 462

Fong v. Commissioner. 76

Foster v. Commissioner. 57

Foxman v. Commissioner 561

Frankfort v. Commissioner. 507

Frazell; U.S. v. 106; 117, 118

Freeland v. Commissioner. 509

Freund, Estate of v. Comm'r 479

Friedman v. Commissioner 410

Fuchs v. Commissioner . 76; 438; 493; 559; 562, 563

G

Gaines v. Commissioner. 88; 291; 297

Gannon v. Commissioner. 491; 501

Garcia v. Commissioner. . .412, 413; 417; 421; 424

Gemini Twin Fund III v. Comm'r. 141

Generes; U.S. v. 304

Gershkowitz v. Comm'r 82, 83; 86

Gibson Products Co. v. U.S.. 175

Gibson Products Co. v. United States. 175

Giffen v. Commissioner 411

Ginsberg v. Commissioner. 417

Ginsburg v. U.S.. . . . . .509; 561

Goatcher v. U.S.. 21

Goldstein, Estate of v. Commissioner 76

Goodman v. Commissioner 286

Gorrill v. Commissioner. 430

Greenberg v. Commissioner 410

Grinnell Corp. v. U.S.. 520

Grodt & McKay Realty, Inc. v. Comm'r 173

Guest v. Commissioner 519

Gulfstream Land and Development Corp. v. Comm'r. 512

H

H. B. Zachry Co. v. Commissioner 105

Hale v. Comm'r. 507; 521

Hale v. Commissioner 128

Hambuechen v. Commissioner. 177; 304

Harkness v. Commissioner. 411

Harris v. U.S.. 21

Hartman v. Commissioner. 413, 414; 419; 423

Hassen v. Commissioner. 337

Hatch's Estate v. Comm'r. 522

Hayden v. Commissioner 79

Heggestad v. Commissioner 302

Hempt Bros., Inc. v. U.S.. 104

Hendler; U.S. v. 197

Hensel Phelps Constr. Co. v. Comm'r. 122

HGA Cinema Trust v. Comm'r 175

Hirsch v. Commissioner 504

Historic Boardwalk Hall, LLC v. Comm'r 321

Hobson v. Comm'r. 286

Hoffman v. Commissioner. 491

Holman v. Commissioner 438; 440

Hornback v. U.S.. . . . . .421, 422

Hunt v. Commissioner. 80

Hutcheson v. Commissioner. 501

I

In re (see name of party) . . . .

Interhotel Co. v. Comm'r 245

Investors Ins. Agency, Inc. v. Comm'r 302

J

Jackson v. Commissioner 175

Jackson v. Commissioner. 515; 570

Jackson Inv. Co. v. Commissioner. 444

Jackson Inv. Co.; Commissioner v.. 444

Jacobs v. Commissioner 444

Jade Trading, LLC v. U.S.. 177

Janklow v. Commissioner 173

Jolin v. Commissioner. 88; 291; 297

Jones v. U.S.. 553

Jupiter Corp. v. U.S.. . . . . .306; 310

K

Kaffie v. Commissioner 491

Kaiser v. Glenn. 522

Kenroy, Inc. v. Comm'r. 118; 127; 129

Ketter v. CIR 410; 413; 418; 420

Ketter v. Commissioner. 410; 413; 418– 420

[References are to pages]

Kimbell v. U.S.. 433
Kintner; U.S. v.. 56
Kintner v. United States. 56
Kirby Lumber Co.; U.S. v.. 80
Knipp v. Commissioner. 493
Kobernat v. Commissioner. 302
Kobor v. U.S.. 129
Krause v. Commissioner 413; 417; 419; 425
Kreidle v. Department of Treasury, IRS. 502
Kuney v. Frank. 416; 423

L

La Rue v. Commissioner. 502, 503
LaBrum & Doak LLP, In re. 201
Lang v. Commissioner. 410
Laport v. Commissioner. 501
Larson v. Commissioner. 56
Leavitt, Estate of v. Comm'r 21
Ledoux v. Commissioner. 507
Lehman v. Commissioner 505
Lehman; Commissioner v.. 505
Lenard L. Politte, M.D., Inc. v. Comm'r. 87
Levasseur; U.S. v.. 412
Levine, Estate of v. Comm'r. 519
Levy v. Commissioner. 141
Lieber v. U.S.. 416
Liebesman v. Commissioner. 420
Linsmayer v. Commissioner. 87
Lipke v. Commissioner 224
Littriello v. United States. 27
Logan v. Commissioner 507
Long v. Commissioner 167; 172; 512; 570
Lusthaus v. Commissioner. 410
Lynch v. Commissioner 302

M

Maddock v. Commissioner. 491
Madison Gas & Electric Co. v. Comm'r. . . .52; 68
Madorin v. Commissioner. 424; 569
Malone v. U.S.. 519
Mammoth Lakes Project v. Comm'r 233
Mangham v. Commissioner 302
Manuel v. Commissioner. 410; 416
Marcus v. Commissioner. 428
Mark IV Pictures, Inc. v. Comm'r. 120
Marriott Int'l Resorts, L.P. v. United States. . . .176
Martin v. U.S.. 509
Maxcy v. Commissioner 559; 563

McCarty v. Cripe. 337
McCauslen v. Commissioner. 522; 563; 592
McDaniel v. Commissioner 504
McDougal v. Commissioner. 120
McManus v. Commissioner. 76
Meinerz v. Commissioner 288; 511
Meyer, Estate of v. Comm'r. 512
Middlebrook v. Comm'r. 417
Middleton v. Commissioner. 503
Miller v. U.S.. . . . . .443; 507
Milliken v. Commissioner. 438
Mitchell v. Commissioner. 492
Morrissey v. Commissioner. 55
Morse v. U.S.. 509
Mushro v. Commissioner. 492, 493

N

National Oil Co. v. Commissioner. 117
Neubecker v. Commissioner. 562
Newman, Estate of v. Comm'r. 83; 86
Nichols v. Commissioner 419
Notice of Proposed Rulemaking. 582
Nowell, Estate of v. Comm'r 476

O

O'Brien v. Commissioner 503
O'Donnell v. Commissioner. 413
Oden v. Commissioner. 106; 141
Oetting v. Commissioner. 304
Offord v. Commissioner. 417
Otey v. Commissioner. 306; 309
Owen v. Commissioner 570

P

Pacheco; U.S. v.. . . . . .118; 127
Palmer v. Commissioner. 122
Panero v. Commissioner. 563
Pappas v. Commissioner. 512
Park Realty Co. v. Commissioner. 309
Paul v. Commissioner 426
Payton v. U.S.. . . . . .410; 413; 430
Peterson v. Gray. 430
Pflugradt v. U.S.. 424
Phillips v. Commissioner. 507
Pietz v. Commissioner 438; 502, 503
Podell v. Commissioner. 67, 68
Poggetto v. U.S.. . . . . .410, 411; 413

[References are to pages]

Pratt v. Commissioner 88; 292; 300; 302; 451

Q

Quick's Trust v. Commissioner 481, 482
Quirk, Estate of v. Commissioner . . . 438; 440; 451

R

Ramos v. United States. 415; 430
Ramos; United States v. 415; 418; 430
Reddig v. Commissioner. 412; 423
Rees; U.S. v. 106
Requard v. Commissioner 509; 563
Resnik v. Commissioner. 67
Rice's Toyota World v. Comm'r. 173, 174
Richardson v. Commissioner. 288; 310
Richlands Medical Ass'n v. Comm'r. 57
Riegelman, Estate of v. Commissioner . . . 481; 491
Rodebaugh v. Commissioner. 431
Roth v. Commissioner. 520
Rudd v. Commissioner. 503
Runkle v. Commissioner. 109

S

Sales v. Commissioner 68
Salina Partnership L.P. v. Comm'r 176
Sargent v. Commissioner. 141; 561
Saviano v. Commissioner 175
Scott v. Commissioner. 286
Scully v. U.S.. . . . . .169; 177
Selfe v. U.S.. 21
Sellers v. Commissioner. 416
Sennett v. Commissioner. 288; 511; 593
Seyburn v. Commissioner 521
Shaheen v. Commissioner 141
Shoenberg v. Commissioner 169; 177
Simons v. Commissioner. 410
Sloan v. Commissioner. 462
Smith v. Commissioner 302
Smith v. Commissioner 423
Smith v. Commissioner 443
Smith, Estate of v. Comm'r 563
Spector v. Commissioner. 305
Spector v. Commissioner. 443
Speelman v. Commissioner 412
Spicker v. Commissioner. 521
Spiesman v. Commissioner 424
St. John v. U.S.. . . . . .118; 127; 129
Stackhouse v. United States. 83

Stafford; U.S. v. 106
Stafford v. United States. 106
Stanback v. Commissioner. 430
Sterenbuch v. Commissioner. 173
Stilwell v. Commissioner. 438; 503
Strangi v. Comm'r. 433
Swiren v. Commissioner. 521

T

Tejon Ranch Co. v. Commissioner. 501, 502
Tennyson v. U.S.. 521
Thompson, Estate of v. Comm'r. 433
Thornley v. Commissioner. 505
Tiberti v. Commissioner 416; 419
Tompkins v. Commissioner 492
Toor v. Westover. 417
Tower; Commissioner v.. 410
Trammell v. Commissioner. 490, 491
Tufts; Commissioner v. . 82; 113; 196; 231; 266; 498
Tunnell v. U.S.. 521
2925 Briarpark, Ltd. v. Comm'r 82

U

U.S. v. (see name of defendant). . . . .
United States v. (see name of defendant). . . . . . .
Universal Research & Dev. Partnership No. 1 v.
    Comm'r. 75
UPS of Am. v. Comm'r 174
Uri v. Commissioner 21

V

Va. Historic Tax Credit Fund 2001 LP v.
    Comm'r. 320; 321
Varner v. Commissioner. 76
Virgil v. Commissioner. 424

W

Walberg v. Smyth 414
Ware v. Commissioner. 507
Weil v. Commissioner 491, 492
Weiss v. Commissioner. 502; 568
Weller v. Brownell. 430
Whipple v. Comm'r 304
Whitmire v. Commissioner 307
Wilmont Fleming Engineering Co. v. Comm'r. .491
Wilson v. Commissioner 76
Wolcott v. Commissioner 507

[References are to pages]

Woodbury v. Commissioner 412; 415; 430
Woodhall v. Commissioner. 481, 482
Woolsey; U.S. v. 507

Y

Yarbro v. Commissioner of IRS 502

Z

Zeeman v. U.S.. 502
Zuckman v. U.S.. 56

TABLE OF STATUTES

[References are to pages]

ILLINOIS

Illinois Compiled Statutes

Title:Ch./Sec.	Page
805:205/8.1 to 205/15	11

FEDERAL STATUTES, RULES, AND REGULATIONS

United States Code

Title:Sec.	Page
26:1(g)	64
26:1(h)	62; 496; 504
26:1(h)(13)	504
26:1(j)	67
26:21	63
26:22	64
26:27	81
26:37	64
26:38	81
26:47	321
26:49(a)(1)(D)(iv)	185
26:57	65
26:59(e)	79; 253
26:59(e)(4)(C)	79
26:61	117; 156
26:61(a)	129
26:61(a)(3)	82
26:61(a)(12)	80; 82
26:67	67
26:83	3; 117– 119; 122; 127; 129; 131, 132
26:83(a)	118; 122
26:83(b)	118; 123–125; 132
26:83(c)	118; 122
26:83(d)	122
26:101	147
26:101(a)	492
26:102	147
26:103	65; 147
26:103(a)	89
26:104	147
26:105	147
26:108	65; 79; 82, 83; 147; 156
26:108(3)(B)	82
26:108(a)	80; 83
26:108(a)(1)(D)	80

United States Code—Cont.

Title:Sec.	Page
26:108(a)(3)	80
26:108(b)	81; 83; 156
26:108(b)(2)(E)	84
26:108(b)(3)	81
26:108(b)(5)	81; 84; 588
26:108(c)	82; 84
26:108(c)(1)	82
26:108(c)(3)(A)	82
26:108(c)(4)	82
26:108(d)(3)	80
26:108(d)(6)	83; 156
26:108(e)(5)	81, 82
26:108(e)(7)	105
26:108(e)(7)(E)	105
26:108(e)(8)	86
26:108(i)	75
26:110	147
26:111	63; 147
26:117	147
26:132	147
26:151	61
26:151(c)	67
26:162	65; 134; 290; 296; 443; 451
26:163	69; 324; 327, 328
26:163(a)	133
26:163(d)	66; 69; 303
26:163(h)	303
26:164	133
26:164(2)	63
26:164(a)	61; 63; 79, 80
26:165	134, 135
26:165(d)	63
26:166	68; 141; 304
26:166(a)	304
26:166(d)	65; 68; 304
26:167	49; 75
26:167(h)	65
26:168	49; 75; 111; 214
26:168(f)(5)	308
26:168(i)(7)	308
26:169	76
26:170	61, 62; 67
26:170(b)	63
26:170(b)(1)(B)	62

[References are to pages]

United States Code—Cont.

Title:Sec.	Page
26:172	61; 68
26:172(d)(4)	65
26:173	79
26:174	75; 133
26:174(a)	79; 253
26:175	63; 67; 76
26:179	65; 75; 78, 79; 589
26:179(b)(3)(A)	78
26:179(b)(3)(B)	79
26:179(d)(1)	78
26:179(d)(8)	78
26:183	64
26:195	76; 133
26:195(a)	133
26:195(b)	78; 133
26:195(c)	134
26:195(d)	78; 133
26:197	540, 541
26:212	61; 63; 134
26:213	63; 67
26:214	63
26:215	63
26:216	63
26:243 to 246	63
26:263	65; 296
26:263A	66; 78
26:263(c)	63; 75; 79; 589
26:264	148, 149
26:265	149
26:265(a)(2)	303
26:267	5; 149; 337; 495
26:267(2)	335
26:267(4)	335
26:267(5)	335
26:267(a)	291
26:267(a)(2)	227; 291; 300; 334; 339
26:267(b)	181
26:267(b)(10)	337, 338
26:267(c)	337
26:267(c)(1)	335
26:267(c)(4)	335, 336
26:267(c)(5)	336
26:267(d)	148; 336, 337
26:267(e)	291
26:267(e)(3)	337
26:269A(b)(2)	22
26:270	64

United States Code—Cont.

Title:Sec.	Page
26:291	65; 508
26:301	20; 23; 570
26:311	23
26:311(b)	517
26:311(b)(1)	517
26:312	23
26:332	142
26:334(b)	142
26:336	32; 526
26:336(b)	517
26:338	32
26:351	18; 37, 38; 42; 74; 99; 102; 104–106; 110; 142; 151; 514; 536; 539; 564, 565; 570
26:351(b)(1)	540
26:351(e)(1)	107
26:356(b)	514
26:357(c)	514, 515
26:358	18; 152; 176
26:358(d)	515
26:358(h)	176
26:361	571
26:362	18; 142
26:367	39; 526
26:367(d)(2)	103
26:368(a)(1)(B)	571
26:368(a)(1)(E)	571
26:368(a)(1)(F)	571
26:401(c)	64
26:401(c)(2)	441
26:404(a)	64
26:408(m)	504
26:408(m)(3)	504
26:441(f)(1)	96
26:441(f)(3)	96
26:442	89
26:444	87; 96, 97
26:444(b)(1)	96
26:444(b)(2)	97
26:444(b)(4)	96
26:446	49; 75; 588
26:446(c)	76
26:447	78
26:447(d)	78
26:448(a)	77
26:448(a)(2)	77
26:448(d)(3)	77
26:448(d)(7)	77

[References are to pages]

United States Code—Cont.

Title:Sec.	Page
26:453. . . . . .49; 75; 308; 311, 312
26:453B(a) 105
26:453B(f) 105
26:453(b) .204
26:453(g) .339
26:453(g)(2) 339
26:461(4). .77
26:461(g) 228; 303
26:461(i)(3) 77
26:464(c). .77
26:464(e)(2) 77
26:465. . . . . .2; 21; 66; 171; 511
26:465(a). .22
26:465(b)(6) 185
26:467. . . . . .201; 303
26:467(c)(2) 509
26:469. . . . . . . .2; 22; 42; 57; 66; 171, 172; 511
26:469(a)(2) 22
26:469(c). .69
26:469(e)(1) 22; 69
26:469(h). .50
26:469(j)(2) 22
26:469(j)(2)(B). 22
26:469(k). .42
26:471 589
26:472 . . . . 75; 589
26:482 431
26:483. . . . . .308; 311
26:501(a). .31
26:512(c). .67
26:542 67
26:611 . . . . 61; 150
26:611(b). .65
26:613 66
26:613A. .150
26:613A(c)(7)(D). 271; 548
26:614 75
26:616(a). .79
26:617 . . . . 63; 79; 508; 588
26:617(a). .79
26:671 to 678. 423
26:671 to 679. 520
26:672 423
26:672(c). 422
26:691.447; 460; 475; 479, 480; 483, 484; 499; 525; 535; 542

United States Code—Cont.

Title:Sec.	Page
26:691(a) .482
26:691(a)(1) 480
26:691(a)(3) 480
26:691(c) .481
26:691(c)(2) 481
26:691(e) .481
26:701 . . . . 1; 19; 44; 59
26:702 . 19; 59; 67; 71; 87; 110; 145; 156; 199; 287; 437; 440; 448; 450; 460
26:702(a). 2; 60–62; 143; 220; 287
26:702(a)(4) 148
26:702(a)(7). 134; 287
26:702(a)(8) 60
26:702(b) 2; 19; 59; 455; 593
26:702(c). .66
26:703 . . . . 59; 87; 110
26:703(2) 2
26:703(a). 61; 145
26:703(a)(1). 2
26:703(a)(2) 61
26:703(b). 1; 12; 48; 59; 75; 588
26:703(b)(1) 79
26:703(b)(2) 79
26:703(b)(3) 79
26:704 . . . . 292; 294–296; 450; 543
26:704(a) 3; 20; 199
26:704(b) . . 3; 15; 20; 47; 54; 72; 86; 90; 120; 166; 170; 178; 183; 186, 187; 189–191; 204; 206; 230–232; 254; 263–265; 308; 319; 337; 426, 427; 430; 432; 503; 580
26:704(b)(2) 200
26:704(c). . . .3; 52; 72–74; 104; 111; 120; 152; 170, 171; 178, 179; 183; 186–189; 191, 192; 194; 197; 199; 203–206; 214–218; 220; 254; 259; 261; 308; 508; 516; 528–530; 532; 534; 544–547; 579, 580; 582; 590–592
26:704(c)(1) 582
26:704(c)(1)(A). . .18; 72; 100, 101; 111; 202, 203; 219
26:704(c)(1)(B) . . 18; 100; 112; 215–217; 219, 220; 582; 591
26:704(c)(1)(B)(i) 581
26:704(c)(1)(B)(iii). 216
26:704(c)(1)(C). 202
26:704(c)(1)(C)(i) 202
26:704(c)(1)(C)(ii) 202
26:704(c)(2) 220

[References are to pages]

United States Code—Cont.

Title:Sec.	Page
26:704(d) . 2; 60; 140; 146; 158; 171; 179; 187; 286; 288; 496; 511; 593	
26:704(e) 200; 308; 411; 414; 426; 432	
26:704(e)(1) 409–412; 414, 415; 423; 428	
26:704(e)(2) 225; 241; 409; 426; 428–432	
26:704(e)(3) 410; 415; 426; 428	
26:705 . .2; 4, 5; 117; 152, 153; 158; 168; 173; 286; 495; 500	
26:705(a). . .85; 159; 161; 163; 167, 168; 198; 209; 483; 499, 500; 510	
26:705(a)(1) 85; 145; 153; 287; 336; 450; 461	
26:705(a)(1)(A). 143; 481	
26:705(a)(1)(B). 143; 147	
26:705(a)(1)(C). 143	
26:705(a)(2). 117; 144; 146	
26:705(a)(2)(A). 144	
26:705(a)(2)(B). .136; 144; 148, 149; 176; 268; 274	
26:705(a)(3). 144; 146; 151	
26:705(b). .167	
26:706 . . . . .60; 87	
26:706(C) 90	
26:706(II) 91	
26:706(a) . . 2; 61; 87; 89; 145; 157; 199; 201; 450; 496; 510	
26:706(b). 2; 48; 54; 76; 96, 97; 588	
26:706(b)(1)(B). 89, 90; 96	
26:706(b)(1)(B)(i). 91	
26:706(b)(1)(B)(ii). 92	
26:706(b)(1)(B)(iii) 93	
26:706(b)(1)(C). 89; 94	
26:706(b)(2). 89	
26:706(b)(3) 92; 296; 301	
26:706(b)(4)(A)(i). 91	
26:706(b)(4)(A)(i)(I). 91	
26:706(b)(4)(B) 91	
26:706(b)(5). 90	
26:706(c) 8; 432; 438; 575; 587	
26:706(c)(1) 201; 223; 560; 575	
26:706(c)(2) 87; 473; 518	
26:706(c)(2)(A). 157; 201; 474; 476; 478; 518	
26:706(c)(2)(A)(i). 496; 510	
26:706(c)(2)(B) 223–225; 500; 519	
26:706(d) 3; 223, 224; 241; 432	
26:706(d)(1). 200; 223	
26:706(d)(2). 200; 223; 227	
26:706(d)(2)(A). 227	

United States Code—Cont.

Title:Sec.	Page
26:706(d)(2)(A)(i) 223	
26:706(d)(2)(B). 227	
26:706(d)(2)(C)(i) 228	
26:706(d)(2)(C)(ii) 228	
26:706(d)(2)(D)(i) 228	
26:706(d)(2)(D)(ii) 228	
26:706(d)(3). 228, 229	
26:707 . . . . .130; 203; 320, 321	
26:707(B) 5; 307	
26:707(a) 2; 4, 5; 88; 105; 120; 130; 289, 290; 293–296; 300; 304; 322	
26:707(a)(1). 289, 290; 303	
26:707(a)(2). . . .137; 290; 305–308; 310; 323; 333	
26:707(a)(2)(A). . .5; 103; 136, 137; 290; 294; 307; 332, 333	
26:707(a)(2)(B) . 101; 103; 290; 293; 307; 311; 320; 331, 332; 569	
26:707(b). 5, 6; 290; 296; 301; 334; 337	
26:707(b)(1) 148; 181; 291; 334; 336, 337	
26:707(b)(1)(B). 567	
26:707(b)(2). 291; 334; 338	
26:707(b)(3) 335	
26:707(c) . . .2; 5; 65; 88; 125; 130; 291; 293–296; 300; 437; 440; 448; 451; 461; 510	
26:708 . . . . 92; 515; 517, 518; 559; 570	
26:708(a). .559	
26:708(b) . . . 8; 223; 296; 301; 308; 513; 518, 519; 522; 551, 552; 559; 562; 566; 568; 570, 571	
26:708(b)(1). 201; 245; 474; 522	
26:708(b)(1)(A). 40; 559; 561; 565	
26:708(b)(1)(B). . .36; 42; 203; 215; 221; 282; 312; 539; 552; 559; 566–568; 570; 572, 573; 579; 582; 588, 589; 591; 593	
26:708(b)(2) 560	
26:708(b)(2)(A). 9; 560; 573; 575, 576	
26:708(b)(2)(B) 9; 36; 560; 583	
26:709 . . . . .76; 135–137; 332	
26:709(a) 135; 333	
26:709(b). 78; 135	
26:721 . 18; 104–106; 117; 119; 122; 128; 130; 151; 292; 306; 512; 515; 536–538; 570	
26:721(a) 3; 99, 100; 102; 106; 108; 539	
26:721(b) . 4; 101, 102; 106–108; 110; 114, 115; 143	
26:721(c). .102	
26:721(d). .103	

[References are to pages]

United States Code—Cont.

Title:Sec. | **Page**

26:722 . . 2–4; 18; 21; 100; 108; 113–115; 141; 143;
152; 163; 168; 206; 292; 499, 500; 512, 513;
515; 538

26:723 . 3, 4; 18; 100; 108–110; 114; 126; 151, 152;
162, 163; 206; 208; 292; 308; 537, 538; 592

26:724 . . . . 4; 72, 73; 100; 110; 593

26:724(a). .73

26:724(b). .73

26:724(c). 73; 110

26:724(d)(3) 110

26:724(d)(3)(A) 74

26:724(d)(3)(B) 74; 110

26:731 . . . 6; 42; 51; 102–104; 114; 150; 154; 216;
219–221; 294; 296; 306; 437; 452; 457; 465;
503; 569; 581

26:731 to 735. 439

26:731 to 736. 292

26:731(a) . 6; 86; 113; 115; 140; 155; 160, 161; 179;
187–189; 196; 208; 443; 454, 455; 457, 458;
465; 503, 504; 512, 513; 516, 517; 577

26:731(a)(1). 22; 146; 150; 444; 457

26:731(a)(2). . . .6; 22; 140; 207; 444; 458; 466; 487

26:731(b) 6

26:731(c) 160; 444

26:731(c)(5) 160

26:732. . . . . .42; 221; 437; 447; 465

26:732(a) 6; 140; 159; 489

26:732(a)(1) 150

26:732(a)(2). 146; 159

26:732(b). . . .6; 140; 222; 464, 465; 579, 580; 589

26:732(c). 6; 467; 557

26:732(d) . . 308; 447, 448; 476, 477; 485–489; 497;
540; 542; 552–557; 589, 590

26:733. . . .2; 85; 113, 114; 141; 144; 149; 165; 168;
196; 437; 500

26:733(2). .218

26:734. . . . . .160; 460

26:734(a) 8

26:734(b).8; 166; 216; 222; 441; 458; 485; 549; 553

26:734(b)(1)(A). 155; 220; 222

26:735. . . . . .110; 468; 487

26:735(a) 6

26:735(b). 6; 522; 592, 593

26:736 . . 7; 437–439; 444; 446; 462, 463; 477; 479;
563

26:736(3). .441

26:736(a) . 7; 440–443; 446–458; 460–469; 477; 481,
482

26:736(a)(1). 7

26:736(a)(2). 7; 150

26:736(b) 7; 439–459; 461–469; 477

26:736(b)(1) 458

26:736(b)(2). 7; 441; 468

26:736(b)(2)(A). 467

26:736(b)(2)(B). 443

26:737. . . . . .100; 112; 216–222; 582; 591

26:737(a) 219, 220; 582

26:737(b). .582

26:737(c)(1) 218

26:741.6–8; 114–116; 166; 477; 487; 495; 503; 505;
512; 569

26:742.2; 4; 141, 142; 198; 475; 483, 484; 495; 527;
580

26:743. .38; 308; 460; 524; 532; 551; 565; 579; 591

26:743(a). 8; 484; 496; 523

26:743(b) . 8; 38; 154; 166; 441, 442; 475; 484–487;
515; 517, 518; 524–529; 531–540; 542–549;
551–555; 589

26:743(d). .524

26:743(e). .524

26:751.7, 8; 104; 114, 115; 166; 442; 445; 447; 453;
455, 456; 460; 477; 486; 495; 500; 503; 505,
506; 509, 510; 515–517; 555

26:751(a) 505, 506; 509

26:751(b). .6; 22; 63; 437; 445–447; 452; 457; 460;
466; 468, 469; 477; 515

26:751(c) .72, 73; 439; 441; 482; 506–508; 532; 543

26:751(d). 73; 506

26:751(d)(2) 72

26:751(d)(2)(A). 509

26:751(d)(2)(B). 509

26:751(d)(2)(C). 509

26:751(d)(2)(D). 509

26:752 . 5; 21; 85, 86; 101; 112; 117; 161; 167; 169;
171, 172; 176; 178; 186, 187; 192, 193; 218;
270; 285; 323; 327, 328; 483; 487; 498; 513;
527; 580

26:752(a) . . 112–114; 141; 143; 168; 180; 196–198;
498–500; 516

26:752(b) . 4; 85; 103, 104; 113; 141; 144; 156; 168;
180; 196, 197; 438; 483; 498; 500, 501; 503;
512; 516; 569; 577; 581

26:752(c). 113; 196, 197; 498

26:752(d) . . 197; 495; 497–499; 503, 504; 519; 527

26:753 481

United States Code—Cont.

Title:Sec.	Page
26:754. . .8; 75; 114; 140; 150; 152–155; 159; 160; 162; 163; 166; 216; 220; 222; 308; 442; 447; 448; 459; 460; 464; 465; 475–479; 481–489; 496; 497; 523–526; 528; 530–533; 535; 537–539; 544; 546; 547; 549; 551–555; 557; 579; 589; 590; 592	
26:755.154; 228; 475; 484; 487; 488; 527; 531; 532; 540–542; 546; 548; 549; 551	
26:761. . . . . .19; 41; 51	
26:761(a). 10; 48; 49; 51; 52; 55	
26:761(a)(2). 50	
26:761(a)(3). 51	
26:761(c). 229; 444	
26:761(e). 474; 517; 518; 526; 570; 571	
26:761(e)(3). 571	
26:761(f). .49	
26:771 to 777 97	
26:851(a). .43	
26:856(c)(1). 31	
26:861 to 865 39	
26:871. 64	
26:871(d). 79	
26:881. 64	
26:901. . . . . .61; 63; 79; 80; 588	
26:901(b)(4). 80	
26:901(b)(5). 80	
26:904 39	
26:906(a). 80	
26:911. . . . . .64; 65; 67	
26:911(d). 441	
26:911(d)(2). 64	
26:931 . . . . .67; 147	
26:951 to 964 . . . . .39; 69	
26:952(a). 69	
26:954 . . . . .67; 69	
26:954(a). 69, 70	
26:995(c). 508	
26:996(f)(1). 508	
26:1001. . . . . .99; 141; 197	
26:1001(a). 140	
26:1001(b). 495; 497, 498	
26:1011 to 1023. . . . . .4; 142	
26:1011(b). 519; 569	
26:1012. . . . . .125; 142; 162; 308; 496; 499; 527	
26:1014. . .142; 162; 164; 475; 483; 484; 487; 489; 499; 525; 527	
26:1014(b)(6). 483	
26:1014(c). 480–482; 535; 542	
26:1015 . . . . .142; 162; 499; 518	

United States Code—Cont.

Title:Sec.	Page
26:1016. .162	
26:1016(a)(2). 545	
26:1017 81	
26:1017(b)(3)(C). 156	
26:1031 . . . . .49; 307; 512; 514; 570	
26:1031(a). 49; 570	
26:1031(a)(1). 514	
26:1031(a)(2)(D). 142; 514	
26:1031(d). 74	
26:1032. . . . . .68; 151–155	
26:1033 . . . . .49; 75, 76	
26:1041. .569	
26:1041(b)(1). 569	
26:1060. . . . . .540, 541	
26:1060(a). 540	
26:1060(b). 540	
26:1060(d)(1). 540	
26:1060(d)(2). 540	
26:1092 .76	
26:1221. . . . . .73; 338; 507; 509	
26:1222. 504	
26:1223(1). 109; 504; 593	
26:1223(2). 142; 593	
26:1231 . . . .62; 73; 109; 116; 287; 505; 509; 527	
26:1231(b). 532; 542	
26:1237 .72	
26:1239 . . . . .291; 334	
26:1239(a). 338, 339	
26:1239(b). 338	
26:1239(c). 338	
26:1239(c)(2). 335	
26:1245 . . . . .105; 508; 543	
26:1246(a) 509	
26:1248(d)(1). 508	
26:1250. .508	
26:1250(a) 504	
26:1250(b)(1). 504	
26:1252. .508	
26:1253. .508	
26:1256 .76	
26:1271 to 1275 303	
26:1271(a)(4). 509	
26:1271(d). 509	
26:1272. . . . . .247; 311	
26:1274 . . . . .308; 311; 330	
26:1278. .508	
26:1348(b) 441	

[References are to pages]

United States Code—Cont.

Title:Sec.	Page
26:1361	10; 15
26:1361(b)(2)	19
26:1361(c)(1)	19
26:1362	19
26:1366	18; 20; 23
26:1366(d)	21
26:1368(b)	23
26:1368(e)	23
26:1371(a)	23
26:1374	20; 23
26:1375	20
26:1399	83
26:1402	65
26:1402(a)(17)	50
26:1491	103
26:1491 to 1494	103
26:1939	411
26:2032	483
26:2032A	494
26:2036(a)	433
26:2036(c)	433
26:2042(2)	493
26:2503(b)	415
26:2701	434
26:2701 to 2704	433; 492
26:2702	434
26:2703	434
26:2703(a)	435
26:2703(b)	435
26:2704	434, 435
26:6012(a)	67
26:6222	59
26:6501(c)(9)	435
26:6662	33; 57; 175
26:6662(a)	449
26:6662(d)(2)(C)(ii)	77
26:6698	51; 57
26:6700	57
26:7519	96, 97
26:7701	41, 42
26:7701(B)	174
26:7701(a)	55
26:7701(a)(3)	55
26:7701(a)(4)	27, 28
26:7701(a)(30)	91
26:7701(a)(42)	74; 110
26:7701(g)	82; 196; 231; 266; 496; 498; 528

United States Code—Cont.

Title:Sec.	Page
26:7701(i)	32
26:7701(o)	173, 174
26:7701(o)(5)(A)	174
26:7704	10; 26; 32; 41; 44; 57
26:7704(a)	43
26:7704(b)	43; 118; 131
26:7704(c)	42–44
26:7704(c)(1)	43
26:7704(c)(3)	43
26:7704(d)	43
26:7704(f)	42
26:7805	27
26:7872	303
26:7874	43, 44

Code of Federal Regulations

Title:Sec.	Page
26:1.61-3	414
26:1.61-6(a)	495; 500
26:1.83-1(a)	123
26:1.83-3(c)	122
26:1.83-3(e)	129
26:1.83-6(a)	125
26:1.83-6(b)	125, 126; 463; 466; 468
26:1.83-6(c)	125
26:1.108-4	81
26:1.108(c)-5	82
26:1.165-9(b)	109
26:1.167(g)-1	109
26:1.170A-1(h)(7)	63
26:1.179-1(f)(2)	79
26:1.179-2(b)(3)(iv)	79
26:1.179-2(c)(2)	79
26:1.351-1(c)(1)	107
26:1.351-1(c)(1)(i)	107
26:1.351-1(c)(1)(ii)	107
26:1.351-1(c)(2)	107
26:1.351-1(c)(4)	107
26:1.351-1(c)(5)	107
26:1.442-1(b)(1)	89
26:1.442-1(b)(2)(ii)	89
26:1.453-9(c)(2)	104
26:1.471-1	509
26:1.482-7	29
26:1.701-2	44, 45; 169
26:1.613A-3(e)(1)	150

[References are to pages]

Code of Federal Regulations—Cont.

Title:Sec.   **Page**

26:1.613A-3(e)(6)(iv) 548
26:1.661(a)-2(f)(1) 518
26:1.691(a)-1(b) 480
26:1.691(a)-2(b) 480
26:1.691(c)-1(a) 481
26:1.691(c)-1(a)(2) 481
26:1.701-1(b)(4)(i) 183
26:1.701-2(a) 45
26:1.701-2(b) 46
26:1.701-2(c) 47
26:1.701-2(e) 44; 47
26:1.701-2(e)(2) 47
26:1.701-2(g) 44
26:1.701-2(h) 44
26:1.702-1(2) 62
26:1.702-1(a) 60, 61; 87
26:1.702-1(a)(1) 62
26:1.702-1(a)(3) 62
26:1.702-1(a)(6) 63
26:1.702-1(a)(8) 62; 64; 71; 287; 548
26:1.702-1(a)(8)(i) 63
26:1.702-1(a)(8)(ii) 64, 65
26:1.702-1(b) 67; 480
26:1.702-1(c)(1) 67
26:1.702-1(ii) 62; 64; 71
26:1.702-2 .68
26:1.703-1(a) 61
26:1.703-1(b)(1) 48; 75
26:1.703-1(b)(2)(iii) 79
26:1.704-1(2) 234; 241
26:1.704-1(3) 234; 241
26:1.704-1(5) 241
26:1.704-1(6) 241
26:1.704-1(a) 231
26:1.704-1(b) 3; 20; 246
26:1.704-1(b)(1)(i) 232
26:1.704-1(b)(1)(iii) 426; 431
26:1.704-1(b)(2) 270
26:1.704-1(b)(2)(i) 233; 246
26:1.704-1(b)(2)(ii)(a) 235
26:1.704-1(b)(2)(ii)(b) 230; 234, 235
26:1.704-1(b)(2)(ii)(b)(2) 236
26:1.704-1(b)(2)(ii)(b)(3) 239, 240
26:1.704-1(b)(2)(ii)(c) 238; 240; 244
26:1.704-1(b)(2)(ii)(d) 238; 242
26:1.704-1(b)(2)(ii)(d)(1) 234; 241
26:1.704-1(b)(2)(ii)(d)(3) 241

Code of Federal Regulations—Cont.

Title:Sec.   **Page**

26:1.704-1(b)(2)(ii)(d)(4) 241
26:1.704-1(b)(2)(ii)(e) 246
26:1.704-1(b)(2)(ii)(f) 239; 244
26:1.704-1(b)(2)(ii)(g) 236; 240; 245
26:1.704-1(b)(2)(ii)(h) 232
26:1.704-1(b)(2)(ii)(i) 245, 246
26:1.704-1(b)(2)(iii)(a) 230; 235; 246, 247
26:1.704-1(b)(2)(iii)(b) 235; 246; 248, 249
26:1.704-1(b)(2)(iii)(c) 235; 246, 247; 249–251
26:1.704-1(b)(2)(iv) 203; 415; 427; 431; 528
26:1.704-1(b)(2)(iv)(a) 251, 252
26:1.704-1(b)(2)(iv)(b) 252, 253; 256
26:1.704-1(b)(2)(iv)(c) 255
26:1.704-1(b)(2)(iv)(d)(2) 256
26:1.704-1(b)(2)(iv)(d)(3) 260
26:1.704-1(b)(2)(iv)(e)(1) 254
26:1.704-1(b)(2)(iv)(e)(2) 256
26:1.704-1(b)(2)(iv)(f) 167; 256; 269
26:1.704-1(b)(2)(iv)(f)(1) 258, 259
26:1.704-1(b)(2)(iv)(f)(5) 256
26:1.704-1(b)(2)(iv)(g)(1) 260
26:1.704-1(b)(2)(iv)(g)(2) 262
26:1.704-1(b)(2)(iv)(g)(3) 261
26:1.704-1(b)(2)(iv)(h) 258
26:1.704-1(b)(2)(iv)(i)(1) 263
26:1.704-1(b)(2)(iv)(k) 241
26:1.704-1(b)(2)(iv)(l) 580; 590
26:1.704-1(b)(2)(iv)(n) 253
26:1.704-1(b)(2)(iv)(o) 263
26:1.704-1(b)(2)(iv)(q) 253
26:1.704-1(b)(3) 231; 264
26:1.704-1(b)(3)(i) 233
26:1.704-1(b)(3)(ii) 264; 335
26:1.704-1(b)(4)(i) 204; 260, 261
26:1.704-1(b)(4)(iv)(f) 170; 178, 179
26:1.704-1(b)(4)(vi) 240; 247
26:1.704-1(b)(5) . 237, 238; 240; 243; 245; 248–251;
                           255; 259; 261–263; 265
26:1.704-1(c) 246
26:1.704-1(d) 288
26:1.704-1(d)(1) 146; 253; 286; 511
26:1.704-1(d)(2) 286–288; 496; 511
26:1.704-1(d)(4) 287
26:1.704-1(e)(1) 253
26:1.704-1(e)(1)(iii) 415
26:1.704-1(e)(1)(iv) 412, 413
26:1.704-1(e)(1)(v) 120; 127; 414; 427

Code of Federal Regulations—Cont.

Title:Sec.	Page
26:1.704-1(e)(2)	256
26:1.704-1(e)(2)(i)	415
26:1.704-1(e)(2)(ii)	414; 416–418
26:1.704-1(e)(2)(iii)	418
26:1.704-1(e)(2)(iv)	419
26:1.704-1(e)(2)(ix)	421
26:1.704-1(e)(2)(v)	417; 419
26:1.704-1(e)(2)(vi)	419
26:1.704-1(e)(2)(vii)	422
26:1.704-1(e)(2)(viii)	424
26:1.704-1(e)(2)(x)	421
26:1.704-1(e)(3)(i)	426; 429, 430
26:1.704-1(e)(3)(ii)	429; 432
26:1.704-1(e)(4)	428
26:1.704-1(e)(4)(i)	425
26:1.704-1(e)(4)(ii)	425, 426
26:1.704-1(f)	260
26:1.704-1(g)	260
26:1.704-1(r)	179
26:1.704-1.4	166
26:1.704-2	170
26:1.704-2(b)(1)	266; 268, 269; 274
26:1.704-2(b)(2)	267; 269
26:1.704-2(c)	267; 269; 274, 275
26:1.704-2(d)	267; 269
26:1.704-2(d)(1)	272
26:1.704-2(e)	270
26:1.704-2(e)(3)	282
26:1.704-2(f)	268
26:1.704-2(f)(2)	284
26:1.704-2(f)(3)	284
26:1.704-2(f)(4)	285
26:1.704-2(f)(6)	283
26:1.704-2(f)(7)	284, 285
26:1.704-2(g)	267; 269; 278
26:1.704-2(g)(1)	279
26:1.704-2(g)(2)	268; 282
26:1.704-2(h)	270
26:1.704-2(h)(1)	280
26:1.704-2(h)(2)	280
26:1.704-2(h)(3)	282
26:1.704-2(h)(4)	280
26:1.704-2(i)	270
26:1.704-2(i)(1)	285
26:1.704-2(j)	275
26:1.704-2(j)(1)(iii)	277

Code of Federal Regulations—Cont.

Title:Sec.	Page
26:1.704-2(j)(2)	283
26:1.704-2(j)(2)(iii)	283
26:1.704-2(k)	270
26:1.704-2(m)	272, 273; 276
26:1.704-3(a)	215; 590
26:1.704-3(a)(1)	203; 205
26:1.704-3(a)(2)	203; 591
26:1.704-3(a)(3)(i)	203; 215; 582
26:1.704-3(a)(5)	203
26:1.704-3(a)(7)	204; 529; 544; 580
26:1.704-3(a)(8)	204
26:1.704-3(a)(8)(i)	205
26:1.704-3(a)(9)	204
26:1.704-3(a)(10)	204, 205
26:1.704-3(b)(1)	206, 207; 210
26:1.704-3(c)(1)	211
26:1.704-3(c)(2)	211
26:1.704-3(c)(3)	211
26:1.704-3(c)(3)(iii)	211
26:1.704-3(c)(4)	204
26:1.704-3(d)	212; 496; 528; 532; 544, 545
26:1.704-3(d)(1)	545
26:1.704-3(d)(2)	213
26:1.704-3(d)(3)	213
26:1.704-3(d)(4)	213
26:1.704-3(d)(5)	212
26:1.704-3(d)(7)	213
26:1.704-3(e)	111; 214
26:1.704-3(e)(2)	111; 214
26:1.704-3(e)(2)(i)	214
26:1.704-3(e)(3)	215
26:1.704-3(e)(3)(ii)	111
26:1.704-3(ii)	214
26:1.704-3(iii)	214
26:1.704-4(a)	215
26:1.704-4(a)(4)	591
26:1.704-4(a)(4)(i)	215
26:1.704-4(b)	215
26:1.704-4(c)	217
26:1.704-4(c)(3)	591
26:1.704-4(d)(2)	217
26:1.704-4(e)	216
26:1.704-4(e)(3)	216
26:1.704-4(f)	217
26:1.704-4(f)(2)	217
26:1.704(b)(1)	170

[References are to pages]

Code of Federal Regulations—Cont.

Title:Sec.   **Page**

26:1.705-1(a) 173; 510
26:1.705-1(a)(1) . 139, 140; 145; 157, 158; 161; 495; 497; 500
26:1.705-1(a)(2) 500
26:1.705-1(b) 167
26:1.705-2 152
26:1.705-2(a) 68; 153
26:1.705-2(b) 153
26:1.705-2(c) 154
26:1.705-2(e) 154
26:1.706-1(a) 61
26:1.706-1(b)(2) 89
26:1.706-1(b)(4)(iii) 94
26:1.706-1(c) 587
26:1.706-1(c)(1)(3) 518
26:1.706-1(c)(2) 157; 224
26:1.706-1(c)(2)(ii) 223–226; 510; 575
26:1.706-1(c)(3)(i) 479
26:1.706-1(c)(3)(ii) 479
26:1.706-1(c)(3)(iv) 474; 563
26:1.706-1(c)(3)(v) 479
26:1.706-1(c)(3)(vi) 474
26:1.706-1(c)(5) 432; 519
26:1.706-1(vi) 479
26:1.707-1(a) 103; 105; 289; 293; 303, 304
26:1.707-1(c) . 88; 291; 297, 298; 301; 335; 451; 573
26:1.707-2 137
26:1.707-3(1) 311
26:1.707-3(a)(1) 311
26:1.707-3(a)(2) 307; 311
26:1.707-3(a)(3) 312
26:1.707-3(a)(4) 312
26:1.707-3(b)(1) 310; 313
26:1.707-3(b)(1)(i) 307
26:1.707-3(b)(1)(ii) 307
26:1.707-3(b)(2) 307; 313, 314
26:1.707-3(c)(1) 307; 310; 313
26:1.707-3(d) 313
26:1.707-3(e) 307
26:1.707-3(f) 311, 312; 314; 316–319
26:1.707-4 . . . . .312; 323
26:1.707-5 312
26:1.707-5(a) 323; 326
26:1.707-5(a)(1) 323; 326
26:1.707-5(a)(2) 330
26:1.707-5(a)(2)(i) 327
26:1.707-5(a)(4) 330

Code of Federal Regulations—Cont.

Title:Sec.   **Page**

26:1.707-5(a)(5) 323–325
26:1.707-5(a)(6) 313
26:1.707-5(a)(6)(i) 324
26:1.707-5(a)(6)(i)(A) 324
26:1.707-5(a)(6)(i)(B) 324
26:1.707-5(a)(6)(i)(C) 324; 326
26:1.707-5(a)(6)(i)(D) 325, 326
26:1.707-5(a)(6)(ii) 325
26:1.707-5(a)(7) 312; 324
26:1.707-5(b)(1) 327
26:1.707-5(b)(1)(ii) 328
26:1.707-5(b)(2)(i) 327, 328
26:1.707-5(b)(2)(iii) 328
26:1.707-5(c) 324
26:1.707-5(d) 326
26:1.707-5(e) 324–327
26:1.707-5(f) 328, 329
26:1.707-6 313
26:1.707-6(a) 330
26:1.707-6(b)(1) 330, 331
26:1.707-6(b)(2) 331
26:1.707-6(b)(2)(i) 331
26:1.707-6(d) 330, 331
26:1.708-1(b) 92; 475
26:1.708-1(b)(1)(i) 479; 518; 561, 562
26:1.708-1(b)(1)(i)(a) 475; 563
26:1.708-1(b)(1)(i)(b) 563
26:1.708-1(b)(1)(ii) . . .518, 519; 552; 565–568; 572
26:1.708-1(b)(1)(iii) 560; 587
26:1.708-1(b)(1)(iii)(b) 560
26:1.708-1(b)(1)(iv) . . . 8; 312; 539; 551, 552; 560; 589, 590
26:1.708-1(b)(1)(v) 552
26:1.708-1(b)(2) 574
26:1.708-1(b)(2)(i) 574
26:1.708-1(b)(2)(ii) 583
26:1.708-1(b)(4) 215
26:1.708-1(b)(ii) 571
26:1.708-1(b)(iv) 591
26:1.708-1(b)(v) 589, 590
26:1.708-1(c)(2) 575
26:1.708-1(c)(3) 576
26:1.708-1(c)(3)(i) 576, 577
26:1.708-1(c)(3)(ii) 576, 577
26:1.708-1(c)(4) 579
26:1.708-1(c)(5) 577; 579
26:1.708-1(c)(6) 580

[References are to pages]

Code of Federal Regulations—Cont.

Title:Sec.	Page
26:1.708-1(d)	583
26:1.708-1(d)(2)(i)	586
26:1.708-1(d)(2)(ii)	587
26:1.708-1(d)(3)(i)	586
26:1.708-1(d)(3)(i)(A)	584
26:1.708-1(d)(3)(i)(B)	585
26:1.708-1(d)(3)(ii)(A)	585
26:1.708-1(d)(3)(ii)(B)	585
26:1.708-1(d)(4)	583
26:1.708-1(d)(5)	586
26:1.708-1(iv)	560
26:1.709-1(b)(1)	135
26:1.709-1(b)(2)	135, 136
26:1.709-1(c)	78
26:1.709-2(a)	135
26:1.709-2(b)	136
26:1.709-2(c)	135
26:1.721-1(a)	102; 105; 306
26:1.721-1(b)	3
26:1.721-1(b)(1)	105; 117; 118; 122; 125; 127, 128
26:1.721-1(b)(2)	125
26:1.731-1(a)	140
26:1.731-1(a)(1)(ii)	161; 302
26:1.731-1(c)(3)	569
26:1.732-1(a)	140
26:1.732-1(d)	476; 486
26:1.732-1(d)(1)(iii)	486
26:1.732-1(d)(1)(iv)	486; 553
26:1.732-1(d)(1)(v)	486; 555
26:1.732-1(d)(1)(vi)	555
26:1.732-1(d)(2)	486
26:1.732-1(d)(4)	557
26:1.732-1(d)(4)(ii)	557
26:1.732-1(e)	555
26:1.732-2(b)	548
26:1.732-2(d)(2)	556
26:1.732-2(d)(3)	556
26:1.734-1(b)	155
26:1.736-1(7)	444
26:1.736-1(a)	563
26:1.736-1(a)(1)	439
26:1.736-1(a)(1)(i)	438
26:1.736-1(a)(1)(ii)	438
26:1.736-1(a)(2)	437; 449
26:1.736-1(a)(3)	450, 451
26:1.736-1(a)(4)	460; 466; 468
26:1.736-1(a)(5)	450, 451; 460, 461

Code of Federal Regulations—Cont.

Title:Sec.	Page
26:1.736-1(a)(6)	439; 479
26:1.736-1(b)(1)	440
26:1.736-1(b)(2)	441, 442
26:1.736-1(b)(3)	442, 443
26:1.736-1(b)(4)	447; 460
26:1.736-1(b)(5)	439; 452
26:1.736-1(b)(5)(i)	453
26:1.736-1(b)(5)(ii)	456
26:1.736-1(b)(5)(iii)	457
26:1.736-1(b)(6)	444, 445; 457–459
26:1.736-1(ii)	453
26:1.737-1(b)(1)	218
26:1.737-1(b)(2)	218
26:1.737-1(b)(3)(ii)	218
26:1.737-1(c)	219
26:1.737-1(c)(1)	219
26:1.737-1(c)(2)(i)	221
26:1.737-1(c)(2)(ii)	220
26:1.737-1(c)(2)(iii)	220
26:1.737-1(c)(2)(iv)	220
26:1.737-1(c)(2)(v)	220
26:1.737-1(d)	220; 222
26:1.737-1(e)	218, 219
26:1.737-2(2)	221
26:1.737-2(a)	221; 583; 591
26:1.737-2(b)(1)	221
26:1.737-2(c)	221
26:1.737-2(d)(1)	221
26:1.737-3(a)	221
26:1.737-3(b)(1)	221
26:1.737-3(b)(2)	221
26:1.737-3(c)	222
26:1.737-3(c)(3)	222
26:1.737-3(c)(4)	222
26:1.737-3(d)	223
26:1.737-3(e)	221
26:1.741-1(c)	512; 515
26:1.742	580
26:1.742-1	483; 499; 535
26:1.743-1(2)	528
26:1.743-1(a)	525
26:1.743-1(b)	447; 460; 484; 524
26:1.743-1(b)(2)(ii)	486; 554, 555
26:1.743-1(d)	527
26:1.743-1(d)(1)	528
26:1.743-1(d)(3)	528, 529
26:1.743-1(e)	527

Code of Federal Regulations—Cont.

Title:Sec.	Page
26:1.743-1(f)	531
26:1.743-1(g)	554, 555
26:1.743-1(g)(1)	548
26:1.743-1(g)(2)(i)	548
26:1.743-1(g)(2)(ii)	548
26:1.743-1(g)(3)	548
26:1.743-1(h)	552; 565; 589, 590
26:1.743-1(h)(1)	539
26:1.743-1(h)(2)	539
26:1.743-1(h)(2)(iv)	539
26:1.743-1(j)(1)	543
26:1.743-1(j)(2)	543
26:1.743-1(j)(3)	544
26:1.743-1(j)(4)	545
26:1.743-1(j)(4)(i)(B)(1)	545
26:1.743-1(j)(4)(i)(B)(2)	545
26:1.743-1(j)(4)(ii)(A)	547
26:1.743-1(j)(4)(ii)(B)	547
26:1.743-1(j)(5)	548
26:1.743-1(k)(1)(i)	553
26:1.743-1(k)(2)(i)	553
26:1.743(g)(5)	549
26:1.751-1(a)(2)	496; 505
26:1.751-1(a)(3)	510
26:1.751-1(b)	7
26:1.751-1(b)(2)(ii)	241
26:1.751-1(c)(1)	507
26:1.751-1(c)(1)(i)	507
26:1.751-1(c)(2)	442
26:1.751-1(c)(4)	508
26:1.751-1(c)(6)(ii)	508
26:1.751-1(d)(2)(i)	509
26:1.751-1(d)(2)(ii)	445; 509
26:1.751-1(f)	496
26:1.751-1(g)	505
26:1.752-1(3)	182
26:1.752-1(a)	180; 327
26:1.752-1(a)(1)	170
26:1.752-1(a)(2)	170; 186
26:1.752-1(b)	168
26:1.752-1(c)	168; 196
26:1.752-1(d)	495; 497
26:1.752-1(d)(1)	180; 195
26:1.752-1(d)(2)	180
26:1.752-1(e)	194; 196
26:1.752-1(f)	179; 194; 196; 580
26:1.752-1(g)	195; 581

Code of Federal Regulations—Cont.

Title:Sec.	Page
26:1.752-1(h)	197
26:1.752-1(j)(2)	182
26:1.752-2	85; 284
26:1.752-2(5)	184
26:1.752-2(a)	170; 178; 180; 182
26:1.752-2(b)	170; 178; 182
26:1.752-2(b)(1)	181; 184
26:1.752-2(b)(1)(i)	182
26:1.752-2(b)(2)	182
26:1.752-2(b)(3)	181
26:1.752-2(b)(4)	173; 175; 181; 184
26:1.752-2(b)(5)	173; 181
26:1.752-2(b)(6)	181; 184
26:1.752-2(c)	182
26:1.752-2(c)(1)	186
26:1.752-2(d)	182
26:1.752-2(d)(2)	185
26:1.752-2(e)	182; 186
26:1.752-2(f)	183, 184
26:1.752-2(g)(1)	185
26:1.752-2(h)(1)	181
26:1.752-2(h)(2)	182
26:1.752-2(j)	182
26:1.752-2(j)(1)	185; 329
26:1.752-2(j)(3)	173; 329
26:1.752-3(a)	170; 178; 187
26:1.752-3(a)(1)	187
26:1.752-3(a)(2)	188
26:1.752-3(a)(3)	171; 179; 188, 189
26:1.752-3(b)	189; 191
26:1.752-3(c)	192
26:1.752-4(b)(2)	180
26:1.752-4(c)	173
26:1.752-4(d)	173
26:1.752-5	580
26:1.752-6	177
26:1.752-6(d)(1)	176
26:1.753-1(a)	482
26:1.753-1(b)	481
26:1.753-3(b)	188
26:1.754-1(a)	553
26:1.754-1(b)	485
26:1.754-1(b)(1)	485; 553
26:1.754-1(c)	485
26:1.755-1(b)(1)(i)	535
26:1.755-1(b)(1)(ii)	532
26:1.755-1(b)(2)(i)	532

Code of Federal Regulations—Cont.

Title:Sec.	Page
26:1.755-1(b)(3)(i)	532
26:1.755-1(b)(3)(ii)	533
26:1.755-1(b)(4)	447; 460; 484; 488; 525; 535
26:1.755-1(b)(5)	536
26:1.755-1(c)	549
26:1.755-1(c)(1)(ii)	155
26:1.755-2	540
26:1.761-1(a)	41
26:1.761-1(c)	229
26:1.761-1(d)	438
26:1.761-1(e)	591
26:1.761-2(3)	54
26:1.761-2(a)(1)	48
26:1.761-2(a)(2)	50
26:1.761-2(a)(2)(iii)	50
26:1.761-2(a)(3)	50, 51
26:1.761-2(a)(3)(iii)	51
26:1.761-2(b)	53
26:1.761-2(b)(2)(i)	48; 53, 54
26:1.761-2(b)(2)(ii)	53, 54
26:1.761-2(b)(2)(ii)(a)	53
26:1.761-2(b)(3)	54
26:1.761-2(c)	54
26:1.761-2(d)	51
26:1.871-10	79
26:1.1001-2	503
26:1.1001-2(4)	519
26:1.1001-2(a)	498
26:1.1001-2(a)(1)	495; 497; 519
26:1.1001-2(a)(2)	82
26:1.1001-2(a)(4)	82
26:1.1001-2(a)(4)(v)	495; 497
26:1.1001-2(c)	519, 520
26:1.1002-1(c)	99
26:1.1011-2	519
26:1.1017-1(a)	81; 84
26:1.1017-1(c)	84
26:1.1017-1(f)	81; 84
26:1.1017-1(g)	84
26:1.1017-1(g)(2)	85
26:1.1017-1(g)(2)(ii)(B)	85
26:1.1031(a)-1(a)(1)	514
26:1.1032-3(a)	68; 151
26:1.1032-3(b)	151
26:1.1032-3(c)	151
26:1.1032-3(e)	151
26:1.1223-1(a)	109

Code of Federal Regulations—Cont.

Title:Sec.	Page
26:1.1245-1(e)(2)	508
26:1.1502-13(c)(1)(i)	550
26:1.7701-1	41, 42
26:1.7704-1	42
26:1.7704-1(a)	43
26:1.7704-1(l)	42
26:1.7704-1(l)(2)	42
26:1.7704-1(l)(4)	42
26:1.7704-2(c)	42
26:1.7704-2(d)	42
26:20.2031-2(h)	491, 492
26:20.2031-3	122; 490, 491
26:25.2503-3(a)	415
26:25.2512-3	490
26:301.6109-1(d)(2)(iii)	591
26:301.7701	27
26:301.7701-1	26
26:301.7701-1(a)(1)	29; 40
26:301.7701-1(a)(2)	27; 29; 40
26:301.7701-1(a)(3)	29
26:301.7701-1(a)(4)	29
26:301.7701-1(c)	29; 57
26:301.7701-1(d)	27; 30; 33
26:301.7701-1(e)	27; 30
26:301.7701-2	37; 41
26:301.7701-2(3)	33
26:301.7701-2(4)	33
26:301.7701-2(5)	33
26:301.7701-2(6)	33
26:301.7701-2(7)	33
26:301.7701-2(a)	57
26:301.7701-2(a)(1)	55
26:301.7701-2(a)(2)	56
26:301.7701-2(a)(3)	56
26:301.7701-2(b)	31; 57
26:301.7701-2(b)(1)	33
26:301.7701-2(b)(8)(i)	34
26:301.7701-2(c)	57
26:301.7701-2(c)(4)	57
26:301.7701-2(d)	34
26:301.7701-3(a)	32, 33
26:301.7701-3(b)(2)	33; 56
26:301.7701-3(b)(2)(ii)	34
26:301.7701-3(b)(3)	31
26:301.7701-3(c)	36; 38
26:301.7701-3(c)(1)	565
26:301.7701-3(c)(1)(iv)	36

Code of Federal Regulations—Cont.

Title:Sec.	Page
26:301.7701-3(c)(2)(iii)	38
26:301.7701-3(c)(v)(A)	31
26:301.7701-3(c)(v)(B)	31
26:301.7701-3(e)	36
26:301.7701-3(f)	33
26:301.7701-3(f)(2)	39
26:301.7701-3(f)(4)	37; 39
26:301.7701-3(g)	37
26:301.7701-3(g)(1)(i)	37
26:301.7701-3(g)(1)(ii)	37
26:301.7701-3(g)(1)(iii)	37
26:301.7701-3(g)(1)(iv)	37
26:301.7701-3(g)(2)	38
26:301.7701-3(g)(3)	38
26:301.7701-4	27
26:301.7701-4(a)	30
26:301.7701-4(b)	30
26:301.7701-4(c)	30
temp:26:1.163-8T	69; 280; 324; 327
temp:26:1.163-9T	69
temp:26:1.263A-1T	66
temp:26:1.367(a)-1T(c)	526
temp:26:1.441-1T(b)(2)	89
temp:26:1.441-3T(c)(2)(i)	96
temp:26:1.441-3T(d)(1)(ii)	96
temp:26:1.444-1T(b)(2)(iii)	97
temp:26:1.448-1T(a)(3)	77
temp:26:1.448-1T(a)(4)	77
temp:26:1.706-1T(a)(1)	90; 93
temp:26:1.706-1T(a)(2)	93
temp:26:1.706-1T(a)(4)	94
temp:26:1.706-1T(d)	93, 94
temp:26:1.706-2T	227
temp:26:1.706-3T	90, 91
temp:26:1.752-1T(j)(3)	114
temp:26:1.755-2T(a)(2)	541
temp:26:1.755-2T(b)(1)	541
temp:26:1.755-2T(b)(2)	541
temp:26:1.755-2T(d)	540
temp:26:1.1060-1T	541
temp:26:1.7874-2T	43
temp:26:1.7874-2T(e)	44

TAX SOURCES

Proposed Treasury Regulations

Sec.	Page
1.1(h)-1	496; 504
1.83-3(e)	119
1.337(d)-3	103
1.465-12	511
1.465-66	511
1.465-66(a)	511
1.702-1(a)(8)	67
1.702-1(ii)	67
1.704-1(b)(2)	86
1.704-1(b)(2)(iv)	90
1.705-2(a)	152; 155
1.705-2(b)(2)(i)	155
1.705-2(b)(2)(ii)	155
1.705-2(c)(1)	155
1.705-2(e)	156
1.706-1(b)(4)	90
1.706-4	91
1.706-4(a)(1)	91
1.706-4(a)(2)	91
1.706-4(c)	91
1.707-5(a)(7)(i)	326
1.707-7 to 1.707-9	332
1.721-1(b)(1)	119; 122
1.721-1(b)(1)(i)	117
1.721-1(b)(2)	119
1.743-2(a)	38
1.743-2(b)	38
1.743-2(c)	38
1.755-1(c)(5)	541
1.755-2(a)(1)	542
1.755-2(a)(2)	542
1.755-2(b)	542
1.755-2(b)(2)	542
1.755-2(b)(i)(1)(B)	543
1.755-2(c)	542
1.755-2(f)	542
1.952-1(g)(1)	68
301.7701	56
301.7701-3(h)	39

TABLE OF ADMINISTRATIVE PRONOUNCEMENTS

References are to page and footnote numbers.

General Counsel's Memorandum
GCM

36702	301n34
38067	302n36
38133	297n26; 301n34
38670	302n42
39043	52n132
39502	552n261
39643	571n77; 572n78
39673	571n72

IRS Announcements
No.

84-102, 1984-45 I.R.B. 21	175n157
88-118, 1988-2 C.B. 450	57n160

IRS Notices
No.

88-75, 1988-2 C.B. 386	42n83
88-99, 1988-2 C.B. 422	66n54
89-37, 1989-1 C.B. 679	103n10
93-2, 1993-1 C.B. 292	103n10
96-39, 1996-2 C.B. 209	71n84
98-11, 1998-1 C.B. 433	71n84
98-35, 1998-2 C.B. 34	71n82; 71n83
99-59, 1999-2 C.B. 761	169n130
99-59, 1999-52 I.R.B. 761	177n163
2000-44, 2000-2 C.B. 255	169n129; 169n130; 169n131; 176n159
2000-44, 2000-36 I.R.B. 255	177n163; 177n164
2001-641, 2001-2 C.B. 316	332n163
2005-43, 2005-24 I.R.B. 1221	119n96
2010-62, 2010-40 I.R.B. 411	174n153

Letter Rulings
Ltr. Rul.

8225069	105n27
8226014	51n122
8301001	105n28

Private Letter Rulings
Priv. Ltr. Rul.

881004	568n47

Private Letter Rulings—Cont.
Priv. Ltr. Rul.

7705028	574n85
7726014	531n203
7748032	462n76
7823013	376n133
7907001	304n51
7930089	462n76
7939005	303n43
7948063	512n124; 565n41
7952057	568n47
8015088	568n52
8024013	428n120
8028113	136n167
8034088	302n36
8116041	570n64
8117210	104n19
8150134	512n124; 565n41
8213051	462n76
8217028	568n47
8228094	569n59
8229034	570n64
8246095	574n85
8252023	568n47
8302108	562n24
8304078	462n76
8314039	167n122
8332031	462n76
8348001	86n182
8350006	168n124
8404027	568n47
8407029	574n83; 574n85
8444069	571n68
8448002	141n6
8517022	568n47
8542044	512n124; 565n41
8605047	583n117
8609021	512n124; 565n41
8619015	574n85
8642003	293n14
8643062	571n68
8851004	566n45
9007045	512n125
9108015	583n117

References are to page and footnote numbers.

Private Letter Rulings—Cont.
Priv. Ltr. Rul.

9130005	80n150
9321047	77n125
9407030	77n125
9412020	513n128; 566n42
9417009	513n128; 566n42
9422034	513n128; 566n42
9501033	77n125
9525058	513n128; 566n42
9525065	513n128; 566n42
9633021	513n128; 566n42
9809003	574n83
9841030	512n124
199935075	75n110

Revenue Procedures
Rev. Proc.

72-13, 1972-1 C.B. 735	56n159
74-17, 1974-1 C.B. 438	56n159
74-33, 1974-2 C.B. 489	94n232; 95n234
83-25, 1983-1 C.B. 689	95n234
84-74, 1984-2 C.B. 736	77n126
92-92, 1992-2 C.B. 505	81n154
93-1, 1993-1 C.B. 313	411n14
93-27, 1993-2 C.B. 343	118n91; 120n104; 127n124; 127n127; 128; 131n143; 131n144; 131n146; 132; 133
95-10, 1995-1 C.B. 501	41n75; 42n86
99-7, 1999-1 I.R.B. 226	35n37
2001-43, 2001-34 I.R.B. 191	131n145; 132n147; 133
2001-43, 2001-43 I.R.B. 191	127n128
2002-16, 2002-9 I.R.B. 572	88n195
2002-38, 2002-22 I.R.B. 103	95n233; 95n234
2002-39, 2002-22 I.R.B. 1046	95n237

Revenue Rulings
Rev. Rul.

55-39, 1955-1 C.B. 403	304n49
56-233, 1956-1 C.B. 51	87n189
56-397, 1956-2 C.B. 599	492n92
57-68, 1957-1 C.B. 207	380n143
57-215, 1957-1 C.B. 208	54n139
57-318, 1957-2 C.B. 362	504n65
58-465, 1958-2 C.B. 376	54n140
59-60, 1959-1 C.B. 237	490n80
60-352, 1960-2 C.B. 208	521n171

Revenue Rulings—Cont.
Rev. Rul.

63-107, 1963-1 C.B. 71	37n48; 55n148
64-56, 1964-1 C.B. 133	106n34
64-155, 1964-1 C.B. 138	515n140; 570n63
65-118, 1965-1 C.B. 30	52n128; 52n129
65-193, 1965-2 C.B. 370	490n80; 490n82
66-94, 1966-1 C.B. 166	286n351
66-95, 1966-1 C.B. 169	298n28
66-264, 1966-2 C.B. 248	562n24
66-325, 1966-2 C.B. 249	559n3; 563n30
67-65, 1967-1 C.B. 168	563n31; 592n152
67-188, 1967-1 C.B. 216	67n58; 522n174
68-79, 1968-1 C.B. 216	67n58
68-79, 1968-1 C.B. 310	62n20
68-196, 1968-1 C.B. 307	423n98
68-289, 1968-1 C.B. 314	522n174
68-609, 1968-2 C.B. 327	490n80; 490n82
69-180, 1969-1 C.B. 183	300n29
70-45, 1970-1 C.B. 17	106n33
70-101, 1970-1 C.B. 278	56n157
70-239, 1970-1 C.B. 74	564n35
70-355, 1970-2 C.B. 51	501n51
71-41, 1971-1 C.B. 211	80n146; 80n147
71-141, 1971-1 C.B. 211	63n26
71-564, 1971-2 C.B. 179	106n35
72-172, 1972-1 C.B. 265	522n174
72-352, 1972-2 C.B. 395	474n20; 518n150
72-504, 1972-2 C.B. 90	303n45; 305n55
73-300, 1973-2 C.B. 215	358n80
73-301, 1973-2 C.B. 215	358n78; 504n64; 507n83
74-40, 1974-1 C.B. 159	495n5; 497n20; 497n25; 503n60
74-71, 1974-1 C.B. 158	65n38
74-175, 1974-1 C.B. 52	288n362
75-1, 1975-1 C.B. 80	519n163; 519n164
75-113, 1975-1 C.B. 19	59n2; 76n118
75-154, 1975-1 C.B. 186	462n76; 462n77
75-194, 1975-1 C.B. 80	433n139; 495n5; 497n20; 497n25; 570n61
75-423, 1975-2 C.B. 260	568n52
75-498, 1975-2 C.B. 29	463n80; 466n84; 468n88
75-523, 1975-2 C.B. 257	69n67
77-137, 1977-1 C.B. 178	568n50
77-304, 1977-2 C.B. 59	67n58
77-309, 1977-2 C.B. 216	531n203
77-310, 1977-2 C.B 217	224n122
77-311, 1977-2 C.B. 218	531n203

Revenue Rulings—Cont.
Rev. Rul.

77-412, 1977-2 C.B.

   223 . . . . 379n141; 392n168; 392n169

77-458, 1977-2 C.B. 220 . 574n84; 574n85; 575n86

78-2, 1978-1 C.B. 202 . . . . 531n203

78-135, 1978-1 C.B. 256 . . . . 512n122

79-51, 1979-1 C.B. 225 . . . . 507n83

79-84, 1979-1 C.B. 223 . . . . 526n182

79-124, 1979-1 C.B. 224 . . . . 526n183

79-205, 1979-2 C.B.

   255 . . . . 114n76; 161n107; 194n227; 196n232;
                      516n142

80-198, 1980-2 C.B. 113 . . . . . . 104n20; 117n84

80-219, 1980-2 C.B. 19 . . . . 52n129

80-234, 1980-2 C.B. 203 . 88n193; 291n10; 297n25

80-235, 1980-2 C.B. 229 . . 106n38; 141n6; 141n7

80-323, 1980-2 C.B. 124 . . . . 515n137

81-38, 1981-1 C.B. 386 . . . . . 570n63; 570n64

81-40, 1981-1 C.B. 508 . . . . . 515n140; 570n63

81-150, 1981-1 C.B. 119 . . . . . 78n130; 134n154

81-153, 1981-1 C.B. 387 . . . . 136n167

81-163, 1981-1 C.B. 433 . . . . 570n61

81-241, 1981-2 C.B. 146 . . . . 358n80

81-261, 1981-2 C.B. 60 . . . . 49n110; 75n109

81-300, 1981-2 C.B. 143 . 292n12; 302n36; 451n50

81-301, 1981-2 C.B. 144 . . . . . 292n13; 451n50

82-213, 1982-2 C.B. 31 . . . . 52n129

83-129, 1983-2 C.B. 105 . . . . . 49n110; 52n131

83-147, 1983-2 C.B. 158 . . . . 493n98

83-148, 1983-2 C.B. 157 . . . . 493n97

83-155, 1983-2 C.B. 38 . . . . 462n78

84-5, 1984-1 C.B. 32 . . . . 175n157

84-11, 1984-2 C.B. 88 . . . . 564n35

84-52, 1984-1 C.B.

   157 . . . . 499n31; 512n124; 513n130; 565n41;
                      566n43

84-52, 1984-2 C.B. 157 . . . . 500n42

84-53, 1984-1 C.B.

   159 . . . . 168n124; 286n352; 495n3; 500n41;
                   501n43; 501n44

84-102, 1984-2 C.B.

   119 . . . . 104n17; 388n163; 390n164

84-111, 1984-2 C.B. 88 . . . . 37n49; 514n135

84-115, 1984-2 C.B.

   118 . . . . . 104n17; 104n21; 516n141; 570n64

84-142, 1984-2 C.B. 117 . . . . 75n112

85-32, 1985-1 C.B. 186 . . . . . 136n166; 136n167

Revenue Rulings—Cont.
Rev. Rul.

86-73, 1986-1 C.B.

   282 . . . . 589n135; 590n137; 592n153

86-101, 1986-2 C.B. 94 . . . . 518n155

86-138, 1986-2 C.B. 84 . . . . 66n49; 71n88

87-50, 1987-1 C.B. 157 . . . . 571n77

87-51, 1987-1 C.B. 158 . . . . . 571n72; 572n78

87-57, 1987-2 C.B. 117 . . 95n235; 95n236; 95n238

87-110, 1987-2 C.B. 159 . . . . 570n63

87-115, 1987-2 C.B. 163 . . . . . 531n203; 532n204

87-120, 1987-2 C.B.

   161 . . . . 114n76; 161n107; 194n227; 196n232

88-77, 1988-2 C.B. 128 . . . . . 172n141; 176n160

88-77, 1988-2 C.B. 129 . . . . 117n81

89-7, 1989-1 C.B. 178 . . . . 66n47; 148n49

89-72, 1989-1 C.B. 257 . . . . 70n74

89-85, 1989-2 C.B. 218 . . . . 551n257

90-16, 1990-1 C.B. 12 . . . . 82n163

91-31, 1991-1 C.B. 19 . . . . 82n160

92-15, 1992-1 C.B.

   215 . . . . 406n192; 407n193; 571n74

92-53, 1992-2 C.B. 48 . . . . 80n151

92-97, 1992-2 C.B.

   124 . . . . 85n178; 86n181; 238n183; 239n188;
                      244n204

92-99, 1992-2 C.B. 35 . . . . 81n153

93-13, 1993-1 C.B. 126 . . . . . 458n65; 458n67

93-80, 1993-2 C.B.

   239 . . . . . . 501n49; 501n51; 503n59; 503n62

93-90, 1993-2 C.B. 238 . . . . 282n339

95-26, 1995-1 C.B. 131 . . . . 176n160

95-37, 1995-1 C.B.

   130 . . . . 513n128; 560n9; 561n20; 566n42

95-41, 1995-1 C.B. 132 . . . . 192n222

95-55, 1995-2 C.B.

   313 . . 11n80; 513n129; 560n9; 561n20; 566n42

96-10, 1996-1 C.B. 138 . . . . . . 148n48; 336n185

96-11, 1996-1 C.B. 140 . . . . 63n24

99-5, 1999-6 I.R.B. 8 . . . . 40n67

99-6, 1999-6 I.R.B. 6 . . . . 40n68; 522n176

99-43, 1999-42 I.R.B.

   506 . . . . 247n219; 247n223; 249n227

99-57, 1999-2 C.B. 628 . . . . 152n66; 152n68

99-57, 1999-2 C.B. 678 . . . . 68n64

1993-2 C.B. 239 . . . . 355n62

2004-59, 2004-1 C.B. 1050 . . . . 565n39

References are to page and footnote numbers.

Technical Advice Memorandum

TAM

8648076 . . . . 358n80
9214011 . . . . 52n133

TABLE OF REGULATIONS

References are to page and footnote numbers.

Proposed Treasury Regulations

Sec.

1.1(h)-1	496n11; 504n68
1.83-3(e)	119n95; 119n98
1.168-5(b)(1)	345n19
1.337(d)-3	103n10
1.465-12	511n120; 511n121
1.465-66	511n120
1.465-66(a)	511n121
1.702-1(a)(8)	68n59
1.702-1(a)(8)(ii)	68n59
1.704-1(b)(2)	86n184
1.704-1(b)(2)(iv)	90n207
1.705-2(a)	152n67; 155n76
1.705-2(b)(2)(i)	155n77
1.705-2(b)(2)(ii)	155n78
1.705-2(c)(1)	155n82
1.705-2(e)	156n83
1.706-1(b)(4)	90n206
1.706-4	91n211
1.706-4(a)(1)	91n213
1.706-4(a)(2)	91n214
1.706-4(c)	91n212
1.707-5(a)(7)(i)	326n137
1.707-7–1.707-9	332n163
1.721-1(b)(1)	119n95; 119n98; 122n112
1.721-1(b)(1)(i)	117n85; 117n86
1.721-1(b)(2)	119n100
1.743-2(a)	38n57
1.743-2(b)	38n58
1.743-2(c)	38n59
1.755-1(c)(5)	541n225
1.755-2(a)(1)	542n227
1.755-2(a)(2)	542n228
1.755-2(b)	542n233
1.755-2(b)(2)	542n231; 542n232
1.755-2(b)(i)(1)(B)	543n234
1.755-2(c)	542n229
1.755-2(f)	542n227
1.952-1(g)(1)	68n60
301.7701	56n159
301.7701-2	39n60
301.7701-3	39n60
301.7701-3(h)	39n62

Temporary Treasury Regulations

Sec.

1.163-8T	69n69; 280n335; 324n120; 324n121; 327n146
1.163-9T	69n69
1.263A-1T	66n54
1.367(a)-1T(c)	526n188
1.441-1T(b)(2)	89n197
1.441-3T(c)(2)(i)	96n241
1.441-3T(d)(1)(ii)	96n240
1.444-1T(b)(2)(iii)	97n245
1.448-1T(a)(3)	77n122
1.448-1T(a)(4)	77n120; 77n123
1.706-1T(a)(1)	90n208; 93n222
1.706-1T(a)(2)	93n223
1.706-1T(a)(4)	94n227; 94n228
1.706-1T(d), Ex. (1)	93n224; 94n225; 94n226
1.706-1T(d), Ex. (6)	94n229
1.706-2T	227n133
1.706-3T	90n210; 91n215
1.752-1T(j)(3)	114n76
1.755-2T(a)(2)	541n223
1.755-2T(b)(1)	541n224
1.755-2T(b)(2)	541n225
1.755-2T(d)	540n222
1.1060-1T	541n226
1.7874-2T	43n90
1.7874-2T(e)	44n93

Treasury Regulations

Sec.

1.61-3	414n28
1.61-6(a)	495n3; 500n41
1.83-1(a)	123n115
1.83-3(c)	122n113
1.83-3(e)	129n136
1.83-6(a)	125n118
1.83-6(b)	125n116; 126n121; 463n80; 466n84; 468n88
1.83-6(c)	125n120
1.108-4	81n157
1.108(c)-5	82n164
1.163-8T	324n128

References are to page and footnote numbers.

Treasury Regulations—Cont.

Sec.

1.165-9(b) 109n54
1.167(g)-1 . . . . 109n54
1.170A-1(h)(7) 63n24
1.179-1(f)(2) 79n138
1.179-2(b)(3)(iv) 79n136
1.179-2(c)(2) 79n135
1.351-1(c)(1) 107n40
1.351-1(c)(1)(i) 107n46
1.351-1(c)(1)(ii) 107n42
1.351-1(c)(2) 107n45
1.351-1(c)(4) 107n43; 107n44
1.351-1(c)(5) 107n41; 107n47
1.442-1(b)(1) 89n200
1.442-1(b)(2)(ii) 89n198
1.453-9(c)(2) 104n22
1.469-1T(g)(2)(i) 22n129
1.471-1 . . . . 509n103
1.482-7 . . . . 29n13
1.613A-3(e)(1) 150n57
1.613A-3(e)(6)(iv) 548n248
1.661(a)-2(f)(1) 518n149
1.691(a)-1(b) 480n41
1.691(a)-2(b), Ex. (1) 480n43
1.691(c)-1(a) 481n48
1.691(c)-1(a)(2) 481n47
1.701-1(b)(4)(i) 183n196
1.701-2 . . . . 44n94; 45n95; 169n131
1.701-2(a) 45n96
1.701-2(b) 46n98; 46n99
1.701-2(c) 47n100; 47n101
1.701-2(e) 44n94; 47n102
1.701-2(e)(2) 47n103
1.701-2(g) 44n94
1.701-2(h) 44n94
1.702-1(a) 60n7; 60n8; 61n9; 87n186
1.702-1(a)(1) 62n19
1.702-1(a)(2) 62n19
1.702-1(a)(3) 62n22
1.702-1(a)(6) 63n26
1.702-1(a)(8) . 62n18; 64n29; 64n31; 64n32; 64n33;
                71n87; 287n355; 548n247
1.702-1(a)(8)(i) 63n27
1.702-1(a)(8)(ii) . . . 62n18; 64n29; 64n30; 64n31;
                64n32; 64n33; 65n37; 71n87
1.702-1(b) 67n58; 480n45
1.702-1(c)(1) 67n57
1.702-2 . . . . 68n66

Treasury Regulations—Cont.

Sec.

1.703-1(a) 61n9
1.703-1(b)(1) 48n110; 75n107
1.703-1(b)(2)(iii) 79n142
1.704-1.4 . . . . 166n118
1.704-1(a) 231n155
1.704-1(b) 3n16; 3n17; 20n123
1.704-1(b)(1)(i) 232n156
1.704-1(b)(1)(iii) 426n115; 431n133
1.704-1(b)(2) 270n315
1.704-1(b)(2)(i) 233n165; 246n212
1.704-1(b)(2)(ii)(a) 235n173
1.704-1(b)(2)(ii)(b) . . 230n150; 234n166; 235n175
1.704-1(b)(2)(ii)(b)(2) 236n176; 236n177;
                236n179; 237n180
1.704-1(b)(2)(ii)(b)(3) 239n187; 240n189
1.704-1(b)(2)(ii)(c) . . 238n184; 240n191; 240n192;
                244n204
1.704-1(b)(2)(ii)(d) . . 238n185; 242n201; 242n202
1.704-1(b)(2)(ii)(d)(1) . 234n167; 234n168; 241n194
1.704-1(b)(2)(ii)(d)(2) . 234n167; 234n168; 241n194
1.704-1(b)(2)(ii)(d)(3) 234n167; 234n168;
                241n194; 241n195
1.704-1(b)(2)(ii)(d)(4) 241n200
1.704-1(b)(2)(ii)(d)(5) 241n200
1.704-1(b)(2)(ii)(d)(6) 241n200
1.704-1(b)(2)(ii)(e) 246n211
1.704-1(b)(2)(ii)(f) 239n186; 244n205
1.704-1(b)(2)(ii)(g) . . 236n178; 240n190; 245n207;
                245n208
1.704-1(b)(2)(ii)(h) . . 232n157; 232n158; 232n159
1.704-1(b)(2)(ii)(i) 245n209; 246n210
1.704-1(b)(2)(iii)(a) . . 230n151; 235n169; 235n170;
                246n213; 246n214; 246n217; 247n222; 247n223
1.704-1(b)(2)(iii)(b) . . 235n171; 246n215; 246n217;
                248n226; 249n227; 249n228
1.704-1(b)(2)(iii)(c) . . 235n172; 246n216; 246n217;
                247n220; 247n221; 249n230; 250n231; 250n232;
                250n233; 250n234; 250n236; 251n237; 251n239
1.704-1(b)(2)(iv) 203n17
1.704-1(b)(2)(iv)(a) . . 251n240; 252n241; 252n242
1.704-1(b)(2)(iv)(b) . . 252n243; 252n244; 252n245;
                253n250; 253n251; 256n259; 431n134
1.704-1(b)(2)(iv)(c) . . 255n255; 255n256; 255n257;
                256n258
1.704-1(b)(2)(iv)(d)(1) 253n250
1.704-1(b)(2)(iv)(d)(2) 256n260; 256n262
1.704-1(b)(2)(iv)(d)(3) 260n272; 260n273;
                260n274

References are to page and footnote numbers.

Treasury Regulations—Cont.

Sec.

1.704-1(b)(2)(iv)(e)(1) 253n251; 254n252; 254n253

1.704-1(b)(2)(iv)(e)(2) 256n261; 256n262

1.704-1(b)(2)(iv)(f) . . 167n119; 256n263; 260n273; 260n274; 269n308; 415n34; 427n119

1.704-1(b)(2)(iv)(f)(1)-(4) 258n265; 259n268

1.704-1(b)(2)(iv)(f)(5) 256n264

1.704-1(b)(2)(iv)(g) . . 260n272; 260n273; 260n274

1.704-1(b)(2)(iv)(g)(1) 260n275

1.704-1(b)(2)(iv)(g)(2) 262n282

1.704-1(b)(2)(iv)(g)(3) 261n276; 261n277

1.704-1(b)(2)(iv)(h) 258n266; 258n267

1.704-1(b)(2)(iv)(i)(1) 263n283

1.704-1(b)(2)(iv)(k) 241n196

1.704-1(b)(2)(iv)(l) . . 528n197; 580n106; 590n139

1.704-1(b)(2)(iv)(n) 253n246; 253n248

1.704-1(b)(2)(iv)(o) 263n284

1.704-1(b)(2)(iv)(q) 253n249

1.704-1(b)(3) 231n154; 264n287; 264n288

1.704-1(b)(3)(i) 233n161; 233n162; 233n163; 233n164

1.704-1(b)(3)(ii) 264n289; 335n174

1.704-1(b)(4)(i) 204n24; 260n275; 261n278; 261n279

1.704-1(b)(4)(iv)(f) . . 170n137; 178n170; 179n171

1.704-1(b)(4)(iv)(r) 179n171

1.704-1(b)(4)(vi) 240n192; 247n218

1.704-1(b)(5), Ex. (1) 265n290

1.704-1(b)(5), Ex. (1)(i) 237n181; 265n291

1.704-1(b)(5), Ex. (1)(ii) 238n182

1.704-1(b)(5), Ex. (1)(ix) 240n191; 243n203

1.704-1(b)(5), Ex. (1)(vi) 243n203

1.704-1(b)(5), Ex. (1)(viii) 245n206

1.704-1(b)(5), Ex. (1)(x) 240n191

1.704-1(b)(5), Ex. (1)(xi) 251n238

1.704-1(b)(5), Ex. (4)(i) 265n291

1.704-1(b)(5), Ex. (5) 248n225

1.704-1(b)(5), Ex. (6) 249n229

1.704-1(b)(5), Ex. (8) 250n235

1.704-1(b)(5), Ex. (9) 248n225

1.704-1(b)(5), Ex. (10)(ii) 249n229; 265n291

1.704-1(b)(5), Ex. (11) 263n283

1.704-1(b)(5), Ex. (13)(i) 261n280

1.704-1(b)(5), Ex. (14)(i) 259n269; 259n270

1.704-1(b)(5), Ex. (14)(ii) 259n271

1.704-1(b)(5), Ex. (14)(v) 255n254

Treasury Regulations—Cont.

Sec.

1.704-1(b)(5), Ex. (18)(vii) 262n281

1.704-1(b)(5), Ex. (18)(viii) 262n281

1.704-1(b)(5), Ex. (19)(iii) 265n291

1.704-1(d) 288n362

1.704-1(d)(1) . 146n36; 286n350; 286n353; 511n116

1.704-1(d)(2) 286n351; 287n356; 287n357; 288n359; 496n14; 511n117

1.704-1(d)(4), Ex. (3) 287n358

1.704-1(e)(1)(iii) 415n36; 415n37; 415n38

1.704-1(e)(1)(iv) 412n17; 412n18; 413n20

1.704-1(e)(1)(v) 120n104; 127n124; 414n32; 414n33; 427n118

1.704-1(e)(2)(i) 415n35; 415n38

1.704-1(e)(2)(ii) 416n41

1.704-1(e)(2)(ii)(a) 416n43; 416n47; 416n48

1.704-1(e)(2)(ii)(b) 417n52

1.704-1(e)(2)(ii)(c) 414n27; 417n58

1.704-1(e)(2)(ii)(d) 417n55; 418n62; 418n63; 418n64

1.704-1(e)(2)(iii) 418n65; 418n66

1.704-1(e)(2)(iv) 419n68; 419n69

1.704-1(e)(2)(ix) 421n78; 421n80; 421n81; 421n82; 421n83

1.704-1(e)(2)(i)-(x) 415n39

1.704-1(e)(2)(v) 417n50; 417n51; 419n71

1.704-1(e)(2)(vi) . 419n72; 419n73; 420n74; 420n75

1.704-1(e)(2)(vii) 422n89; 422n90; 422n91; 422n92; 422n93; 422n94

1.704-1(e)(2)(viii) . . 424n100; 424n102; 424n104; 425n105

1.704-1(e)(2)(x) 421n86

1.704-1(e)(3)(i)(b) . . . 426n116; 426n117; 429n127

1.704-1(e)(3)(i)(c) . . . 430n128; 430n129; 430n130

1.704-1(e)(3)(ii) 429n124

1.704-1(e)(3)(ii)(a), Ex. (1) 429n125

1.704-1(e)(3)(ii)(a), Ex. (2) 429n125

1.704-1(e)(3)(ii)(a), Ex. (3) 429n125

1.704-1(e)(3)(ii)(c) 432n135

1.704-1(e)(4) 428n123

1.704-1(e)(4)(i) 425n107

1.704-1(e)(4)(ii) 426n111

1.704-1(e)(4)(ii)(a) 425n108; 425n109

1.704-1(e)(4)(ii)(b) 425n110

1.704-2 . . . . 170n137

1.704-2(b)(1) 266n292; 268n302; 269n304; 274n322; 274n323

References are to page and footnote numbers.

Treasury Regulations—Cont.

Sec.

1.704-2(b)(2) 267n296; 269n307; 269n309
1.704-2(c) . 267n298; 269n305; 274n324; 275n325; 275n326
1.704-2(d) 267n297; 269n306
1.704-2(d)(1) 272n318; 273n319
1.704-2(e) 270n314
1.704-2(e)(3) 282n340
1.704-2(f) 268n300
1.704-2(f)(2) 284n345
1.704-2(f)(3) 284n344
1.704-2(f)(4) 285n347
1.704-2(f)(6) 283n342
1.704-2(f)(7), Ex. (1) 285n348
1.704-2(f)(7), Ex. (2) 284n346
1.704-2(g) . . 267n299; 269n310; 278n330; 278n331
1.704-2(g)(1) 279n333
1.704-2(g)(2) 268n301; 282n341
1.704-2(h) 270n311
1.704-2(h)(1) 280n336
1.704-2(h)(2) 280n334
1.704-2(h)(3) 282n338
1.704-2(h)(4) 280n337
1.704-2(i) 270n312
1.704-2(i)(1) 285n349
1.704-2(j) 275n326
1.704-2(j)(1)(iii) 277n329
1.704-2(j)(2) 283n342
1.704-2(j)(2)(iii) 283n343
1.704-2(k) 270n313
1.704-2(m), Ex. (1)(i) 272n317; 273n320
1.704-2(m), Ex. (4)(i) 276n327
1.704-2(m), Ex. (4)(ii) 276n328
1.704-3(a) 215n66; 590n140
1.704-3(a)(1) . . . 203n12; 203n13; 205n28; 205n29
1.704-3(a)(2) . . 203n14; 203n15; 203n16; 591n144
1.704-3(a)(3)(i) 203n17; 215n65; 582n114
1.704-3(a)(5) 203n18
1.704-3(a)(7) . 204n20; 204n22; 529n200; 544n239; 580n107
1.704-3(a)(8) 204n21
1.704-3(a)(8)(i) 205n27
1.704-3(a)(9) 204n23
1.704-3(a)(10) 204n25; 205n32
1.704-3(b)(1) 206n34; 207n38; 210n43
1.704-3(c)(1) 211n44; 211n45
1.704-3(c)(2) 211n46
1.704-3(c)(3) 211n50

Treasury Regulations—Cont.

Sec.

1.704-3(c)(3)(iii) 211n47; 211n48; 211n49
1.704-3(c)(4) 204n19
1.704-3(d) . . . 212n51; 496n8; 528n195; 532n207; 544n237; 545n244
1.704-3(d)(1) 545n242
1.704-3(d)(2) 213n54
1.704-3(d)(3) 213n55
1.704-3(d)(4) 213n53
1.704-3(d)(5) 212n52
1.704-3(d)(7), Ex. (1) 213n56
1.704-3(e) 111n63; 214n57
1.704-3(e)(2) 111n64; 214n58; 214n59
1.704-3(e)(2)(i) 214n60
1.704-3(e)(2)(ii) 214n60
1.704-3(e)(2)(iii) 214n60
1.704-3(e)(3) 215n61
1.704-3(e)(3)(ii) 111n65
1.704-4(a) 215n63; 356n64
1.704-4(a)(4) 591n143
1.704-4(a)(4)(i) . 215n62; 215n63; 356n63; 356n64
1.704-4(b) 215n64; 356n65
1.704-4(c) 217n73
1.704-4(c)(3) 591n141; 591n142
1.704-4(d)(2) 217n72
1.704-4(e) 216n68; 216n70
1.704-4(e)(3) 216n71
1.704-4(f) 217n74
1.704-4(f)(2), Ex. (1) 217n75
1.704(b)(1)-(2)(iv) 170n138
1.705-1(a) 173n147; 510n114
1.705-1(a)(1) 139n2; 140n4; 145n32; 157n93; 158n94; 161n104; 359n81; 495n6; 497n21; 500n40
1.705-1(a)(2) 500n37
1.705-1(b) 167n122
1.705-1(b), Ex. (1) 167n120
1.705-1(b), Ex. (3) 167n121
1.705-2 . . . . 152n67; 152n69
1.705-2(a) 68n63; 153n71
1.705-2(b) 153n72
1.705-2(c) 154n73
1.705-2(e) 154n74
1.706-1(a) 61n10
1.706-1(b)(2) 89n198
1.706-1(b)(4)(iii) 94n231
1.706-1(c) 587n132
1.706-1(c)(1)(3) 518n152

References are to page and footnote numbers.

Treasury Regulations—Cont.

Sec.

1.706-1(c)(2) 157n93; 224n123

1.706-1(c)(2)(ii) 223n111; 223n116; 224n118;
223n129; 226n130; 510n112; 575n90

1.706-1(c)(3)(i) 479n39

1.706-1(c)(3)(ii) 479n35; 479n36

1.706-1(c)(3)(iv) 474n19; 563n31

1.706-1(c)(3)(v) 479n37

1.706-1(c)(3)(vi), Ex. (3) 474n19

1.706-1(c)(3)(vi), Ex. (4) 479n35

1.706-1(c)(5) 432n137; 519n157

1.707-1(a) 103n11; 105n26; 289n1; 293n15;
303n44; 303n46; 304n48; 304n49

1.707-1(a)(1) 105n25

1.707-1(c) 88n191; 291n9; 297n24; 301n33;
335n175; 451n52; 573n80

1.707-1(c), Ex. (2) 298n28

1.707-1(c), Ex. (3) 297n26

1.707-1(c), Ex. (4) 298n27

1.707-2 . . . . 137n171

1.707-3(a)(1) 311n84

1.707-3(a)(2) . . . 307n68; 307n69; 311n86; 311n87

1.707-3(a)(3) 312n89; 312n90

1.707-3(a)(4) 312n93

1.707-3(b)(1) 310n81; 310n82; 313n98

1.707-3(b)(1)(i) 307n64

1.707-3(b)(1)(ii) 307n65

1.707-3(b)(2) 307n66; 313n99; 314n104

1.707-3(c)(1) 307n67; 310n83; 313n100

1.707-3(d) 313n101

1.707-3(e) 307n62

1.707-3(f) 311n85

1.707-3(f)(1) 311n85

1.707-3(f), Ex. (2) 312n88

1.707-3(f), Ex. (3) 316n106

1.707-3(f), Ex. (3)(iii) 316n105

1.707-3(f), Ex. (4) 314n102

1.707-3(f), Ex. (5) 317n107

1.707-3(f), Ex. (7) 318n108

1.707-3(f), Ex. (8) 319n110

1.707-4 . . . . 312n91; 323n116

1.707-5 . . . . 312n94

1.707-5(a) 323n117; 326n134

1.707-5(a)(1) 323n119; 326n136; 326n140

1.707-5(a)(2) 330n156

1.707-5(a)(2)(i) 327n141

1.707-5(a)(4) 330n157

1.707-5(a)(5) 323n119; 324n120; 325n132

Treasury Regulations—Cont.

Sec.

1.707-5(a)(6) 313n96

1.707-5(a)(6)(i) 324n124

1.707-5(a)(6)(i)(A) 324n125

1.707-5(a)(6)(i)(B) 324n126

1.707-5(a)(6)(i)(C) 324n128; 326n138

1.707-5(a)(6)(i)(D) 325n129; 326n139

1.707-5(a)(6)(ii) 325n130

1.707-5(a)(7) 312n95; 324n127

1.707-5(b)(1) 327n143

1.707-5(b)(1)(ii) 328n150

1.707-5(b)(2)(i) 327n144; 327n145; 328n147

1.707-5(b)(2)(iii) 328n148

1.707-5(c) 324n120; 324n121

1.707-5(d) 326n135

1.707-5(e) 324n123

1.707-5(e), Ex. (2) 327n142

1.707-5(e), Ex. (5) 325n131

1.707-5(e), Ex. (6) 326n133

1.707-5(f), Ex. (10) 328n149

1.707-5(f), Ex. (11) 329n151

1.707-6 . . . . 313n97

1.707-6(a) 330n154

1.707-6(b)(1) 330n156; 330n157; 331n158

1.707-6(b)(2) 331n160; 331n161

1.707-6(b)(2)(i) 331n159

1.707-6(d), Ex. (1) 330n155

1.707-6(d), Ex. (2) 331n162

1.708-1(b) 92n220

1.708-1(b)(1)(i) . 479n34; 561n14; 561n15; 561n19;
562n21; 562n25

1.708-1(b)(1)(i)(a) 475n22; 518n154; 563n29

1.708-1(b)(1)(i)(b) 475n22; 563n32

1.708-1(b)(1)(ii) . . . 518n153; 519n158; 552n263;
552n264; 565n41; 566n44; 566n45; 567n46;
568n48; 568n51; 571n77; 572n79

1.708-1(b)(1)(iii) 560n7; 560n8; 587n131

1.708-1(b)(1)(iii)(b) 560n10

1.708-1(b)(1)(iv) . 8n68; 215n66; 312n92; 539n216;
551n258; 552n260; 560n7; 560n8; 560n11;
589n136; 590n138

1.708-1(b)(1)(v) 552n259; 589n135; 590n137

1.708-1(b)(2) 574n85

1.708-1(b)(2)(i) 574n81; 574n82

1.708-1(b)(2)(ii) 583n117; 583n118; 583n119;
583n120

1.708-1(b)(iv) 591n149

1.708-1(c)(2) . . . 575n87; 575n88; 575n89; 575n91

References are to page and footnote numbers.

Treasury Regulations—Cont.

Sec.

1.708-1(c)(3) 576n94
1.708-1(c)(3)(i) 576n93; 576n95; 577n100
1.708-1(c)(3)(ii) 576n93; 577n96
1.708-1(c)(4) 579n102
1.708-1(c)(5), Ex. (3) 577n97; 577n99
1.708-1(c)(5), Ex. (5) 579n104
1.708-1(c)(6) 580n108
1.708-1(d) 583n121
1.708-1(d)(2)(i) 586n129
1.708-1(d)(2)(ii) 587n130
1.708-1(d)(3)(i) 586n127
1.708-1(d)(3)(i)(A) 584n123
1.708-1(d)(3)(i)(B) 585n124
1.708-1(d)(3)(ii)(A) 585n125
1.708-1(d)(3)(ii)(B) 585n126
1.708-1(d)(4) 583n122
1.708-1(d)(5), Ex. (7) 586n128
1.709-1(b)(1) 135n161
1.709-1(b)(2) 135n162; 136n166
1.709-1(c) 78n128; 78n129
1.709-2(a) 135n163; 135n164; 136n165
1.709-2(b) 136n168; 136n169
1.709-2(c) 135n160
1.721-1(a) 102n4; 104; 105n25; 306n58
1.721-1(b) 3n23
1.721-1(b)(1) . . 105n31; 117n85; 117n86; 118n88;
                  122n112; 125n118; 128n130
1.721-1(b)(2) 125n119
1.731-1(a) 140n4
1.731-1(a)(1) 366n110
1.731-1(a)(1)(i) 362n93
1.731-1(a)(1)(ii) 161n103; 302n38; 353n61;
                  359n82
1.731-1(c)(3) 569n54; 569n55
1.731-2 . . . . 348n31
1.731-2(b)(1) 349n37
1.731-2(b)(2) 349n39
1.731-2(b)(3) 349n38
1.731-2(c)(3)(i) 348n35
1.731-2(c)(3)(ii) 349n36
1.731-2(d)(1)(i) 350n44
1.731-2(d)(1)(ii) 351n46
1.731-2(d)(2) 350n45
1.731-2(e)(2)(i) 351n52
1.731-2(e)(2)(ii) 351n53
1.731-2(f)(1)(i) 351n55
1.731-2(h) 352n58

Treasury Regulations—Cont.

Sec.

1.731-2(h)(1) 352n59
1.731-2(h)(3) 352n60
1.731-2(j), Ex. (1) 349n40
1.731-2(j), Ex. (2) 349n41
1.731-2(j), Ex. (6) 352n57
1.732-1(a) 140n4; 362n93
1.732-1(c)(1) 361n90
1.732-1(c)(2) 361n91; 361n92
1.732-1(c)(4) 370n119; 371n121; 372n122
1.732-1(d) 476n25; 486n69
1.732-1(d)(1)(iii) 486n70
1.732-1(d)(1)(iv) 486n71; 553n271
1.732-1(d)(1)(v) 486n73; 555n273
1.732-1(d)(1)(vi) 404n187; 404n188; 555n274
1.732-1(d)(2) 486n74
1.732-1(d)(4) 364n95; 557n283
1.732-1(d)(4), Ex. (1) . 364n96; 557n284; 557n286
1.732-1(d)(4), Ex. (2) . . . 364n96; 557n284
1.732-1(d)(4)(ii) 557n285
1.732-1(d)(5) 364n97
1.732-1(e) . . 383n155; 555n277; 556n278; 556n279
1.732-2(b) 548n249; 548n250; 548n251
1.732-2(d)(2) 556n280; 556n281
1.732-2(d)(3) 556n282
1.732-3 . . . . 357n69
1.732(c) 370n117; 370n118
1.734-1(b) 155n81
1.734-1(e) 399n186
1.735-1(b) 369n115
1.736-1(a) 563n32; 563n33
1.736-1(a)(1) 439n14
1.736-1(a)(1)(i) 366n108; 438n6
1.736-1(a)(1)(ii) . . . 438n7; 438n8; 438n9; 438n10
1.736-1(a)(2) 366n107; 437n5; 449n47
1.736-1(a)(3) 450n48; 451n51
1.736-1(a)(4) 460n73; 466n85; 468n89
1.736-1(a)(5) . . . 450n49; 451n53; 460n72; 461n75
1.736-1(a)(6) 439n13; 479n38
1.736-1(b)(1) 440n16; 440n18
1.736-1(b)(2) 441n23; 441n24; 442n25
1.736-1(b)(3) . . 442n26; 443n27; 443n28; 443n29;
                  443n31
1.736-1(b)(4) 447n43; 460n70
1.736-1(b)(5) 439n12; 452n54; 453n55
1.736-1(b)(5)(i) 453n56; 453n57; 455n58
1.736-1(b)(5)(ii) 453n56; 456n59; 456n60

References are to page and footnote numbers.

Treasury Regulations—Cont.

Sec.

1.736-1(b)(5)(iii) 457n61; 457n62

1.736-1(b)(6) . . . 344n9; 344n10; 444n37; 444n38; 445n39; 445n40; 457n63; 458n66; 458n67; 459; 459n68

1.736-1(b)(7) 444n37

1.736-1(b)(7), Ex. (2) 344n9

1.737-1(b)(1) 218n79

1.737-1(b)(2) 218n80

1.737-1(b)(3)(ii) 218n81

1.737-1(c) 219n84

1.737-1(c)(1) 219n85

1.737-1(c)(2)(i) 221n96

1.737-1(c)(2)(ii) 220n90

1.737-1(c)(2)(iii) 220n91

1.737-1(c)(2)(iv) 220n92

1.737-1(c)(2)(v) 220n93

1.737-1(d) 220n94; 222n107

1.737-1(e), Ex. (1) 219n89

1.737-1(e), Ex. (2) 218n83

1.737-2(a) . . 221n97; 583n116; 591n145; 591n146

1.737-2(b)(1) 221n98

1.737-2(c) 221n99

1.737-2(d)(1) 221n100

1.737-2(d)(2) 221n100

1.737-3(a) 221n101

1.737-3(b)(1) 221n102

1.737-3(b)(2) 221n103

1.737-3(c) 222n105

1.737-3(c)(3) 222n106

1.737-3(c)(4) 222n108

1.737-3(d) 223n109

1.737-3(e), Ex. (1) 221n104

1.741-1(c) 512n123; 515n137

1.742-1 . . . . . 483n62; 499n34; 499n35; 535n212; 580n106

1.743-1(a) 525n180

1.743-1(b) 447n44; 460n71; 484n65; 524n177

1.743-1(b)(2)(ii) 486n72; 554n272; 555n275; 555n276

1.743-1(d) 527n191

1.743-1(d)(1) 528n194

1.743-1(d)(2) 528n194

1.743-1(d)(3) 528n198

1.743-1(d)(3), Ex. (2) 529n199

1.743-1(e) 527n190

1.743-1(f) 531n201; 531n202

1.743-1(g) 554n272; 555n275; 555n276

Treasury Regulations—Cont.

Sec.

1.743-1(g)(1) 548n249

1.743-1(g)(2)(i) 548n250

1.743-1(g)(2)(ii) 548n251

1.743-1(g)(3) 548n252

1.743-1(h) . . . 552n260; 565n36; 565n37; 565n38; 589n135; 590n138

1.743-1(h)(1) 539n215

1.743-1(h)(2) 539n217

1.743-1(h)(2)(iv) 539n218

1.743-1(j)(1) 543n235

1.743-1(j)(2) 543n236

1.743-1(j)(3) 544n238

1.743-1(j)(4) 545n240

1.743-1(j)(4)(i)(B)(1) 545n241

1.743-1(j)(4)(i)(B)(2) 545n243

1.743-1(j)(4)(ii)(A) 547n245

1.743-1(j)(4)(ii)(B) 547n246

1.743-1(j)(5) 548n247

1.743-1(k)(1)(i) 553n268

1.743-1(k)(2)(i) 553n269

1.743(g)(5) 549n254

1.751-1(a)(2) 496n10; 505n78

1.751-1(a)(3) 510n109

1.751-1(b) 7n53; 381n147

1.751-1(b)(1)(i) 376n130; 379n140

1.751-1(b)(1)(ii) 380n143

1.751-1(b)(2) 376n131; 381n148; 382n150

1.751-1(b)(2)(ii) . . . 241n199; 384n158; 384n159; 384n160

1.751-1(b)(2)(iii) . . . 376n132; 382n149; 382n151

1.751-1(b)(3) 376n131; 381n148; 382n150

1.751-1(b)(3)(ii) 384n158; 384n159

1.751-1(b)(3)(iii) . . . 376n132; 382n149; 382n151

1.751-1(b)(4)(i) 380n145

1.751-1(c)(1) 507n83

1.751-1(c)(1)(i) 377n134; 507n84

1.751-1(c)(2) 442n25

1.751-1(c)(3) 378n137

1.751-1(c)(4) 391n166; 508n89

1.751-1(c)(4)(i) 391n167

1.751-1(c)(5) 391n166

1.751-1(c)(6)(ii) 508n90

1.751-1(d)(2)(i) 509n103

1.751-1(d)(2)(ii) 445n41; 509n106

1.751-1(f) 496n10

1.751-1(g) 505n79

Treasury Regulations—Cont.

Sec.

1.751-1(g), Ex. (2)(c) 380n142

1.751-1(g), Ex. (2)(d)(1) 376n132; 382n151; 383n152

1.751-1(g), Ex. (2)(d)(2) 383n157

1.751-1(g), Ex. (2)(e)(1) 384n158

1.751-1(g), Ex. (3)(c) 376n132; 382n151

1.751-1(g), Ex. (3)(d)(1) 376n132; 382n151; 383n152

1.751-1(g), Ex. (3)(e)(1) 384n158

1.752-1(a) 180n178; 327n141

1.752-1(a)(1) 170n132

1.752-1(a)(2) 170n133; 186n210

1.752-1(b) 168n125

1.752-1(c) 168n126; 196n237

1.752-1(d) 495n5; 497n20; 497n25

1.752-1(d)(1) 180n176; 195n229

1.752-1(d)(2) 180n177

1.752-1(e) 194n226; 196n231; 196n234

1.752-1(f) . . 179n173; 194n227; 196n232; 580n109

1.752-1(g) 195n228

1.752-1(g), Ex. (2) 581n110

1.752-1(h) 197n241; 197n244

1.752-1(j)(2) 182n191

1.752-1(j)(3) 182n191

1.752-2 . . . . 85n180; 284n345

1.752-2(a) . . 170n134; 178n166; 180n179; 182n192

1.752-2(b) 178n167; 182n193

1.752-2(b)(1) 181n180; 184n199; 184n200

1.752-2(b)(1)(i)-(v) 182n194

1.752-2(b)(2) 182n195

1.752-2(b)(3) 181n181

1.752-2(b)(4) 173n143; 175n155; 181n182; 184n202

1.752-2(b)(5) 173n144; 181n183; 184n200

1.752-2(b)(6) 181n184; 184n201

1.752-2(b)-(j) 170n135

1.752-2(c) 182n188

1.752-2(c)(1) 186n209

1.752-2(d) 182n189

1.752-2(d)(2) 185n203

1.752-2(e) 182n187; 186n208

1.752-2(f), Ex. (1) 183n197

1.752-2(f), Ex. (2) 184n198

1.752-2(g)(1) 185n207

1.752-2(h)(1) 181n185

1.752-2(h)(2) 182n186

1.752-2(j) 182n190

Treasury Regulations—Cont.

Sec.

1.752-2(j)(1) 185n205; 185n206; 329n153

1.752-2(j)(3) 173n144; 329n153

1.752-3(a) 170n136; 178n169; 187n211

1.752-3(a)(1) 187n212

1.752-3(a)(2) 188n213

1.752-3(a)(3) 171n139; 179n172; 188n215; 188n216; 188n217; 189n218; 189n219

1.752-3(b), Ex. (1) 189n220

1.752-3(b), Ex. (2) 191n221

1.752-3(c) 171n139; 189n219

1.752-3(c), Ex. (3) 192n223

1.752-4(b)(2) 180n174

1.752-4(c) 173n145

1.752-4(d) 173n146

1.752-5 . . . . 581n109

1.752-6 . . . . 177n162

1.752-6(d)(1) 176n158

1.752-7 176

1.753-1(a) 482n54

1.753-1(b) 481n52

1.753-3(b) 188n214

1.754-1(a) 393n171; 553n267

1.754-1(b) 485n66

1.754-1(b)(1) 408n195; 485n68; 553n265

1.754-1(c) 485n67

1.755-1(a) 397n180

1.755-1(a)(1)(iii) 406n190

1.755-1(b)(1)(i) 535n211

1.755-1(b)(1)(ii) 532n206

1.755-1(b)(2)(i) 532n208

1.755-1(b)(3)(i) 532n209

1.755-1(b)(3)(ii) 533n210

1.755-1(b)(4) . . 447n44; 460n71; 484n65; 488n77; 525n181; 535n213

1.755-1(b)(5) 536n214

1.755-1(c) 364n99; 397n179; 549n253

1.755-1(c)(1)(i) 398n182

1.755-1(c)(1)(ii) 155n81; 397n181

1.755-1(c)(2) 398n183

1.755-1(c)(3) 398n184

1.755-1(c)(4) 405n189

1.755-2 . . . . 540n219

1.761-1(a) 41n72

1.761-1(c) 229n149

1.761-1(d) 341n1; 343n8; 347n24; 347n27; 368n112; 438n9

1.761-1(e) 591n147

Treasury Regulations—Cont.

Sec.

1.761-2(a)(1)	48n107; 48n108
1.761-2(a)(2)	50n119
1.761-2(a)(2)(iii)	50n120
1.761-2(a)(3)	50n121; 51n124
1.761-2(a)(3)(iii)	51n123
1.761-2(b)(2)(i)	48n106; 53n134; 54n142
1.761-2(b)(2)(ii)	53n135; 54n143
1.761-2(b)(2)(ii)(a)	53n136
1.761-2(b)(2)(ii)(b)	53n136
1.761-2(b)(3)	54n142; 54n143; 54n145; 54n146; 54n147
1.761-2(c)	54n137; 54n138; 54n141; 54n144
1.761-2(d)	51n125
1.871-10	79n142
1.1001-2	503n63
1.1001-2(a)	498n26
1.1001-2(a)(1)	495n4; 497n19; 497n24; 519n160
1.1001-2(a)(2)	82n162
1.1001-2(a)(4)	82n159; 519n160
1.1001-2(a)(4)(v)	495n5; 497n20; 497n25
1.1001-2(c), Ex. (3)	519n160
1.1001-2(c), Ex. (4)	519n160
1.1001-2(c), Ex. (5)	521n167
1.1002-1(c)	99n2
1.1011-2	519n162
1.1017-1(a)	81n155; 84n171
1.1017-1(c)	84n171; 84n173
1.1017-1(f)	81n157; 84n173
1.1017-1(g)	84n172; 84n174
1.1017-1(g)(2)	85n175
1.1017-1(g)(2)(ii)(B)	85n176
1.1031(a)-1(a)(1)	514n133
1.1032-3(a)	68n61; 68n62; 151n60
1.1032-3(b)	151n61
1.1032-3(c)	151n62
1.1032-3(e), Ex. (5)	151n63
1.1223-1(a)	109n52
1.1245-1(e)(2)	508n89
1.1502-13(c)(1)(i)	550n255; 551n256
1.1502-34	357n69
1.7701-1 *et seq.*	41n75; 42n86
1.7704-1(a)	43n87
1.7704-1(l)	42n81
1.7704-1(l)(2)	42n84
1.7704-1(l)(3)	42n82
1.7704-1(l)(4)	42n85
1.7704-2(c)	42n82

Treasury Regulations—Cont.

Sec.

1.7704-2(d)	42n82
20.2031-2(h)	491n88; 491n89; 492n90
20.2031-3	122n107; 490n79; 491n85
25.2503-3(a)	415n40
25.2512-3	490n79
301.6109-1(d)(2)(iii)	591n148
301.7701-1-301.7701-3	26n1
301.7701-1(a)(1)	29n8; 40n70
301.7701-1(a)(2)	27n5; 29n9; 29n10; 40n71
301.7701-1(a)(2)(c)(1)	27n2
301.7701-1(a)(3)	29n11; 29n12
301.7701-1(a)(4)	29n15
301.7701-1(c)	29n14; 57n161; 57n162
301.7701-1(d)	27n4; 30n20; 33n32
301.7701-1(e)	27n4; 30n20
301.7701-2	37n47; 41n73
301.7701-2(a)	57n164
301.7701-2(a)(1)	55n151
301.7701-2(a)(2)	56n152; 56n153
301.7701-2(a)(3)	56n154
301.7701-2(b)	31n22; 57n164
301.7701-2(b)(1)	33n29
301.7701-2(b)(3)	33n29
301.7701-2(b)(4)	33n29
301.7701-2(b)(5)	33n29
301.7701-2(b)(6)	33n29
301.7701-2(b)(7)	33n29
301.7701-2(b)(8)(i)	34n35
301.7701-2(c)	57n164
301.7701-2(c)(4)	57n164
301.7701-2(d)	34n36
301.7701-3	37n47
301.7701-3(a)	32n27; 33n28
301.7701-3(b)(2)	33n33
301.7701-3(b)(2), Ex. (2)	56n154
301.7701-3(b)(2)(ii)	34n34
301.7701-3(b)(3)	31n21
301.7701-3(c)	36n43; 38n54
301.7701-3(c)(1)	565n40
301.7701-3(c)(1)(iv)	36n44; 36n45
301.7701-3(c)(2)(iii)	38n56
301.7701-3(c)(v)(A)	31n23
301.7701-3(c)(v)(B)	31n24
301.7701-3(e)	36n39; 36n41
301.7701-3(f)	33n30
301.7701-3(f)(2)	39n63; 39n64

References are to page and footnote numbers.

Treasury Regulations—Cont.

Sec.

301.7701-3(f)(4), Ex. (1) 37n52

301.7701-3(f)(4), Ex. (2) 39n65

301.7701-3(f)(4), Ex. (3) 39n66

301.7701-3(g) 37n46

301.7701-3(g)(1)(i) 37n48

301.7701-3(g)(1)(ii) 37n49

301.7701-3(g)(1)(iii) 37n50

301.7701-3(g)(1)(iv) 37n51

Treasury Regulations—Cont.

Sec.

301.7701-3(g)(2) 38n54

301.7701-3(g)(3) 38n55

301.7701-4 . . . . 27n6

301.7701-4(a) 30n16

301.7701-4(b) 30n19

301.7701-4(c) 30n17; 30n18

INDEX

[References are to sections.]

A

ACCOUNTING
Generally . . . 3.01
Method (See ACCOUNTING METHOD)
Taxable income, computation of (See INCOME, subhead: Taxable income, computation of)
Taxable year (See TAXABLE YEAR)

ACCOUNTING METHOD
Generally . . . 3.03[B]
Cash method, disallowance of
   C corporation as partner . . . 3.03[B][1]
   Farming partnerships with corporate partner . . . 3.03[B][3]
   Tax shelter partnerships . . . 3.03[B][2]

ACQUISITION OF PARTNERSHIP OR LIMITED LIABILITY COMPANY INTEREST BY CONTRIBUTION
Generally . . . 4.01
Allocation of income, gain, loss and deduction attributable to contributed property . . . 4.03[E]
Amortization
   Organization expenses, of . . . 4.06[B]
   Start-up expenses, of . . . 4.06[A]
Assets produced by personal services . . . 4.02[B][4]
Basis rules
   Limited liability company's basis in contributed property . . . 4.03[C]
   Member's basis in partnership or limited liability company interest . . . 4.03[A]
   Partner's basis in partnership or limited liability company interest . . . 4.03[A]
   Partnership's basis in contributed property . . . 4.03[C]
Cancellation of partnership or limited liability company debt . . . 4.02[B][3]
Capital interest received for contribution of services
   Generally . . . 4.05[B]
   Basis of service partner's in partnership interest . . . 4.05[B][4]
   Deduction for payments to service partner or member . . . 4.05[B][5]
   Election to include income under Section 83(b) . . . 4.05[B][3]
   Gain or loss, recognition of . . . 4.05[B][6]
   Loss or gain, recognition of . . . 4.05[B][6]
   Payments to service partner or member, deduction for . . . 4.05[B][5]
   Unvested interests . . . 4.05[B][2]
   Value of interest received . . . 4.05[B][1]
Characterization rules . . . 4.03[D]
Disguised organization and syndication expenses . . . 4.06[D]
Distributions of contributed property . . . 4.03[F]
Future profits, receipt of interest in
   Generally . . . 4.05[C]

ACQUISITION OF PARTNERSHIP OR LIMITED LIABILITY COMPANY INTEREST BY CONTRIBUTION—Cont.
Future profits, receipt of interest in—Cont.
   Campbell decision . . . 4.05[C][2]
   Diamond decision . . . 4.05[C][1]
   Revenue Procedures 93-27 and 2001-43 . . . 4.05[C][3]
   Service's current position . . . 4.05[C][3]
Gain or loss
   Investment company, gain recognized on contribution of property to . . . 4.02[C]
   Nonrecognition rule . . . 4.02[A]
   Recognition of . . . 4.05[B][6]
Holding periods
   Limited liability company's basis in contributed property . . . 4.03[C]
   Member's basis in partnership or limited liability company interest . . . 4.03[B]
   Partner's basis in partnership or limited liability company interest . . . 4.03[B]
   Partnership's basis in contributed property . . . 4.03[C]
Installment obligations . . . 4.02[B][1]
Liabilities
   Generally . . . 4.04
   Accounts payable of contributed business, assumption of . . . 4.04[F]
   Contributing partners' or members' liabilities
      Decrease in individual liabilities, effect of . . . 4.04[D]
      Gain recognized when liabilities exceed contributing partner's or member's basis . . . 4.04[E]
   General treatment of changes in partners' or members' liabilities . . . 4.04[A]
   Limited liability companies, effect of change in liabilities on . . . 4.04[C]
   Noncontributing partners or members, effect of change in liabilities on . . . 4.04[B]
   Partnership, effect of change in liabilities on . . . 4.04[C]
Loss (See subhead: Gain or loss)
Nonrecognition rule . . . 4.02[A]
Organization expenses
   Amortization of . . . 4.06[B]
   Disguised organization and syndication expenses . . . 4.06[D]
   Syndication expenses, disguised organization and . . . 4.06[D]
Personal notes . . . 4.02[B][5]
Personal services, assets produced by . . . 4.02[B][4]
Property, defined . . . 4.02[B]
Right to use property . . . 4.02[B][2]
Services, contribution of
   Generally . . . 4.05[A]

I-1

[References are to sections.]

**ACQUISITION OF PARTNERSHIP OR LIM-
ITED LIABILITY COMPANY INTEREST BY
CONTRIBUTION**—Cont.
Services, contribution of—Cont.
  Capital interest received for services (See sub-
    head: Capital interest received for contribu-
    tion of services)
  Future profits, receipt of interest in (See sub-
    head: Future profits, receipt of interest in)
Start-up expenses, amortization of . . . 4.06[A]
Syndication expenses
  Disguised organization and . . . 4.06[D]
  Nondeductibility of . . . 4.06[C]

ADVANCES
Basis adjustments, order of . . . 5.01[F][5]
Current distributions . . . 8.03[B]

ALLOCATIONS
Basis adjustments
  Contributing partner, distributions to
    . . . 6.02[C][3]
  Noncontributing partner, distributions to
    . . . 6.02[B][1]
  Sale or exchange of partnership or limited li-
    ability company interest (See SALE OR EX-
    CHANGE OF PARTNERSHIP OR LIM-
    ITED LIABILITY COMPANY INTEREST,
    subhead: Allocations)
  Section 754 election . . . 8.07[A]
Basis to distributed property . . . 8.04[E]
Contributed property, attributable to
  Generally . . . 4.03[E]; 6.02
  Noncontributing partner, distributions to (See
    subhead: Noncontributing partner, distribu-
    tions to)
  Reasonable allocation methods (See subhead:
    Reasonable allocation methods)
Contributing partner, distributions to
  Generally . . . 6.02[C]
  Basis adjustments . . . 6.02[C][3]
  Distributions not subject to Section 737 rules
    . . . 6.02[C][2]
  Net pre contribution gain, computation of
    . . . 6.02[C][1]
Family partnerships (See FAMILY PARTNER-
  SHIPS, subhead: Allocation of partnership income
  among family members)
Income, of
  Generally . . . 1.02[B][2][d]; 4.03[E]
  Partner's death, pre-1998 rules . . . 11.02
Interest changes
  Generally . . . 6.03; 6.03[A]
  Cash-basis items, special rule for allocation of
    . . . 6.03[C]
  Partnership agreement . . . 6.03[E]
  Tiered partnerships . . . 6.03[D]
  Varying-interest rule . . . 6.03[B]
Losses, of . . . 1.02[B][2][d]; 4.03[E]
Noncontributing partner, distributions to
  Generally . . . 6.02[B]
  Anti-abuse rule . . . 6.02[B][2]
  Basis adjustments . . . 6.02[B][1]

ALLOCATIONS—Cont.
Nonrecourse liabilities, allocations of items attribut-
  able to
  Generally . . . 6.08
  Minimum-gain chargeback . . . 6.08[G]
  Nonrecourse borrowings . . . 6.08[F]
  Nonrecourse deductions . . . 6.08[B], [D]
  Partner nonrecourse debt . . . 6.08[H]
  Partnership minimum gain . . . 6.08[C], [E]
  Regulatory overview . . . 6.08[A]
  Safe-harbor rules . . . 6.08[B]
Partnership agreement
  Change in partners' interest under
    . . . 6.03[E]
  Defined . . . 6.04[B]
  Valid partnership agreement, absence of
    . . . 6.04[C]
Reasonable allocation methods
  Generally . . . 6.02[A]
  Aggregation rules . . . 6.02[A][4]
  Remedial allocation . . . 6.02[A][3]
  Securities partnerships . . . 6.02[A][5]
  Small disparities . . . 6.02[A][4]
  Traditional method
    Generally . . . 6.02[A][1]
    Curative allocations, with
      . . . 6.02[A][2]
Special allocations
  Generally . . . 6.04; 6.04[A]
  Partnership agreement
    Defined . . . 6.04[B]
    Valid partnership agreement, absence of
      . . . 6.04[C]
Transitory allocations . . . 6.05[B][3]

AMORTIZATION
Basis adjustment effect on . . . 12.08[I][2]
Organization expenses, of . . . 3.03[C]; 4.06[B]
Start-up costs, of . . . 3.03[D]
Start-up expenses, of . . . 4.06[A]

ANTI-ABUSE RULES
Generally . . . 2.05
Abuse of entity rule . . . 2.05[C]
Allocations attributable to contributed property
  . . . 6.02[B][2]
Circumstances analysis, facts and . . . 2.05[B]
Facts and circumstances analysis . . . 2.05[B]
Marketable securities, distributions of
  . . . 8.02[A][6]
Recourse liabilities . . . 5.06[C]
Subchapter K, transactions inconsistent with intent
  of . . . 2.05[A]

AT-RISK RULES
Loss limitation under . . . 1.02[B][2][f]
Passive activity rules and, interaction with
  . . . 5.03[C]

B

BAD DEBTS
Nonpartner capacity, transactions in which partner
  acts in . . . 7.04[A][1]

[References are to sections.]

BASIS ADJUSTMENTS
Generally . . . 1.01[J]
Allocations attributable to contributed property
  . . . 6.02[B][1]
Continuing adjustments to partner's basis
    Generally . . . 5.01[C]
    Decreases in basis (See subhead: Decreases in
      basis)
    Increases in basis
        Depletion deductions . . . 5.01[C][5]
        Tax-exempt income, for . . . 5.01[C][2]
      Taxable income or loss, for . . . 5.01[C][1]
Debt as discharged . . . 5.01[D]
Decreases in basis
    Depletion deductions . . . 5.01[C][6]
    Distributions, for . . . 5.01[C][4]
    Nondeductible expenditures, for
      . . . 5.01[C][3]
Distributions to partners (See DISTRIBUTIONS TO
  PARTNERS OR MEMBERS, subhead: Basis ad-
  justment)
Exchange or sale of partnership . . . 5.01[E]
Increases in basis
    Depletion deductions . . . 5.01[C][5]
    Tax-exempt income, for . . . 5.01[C][2]
Liquidation of partnership interest . . . 5.01[E]
Order of basis adjustments
    Generally . . . 5.01[F]
    Advance or draw taken . . . 5.01[F][5]
    Cash distributions, gain recognized on
      . . . 5.01[F][3]
    Distributed property . . . 5.01[F][2]
    Draw taken, advance or . . . 5.01[F][5]
    Encumbered property contributed or distributed
      . . . 5.01[F][6]
    Loss-deduction limitation . . . 5.01[F][1]
    Marketable securities . . . 5.01[F][4]
Sale of corporate partner's stock
    Generally . . . 5.01[C][7]
    Distribution to another partner
      . . . 5.01[C][7][b]
    Section 754 election not in effect, upon
      . . . 5.01[C][7][a]
Sale or exchange of partnership or limited liability
  company interest (See SALE OR EXCHANGE
  OF PARTNERSHIP OR LIMITED LIABILITY
  COMPANY INTEREST, subhead: Basis adjust-
  ments)
Section 743(b) basis adjustment (See SALE OR EX-
  CHANGE OF PARTNERSHIP OR LIMITED
  LIABILITY COMPANY INTEREST, subhead:
  Section 743(b) basis adjustment)
Taxable income or loss, for . . . 5.01[C][1]
Tiered partnership
    Distributions by . . . 8.07[D]
    Transfers of interests . . . 12.08[E]

**BASIS OF PARTNERSHIP OR LIMITED LI-
ABILITY COMPANY INTEREST**
Generally . . . 1.01[E]; 5.01

**BASIS OF PARTNERSHIP OR LIMITED LI-
ABILITY COMPANY INTEREST**—Cont.
Acquisition of interest by contribution (See ACQUI-
  SITION OF PARTNERSHIP OR LIMITED LI-
  ABILITY COMPANY INTEREST BY CONTRI-
  BUTION, subhead: Basis rules)
Adjustments (See BASIS ADJUSTMENTS)
Alternative method for determining basis . . . 5.02
Capital account, relation of partner's basis and
  . . . 5.01[I]
Death of partner or member (See DEATH OF
  PARTNER OR MEMBER, subhead: Basis)
Decreases in (See BASIS ADJUSTMENTS, sub-
  head: Decreases in basis)
Determination of basis
    Generally . . . 5.01[A]
    Alternative method . . . 5.02
    Initial basis . . . 5.01[B]
    Partnership's basis in its assets . . . 5.01[G]
Increases in basis adjustments
    Depletion deductions . . . 5.01[C][5]
    Tax-exempt income, for . . . 5.01[C][2]
Inside and outside basis
    Generally . . . 5.01[H]
    Equivalence of
        Events upsetting . . . 5.01[H][1]
        Restoring equivalence . . . 5.01[H][2]
        Section 754 election . . . 5.01[H][2]
Liabilities of partnership, effect of (See LIABILI-
  TIES OF PARTNERSHIP)
Outside basis (See subhead: Inside and outside ba-
  sis)
Sale or exchange of partnership interest
  . . . 12.02[B]
Section 705(b) . . . 5.02

BUSINESS FORM
C corporations . . . 1.02[A][1]
Changes in (See TERMINATION OF PARTNER-
  SHIP OR LIMITED LIABILITY COMPANY,
  subhead: Changes in business form)
Choice of business form, factors for consideration in
    Generally . . . 1.02[B]
    Nontax factors (See subhead: Nontax factors in
      choice of business form)
    Tax factors (See subhead: Tax factors in choice
      of business form)
Co-ownership . . . 1.02[A][7]
Limited liability companies . . . 1.02[A][6]
Limited liability partnerships . . . 1.02[A][5]
Limited partnerships . . . 1.02[A][4]
Nontax factors in choice of business form
    Capital structure . . . 1.02[B][1][c]
    Control arrangements, management and
      . . . 1.02[B][1][b]
    Death or withdrawal of owner
      . . . 1.02[B][1][e]
    Limited liability . . . 1.02[B][1][a]
    Management and control arrangements
      . . . 1.02[B][1][b]
    Transferability of interests . . . 1.02[B][1][d]
    Withdrawal of owner, death or
      . . . 1.02[B][1][e]

[References are to sections.]

BUSINESS FORM—Cont.
Partnerships . . . 1.02[A][3]
Prevalent business forms . . . 1.02[A]
S corporations . . . 1.02[A][2]
Tax factors in choice of business form
    Capital contributions . . . 1.02[B][2][a]
    Distributions . . . 1.02[B][2][g]
    Income
        Allocations of . . . 1.02[B][2][d]
        Taxation of . . . 1.02[B][2][c]
    Losses
        Allocations of . . . 1.02[B][2][d]
        At-risk rules, limitation under
          . . . 1.02[B][2][f]
        Basis limitation on deductibility of
          . . . 1.02[B][2][e]
        Passive activity rules, limitation under
          . . . 1.02[B][2][f]
        Taxation of . . . 1.02[B][2][c]
    Ownership restrictions . . . 1.02[B][2][b]

C

CAPITAL ACCOUNT
Generally . . . 6.06; 6.06[A]
Adjustments
    Assumed partnership liabilities . . . 6.06[C]
    Book value and tax basis disparities of contrib-
      uted or revalued property . . . 6.06[F]
    Contributions of property, for
        Generally . . . 6.06[B]
        Book value and tax basis disparities be-
          tween . . . 6.06[F]
        Tax basis and book value disparities be-
          tween . . . 6.06[F]
    Disallowed losses . . . 6.06[G]
    Distributions of partnership property
      . . . 6.06[B]
    Employee benefit plan contributions
      . . . 6.06[H]
    Guaranteed payments . . . 6.06[H]
    Noncapital expenditures . . . 6.06[G]
    Nondeductible expenditures . . . 6.06[G]
    Promissory notes . . . 6.06[D]
    Revaluations of partnership property
        Generally . . . 6.06[E]
        Book value and tax basis disparities be-
          tween . . . 6.06[F]
        Tax basis and book value disparities be-
          tween . . . 6.06[F]
    Tax basis and book value disparities of con-
      tributed or revalued property . . . 6.06[F]
Partner's basis, relationship between . . . 5.01[I]

C CORPORATIONS
Business forms . . . 1.02[A][1]

CHARITABLE CONTRIBUTIONS
Sale or exchange of partnership or limited liability
    company interest . . . 12.06[L]

CHILDREN
Family partnerships, partner status of minor children
    in . . . 9.04

**CLASSIFICATION OF ENTITIES FOR TAX
   PURPOSES**
Generally . . . 2.01
Anti-abuse rules (See ANTI-ABUSE RULES)
Business entity, defined . . . 2.02[C]
Classification regulations, overview of
    Generally . . . 2.02[A]
    Domestic ventures (See subhead: Domestic
      business entity, classification of)
    Election procedures
        Generally . . . 2.02[F]
        Classification, change in . . . 2.02[G][1]
    Foreign ventures (See subhead: Foreign busi-
      ness entities, classification of)
Corporations
    Per se corporations
        Domestic entities . . . 2.02[D][1]
        Foreign entities . . . 2.02[E][2]
    Publicly traded partnership rules (See subhead:
      Publicly traded partnership rules)
    Unincorporated associations . . . 2.07
Domestic business entity, classification of
    Generally . . . 2.02[A][1], [D]
    Grandfather rules . . . 2.02[D][4]
    Per se corporations . . . 2.02[D][1]
    Single-owner entities . . . 2.02[D][2]
    Two or more owners, entities with
      . . . 2.02[D][3]
Election procedures
    Generally . . . 2.02[F]
    Classification, change in . . . 2.02[G][1]
    Partnership taxation provisions, elections to be
      excluded from (See PARTNERSHIPS
      (GENERALLY), subhead: Elections to be
      excluded from tax rules)
Entity, defined . . . 2.02[B]
Existence of entity, determination of . . . 2.03
Foreign business entities, classification of
    Generally . . . 2.02[A][2], [E]
    Division of partnership, classification following
      . . . 2.02[E][6]
    Grandfather rules . . . 2.02[E][3]
    Limited liability defined . . . 2.02[E][1]
    Per se corporations . . . 2.02[E][2]
    Single-owner foreign entities . . . 2.02[E][4]
    Termination of partnership, classification fol-
      lowing . . . 2.02[E][6]
    Two or more owners, entities with
      . . . 2.02[E][5]
Grandfather rules
    Domestic entities . . . 2.02[D][4]
    Foreign entities . . . 2.02[E][3]
Number of members, change in . . . 2.02[G][2]
Partnership, classification of
    Division, classification following
      . . . 2.02[E][6]
    Partnership taxation provisions, elections to be
      excluded from (See PARTNERSHIPS
      (GENERALLY), subhead: Elections to be
      excluded from tax rules)
    Publicly traded partnership rules (See subhead:
      Publicly traded partnership rules)

[References are to sections.]

CLASSIFICATION OF ENTITIES FOR TAX PURPOSES—Cont.

Partnership, classification of—Cont.

   Termination, classification following . . . 2.02[E][6]

Per se corporations

   Domestic entities . . . 2.02[D][1]

   Foreign entities . . . 2.02[E][2]

Pre-1997 rules . . . 2.07

Publicly traded partnership rules

   Generally . . . 2.04

   Definition . . . 2.04[B]

   Effective date of final regulations . . . 2.04[A]

   Foreign partnership . . . 2.04[D]

   Qualifying passive-type income not taxed as corporation . . . 2.04[C]

Single-owner entities

   Domestic entities . . . 2.02[D][2]

   Foreign entities . . . 2.02[E][4]

Two or more owners, entities with

   Domestic entities . . . 2.02[D][3]

   Foreign entities . . . 2.02[E][5]

Unincorporated associations . . . 2.07

CONSOLIDATION. (See TERMINATION OF PARTNERSHIP OR LIMITED LIABILITY COMPANY, subhead: Merger or consolidation)

CONSTRUCTIVE DISTRIBUTIONS

Decrease in partner's share of partnership liabilities, money distribution upon . . . 8.02[B]

Disproportionate distributions, computation of gain or loss in . . . 8.06[B][3]

Money distribution upon decrease in partner's share of partnership liabilities . . . 8.02[B]

CONTRIBUTIONS TO PARTNERSHIP OR LIMITED LIABILITY COMPANY

Generally . . . 1.01[D]

Acquisition of interest by contribution (See ACQUISITION OF PARTNERSHIP OR LIMITED LIABILITY COMPANY INTEREST BY CONTRIBUTION)

Capital account adjustments

   Generally . . . 6.06[B]

   Book value and tax basis disparities between . . . 6.06[F]

   Tax basis and book value disparities between . . . 6.06[F]

Capital contributions, tax consequences of . . . 1.02[B][2][a]

Disguised sale, contributions with related distribution treated as (See DISGUISED SALES)

Partner-partnership transactions treated as . . . 7.01[F]

Property, contributions of

   Allocations attributable to contributed property (See ALLOCATIONS, subhead: Contributed property, attributable to)

   Characterization of gain or loss on disposition of . . . 3.02[D]

CONTROLLED AND RELATED PARTNERSHIPS, SALES AND EXCHANGES INVOLVING

Accrued expenses, deductions for . . . 7.05[F]

Control under Section 707(b), defined . . . 7.05[B]

Gain treated as ordinary income

   Depreciable property . . . 7.05[E]

   Property not capital asset to purchaser, if . . . 7.05[D]

Loss deductions, limitation on . . . 7.05[C]

Tax-motivated transactions . . . 7.05[A]

CONTROLLED FOREIGN CORPORATION

Income, characterization of . . . 3.02[C][2]

CO-OWNERSHIP

Business forms . . . 1.02[A][7]

CORPORATIONS

Basis adjusted property, contributions of . . . 12.08[G]

C corporations . . . 1.02[A][1]

Classification for tax purposes (See CLASSIFICATION OF ENTITIES FOR TAX PURPOSES, subhead: Corporations)

Contribution of basis adjusted property . . . 12.08[G]

Nonrecognition transactions involving exchanges of partnership or limited liability company interests (See SALE OR EXCHANGE OF PARTNERSHIP OR LIMITED LIABILITY COMPANY INTEREST, subhead: Corporations)

S corporations . . . 1.02[A][2]

Termination of partnership or limited liability company upon change to . . . 13.03[B]

CURRENT DISTRIBUTIONS

Generally . . . 8.03

Advances against partner's expected distributive share . . . 8.03[B]

Draws against partner's expected distributive share . . . 8.03[B]

Gain or loss . . . 8.01[A][1]

Liquidating distributions distinguished . . . 8.01[B]

Loss or gain . . . 8.01[A][1]

Money distributions . . . 8.03[A], [D]

Property distributions . . . 8.03[C], [D]

Special basis in distributed property under Section 732(d) . . . 8.03[E]

Tax consequences to partnership . . . 8.03[F]

D

DEATH OF PARTNER OR MEMBER

Allocation of income for year of partner's death, pre-1998 rules . . . 11.02

Basis

   Distributed property, Section 732(d) election for . . . 11.04[B][2]

   Partnership or limited liability company property, of . . . 11.01[B][4]; 11.04[B]

   Section 732(d) election for distributed property . . . 11.04[B][2]

   Section 754 election . . . 11.04[B][1]

[References are to sections.]

DEATH OF PARTNER OR MEMBER—Cont.

Basis—Cont.

    Successor's interest, of . . . 11.01[B][3];
      11.04[A]

    Summary of effect . . . 11.04[B][3]

Estate taxation

    Generally . . . 11.01[B][5]

    Valuation of partnership or limited liability
      company interest, determination of (See sub-
      head: Valuation of partnership or limited
      liability company interest, determination of)

Income-in-respect-of-a-decedent rule (See INCOME-
    IN-RESPECT-OF-A-DECEDENT (IRD))

Losses, deduction of . . . 6.09[B]

Nonrecognition transaction, exchange of interests in
    . . . 12.06[J]

Nontax considerations in choice of business form
    . . . 1.02[B][1][e]

State law considerations

    General partnerships . . . 11.01[A][1]

    Limited liability company . . . 11.01[A][3]

    Limited partnerships . . . 11.01[A][2]

Tax considerations

    Generally . . . 11.01[B]

    Basis (See subhead: Basis)

    Estate taxation . . . 11.01[B][5]

    Liquidation

      Deceased partner or member's interest, of
        . . . 11.01[B][6]

      Partnership or limited liability company,
        of . . . 11.01[B][9]

    Sale of decedent's interest

      Remaining partners or members, to
        . . . 11.01[B][7]

      Third party, to . . . 11.01[B][8]

    Successor joins partnership or limited liability
      company . . . 11.01[B][10]

    Tax year closes for deceased partner or mem-
      ber . . . 11.01[B][1]

    Terminates partnership or limited liability com-
      pany . . . 11.01[B][2]

Valuation of partnership or limited liability company
    interest, determination of

    Generally . . . 11.05

    Insurance-funded agreements

      Cross-purchase agreements
        . . . 11.05[A][1]

      Redemption agreements . . . 11.05[A][2]

    Partnership or limited liability company agree-
      ments, effects of . . . 11.05[A]

    Section 2032A . . . 11.05[B]

    Special valuation rules . . . 11.05[B]

DEBT

Basis adjustments for discharge of indebtedness
    . . . 5.01[D]

Cancellation of partnership or limited liability com-
    pany debt . . . 4.02[B][3]

Discharge of indebtedness

    Generally . . . 3.03[F][2]

    Basis adjustments for . . . 5.01[D]

    Depreciable property, basis reduction election
      . . . 3.03[F][2][c], [F][2][f]

DEBT—Cont.

Discharge of indebtedness—Cont.

    Partnership interest

      Basis of . . . 3.03[F][2][g]

      Exchange of . . . 3.03[F][2][h]

    Purchase price adjustment . . . 3.03[F][2][a]

    Qualified real property business indebtedness
      . . . 3.03[F][2][d]

    Separate partner treatment of debt-discharge
      rules . . . 3.03[F][2][e]

    Tax attributes, reduction of . . . 3.03[F][2][b]

DEDUCTIONS

Accrual-method deductions, deferral of . . . 7.01[D]

Accrued expenses, for . . . 7.05[F]

Basis limitation on deductibility of losses
    . . . 1.02[B][2][e]

Depletion deductions

    Decreases in basis . . . 5.01[C][6]

    Increases in basis adjustments . . . 5.01[C][5]

Distributive shares (See DISTRIBUTIVE SHARES,
    subhead: Losses, deduction of)

Loss limitation

    Controlled and related partnerships, sales and
      exchanges involving . . . 7.05[C]

    Order of basis adjustments . . . 5.01[F][1]

Nonrecourse deductions . . . 6.08[B], [D]

Payments to service partner or member
    . . . 4.05[B][5]

Sale or exchange of partnership property, effect on
    loss deductions of . . . 12.05

DEPRECIABLE PROPERTY

Basis reduction, election to . . . 3.03[F][2][c],
    [F][2][f]

Expense cost, election to . . . 3.03[E]

Gain treated as ordinary income . . . 7.05[E]

DISGUISED SALES

Generally . . . 7.04[D]

Debt-financed disguised sales . . . 7.04[D][5]

Disclosure of transactions . . . 7.04[D][8]

Encumbered property, transfers of

    Generally . . . 7.04[D][4]

    Nonqualified liabilities . . . 7.04[D][4][b]

    Qualified liabilities . . . 7.04[D][4][a]

Partnership interest, of . . . 7.04[D][7]

Partnership to partner, by . . . 7.04[D][6]

Payments not included in . . . 7.04[D][3]

Regulatory overview . . . 7.04[D][1]

Tests for determining whether disguised sale occurs
    . . . 7.04[D][2]

**DISTRIBUTIONS TO PARTNERS OR MEM-
    BERS**

Generally . . . 1.01[G]; 8.01; 8.01[A]

Basis

    Corporate partner stock distributions to other
      partners . . . 5.01[C][7][b]

    Decrease in basis . . . 5.01[C][4]

    Distributed property in distributee partner's
      hands, of . . . 8.01[A][3]

    Distributee partner's interest in partnership, of
      . . . 8.01[A][2]

[References are to sections.]

DISTRIBUTIONS TO PARTNERS OR MEMBERS—Cont.

Basis—Cont.
Undistributed property, partnership's basis in . . . 8.01[A][6]
Basis adjustment
Generally . . . 8.07; 8.07[F]
Allocation under Section 754 election . . . 8.07[A]
Carry forward of unusable basis adjustments . . . 8.07[C]
Cash distribution, recognition of gain on . . . 8.07[B][1]
Computation under Section 754 election . . . 8.07[A]
Distributed property changes . . . 8.07[B][3]
Liquidating distribution, recognition of loss on . . . 8.07[B][2]
Marketable securities, distributions of . . . 8.02[A][5]
Section 732(d), under . . . 8.07[B][4]
Section 751(b) . . . 8.07[E]
Tiered partnerships, distributions by . . . 8.07[D]
Unusable basis adjustments, carry forward of . . . 8.07[C]
Capital account adjustments . . . 6.06[B]
Character of distributed property . . . 8.01[A][4]
Character of partner's gain or loss on disposition of distributed property
Generally . . . 8.05
Inventory . . . 8.05[A]
Recapture property . . . 8.05[B]
Unrealized receivables . . . 8.05[A]
Constructive distributions (See CONSTRUCTIVE DISTRIBUTIONS)
Contributions of property, distributions associated with
Generally . . . 4.03[F]; 8.02[C]
Disguised sales (See DISGUISED SALES)
Corporate partner, distributions of stock to . . . 8.02[D]
Current distributions (See CURRENT DISTRIBUTIONS)
Deceased partner's successor, payments to . . . 8.01[A][7]
Disposition of distributed property, character of gain or loss on (See subhead: Character of partner's gain or loss on disposition of distributed property)
Disproportionate distribution rules
Generally . . . 8.06
Gain or loss
Computational steps . . . 8.06[B][1]
Constructive distributions where partner's share of partnership liabilities decrease . . . 8.06[B][3]
Noncash distributions . . . 8.06[B][2]
Liquidation of entire partnership, distributions in . . . 8.06[D]
Recapture property, distributions involving . . . 8.06[C]
Transactions not treated as . . . 8.06[A]

DISTRIBUTIONS TO PARTNERS OR MEMBERS—Cont.

Gain or loss
Current distributions . . . 8.01[A][1]
Disposition of distributed property, character of gain or loss on (See subhead: Character of partner's gain or loss on disposition of distributed property)
Disproportionate distribution rules (See subhead: Disproportionate distribution rules)
Liquidating distributions . . . 8.01[A][1]
Holding period . . . 8.01[A][4]
Inventory
Character of partner's gain or loss on disposition of . . . 8.05[A]
Disproportionate distribution rules (See subhead: Disproportionate distribution rules)
Liquidating distributions (See LIQUIDATING DISTRIBUTIONS)
Loss (See subhead: Gain or loss)
Marketable securities, distributions of
Generally . . . 8.02[A]
Anti-abuse rule . . . 8.02[A][6]
Basis adjustment . . . 8.02[A][5]
Defined . . . 8.02[A][1]
Gain recognition rule, distributions not subject to . . . 8.02[A][3]
Investment partnerships, exception for . . . 8.02[A][4]
Money distribution reduced by partner's share of appreciation . . . 8.02[A][2]
Recapture property
Character of partner's gain or loss on disposition of . . . 8.05[A]
Disproportionate distribution rules . . . 8.06[C]
Retiring partner, payments to . . . 8.01[A][7]
Sale or exchange of partnership or limited liability company interest (See SALE OR EXCHANGE OF PARTNERSHIP OR LIMITED LIABILITY COMPANY INTEREST, subhead: Distributions of partnership or limited liability company interest)
Section 751 property, distributions changing partner's share of . . . 8.01[A][5]
Tax factors in choice of business form . . . 1.02[B][2][g]
Unrealized receivables
Character of partner's gain or loss on disposition of . . . 8.05[A]
Disproportionate distribution rules (See subhead: Disproportionate distribution rules)

DISTRIBUTIVE SHARES
Generally . . . 1.01[C]; 6.01[A]
Advances against partner's expected . . . 8.03[B]
Allocations (See ALLOCATIONS)
Capital account (See CAPITAL ACCOUNT)
Draws against partner's expected . . . 8.03[B]
Losses, deduction of
Generally . . . 6.09[A]
Death, effect of . . . 6.09[B]
Gift, effect of . . . 6.09[B]
Sale, effect of . . . 6.09[B]

[References are to sections.]

DISTRIBUTIVE SHARES—Cont.

Losses, deduction of—Cont.

    Termination, effect of . . . 6.09[B]

Partner-partnership transactions included in
   . . . 7.01[F]

Substantial economic effect test (See SUBSTAN-
TIAL ECONOMIC EFFECT TEST)

Taxable year . . . 6.01[B]

DRAWS

Basis adjustments, order of . . . 5.01[F][5]

Current distributions . . . 8.03[B]

Services or use of capital, payments for
   . . . 7.03[E]

E

ELECTIONS

Generally . . . 2.02[F]

Classification, change in . . . 2.02[G][1]

Depreciable property

    Basis reduction . . . 3.03[F][2][c], [F][2][f]

    Expense cost, election to . . . 3.03[E]

Income (See INCOME, subhead: Elections affecting
partnership or limited liability company income)

Large partnerships, simplified flow through for election of . . . 3.05

Partnership taxation provisions, elections to be excluded from (See PARTNERSHIPS (GENER-
ALLY), subhead: Elections to be excluded from
tax rules)

Section 83(b), election to include income under
   . . . 4.05[B][3]

Section 732(d) election (See SALE OR EX-
CHANGE OF PARTNERSHIP OR LIMITED
LIABILITY COMPANY INTEREST, subhead:
Section 732(d) election)

Section 754 election

    Basis adjustments

        Allocation . . . 8.07[A]

        Computation . . . 8.07[A]

    Death of partner or member . . . 11.04[B][1]

    Making and reporting . . . 12.08[M]

    Reporting, making and . . . 12.08[M]

    Restoring equivalence . . . 5.01[H][2]

    Sale of corporate partner's stock
       . . . 5.01[C][7][a]

Taxable year . . . 3.04[F]

Tax consequences . . . 13.06[B]

ENCUMBERED PROPERTY

Disguised sales (See DISGUISED SALES, subhead:
Encumbered property, transfers of)

Partner's share of partnership liabilities related to
(See LIABILITIES OF PARTNERSHIP, subhead:
Encumbered property)

ENTITIES (See CLASSIFICATION OF ENTITIES
FOR TAX PURPOSES)

ESTATE TAXATION

Generally . . . 11.01[B][5]

Family partnership . . . 9.07

ESTATE TAXATION—Cont.

Valuation of partnership or limited liability company
interest, determination of (See DEATH OF PART-
NER OR MEMBER, subhead: Valuation of partnership or limited liability company interest, determination of)

**EXCHANGE OF PARTNERSHIP OR LIMITED
LIABILITY COMPANY INTEREST** (See
SALE OR EXCHANGE OF PARTNERSHIP OR
LIMITED LIABILITY COMPANY INTEREST)

F

FAMILY PARTNERSHIPS

Generally . . . 9.01

Allocation of partnership income among family
members

    Generally . . . 9.06

    Disproportionate allocation, reallocation for
       . . . 9.06[D]

    Donor's services, reallocation for reasonable
       value of . . . 9.06[C]

    Gift, allocation in year of . . . 9.06[E]

    Indirect gifts

        Generally . . . 9.06[B]

        Intrafamily sales treated as . . . 9.06[A]

Capital interest acquired by gift, partner status
where

    Generally . . . 9.02[C]

    Donee as real owner . . . 9.02[C][2]

    Donor as real owner . . . 9.02[C][1]

    Limited partnership interest acquired by gift
       . . . 9.02[C][3]

    Tax-avoidance motive in gift of partnership
       interest . . . 9.02[C][4]

Estate tax considerations . . . 9.07

Gifts

    Allocation in year of . . . 9.06[E]

    Capital interest acquired by gift, partner status
       where (See subhead: Capital interest ac-
       quired by gift, partner status where)

    Indirect gifts

        Generally . . . 9.06[B]

        Intrafamily sales treated as . . . 9.06[A]

    Sales of partnership interests . . . 9.05

Gift tax considerations . . . 9.07

Minor children, partner status of . . . 9.04

Partner status, establishment of

    Generally . . . 9.02

    Capital as material income-producing factor
       . . . 9.02[B]

    Capital interest acquired by gift (See subhead:
       Capital interest acquired by gift, partner sta-
       tus where)

    Minor children, of . . . 9.04

    Section 704(e)(1) . . . 9.02[B]

    Subjective test of partner status . . . 9.02[A]

    Trustees, of . . . 9.03

Sales of partnership interests

    Generally . . . 9.05

    Intrafamily sales treated as indirect gifts
       . . . 9.06[A]

[References are to sections.]

FAMILY PARTNERSHIPS—Cont.
Trustees, partner status of . . . 9.03

FOREIGN TAXES
Partners, elections made by . . . 3.03[F][1]

G

GIFTS
Family partnerships (See FAMILY PARTNER-
SHIPS, subhead: Gifts)
Limited liability company interest, of . . . 12.06[K]
Partnership interest, of . . . 12.06[K]

GIFT TAXATION
Family partnership . . . 9.07

GOODWILL
Allocation to . . . 12.08[H]
Liquidating payments . . . 10.01[C][2]

GROSS INCOME
Partner's share of partnership, determination of
. . . 3.02[B]

GUARANTEED PAYMENTS
Capital, payments for use of (See subhead: Services
or use of capital, payments for)
Capital account adjustments . . . 6.06[H]
Partner-partnership transactions
Generally . . . 7.01[E]
Services or use of capital, payments for (See
subhead: Services or use of capital, pay-
ments for)
Services or use of capital, payments for
Generally . . . 7.03[B]
Bonuses . . . 7.03[E]
Character . . . 7.03[C]
Draws . . . 7.03[E]
Gross income, payments computed from
. . . 7.03[D]
Profits, payments dependent on . . . 7.03[E]
Tax consequences . . . 7.03[A]

I

INCOME
Allocations of
Generally . . . 1.02[B][2][d]
Partner's death, pre-1998 rules . . . 11.02
Characterization (See subhead: Partnership-level
characterization)
Contributed property, character of gain or loss on
disposition of . . . 3.02[D]
Controlled foreign corporation income, character of
. . . 3.02[C][2]
Elections affecting partnership or limited liability
company income
Generally . . . 3.03[A]
Accounting method (See ACCOUNTING
METHOD)
Amortization
Organization expenses, of . . . 3.03[C]
Start-up costs, of . . . 3.03[D]

INCOME—Cont.
Elections affecting partnership or limited liability
company income—Cont.
Expense cost of depreciable property, election
to . . . 3.03[E]
Partner-level elections
Generally . . . 3.03[F]
Foreign tax credit . . . 3.03[F][1]
Indebtedness, discharge of (See DEBT,
subhead: Discharge of indebtedness)
Gross income, determination of partner's share of
partnership . . . 3.02[B]
Partnership-level characterization
Generally . . . 3.02[C]
Contributed property, character of gain or loss
on disposition of . . . 3.02[D]
Controlled foreign corporation income, charac-
ter of . . . 3.02[C][2]
Effect of . . . 3.02[C][1]
Separately stated items
Generally . . . 3.02[A]
Partner's return, items subject to limitations on
. . . 3.02[A][4]
Partner's tax liability, items affecting
. . . 3.02[A][3]
Regulations, items specified in . . . 3.02[A][2]
Section 702, items specified in . . . 3.02[A][1]
Taxable income, computation of
Generally . . . 1.02[B][2][c]; 3.02
Gross income, determination of partner's share
of partnership . . . 3.02[B]
Partnership-level characterization (See sub-
head: Partnership-level characterization)
Separately stated items (See subhead: Sepa-
rately stated items)

**INCOME-IN-RESPECT-OF-A-DECEDENT
(IRD)**
Generally . . . 11.03[A]
Partnership or limited liability company interest,
attributable to
Generally . . . 11.03[B]
Allocation of basis adjustments among partner-
ship assets . . . 12.08[F][1]
Assets would be income-in-respect-of-a-
decedent if held by decedent
. . . 11.03[B][2]
Liquidating payments . . . 11.03[B][1]

**INTEREST IN PARTNERSHIP OR LIMITED
LIABILITY COMPANY**
Acquisition of (See ACQUISITION OF PARTNER-
SHIP OR LIMITED LIABILITY COMPANY
INTEREST BY CONTRIBUTION)
Basis (See BASIS OF PARTNERSHIP OR LIM-
ITED LIABILITY COMPANY INTEREST)
Exchange of (See SALE OR EXCHANGE OF
PARTNERSHIP OR LIMITED LIABILITY
COMPANY INTEREST)
Partners' interest, determination of
Generally . . . 6.07; 6.07[A]
Factors considered in . . . 6.07[B]

[References are to sections.]

INTEREST IN PARTNERSHIP OR LIMITED LIABILITY COMPANY—Cont.

Sale of (See SALE OR EXCHANGE OF PARTNERSHIP OR LIMITED LIABILITY COMPANY INTEREST)

INVENTORY

Character of partner's gain or loss on disposition of . . . 8.05[A]

Disproportionate distribution rules (See DISTRIBUTIONS TO PARTNERS OR MEMBERS, subhead: Disproportionate distribution rules)

Sale or exchange of partnership interest . . . 12.03[A][2]

INVESTMENT COMPANY PARTNERSHIPS

Gain recognized on contribution of property to . . . 4.02[C]

Marketable securities, distributions of . . . 8.02[A][4]

IRD (See INCOME-IN-RESPECT-OF-A-DECEDENT (IRD))

L

LARGE PARTNERSHIPS

Simplified flow through for election of . . . 3.05

LEASES (See LOANS AND LEASES)

LIABILITIES OF PARTNERSHIP

Generally . . . 5.04[A]

Basis of partnership interest, effect on

Generally . . . 5.03[A]

At-risk and passive activity rules, interaction with . . . 5.03[C]

Nonrecourse liabilities in tax-sheltered investments . . . 5.03[B]

Passive activity and at-risk rules, interaction with . . . 5.03[C]

Tax-sheltered investments, nonrecourse liabilities in . . . 5.03[B]

Capital account adjustments . . . 6.06[C]

Changes in partner's share of

Addition of partner . . . 5.08[C]

Amount of partnership liability, changes in . . . 5.08[B]

Encumbered property (See subhead: Encumbered property)

Events that change partner's shares . . . 5.08[A]

Loss of partner . . . 5.08[C]

Sale or exchange of partnership interest . . . 5.08[E]

Constructive distributions upon decrease in partner's share of (See CONSTRUCTIVE DISTRIBUTIONS)

Contingent liabilities . . . 5.04[C]

Encumbered property

Contributions of . . . 5.08[D][1]

Distribution of . . . 5.08[D][2]

Payments on excess encumbrance . . . 5.08[D][4]

LIABILITIES OF PARTNERSHIP—Cont.

Encumbered property—Cont.

Value of property, limitation of encumbrance to . . . 5.08[D][3]

Loans treated as capital contributions . . . 5.04[E]

Obligations treated as liabilities under regulations Section 1.752-7 . . . 5.04[D]

Partner's share of liability, determination of

Generally . . . 5.05[A]

Assumption of partnership or partner debt . . . 5.05[C]

Changes in (See subhead: Changes in partner's share of)

Nonrecourse liabilities

Allocation rules coordinated . . . 5.07[A]

Computation . . . 5.07[B]

Recourse liabilities (See RECOURSE LIABILITIES)

Related persons, interests of . . . 5.05[B]

Sham liabilities . . . 5.04[B]

Thin partnerships . . . 5.04[E]

LIMITED LIABILITY COMPANIES (LLCs)

Acquisition of interest by contribution (See ACQUISITION OF PARTNERSHIP OR LIMITED LIABILITY COMPANY INTEREST BY CONTRIBUTION)

Basis of interest in (See BASIS OF PARTNERSHIP OR LIMITED LIABILITY COMPANY INTEREST)

Business forms . . . 1.02[A][6]

Cancellation of debt . . . 4.02[B][3]

Computing and reporting income from . . . 1.01[B]

Contributions to (See CONTRIBUTIONS TO PARTNERSHIP OR LIMITED LIABILITY COMPANY)

Death of partner or member . . . 11.01[A][3]

Deceased owner's estate . . . 1.01[H]

Distributive shares . . . 1.01[C]

Elections affecting income (See INCOME, subhead: Elections affecting partnership or limited liability company income)

Exchange of (See SALE OR EXCHANGE OF PARTNERSHIP OR LIMITED LIABILITY COMPANY INTEREST)

Owner-entity transactions . . . 1.01[F]

Payments to retiree . . . 1.01[H]

Reporting and computing income from . . . 1.01[B]

Rules governing taxation, overview of . . . 1.01

Sale or exchange of (See SALE OR EXCHANGE OF PARTNERSHIP OR LIMITED LIABILITY COMPANY INTEREST)

Subchapter K, aggregate and entity principles of . . . 1.01[A]

Taxable year (See TAXABLE YEAR)

Termination of (See TERMINATION OF PARTNERSHIP OR LIMITED LIABILITY COMPANY)

LIMITED LIABILITY PARTNERSHIPS (LLPs)

Business forms . . . 1.02[A][5]

[References are to sections.]

LIMITED PARTNERSHIPS
Business forms . . . 1.02[A][4]
Death of partner or member . . . 11.01[A][2]
Limited liability partnerships . . . 1.02[A][5]

LIQUIDATING DISTRIBUTIONS
Generally . . . 8.04
Basis allocation to distributed property . . . 8.04[E]
Current distributions distinguished . . . 8.01[B]
Deficit capital accounts (See SUBSTANTIAL ECO-
   NOMIC EFFECT TEST, subhead: Deficit capital
   accounts)
Disproportionate distribution rules . . . 8.06[D]
Distributions, basis adjustments related to
   . . . 8.07[B][2]
Gain or loss
   Generally . . . 8.01[A][1]; 8.04[B]
   Determination . . . 8.04[C]
   Money distribution . . . 8.04[A]
   Reporting . . . 8.04[C]
Loss (See subhead: Gain or loss)
Money distribution, recognition of gain on
   . . . 8.04[A]
Positive capital account balances, of . . . 6.05[A][2]
Property distributions . . . 8.04[D]

LIQUIDATING PAYMENTS
Generally . . . 10.01
Cash liquidating payments, series of
   Generally . . . 10.02
   Section 736(a) (See subhead: Section 736(a))
   Section 736(b) (See subhead: Section 736(b))
Classification of . . . 10.01[B]
Gain or loss, computation of
   Section 736(a) . . . 10.02[C]
   Section 736(b) . . . 10.02[B]
Income-in-respect-of-a-decedent rule
   . . . 11.03[B][1]
Loss or gain, computation of
   Section 736(a) . . . 10.02[C]
   Section 736(b) . . . 10.02[B]
Noncash liquidating payments . . . 10.03
Payments governed by Section 736 . . . 10.01[A]
Section 736(a)
   Generally . . . 10.01[D]
   Amount of payments, determination of
      . . . 10.01[D][1]
   Determination . . . 10.02[A]
   Gain or loss, computation of . . . 10.02[C]
   Loss or gain, computation of . . . 10.02[C]
   Lump-sum liquidating payment, taxation of
      . . . 10.01[D][3]
   Taxation of . . . 10.01[D][2]
Section 736(b)
   Generally . . . 10.01[C]
   Determination . . . 10.02[A]
   Gain or loss, computation of . . . 10.02[B]
   Goodwill, limited exclusion for
      . . . 10.01[C][2]
   Loss or gain, computation of . . . 10.02[B]
   Taxation of . . . 10.01[C][3]
   Unrealized receivables, limited exclusion for
      . . . 10.01[C][2]

LIQUIDATING PAYMENTS—Cont.
Section 736(b)—Cont.
   Valuing partner's share of partnership property
      . . . 10.01[C][1]

**LIQUIDATION OF PARTNERSHIP OR LIM-
   ITED LIABILITY COMPANIES INTEREST**
Basis adjustments . . . 5.01[E]

LLCs (See LIMITED LIABILITY COMPANIES
   (LLCs))

LLPs (See LIMITED LIABILITY PARTNERSHIPS
   (LLPs))

LOANS AND LEASES
Capital contributions, treatment as . . . 5.04[E]
Nonpartner capacity, transactions in which partner
   acts in . . . 7.04[A]
Nonrecourse loans . . . 5.06[F]

LOSSES
Acquisition of partnership or limited liability com-
   pany interest by contribution (See ACQUISITION
   OF PARTNERSHIP OR LIMITED LIABILITY
   COMPANY INTEREST BY CONTRIBUTION,
   subhead: Gain or loss)
Allocations of . . . 1.02[B][2][d]
At-risk rules, limitation under . . . 1.02[B][2][f]
Basis limitation on deductibility of
   . . . 1.02[B][2][e]
Computation of (See SALE OR EXCHANGE OF
   PARTNERSHIP OR LIMITED LIABILITY
   COMPANY INTEREST, subhead: Gain or loss,
   computation of)
Contributed property, character on disposition of
   . . . 3.02[D]
Current distributions . . . 8.01[A][1]
Deductibility of (See DEDUCTIONS)
Disallowed losses . . . 6.06[G]
Disposition of distributed property (See DISTRIBU-
   TIONS TO PARTNERS OR MEMBERS, sub-
   head: Character of partner's gain or loss on dispo-
   sition of distributed property)
Disproportionate distribution rules (See DISTRIBU-
   TIONS TO PARTNERS OR MEMBERS, sub-
   head: Disproportionate distribution rules)
Distributive share (See DISTRIBUTIVE SHARES,
   subhead: Losses, deduction of)
Economic risk of . . . 5.06[A]
Liquidating distribution (See LIQUIDATING DIS-
   TRIBUTIONS, subhead: Gain or loss)
Partnership liabilities, changes in partner's share of
   . . . 5.08[C]
Passive activity rules, limitation under
   . . . 1.02[B][2][f]
Section 736(a) . . . 10.02[C]
Section 736(b) . . . 10.02[B]
Section 743(b) basis adjustment . . . 12.08[I][1]
Section 751 property (See SALE OR EXCHANGE
   OF PARTNERSHIP OR LIMITED LIABILITY
   COMPANY INTEREST, subhead: Section 751
   property, characterization of gain or loss on)
Suspended losses . . . 13.06[G]

[References are to sections.]

LOSSES—Cont.
Taxation of . . . 1.02[B][2][c]

M

MEMBER-LIMITED LIABILITY COMPANIES TRANSACTIONS (See PARTNER-PARTNERSHIP TRANSACTIONS)

MERGER OR CONSOLIDATION. (See TERMINATION OF PARTNERSHIP OR LIMITED LIABILITY COMPANY, subhead: Merger or consolidation)

N

NONRECOGNITION RULE
Acquisition of partnership or limited liability company interest by contribution . . . 4.02[A]
Sale or exchange of partnership or limited liability company interest (See SALE OR EXCHANGE OF PARTNERSHIP OR LIMITED LIABILITY COMPANY INTEREST, subhead: Nonrecognition transaction, exchange of interests in)

NONRECOURSE LIABILITIES
Allocations of items attributable to (See ALLOCATIONS, subhead: Nonrecourse liabilities, allocations of items attributable to)
Partner's share of liability
    Allocation rules coordinated . . . 5.07[A]
    Computation . . . 5.07[B]
Tax-sheltered investments . . . 5.03[B]

O

ORGANIZATION EXPENSES
Amortization of . . . 3.03[C]; 4.06[B]
Disguised organization and syndication expenses
    . . . 4.06[D]
Syndication expenses, disguised organization and
    . . . 4.06[D]

P

PARTNER-PARTNERSHIP TRANSACTIONS
Generally . . . 7.01
Accrual-method deductions, deferral of . . . 7.01[D]
Contributions, transactions treated as . . . 7.01[F]
Disguised sales (See DISGUISED SALES)
Distributive share, transactions included in
    . . . 7.01[F]
Nonpartner capacity, transactions in which partner acts in
    Generally . . . 7.01[A]; 7.04
    Bad debts . . . 7.04[A][1]
    Determination as to whether partner acting in partner or nonpartner capacity . . . 7.02
    Disguised payments for services or property, transactions treated as . . . 7.04[E]
    Disguised sales, transactions treated as (See DISGUISED SALES)

PARTNER-PARTNERSHIP TRANSACTIONS—Cont.
Nonpartner capacity, transactions in which partner acts in—Cont.
    Guaranteed payments, treatment of (See GUARANTEED PAYMENTS)
    Loans and leases . . . 7.04[A]
    Recharacterization of transactions . . . 7.01[B]
    Sales . . . 7.04[C]
    Services . . . 7.04[B]
Sales and exchange transactions
    Controlled partnerships, involving (See CONTROLLED AND RELATED PARTNERSHIPS, SALES AND EXCHANGES INVOLVING)
    Losses and capital gains, treatment of
    . . . 7.01[C]
    Nonpartner capacity, transactions in which partner acting in . . . 7.04[C]
    Related partnerships, involving (See CONTROLLED AND RELATED PARTNERSHIPS, SALES AND EXCHANGES INVOLVING)

PARTNERS
Death of (See DEATH OF PARTNER OR MEMBER)
Family partnerships, status as partner in (See FAMILY PARTNERSHIPS, subhead: Partner status, establishment of)
Retirement of partners . . . 8.01[A][7]
Successor partners (See SUCCESSOR PARTNERS)

PARTNERSHIPS (GENERALLY)
Acquisition of interest by contribution (See ACQUISITION OF PARTNERSHIP OR LIMITED LIABILITY COMPANY INTEREST BY CONTRIBUTION)
Basis of interest in (See BASIS OF PARTNERSHIP OR LIMITED LIABILITY COMPANY INTEREST)
Business forms . . . 1.02[A][3]
Cancellation of debt . . . 4.02[B][3]
Classification of
    Division, classification following
    . . . 2.02[E][6]
    Termination, classification following
    . . . 2.02[E][6]
Computing and reporting income from . . . 1.01[B]
Contributions to (See CONTRIBUTIONS TO PARTNERSHIP OR LIMITED LIABILITY COMPANY)
Deceased owner's estate . . . 1.01[H]
Distributive shares . . . 1.01[C]
Elections affecting income (See INCOME, subhead: Elections affecting partnership or limited liability company income)
Elections to be excluded from tax rules
    Generally . . . 2.06[A]
    Effective date . . . 2.06[G]
    Effect of election . . . 2.06[C]
    Entities eligible for election
        Generally . . . 2.06[B]

[References are to sections.]

PARTNERSHIPS (GENERALLY)—Cont.
Elections to be excluded from tax rules—Cont.
  Entities eligible for election—Cont.
    Extraction, partnerships for
      . . . 2.06[B][2]
    Investment partnerships . . . 2.06[B][1]
    Production, partnerships for
      . . . 2.06[B][2]
    Securities dealers, organizations of
      . . . 2.06[B][3]
    Use of property, partnerships for
      . . . 2.06[B][2]
    Intent, election by showing . . . 2.06[E]
    Partial exclusion election . . . 2.06[F]
    Procedure for making election . . . 2.06[D]
    Revocation . . . 2.06[G]
Exchange of (See SALE OR EXCHANGE OF
  PARTNERSHIP OR LIMITED LIABILITY
  COMPANY INTEREST)
Family partnerships (See FAMILY PARTNER-
  SHIPS)
Investment company partnerships
  Gain recognized on contribution of property to
    . . . 4.02[C]
  Marketable securities, distributions of
    . . . 8.02[A][4]
Liabilities of partnership (See LIABILITIES OF
  PARTNERSHIP)
Limited liability partnerships . . . 1.02[A][5]
Limited partnerships (See LIMITED PARTNER-
  SHIPS)
Owner-entity transactions . . . 1.01[F]
Payments to retiree . . . 1.01[H]
Publicly traded partnerships taxed as corporations
  (See CLASSIFICATION OF ENTITIES FOR
  TAX PURPOSES, subhead: Publicly traded part-
  nership rules)
Reporting and computing income from . . . 1.01[B]
Rules governing taxation, overview of . . . 1.01
Sale or exchange of (See SALE OR EXCHANGE
  OF PARTNERSHIP OR LIMITED LIABILITY
  COMPANY INTEREST)
Subchapter K, aggregate and entity principles of
  . . . 1.01[A]
Taxable year (See TAXABLE YEAR)
Termination of (See TERMINATION OF PART-
  NERSHIP OR LIMITED LIABILITY COM-
  PANY)
Tiered partnerships (See TIERED PARTNERSHIPS)

PASSIVE ACTIVITY RULES
At-risk rules and, interaction with . . . 5.03[C]
Loss limitation under . . . 1.02[B][2][f]

PROFITS INTEREST (See ACQUISITION OF
  PARTNERSHIP OR LIMITED LIABILITY
  COMPANY INTEREST BY CONTRIBUTION,
  subhead: Future profits, receipt of interest in)

PROMISSORY NOTES
Capital account adjustments . . . 6.06[D]

PROPERTY
Allocations attributable to contributed property (See
  ALLOCATIONS, subhead: Contributed property,
  attributable to)
Defined . . . 4.02[B]
Depreciation (See DEPRECIABLE PROPERTY)
Disguised payments for . . . 7.04[E]
Disposition of distributed property (See DISTRIBU-
  TIONS TO PARTNERS OR MEMBERS, sub-
  head: Character of partner's gain or loss on dispo-
  sition of distributed property)
Encumbered property
  Disguised sales (See DISGUISED SALES,
    subhead: Encumbered property, transfers of)
  Partner's share of partnership liabilities related
    to (See LIABILITIES OF PARTNERSHIP,
    subhead: Encumbered property)
Recapture property
  Character of partner's gain or loss on disposi-
    tion of . . . 8.05[A]
  Disproportionate distribution rules
    . . . 8.06[C]
Revaluation of partnership property (See REVALU-
  ATIONS OF PARTNERSHIP PROPERTY)
Right to use property . . . 4.02[B][2]
Section 751 property (See SALE OR EXCHANGE
  OF PARTNERSHIP OR LIMITED LIABILITY
  COMPANY INTEREST, subhead: Section 751
  property, characterization of gain or loss on)

PUBLICLY TRADED PARTNERSHIP (See
  CLASSIFICATION OF ENTITIES FOR TAX
  PURPOSES, subhead: Publicly traded partnership
  rules)

R

RECAPTURE PROPERTY
Character of partner's gain or loss on disposition of
  . . . 8.05[A]
Disproportionate distribution rules . . . 8.06[C]

RECHARACTERIZATION RULES
Nonpartner capacity, transactions in which partner
  acts in . . . 7.01[B]
Sale or exchange of partnership interest . . . 12.07

RECOURSE LIABILITIES
Generally . . . 5.06
Anti-abuse rules . . . 5.06[C]
Economic risk of loss . . . 5.06[A]
Interest on nonrecourse debt, obligation to pay
  . . . 5.06[E]
Nonrecourse loan to partnership . . . 5.06[F]
Obligations satisfied . . . 5.06[D]
Payment obligations of partners . . . 5.06[B]

**RELATED PARTNERSHIPS, SALES AND EX-
  CHANGES INVOLVING** (See CONTROLLED
  AND RELATED PARTNERSHIPS, SALES AND
  EXCHANGES INVOLVING)

RETIREMENT OF PARTNER
Distribution rules . . . 8.01[A][7]

[References are to sections.]

RETIRING PARTNER/MEMBER OR DECEDENT'S SUCCESSOR, LIQUIDATING PAYMENTS TO (See LIQUIDATING PAYMENTS)

REVALUATIONS OF PARTNERSHIP PROPERTY
Generally . . . 6.06[E]
Book value and tax basis disparities between . . . 6.06[F]
Tax basis and book value disparities between . . . 6.06[F]

S

SALE OR EXCHANGE OF PARTNERSHIP OR LIMITED LIABILITY COMPANY INTEREST
Generally . . . 1.01[I]; 12.01
Allocations
    Goodwill, to . . . 12.08[H]
    Partnership assets, allocations of basis adjustments among
        Generally . . . 12.08[F]
        Carryover basis transaction . . . 12.08[F][2]
        Income-in-respect-of-a-decedent . . . 12.08[F][1]
Basis adjustments
    Generally . . . 5.01[E]; 12.08[A]
    Affiliated groups of corporations, sale of partnership interests between members of . . . 12.08[K]
    Allocations (See subhead: Allocations)
    Applicability of basis adjustment rules . . . 12.08[C]
    Contribution of basis adjusted property to partnership or corporation . . . 12.08[G]
    Electing to adjust . . . 12.08[B]
    Section 732(d) election (See subhead: Section 732(d) election)
    Section 743(b) basis adjustment (See subhead: Section 743(b) basis adjustment)
    Section 754 election, making and reporting . . . 12.08[M]
    Tiered partnerships, transferring interest in . . . 12.08[E]
    Transfers terminating partnerships . . . 12.08[L]
Controlled partnerships, sales and exchanges involving (See CONTROLLED AND RELATED PARTNERSHIPS, SALES AND EXCHANGES INVOLVING)
Corporations
    Affiliated groups of corporations, sale of partnership interests between members of . . . 12.08[K]
    Basis adjusted property, contributions of . . . 12.08[G]
    Contribution of partnership or limited liability company interest to . . . 12.06[D]
    Conversion of corporation to partnership or limited liability company . . . 12.06[E]

SALE OR EXCHANGE OF PARTNERSHIP OR LIMITED LIABILITY COMPANY INTEREST—Cont.
Corporations—Cont.
    Distributions of partnership or limited liability company interest by . . . 12.06[G]
Deductions for losses . . . 12.05
Distributions of partnership or limited liability company interest
    Corporation, by . . . 12.06[G]
    Estate, by . . . 12.06[I]
    Partnership, by . . . 12.06[H]
    Section 743(b) adjustment . . . 12.08[J]
    Trust, by . . . 12.06[I]
Gain or loss, computation of
    Generally . . . 12.02
    Abandonment interest . . . 12.02[D]
    Amount realized
        Generally . . . 12.02[A]
        Deficit-capital-account effect on . . . 12.02[E]
    Basis . . . 12.02[B]
    Character of loss . . . 12.02[D]
    Deficit-capital-account effect on amount realized . . . 12.02[E]
    Holding period . . . 12.02[F]
    Portion of partner's interest . . . 12.02[C]
    Section 751 property, characterization of gain or loss on (See subhead: Section 751 property, characterization of gain or loss on)
    Tax rate . . . 12.02[F]
    Worthless interest . . . 12.02[D]
Goodwill, allocations to . . . 12.08[H]
Losses
    Computation of (See subhead: Gain or loss, computation of)
    Deduction of . . . 6.09[B]
Nonrecognition transaction, exchange of interests in
    Generally . . . 12.06
    Another partnership, contributing partnership or limited liability company interest to . . . 12.06[F]
    Charitable contributions . . . 12.06[L]
    Conversions of partnership to limited liability company interest and vice versa . . . 12.06[B]
    Corporations, transactions involving (See subhead: Corporations)
    Death of partner, transfers at . . . 12.06[J]
    Different partnerships, exchange of interests in . . . 12.06[C]
    Distributions of partnership or limited liability company interest (See subhead: Distributions of partnership or limited liability company interest)
    Gifting of partnership or limited liability company interest . . . 12.06[K]
    Same partnership, exchange of interests in . . . 12.06[A]
Partner-partnership transactions
    Losses and capital gains in, treatment of . . . 7.01[C]

[References are to sections.]

SALE OR EXCHANGE OF PARTNERSHIP OR LIMITED LIABILITY COMPANY INTEREST—Cont.

Partner-partnership transactions—Cont.
    Nonpartner capacity, transactions in which partner acting in . . . 7.04[C]
Partner's share of liabilities . . . 5.08[E]
Recharacterization . . . 12.07
Related partnerships, sales and exchanges involving (See CONTROLLED AND RELATED PARTNERSHIPS, SALES AND EXCHANGES INVOLVING)
Section 732(d) election
    Generally . . . 12.09
    Disproportionate distributions of Section 751 property, effect of election on . . . 12.09[A]
    Making election . . . 12.09[B]
    Mandatory adjustments . . . 12.09[C]
Section 743(b) basis adjustment
    Amortization, effect of basis adjustment on . . . 12.08[I][2]
    Computation of . . . 12.08[D]
    Cost recovery, effect of basis adjustment on . . . 12.08[I][2]
    Depletion, effect of basis adjustment on . . . 12.08[I][2]
    Distributions of property for which Section 743(b) adjustment has been made . . . 12.08[J]
    Gain or loss, effect of basis adjustment on . . . 12.08[I][1]
    Income, effect of basis adjustment on . . . 12.08[I][1]
    Tax consequences of . . . 12.08[I]
Section 751 property, characterization of gain or loss on
    Generally . . . 12.03
    Definition of . . . 12.03[A]
    Inventory . . . 12.03[A][2]
    Reporting requirements . . . 12.03[B]
    Unrealized receivables . . . 12.03[A][1]
Section 754 election, making and reporting . . . 12.08[M]
Tax year, effects of . . . 12.04

S CORPORATIONS
Business forms . . . 1.02[A][2]

SECURITIES
Basis adjustments, order of . . . 5.01[F][4]
Distributions of (See DISTRIBUTIONS TO PARTNERS OR MEMBERS, subhead: Marketable securities, distributions of)

SERVICES
Assets produced by personal services . . . 4.02[B][4]
Capital interest received for contribution of (See ACQUISITION OF PARTNERSHIP OR LIMITED LIABILITY COMPANY INTEREST BY CONTRIBUTION, subhead: Capital interest received for contribution of services)

SERVICES—Cont.
Contribution of (See ACQUISITION OF PARTNERSHIP OR LIMITED LIABILITY COMPANY INTEREST BY CONTRIBUTION, subhead: Services, contribution of)
Current position . . . 4.05[C][3]
Disguised payments for . . . 7.04[E]
Donor's services, reallocation for reasonable value of . . . 9.06[C]
Guaranteed payments for (See GUARANTEED PAYMENTS, subhead: Services or use of capital, payments for)
Nonpartner capacity, transactions in which partner acts in . . . 7.04[B]
Payments to service partner or member . . . 4.05[B][5]

SOLE PROPRIETORSHIP
Termination of partnership or limited liability company upon change to . . . 13.03[A]

START-UP COSTS
Amortization of . . . 3.03[D]; 4.06[A]

SUBCHAPTER K
Aggregate and entity principles . . . 1.01[A]
Entity principles, aggregate and . . . 1.01[A]
Transactions inconsistent with intent of . . . 2.05[A]

SUBSTANTIAL ECONOMIC EFFECT TEST
Generally . . . 6.05
Deficit capital accounts
    Generally . . . 6.05[A][3]
    Deficit-restoration requirement
        Generally . . . 6.05[A][3][a]
        Exceptions to (See subhead: Exceptions to deficit-restoration requirement)
Economic-effect test
    Economic-effect equivalence . . . 6.05[A][4]
    Liquidating distributions
        Deficit capital accounts (See subhead: Deficit capital accounts)
        Positive capital account balances, of . . . 6.05[A][2]
    Partial economic effect . . . 6.05[A][5]
    Partnership agreement, provisions required in . . . 6.05[A][1]
    Provisions required in partnership agreement . . . 6.05[A][1]
Exceptions to deficit-restoration requirement
    Alternate economic-effect test . . . 6.05[A][3][b][i]
    Partial obligation to restore deficit . . . 6.05[A][3][b][ii]
    Reduction of obligation . . . 6.05[A][3][b][iii]
Substantiality test
    Generally . . . 6.05[B]
    After-tax economic consequences rule . . . 6.05[B][1]
    Shifting tax consequences . . . 6.05[B][2]
    Transitory allocations . . . 6.05[B][3]

[References are to sections.]

SUCCESSOR PARTNERS

Admission as partner . . . 11.01[B][10]

Basis of successor's partnership or limited liability company interest . . . 11.01[B][3]; 11.04[A]

Distribution rules . . . 8.01[A][7]

SYNDICATION EXPENSES

Disguised organization and . . . 4.06[D]

Nondeductibility of . . . 4.06[C]

T

TAXABLE YEAR

Generally . . . 3.04

Adoption of . . . 3.04[B]

Business purpose for fiscal tax year

    Generally . . . 3.04[D]

    Gross receipts test

        Generally . . . 3.04[D][1]

        Business purpose when not satisfied . . . 3.04[D][2]

    Natural business year . . . 3.04[D][1]

Changes of . . . 3.04[B]

Deceased partner or member, for . . . 11.01[B][1]

Distributive shares . . . 6.01[B]

Election . . . 3.04[F]

52-53-week taxable year . . . 3.04[E]

Sale or exchange of partnership interest . . . 12.04

Selection of partnership tax year

    Generally . . . 3.04[C]

    Least-aggregate-deferral rule . . . 3.04[C][3]

    Majority-interest taxable year rule . . . 3.04[C][1]

    Principal-partners rule . . . 3.04[C][2]

Termination of partnership or limited liability company . . . 13.06[A]

Timing of partner's share of partnership income . . . 3.04[A]

TAXATION (GENERALLY)

Attributes, reduction of . . . 3.03[F][2][b]

Business form, choice of (See BUSINESS FORM, subhead: Tax factors in choice of business form)

Classification of economic relationships (See CLASSIFICATION OF ENTITIES FOR TAX PURPOSES)

Current distributions . . . 8.03[F]

Death of partner or member (See DEATH OF PARTNER OR MEMBER, subhead: Tax considerations)

Estate taxation (See ESTATE TAXATION)

Foreign tax credit . . . 3.03[F][1]

Gift tax considerations . . . 9.07

Income, of (See INCOME, subhead: Taxable income, computation of)

Losses, of . . . 1.02[B][2][c]

Lump-sum liquidating payment . . . 10.01[D][3]

Partnership taxation provisions, elections to be excluded from (See PARTNERSHIPS (GENERALLY), subhead: Elections to be excluded from tax rules)

Section 736(a) payments . . . 10.01[D][2]

Section 736(b) payments . . . 10.01[C][3]

TAXATION (GENERALLY)—Cont.

Section 743(b) basis adjustment . . . 12.08[I]

Taxable year (See TAXABLE YEAR)

Termination of partnership or limited liability company (See TERMINATION OF PARTNERSHIP OR LIMITED LIABILITY COMPANY, subhead: Tax consequences)

TERMINATION OF PARTNERSHIP OR LIMITED LIABILITY COMPANY

Generally . . . 1.01[K]; 13.01

Business form, changes in (See subhead: Changes in business form)

Cessation of business or financial activities

    Generally . . . 13.02

    Tax consequences . . . 13.06[C]

Changes in business form

    Generally . . . 13.03

    Conversion of interests within partnership . . . 13.03[C]

    Conversion partnership to limited liability company and vice versa . . . 13.03[D]

    Corporation, change to . . . 13.03[B]

    Sole proprietorship, change to . . . 13.03[A]

Classification following . . . 2.02[E][6]

Consolidation (See subhead: Merger or consolidation)

Conversion of interests (See subhead: Merger or consolidation)

Death of partner or member . . . 11.01[B][2]

50 percent sale or exchange rule

    Generally . . . 13.04

    Capital interest, determination of . . . 13.04[B][1]

    Determination of whether 50 percent of profits and capital are transferred . . . 13.04[B]

    Nontaxable transfers considered exchanges . . . 13.04[A][2]

    Profits interest, determination of . . . 13.04[B][2]

    Sale or exchange requirement . . . 13.04[A]

    Tiered partnerships . . . 13.04[A][3]

    Transfers not causing termination . . . 13.04[A][1]

Losses, deduction of . . . 6.09[B]

Merger or consolidation

    Continuity of partnership or limited liability company . . . 13.05[A]

    Division of partnership or limited liability company . . . 13.05[C]

    Tax consequences . . . 13.05[B]

Sale or exchange

    Basis adjustments . . . 12.08[L]

    50 percent sale or exchange rule (See subhead: 50 percent sale or exchange rule)

    Tax consequences . . . 13.06[D]

Tax consequences

    Assets deemed contributed to new partnership . . . 13.06[D]

    Assets deemed distributed . . . 13.06[C]

    Cessation of business . . . 13.06[C]

    Character of partnership property following termination . . . 13.06[F]

**TERMINATION OF PARTNERSHIP OR LIM-
ITED LIABILITY COMPANY**—Cont.
Tax consequences—Cont.
  Elections . . . 13.06[B]
  Holding period for assets following termination
    . . . 13.06[E]
  Merger or consolidation, of . . . 13.05[B]
  New partnership, assets deemed contributed to
    . . . 13.06[D]
  Suspended losses . . . 13.06[G]
  Taxable year . . . 13.06[A]

THIN PARTNERSHIPS
Generally . . . 5.04[E]

TIERED PARTNERSHIPS
Basis adjustments
  Distributions by tiered partnership
    . . . 8.07[D]
  Transfers of interests in tiered partnerships
    . . . 12.08[E]
Change of interests in . . . 6.03[D]
50 percent sale or exchange rule . . . 13.04[A][3]

TRUSTEES
Family partnerships, partner status in . . . 9.03

TRUSTS
Distributions of partnership or LLC interest by
  . . . 12.06[I]

U

UNREALIZED RECEIVABLES
Character of partner's gain or loss on disposition of
  . . . 8.05[A]
Disproportionate distribution rules (See DISTRIBU-
  TIONS TO PARTNERS OR MEMBERS, sub-
  head: Disproportionate distribution rules)
Liquidating payments . . . 10.01[C][2]
Sale or exchange of partnership interest
  . . . 12.03[A][1]

V

VALUATION (See DEATH OF PARTNER OR
  MEMBER, subhead: Valuation of partnership or
  limited liability company interest, determination
  of)